RESEARCH METHODS IN PSYCHOLOGY

SECOND EDITION

edited by
Glynis M. Breakwell, Sean Hammond
and Chris Fife-Schaw

SAGE Publications
London • Thousand Oaks • New Delhi

Editorial arrangement © Glynis M. Breakwell,
Sean Hammond and Chris Fife-Schaw 2000
Chapter 1 © Glynis M. Breakwell 2000
Chapter 2 © Glynis M. Breakwell and David Rose 2000
Chapter 3 © Martyn Barrett 2000
Chapter 4 © Alyson Davis and David Rose 2000
Chapter 5 © Sarah L. Wilson 2000
Chapter 6 © Chris Fife-Schaw 2000
Chapter 7 © Chris Fife-Schaw 2000
Chapter 8 © Jennifer Brown and Julie Barnett 2000
Chapter 9 © John Everatt 2000
Chapter 10 © Evanthia Lyons and Xenia Chryssochoou 2000
Chapter 11 © Chris Fife-Schaw 2000
Chapter 12 © Chris Fife-Schaw 2000
Chapter 13 © Sean Hammond 2000
Chapter 14 © David Rose 2000
Chapter 15 © Paul Barrett and Paul Sowden 2000
Chapter 16 © Jill Wilkinson 2000
Chapter 17 © Glynis M. Breakwell 2000
Chapter 18 © Adrian Coyle 2000
Chapter 19 © Evanthia Lyons 2000
Chapter 20 © Margaret Wilson and Sean Hammond 2000
Chapter 21 © Glynis M. Breakwell and Peter Wood 2000
Chapter 22 © Lynne J. Millward 2000
Chapter 23 © David Uzzell 2000
Chapter 24 © Peter Simpson 2000
Chapter 25 © Chris Fife-Schaw 2000
Chapter 26 © Sean Hammond 2000
Chapter 27 © Chris Fife-Schaw 2000
Chapter 28 © Peter Wood

First edition published as *Research Methods in Psychology* in 1995.
Reprinted 1995, 1997, 1998
This edition first published 2000. Reprinted 2001, 2002

 SAGE Publications Ltd
6 Bonhill Street
London EC2A 4PU

SAGE Publications Inc
2455 Teller Road
Thousand Oaks, California 91320

SAGE Publications India Pvt Ltd
32, M-Block Market
Greater Kailash – I
New Delhi 110 048

British Library Cataloguing in Publication data

A catalogue record for this book is available from the British Library

ISBN 0 7619 6590 4
ISBN 0 7619 6591 2 (pbk)

Library of Congress catalog record available

Typeset by Mayhew Typesetting, Rhayader, Powys
Printed in Great Britain by The Cromwell Press Ltd, Trowbridge, Wiltshire

Contents

Contributors

Julie Barnett is a Research Fellow in the Psychology Department at the University of Surrey. She obtained her degrees at Loughborough and Surrey. Her PhD was concerned with the effects of asking sensitive questions in questionnaires. Her research interests include risk perception and communication, identity, and the relationships between research methodologies and the development of theory.

Martyn Barrett is Professor of Psychology at the University of Surrey. He obtained his degrees at Cambridge and Sussex in the 1970s. He has worked extensively on the development of language in children and on the development of children's drawings. More recently he has been working on the development of national and ethnic identity in childhood and adolescence and the development of prejudice and stereotyping in children and adolescence. Over the years, Professor Barrett has received numerous grants from the ESRC, the Commission of the European Communities, the Nuffield Foundation, and various other bodies, and he regularly publishes and presents papers at national and international conferences.

Paul Barrett is Chief Scientist at the State Hospital, Carstairs where he is involved in research on the assessment of mentally disordered offenders. His primary research interests are in the electrophysiological aspects of assessment particularly where they relate to personality and cognitive functioning. He also has a major interest in theoretical and applied psychometrics and has developed this interest in a number of fields including occupational psychology and forensic psychology.

Glynis M. Breakwell is Professor of Psychology, Head of the School of Human Sciences and Pro-Vice-Chancellor (Research and Enterprise) at the University of Surrey. She currently conducts research in identity processes and social representations; risk communication; and military psychology. Most of her research has been funded by ESRC but also latterly by the EC and various government departments. She has published 19 books and many journal articles in social psychology.

Jennifer Brown is a Reader in the Department of Psychology and is the Director of the Forensic Psychology Masters programme. Her research interests are in the field of occupational stress and organisational culture in the police. She has also undertaken research into psychological aspects of police investigative activity such as distinguishing between true and false rape allegations. She was formerly Head of Research at the Hampshire Constabulary, and also a

Principal Lecturer at the University of Portsmouth's Institute of Police and Criminological Studies.

Xenia Chryssochoou is a Lecturer in Social Psychology at the University of Surrey. She obtained her degrees from Athens and Paris and her PhD was concerned with national and European identity. She previously lectured in France at the University of Paris V and at the University Institute for Teacher Training (Reims). She is interested in intergroup relations as well as group formation. In particular she is studying how identity issues and social justice issues affect the relationships between groups in the context of a multinational, multi-ethnic and multicultural society.

Adrian Coyle is a Senior Lecturer in Psychology at the University of Surrey. He obtained his degree in psychology from University College Dublin and his PhD from the University of Surrey. Before taking up his present post, he worked in HIV/AIDS research, counselling and education in university and NHS settings. He is currently part of the team which runs the University of Surrey's Practitioner Doctorate in Psychotherapeutic and Counselling Psychology. His primary research interests are in lesbian and gay psychology (mostly within a social psychological framework) and – with colleagues from Loughborough University and the University of Surrey – he was instrumental in establishing a Lesbian and Gay Psychology Section within the British Psychological Society in 1998. His other research interests and publications cover the domains of feminist psychology, counselling psychology and HIV/AIDS, and he is committed to the dissemination and development of qualitative approaches to psychological research.

Alyson Davis is a Senior Lecturer in Psychology at the University of Surrey. She obtained her degree in psychology from Sussex before taking a PGCE. Her PhD was awarded by the University of Birmingham which she completed before taking up a Lectureship in Educational Psychology at the same institution. She then took up a Lectureship in Child Psychology at the Institute of Education before assuming her current post in the Department. She has research interests in children's representations (drawing, writing and number) and in the development of pretence and imagination.

John Everatt is a Lecturer in Psychology at the University of Surrey. He obtained his BSc (Hons) Psychology degree from Newcastle Polytechnic and his PhD from the University of Nottingham. His lecturing roles have included teaching research methods and statistics, and cognitive and educational aspects of psychology. His PhD investigated individual differences in reading, an area of research which he continued to study while working at the University of Wales, Bangor (particularly when working with the Dyslexia Unit at the same institution), and which he has further developed since joining the Department of Psychology at Surrey. He has been involved in several research council and charity funded projects, given numerous talks at conferences, research seminars and charity-organised meetings, and authored many journal articles and book chapters in the area; he has recently edited the book *Reading and Dyslexia: Visual and Attentional Processes*, and is an Executive Editor on the journal *Dyslexia: An International Journal of Research and*

Practice. He has also acted as research consultant on a number of research projects within health/clinical fields associated with psychology (e.g. attitudes to health, assessments of pain management procedures, and surveys of health care workers), and was a statistics adviser on the Research and Development Committee of a local National Health Service Trust.

Chris Fife-Schaw is a Senior Lecturer in Psychology at the University of Surrey. He obtained his degrees at Newcastle, Strathclyde and Sheffield Universities in the late 1970s and early 1980s. His PhD was concerned with the notion of rationality in voting decisions. Since 1984 he has worked in the Department on several research projects concerned with young people: the first about young people's attitudes to new technology, the second on the political and economic socialisation of young people and the third on the impact of AIDS/HIV on the general population of young people. He now lectures in social psychology, research methods and structural equation modelling and his research interests are in risk perception, models of behavioural regulation, and developing alternative measures of attitudes that do not involve questionnaires.

Sean Hammond is the Head of the Clinical Decision Making Support Unit at Broadmoor Hospital. His primary interests are in forensic and health psychology and he has particular expertise in psychometrics and multivariate statistics. Current work involves risk assessment of mentally disordered offenders and the development of procedures for assessing sex offenders. He has been a research consultant to a number of companies and NHS trusts. He is currently a visiting Reader in Psychology at the University of Surrey and is a research consultant on both the offender profiling programme of the Behavioural Science Section of Surrey Police Force and on the psychiatric risk assessment, management and audit programme for the Surrey–Hampshire Borders NHS Trust.

Evanthia Lyons is a Senior Lecturer in Psychology at the University of Surrey. She obtained her degrees at Bedford College and Institute of Education, University of London. Her doctoral research was concerned with social psychological processes involved in adolescent everyday decision making. Since then she has carried out research into the development of national identities in children, the role of social memories in maintaining inter-group conflicts, and processes involved in the construction of European identities and citizenship. Much of her work uses cross-national designs. She currently teaches social psychology and qualitative research methods at masters and doctoral level.

Lynne J. Millward is a Senior Lecturer in Psychology at the University of Surrey. She obtained her degrees from Exeter and Kent and her PhD was concerned with identity processes, group formation and change, and the relationship between cognition and affect. Prior to joining the Department she worked as an occupational psychologist in a management consultancy practice in London where she specialised in the design and implementation of selection, training and assessment procedures. Her current research interests include the social psychology of work, group processes, identity dynamics, sexuality and the relationship between thoughts, feelings and behaviour.

David Rose is a Reader in Psychology at the University of Surrey. He holds degrees in psychology, neurophysiology and the history and philosophy of science from Bristol and Cambridge Universities, and is interested in wide areas of brain research, visual perception, cognition, philosophy of mind and philosophy of science. His recent research has centred mainly on visual psychophysics, but he also has experience in broad areas of neuroscience and is currently extending his investigations to theories of consciousness. He has undertaken consultancy work for the government and industry and has collaborated with researchers in a dozen other universities across the UK and the USA, supported by funds from the Wellcome Trust, the SERC, the MRC, the NIH, the NSF and the Royal Society among others. He has edited two books, *Models of the Visual Cortex* and *The Artful Eye*, is on the Editorial Board of the *Journal of Intelligent Systems*, and is a consultant referee for numerous academic journals and publishers, and for the media.

Peter Simpson is a Lecturer in Psychology at the University of Surrey. He obtained degrees from Leeds, Sussex and Cambridge. He has carried out research on visual attention and recognition, and problem solving in science and engineering education. He has worked on the design of computer interface languages, and musical acoustics and instrument design. He is currently investigating factors in auditory space perception, the provision of synthetic speech aids for the disabled, and laterality effects in the planning and performance of safety critical skills.

Paul Sowden obtained his BSc and PhD from the University of Surrey. His PhD explored perceptual learning, and its role in acquiring complex discrimination skills. He was subsequently appointed as a Research Fellow at the University of Surrey conducting NHS-funded research into perceptual learning and computer-aided decision making in breast cancer screening. Following this he was appointed as a University Tutor and then as a Lecturer at Surrey. He currently lectures on perception, biological bases of psychology, and psychophysiological research methods. His general research interests are in the areas of perception and cognition, ergonomics and biological psychology. More specifically his recent publications have included articles on: visual processing; perceptual learning and the plasticity of the human brain; perceptual expertise, especially perception of medical images; training people to acquire complex perceptual skills; colour perceptions; and the use of colour in computer displays.

David Uzzell is Professor of Psychology at the University of Surrey. He holds degrees in geography, psychology and social psychology from the Universities of Liverpool, Surrey and London (LSE) Universities. He is Director of the MSc in Environmental Psychology and specialises in applied research on environmental and heritage education and interpretation, architectural assessment, safety and security, transport and sustainability. He is currently undertaking research on: transport, air pollution and health and the development of sustainable transport policies; social exclusion and sustainability; intergroup conflict between user groups of shared use cycleways and footpaths; safety and security in European railway stations. He is President of the International Association for People–Environment Studies (IAPS) and a Fellow of the British Psychological Society. He recently published, with R. Ballantyne, *Contemporary Issues in Heritage and Environmental Interpretation* (The Stationery Office).

Jill Wilkinson was a Lecturer in Psychology at the University of Surrey. She is a Chartered Counselling Psychologist and a Chartered Health Psychologist and also runs an independent clinical practice. Her particular interests are in cognitive aspects of social behaviour in schizophrenia and in the psychological effects of ill-health. Her teaching includes assessment in health and clinical settings, the psychological therapies and therapeutic skills.

Margaret Wilson is a Lecturer in Psychology at the University of Kent. She has an MSc in environmental psychology and a PhD in Psychology from the University of Surrey. She has worked in several areas of applied social psychology, as well as undertaking theoretical and methodological research. Her research interests are in social, environmental and investigative psychology. She is also interested in Facet Theory and qualitative research methods, and has been instrumental in developing the use of open-ended sorting procedures.

Sarah L. Wilson is a Senior Lecturer in Health Psychology in the Department of Psychological Medicine at the University of Glasgow. She graduated from Swansea and studied for her doctorate at the Institute of Psychiatry. She is a neuropsychologist as well as a health psychologist, and since 1980 has been engaged in research involving severely physically disabled and brain-injured people. Areas of research include computer-based assessment, the role of psychological factors in rehabilitation, recovery from very severe brain injury and, most recently, the treatment of patients in vegetative state.

Peter Wood was a Lecturer in Psychology and Chartered Occupational Psychologist at the University of Surrey. He graduated in psychology from Manchester University, and received his PhD from Loughborough University. A large part of his earlier career was spent at Loughborough in the Department of Ergonomics, and subsequently in the Department of Social Sciences, undertaking research in vehicle ergonomics, consumer safety and stress behaviour. He also spent three years in industry working for the Ford Motor Company on vehicle safety systems. Over more recent years his interests have broadened into the general area of I/O Psychology, and he is currently Course Director of the MSc in Occupational and Organisational Psychology. Research interests include shift work, organisational commitment, and occupational stress.

Preface to the Second Edition

For editors of any textbook, being invited to produce a second edition of your book is very flattering. It indicates that you must have done something right, certainly enough to make your publishers feel that their faith in you has been rewarded and that they think the book will continue to be a success. This poses something of a dilemma, however. Do you leave the book essentially unchanged or do you opt for a substantial rewrite? It would be tempting to think that since the book has been reasonably successful, doing next to nothing will do. More realistically, though, no book is so good that it could not be improved and, of course, in the behavioural sciences things move on.

In this second edition the major changes are in the form of the addition of new chapters dealing with topics not covered in the first edition. There are two new chapters to do with the nature of samples. John Everatt contributes a new chapter on working with special groups (for example, people with particular medical conditions). Often researchers are interested in psychological aspects of people with particular sets of circumstances or characteristics that make adopting traditional methods either inappropriate or impractical. John discusses these issues and suggests some alternative approaches. Another common concern, particularly of social psychologists, is to study differences and similarities between people from different cultures. Such research brings with it a whole range of concerns about whether what you are doing as a researcher means the same thing in all the cultures you study. This potentially adds considerable ambiguity to your data and these and related issues are addressed directly in a new chapter by Evanthia Lyons and Xenia Chryssochoou.

Recent years have seen the continued rise in importance of qualitative modes of data analysis. Traditional research methods courses with an exclusive emphasis on hypothesis testing and statistical analyses are rapidly becoming a thing of the past. Though the first edition dealt with some of these issues we have included a new chapter by Evanthia Lyons on content analysis strategies and have substantially revised those chapters dealing with qualitative research approaches. Finally, we have added a new chapter on structural equation modelling (SEM). This may seem like a rather specialised statistical topic for a general research methods textbook but it is included primarily because of the philosophical orientation to research that accompanies its use. If applied appropriately it can encourage a rigorous and systematic approach to theory testing – something we believe is to be encouraged.

All the chapters carried over from the first edition have been revised and updated. For some chapters, such as those dealing with statistical and design matters, the revisions are modest since there have been few major developments in recent years that would challenge what are now well-established knowledge bases. For others, such as the chapters on Facet Theory and the relationship between theory and method, we have taken the opportunity to substantially restructure the chapters to reflect changes in the way people are thinking about these topics.

As with the first edition, our goal remains to provide readers with a gentle introduction to each topic, with hopefully enough explanation of the main issues that the reader will be able to dig deeper into more specialised texts without feeling lost. All the chapters conclude with pointers to further reading which we encourage readers to take advantage of.

PART I

1

Introducing Research Methods in Psychology

Glynis M. Breakwell

Contents

1.1 OBJECTIVES OF THE BOOK

The purpose of this book is to offer students at the undergraduate and post-graduate levels a reasonably comprehensive introduction to the research methods which can be used in the exploration of psychological processes. Like any science, psychology is concerned with identifying how processes operate. A process here is defined as a series of changes. The task of the psychological researcher is to plot patterns of changes in any one variable and to describe the relationships between changes in that variable and changes in others. Theories essentially specify the principles or rules which predict these relationships. The variables which interest theorists in psychology lie at intraindividual, inter-personal and societal levels of analysis. They range from the biochemical and genetic, through the physiological, to the cognitive and affective, and beyond to interpersonal networks and communication, and further still to social power hierarchies and ideologies. In so far as the psychological processes they study are influenced by the material context or physical environment, many psycho-logists see these also as a target of their analysis. Such diversity of subject matter requires a diversity of research methods. Students of psychology are therefore usually subjected to research methods training which is simul-taneously both broader and more intensive than in virtually any other science.

This book is designed to provide the basic information a student might need about each of the common research strategies used to examine psychological processes. How to conduct experiments and the nature of quasi-experimental designs for data collection are described. Classic methods of direct observation are depicted. Psychophysical and psychophysiological procedures are cata-logued. Survey techniques are presented. Questionnaire design, psychometric techniques and interviewing are all reviewed. Ethnography and action research are introduced. Alongside these popular and well-rehearsed approaches, others that are less frequently used or that are relatively new are also explained. These include single case experimental designs, discourse analysis, focus groups, diary techniques, simulation and cross-cultural analysis. We have included such a wide range of approaches because we believe that it is only by knowing most, if not all, of what could be used to address a particular research problem that the researcher can make appropriate methodological choices. In presenting these approaches, we have tried to be value-neutral: we do not play favourites; there are no methodological heroes or design villains in this text. Each approach is presented as fairly as possible and there is no attempt to proselytise any one in particular. In fact, the assumption underlying this collection of approaches is that the usefulness of any method can only be judged against the nature of the research question that you wish to answer. More importantly, it is assumed that all methods have weaknesses and limitations. Therefore, it is argued that theorists will want to have recourse to a variety of methods that they will need to implement in an integrated fashion (see Chapter 2).

1.2 STRUCTURE OF THE BOOK

Each chapter attempts to present a practical guide to the research approach it covers. The object is to demythologise where necessary, to systematise and summarise succinctly relevant information, and to offer advice which will be useful when you try to use the approach yourself. Each chapter should provide you with enough information so that you can judge whether that approach will be of any use to you in addressing a particular research problem. Typically, the chapters are structured so as to introduce the approach, illustrate its potential and the details of using it, identify its weaknesses (where possible showing how they can be overcome), and suggest further literature which can be used to acquire a better understanding of it.

As is evident from the contents pages, the book begins with the issues surrounding the relationship between theory building concerning psychological processes and research methodology. It also provides a thorough examination of the practical and ethical issues involved in planning and executing any research. Having done this, it goes on to focus upon how to structure data collection, presenting both the principles which need to be understood when trying to measure a psychological variable and the prime types of research design which can be employed. This part of the book also includes a chapter on facet theory which in reality is not a theory but a meta-theoretical approach which tries to show how researchers can be more systematic in defining their hypotheses and operationalising variables. The subsequent chapters contain the descriptions of what might be called data elicitation techniques. Mostly, these include details of the types of data which the technique yields and what forms of data analysis are necessary to make sense of them. These include psychophysiological data as well as self-report and individual and interpersonal behavioural data. There is also a chapter on computer simulation as a method of data generation and modelling. The closing chapters explain the nature of the assumptions underlying bivariate, multivariate and meta-analytic statistical approaches. The purpose of these chapters is not to provide detailed explanations of specific statistical tests. The object is to explain the logic which should dictate which statistical test you should choose to use and what this sort of test is capable of telling you about your data. A basic understanding of statistical assumptions is often slow to mature and can be delayed by dealing too soon with the mathematical details of specific tests. Here, the reader is introduced to these fundamental statistical assumptions in a way which shows how they are linked to types of research design and levels of measurement and, perhaps, this makes them more comprehensible. Readers needing detailed information on specific statistical tests are directed to appropriate alternative texts.

Given the variety of approaches covered in this book, we expect that it will be useful throughout the course of an individual's research training. Chapters which are not used at an undergraduate level may well be central to a postgraduate course or be valuable later when considering further research activity. Effectively the book can be used in modules, and progress towards a thorough understanding and skilled use of these various approaches can be achieved in easy stages. As a reference text for more experienced researchers, the book has been written as far as possible so as to incorporate current and recent developments. This is done in the hope that this book can be used as a resource in the process of continuing professional development.

2

Research: Theory and Method

Glynis M. Breakwell and David Rose

Contents

2.1 THEORY BUILDING AND THEORY TESTING

2.1.1 The importance of theories

Why do we do research? Once the superficial retorts to this question, such as to keep a job or to get good coursework marks, are out of the way, the serious answer would be: we do research to find out what has happened, how it happened, and, if possible, why it happened. We use 'happened' rather than 'happening' because by the time we have recorded something it is inevitably in the past tense. But there is more: once we have some idea of the kinds of things that may happen, in other words we have a **theory**, we can use that theory to predict what will happen in the future. If we also understand why things happen the way they do, we may even be able to improve the future by intervening in the world. Knowledge is power, knowledge is stored in the form of theories, and as Kurt Lewin once said: 'nothing is as powerful as a good theory'.

It could be argued that research is not inevitably tied to formal theory building or theory testing. Some researchers self-consciously eschew the construction of theory for philosophical reasons. They use their research to describe in detail specific happenings without any attempt to use these as instances to illustrate or test some general underlying explanatory framework. Other researchers ignore theory because they do their research for purely practical reasons. They think they only need to know what has happened in order to decide what they (or their clients) should do next.

In response, we can argue that even those researchers who have no time for formal theories are in fact working with implicit theories. Any set of ideas about the relationships between variables can be called a theory. At an informal level, we build theories all the time. In fact, George Kelly (1955), when he developed the theory of personal constructs to explain personality and cognitive processes, based his argument on the metaphor of 'man the scientist'. Kelly suggested that we all behave as scientists in so far as we are inveterate constructors of theories. They help us to navigate in the world by letting us explain to ourselves what we think is happening and why it is happening. Informal theories of this type are particularly valuable because we invariably use them as the basis for predicting what will happen next.

So, for instance, you might observe events which lead you to conclude that men in their late teens or early twenties are more likely than other people to drive their cars aggressively and erratically, with their windows open, with heavy bass music blaring, on sunny days. From this you might generate an informal theory that attributes their driving behaviour to their age or possibly some interaction of their age with the music and the sunshine. As a naïve scientist, you are not obliged to test your theory. You can go ahead to predict from it that young men playing audible music on sunny days are more likely to be a danger to you and adjust your own behaviour accordingly. Theory building of this sort has survival value – though when it goes wrong it also has the capacity seriously to endanger you. Such theories can mislead you, directing you to cues in the situation which are irrelevant. Your sunny day, music-loving bad driver theory is only really valuable if it turns out that in the rain young men are at least as good as any other driver. However, Kelly pointed out that the erroneous theory is usually just a staging post to a better version. As naïve scientists, we are mostly willing to refine our theories on the basis of new information which proves the earlier versions wrong.

The implicit theories which inform some research have the same sort of power to both aid and hinder survival. Even while they remain unmentioned, these implicit theories direct the attention of the researcher to focus on some things rather than others, to use certain research approaches rather than others, and to try this rather than that form of analysis. In most cases, it would be better if the researcher did articulate these implicit theories. By doing so, it is possible to analyse their logical weaknesses (e.g. inconsistencies) and their substantive weaknesses (e.g. omission of important variables). Some researchers resist making their implicit theories explicit because they do not see their task as theory building. Yet this is actually a poor excuse. It does not really preclude the need to specify what theoretical assumptions underlie your work. Since these assumptions will inevitably affect what you do, they should be described so that other researchers can judge how far your research activities and findings are influenced by them (e.g. Dobson and Rose, 1985). Researchers who do try to lay bare these underlying assumptions often find that the discipline needed to articulate them has the effect of bringing about for themselves a new understanding of their research problem. Essentially, whether you see yourself as a theory builder or not, it is always useful to examine the implicit theories which affect your research.

2.1.2 The basic construction of a theory

The process of formal theory building was traditionally supposed by philosophers of science to proceed in an orderly manner from description, to taxonomy, and thus to testable causal hypotheses. This would mean that the first task of the theorist is to describe the phenomena of interest thoroughly and systematically. The next task is to categorise phenomena, showing how specific instances are characterised by common attributes which make them capable of being treated in some sense as equivalent to each other. Such categorisation is one way of ordering the plethora of data which are generated whenever descriptions are not pre-structured. The categorisation scheme can be labelled as a theoretical construct. Learning theory has categorised phenomena to generate two very salient constructs: stimuli and responses. To the behaviourist, all phenomena at any one moment can be categorised as either a stimulus or a response. By this act of definition, suddenly the multitudinous world is dichotomised, order is imposed and it is our task to explain the relationship between stimulus and response.

Once the taxonomy is complete, the theorist's next task entails stating how one category of phenomena is related to another. The description of a single set of relationships between phenomena does not become a theory unless general principles about the relationships of similar phenomena are formulated. To say, 'The woman kicked the dog after he bit her and he was never found to bite her again', is a description of a pattern of events: it is not a theory. But if one were to say, 'The woman punished the dog for biting and he never did it again', there remains only one further step towards generalisation before a theory comes into being: 'Punishment of a behaviour leads to the diminution of that behaviour.' The result is a recognisable basic tenet of learning theory (to be much qualified later by statements about the frequency of punishment, the temporal relationship of the punishment to the behaviour, and the availability of alternative rewards for the behaviour). Basic theories are sets of what might be called **relational rules**. The relational rule specifies how variation in one theoretical construct is related to variation in one or more others.

2.1.3 The nature of explanation

An explanation can be of two sorts: the mechanistic or process variety or the functional variety. The **mechanistic or process explanation** accounts for a phenomenon in terms of phenomena which are its precursors. It is usually in the form: if A and B occur, then C will follow. In contrast, the **functional**

explanation accounts for a phenomenon in terms of the consequences it has. It is usually in the form: A occurs in order that B will follow. The functional explanation assumes that the phenomenon to be explained is purposive, intentional or teleological (i.e. it occurs to achieve some goal).

Another way of talking about the distinction between the mechanistic and functional types of explanation is to say that the former is concerned with causes and the latter with reasons: with how as opposed to why. Traditional theories, e.g. in physics, tend to deal only with the first of these. However, psychological theories use both types of explanation. Some theorists use both explanatory forms to account for a single psychological process. For instance, in studying altruism (helping or pro-social behaviour) researchers have found that people are less likely to offer someone help if they perceive that person to be in need because he or she has made too little effort, not used his or her own ability and not chosen to get out of the difficulty when it was possible to do so. One explanation of helping suggests that people see the need for assistance, then assess whether the individual is responsible for his or her own predicament; if he or she is responsible this leads to anger and no helping, but if that individual is deemed not to be responsible this leads to sympathy and helping. This is clearly a mechanistic explanation. Another explanation of helping suggests that people are unwilling to help an unfortunate whom they see to be the origin of his or her own fate because they wish to punish the miscreant for failures of effort or judgement. In this explanation the punishment (i.e. failure to help) serves the function in some way of exacting restitution and may warn others that such slack behaviour is unacceptable and not rewarded with help. It should be noted that these two explanations of the same phenomenon are not mutually exclusive. The functional explanation may serve to account for the anger, so central to the mechanistic explanation, which is aroused when the needy are shown not to have tried to shift for themselves.

2.1.4 Building more complex theories

This mixing of mechanistic and functional explanations is common in psychological theories. It may emanate, in part, from the way psychological processes and thus psychological theories often traverse many levels of analysis. We would argue (Breakwell, 1994; Rose and Dobson, 1985; 1989) that psychologists should be building theories which encompass processes at the intrapsychic (i.e. physiological, cognitive, affective and oretic) level, the interpersonal level and the societal level of analysis. But we are currently a long way away from the grand theory in psychology. We have low or middle range theories designed to explain relatively narrow bands of phenomena. Thus, for instance, we have theories of aggression distinct and separate from theories of altruism when common sense might think them to be in some way connected. These low-level theories, while they may offer a detailed mechanistic explanation of their target phenomena, tend to rely upon what Israel (1972) called 'stipulative statements' that concern assumptions about the nature of the individual, the nature of society and the nature of the relationship between the individual and society. These stipulative statements are often functionalist (for example, a variety of social Darwinism as illustrated in the theory of altruism described above). This results in a strange mélange of explanatory types being moulded together in many psychological theories – made more strange by the fact that some significant element of the explanation remains unsaid. Those elements which lie at a different level of analysis from that of the main theory will reside at the margin, unexamined and untested.

Just as mechanistic and functional explanations are not so simple to keep apart, the distinction between theories built from induction and theories developed through deduction is not easy to maintain in practice. **Induction** entails inferring a general law from particular instances (for example, the theory about young men drivers given above). **Deduction** entails drawing from the general an inference to the particular. In practice, theory building is a messy, iterative process. Relational rules that seem to be valid are usually crafted by successive approximation. This process of approximation will involve both deductive and inductive reasoning (Oldroyd, 1986). You may well, for instance, in developing a theory of how identity processes which concern self-esteem affect memory capacity, set off by cataloguing the range of examples of instances where memory capacity has been shown to be greater for self-relevant information and where it has been proven to be more accurate for information which is positive about the self. From this you might induce a generalisation: the memory for self-evaluative information will be greater and more accurate if that information is positive than if it is negative. From this generalisation, you might go on to deduce that memory for exam results will be better if they are the individual's own results and especially if they were good results.

In summary, the process of induction allows us to produce theoretical generalisations which are based on evidence about a range of specific instances; one reason for doing research is to collect this evidence. The process of deduction allows us to derive specific predictions from those generalisations, and another reason for doing research is to test these predictions.

2.1.5 Theory testing

For a long time, it was thought that theory testing involves showing that a theory gives rise to accurate predictions about what will happen under a particular set of circumstances. However, this method is not really convincing, since it can never prove that the theory will always be right under every possible set of circumstances, no matter how many times it is tested. Instead, it has been suggested that what we should do in testing a theory is to try to prove it wrong (Popper, 1959). By showing where a theory is wrong, we show which bits need to be replaced and in most cases we also show what needs to be substituted. Research designed to test a theory will be organised so as to show whether a prediction deduced from that theory is wrong. This would **falsify** the theory. If we fail to disprove the prediction, the theory survives to face another test. Research can never prove a theory, it can merely accumulate examples of where the theory has not been disproven. The reason a theory cannot be proven in absolute terms is that it must entail generalisation and the empirical research can only ever sample specific instances of that generality. A good theory is one which survives intact through many sincere and severe attempts at falsification.

One problem with this approach is that theories may survive because they are not strictly falsifiable. Some theories are unfalsifiable because they rest upon a tautology. For instance, some critics of learning theory would argue that one of its fundamental assertions cannot be falsified because the concept of a reinforcer is defined in a tautological way. Thus a reinforcer is defined as anything which acts to increase the frequency of a response. The theory then goes on to state that responses which are reinforced increase in frequency. The circularity in the argument is clear when the theory is reduced to its fundamentals in this way. Such a tautology means that the theory cannot be tested because a key concept cannot be operationally defined independently.

Another problem example is the Freudian theory of ego-defence mechanisms, which cannot be falsified for a different reason. In this case, the theory attempts to explain how the conscious mind protects itself from material which must remain in the unconscious or preconscious mind. Freud explained that such material is handled by a series of ego-defence mechanisms (such as sublimation, displacement, regression, fixation, etc.). What makes this aspect of psychoanalytic theory untestable is the fact Freud offers such an array of defence mechanisms that it is impossible to formulate a test of the operation of one which would not be potentially abrogated by the operation of another. For instance, one might set out to test the notion of sublimation which would say that an unacceptable unconscious impulse driven by the id should be translated into one which is socially acceptable before it could gain access to the conscious mind. The first problem the empiricist would have is in knowing that the impulse existed at all. The second would be that the impulse need not be dealt with by sublimation: it could be treated through reaction formation. This would mean that even if you established when the impulse was occurring and monitored no evidence of sublimation, you would not have falsified the theory because the impulse had been dealt with by another equally valid defence mechanism. Freud basically produced what could be called an **overdetermined** model: a theory which allows multiple determiners of outcomes in such a way that no single determiner can be empirically proven to be irrelevant.

2.1.6   Advanced theory structures

Other problems with falsifiability appear when we consider theories in advanced areas of research. Although induction can give us our initial ideas when we first begin to investigate a fresh research field, delving further into an already established area of research requires new skills entirely. Deductive skills will serve for testing simple theories, but in advanced areas of research the theories have been built into complex structures, with many levels and enormous ranges of applicability.

Some philosophers have divided the components of such theories into two types: the fundamental 'hard core' of assumptions and presuppositions that are basic to the whole enterprise, and a collection of auxiliary **hypotheses** that derive from the hard core and make predictions about what will happen in particular situations (Lakatos, 1970). The whole complex is known as a **research programme**. Everyday research concerns tests of the auxiliary hypotheses, and the more the programme generates new hypotheses, and the more these find empirical support, the more 'progressive' the research programme is said to be.

A single experiment is however not sufficient to falsify a complex theory: instead, only a series of negative results (failed predictions), together with a paucity of new ideas stemming from within the programme, can suggest that the programme is 'degenerative'. Only after a period of such degeneration may the situation be considered so bad that it is necessary to revise or even reject the whole theory.

Of course, in practice it is difficult to judge when this latter course of action is necessary. This is because one of the characteristics of a complex theory structure is that it can be so easily modified by adding or subtracting new components. In fact a fundamental problem with these structures is that just about any negative or unexpected empirical result can be accommodated by adding *ad hoc* hypotheses to the theory. This is known as the **Duhem–Quine thesis**.

For example, the presupposition that children learn by copying others might lead to the hypothesis that children who view violent cartoons on television will subsequently show similar antisocial behaviour. Suppose then that observations of a group of 10-year-olds who regularly watch 'Tom and Jerry' cartoons reveal no difference in some measure of violent social behaviour, when compared with 10-year-olds who do not watch 'Tom and Jerry'. The theorist can then say: ah, well, the antisocial behaviour will only be revealed later, when the child enters adolescence and encounters more testing situations such as gang fights. Or: the cartoons do have the predicted effect but only on children of a particular age, for example below 10 years old, because by age 10 the children have learned the difference between cartoons and reality. Or: only cartoons involving violence between humans will lead to antisocial behaviour. And so on. In each of these cases, the theorist has added an additional hypothesis after the facts of the experiment have become known. These hypotheses act to save the core tenets of the theory from falsification (disproof), by making the theory a little bit more complicated. Although in principle we should not allow such *post hoc* theorizing, it is inevitable, given that life is complicated and a correct theory will therefore need to be complex also, if it is to specify in exact detail what will happen when and under what circumstances. However the indefinitely large number of these possible *ad hoc* hypotheses does make it very difficult to disprove a theory conclusively.

2.1.7 Testing a theory structure

Although psychology as a whole does not yet have a single grand unifying theory, many of the theories you encounter will nevertheless be so complex as to render simple interpretation and methods inadequate. This fact has several consequences for research methodology in those situations.

First, the choice of which observations it is worthwhile to make is informed by the background knowledge that has already been built up in that field. This requires you to know not only what observations have already been accrued, but also which theories and hypotheses are still under development and are worthy of further investigation.

Second, the meaning of any new observations you make depends on the background theory: you have to interpret your empirical findings in the light of the theory. For example criminal behaviour can appear very different, depending whether your underlying theory of behaviour is genetic or behaviourist or whatever: are violent criminals just basically evil, or victims of their hormones, or morally corrupted by a corrupt society around them, or copying the example set by their violent parents, or suffering from brain damage?

You also have to know what the implications of the observation are for the whole structure of the theory: for example is an unexpected observation inconsistent only with the particular hypothesis you are testing, or does it count against the underlying assumptions of the whole theory? In other words, does the failure of prediction arise because the fundamental tenets of the whole approach are wrong, or merely one of the auxiliary hypotheses – and if so which one? How can you tell? Falsifiability becomes problematic when there are so many interacting hypotheses, data bases and collateral assumptions that any one of them might be in error, so throwing your prediction out.

Take for example Bandura's (1997) theory of self-efficacy, which states that people vary in the extent to which they believe that they can achieve whatever they set out to do (i.e. they vary in self-efficacy). People who have high self-efficacy expectancies are healthier, more effective and generally more successful than those with low self-efficacy expectancies. From this theory we may derive a hypothesis that a person who is high in self-efficacy and who becomes ill will be more likely to take medication to cure the condition. However, this behaviour will only take place if the person has a belief that the medication will be efficacious. A method of testing this hypothesis is to monitor whether people with high self-efficacy who become ill are actually more likely to take medicine when advised to do so. Suppose however we find they do not. Is this because Bandura's theory is wrong, because our hypothesis is wrong, because the independent variables (Chapter 4) of self-efficacy and belief in the medication have been indexed inappropriately, or because our method of measuring behaviour was inadequate or inappropriate?

All predictions also have a *ceteris paribus* clause attached: they assume that no extraneous variables or factors will interfere with the observations or invalidate them in any way. It is a frequent occurrence for data not to be as expected, and perhaps the commonest way of explaining the anomaly is to postulate an extra variable that is affecting the outcome. In the above example, for instance, people might not take medicine voluntarily because they have an additional belief, such as that medication in general does not work, or is immoral on religious grounds, or would cause too many side-effects. Controlled experiments that are designed to reveal any such extraneous variable are accordingly often performed on an *ad hoc* basis after the main body of observations have been made.

Third, the empirical methods used are themselves theory relative. It is not possible to divide science into theory and observation, as was claimed by **positivist** philosophers earlier in this century. Although empirical science worships the idol of the 'neutral' observer who is an unbiased recorder of Nature, in practice this standard is an unattainable ideal. Thus we all have some idea of what we might find when we make an observation, and in many cases we know what we want to find. The techniques of 'blind' experimentation have been developed to help cope with exactly this problem (see Chapter 4).

Additionally, the very measuring instruments we use have been developed under particular theoretical backgrounds; their construction depends upon a whole network of theoretical assumptions about the nature of the materials used and the way these interact with the subjects of the experiment. For example, psychoanalytic theory developed the Rorschach inkblot test as an instrument to facilitate behaviour sampling. Responses to this test have been used to make inferences about a person's 'personality' type. However, the results do not make sense under modern personality theory, which instead uses complex statistical analyses of responses to a much wider variety of simpler but more strictly defined tests (e.g. questionnaires). The kinds of personality categories recognised under psychoanalytic theory are not commensurate with those of alternative theories. Another example would be trying to assess memory ability by presenting nonsense syllable pairs on a memory drum to see how many associations can be remembered. This makes sense under behaviourism; but under Gestalt theory, or modern cognitive theory, the number of associations is just not interesting: instead it is the emergent, holistic and semantic organisational properties of memory that are relevant, and the kinds of tests that are considered appropriate are very different (e.g. structuring in free recall). Moreover, under some theories there is no such thing as a 'nonsense syllable': all stimuli are taken to have meaning.

The idea that the interpretation of the data generated always depends upon a network of background theory does not just apply to the 'apparatus' by which we interact with the subject; it is no less true of the quantitative numerical techniques we use to analyse the data (Lamiell, 1995). For example the basic methods of statistics were developed under positivist principles, which are now considered obsolete. They assume that theory-neutral observations can be made by unprejudiced objective impartial observers. The process of using statistics thus creates a delusion of certainty that makes it all too easy for us to fall into the trap of letting the empirical results and the significance levels of the associated analyses tell us what to believe. You should not allow yourself to be dominated by the probability level in deciding what conclusions to draw. Quantitative results have to be interpreted in the light of a whole lot of background knowledge, theory and opinion.

Finally, an established theory will have accreted to itself the results of numerous empirical tests, some of which support the theory and some of which do not. If the supporting evidence comes from many different sources and is of many different types, the convergence on to the same conclusion from all these sources is regarded as making the theory stronger or more valid than if the evidence comes from repeated observations all of the same type (if only because the latter might be caused by some artefact or error in the method). Predicting new observations is also generally regarded as carrying more weight than fitting retrospectively an old body of observations. False predictions of the theory are categorised as **anomalies**, and most advanced theories bear a number of these – although not all the supporters of the theory will necessarily admit their existence. This is because evidence is not always accepted at face value, if only because experiments are complicated and not perfectly reliable. It is only with years of hindsight that empirical outcomes can be classified as valid or invalid, in the light of which theory has turned out to be the correct one (Lakatos, 1970). In the interim, it is conventional to live with the anomalies, provided they are not too many in number or too crucial and convincing.

Periods in which scientists beaver away collecting data under a generally accepted theory have been described as **normal science** (Kuhn, 1962). Complete rejection of such generally accepted theories does not usually occur unless there exists an alternative or competing theory (as well as many anomalies in the old theory). Until such arrives, researchers have no real alternative but to carry on using the old theory, despite all its faults. When another theory exists, it predicts a pattern of results that differs from the pattern predicted by the old theory. If the new pattern fits the actual data better, the new theory is likely to be adopted (allowing also for the other criteria for theory acceptance outlined below). Once such a **revolution** or **paradigm shift** occurs, the meaning of all the empirical results is reinterpreted: what previously appeared to be peculiar if not downright bizarre data may now be seen to be understandable, given the new theory. So previous anomalies are now consonant with expectation, in that they can be deductively related to the covering laws (relational rules) in the new theory. Any observations that remain unexplained become anomalies under the new theory; adoption of the new theory is intended to reduce the number of anomalies as much as possible. Positivist philosophers suggested one could simply count up the number of successful empirical predictions of a theory, subtract the number of anomalies, and pick the theory with the highest score. However this assumed all observations carry equal weight and each is an isolated nugget of fact. Instead, observations fit together to form a pattern, and the links between them should form a logically **coherent** structure.

The psychological process of reinterpreting and reorganising the whole set of empirical data has been likened to the Gestalt-like change in perception and understanding that can occur in individual knowledge following an act of 'insight' (Kuhn, 1962). A novel synthesis of the data into a new pattern is usually presented in the form of a **review article** and brings great credit to its originators. While you will almost always undertake a 'literature review' as part of any research project, in which you summarise the extant findings in the field, if you perceive a novel pattern by which more of the data can be accounted for by some new theory than by any existing theory, your contribution will be highly valued.

We have discussed theory testing as involving primarily empirical testing and observation, but given the existence of complex theory structures and the Duhem–Quine thesis, reliance on simple observational evidence is clearly not enough. The alternative is to use **rationalist** principles alongside empiricist ones: theories can be evaluated according to several non-empirical criteria, such as their parsimony, ease of communication, flexibility, fruitfulness, insightfulness, internal consistency, simplicity, elegance, breadth, and so on. Such principles are used implicitly by all scientists and are actually a central reason for the success of science. No one criterion alone is sufficient: a judicious and balanced combination of arguments should guide one's choice.

Consider **simplicity** for example. A corollary of the Duhem–Quine thesis is that any given set of data can in principle be explained by an infinite number of theories. The thesis states that theories can be elaborated to any degree of complexity we wish. It is therefore possible to take almost any theory and by adding sufficient auxiliary hypotheses modify that theory so it can explain a particular set of data. In such cases, our choice of which theory to adopt is 'underdetermined' by the data, since the data do not point unequivocally to one theory and one theory only. The normal response to this problem is to choose the simplest theory, applying what is called **Occam's razor** (sometimes spelt **Ockham's** razor), which states that we should not multiply hypotheses needlessly. A problem with simplicity is that it assumes that the complexity of a theory can be measured in some objective way so that different theories can be compared. However, advanced theory structures differ so much qualitatively as well as in their quantitative 'complexity' that comparison by any single common yardstick may in practice be impossible. Thus theories are often **incommensurable** because their underlying purposes and assumptions are different; they have different criteria for their own success, since their aims and intended context of application are very different. Theory comparison and selection may then appear a matter of subjective judgement.

2.1.8   The meaning of theories

The notion that a theory can be successful for a period of time, and can then be replaced by a totally different and incommensurable theory that is even more successful, leads to the question of why the first theory should have been successful at all, given that it was wrong. Research into scientific practice itself has shown that science is not so different from other spheres of life: it is a social activity, and the choice of which theory to believe, which data to accept as correct, which professor or department to rely on, is as much a matter of attitude and opinion formation as is any other psychological belief. Personal and social factors cannot be excluded from science. At its most extreme, this school of opinion (known as the **strong programme in the sociology of knowledge**) denies that any theory describes an objective reality: it is just a matter of socially reached consensus among the scientific community as to what to believe (**relativism**).

Other researchers treat theories as useful ways of predicting what will happen under given circumstances, but without making any claim one way or the other as to whether the theories describe an actual 'reality' (this attitude is variously called pragmatism, operationalism or instrumentalism). This issue is still the subject of intense debate in the philosophy of science. Moderating voices accept the (empirically observed) fact that social factors do operate in science, but that objective empirical data about the world play their part too: the social factors are not the sole determinants of theory acceptance or rejection. Thus although interpersonal disputes play a crucial part at the cutting edge of research, where the truth is still uncertain, in the long run scientists are kept on the right path by some kind of objective reality operating via the empirical observations (e.g. Oldroyd, 1986; Hull, 1988; Kitcher, 1993; Klee, 1997).

The Duhem–Quine thesis and the strong programme in the sociology of knowledge have led some people to conclude that relativism is the norm. Thus although everybody starts out believing that there is an absolute truth about how the world is, and there is a single correct answer to every problem, which it is science's job to find, we soon realise that life is more complicated, that people in positions of authority can hold differing opinions (often diametrically opposed) and that no one can be 100% sure about anything. Most research students reach a point when they realise that observations are not pure nuggets of truth, and that they all depend upon a network of assumptions (about the nature of the measuring instrument, the theoretical and observational presuppositions from which the hypotheses were derived, and so on, as explained above). At this point it is important not to despair; life goes on and science does work. You have to realise that all beliefs have pros and cons, that whatever theory you adopt will have some evidence and arguments in favour of it and some against. You have to decide which theory to believe in, otherwise you cannot act. You will select what is in your opinion the best theory, given the currently available theories and evidence. However, your choice of theory should not be adhered to as a dogma that cannot be contradicted. You must adopt a flexible attitude: you must realise that your choice is provisional, and you must always be ready to change your belief in the light of new evidence and arguments.

Nowadays, there is increasing appreciation of the complexity of psychological systems and processes. Psychologists and biologists look for particular *causal* mechanisms, rather than for universal covering laws (e.g. Bechtel and Richardson, 1993). This avoids the problems of the grand theory structures outlined above. The idea is still to explain the phenomena that are observed, but to give understanding of how and why they arise, in terms of what causes them, not which universal law of nature they are deductively in accordance with. The idea of simple universal laws arose within seventeenth century physics; more recently however we have come to realise that biological systems are too complex to analyse using the same methods, and entirely different principles are called for. Functional explanations as well as mechanistic ones (section 2.1.3) must be given together. People and animals evolved and survived within a chaotically changing range of environments that have shaped and altered us over the aeons in ways that no simple law will describe. Our aims as psychologists therefore have to be to explain the particulars of mental life and behaviour we encounter in terms of the individual people we are observing, their constitutions and their immediate and past circumstances. To do so we have to use multiple methods, both rationalist and empiricist in nature. It is to this end that many of the new methods described in the following chapters of this book are directed.

2.2   MATCHING METHODOLOGIES TO THEORY

Different types of theory have to be tested using different types of research method. The nature of the theory limits the range of research methods which can be meaningfully used to test it. For example, a theory explaining variation in visual acuity is likely to need to measure acuity using some psychophysical technique (see Chapter 14). However, the extent of these limitations should not be overestimated. Most psychological theories can be tested using more than one method. In fact, it is advisable to try to test a theory using a variety of methods in order to prove that it is no artefact of the method which results in the theory being supported.

A piece of research can differ along a series of four independent dimensions:

1   type of data elicited
2   technique of data elicitation
3   type of design for monitoring change
4   treatment of data as qualitative or quantitative.

2.2.1   Type of data elicited

In psychological research the data can vary in origin: they can be intra-personal (e.g. genotypic information, cognitions, emotions, etc.); or inter-individual (e.g. friendship networks, communication patterns, etc.); or societal (e.g. institutional hierarchies, ideological systems, etc.).

2.2.2   Technique of data elicitation

Data can be elicited directly or indirectly from a target. Direct elicitation methods would include any stimulus to self-report (e.g. interviewing, self-completion questionnaires, etc.) or self-revelation through behaviour (e.g. role-play, performance on tasks, etc.). Indirect elicitation methods would include techniques that rely upon the researcher observing behaviour (e.g. participant observation) or using informants about the target's behaviour, thought or feelings (e.g. archival records, witnesses, etc.).

Data elicitation can vary in terms of the amount of control exerted by the researcher upon a target. This control can be manifest in restrictions imposed upon the freedom of the target to give information (e.g. forced-choice options rather than open-ended responses to questions). It can be evident in the extent to which the target is manipulated (e.g. in experiments through the creation of artificial contexts or in surveys through the use of cover stories designed to mislead the target about the purpose of the study).

2.2.3   Type of design for monitoring change

A central task for psychological theories is to explain change. Researchers whose objective is to identify and explain change have a choice of three main classes of design for data collection: longitudinal, cross-sectional or sequential. A **longitudinal design** involves data being collected from the same sample of individuals on at least two occasions. The interval between data collections and the number of data collections vary greatly: the research can be contained in a few days or spread over several decades. A longitudinal design allows researchers to establish changes in individuals over time as the sample ages or experiences some identifiable alteration in experience. In experimental parlance, a longitudinal design might be called a repeated measures design (see Chapter 4). A **cross-sectional** design involves eliciting information at a single time from people in a number of different conditions that are expected to be significant to the change. Often this means studying people in different age cohorts because, particularly in theories of developmental psychology, age is deemed to be a major determinant of change. The term 'age cohort' refers to the total population of individuals born at approximately the same time, which is usually taken to mean in the same calendar year. The cross-sectional design permits age-related changes to be gauged.

A **sequential** design will choose samples from a particular condition (e.g. a specific age cohort) but will study them at different times. The periodicity in sequential data gathering varies across studies. A simple sequential design might involve sampling the 21-year-old cohort of 1989, the 21-year-old cohort of 1979, and the 21-year-old cohort of 1969. This type of design would be targeted at revealing whether changes in a particular age group are affected by factors which are associated with their specific socio-historical era.

When studying patterns of change that are age-related there are always three factors which could possibly explain observed relationships: development tied to the ageing of the individual; characteristics associated with the particular age cohorts studied; and impact of the specific time of measurement. **Time of measurement** is the term suggested by Schaie (1965) to refer to the set of pressures upon the individual generated by the socio-environmental context at the point data are collected. The difficulty facing researchers interested in explained age-related changes lies in establishing which of these three factors is the source of change. The strategy adopted by most researchers is to keep one of the factors constant. For instance, the longitudinal design keeps the cohort constant. The cross-sectional design keeps the time of measurement constant. The sequential design keeps the chronological age constant. Of course, this means that explanation of any observed age-related trend remains problematic since these designs always leave two of the three explanatory factors free to vary simultaneously. Irrespective of which of these three designs is adopted, two explanatory factors will be confounded. This represents the major methodological drawback in using such relatively simple designs.

There is a secondary problem. By holding one factor constant, the design obviously rules out the possibility of exploring the effects of that factor in interaction with the others. Yet, in virtually all complex systems of change, one would expect interaction effects between developmental, cohort and time of measurement factors. The solution to this fundamental methodological problem has been to integrate the three design types in what is known as a **longitudinal cohort sequential** design. This combines the longitudinal follow-up of a series of cohorts first sampled simultaneously as in a cross-sectional study with the sequential addition of new cohorts of the same ages to the study at each subsequent data collection point.

Even if a researcher believes the psychological construct under investigation is not influenced by the chronological maturation of the individual and not affected by the socio-historical context of the data collection, the burden of proof rests upon that researcher to show that they are not important. It used to be thought that only a developmental psychologist really needed to consider whether to use a cohort sequential longitudinal design. Now, particularly as lifespan development becomes an accepted stipulative adjunct to most theories of psychological functioning, all researchers need to understand the implications of these different types of design.

2.2.4   Treatment of data as qualitative or quantitative

Research methods can be differentiated according to whether data are submitted to a qualitative or quantitative treatment. A **qualitative treatment** describes what processes are occurring and details differences in the character of these processes over time. A **quantitative treatment** states what the processes are, how often they occur, and what differences in their magnitude can be measured over time.

It is important to reiterate that these four dimensions on which a piece of research can be described are independent of each other. Data type, elicitation technique, the design for monitoring change, and the qualitative or quantitative treatment of the data can be put together in many varieties. For instance, it is possible to use a qualitative treatment of data acquired as part of an experiment conducted in a longitudinal study.

A researcher, in structuring a study along these four dimensions, will have to make hard decisions. The decisions will in part be determined by whether theory building is at an inductive or deductive phase. A broader range of data types, elicitation techniques with lower control, cross-sectional designs, and qualitative treatment of data may be most appropriate in the early inductive phase. The deductive phase leading to testable predictions is likely to be linked to the narrowing of data types, direct and controlled data elicitation, a mixture of change monitoring designs, and the quantitative treatment of data. Sadly the decision is also too often influenced by preconceptions, prejudices and fears. Researchers get trapped into one methodological approach (i.e. a package of one type of data, one elicitation technique, one design, and one data treatment). Once a routine sets in this can be easier than getting to know (or even remembering) how to do the other things. Also, of course, often researchers acquire their reputation on the basis of using a specific sort of methodology. To relinquish it is tantamount to abandoning their claim to fame. The solution may lie in practising eclecticism of methodology from an early stage in a research career.

Such eclecticism is fostered by forcing yourself, when faced with the task of constructing any study to test a hypothesis deduced from your theory, to provide at least two realistic alternative methodologies. Then weigh the pros and cons of each. Work out the differences between what they will tell you. In most cases, even minor variations of methodology will substantially affect what you can conclude. Ultimately, researchers have to choose between alternative feasible methodologies in the full knowledge of what they might lose by passing over those which they reject. The chapters in this book make an attempt to help you to see what are the strengths and weaknesses of various techniques, designs and data treatments.

2.3   INTEGRATING FINDINGS FROM DIFFERENT METHODOLOGIES

If you understand different methodologies and use them in concert, there comes a point when you must ask yourself: how do I put the findings from one methodology together with those from another? The easy answer focuses upon the theory. Assuming that each methodology is used to test one or more hypotheses derived from the theory, as long as the various methodologies yield conclusions which are compatible with the theory there is no problem. They are merely vehicles for theory testing; they may travel by different routes but they get to the same destination ultimately.

The problems arise when different methodologies produce contradictory or inconsistent conclusions about the hypothesis tested. In the baldest terms, one may support the hypothesis, whereas another may generate evidence which indicates that it is incorrect. The first step in this situation is to check that the methodologies were both executed properly. If they were, you should, if possible, collect further data using the same methodologies. If the inconsistent result is repeated, it is necessary to examine whether there is some identifiable attribute differentiating between the methodologies which could explain their inconsistent results. If such an attribute can be identified, it should be incorporated into another study in a controlled way so that its effect can be studied systematically. This may support the introduction of some caveat into the original hypothesis. If no such attribute can be identified, the hypothesis should be retested using a series of completely different methodologies. If these yield contradictory evidence, it is reasonably certain that the hypothesis will need to be reformulated. The combination of evidence from the various methodologies should show where its limitations lie and point to an appropriate revision.

Obviously, all this procedure of iterative data collection takes time and resources. The researcher will have to decide whether this aspect of the theory is sufficiently important to merit such effort. If the procedure is not followed, it is essential that the original finding which refuted the hypothesis is treated seriously. The temptation to dismiss the finding in such a situation must be resisted. There are many siren voices which will offer ways of discounting the finding in terms of the relative merits of the methodologies. Unless you clearly stated on an *a priori* basis that one methodology would be given priority in the event of inconsistencies in the findings, the methodologies must be treated retrospectively as having equivalent standing.

When there are inconsistent results, an integrated approach to the use of several methodologies may be inconvenient but it also has great advantages. Every methodology has its limitations. The nature of these limitations differs. Using a series of methodologies allows you to compensate for the weaknesses of one methodology in a domain by supplementing or complementing it with another methodology which is stronger in that domain. The development of a coherent strategy for integrating methodologies, designed to test clearly defined hypotheses comprehensively, is the basic foundation for researching psychological processes.

2.4 FURTHER READING

The following are good general discussions of approaches to researching psychological processes: Kelly (1955) *The Psychology of Personal Constructs*, Vols 1 and 2; Breakwell (1994) 'The echo of power: an integrative framework for social psychological theorising', which appeared in *The Psychologist*; and Schaie's (1965) 'A general model for the study of developmental problems', which appeared in the *Psychological Bulletin*. Excellent introductions to the general problems of scientific method are given by Chalmers (1999) *What Is This Thing Called Science?* and Papineau (1996) 'Philosophy of science' in *The Blackwell Companion to Philosophy*. The application of these methods to psychology is most directly discussed by Bechtel (1988) in his *Philosophy of Science: An Overview for Cognitive Science*.

3

Practical and Ethical Issues in Planning Research

Martyn Barrett

Contents

3.1   INTRODUCTION

This chapter is concerned with the practical and ethical issues which need to be considered when planning psychological research systematically. There are many different issues which need to be taken into account if a piece of psychological research is to achieve its intended goal, and each of these issues requires careful decisions to be made during the course of the planning process. Of necessity, this chapter will have to discuss these issues and decisions in a particular sequence. However, it is important to bear in mind that these decisions are not independent of one another, and that making one decision can have important implications for other decisions (for example, choosing to use a particular statistical procedure may have implications for the minimum size of sample which ought to be used, or an ethical decision concerning the invasion of privacy might lead one to choose interviewing rather than naturalistic observation for collecting data). This complex interdependence means that the process of planning psychological research does not consist of a simple linear sequence of decisions. Instead, as we seek operational definitions of the theoretical concepts that are contained in the hypotheses which we wish to test by means of our research, we are of necessity having to think simultaneously about possible ways of measuring these concepts in particular types of settings with various types of subjects, and thus also have to think about whether we have access to those subjects and whether it is feasible to collect such data on an appropriate timescale with the resources which are available to us in a way that can be analysed by the types of statistics which are pertinent to testing the hypotheses from which we started out. This complex interdependence of the various decisions which together comprise the planning process should be borne in mind throughout this chapter.

To a certain extent, many of the issues which will be discussed in this chapter might appear to be a matter of simple common sense. However, if this is the case, it is surprising how often such common sense fails researchers, particularly those early in their careers. There are all sorts of pitfalls which can bedevil psychological research and can prevent that research from achieving its intended goals. The hope is that this chapter will at least help to sensitise the beginning researcher to some of the major pitfalls.

3.2   FORMULATING RESEARCH QUESTIONS

3.2.1   Selecting a topic to study

When planning a piece of psychological research, there is of course one particular step which needs to be taken first, and that is to identify and select a topic to study. There are all sorts of reasons why psychologists choose to study particular topics. They might do so because of a personal interest in the topic or because they make a value judgement about the importance of that topic. Or a topic may be chosen for a theoretical reason, perhaps because the researcher has spotted an assumption or a prediction made by a particular theory which has never been tested empirically. Alternatively, the researcher may have a concern with a particular social problem and wants to contribute towards the resolution of that problem, or wishes to help improve the quality of life for a particular group of individuals. All of these reasons are equally valid. Essentially, they all boil down to an assessment that the topic which has been chosen is either interesting, important or useful.

However, from a practical point of view, it is crucial to also take into account a further criterion when selecting a particular topic to investigate: is it realistic and feasible to conduct research into this topic, given the practical and ethical restrictions on what the researcher is able to do? In order to derive an answer to this question, though, it is essential to move on from the general topic to the formulation of the specific questions concerning that topic which will be addressed by means of the research, so that the researcher can work out precisely what is required in practice in order to answer those questions, and can then work out whether or not these requirements can be met.

3.2.2   The need to formulate specific research questions

To take an example, the researcher might believe that aggression in children is an important topic to study. However, selecting this general topic for research is not sufficient to enable us to say whether the intended research is or is not feasible. Firstly, it is necessary to state exactly what it is that the researcher wants to find out about this topic. For example, does the researcher want to discover how aggressive behaviour in children varies as a function of age, or the factors which cause children to be aggressive to others, or the responses which children's aggressive behaviour elicits from other people, or what? Notice that in all cases, if the researcher's goal is to discover something about the topic which has been selected, then it is always possible to state that research goal in the form of a question. How does children's aggressive behaviour vary as a function of age? What are the factors which cause children to be aggressive to others? What are the responses which children's aggressive behaviour elicits from other people? If the intended goal of the research cannot be formulated as an explicit question, or as a series of such questions, then that research does not have a coherent goal.

Let us pursue our hypothetical example a little further. Let us assume that the researcher decides that the question to be addressed by means of the research is the relatively mundane one of: how does children's aggressive behaviour vary as a function of age? Notice that it is clearly impossible for any researcher to study children's aggressive behaviour in all contexts at all ages. Consequently, in order to assess the feasibility of the research, the researcher now needs to qualify the research question further by stipulating the appropriate contexts which are of interest. For example: how does children's aggressive behaviour in the school playground/in the home/in the streets/etc. vary as a function of age? The feasibility of the study can now begin to be assessed against the criterion of whether the researcher can obtain access to children in the contexts which are of interest. The researcher also needs to specify the ages of the children who would be studied. Would the study cover children of all ages (is this feasible?) or just children of particular ages (if so, of what ages, and does the researcher have access to children of those ages?)? In addition, notice that the term 'aggressive behaviour' must also be defined in order to assess the feasibility of the research. For example, does 'aggressive behaviour' include inflicting psychological injury on others, as well as physical injury? If so, is it feasible to assess whether or not psychological injury has been inflicted? Also, must aggressive acts be intentional? If so, is it feasible to assess intentionality in children of the ages which would be studied?

Ethical considerations must also play a role in assessing the feasibility of studying this topic. For example, most people today would consider it unethical for a psychologist to deliberately elicit aggressive behaviour from children so that the characteristics of that behaviour can be studied. This would not be feasible on ethical rather than practical grounds. However, in the past, different ethical standards have applied. For example, Bandura's classic studies into aggressive behaviour in children, which were conducted in the late 1950s and early 1960s, entailed the provision of role models of aggressive behaviour for children to imitate (see Bandura and Walters, 1963). Thus, the ethical considerations which are used to evaluate the feasibility of a piece of research inevitably change over time, and past practices should not be used as an automatic guide to what is ethically acceptable today. It should be clear from the example given here that, in order to decide whether or not a particular topic which has been selected for investigation passes the criterion of feasibility, it is essential to formulate not just research questions, but highly specific research questions.

However, there is also an additional reason why it is necessary to formulate specific research questions at the outset of the planning process. This is so that the researcher can ensure, during the course of planning, that the data which are collected will actually address the research questions which are of interest. There is very little point in jumping directly from the identification of a general topic to the collection of data, and then trying to articulate specific questions about that general topic afterwards. Such a procedure is extremely unlikely to result in any of the data which are collected being appropriate for addressing the particular questions which the researcher will really want to ask about that topic. Instead, in order to ensure that the data which are collected are relevant to answering the specific questions which are of interest to the researcher, it is vital to use the specific research questions themselves to inform the design of the research from the outset, so that the researcher can be certain that the data which are collected will actually answer those questions.

3.2.3 Strategies to adopt when formulating specific research questions

When thinking about specific research questions, several strategies may be used to ensure that the questions which are formulated are suitable for the further planning purposes for which they are required. First of all, it is always helpful to formally articulate research questions in words. If you cannot articulate these questions in words, they are unlikely to lead to any productive research. Secondly, the articulated questions should contain specifications of the particular situations or conditions in which the phenomena of interest would be studied, as well as specifications of the precise type of subjects who would be used in the research.

Thirdly, it is important to articulate these questions in such a way that they can be addressed by means of a specified type of empirical evidence. This is achieved by providing **operational definitions** of the concepts which are included in the research question. An operational definition of a concept is a statement of the activities or operations which are needed to measure that concept in practice (or, in the case of an independent variable, a statement of the activities or operations which are needed to manipulate that variable in practice). For example, if the research question is 'How does children's aggressive behaviour vary as a function of age?', we obviously need an operational definition of the concept of 'aggressive behaviour', that is, a statement of how it would be measured in practice. For example, it might be defined operationally as 'any behaviour which two or more independent adult observers classify as having aggressive intent' or as 'any behaviour which, when a video recording of it is played back to the child and the child is questioned about it, the child admits was intended to hurt another person'. Similarly, if a research question contains references to subjects' personalities or intelligence, the concepts of 'personality' and 'intelligence' could be operationally defined as the measures which are obtained by using a particular personality test (such as the EPQ) or intelligence test (such as the WISC-R), respectively.

A fourth point to bear in mind when formulating specific research questions is that all such questions must be empirically testable. For example, 'Do different people have the same subjective experience of the colour red?', 'Does the human foetus have a conscious mind?', and 'If a child believes in God, is that a true or a false belief?' are all empirically untestable questions. These questions are untestable because at least one of the concepts which each question contains cannot be given a satisfactory operational definition (the concepts 'subjective experience', 'conscious mind of a foetus' and 'God', respectively). Thus, the testability of research questions is very closely linked to whether or not it is possible to provide adequate operational definitions of their constituent concepts.

3.2.4   Choice of possible research methods

Having identified the specific research questions, and having established adequate operational definitions of the concepts, the researcher is then in a position to be able to select possible research designs and methods of data collection which could be used to obtain the data to address these questions. For example, let us suppose that our hypothetical researcher has decided to investigate aggression in children by trying to answer the specific research question 'Do 7-year-old children produce more aggressive acts than 5-year-old children in the school playground?', and has operationally defined 'aggressive acts' as 'any act which two or more independent adult observers classify as having aggressive intent'. In that case, the researcher is now in a position to choose either a cross-sectional or a longitudinal research design for studying the children at the two different ages, and is able to choose naturalistic observation as an appropriate method for collecting the data.

The specific considerations which should motivate the choice of any particular research design and any particular method of data collection at this point in the planning process are beyond the scope of the present chapter. The reader is therefore referred to the contents of the other chapters in this book in order to find out how particular research questions and particular operational definitions should feed into the decision to use or not to use any particular research design or method.

For present purposes, however, let us assume that the bridge has now been made from the specific research question to the possible research designs and possible methods of data collection.

3.2.5   The literature review

So far in this chapter, no mention has been made of the role which the literature review ought to play in planning a piece of psychological research. Obviously, though, a thorough review of the literature is an essential component of planning research into any topic. The literature contains accounts of all the existing psychological theories and concepts which can be used to generate or to structure research ideas; of the findings which have been obtained by previous researchers and which can therefore be either assumed and built upon, or questioned, when planning further research into that topic; of the arguments and lines of thinking which have proved profitable to previous researchers and which may therefore prove profitable to pursue further; and of the blind alleys down which previous researchers have gone and which therefore ought to be avoided.

Furthermore, the existing literature is an enormously rich repository which contains a massive amount of information about the topics which have been investigated in the past, about the specific research questions which have been asked by previous researchers, about the operational definitions which have been adopted in previous studies, and about the research designs and methods which have been used by previous researchers. Thus, the existing literature can be used as a invaluable source from which to mine all sorts of research topics, research questions, operational definitions, research designs and methods, all of which can be used to inform the process of planning research.

3.2.6   Accessing the relevant literature

There are two principal ways in which to access the literature relevant to any given topic. The first is to use a standard abstracting source. The most useful such source for the research psychologist is *Psychological Abstracts*. This contains the abstracts of the articles which appear in virtually all of the journals which publish psychological research. Nowadays, most psychologists access *Psychological Abstracts* in a computerised form which is called PsycLit. This contains the abstracts of psychology journal articles on a CD-ROM, which can

matically by typing into the computer the key words which
in which you are interested. The system then displays the
articles which have been located, and by reading these
ly possible to work out whether or not any given article is of
to merit reading in full (if your own library does not
journal in which an article appeared, it may be possible for
obtain it for you through their inter-library loans system).

An alternative way of searching the literature is to begin from the reference lists of the central textbooks that have been written on the topic in which you are interested. It is often useful to begin by picking out from these reference lists the most recent major review articles which have been written on the topic in which you are interested, as well as any recent empirical articles which seem to be particularly important. The reference lists of both types of articles can then be used to locate other relevant empirical articles, and the reference lists of these empirical articles can be used to locate further empirical articles. If you use this method of accessing the literature, however, you should bear in mind that there is usually, at the very least, a two-year lag between articles being published in journals and those articles being picked up by and referred to in textbooks. Consequently, this method of searching the literature must always be accompanied by a systematic search through the most recent issues of all the major journals which publish articles on the topic in which you are interested, to ensure that you pick up on any article which has not yet penetrated the textbooks.

Whichever method is used to locate the relevant literature, that literature should then be used to inform the entire planning process, from the selection of an appropriate topic, through the formulation of specific research questions and operational definitions, to the identification of the possible research designs and methods which could be used to address those research questions.

3.3 ASSESSING THE PRACTICAL FEASIBILITY OF THE RESEARCH

Having reached this point, the research is now sufficiently well articulated to enable the researcher to assess the practical feasibility of conducting the research. This assessment may well lead the researcher to reject some possible designs or methods, or even to revise some of the operational definitions or research questions, if these now prove not to be feasible on purely practical grounds. It is therefore essential that, at this point, the researcher systematically thinks through all of the following issues.

3.3.1 Subjects required for the research

First of all, the researcher must think through the issue of subject availability. What type of subjects, with what particular characteristics, will the research require? Will these subjects need to be in any particular location, situation or context for the research to take place? How many subjects are needed? In answering this last question, account should be taken of the power of the statistical methods which are to be used to analyse the data, and power tables, which are sometimes included at the back of statistics textbooks, should be consulted in order to help determine an appropriate sample size (see Chapter 25). Finally, are such subjects in this number available to the researcher?

If the answers to all of these initial questions are satisfactory, further questions then need to be asked. Are the subjects themselves willing to participate in the research? If payment is required in order to entice the subjects into participation, is the necessary budget available?

In thinking about this issue of subject availability, there are many factors which need to be borne in mind. For example, there are the problems of uncontrolled **subject attrition** (i.e. subjects dropping out of the study while it is in progress) and **subject non-compliance** (i.e. subjects not complying with the research procedure). Subject attrition and non-compliance are not always a consequence of subjects being bloody-minded. In large scale longitudinal studies, for example, which take place over a period of many years, it is perhaps inevitable that at least some subjects in the study will move home, fall ill, or even die during the course of the study. Of course, if there are high levels of subject attrition or non-compliance, this leads to the sample of subjects becoming systematically biased, either for lack of mobility, or for staying power, or for willingness to cooperate with the research procedure. Furthermore, it is always possible that such characteristics are related in a systematic manner to the psychological phenomena which are being studied. The problem of non-compliance can be particularly serious in research which involves questionnaires about a sensitive topic being mailed to subjects for completion and return. Such questionnaires may only have a return rate somewhere in the region of 10–40%. This rate of self-selection from a sample which was originally constructed on systematic principles represents a very serious biasing of the sample which will inevitably affect the generalisability of the findings which are obtained.

There are, however, some general precautions which can be taken by the researcher concerning subject attrition and non-compliance. Firstly, the sample which is planned should always be large enough to allow for possible attrition and non-compliance. Secondly, when recruiting subjects, the researcher should always try to make participation in the study sound as interesting as possible; it is important to emphasise any parts of the study that might be especially interesting to subjects themselves. Avoid saying that participating in the study is a way of 'doing your bit for science'; this is not a formula which wins over hesitant subjects. Thirdly, you should assure potential subjects of complete confidentiality and anonymity of their results where necessary. Fourthly, you can offer to inform the subjects of the eventual outcome of the research; this may be done by producing a simple written summary of the research findings at the end of the study in jargon-free language, which can be sent to the subjects who participated in the research.

In some cases, the recruitment of subjects for the study can depend upon certain key individuals, or 'gatekeepers', who have to give their permission and co-operation in order for the subjects who are the target of the research to be used. Perhaps the two most common types of gatekeepers are the headteachers of schools, who control access to the children in their schools, and doctors, who can provide access to patients. Obviously, the feasibility of the research will then depend upon winning over the co-operation of these gatekeepers. Gatekeepers can have both disadvantages and advantages. For example, it may be difficult to win a headteacher over to the idea of a study of playground aggression if that headteacher maintains that no aggressive behaviour ever occurs in the playground of his or her school. However, once a headteacher has been won over, the researcher will then have open access to the very large numbers of children who attend that school (and will not have to recruit each and every subject individually).

Because the feasibility of such studies depends crucially upon the co-operation of the gatekeeper, it is always extremely important to ensure that gatekeepers are treated with courtesy. It is important that gatekeepers are only approached after the researcher has fully thought through all the precise details of what needs to be done in the study, so that the researcher is able to answer any questions concerning the study which may arise when discussing the research with the gatekeeper. This presents a professional image which helps to inspire the gatekeeper's confidence in the researcher. Again, during such discussions, the purpose of the study should be made to sound interesting, and the researcher can offer to send the gatekeeper a written summary of the findings of the research when the study has been completed.

One problem which can be unintentionally caused by gatekeepers is that they take it upon themselves to select which particular subjects are used in the research. For example, if the research requires schoolchildren to be tested individually outside their classroom, teachers may select only their brightest children to send to the researcher, hoping to impress the researcher with their abilities. However, such a process obviously results in a biased sample being used for the research. Thus, it is always sensible for the researcher to plan a systematic method for selecting which particular subjects should participate in the research (e.g. picking every other child from the class register irrespective of their ability), and to agree this plan with the gatekeeper at the outset.

3.3.2 Equipment and materials required for the research

In assessing the practical feasibility of the research, the researcher must also consider very carefully all the equipment and materials which are needed for the study to take place. If any special materials or equipment are needed, does the researcher already have them or not? If not, and if they have to be specially purchased or constructed, are the necessary funds available for these purposes? If the funds are not available, could the materials or equipment be borrowed from or used at another institution or department of psychology? If materials have to be specially designed, or if equipment has to be specially constructed, can this be done on an appropriate timescale? Can such purpose-built equipment be properly tested to eliminate any possible teething and technical problems which it might have so that it will be fully functional by the time that it is needed?

Finally, under this heading, the researcher should consider whether he or she needs time to learn how to use the relevant materials and/or equipment. For example, it can take a lot of time for a novice to learn how to customise computer software (e.g. for presenting visual stimuli to subjects, or for recording subjects' reaction times) or to learn how to administer and score a standardised psychometric test. If time is required for mastering the materials or the equipment, it is important that the timetable for the research is drawn up in such a way that it allows an adequate amount of time for these purposes.

3.3.3 Consumable items required for the research

The researcher also needs to think through, at the planning stage, all the consumable items which will be needed for the research (i.e. items which will be completely used up during the course of conducting the research). It is important that all consumables are properly costed to ensure that the funds which are required in order to conduct the research do not exceed the total budget available for the research. For example, any photocopying (of, for example, interview schedules or questionnaires), postage (for mailing out postal questionnaires), video or audio recording tapes, computer disks, computer printing, etc. should all be properly costed out in order to ascertain whether the budget is sufficient for conducting the research.

3.3.4 Other costs which may be incurred by the research

Finally, there may be other costs involved in conducting the research. For example, will the researcher be able to conduct all the work on his or her own? If it is necessary for the researcher to have assistance from others in conducting the research, and if the people who provide this assistance need to be paid for their time, are the funds available to pay these people at the appropriate rate? For example, if the researcher needs help to collect the data (e.g. to help interview subjects, to make independent observations of subjects, or to act as stooges in an experiment), or if assistance is needed in coding the data (e.g. for running checks on the reliability of the coding), it may be necessary to pay the people who provide this help. If so, the total number of hours of assistance which will be needed must be properly costed in advance, in order to see whether the research can be conducted within the budget which is available.

Also, if the researcher and/or any person assisting them needs to travel from their normal place of work to another location in order to test subjects (e.g. to a school or to a hospital), this will require funds to cover the costs of the travel and of any subsistence which might be needed by the researchers (such as food or overnight accommodation). Once again, the costs which are involved need to be worked out in advance, taking into account the location of the subjects, the size of the sample, and the length of time that it will take to collect the data from each subject. Once again, the research will only be feasible if the total budget which is available to the researcher is able to cover these costs.

3.3.5 Pilot work

Let us assume that the researcher has run through all the preceding checks on subject availability and access, the availability of materials and equipment, and the availability of the funds which are needed to cover consumable costs, research assistance costs, and travel and subsistence costs. If all of these considerations indicate that the research is feasible, it is often extremely useful to then conduct pilot work, in order to try out the methods, materials, equipment, etc. in advance of running the full-scale study itself.

Such pilot work should be conducted using a smaller group of subjects who have similar characteristics to those of the subjects who will be used in the main study itself. Pilot work can be used to test out the various operational definitions and research methods which are still under active consideration, and to see if some of these methods and definitions are more useful or are simpler to administer than others. Pilot work can also be used to establish whether subjects understand instructions, to ascertain how much time it takes to test each subject, to obtain practice in administering all the tasks and in making all the necessary measurements (ideally, the researcher should be trained to saturation before the main study commences, so that any training effects do not contaminate the main study itself), to find out whether tasks are sufficiently sensitive to discriminate amongst subjects, to examine whether the measures which are being made have stable measurement properties (i.e. are reliable), etc.

It is often the case that, if a variety of different possible research methods and operational definitions have still been under active consideration up to this point in the planning process, the pilot work helps to sort out the more useful and reliable methods and definitions, thereby facilitating the final selection by the researcher of those particular methods and definitions which will be used in the main study itself.

3.3.6 Identifying the statistical analyses needed and rechecking the sample size

Once the research design, operational definitions, and methods of data collection have been selected for use in the study, it is then essential for the researcher to identify in advance the types of data which will be collected, and the types of statistical analyses which will be performed on those data in order to answer appropriately the research questions which have been posed. The choice of statistical analyses will be determined by the research design, by the type of data which will be collected, and by the research questions which are being asked (see Chapters 25 and 26). Having selected appropriate methods of analysing the data, it is then necessary, at the planning stage, to check back to the sample size which is being planned, and to the availability of the subjects who are required for the study. It is vital to do this, in order to ensure that sufficient data will be collected from a large enough sample to enable the proposed statistical analyses to detect the relationships and effects which are being sought, assuming they are present in the data.

3.3.7 Formulating a timetable

Another aspect of planning research systematically is to formulate an explicit timetable for the research. This timetable needs to contain all the intermediate staging posts, and their deadlines, which will punctuate the research (e.g. when the data collection will begin and end, when data coding will begin and end, when the statistical analyses will be conducted, when the writing-up of the research will take place, etc.). In producing this timetable, it is essential to adopt a realistic stance, and to allow sufficient time for all the component activities which are involved, including any final piloting that may be required, the time that may be required for training additional researchers, the time needed for recruiting subjects, the time needed for testing all subjects or for collecting all data (Does this involve testing all subjects simultaneously, or in sequence? Will you have to wait for subjects to make their returns of a mailed questionnaire through the post? Is it necessary to build in time for the replacement of subjects who fail to attend for testing or fail to reply? etc.), the time which is needed for debriefing subjects, transcribing any data from audio or video recordings, coding the data, running reliability checks upon the data coding, entering the data into the computer, analysing the data, interpreting the results of the analyses, and writing the report.

Having produced this explicit timetable which contains a realistic estimate of the amounts of time needed for all the component activities, it is then necessary to go back yet again and recheck the availability of subjects, equipment and all other resources which will be used for the research. In particular, it is essential to check that subjects, equipment and resources will be available at the times which are required according to the timetable that has been worked out. After all, if the subjects, for example, are not available for testing when the timetable stipulates (e.g. if schoolchildren are required for testing during a school's summer vacation), then, quite simply, it will not be feasible to conduct the research on that timetable. If there are any problems concerning subject, equipment or resource availability, then it is necessary for the researcher to revise either the timetable or the content or structure of the study itself so that it fits into a feasible timetable.

3.3.8 Conclusions

Assessing the practical feasibility of a piece of research is clearly a complex activity. Not only are there many different aspects of the research that need very careful checking in order to ensure that the research is feasible in practice; in addition, if the research proves unfeasible on just one count, it may be necessary to revise the entire study. Nevertheless, having planned a piece of research through to this level of detail, if it turns out not to be feasible to run the study as planned, it is always worth considering the possible modifications which could be made to it before abandoning it entirely and starting from scratch once again (for example, other possible sources of subjects could be tried, extravagant but unnecessary costs could be cut back, the timetable for the study could be extended, etc.).

3.4 ASSESSING THE ETHICAL FEASIBILITY OF THE RESEARCH

In the preceding section, we considered issues concerning the practical feasibility of a piece of research. The present section considers issues which are to do with the ethical feasibility of a piece of research. It is quite possible that a research study is feasible on practical grounds, but is unfeasible because it would be judged to be unethical to conduct that study. The criteria which ought to be used by psychologists in order to assess whether a particular study is or is not ethically acceptable have been formalised in statements issued by the British Psychological Society (1993) and by the American Psychological Association (1992) (see section 3.8). Any person who is intending to conduct psychological research should obtain a copy of, and should study in full, one or other of these two statements (or an equivalent statement which has been issued by a corresponding professional body). The addresses from which the BPS and the APA statements may be obtained are given at the end of this chapter. The following account draws heavily upon the principal criteria which are contained in the BPS statement.

3.4.1 The protection and welfare of participants

A fundamental principle which underpins all ethical codes relating to psychological research is that psychologists must always consider the welfare of the subjects who participate in their research, and must protect them from being either physically or mentally harmed by the research process. In practice, this means that the risk of harm to someone who participates in a psychological study should normally never be greater than the risks which that person would encounter during the course of their normal lifestyle. If there are any aspects of the study which might result in any harm or undesirable consequences for the subjects, the researcher has a responsibility to identify and remove or correct these consequences. If this is not possible, and if there is a risk that the participants in the research will suffer in some way, either physically or psychologically, as a result of the research, then that research would normally be considered to be ethically unacceptable.

Of course, there are certain types of psychological research where the risk of harm, unusual discomfort, or other negative consequences for the subject's future life might occur or might be greater than in everyday life (for example, in certain types of psychopharmacological studies, there may be unanticipated side-effects of the drugs which are administered to subjects). In such cases, the researcher must always obtain the disinterested approval of independent advisers before the research takes place (usually this advice is obtained from an independent ethics committee, either of the university or of the hospital in which the research is based). In addition, in such cases, the participants must be fully informed of the possible risks to them, and real informed consent must be given by each subject individually.

3.4.2 The principle of informed consent

More broadly, the BPS ethical principles stipulate that, wherever it is possible, researchers should inform participants in psychological research of all aspects of that research which might reasonably be expected to influence their willingness to participate in that research; in addition, researchers should normally always explain any aspect of the research about which a participant inquires. Thus, when a subject agrees to participate in a study, that person's consent should normally be informed by knowledge about the research. This is the principle of informed consent.

In some cases, of course, subjects may be unable to give informed consent. This is the case whenever the research involves either young children or adults with impairments in understanding and/or communication. In such cases, informed consent should instead be given either by parents or by those in *loco parentis*. In addition, it may be necessary in such cases (depending upon the potential risks to the participants) to also obtain advice and approval from an independent ethics committee. If such permission and/or such approval cannot be obtained, then the study would be considered to be ethically unacceptable and ought to be either revised or abandoned.

It is important to bear in mind, when considering the application of the principle of informed consent, that a researcher is often in a position of authority or influence over the participants. This position should never be used to pressurise the participants to take part in, or remain in, an investigation. Similarly, the payment which may be offered to subjects should not be used to induce them to accept risks which they would not normally accept in their everyday life without payment.

3.4.3 The use of deception

In the case of some psychological studies, however, it is simply not possible to tell the subjects everything which they could be told about the study because, if they had knowledge about the actual purpose of the investigation, they might alter those critical aspects of their behaviour which are of interest to the investigator, thereby undermining the purpose of the study. Alternatively, it is sometimes simply impossible to study a particular psychological process without deliberately misleading the subjects. According to the BPS ethical principles (section 4.1), the basic guidelines which should be followed in all such situations are the following: 'The withholding of information or the misleading of participants is unacceptable if the participants are typically likely to object or show unease once debriefed. Where this is in any doubt, appropriate consultation must precede the investigation. Consultation is best carried out with individuals who share the social and cultural background of the participants in the research, but the advice of ethics committees or experienced and disinterested colleagues may be sufficient.'

However, the BPS principles also add that the intentional deception of subjects ought to be avoided wherever this is possible. Consequently, the researcher should always first consider whether there are alternative procedures available which do not require deception. If no such alternatives are available, and if it is judged that the intended deception is an ethically permissible procedure, then the subjects should be debriefed at the earliest opportunity.

3.4.4 The debriefing of subjects

In all studies where subjects are aware that they have taken part in an investigation, after the data have been collected, the subjects should be given any information which they might need or request concerning the nature of the study. The researcher should also discuss with the subjects their experience of the research process, so that if there are any unintended or unanticipated effects of the research, these can be monitored. Researchers also have a responsibility to ensure that, if any active intervention is required to negate the effects of an investigation upon a subject, such intervention should be provided before the subjects leave the research setting. Consequently, when drawing up the timetable for the research for the purposes of assessing whether or not the research will be feasible on practical grounds, sufficient time must be built into that timetable to allow for the debriefing of subjects after testing wherever this may be necessary.

3.4.5 Subjects' right to withdraw from an investigation

Researchers should also make it clear to subjects at the outset of the study that they have a right to withdraw from the research at any time, irrespective of whether or not payment or any other inducement has been offered. In the case of children, their avoidance of the testing situation ought to be taken as evidence of a failure to consent to the research procedure, and should be acknowledged.

Furthermore, the BPS ethical principles state that subjects should always have the right to withdraw any consent which they may have given previously to participate in the study, either in the light of their experience of the investigation, or as a result of their debriefing. In such cases, subjects also have a right to require that any data pertaining to themselves, including any recordings, be destroyed. Obviously, if a sufficient number of subjects exercise this right in any individual study, a sampling bias will be introduced to the study which could limit the generalisability of the results. However, this is a limitation which the researcher must accept, as the retention and use of the data which were provided by a subject who has subsequently withdrawn his or her consent is an ethically unacceptable practice.

3.4.6 The invasion of privacy in observational research

Research which is based upon the naturalistic observation of subjects in their everyday settings raises particular ethical concerns, because in such studies, informed consent may not be given by the subjects. Such studies must, therefore, respect the privacy and psychological wellbeing of the subjects who are studied. Furthermore, if consent is not obtained in advance, observational research is only acceptable in places and situations where those observed would expect to be observed by strangers. Particular account should be taken of local cultural values, and of the possibility that the subjects might consider it to be an invasion of their privacy to be observed whilst believing themselves to be unobserved, even though they are in a normally public place.

3.4.7 Confidentiality and the anonymity of data

The BPS ethical principles also stipulate that all information which is obtained about a subject during an investigation must be confidential unless it has been agreed otherwise in advance. All participants in psychological research have a right to expect that the information which they provide will be treated confidentially and, if published, will not be identifiable as theirs. If such confidentiality or anonymity cannot be guaranteed, then the participant must be warned of this before he or she agrees to participate in the study.

In addition, it should be noted that, in the UK, when data about an individual person are stored on a computer in such a form that the individual is identifiable, then the person storing those data must comply with the provisions of the Data Protection Act 1984. This involves registering with the Data Protection Registrar, for which registration forms are available from the Registrar's Office. For researchers who work within an institution, such as a university, there is often an institutional administrator handling these matters. The Data Protection Act is designed to ensure that those who record and use personal information on computers are open about that use and follow sound and proper practices.

3.4.8 Conclusions

From the preceding account, it should be clear that there are not only many practical considerations which need to be borne in mind while planning psychological research; there are also many different ethical considerations which too have to be accommodated if the planned research is to be ethically feasible. If the research which is being planned requires any of the preceding ethical principles to be violated in an unacceptable manner, then that research must be assessed as being ethically unfeasible. However, should a study be judged to be unacceptable on ethical grounds, having reached this point in the planning process, it is always worth reconsidering those specific aspects of the study which have been found to be problematic in order to see whether there are any alternative procedures which may be adopted which would be ethically acceptable. But if no such alternative procedures are available (and remember that any such alternative procedures would also have to be assessed as being feasible on practical as well as ethical grounds), then the researcher is obliged to abandon the research which has been planned.

3.5 CONSIDERING THE POSSIBLE OUTCOMES OF THE RESEARCH IN ADVANCE

Finally, it can help to focus the mind while planning a piece of research to consider the possible outcomes of the research in advance. To this end, it is useful to break down possible outcomes into those things which will be delivered immediately upon the completion of the research, and the longer term outcomes which might emerge eventually from the work.

Things which are immediately deliverable upon completion of the research would include: the answers to the specific research questions which the research was designed to provide; and the immediate research report (whether this is in the form of a final-year undergraduate research project report, an MSc thesis, or an end-of-project report for a funding agency).

Longer term products of the research could include: any further studies which might be required to clarify or to extend the results which will be obtained (focusing upon further studies which might be required for clarification purposes can be an extremely useful process for thinking through the limitations of the planned study); any applied policy recommendations which might be able to be made on the basis of the research to relevant authorities; and the publication of the findings of the research. Publication should, under normal circumstances, always be regarded as the proper endpoint of research. For it is only when research is published that it enters the public domain, becomes available to the scientific community, and can be properly regarded as contributing to the general scientific understanding of the issues which it has been designed to study.

3.6 APPLYING FOR RESEARCH FUNDING

As noted earlier, an important part of the process of planning research is working out the costs which will be incurred in carrying out the planned research (e.g. the costs of your equipment and materials, of your consumable items, of any research assistance, of your travel expenses, etc.). If you do not have sufficient funds yourself in order to be able to cover all of these costs, you will need to apply for the money from a research funding source in order to be able to carry out the research. In some departments of psychology, students are able to apply for funds from a specific budget to cover the costs of conducting their research; alternatively, you may be thinking about applying for funding to an external organisation such as a research council or a charity in order to obtain a more substantial sum of money than an internal source will allow. Or, if you are a student who wishes to conduct the planned research for your PhD, you may need to apply to a research council or some other body to cover not only your research costs but also your university registration fees and your maintenance.

If you are intending to apply for funding, there are a few useful rules which you should always try to follow. First, you should always read very carefully the detailed notes which accompany any application form, in order to see whether the terms of reference of the funding body or funding scheme apply to the particular piece of research which you wish to conduct. Sometimes, funding bodies specify that they will only fund research on certain specific topics; sometimes they specify that, while they are willing in principle to fund research in any number of areas, priority will nevertheless be given to projects on particular topics. Obviously, if you wish to maximise your chances of being awarded the funding, you should always make sure that your project or area of research closely matches the topics or priority areas specified by the funding body to which you are applying. The reality is that applying for external research funding is a fiercely competitive process these days, and if you ignore the funding priorities of the bodies to which you are applying, your application is very unlikely to be successful.

Second, when reading the guidance notes which accompany the application form, look to see if there are any particular features of proposals which are encouraged by or are of special interest to the funding body (e.g. involving a partner from another discipline). Here, if it is at all possible to build these favourable features into your own proposal (but without compromising the scientific and methodological integrity of your research, of course!), you should always try to do so. Such a strategy can only enhance the prospects of a successful outcome.

Third, if you have planned your research properly, you should be able to give very precise details in the application about exactly what it is you are going to be doing. Under most circumstances, these details should minimally include: an indication of the existing body of research which you have drawn upon in developing the proposed research; the specific research questions which the research will address, and why these are interesting or important; the research methods which are going to be used and the motivation for using these particular methods; exact details of the sample characteristics and size (and if there are any possible questions about your access to the sample, copies of letters of support from potential gatekeepers might usefully be included); the type of equipment and materials which will be used; the role and content of any pilot work in the research; the methods of statistical analysis that will be used to analyse the data; any ethical issues that may be involved in conducting the research and how you will ensure that your research complies with an established set of ethical guidelines (and if there are any major ethical issues entailed by your research, a copy of a letter from an ethical committee granting you permission to conduct the research might also be usefully included); the timetable on which the various phases of the research will be conducted; the outputs and deliverables of the research, including your plans for disseminating the findings of the research through conference presentations and publications; and how your research will be useful, and to whom (for example, whether your research will be useful to other researchers; to particular groups of people such as social workers, teachers, clinical psychologists, etc.; or to organisations such as a particular government department or a local authority).

Fourth, in writing the proposal, be open about any obvious problems which the research might encounter, and explain how you will tackle these problems if they do occur. Your application and proposal will almost certainly be read by someone who has a good understanding of the realities of the research process, and they will know only too well that research does not always proceed as planned. So they will be looking to see if you are being realistic in your plans, and whether you give any evidence in your application that you will be able to respond appropriately to problems if these do occur.

Fifth, always make sure that you fill in the application form exactly as required and to the letter. If you cannot even follow the simple instructions for filling in an application form, the funding body will have very little confidence in your ability to execute a piece of original research, and they may even reject your application without considering it properly if you fail to provide information which they regard as crucial for evaluating the application.

Sixth, always type or word-process your application: it is a nightmare for a referee to try to read and evaluate a handwritten proposal. The presentation and appearance of an application is extremely important, and poor presentation is highly likely to affect the judgement which a referee forms of your proposal. Correct spelling and use of grammar are important too.

Finally, if you are posting your application close to a specified deadline, it is always sensible to obtain proof of posting, just in case there are any unexpected postal delays which might lead to your application arriving after the specified deadline. It should go without saying that the application should arrive before the stated deadline. Many bodies will simply ignore applications that arrive late.

3.7   A FINAL TIP: THE INEXORABLE RULE OF SOD'S LAW

Sod's Law, expressed metaphorically, is: if you drop a piece of buttered toast, it will always land on the floor buttered side down. Expressed more directly, Sod's Law is: if anything can possibly go wrong, it will go wrong.

As any experienced researcher will be able to tell you, in scientific research the rule of Sod's Law is inexorable. There is very little that can be done to thwart it, except to form an appropriate mental set at the very outset of the planning process, to think through every single aspect of the research in advance in minute detail, and then to double-check and triple-check everything before the research is ready to roll. While these activities in themselves may not necessarily thwart Sod's Law, they will at least enable you to congratulate yourself on those rare occasions that you manage to evade its worst consequences.

3.8   BPS AND APA ADDRESSES

A copy of the British Psychological Society's *Ethical Principles for Conducting Research with Human Participants* (1993) may be obtained from: The British Psychological Society, St Andrews House, 48 Princess Road East, Leicester LE1 7DR, UK.

A copy of the American Psychological Association's *Ethics Code* (1992) may be obtained from: APA Order Department, American Psychological Association, 750 First Street, NE, Washington DC 20002-4242, USA.

3.9   FURTHER READING

Detailed discussions of the various issues which are involved in selecting research topics, formulating specific research questions, and formulating operational definitions of concepts, are contained in Kerlinger (1973) *Foundations of Behavioural Research* and Selltiz et al. (1976) *Research Methods in Social Relations*. The book by Selltiz et al. also contains excellent discussions of the issues involved in assessing both the practical and the ethical feasibility of psychological research, while Shaughnessy and Zechmeister (1994) *Research Methods in Psychology* contains a very good discussion of the APA ethical guidelines.

PART II

4

The Experimental Method in Psychology

Alyson Davis and David Rose

Contents

4.1 INTRODUCTION

Psychological research has two major goals. The first is to provide a description of human behaviour and its underlying psychological processes and the second is to provide an explanation for that behaviour. The task of generating sufficient evidence to enable the descriptive task of research is well met by many different systematic research methods including experiments. However, the uniqueness and power of the experimental method is that it allows us to address the problem of explanation. It goes beyond the descriptive problem towards providing answers as to how and why that behaviour comes about. In other words, by using experiments it is possible to answer questions about the causes of behaviour. For this reason both undergraduate and postgraduate students receive substantial training in the principles of experimental design and carrying out experiments for themselves. Is this time well spent? The purpose of this chapter is to convince you that the answer is 'yes'. We shall outline the basic tenets of the experimental method and principles of designing experimental research in an attempt to justify the widespread use of experiments within psychology. In doing so, we will concentrate on the reasons why the principles should be adhered to (most but not all of the time), for the sake of psychological theory and not just in the interests of 'good science'.

4.2 EXPERIMENTATION AND THE SCIENTIFIC METHOD

Historically, the widespread use of experiments in psychological research began in nineteenth century German psychophysics, in particular with Helmholtz's (1866) empirical studies of visual perception and Wundt's founding of the first experimental psychology laboratory in 1879. The methodology of experimental design then developed with the rise of statistics and behaviourism earlier in this century (e.g. Fisher, 1935; Skinner, 1953). Since then the use of experiments in psychological research has become synonymous with psychology's acceptance as a scientific discipline. This said, these early influences have also led to experimental methodology being associated with a mechanistic approach to human thinking and behaviour. While there is a relationship between method and theory, most psychologists who adopt experimental methodology are testing theories far removed from behaviourist learning theory and are interested in precisely those unobservable mental processes which the behaviourists found so abhorrent. Nevertheless, there are some basic assumptions underlying experimentation in terms of its relationship with the scientific method which must be accepted by the researcher in adopting experimental methodology.

The method by which experiments seek out the causes of human behaviour assumes acceptance of a deterministic and atomistic framework, whereby behaviour and its causes are both seen as being objectively specifiable and divisible into discrete units. Moreover, the complexity of real-life stimuli and responses can be simplified, controlled and quantified without losing the meaningfulness of the results. On these grounds alone some psychologists reject the experimental method as an unacceptable and inappropriate research methodology and propose instead alternative methodologies (see for example Chapter 23). Therefore, from the outset it must be appreciated that in using experiments in research you are adopting a methodology which like any other method carries with it acceptance of certain ruling principles.

4.3 WHAT IS AN EXPERIMENT?

In the popular television series 'The Good Life' one of the leading characters, Tom, is seen in the kitchen contemplating a row of three seed boxes. He declares to his wife his intention of carrying out an experiment into the effects of talking to his plants. All the boxes contain the same seeds. The seeds in box A, he announces, are to be spoken to for 10 minutes every morning in a calm, gentle manner. The seeds in box B are to be shouted at for the same length of time, while those in box C are to be ignored and not spoken to at all. Not perhaps, you may say, cutting-edge science but it serves a purpose very well as providing an example against which to test the formal definition of an experiment.

Is Tom carrying out an experiment? At the minimal level he is, not a perfect one, but one which meets the basic criteria. As mentioned briefly in the introduction an experiment is a test of cause–effect relationships by collecting evidence to demonstrate the effect of one variable on another. In its simplest form, two groups of people are treated in exactly the same way except for one (the **experimental** or **differential treatment**) and any observed difference between the groups is then attributed to the different treatment. Tom has these basic ingredients in his three seed boxes. He is testing the effect of speech (a variable) on another variable (growth rate of the seeds). He treats his groups of participants (seed boxes) in exactly the same way except for one (whether they are spoken to kindly or shouted at). In fact, he goes one step further by introducing a different level of his variable by including a control condition whereby one box is not spoken to at all. There are, of course, many questions which would have to be answered in order to evaluate the appropriateness of Tom's experimental design – such as whether all the seeds are of equivalent gestation, and whether they would all be kept under the same conditions of lighting – but the essential ingredients for an experiment are present. In later sections we shall unpack in some detail what these ingredients are but first we need to take a step back and ask how experiments come about.

Experiments do not design themselves simply by following a set of rules. They are designed as a means of answering questions, of testing hypotheses and predictions about the psychological world. All of us carry theories about why people behave and think the way they do, and the following is a series of hypotheses or predictions which serve as illustrations:

- Watching aggressive television programmes makes people more aggressive.
- Men believe they are better car drivers than women.
- Children who are sensitive to rhyme in early childhood make better progress in learning to read than those who do not.
- Mothers who concentrate their babies' attention on objects are more likely to have children whose early vocabulary comprises nominals than mothers who do not.
- Remembering a list of items is easier if the list is read twice rather than once.

At one level these are all hypotheses, in that they predict some relationship between the different variables (e.g. type of television and aggressive behaviour, sex and driving ability, reading ability and academic progress etc.). Hypotheses are formal statements of predictions derived from evidence from earlier research and theory, or simply the result of a hunch. All these examples lie in the realm of psychological enquiry and yet not all lend themselves particularly well to the experimental method. Why? The crux of making decisions about appropriate methodology is the appropriateness of a particular method for addressing a particular type of research question. For example, in the case of men's belief about sex differences and driving skills, the example is formulated as a hypothesis but not one in which an experimental design would be most appropriate since the question is about belief rather than behaviour. This kind of attitudinal claim lends itself to questionnaire and survey methodology rather than experimentation. Similarly, the example about children's early vocabulary illustrates another way in which experimental methodology is not necessarily the most appropriate. By definition, natural language is not easily manipulated, and yet the hypothesis as stated is empirically testable, by means of systematic observation alone without experimental intervention. The final example is the most obvious case for experimental testing under classic experimental design since it would be relatively simple to compare groups of people who were given differential levels of repetition of an initial list to remember and compare their performance.

However, the relevance of the experimental method to these and any other hypotheses is that whereas other methods would establish the existence of the relationship being claimed, one cannot address the question of causality without appeal to experimentation. For this reason we now turn to a more detailed look at causal relationships and how they can be established using experiments.

4.4 CAUSALITY AND EXPERIMENTATION

Psychology students are reminded repeatedly of the dangers of inferring causality from a correlation. It is a lesson well worth learning since the pitfalls are not always obvious. The correlation may be spurious or caused by a third variable that affects both the first two (a 'common cause'). An example should help illustrate this point. In 1993 the truancy figures in secondary schools increased and during the same period school examination scores likewise increased. While it seems counter-intuitive that non-attendance at school causes improved exam performance, we might have been tempted to accept it had the correlation been a negative one. In addition, what right have we to interpret the correlation as suggesting truancy causes good exam scores: why not good exam scores causing truancy? There is no principled way of inferring the direction of causality from the correlation alone; other factors must be considered. We can extend this example even further. Thus during the same period there was increased global warming, increased crime in Moscow, and increased ageing in pet hamsters. Truancy levels can correlate with many other phenomena, and we cannot just choose one at random and then draw conclusions. The principle remains the same: causality needs to be established over and above the description of an existing relationship between two variables. How can this be achieved?

The most commonly used technique in psychological experiments is the canon put forward by the philosopher Mill (1874) – the **method of difference**. Using this method one applies a test twice (say, to the same people twice each, or to two groups of people: see below). These test applications are identical except in only one respect and any observed differences in the participants' performance can then be attributed to the difference in treatment. Careful use of this method should indicate whether or not the particular treatment that is being varied can have a causal influence on behaviour (other factors might of course intervene in more complex situations; see Lipton, 1991). But in principle the aim of establishing causality is to provide an explanation that is the only explanation for the observed phenomenon.

4.5 VARIABLES

Variables and the control and manipulation of variables are central both to defining what constitutes an experiment and to distinguishing a good experiment from a weak one. A variable is any characteristic that can vary across people or situations that can be of different levels or type. Thus in the list of examples given above aggressive behaviour, type of television, sex, driving ability, age, reading ability are all types of variable. There are two basic kinds – independent variables and dependent variables. This distinction is central to experimental design and so we shall take each in turn.

4.5.1 Independent variables

The **independent variable** is that which the experimenter manipulates or controls and as such is the variable in whose effect the researcher is interested. It is the one that differs between the treatments in Mill's method of differences, described above. The experimental hypothesis proposes that the independent variable will actually cause the change in the behaviour being measured (dependent variable). For example, from our selection of illustrations the hypotheses suppose that the type of television viewed will determine the levels of aggression, and likewise that phonological skill will determine reading ability. Note that, in principle, variables may be independent or dependent depending on the formulation of the research hypothesis: they can be causes or effects. In practice, however, some variables such as sex and age are fixed – that is, they are outside the experimenter's control.

One way of classifying independent variables is in terms of those which can be quantified in some way in that the experimenter can determine the amount or levels presented in the study, such as amount of drug administered or time allowed to perform a task. Such variables are termed **quantitative**. In contrast, other independent variables differ in kind and are termed **categorical**. Examples of qualitative, categorical independent variables include the race and sex of people chosen, type of drug administered and type of experimental instructions given. The conditions of an experiment refer to the levels of independent variable received by the participants, or the levels of treatment. True experiments require at least two conditions in order that variable manipulation can occur but in principle there is no limit to the maximum number of conditions (see Chapter 11 for further discussion on levels of measurement).

4.5.2 Dependent variables

Essentially, the dependent variable is the behavioural measure made by the experimenter; it is the outcome which may or may not, depending on the hypothesis, be predicted to depend on the independent variable. Thus in our earlier examples, aggressive behaviour, reading ability, early vocabulary and driving ability are all examples of dependent variables. In the same way that independent variables must be carefully selected so that they can be easily and systematically controlled within the experiment, so must the dependent variable be selected so that it can be sensibly and meaningfully measured. The dependent variable must not only be measurable with enough sensitivity to detect some effect that stands up to statistical testing but also be sensitive to alterations in the level of the independent variable. Thus, in the example of our aggressive television experiment we have within our theoretical stance an assumption that the amount of aggressive programme exposure will impact on the amount of aggressive behaviour resulting from this. To test this we would need to plan very carefully how aggressive behaviour was to be measured in our experiment to pick up our predicted experimental effects.

The fundamental problem of deciding on an appropriate dependent variable stems from the very nature of psychological enquiry. Most psychological research is interested in outcome measures which are only indirectly related to the psychological process in which we are interested. Much present-day research is dealing with questions about mental processes which are not directly observable but where some behavioural measure is taken as being symptomatic of some underlying process. It is this inferential nature of psychological research which makes it so difficult. Learning, problem solving, developmental change and so on cannot be directly observed and so even the most clearly specifiable of problems needs great care in the selection of our outcome measure. One way of addressing this issue is by the use of an **operational definition** of the dependent variable, where one makes an explicit statement about the precise way in which observed behaviour is going to be scored or categorised as the dependent variable. In the case of our aggressive behaviour following violent television we would need to specify what constitutes aggression – whether it be acts of physical violence against others or against objects or verbal aggression.

The difficulties of precision in designing experiments cannot really be appreciated by reading textbooks or even scientific journal articles: direct personal experience however is very effective! Developmental psychologists are interested in the development of babies' ability to retrieve hidden objects since there are theoretical reasons for supposing that this provides some measure of the baby's general level of cognitive development (Piaget, 1952a). As such there is a relatively large literature reported in the scientific journals on the infant's reaction to hidden objects. Such experiments involve a dependent variable which measures whether or not the infant retrieves or searches for an object when it is hidden in various locations and means of concealment. It sounds simple enough; the reality, however, is far from simple. For example, what constitutes an effective attempt at search? The 9-month-old infant will move his or her hands around and in doing so displace the cover: is this searching behaviour? Likewise he or she may wait some time, cry, giggle, look around and then move towards an object, pick it up, drop it and even replace it. How can such behaviour be classified? It is tempting to suppose that these difficulties arise out of attempting experiments with types of people who are implicitly difficult to work with.

The problem, we suspect, is much more fundamental to all forms of experimental research. Working with infants and young children simply makes explicit those problems of defining psychological measurement in general. For example, adult participants often adopt particular stances with regard to the experiment, which depend on what they think of you, of psychology, or of science in general. This is known as **subject bias**. Disgruntled, depressed or downright antisocial people (i.e. anyone who doesn't like you) may deliberately fail to conform to the experimental instructions, often in subtle and undetectable ways. Conversely, most people are happy to comply, but go to the opposite extreme. They wish to do what they are supposed to, and to do it well – but they form assumptions about exactly what it is they are supposed to do. The instructions given to participants usually deliberately leave out the real reason for doing the experiment, because if the participants know, they will adapt their performance in ways they think appropriate to your aims, rather than just behaving as they would normally (see Chapter 3 for discussion of the ethical issues that arise here). In the absence of reasons, people often make up their own; they try to guess what you want from the experiment, and they then behave according to their false presumption about the real situation. For example, a common test of 'creativity' is to ask someone to write down as many uses for a brick as they can think of in one minute. Suppose the participant does not know this is a straightforward quantitative test of creativity, but guesses it to be a personality test, and so guesses it is the content of the ideas that will be analysed, not simply their number. Any unpleasant ideas that occur, such as 'hit an old lady over the head with the brick and steal her purse', will thus be suppressed on the assumption they will create a negative opinion of the thinker. This might be true, but from the experimenter's point of view the test will be covertly flawed, in that it no longer gives a true measure of the individual's creativity.

In experiments, as in all systematic research, the stakes are very high. Claiming psychological causality on the basis of poorly designed studies renders experiments worthless at best and potentially damaging at worst. These difficulties can be formalised by using the concepts of reliability and validity. **Reliability** refers to the consistency or stability of any experimental effect. The most common technique for establishing reliability is by replication. If the same experimental design leads to the same results on subsequent occasions and using different samples then the experiment is said to be reliable. Typically, however, experimenters do not replicate their own experiments on more than one occasion for pragmatic reasons and so reliability is commonly established by other researchers replicating a particular experimental paradigm within their own research.

Unfortunately, evidence suggesting that an experiment is reliable is no guarantee of its validity. **Validity** refers to whether or not an experiment explains what it claims to explain: in other words, the truth of the causality which is being inferred. Validity can be dealt with to some extent by providing adequate operational definitions although these can sometimes be reduced to rather unhelpful truisms such as the frequently cited claim that 'intelligence is what intelligence tests measure'. The importance of validity in psychological experimentation cannot be overstressed, not only because of its status as a basic tenet of experimental method but also because of the very real human consequences which potentially arise when claims of causality arise from an invalid dependent measure. An example comes from the work of Milgram (1974) where, in a series of famous experiments on obedience, he asked people to administer electric shocks to other people when they failed to get simple learning problems correct (the 'victims' were confederates of the experimenter who were just acting and were, in fact, not shocked). Usually over half of the participants would end up administering apparently dangerous levels of electric shock to the 'victims' when told to do so. Milgram concluded that these studies had demonstrated high levels of obedience to authority in many apparently ordinary people. The validity problem here is that it is unclear that obedience, and obedience alone, was the cause of the people's behaviour. Some may have 'seen through' the experiment and some may have felt that no serious academic could actually allow people to be hurt in an experiment. Milgram has also been criticised for creating an extremely stressing and distressing novel experimental environment that does not mirror 'real-world' situations at all. The debate about the value and validity of Milgram's work continues even to this day.

A further issue related to the selection and measurement of the dependent variable is that of floor and ceiling effects. A **floor effect** occurs where a null result emerges because the majority of the participants score at the very bottom end of the scale. A floor effect may well emerge simply because the task is too difficult for the participants and the experiment is thus insensitive to changes in the independent variable. An obvious example is a psycho-physical task where the stimulus is too weak to be detected. If the purpose of the experiment is to compare people's sensitivity to lights of different colours, but all the colours are below threshold, no meaningful data will be obtained.

Ceiling effects are the converse of floor effects and are found when people score too close to the top of the scale. Continuing with the example, if all the coloured lights are so bright as to be clearly visible, the task would be too easy and therefore result in a ceiling effect. Floor and ceiling effects can, we emphasise, be obtained with any task whose dependent variable cannot track the full range of the independent variable. Unfortunately, preventing floor and ceiling effects involves more than common sense and a good grasp of the relevant scientific literature. It is almost always necessary to carry out pilot studies to check the appropriateness of your subject pool and variables before carrying out the experiment proper. In addition, Chapter 14 describes techniques for adjusting the difficulty of a task continually during the experiment to keep the subject's responses near the middle of the available response scale, so that floor and ceiling effects never occur.

4.6 EXPERIMENTAL MANIPULATION AND CONTROL

The power of the experimental technique rests on its ability to assure that only the independent variable is permitted to vary systematically across the conditions of the experiment. Where one or more other variables unintentionally vary alongside the manipulated variable this results in **confounding**.

Confounding of variables can render an experiment useless since it makes the results uninterpretable. An example should make this clear. Suppose you were investigating the effects of different techniques of teaching reading to children. To do this three teachers are trained in three different techniques and the children's reading ability is assessed before and after receiving one of the three methods. Any observed differences are then attributed to differences in teaching method. However, there are real difficulties in making such claims because the variable 'teacher' is confounded with the manipulated variable 'method'. In other words, one cannot distinguish whether any effects arise out of teacher differences or differences in teaching method. Even where it seems intuitively unlikely that a confounding matters, the danger is a very real one. In the above example the confounding would be serious since there is, in fact, good evidence to suggest that individual teachers can have differential effects on children's performance (Tizard et al., 1988).

Some confoundings are obvious while others are far more subtle yet equally damaging to the strength of the experiment. Even in laboratory settings confoundings can easily occur, such as testing people at different times of the day where the dependent variable is very sensitive to fatigue effects. As these examples demonstrate, the more closely related the confounded variable is to the independent variable the more serious the consequences. Recognising confoundings after data have been collected is too late – the experiment is already ruined. Therefore checking for possible confoundings before running the experiment is essential.

4.7   BASIC EXPERIMENTAL DESIGNS

There are two fundamental experimental designs (which form the basis of all the more complex designs) and which differ according to the way in which they deal with the control of subject variation. The methods are **between-subject design** and **within-subject design**. These terms are synonymous with the labels **independent** (or **separate**) and **related** (or **repeated**) groups (or measures) designs. If two or more totally separate groups each receive different levels of the independent variable then this constitutes a between-subject design. In contrast, if the same group of people receive all the various conditions or levels of the independent variable then this is an instance of within-subject design. Both these methods carry advantages and disadvantages and the selection of basic design must rest on the nature of the research hypothesis as well as pragmatic concerns.

You should note that while it is no longer considered appropriate to refer to participants in experiments as 'subjects', the terms for types of experimental design have yet to change. We will continue to refer to between-subject designs and within-subject designs here for the sake of consistency with other texts.

4.7.1   Between-subject designs

Allocating people to different conditions within an experiment rather than presenting people with all the experimental conditions consecutively is the most common experimental paradigm used in experimental psychology. Immediately, this method poses a threat to the power of the experiment because by definition there are different people in each group and these groups may share different characteristics at the outset of the experiment which will influence their performance. Let us take the example of the children in our earlier hypothetical experiment who are in three different classes each receiving a different method of being taught to read. In the discussion of confounding variables it was pointed out that there is a risk of teacher differences interfering with teaching method effects. In addition to this possibility there is also a chance that the three groups of children differed before the introduction of the different teaching problems. Perhaps the groups differ by chance, one class being significantly more able than the others, or they may differ by some predetermined factor such as the type of teaching method they received in an earlier class. So, how can this type of problem be overcome? The answer is by adhering to a fundamental principle of experimental design known as randomisation.

4.7.2   Randomisation

Randomisation is a technique to ensure that as few differences as possible exist between different subject groups by giving every subject an equal chance of being allocated to each of the experimental conditions. Procedurally, randomisation is relatively straightforward to achieve. One assigns arbitrary numbers to each subject and literally pulls out these numbers from a hat. In a two-group design with 10 people in each group the people corresponding to the first 10 numbers selected would constitute one group and the second 10 the other group. The mechanics of this procedure is simplified by the use of random number tables found in most statistics textbooks or generated on a computer. Other methods of attaining random allocation to groups can be used such as tossing a coin, or in the case of our classes of schoolchildren, alphabetical lists of children's names might be used. The precise method is irrelevant as long as the procedure ensures that each individual has an equal chance of appearing in each of the experimental groups.

It is important to note that this procedure does not eliminate or even reduce individual differences: it simply distributes those differences randomly between the groups. So continuing our example, those children whose previous reading experience might facilitate their performance in the experiment appear in all the groups in roughly equal numbers. The ideal being aimed at is of totally equal distribution but because allocation is done on a random probabilistic basis this can never be guaranteed. But, because the chance of a very biased distribution is very small indeed, randomisation of participants is an important step in setting up even the smallest of experiments.

As the number of people in an experiment increases, so does the likelihood of attaining an equal distribution of those subject variables which might interfere with the causal relationship being tested for. For this reason, psychologists generally regard an experiment as more reliable if there are large numbers of people involved (see Chapter 25 for additional statistical justifications for large samples.) Consider the extreme opposite case. If there were only one subject in each group, different outcomes might be due to individual differences in reaction to the independent variable, rather than reflecting any general reaction, principle or law that applies to all people and that can thus be used in the future to make predictions or decisions.

Despite the strength of randomisation as a technique and its relative ease of implementation, it is surprising how many experiments remain uninterpretable because of the researcher's failure to ensure random distribution of people across groups. See also Chapter 6 for a discussion of quasi-experimental designs.

4.7.3 Matching

The sensitivity of an experiment refers to its ability to pick up any effect of the independent variable. Sometimes experimental effects may be very small and yet of great psychological significance. A classic example of such a situation is in sex differences. On most measures males and females do not respond differentially: the similarities far outweigh the differences. However, those psychological areas in which one sex outperforms the other are of great psychological interest but the actual size of the effects can be very slight indeed. Therefore, researchers interested in this area must make sure that the experiment is designed to be maximally sensitive.

Randomisation of participants to experimental groups will guard against certain error but will not increase sensitivity. All is not lost, however, since there are steps which will achieve this, namely various means of matching participants. If we take our example of a group of schoolchildren embarking on their different programmes of being taught to read, there are many instances of existing differences between those children which might interfere with our ability to assess the effectiveness of the different programmes. Prior reading training is one we have already mentioned, but other factors such as intelligence and age are also potentially significant. When running experiments with children, age is a difficult variable to deal with because development is so rapid in early childhood that even a six-month age difference between two children might exert a significant effect on the child's performance. Therefore, we would want to be sure that the children in each condition were of a similar age.

Randomisation of our class of children would help ensure that the average age of our groups was similar but we may need to do more than that. Where there is reason to believe that some variable which is not manipulated by the experiment may exert an effect then it is necessary to take the additional step of actually matching children. In the case of age, we would make sure that for each subject in group A there was a child of the exact chronological age (in years and months) in each of groups B and C. Furthermore, if intelligence were a concern to us then we might take a further step of assessing IQ on some standardised test and then match children across groups according to IQ. When these kinds of precautions are taken then the probability of revealing a true causal relationship between our independent variable of teaching method and our dependent variable of reading performance is dramatically increased.

A numerical example may make this clear. Suppose we have two groups with three people in each who participate in an experiment that gives a numerical score outcome reflecting their level of performance. We obtain scores from the first group of 1, 26 and 39, and from the second group 2, 27 and 40. The mean scores of the two groups are 22 and 23 respectively – a difference, but one so small compared to the variability between people within each group that we would probably not credit that it tells us anything meaningful or reliable about whether there is a real difference between the two groups. Now consider however what would have happened had the participants been matched, and if one pair of participants had scored 1 and 2, the second pair 26 and 27, and the third pair 39 and 40. In each case there is a consistent difference such that people in the second group scored higher. The difference in scores is only 1, but it is so consistent we would be much more likely to believe there is an actual difference between the two groups. The experiment is much more sensitive with the matched-pair design.

The importance of matching becomes more salient when the experiment comprises very different participant groups. Suppose the experiment is comparing some kind of treatment intervention on groups of people with some disability such as autism, schizophrenia, dyslexia or Down's syndrome. How can these people be matched? The answer to this lies very much in the realm of the experimental hypothesis. We shall use the example of dyslexia to highlight some of the traditional matching techniques and point out how these have recently been improved.

Some people, who have average or significantly above average IQs, have pronounced difficulties with reading and writing. The term 'dyslexia' is often applied to these people to describe this paradoxical gap between their intelligence and their literacy skills. The theoretical debate around the causes of dyslexia has assumed a specific cognitive or neuropsychological deficit and not surprisingly has been the focus of many research studies and experiments. The typical experimental paradigm has been to take a group of people with reading difficulties and compare them with people of the same age and intelligence. Thus the groups were matched for mental age and the experiments then went on to probe the nature of the reading difficulty of the dyslexic group.

More recently, however, research by Bryant and colleagues has criticised this approach on both methodological and theoretical grounds (Bryant and Bradley, 1985). The traditional approach assumes that reading difficulties are caused by some deficit but the methodology used does not allow us to distinguish cause and effect. As Bryant points out, reading difficulties not only have causes but also exert effects: a person with reading difficulties will be less able to deal with other aspects of the world because print is so endemic to everyday life. While experimental methods employing the mental age matched design allow us to look at causal relationships, they do not allow us to decide which is the cause and which is the effect. A beautifully simple way around this problem is to introduce an additional matched group of people – those who are matched with the people with dyslexia according to reading age – which is precisely what Bryant did in his series of experiments. This way, differences between people at the same level of reading ability might truly reveal something about the nature of the 'deficit'.

One reason why we particularly like this example is that it shows that changes in methodology are not introduced purely in the interests of better scientific method such as enhancing the sensitivity of the test. They have real and sometimes very dramatic theoretical consequences. It also illustrates how generations of scientists accept particular methods without noticing the flaws in current procedure.

4.7.4 Within-subject designs

Some types of experiment solve the problem of differences between people and the need for matching by using the same people in each of the experimental conditions. Within-subject designs, as they are called, have one very obvious advantage since each individual acts as his or her control. When the same person performs quite differently under each of the treatments then the effect of the independent variable is very clear indeed, but this method carries with it some disadvantages which in some cases make the method inappropriate but in others can be dealt with by following certain precautions.

The first problem which within-subject designs pose is that which arises because by definition the different levels or tasks in the experiment must be completed serially, one after another. The serial nature of testing can easily give rise to **order effects**, where doing one task first and another second influences the person's performance. A clear example might be a task involving high levels of concentration, such as an auditory discrimination task in which two words are simultaneously presented in each ear and the participant has to identify one on the basis of some given criterion which differs in each experimental condition. In such a situation, the participant is quite likely to show an incremental improvement from one condition to the next as they gain experience with the nature of the task, such that performance in the first condition would always be inferior to performance in later conditions. Any experiment in which familiarity with the experimental setup and procedure can grow is at risk of showing order effects which will distort the interpretation of the results. Similarly, fatigue and boredom can also increase over time and affect the outcome. Moreover, these types of order effect will arise regardless of the precise sequencing of conditions since they arise simply out of the fact that one condition must be first, second, third and so on.

A more specific kind of difficulty arising out of order of presentation is the potential for **carry-over effects**. These come into play when performance on one condition is dependent in part on the conditions which precede it; this runs the risk of lowering the experiment's validity. Carry-over effects can be characterised in a number of ways. The first is where the participant gains experiment-relevant skills in one task which spill over into the next task presented. So in a two-condition (A and B) experiment let us suppose that while undertaking A the subject picks up skills which will enhance performance on B. When presented as AB order, the participant's score on B will be artificially inflated compared with the same experiment run as a between-subject design.

Another common carry-over situation is when two tasks differ in difficulty. Suppose task A is easy and task B difficult, and you intend to assess people's abilities on each task by using a power measure such as how quickly they finish or how many problems they solve correctly. An individual who does task A first will get the impression the experiment is easy, and will therefore approach task B with that in mind: this individual will work quickly and therefore make many mistakes. Conversely, the individual who does task B first will come to think the experiment difficult, and will therefore perform slowly and carefully when it is time to do task A. The participants may thus score differently on task A, depending on whether it was attempted first or second, and the same may be true for task B. So which is the appropriate score on each task? From the theoretical point of view, it is also interesting to ask what 'skills' the participants acquired or developed during the first task that they then use to do the second task.

A further scenario is where experience of one task actually creates a situation where the participant reinterprets the meaning of the experiment and the experimenter's intentions (either rightly or wrongly) and therefore changes their behaviour on all subsequent tasks. Examples of this latter type are particularly common when testing young children's cognitive understanding and indeed have been exploited in developmental psychology for their theoretical interest (see Davis, 1991 for further discussion). One familiar example is in testing young children's understanding of number. Piaget (1952b) showed how children under the age of 5 or 6 often report that the number of objects in a row actually changes simply because an adult (acting as experimenter) spreads the row of objects out so that the row appears longer. This phenomenon is said to arise because the young child does not understand number invariance or number conservation. It is a very powerful and convincing effect to witness. It is even more striking if one then retests the child and, instead of the adult spreading out the row, the adult picks up a teddy bear and the teddy is seen as spreading out the row of objects. Experiment after experiment has shown how children who fail to conserve when the transformation is undertaken by an adult, change to give conserving responses when a cuddly toy performs the action. Furthermore, these studies show significant carry-over effects. If children are tested in the teddy bear condition first then they are more likely to give correct conserving responses on the adult condition than children who are given the reverse order of presentation. Note the difference between order effect and carry-over effect here; it is not that children show an improvement from first to second task but that they show improvement only with a particular sequence of conditions.

So, we have been trying to suggest that carry-over effects can be of theoretical interest rather than simply viewing them as experimental pitfalls to be avoided at all costs. This said, they can only provide valuable insight if the experiment is designed so that they can be recognised. In the number conservation examples above the relevant experimental manoeuvre employed was that of **counterbalancing**: half the children were given the Piagetian version of the task first followed by the modified task involving the toy, and the other half were given the toy condition followed by the standard Piagetian condition. In a two-treatment design, this AB, BA counterbalancing is effective, efficient and easy to implement. Both order and carry-over effects can be readily recognised.

But what of more complex designs involving many levels of the independent variable? True counterbalancing becomes very unwieldy as the

		Order		
Subject 1	A	B	C	D
Subject 2	B	C	D	A
Subject 3	C	D	A	B
Subject 4	D	A	B	C
Subject 5	A	B	C	D
Subject 6	B	C	D	A
Subject 7	C	D	A	B
Subject 8	D	A	B	C
Subject 9	A	B	C	D
- - - - -	- -	- -	- -	- -
Subject *n*	D	A	B	C

FIGURE 4.1   *Counterbalancing by Latin squares*

number of conditions increases: three conditions give six different orders and five generate 120! Consequently, researchers using more than three or four treatments will settle for **incomplete counterbalancing** as in **Latin-square design**. A Latin square ensures that each level or condition appears equally in each position (Fisher, 1935). An example with four levels of treatment (A, B, C and D) is shown in Figure 4.1. Such an experiment would require at least four participants or multiples of four so that they are evenly divided among the four possible orders of treatment. It is worth noting that in a design as complex as this, any carry-over effects are being controlled for by being randomly distributed across the experiment and are not likely to be clearly apparent as in a two-condition design (AB, BA) unless very large numbers of people were being tested.

We have organised section 4.7 along the dichotomy of between-subjects versus within-subjects design. Like many of the other concepts that have been considered this is an oversimplification and to some extent a fairly arbitrary distinction made in the interests of ease of presentation and learning. In practice many experiments involve the use of both within-subject and between-subject measures. These mixed designs are increasingly common as access to complex statistical analysis becomes more available on personal computers. This said, it is not the case that complex design is on the increase simply for pragmatic reasons: there are good theoretical grounds for this change. Psychological processing is a multivariate activity: there is probably not one single phenomenon in psychology which can be described by appeal to a single variable.

4.8   EVALUATING THE EXPERIMENTAL METHOD

Throughout this chapter we have avoided having a section on advantages and disadvantages of the experimental method; however, the discussion which follows might well have fallen under such a heading. Although the whole enterprise of experimental design rests on quantification we would argue that the decision about what type of methodology is employed is not easily quantifiable. The decision rests on the nature of the research question, one's own experience and expertise and a host of other essentially qualitative factors. Some questions do literally cry out for experimental investigation and it would be plain silly in some instances to use other methodologies. But our own personal view of progression in psychology is not one where experimental methodology continues to be more and more sophisticated, thus squeezing out alternatives.

There are two issues at stake: one is whether or not the experimental method has a significant role to play in psychological research, and the second is the subtlety of our ability to combine different methodologies. In the pursuit of causal explanations, experimental methods are identified as the only way of achieving such goals, but there is a certain arrogance attached to this claim because it tends to blur the unavoidable fact that there is little point in searching for causality unless we can be sure that a meaningful relationship exists which warrants our efforts to determine cause and effect in the first place. It is quite possible to follow the rules of experimental methodology to answer a ridiculous question in just the same way as a computer will calculate the average gender of people. The suggestion we are making is that the experimental method is dependent for its success on living alongside other methodologies for one very simple reason. The weaknesses of the key alternative to experimentation, namely correlational techniques, can be complemented by the strengths of the experimental method and vice versa (see Bryant, 1990 for a full discussion of this point).

Experiments are frequently criticised (and rightly so) for the fact that they lack **ecological validity**. Findings generated in laboratory conditions where behaviour must be tightly controlled may not tell us anything interesting about life outside the laboratory. In other words they lack **external validity**. However, they are a good way, in fact the only way, of answering causal questions. Correlational studies, on the other hand, tell us very little about the causes of relationships between events, but they can be carried out in natural 'real-life' settings and so tell us a good deal about people's normal behaviour. There are a few, but very powerful, instances where researchers have capitalised on the dovetailing characteristics of combined methodologies to great effect (see for example Bryant and Bradley, 1985).

4.9 CONCLUSIONS

We hope that in the course of this chapter we have not only highlighted the issues one needs to be aware of when designing effective psychological research but also gone some way in explaining why the experimental method has a real contribution to offer. Yet there is a sense in which one feels 'but life is not like that' when trying to define the ideal control condition or a readily measurable dependent variable. One of the overriding difficulties of the experimental method is that the ideal often is humanly impossible as in the case where it would be too time-consuming or where certain groups, conditions or variables literally do not exist. Sometimes it is not possible to meet the criteria formally demanded by experimental designs discussed here and we have to resort to quasi-experimental methods or adopt alternative methodologies entirely.

Furthermore, because scientific research is a human endeavour, researchers themselves as much as their participants get involved in chains of unavoidable events which mean that the most clearly defined of objective plans get waylaid. Even Skinner, as a disciple of objective methodology, laid down some less than scientific principles of the pragmatics of carrying out research, in a talk about his own experiences (for a discussion of these see Christensen, 1988).

Does the fact that our research will fall short of logical purity negate the whole exercise of striving for systematic objective study? The answer must be a definite 'no'. There is such a thing as good evidence and experimental methodology is currently one of the best research tools we have at our disposal to uncover it.

4.10   FURTHER READING

There is no shortage of good textbooks on experimental design issues but the following are very helpful and clear. Christensen's (1988) *Experimental Methodology* is a good detailed guide to the principles of experimental design. Keppel and Saufley's (1980) *Introduction to Design and Analysis: A Student's Handbook* outlines the main types of experimental design alongside appropriate techniques for analysis.

5

Single Case Experimental Designs

Sarah L. Wilson

Contents

5.1 INTRODUCTION: WHAT ARE SINGLE CASE EXPERIMENTS?

Single case experiments are scientific investigations in which the effects of a series of experimental manipulations on a single participant are examined. An example of the application of single case experimental method would be the assessment of the effects of one or more treatments on one individual. Single case experimental research should not be confused with case studies. Case studies are retrospectively written reports of observations on individuals, which may raise questions that initiate research; single case experiments are, of course, prospectively planned.

The origins of single case methodology are in clinically based research, stemming from the work of people like M.B. Shapiro in the 1950s and J.B. Chassan in the 1960s. Today, there is still very much a clinical focus in the application of single case methodology. Examples of its use include the evaluation of behaviour modification and skill training programmes, assessment of drug effects and examining the effects of treatments in physical rehabilitation.

5.2 PROBLEMS WITH THE GROUP COMPARISON APPROACH

In applied research programmes such as these there can be objections, limitations and practical issues associated with the use of group comparison methods (see also Chapter 7).

5.2.1 Numbers of cases

If the purpose of the study is to examine the effect of treatment on a particular disorder or syndrome, there may be difficulties in collecting sufficient numbers of patients in order to match patients' variables, which may interact with the treatment under investigation (e.g. age, pathology, personality characteristics, IQ, social class), in order to make a control group feasible. In some of the rarer syndromes, e.g. vegetative state (Wilson and McMillan, 1993), collecting sufficient cases for an experimental group can prove problematic, even when the research is based at centres which specialise in that particular type of patient; yet shortage of patients does not mean that the necessity for research is any less.

There are two methods to overcome the participant shortage problem and enable group comparison approaches: either by carrying out the research over an extended period of time, or by using a multi-centred study. Both approaches present practical problems, however. Using an extended period for the research can present funding problems and the research may also be vulnerable to changes in the institution within which it is set, e.g. changes in care philosophy. The use of a multi-centred approach can bring problems such as matching care environments and treatment philosophies, maintaining consistent style amongst the researchers and dealing with the practical difficulties in administering such a project.

5.2.2   Maintaining an uncontaminated control group

Circumstances may exist where, for the best possible reasons, relatives of participants in the control group or care staff may attempt to use the experimental treatment on members of the control group. This may be a particular risk when relatives are participants in the treatment regime for the experimental group and may talk to other families. Such situations occur from a desire to help, even when the treatment is of unproven worth, and are most likely in conditions where proven treatments are rare.

A strategy to cope with this problem in a group comparison study would be to obtain the control group from another centre, giving due consideration to the issues already discussed in relation to multi-centred studies. Even with this approach, however, there may be a risk of contamination.

5.2.3   Evaluation of individual treatment programmes

There are circumstances in which the use of any approach other than single case methodology is inappropriate. A specific example is where a treatment regime has been designed with the problems of one individual in mind and there is a need to empirically establish the efficacy of the treatment or treatments in question with respect to that individual. Such circumstances can occur, for example, where behaviour modification programmes are being used.

5.2.4   Obscuring individual outcomes in group averages

In any group of experimental participants, there may be homogeneity for particular variables, e.g. diagnosis, age and duration of illness; however the group could be entirely heterogeneous for other factors which could interact with the treatment, e.g. history, attitudes, environment. This would lead to differences in treatment outcome within the group and the average response would not reflect any individual in the group.

5.2.5   Generalising findings to practice

In practice, the clinician may wish to apply the results of group research to assist in the treatment of individual cases. In their review of the limitations of group designs in applied research Bergin and Strupp (1972) noted two particular limitations in generalising results from group research to individual cases. One problem is that of inferring from the results for a relatively homogeneous group as representatives of a given population; the other is generalising from the average response of a heterogeneous group to a particular individual.

The problem of homogeneity arises because, particularly when dealing with clinical or educational research, it is very difficult to achieve a proper random sample that will be truly representative of the whole population being investigated. The sample will be biased by the admission and treatment or management policies of the institution from which the sample is being drawn or the characteristics of the population in its catchment area. One of the major criticisms of Freud's work, for example, is that his studies are based on middle class Viennese subjects. On the other hand if the sample is truly heterogeneous, the greater is the difficulty in applying the results to one individual, and the specific effects of a given treatment on one individual with a particular set of problems become lost in the average (Barlow and Hersen, 1984: 54). For example, a treatment for depression may alleviate severe agitation and terminal sleep disturbance but have a deleterious effect on psychomotor retardation and depressive delusions. If the results from a heterogeneous population were to be considered as a whole, the adverse findings could be masked in the population mean, with potentially dangerous consequences if the clinician in question was dealing with a patient with psychomotor retardation and depressive delusions.

Studies using heterogeneous populations and therefore having large inter-individual variability may have results where some participants produce marked improvements and others get worse. The resulting average improvement is statistically significant but weak in terms of its clinical significance.

5.2.6 Within-subject variability

Classically, group comparison studies require measurement pre-treatment and measurement post-treatment. The changes which occur within individuals during treatment may also yield valuable information: for example, the point at which treatment effects take place and whether they are sustained.

5.2.7 Ethical issues

One of the major sources of contention in research evaluating treatments is that of the ethics of withholding the treatment from the control group. The objections, which can arise from clinicians, relatives and, of course, the patients, are that those in the control group may not have the opportunity to benefit from the treatment in question or may actually suffer as the result of being included in the control group. The argument that the value of the treatment in question is unproven, hence the need for the study, is one that may have little impact.

5.3 GENERAL ISSUES IN SINGLE CASE RESEARCH

There are several issues to be considered when single case methodology is to be applied. Firstly there is the point which follows on from those concerning applying the results from group studies to individual cases in that there are equal problems in extrapolating from the results of single case studies to groups. One single case experimental study can be used to gain information about the participant and to produce hypotheses for further investigation with further single cases or with groups. If however the same experiment is repeated several times with similar participants then a base for generalisation from single case studies can be created (Barlow and Hersen, 1984: 56). In other words, single cases can be grouped.

An example of this can be found in Wilson et al. (1996a) where a meta-analyis was carried out on a series of 24 single case experiments which examined the immediate effects of sensory stimulation treatment on patients diagnosed as being in the vegetative state, to evaluate the effectiveness of the treatment when the patients were considered as a group. As half of these patients later emerged from the vegetative state and half did not, a meta-analytic approach with these single case data was also used to relate behaviour whilst still in a vegetative state to eventual outcome (Wilson et al., 1996b).

Single case methodology is not only suitable for studies where the effects of experimental manipulations are to be investigated. It can also be applied in studies where the aim is to gather a natural history. An example of this would be studying recovery from brain injury in a group of people who are heterogeneous in terms of variables which can influence the course of recovery such as nature and site of injury, time since injury, treatment regimes and demographic variables; who are sufficiently numerous to allow grouping for particular variables; and where individual recovery courses are also of intrinsic interest (Powell and Wilson, 1994).

5.4 PREPARING A SINGLE CASE EXPERIMENT: MEASURES, DESIGNS AND PHASE LENGTHS

Having identified the topic of research, i.e. what experimental manipulations are to be tried on which person, the three preparatory tasks are:

1   the selection of appropriate methods of serial measurement
2   the selection of an experimental design
3   deciding on the criteria for determining the lengths of the phases of the experiment.

5.4.1 Selection of serial measures

The measurement selected must of course be appropriate for the aspect of behaviour which is to be experimentally manipulated. More than one method of measurement can be selected; all methods selected should meet the classical criteria of validity (i.e. the assessment measures that which it is purported to measure) and reliability. **Test–retest reliability** requires that repeated assessments will produce identical results if the subject is in an unchanged condition; that is, if there has been no change in the subject's state there will be no change in the results from the assessment. **Inter-rater reliability** requires that if two people are assessing the same subject at the same time but independent of each other then they will produce the same results. Inter-rater reliability is relevant when more than one person is to be carrying out the assessment; also in the situation when one person is responsible for carrying out the assessments over a long period, when drift from the agreed form can occur. Procedures such as having training sessions for the assessors can help achieve good inter-rater reliability, and having clear, well-documented instructions for the assessment procedure is important for maintaining both forms of reliability. The assessment procedure should also be sufficiently sensitive to detect change when it occurs.

If the assessment selected has elements of skilled performance (Sunderland, 1990), then improvements may occur through practice. In order to minimise the effects of practice, a procedure can be adopted of using a prolonged initial baseline phase in which the assessment may be applied a number of times until the initial improvement in performance levels off, or alternatively of providing some additional initial practice sessions to allow the person to become familiar with the assessment procedure. Sunderland also recommends that the use of several attempts at the target task for each assessment and taking the best score should be considered to minimise the effects of any stray variations in performance; he also offers the caveat that in this case the serial assessment used should be brief in order to maintain motivation.

5.4.2 Selection of an experimental design

Whatever form of single case design is used it is of prime importance that only one variable should be changed at a time, as when more than one variable is manipulated simultaneously it is impossible to determine how much and in what way each variable contributes to any behaviour change.

5.4.3 A-B designs

The A-B design is the simplest experimental design in which the target behaviour is clearly specified and measurements are carried on throughout both A and B phases. Phase A is the baseline phase during which the natural occurrence of the target behaviour or behaviours is monitored; in phase B the treatment variable is introduced (Barlow and Hersen, 1984). A hypothetical example of an A-B design is illustrated in Figure 5.1.

There is however an important reservation concerning the clinical application of the A-B design; this is that it may not be possible to tell whether any behaviour change that occurs following onset of the treatment results from the treatment *per se* or from spontaneous changes that are part of the recovery process. This issue is particularly germane when there is only weak evidence of an experimental effect, i.e. only a slight and gradual acceleration of the recovery curve is seen. One possible way of overcoming this problem is by the use of a **control variable**. A control variable would be another aspect of behaviour which would be as susceptible to the effects of recovery as the experimental variable, but not susceptible to the effects of the treatment. If the effects found following treatment were due to spontaneous recovery then the curves for the treatment and control variables should be parallel.

Another variation on the A-B design is the A-B withdrawal design or A-B-A design, where the treatment given in B is withdrawn for the second A phase. If, following the baseline phase A, behaviour changed during treatment phase B and then returned to baseline levels when it was withdrawn during the second A phase, then there is a high degree of certainty that the behaviour change was

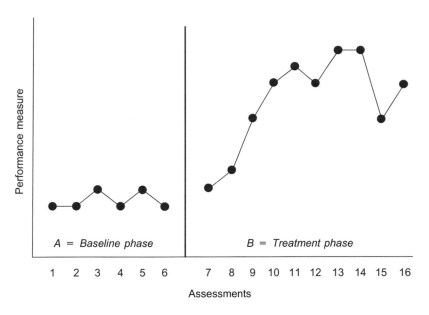

FIGURE 5.1   *Example of an A-B design*

the result of the treatment given in phase B (Barlow and Hersen, 1984). Worthington (1995) comments that in a true A-B-A design, the second A phase should incorporate the same procedure used in the B phase but applied to an alternative and incompatible behaviour, but in practice this procedure is rarely used other than in behaviour modification. A hypothetical example of an A-B-A design experiment is given in Figure 5.2. There are problems with the use of this design. One is the ethical dilemma in the clinical setting of withdrawing a treatment. Another problem is that if the individual has had a form of training (e.g. spelling, doing up buttons) in the B phase, it may not be possible (or desirable) to undo that learning for the subsequent A phase and carry-over effects from the B phase to the subsequent A phase may be seen.

The ethical dilemma of treatment withdrawal may be dealt with by using the A-B-A-B design; this design finishes with a treatment phase which can then be extended beyond the end of the study, but a phase of withdrawal does allow the opportunity for the efficacy of the treatment given in the B phases to be evaluated. Specifically the phases are baseline (A), treatment (B), withdrawal of treatment (A), treatment (B). This design gives two opportunities for demonstrating the effects of the treatment over the target behaviour after the initial A to B comparison: specifically B to A and then A to B. A hypothetical example of an A-B-A-B design is given in Figure 5.3.

There are other variations on the A-B-A-B design, for example having many treatment and baseline phases (A-B-A-B-A-B-A-B-A-B) or incorporating another treatment (A-B-A-C-A-B-A-C). In clinical settings, however, there may be circumstances in which it can appear unreasonable to other caregivers to withdraw an apparently successful treatment, even if it is going to be applied again, when the treatment in question has had the apparent effect of eliminating

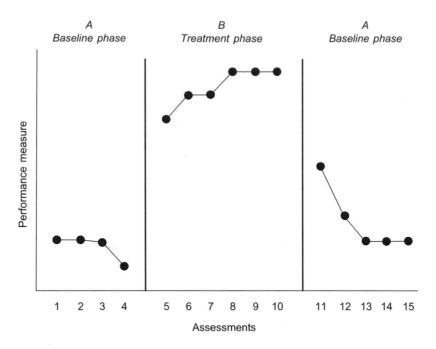

FIGURE 5.2   *Example of an A-B-A design*

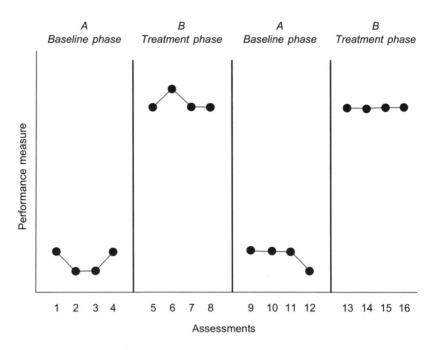

FIGURE 5.3   *Example of an A-B-A-B design*

an unpleasant behaviour. Yule (1987) describes the A-B-A-B design as probably not appropriate for demonstrating experimental control over the acquisition of new skills because of the difficulties in reversing behaviours that have become established; its greatest value is probably where the occurrence of an already existing skill is being manipulated. It must also be borne in mind, whether using A-B-A-B, A-B-A-C-A or other variants of the design, that behaviour may not return to pre-treatment baseline levels in second and subsequent A phases, making it difficult to achieve an unequivocal evaluation of treatment effects (Worthington, 1995).

5.4.4 Multiple baseline designs

There are clearly occasions when the use of withdrawal designs is impractical, such as when treatments cannot be withdrawn or reversed due to practical or ethical reasons or problems in co-operation with other caregivers. In drug studies the effects of active medication may persist into the placebo phase. Multiple baseline designs (Baer et al., 1968) can be used in situations where withdrawal or reversal of treatments is not feasible.

In using a multiple baseline design, a number of different aspects of behaviour are identified and measured over a period of time to provide baselines against which changes can be measured. An example would be from a study of the effects of social skills training for mildly and moderately retarded adults (Bates, 1980), the aspects of behaviour being introductions and small talk, asking for help, differing with others and handling criticism. Once the baselines are established, the experimenter then applies an experimental variable (treatment) to one of the behaviours. After an appropriate length of time, treatment is also applied to a second behaviour, leaving the remaining behaviours untreated, and so on until all behaviours are being treated. Treatment is not applied to any behaviour until a stable baseline has been achieved for that behaviour. A hypothetical example of a multiple baseline design is given in Figure 5.4. The purpose of this design is to demonstrate the power of the experimental variable (treatment) in that each behaviour should maximally change only after the experimental variable is applied to it and those behaviours which are untreated should remain unchanged. If change only occurs in each behaviour after the experimental variable has been applied then efficacy can be assumed.

The multiple baseline design can be conceptualised as a series of separate A-B designs; for each behaviour, the baseline is the A phase and the treatment is the B phase. As a consequence the limitations of the A-B design apply; without withdrawal of treatment the controlling effects on the target behaviours are not clearly demonstrated. The effects of the treatment are inferred from the lack of change in the untreated behaviours and this assumption is based on the premise that the targeted behaviours are independent of one another. If the targeted behaviours co-vary then the treatment effects must be called into question. For a convincing demonstration of treatment effects, Barlow and Hersen (1984: 212) recommend a minimum of three to four baselines should be used if practical and experimental considerations permit.

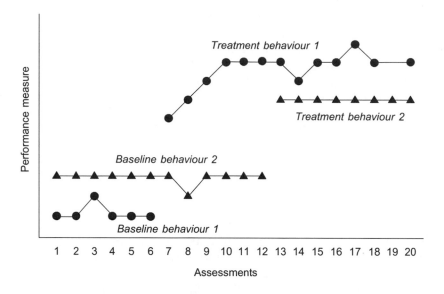

FIGURE 5.4   *Example of a multiple baseline design (across behaviours)*

There are three basic types of multiple baseline design. The one that has already been described as part of the general discussion is the multiple baseline across behaviours; this design is defined by Barlow and Hersen (1984) as the sequential application of a treatment variable to independent behaviours within the same individual. The two other types of design are multiple baseline across subjects and multiple baseline across settings.

In the **multiple baseline across subjects design**, a specified treatment is applied in sequence to a series of matched subjects who share the same environmental conditions (Barlow and Hersen, 1984). Each subject is assessed using the same measure(s) and as the treatment is applied to succeeding subjects, so the baseline for each individual increases in length. An example of the application of this design would be evaluating the effects of a behaviour management regime on children who have episodes of urinary incontinence. In this design only one behaviour is being investigated but this does not preclude gaining further information by monitoring other behaviours at the same time.

Barlow and Hersen (1984) define the **multiple baseline across settings design** as when a treatment variable is applied sequentially to the same behaviour across different and independent settings in the same subject. In this design, a single person is used and a single behaviour is investigated; baseline measures are obtained for that behaviour in different environmental settings. The treatment variable is then applied in one environmental setting after the other. An example of the application of this design is provided by Kirchner et al. (1980) who examined the effects of the introduction of a police helicopter patrol on burglary rates in two high density residential areas. Kirchner et al. also incorporated an A-B-A withdrawal element into their design so the effects of withdrawing the helicopter patrol could be seen.

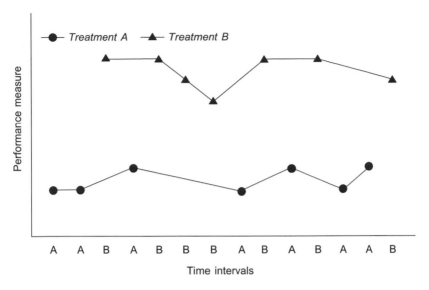

FIGURE 5.5 *Example of an alternating treatments design comparing treatments A and B*

5.4.5 Alternating treatments design

This design has been proposed as a method of assessing the relative effectiveness of two (or more) treatments or conditions and is suggested as an alternative to the use of the between-groups comparison. This design is applied by the rapid alternation of two or more treatments or conditions within a single subject (Barlow and Hersen, 1984). Rapid, in this context, is not defined necessarily in terms of a fixed period of time such as every hour; it could be that every time the patient is seen an alternate treatment is given. This design does not require a baseline period and the sequence of treatments should be decided on a random basis. Figure 5.5 illustrates a hypothetical study conducted using an alternating treatments design, showing that relative efficacy can be established by comparing data points from different treatments.

The alternating treatments design does have the advantages of not requiring withdrawal of treatment, of producing utilisable data more rapidly than A-B-A withdrawal designs, and of not being sensitive to background trends in behaviour because the treatments are applied in the context of what is happening at the time. The major disadvantage is the possibility that the treatments may interact or interfere with each other; also in a clinical situation it is unusual to alternate treatments, and the other forms of single case design provide scenarios closer to clinical practice.

This type of design has been used to evaluate the effects of aromatherapy and massage on disturbed behaviour in four patients suffering from dementia (Brooker et al., 1997). The rationale for its use stems from the variability of the behaviour of dementia sufferers over time; thus if the treatments had been given in blocks rather than being randomised, even if the order of the treatment blocks was randomised, it could be argued that differences between the responses to treatments could be due to deterioration in the patient's condition rather than the relative efficacies of the treatments. Four treatment conditions were used in this study: aroma only, massage only, aroma and massage, and no treatment; eight to twelve trials of each treatment condition were given in randomised order over a three-month period. Efficacy was evaluated using behavioural scales to assess agitated behaviour administered after the treatment sessions.

5.4.6   Simultaneous treatments design

This approach permits the evaluation of two (or possibly more) treatments in the same experimental phase and also does not require the withdrawal of a treatment (Kazdin and Hartman, 1978). It is accomplished by giving both treatments on a daily basis, taking care to balance between the treatments to ensure there is equal representation during the experimental phase for time of treatment (e.g. morning versus afternoon) and also therapists (if there is more than one), since both these variables could influence response to treatment. This approach permits a rapid comparison of the treatments. In cases where the individual concerned is recovering (e.g. following brain injury) or deteriorating (e.g. as in dementia), this design also provides a control for the effects that changes in the patient's condition may have on performance. An evaluation in parallel of two sensory stimulation treatment protocols, in which there was random assignment as to which protocol was used in the morning session and which in the afternoon for each day, is reported in Wilson et al. (1993).

5.4.7   Randomisation

Apart from the examples given in the two previous sections there are other ways in which randomisation can be incorporated in single case experiments. Randomisation can be used to control for extrinsic factors which may influence the subject's behaviour, e.g. weather, environmental noise and other daily activities, and also internal factors such as diurnal variations in wakefulness and degree of hunger. Careful consideration must be given however to factors which constrain the use of randomisation, for example there may be constraints as to when a particular treatment may be administered or as to the length of phases of the experiment or the time that has to be allowed for carry-over effects of a particular treatment to subside. Such constraints do not necessarily preclude the use of randomisation, however. In a simple A-B-A design, for example, the time available for the experiment can be divided into blocks and randomisation can be used to determine in which time block each phase commences, but this could be operated within the constraints imposed by the minimum number of blocks required for each phase (Edgington, 1996). In a multiple baseline design, the timing of the commencement of individual intervention phases can similarly be randomly determined.

5.4.8   Initial baseline

The function of the baseline is to provide a standard by which the effects of treatment can be evaluated. Barlow and Hersen (1973) stated that a minimum of three separate observation points should be plotted to establish a trend in the data.

The ideal baseline is a stable one, where there is no discernible upward or downward trend in the data and so subsequent treatment effects are clearly seen. Another type of baseline shows a trend in behaviour that is in the opposite direction to the treatment effect; this sort of baseline is also acceptable since if there is a treatment effect it will quite clearly be demonstrated by reversing the trend in the data. One problematic type of baseline is where the trend in the data is in the same direction as the expected treatment effect and therefore it will be difficult to distinguish treatment effects from spontaneous change. Other problematic types include: alternating high and low trends, U-shaped, inverted U-shaped, and unstable which shows no particular pattern at all. One method of dealing with such problematic baselines is to continue them until a level trend has been achieved; this strategy may not be practicable however and it may be necessary to stipulate a maximum duration of the baseline period. Some simple statistical tests which can be applied to examine baseline data for randomness, for cyclical variation, and for trends in the mean or variability are described in Morley and Adams (1989).

5.4.9 Subsequent phases

The same recommendation applies to experimental phases: that the phase should be of sufficient length to show a lack of trend and a constant range of variability. Carried to its natural conclusion this would mean that different phases could have markedly differing lengths; however relative equivalence of phase lengths is desirable (Barlow and Hersen, 1984). It is recognised, as with baseline length, that ethical or practical considerations may place limitations on duration of phases.

5.5 PERFORMING THE EXPERIMENT

Once the objective of the study has been established and a protocol decided upon, then the process of data collection can commence. The procedures used should, of course, be carefully recorded. It is important that any external events that occur during the course of the experiment which may influence the outcome are carefully noted, e.g. changes in state of health and major life events.

5.6 DATA ANALYSES

There are two ways in which to deal with data from single case experiments: one is visual inspection, the other is performance of statistical tests. It is sometimes useful to use both approaches, but sometimes visual inspection alone will suffice.

5.6.1 Visual inspection

The data should be presented as a graph. In the first instance a graph should be drawn including all the data points. It may prove useful subsequently if there is high variability in the data to produce graphs with smoothed curves by blocking the data; however, care should be taken to avoid distorting the results. Scales for the axes should also be selected with care. Too large a scale will flatten out any treatment effects and too small a scale might suggest that the data are more variable than is actually the case. Different approaches to the graphical presentation of single case data are described by Morley and Adams (1991).

The use of visual inspection alone may be appropriate, when what is required is to show whether there has been a treatment effect and that the treatment effect is clearly discernible. There are other occasions, for example when the data are variable, when it is difficult to discern whether there is a treatment effect, and then statistical analysis is called for. It must be remembered that in clinical applications, there can be a difference between statistical significance and clinical significance. Occasions have been noted when behaviour changes which were too small to be significant statistically did have clinical significance, and also when behaviour changes which did reach statistical significance were not judged to have been clinically significant.

5.6.2 Serial dependency

Data collected in single case experiments *may* exhibit what is described as serial dependency; that is, successive observations may be related to one another so that preceding observations can be used to predict succeeding ones. Parametric tests such as F and t are based on the assumption that observations are independent of one another; the use of serially dependent data can significantly bias F- and t-tests leading to both type I and type II errors (see Chapter 25).

Serial dependency can be detected by the use of a statistical procedure known as **autocorrelation**. Autocorrelation refers to a correlation between data points separated by a particular interval. If an interval of one is used, the first observation is paired with the second, the second observation is paired with the third, the third with the fourth and so on. The correlation coefficient r is then calculated and examined for significance. Usually testing for autocorrelation with an interval (or lag) of one is sufficient to test for serial dependency, although a more sensitive analysis may be obtained by performing auto-correlations with different intervals. For example, using an interval of three, the first observation would be paired with the fourth, the second with the fifth and so on. It is recommended that autocorrelations should be calculated separately for data from the different phases of the experiment as treatment may affect dependency. Procedures have been suggested (Barlow and Hersen, 1984: 294–5) to allow the use of t and F with data that have been found to be serially dependent. An example is, in an A-B-A-B design, to combine the data from the two A phases and compare them with the data from the two B phases. The rationale for this is that the data from the first A phase would probably be more highly correlated with the data from the first B phase than with the data from the second A phase, since autocorrelations tend to decrease with distance. Not all statistical techniques that can be used to assess single case data are sensitive to serial dependency however.

5.6.3   Statistical analyses

Once the possibility of serial dependency in the data has been excluded, a *t*-test can be used to analyse the data from an A-B design. The usual application of *t*-tests is to data from group studies; in related *t*-tests, repeated observations on the same people under two conditions are compared so that the effect of the conditions (or treatments) on the measure can be determined. Likewise, in independent *t*-tests, two groups of people are used and they are compared on a particular measure so that the effect of belonging to a particular group is evaluated.

In single case research, independent *t*-tests can be used to compare scores from a particular measure taken in the baseline phase with scores from that same measure taken during the treatment phase, so instead of comparing scores from groups of people we are comparing scores from groups of assessment sessions. Related *t*-tests can be applied when the design requires comparison of scores from two different conditions within a session, for example comparison of pre-treatment and post-treatment scores. Instead of comparing two scores for each person, we are comparing two scores for each assessment session. Where A-B-A-B or A-B-A-C type designs are used then analysis of variance can be applied to compare the data from the different phases.

There is a further consideration for the use of analyses such as these which test the differences in means if there are marked trends in the different phases. If the baseline and treatment phases both have a marked trend in the same direction, then the means are bound to be significantly different. For example, if there is a continuous upward trend, the data points from the B phase will all exceed the data from the A phase; the significance of the result will be a reflection of the trend. On the other hand, if a situation occurs such as a downward trend in the baseline phase and an upward trend in the treatment phase, there may not be a significant difference between the means, yet the treatment will have clearly had an effect. Trends in phases of the data can be examined quickly by use of the split-middle technique (White, 1972). The procedure is described in detail in Barlow and Hersen (1984).

Time series analysis can be used to examine trends in the data and also changes in level. This technique provides a *t*-test that is appropriate when there is serial dependency in the data, and is also not dependent on having stable baselines; it is dependent on having a relatively large number of data points however. This technique and the application of randomisation tests are also discussed in detail in Barlow and Hersen (1984). Sunderland's comment on the utility of statistical analyses in single case studies (even having excluded the possibility of serial dependency) is that

the results should still be treated with a little caution as these statistical procedures are being used in a context for which they were not originally designed and other less important assumptions are still violated. It is therefore best to treat them as a way of describing the strength of any effects suggested by the graphical analysis, and no great reliance should be placed on the exact size of the probability values calculated. (1990: 190–1)

5.7 FURTHER READING

Barlow and Hersen's (1984) *Single Case Experimental Designs* is, to my knowledge, the most comprehensive, extensive and well-known textbook on the subject. Yule's (1987) chapter on the evaluation of treatment programmes which appears in Yule and Carr's *Behaviour Modification for People with Mental Handicaps* is a readable introductory chapter, well illustrated with examples from published studies. Also worth a look is Sunderland's (1990) article on single case experiments in neurological rehabilitation: it is an accessible paper, written from a practical viewpoint, which describes the stages of single case research. For further reading on the use of randomisation in single case experiments, Edgington (1996) is recommended. Finally, a recently published textbook by Franklin et al. (1997) called *Design and Analysis of Single Case Research* contains some useful examples and decision trees to help you choose appropriate statistics for single case research problems.

6

Quasi-Experimental Designs

Chris Fife-Schaw

Contents

6.1 INTRODUCTION

In Chapter 4 the basics of classical experimental designs were discussed. Most textbooks and degree courses stress the value of doing experiments since they offer the most clear-cut route to testing hypotheses about causes and effects. The experimenter has control over the relevant independent variables and allocates participants to conditions at random in an attempt to make sure that they know exactly what is responsible for the changes they observe.

This is to be contrasted with observational and correlational approaches, where we can observe that two variables appear related to one another but it is difficult to determine whether there is a causal relationship between the variables (one 'causes' the other) or some third variable is responsible for the observed relationship (see Chapter 25). Although this state of affairs may seem less than satisfactory – after all, we usually want to be able to say what caused what – correlational studies are often the best we can hope for in many real-world domains. Practical considerations limit the amount of control we can expect to have in such situations, so we have to be careful whenever we try to interpret relationships between variables.

In between correlational and experimental approaches lie two other kinds of approach: the **pre-experiment** and the **quasi-experiment**. Pre-experiments are not regarded as particularly useful but are informative in the sense that they highlight the positive virtues of quasi-experiments. Pre-experiments are best illustrated by an example.

6.2 PRE-EXPERIMENTS

I once attended a course on rapid reading in an attempt to increase the speed with which I could get through paperwork. The university was pleased to supply such training as it would help the staff perform better and this would, in turn, help the university to be more efficient. A consultant was hired to do the training. With the current political concern to evaluate everything, the consultant felt obliged to conduct an experiment to see if the training had actually worked. Before the training started we were given a report to read and we were asked to time our reading of it and answer some factual questions about the report's content. Having done this, the training went ahead and at the end of the day we were tested on our reading again. So that the times and test scores would be readily comparable we read the same text and answered the same questions. Needless to say reading speed had increased dramatically (four times quicker in my case) and accuracy remained high. The consultant, with obvious satisfaction, declared the day a success.

The problem here, of course, is that we do not really know if the training had any effect on reading speed at all. Whether we have been able to accurately detect the effect of the training is referred to as the **internal validity** of the experiment.

There are several problems with this procedure which challenge its internal validity even though at first sight it looks like a reasonable thing to have done. First, the test materials were the same on both occasions and since we had seen them only about 7 hours previously there is a strong possibility that we would remember the content. Thus improvements may be reflecting memory for the material rather than increased reading speed. It is obviously easier to read something quickly if you already know what it is about. The same applies to the 'test' questions. Such threats to the experiment's internal validity are called **testing effects**. In all sorts of studies, repeatedly exposing participants to the test materials is likely to make them familiar with them and less anxious about what they have to do. Such effects tend to inflate post-test scores.

In fairness, were the consultant to have used a different report and different test questions, it would have been even more difficult to know what any differences in reading speed could be attributed to. The second text might be naturally easier to read or, possibly, more difficult.

A second problem concerns what are called **maturational effects**. Merely having the time to concentrate on reading speed even without experiencing the training may have led to improvements. As none of those tested had been allowed to spend the day thinking about rapid reading without being trained, we do not really know whether the training *per se* had an effect.

Another problem concerns **sample selection**. All those present felt that they had a reading speed problem and, at least at the start of the day, were motivated to improve. You had to volunteer for the course and there was no external pressure on people to attend. Having put a day aside to improve performance, not trying hard to improve would have been somewhat perverse. This factor, in conjunction with the potential maturational effects noted above, may have served to increase scores on the retest. Again, we cannot really say how effective the training was, and even if it was effective here, it might be somewhat less useful when people are not so keen to be trained. This latter point refers to the **external validity** of the study: just how generalisable are the findings? If training works, does it only work for very committed people?

It should be noted that all of these problems are concerned with the experiment (as a pre-experiment) and do not say anything about the virtues of the course. It may have worked very well or it may not. Whichever is the case, this study shed very little light on the issue. This is obviously not an ideal way to demonstrate that the training package increased reading speed.

Other common forms of pre-experiment are commonly found in news stories where some sort of intervention has to be evaluated. A crude example would be to see if peer teaching improved computing skills by comparing children's exam performances in schools that had adopted peer teaching with ones that had maintained traditional teacher-led methods. At one level this looks like a legitimate comparison between treatment groups – one that gets peer teaching and one that does not. Clearly a true controlled experiment is not possible as it would be ethically and politically unacceptable to randomly allocate children to schools and thus to the 'treatment' conditions.

Numerous problems follow in interpreting any differences that are observed between the groups. First, there is the question of whether the schools are comparable. Perhaps the schools that adopt peer teaching simply have more able or more socially advantaged children in them. Those children from higher socio-economic backgrounds may be expected to have home computers and thus be more computer literate, for instance. There is also a possibility that some event, such as a cutback in funds for computer maintenance, may occur in one school and not another. Such a sudden change in one of the groups is known as a **history effect** and may lead to a difference between the groups which is not attributable to the treatment (here peer teaching) but is due to something else.

6.3 QUASI-EXPERIMENTS

Many of the problems discussed in relation to pre-experiments reduce the degree of certainty you can have that the 'treatment' actually caused the observed differences in the dependent variable of interest (i.e. the study's internal validity). Because of this, it is rare to see pre-experiments in high status academic journals. However, many of the research questions that we would like to answer simply cannot be answered by resorting to true experiments. This is usually because either we cannot randomly allocate participants to treatment conditions or it would be unethical to do so. Chapter 5 has already dealt with some of the more obvious medically related ethical problems of withholding a potentially beneficial treatment from patients. With less sensitive topics, even where withholding a treatment is not a problem, random allocation may simply be practically impossible. In the computer skills example above, for instance, we could not randomly allocate children to the schools.

Quasi-experiments should not be seen, however, as always inferior to true experiments. Sometimes quasi-experiments are the next logical step in a long research process where laboratory-based experimental findings need to be tested in practical situations to see if the findings are really useful. Laboratory-based experiments often reveal intriguing insights yet the practical importance, or substantive significance, of these can only be assessed quasi-experimentally. Laboratory studies may have shown that under certain highly controlled conditions, peer teaching improves computer test scores, but the 'real' issue is whether peer teaching is good for children in their schools. This is a question about the **external validity** of the laboratory-based studies.

Three classical quasi-experimental designs exist which attempt to overcome these threats to internal validity discussed above. What is presented below is a summary of the three prototypical designs; many variations of these are possible (see Cook and Campbell, 1979). Many of the principles involved are common to those discussed in Chapter 5 on single case designs and you should read that chapter as well if you are intending to design your own quasi-experimental study. It should be noted that quasi-experimental approaches, in common with true experiments, assume that there is a 'true' answer to the question of what causes the changes in the dependent variable.

6.4 NON-EQUIVALENT CONTROL GROUP (NECG) DESIGNS

As we saw in the example of the computer skills, the two groups (as defined by which school they attended) may not have been comparable. The intervention of peer teaching (the treatment) may have had an effect on test scores but we cannot be sure that the peer teaching group were not already better at computing, prior to the inception of the new programme. The non-equivalent control group design (NECG) overcomes this by requiring a pre-test of computing skill as well as a post-test. The pre-test allows us to have some idea of how similar the control and treatment group were before the intervention.

Figure 6.1 shows a range of possible outcomes from a simple NECG design. In graph A the control group starts off scoring less than the treatment group, reflecting the non-equivalence of the two groups; finding a control group with exactly equivalent scores in a quasi-experimental design is difficult. Both groups improve after the intervention but the treatment group has clearly improved more than the control group. This is quite a realistic picture to find in studies of educational interventions like the computer skills study discussed earlier. We would expect the control group to improve a bit as, after all, they are still being taught and are maturing. If the treatment had an effect, then scores should have improved more than might have been expected if the

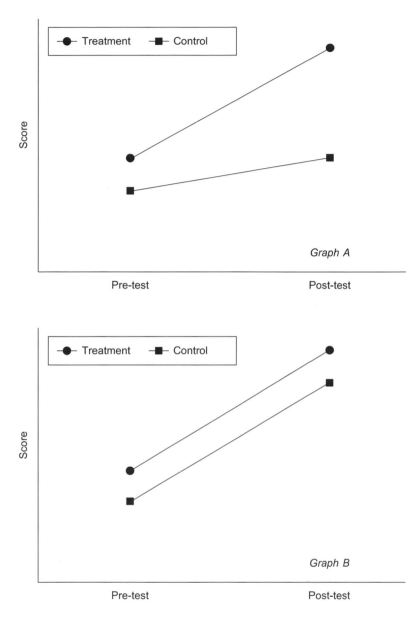

FIGURE 6.1 *Non-equivalent group designs*

intervention had not taken place. Graph B shows what might have happened if the treatment had no effect. Scores in both groups changed about the same amount.

The graphs in Figure 6.1 are prototypical and reflect improvements over time. It is, of course, possible for all sorts of patterns to be found. Non-equivalent controls may outscore the treatment group at the pre-test; they may even be equal. Perhaps a treatment serves to allow the treatment group to 'catch up' with the controls. The treatment might *decrease* scores. There are many possibilities. In all cases you are looking for an interaction between treatment condition (treatment vs. control) and time of measurement (pre-test vs. post-test). You would obviously test for such an interaction statistically (see Chapter 26), but by plotting graphs like these you should observe lines of differing gradients; parallel lines usually indicate no treatment effect (but see below).

6.4.1 Problems with NECG designs

Almost by definition, NECG designs suffer from potential sample **selection biases**. In studies of 'alternative' therapeutic interventions in particular, there is often a problem that those who get a new treatment had actually sought it out, perhaps because traditional treatments had not worked for them. Such people may be highly motivated to see the new treatment succeed and might have ideological objections to existing treatments. There is also the possibility that those offering the therapy may select people they believe would benefit from it or who they think will comply with the regimen. Those who are thought likely to be 'difficult' cases, or for whom the disease may have progressed too far, might not be selected and may even end up appearing in the control group.

Clearly it would be unethical to refuse a new treatment to those who want it or to force those content with existing treatments to receive a new and presumably still untested treatment. However, where possible, you should attempt to have control over, or at least full knowledge of, how the samples are selected. Be aware that those whose efforts are being evaluated may have a vested interest in the outcome of your study.

Even though we have pre-test measures on which we can compare samples, this does not guarantee that the two groups were truly equivalent before the treatment started. If one group was more able or brighter, maturation may proceed at a faster rate in that group than the other. We might expect, for instance, that children's computer skills improve with age (maturation) and that more able kids learn these skills more quickly and easily. Were the treatment group to contain proportionately more high ability children, group differences may arise out of these differential rates of maturation rather than exposure to the peer teaching method. This is referred to as a **selection/ maturation interaction**. As the pre-test is usually only used to compare groups on the dependent variable, such a problem may remain undetected. One obvious solution would be to measure variables that might conceivably lead to differential maturation rates at the pre-test (e.g. IQ) though this naturally increases demands on participants.

Statistical regression towards the mean is another phenomenon which may influence interpretation of the data. Regression towards the mean is reflected in very high pre-test scorers scoring lower at post-test and very low pre-test scorers scoring higher at post-test. If we are studying people who score at the extremes on the dependent variable we may mistake changes at post-test for this natural regression to the mean. Why this happens is a little difficult to grasp at first but depends on the fact that our test measures will naturally contain some errors (see Chapter 11). Cook and Campbell (1979) use an everyday example which is fairly easy to understand; what appears here is merely an embellished version of their example.

If we have an ability test, say like an exam, we might do worse than our 'true' ability would merit because we were distracted by other students, we were extremely badly hung over (worse than usual) and we had revised the topics which did not come up on the paper. We know that if we took an exam for the same subject again we might expect to do better next time, more accurately reflecting our ability. This is because we would expect these sources of error (failures to record our true ability) to be less likely to *all* co-occur next time around. Similarly, if we were very lucky, the exam might only contain questions on the topics we had revised and we might be fortunate enough to sit the exam on the only day of the year when we were not hung over and everybody behaved themselves in the exam hall. This time we might get a mark that somewhat overstated our true ability in the subject. However, we probably would not expect to be so lucky if we took the exam again without further revision.

Across a sample of people, those with mid range scores are likely to be about equally influenced by these errors (inflating and reducing scores) so they would cancel out on average, leading to no systematic bias in our experiment. People at the extremes, however, are *less likely* to score more extremely on being retested as some of those who had extreme scores at pre-test will have done so because their scores had already been inflated (or reduced) by large errors. Since extremely large errors are relatively less likely than moderate size errors, two consecutive large errors in the same direction are very unlikely. This means that post-test scores will tend towards the population's mean score.

For quasi-experiments, this is a particular problem when the treatment group has been selected because of people's low scores on the dependent variable (e.g. selecting people with poor computing skills for the peer teaching method). The simplest way to guard against this (though easier said than done) is to ensure that your control group is also drawn from the pool of extreme scorers. The ethics of denying an intervention to children who are particularly bad at computing are clearly an issue here. The problem is also more likely to influence results if your dependent measure has low test–retest reliability. The less reliable the measure (i.e. the more error-prone it is) the more there is likely to be regression to the mean.

Finally, for now, **history effects** can affect the validity of NECG studies. If some event, in addition to the treatment intervention, occurs between pre-test and post-test in one group only, then it is not clear what any group differences at post-test should be attributed to. For example, an evaluation of a persuasive campaign to promote commuting to work by urban railways in different cities may be invalidated if the 'treatment' city suffers from road travel chaos caused by unanticipated roadworks on the main commuter routes during the period of the study. People may flock to the trains but only because driving to work (their preferred method) was nearly impossible.

You should be aware that history, selection and maturation effects can work both to enhance group differences *and* to obscure them.

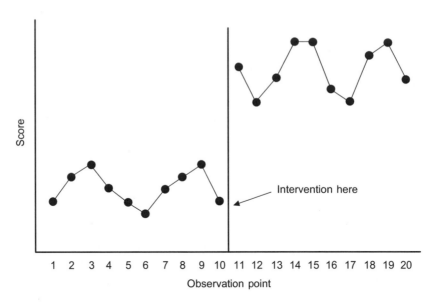

FIGURE 6.2 *Example time series data*

6.5 TIME SERIES DESIGNS

Time series designs involve having only one sample but taking measurements of the dependent variable on three or more occasions. Such designs are sometimes referred to as **interrupted time series** designs as the treatment intervention 'interrupts' an otherwise seamless time series of observations. Figure 6.2 gives an illustration of some hypothetical time series data.

   As you can see, the main feature that you are looking for when collecting time series data is that the only substantial change in scores coincides with the intervention. The virtue of such a design is that it is relatively less likely that short term historical events (i.e. **history effects**) will either (a) co-occur with the treatment and/or (b) have a lasting effect over time. It is also unlikely that small differences pre- and post-intervention will be maintained if the treatment really has no effect. Any maturation effects should be reflected in gradual trends in time series data and not radical changes occurring at the same time as the intervention.

   For time series studies to work well, multiple data collection/observation points are required. It is difficult to detect trends of any kind with just three observation points so, where possible, opt for as many observation points as is realistic but pay due regard to participant fatigue, boredom and irritation.

6.5.1 Problems with time series designs

Time series studies potentially suffer from the threat of **testing effects** to their validity. As these studies, by definition, require repeated administration of the same dependent measures, there is a tendency for people to gradually do better as time goes on. This is a separate phenomenon from **maturation effects** as testing effects arise out of familiarity with the measurement procedures. When presented with a novel test, for instance, we usually do not know what is required and may be anxious about our performance. Repeated exposure to the test material should reduce these anxieties and allow us to perform better. It is also possible that respondents might come to know what they are being asked about and develop more efficient answering strategies, allowing them to respond more quickly. This is especially a problem where measurements are timed.

The net impact of testing effects is that, if the *magnitude* of the treatment effect itself is small, it may get swamped by the testing effects. If the size of the treatment effect is relatively large there will be little problem in determining that the treatment actually had an effect.

Another potential problem concerns **instrumentation effects**. These refer to changes in accuracy of measurements over time. One good example would be the reporting of crimes. Over time the likelihood of reporting (and the police recording) crimes changes as a function of changes in the social representation of the crimes rather than their frequency *per se*. What may have been regarded as common assault in the past may come to be seen as a racially motivated attack in more enlightened times. Similarly, women are now encouraged to report sexual attacks and the social opprobrium that used to follow a claim of rape is now somewhat reduced, though still present. What this is really about is a change in the way the measures are taken and their relative accuracy. Studies that involve measures taken by observers are particularly at risk from instrumentation effects as observers learn how to use the coding schedule more efficiently or, more likely (and worse), become fatigued by the schedule and attempt their own reinterpretation of it.

Subject or participant mortality refers to the loss of participants from your study over time. Time series studies, especially those that cover long periods, are prone to participant mortality problems which are usually outside the experimenter's control. Some participants may indeed die during the study, but it is more normal that some will drop out through boredom or a lack of interest or perhaps because they move house. If you do not have a large sample to start with you run the risk that you will have too few people left at the end of the study to enable you to draw any reliable conclusions at all.

Participant mortality would not be such a great problem were it a truly random event. However, reasons for leaving that are related to the nature of the study (e.g. a lack of interest in the research topic or the intrusive nature of the measures) can lead to a situation where the surviving sample becomes progressively more biased in favour of showing that the treatment works. Say you were trying to evaluate the effect of a local waste recycling advertising campaign and had started regular assessments of how much waste people recycled. Even if you started with a fairly representative sample of the population, you might well find that by the time you had started the adverts and were collecting post-intervention observations, only environmentally committed people were still ready and willing to help you with the project. In all likelihood, your estimates of average post-intervention waste recycling behaviour would be considerably higher than the pre-intervention average, but this would be mainly due to sample mortality rather than the adverts.

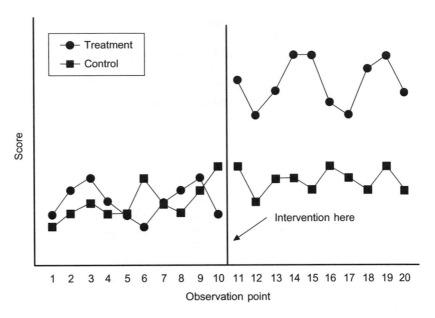

FIGURE 6.3   *Time series with non-equivalent control group*

Careful mapping of sample survivors' pre- and post-intervention behaviour would overcome this problem but this is naturally a rather unsatisfactory solution since such a campaign was presumably intended to change the behaviour of the less environmentally committed people who were lost to the study. Needless to say, strenuous efforts need to be made to maintain the sample.

6.6   TIME SERIES WITH NON-EQUIVALENT CONTROL GROUP (TSNECG) DESIGNS

Many of the problems associated with time series and NECG designs are neatly overcome by the combination of the two approaches in the TSNECG design, sometimes also called the **multiple time series design**. An extended series of data collection points are used with both the treatment group and the non-equivalent control. Figure 6.3 illustrates what we would hope to find if there really was a strong treatment effect.

While it is clear from Figure 6.3 that there is variability in scores over time and that there appears to be a gradual improvement in scores in the control group, potentially via testing, instrumentation or maturation effects, the post-intervention scores for the treatment group are considerably higher than for the controls.

6.6.1   Problems with TSNECG designs

The price to be paid for minimising so many threats to validity is all-round increased cost and the need to study many more people. This is not a problem when conducting research on existing archival data but may be a serious problem if you intend to collect fresh data.

Differential sample mortality in the two groups can be a problem. If people who are somewhat apathetic to the study are differentially more likely to be lost from one group than the other, then group differences may be artificially enhanced or constrained. It is also possible with studies that last for some period of time that the control group will become exposed to, or aware of, the treatment. People in the two groups may mix and discuss the intervention, and control group members may either seek the treatment for themselves or withdraw from the study through becoming aware that they may never be exposed to the treatment or intervention.

Sometimes, merely being aware of the existence of a 'problem' that needs treating may change behaviours of control group members. If control group members come to feel that they are being deliberately disadvantaged in some way they may choose to perform less well when measurements are taken. This may be a serious problem when researchers are heavy-handed and insensitive in the way they handle people. Alternatively, control group members may compensate for not receiving the treatment by trying harder to perform well. This is called **compensatory rivalry** and would serve to obscure true treatment effects.

TSNECG designs are not immune to the other threats to validity discussed earlier, especially if the magnitude of the treatment effect is weak and the variability between scores on successive observations is relatively high. In common with the single case designs discussed in Chapter 5, detecting a treatment effect is easiest when it is possible to establish a fairly clear-cut stable baseline in both the control group and the treatment group prior to the intervention. As with true experiments, it may be necessary to increase sample sizes substantially in order to provide the necessary statistical power to detect these weak effects.

6.7 MODIFICATIONS TO THE BASIC DESIGNS

The basic designs described here are really the tip of the iceberg in terms of possibilities. With NECG designs there is no necessity that there only be two treatment conditions (treatment and control). It is perfectly possible to have different levels of the treatment or combinations of treatments in one design. For example, we might extend the computer skills example to include a control (traditional teaching) group, a group that had two periods a week of peer teaching and one that had three per week. In fairness to traditional methods of teaching, we might also divide the control group into one that had two periods per week and one that had three periods. Clearly, this new design is much more useful to curriculum developers since it not only tells us whether peer teaching is better than traditional methods but also whether spending more time on computing yields worthwhile increases in skill level. Assuming we had enough schools prepared to help, we could even add a group that gets both traditional and peer teaching for a total of three periods.

Sometimes concerns about **testing effects** may lead us to believe that post-test measures will be unduly influenced by people having completed the pre-test. An example might be of a knowledge test with a short period between pre- and post-test. In such a situation we might expect people to remember the items, thus inflating the apparent power of any intervention. It is also often the case that merely asking people about some aspect of their lives changes their behaviour in that domain. For instance, merely asking about your waste recycling activities might make you think that you ought to recycle more waste. Somebody showing interest in your behaviour may change it. This is called the **Hawthorne effect** after the electricity plant in Illinois where the phenomenon was first formally described in studies on attempts to enhance worker performance (Roethlisberger and Dickson, 1939). It is possible to get over both sorts of problem by using separate pre- and post-test samples so that different individuals take the pre- and post-tests. This approach is only sensible if you have a large pool of people from which to draw your samples and you can draw them by some fairly random procedure.

For time series designs and TSNECG designs it is possible to adopt some of the treatment withdrawal designs described in Chapter 5. These involve intervening with the treatment and then, at a later point, withdrawing it and observing a subsequent fall in scores on the dependent measure. This approach works best when the treatment is not expected to have a lasting effect on the dependent variable and has to be 'maintained' in some sense for the effect to be shown. An example might be to evaluate the effectiveness of camera-based speed checks on stretches of road. Speeds could be monitored surreptitiously for some period before erecting the camera systems then, after a period with the cameras in place, they could be removed to see if speeds gradually increased in their absence. Like the single case A-B-A-B design (Chapter 5) the cameras could be re-erected later to see if speeds fell again.

6.8 CONCLUSIONS

Having read through this chapter and followed all the potential problems associated with each quasi-experimental design, you might be forgiven for concluding that such approaches are too fraught with difficulties to make them worthwhile. The difficulties, however, are inevitable whenever you forgo experimental control in order to do research outside the laboratory. What I hope to have shown you is that there are some rigorous methods available and, while they will not necessarily lead you to unambiguous answers to your research questions, they do at least highlight the likely threats to validity. If you know where potential interpretative problems lie then you can address them and make some estimate of the likely impact these could have had on the results of your study. Quasi-experiments, providing they are conducted with due care, can be the most powerful available means by which to test important hypotheses.

6.9 FURTHER READING

The classic text in this area is Donald Campbell and Julian Stanley's (1966) *Experimental and Quasi-Experimental Designs for Research*. This is a very short book of only 70 pages which had first appeared as a chapter in Gage (1963). It is the place where quasi-experimental designs were first comprehensively explained. Thomas Cook and Donald Campbell (1979) produced a more detailed text called *Quasi-Experimentation: Design and Analysis Issues for Field Settings*. This contains discussions of the major designs and a few more as well as information about the appropriate statistical models to be used with each design.

7

Surveys and Sampling Issues

Chris Fife-Schaw

Contents

7.1 INTRODUCTION

This chapter will cover two topics: sampling issues and the use of survey techniques. These two topics are dealt with in some depth in sociology and political science and, though psychologists regularly conduct surveys, it is fair to say that psychologists' surveys might benefit from the methodological sophistication found elsewhere in the social sciences.

Conceptually, surveys and sampling techniques are not tied to any particular philosophical viewpoint. Those adopting a hypothetico-deductive approach will be concerned to sample appropriately, as will those taking a more constructivist perspective. Whenever the goal is to make statements about a group of people then, unless you approach all the members of that group, how you draw your sample of that group will have an impact on how much confidence you can have in the generalisability of your findings.

Similarly, surveys are not tied to any particular data gathering technique. Whilst questionnaire and structured interview surveys are most common, it is perfectly possible to collect qualitative data within a survey. Even experimental investigations can be done using survey techniques though these are still quite rare (but see Gaskell et al., 1993). Physiological and other, more invasive, measures can also be collected in certain types of survey providing the resources to get respondents to a suitable testing site are available.

7.2 BASIC SURVEY DESIGNS

Chapter 2 has already outlined many of the 'meta-design' issues involved in designing studies but these are especially relevant in survey design and well worth considering in more detail. Within limits, researchers are free to design their surveys in any way they wish, though there are a number of well understood designs that you should consider before embarking on a new design. Moser and Kalton (1971) is still the most widely regarded guide to survey design and those wishing to get a more technical appreciation of survey issues should look at this text.

7.2.1 Cross-sectional surveys

This is the simplest survey design as it involves approaching a sample of respondents once only. Since the sample is regarded as a cross-section of the population(s) under study it is possible to make comparisons between subgroups (e.g. males vs. females, older vs. younger people, etc.) and look for relationships between variables (see Chapter 25).

Advantages By far the greatest advantage is the relatively low cost associated with gathering the data. All other things being equal, response rates are generally higher than for other procedures. You can devise your study and get the results in a fairly short period. Conclusions can be drawn and published quickly in time for other agencies to make use of your data for policy change purposes, etc.

Disadvantages The data are unduly susceptible to **time of measurement** effects. These are influences on responses that are due to immediate historical events. For example, attitudes towards using public transport might be changed dramatically by a major rail crash on the morning that your survey takes place. In a more subtle manner, media attention on the topic of your study may influence responses to some of your items. Often only a part of your sample (e.g. TV watchers) will be exposed to this and you may not know which part has been so exposed. Sometimes this may seem like a good thing since you may be interested in media influences on attitudes but, since this is really a hypothesis about *change*, then the cross-sectional design is not really appropriate.

7.2.2   Time series surveys

These are best thought of as a series of cross-sectional surveys on the same topic using the same (or very similar) survey instruments. Having selected a suitable period for separating the surveys, you draw a new sample for each wave of questioning. Opinion polls such as the regular polls reported in national newspapers are usually part of time series surveys. Monthly assessments of support for the political parties can be plotted to see if levels of support have changed systematically in response to political/historical events that occurred between waves of questioning.

Advantages   The principal aim is to assess the impact of time of measurement effects. In the poll example, the research questions are usually about whether historical events changed responses. Did that train crash have a lasting impact on willingness to travel by train?

Disadvantages   Studies are expensive to mount since you need multiple samples of around the same size as a single cross-sectional survey if you want accurate measures of key variables.
   Cohort effects can become confounded with time of measurement effects. Although each sample is assumed to be equally representative of the relevant population they may well differ from one another as a result of simply being a different cohort of people. Problems arise when trying to attribute differences to historical events and these events alone. The observed differences may just reflect the fact that you are asking a different cohort of people for their responses.

7.2.3   Longitudinal designs

Longitudinal designs involve drawing a single sample and measuring their responses on more than one occasion. Any number of recontacts are possible in theory and these designs are especially useful for tracking developmental changes and the psychological impact of life events, etc.

Advantages   The main advantage is the ability to follow individuals and to monitor the impact of events on responses. They permit the study of **age-related development**. Since changes can be monitored within individuals, the problems of cohort effects are removed. An increase in score on a variable can be compared with the *same individual's* score at an earlier time.

Disadvantages   **Time of measurement** effects can be confused with **age-related development**. If historical events serve to increase values of some variable you are interested in, observed increases that are in line with the increased age of respondents may be misinterpreted as developmental trends rather than the historical effects they really are.

Apart from the obvious increased cost over cross-sectional studies, these designs suffer from **sample attrition**. At each subsequent wave of questioning some people will drop out of your study, leaving a reduced sample of people to provide usable data at all points in the study. The people who stay with the survey may be a biased sample. While you may start with a fairly representative sample, those who stay with you may be systematically different from those who leave. They may be more interested in the topic of the research, they may be more compliant, they may be the kinds of people who do not move house often, etc.

Attracting people to the study in the first place may be more difficult if they are forewarned about future contacts. Some people may be happy to fill in one questionnaire but unwilling to commit themselves to filling in four. As you will have to have some way of identifying respondents so you can recontact them, anonymity of responses cannot be claimed. A significant number of people will be put off by this especially if the topic of study is in any way sensitive.

Another difficulty concerns **sample conditioning**. People who are studied on several occasions soon come to know what is required of them and the types of questions that will be asked. Because of this they may no longer be 'naïve' respondents and some may intentionally attempt to find out more about the research topic.

Really long term longitudinal studies (e.g. the National Child Development Study) require long term commitment of resources from funding agencies. Such far-sighted generosity in the face of the possibility that the study may fail to reveal anything of interest makes this approach comparatively rare.

7.2.4 Longitudinal cohort sequential designs

In the above discussion three sources of influence on responses have been mentioned: age-related change, time of measurement effects and cohort effects. Cross-sectional designs keep time of measurement constant; time series designs usually keep age-related changes constant by using similarly aged samples; and longitudinal designs keep the cohort constant. This means that interpreting data from any of these designs always leaves two of these three possible influences free to have 'caused' the observed responses and often we cannot tell exactly which is most influential.

The longitudinal cohort sequential design (LCSD) attempts to overcome this by combining elements of all three designs into one much larger design. Some cohorts of respondents are studied longitudinally while other new cohorts are added at a later date for comparative purposes. Figure 7.1 gives an example of such a design from the Social and Psychological Consequences of AIDS/HIV for 16–21-Year Olds Study (Breakwell and Fife-Schaw, 1992). In this diagram you can see that age-related effects can be assessed by comparing longitudinal changes in different cohorts. For instance, is a change observed between D_{16} and D_{17} also present when E_{16} is compared with E_{17}? Cohort effects are indicated if, at all stages in the study, the rank ordering of cohorts on a particular measure remains the same. Time of measurement

1989	1990	1991
		F_{16}
	E_{16}	E_{17}
D_{16}	D_{17}	D_{18}
C_{17}	C_{18}	C_{19}
B_{18}	B_{19}	B_{20}
A_{19}	A_{20}	A_{21}

FIGURE 7.1   *An example longitudinal cohort sequential design (LCSD)*

effects can be estimated by comparing responses in cohorts across time. If some event has a broad impact on responses, changes between, for instance, D_{16} and D_{17} should also be observed between A_{19} and A_{20} and likewise in cohorts B and C. While there are more pure and complicated versions of this design (see Breakwell and Fife-Schaw, 1994) this basic model allows the possibility in principle of investigating interactions between these effects.

Advantages   The potential to investigate main effects and possible inter-actions between age-related, time of measurement and cohort effects are the LCSD's main advantages.

Disadvantages   As with the standard longitudinal design, sample attrition remains a problem. This is even more apparent when you want to compare a new cohort, which has yet to suffer attrition through repeated contact, with an older one which has been depleted. Comparisons between such cohorts need to be conducted with considerable caution.

Although the LCSD is a very powerful design, interpreting analyses may be somewhat less easy than implied above. Often real effects are weak or inter-actions between effects are complex. Whilst there would be no scope for detecting them with some of the other survey designs, considerable analytical sophistication is required to make sense of data generated by such a design.

7.3   SAMPLING ISSUES

Before commencing any study you should ask yourself whether the nature of your sample will matter for any conclusions you might want to draw from it. If you are studying a perceptual or neurophysiological phenomenon, you may think that all humans are likely to be similar and that any collection of people willing to do your experiment will be OK. For many such phenomena this may be a safe assumption, but there will always be the odd exception and the problem is that you may not know when you have found that exception. If you assume that any subject will be as appropriate as any other, then you should at least be aware that you are making this assumption. For most other psychological phenomena, *who* you study does matter.

As well as mattering from a substantive theoretical viewpoint, good sampling is required if inferential statistics are to be used. Many commonly used statistical tests *assume* you have drawn random samples and use **sampling**

theory to estimate the 'significance' of any effects you find. Poor sampling introduces unknown sources of error into these calculations so that statistical results may prove difficult to interpret.

7.3.1 Estimating population parameters

In most common applications of survey techniques the aim is to estimate the size of something in the population – a **population parameter**. A crude example might be to estimate the average adult female height and the amount of variation there is around this average. As it would not be possible to ask everyone, you would need to draw a representative sample of females and measure their heights. In your sample you would be able to find the mean height and the standard deviation quite easily. Let's say they came out at 160 cm and 25 cm respectively.

These two figures, the mean height and the standard deviation, are called **sample statistics** since they refer to your sample. Normally you do not really want to know about the mean and standard deviation in your particular sample, you want to estimate the mean in the population. To do this you treat your sample mean and standard deviation as *estimates* of the true population mean and standard deviation. These 'true' quantities are referred to as **population parameters**. While your mean score is acceptable as an estimate of the population mean, the formula for estimating the population standard deviation is as follows:

$$\text{estimated standard deviation} = \sqrt{\left[\frac{\sum X^2 - (\sum X)^2/n}{n-1}\right]}$$

The X terms in this equation are the raw observations (heights) and n refers to the size of your sample. You should note that the $n-1$ term in this equation corrects for the fact that the variability of scores in your sample is likely to be smaller than it really is in the population. As sample size increases, so the impact of subtracting 1 from the sample size has less effect on the estimate.

Unless you have the opportunity to draw a new sample, this estimate is the best you have of the true population mean and standard deviation. In reality the true population mean might be 162.5 cm and the standard deviation, 27.5 cm. Your sample, because it is a sample, is always likely to yield a less than perfectly accurate estimate of the population parameter.

It is important to recognise that any summary statistics, including statistics such as correlations, variances and regression weights, are best thought of as **parameter estimates**. The accuracy of these estimates, as with our mean height example, will depend on how well the relevant constructs were measured, how well the sampling was done and how large the sample is.

7.3.2 Sample size – the bigger the better?

When attempting to make parameter estimates, it is usually the case that the bigger the sample (assuming it to have been drawn appropriately) the better the estimates. As sample sizes increase the standard error associated with any parameter estimate gets smaller.

Standard errors of parameter estimates are very important for the confidence you can have in the estimates themselves. If you took lots of random samples and calculated the means within each you would end up with a distribution of sample means. In most cases this distribution would be a normal distribution. The standard deviation of this distribution (not the distribution of raw scores in the sample) can be calculated from information you have gained from just one sample using the following formula. The standard deviation $\sigma_{\bar{X}}$ of the distribution of sample means is called the **standard error** (SE) of the mean $\bar{X}$.

$$\text{est. SE of } \bar{X} \text{ or est. } \sigma_{\bar{X}} = \frac{\text{est. } \sigma}{\sqrt{n}}$$

where σ is the population standard deviation and n is the sample size. Again, this is an estimate of a population parameter. We didn't collect all possible samples so we are estimating the standard error. As with the standard deviation of raw scores we can use the standard error to indicate how likely it is that the population mean lies between particular values. For instance if the mean female height in a *sample* of 25 women was 160 cm and the estimated population standard deviation was 25 cm then the standard error of the mean would be:

$$\frac{25}{\sqrt{25}} = 5$$

We know from the theory of normal distributions that 95% of the scores in a normal distribution lie between the mean and 1.96 standard deviations from the mean. In our example this indicates there is a 0.95 probability that the population mean lies somewhere between 169.8 (160 + (1.96 × 5)) and 150.2 (160 − (1.96 × 5)). This gives us some **confidence limits** so that if we are asked what the population mean height is we can say we are fairly (95%) certain that it lies somewhere between 150.2 and 169.8.

The standard error of the mean decreases with increased sample size. If we had sampled 100 women yet still achieved a mean of 160 cm and an estimated population standard deviation of 25 cm the new standard error of the mean would be:

$$\frac{25}{\sqrt{100}} = 2.5$$

Now we are 95% certain that the population mean lies somewhere between 155.1 and 164.9 – somewhat less of a range than before (9.8 vs 19.6 cm). Note that we have had to collect four times as many data to halve the size of the 95% confidence limit interval. In reality you will have limited resources, and drawing very large samples may well be out of the question. However, it would be unwise to rush ahead with a study using a small sample if it was likely to lead to parameter estimates that carried unhelpfully large standard errors.

This example has used mean height as the population parameter of interest. Obviously this is not a psychological variable but the principles illustrated here would apply equally to any psychological variable. Any parameter estimated from sample data (e.g. a mean score, a correlation, a variance, a ratio, etc.) will have an associated standard error (calculated with differing formulae) which you should always seek to make as small as is practical. The standard error is an estimate of how much **sampling error** you have.

7.4 SAMPLING STRATEGIES

How do you select the sample? This decision will depend on the type of measurements you want to make, the nature of the population being studied, the complexity of your survey design and the resources available.

The first stage in any survey is to define the population from which you want to draw your sample. This is a decision that should be based on theoretical considerations. For example, you might be interested in the effects of youth unemployment on psychological wellbeing and thus need to study samples from the population of employed and unemployed youth. Or, you might have a developmental hypothesis that some cognitive abilities changed around the seventh or eighth year, so you might sample from the population of children aged 5, 7, 9 and 11, etc.

For most sampling strategies you will need a **sampling frame** which is a list of all the members of the population from which you can then draw your sample. This might sound easy at first but practical restrictions often curb your initial ambitions.

A truly representative survey of employed and unemployed young people in the UK is likely to prove very expensive and even more so if you intend to interview respondents. Assuming you really intend to get a representative sample of young people, then you would need to be prepared to travel to the Scottish Islands as well as the Scilly Isles. You would also need access to prisons and psychiatric hospitals, and then there is the question of whether people temporarily staying abroad should be included. What will you do about those who are seriously ill, or too disabled to respond, or homeless, or perhaps cannot speak English sufficiently well to understand your questions?

Similarly in the developmental example, your theory is probably not restricted in its applicability to UK children. Developmental theories often attempt to be universally applicable and you are unlikely to intend to draw a representative sample of the world population of children. If you resort to surveying children in local schools, can you be sure that they really do represent all children? Perhaps the local schools draw on predominantly middle class, socially advantaged areas. Perhaps they do not contain many children from ethnic minority groups. In both cases you would probably have to limit the scope of your study and restrict yourself to populations that you can reasonably get access to. Be aware that this puts restrictions on the degree to which you make generalisations based on your data.

7.5   CLASSICAL SAMPLING STRATEGIES

7.5.1   Simple random samples (SRS)

As the name suggests, the aim here is to achieve a sample where each person in the sampling frame has an equal chance of being selected for the survey. There are many ways to obtain a simple random sample (also sometimes called a **probability sample**). The first is to put all the names into a hat or tombola and simply draw out as many names as you need for the sample. This is reasonable when you have a small sampling frame, but if you had a list with 10,000 names on it you would have to write them all on to bits of paper first and this could be very time-consuming. You could number all the names in your population listing and use a random number generator but you must ensure that once a name is selected it cannot then be selected again. This is called **sampling without replacement** and is normal practice.

An alternative approach involves defining a **sampling interval** that you use to select potential respondents from the sampling frame. Let us say you have a sampling frame that contained 1600 names and you wanted a random sample of 200 to receive your questionnaire. The sampling interval here would be 1600/200 = 8. The next step is to use random number tables to select a number between 1 and 8 to give the **seed** number to start with. Say you get a 5. You would select the 5th person on the list, then the 13th (5 + 8), then the 21st (13 + 8) and so on. Strictly speaking, this procedure is not truly random sampling since once the 5th person has been selected the 4th and 6th cases cannot be selected as the order of the list determines who is now selected. However, for most purposes these procedures produce samples that are as good as those using tombola-type procedures.

Advantages   The SRS permits the full use of conventional statistical techniques. In many respects the SRS is to be regarded as the 'ideal' sampling strategy when parameter estimates are being made.

Disadvantages   SRS approaches are somewhat cumbersome when you wish, say, to sample from the whole of the UK. Interviewers would need to be sent to all corners of the country possibly to conduct only one or two interviews. While, generally speaking, an SRS will be representative of the population as a whole, any particular sample may not contain people with certain key characteristics. For instance, by chance you may fail to survey anyone from very high income groups and this might be important if your survey concerned attitudes towards charity donations.

7.5.2   Stratified random sampling

The stratified random sampling procedure addresses one of the disadvantages of the SRS approach by initially dividing the sample into **strata** or separate subpopulations. In the above example we might use Census information to divide the sampling frame up into people who live in high, medium and low income areas (what counted as 'high', 'medium' and 'low' would need to be carefully defined first). Once done, simple random samples are drawn from within these three strata. The three strata do not contribute an equal number of people to the sample but a number in proportion to the expected, or known, sizes of these strata in the population. There are proportionately fewer high earning people than low earners and your eventual sample must reflect these proportions as accurately as possible.

Advantages   The procedure increases the likelihood that key groups end up being in your sample whilst still maintaining much of the random element that is desirable for parameter estimation. Stratification also lowers the standard error of estimates by removing the effect of between-strata variation (see Moser and Kalton, 1971 for a more technical discussion of this design).

Disadvantages   In many cases you will not have the necessary information with which to create the strata. It would be unwise, for instance, to use foreign sounding names as the basis for dividing population lists up in terms of ethnicity. Information on ethnicity is usually unavailable in population listings with the notable exception of those based on the Census. This lack of information may well apply to the key variables of interest in your study.

7.5.3   Cluster sampling procedures

This approach gets over the difficulties of travelling distances and costs associated with the SRS approach by first selecting a smaller number of clustering units and then drawing the sample from within these smaller units. You might wish to sample schoolchildren's attitudes towards exams but it would be impractical to use an SRS design to achieve this. Instead you could select schools as clustering units. These would be selected at random and then all pupils within these schools would be sampled. For the purposes of increasing the accuracy of any estimates you wish to make it is usually better to have a larger number of small clustering units than to have a small number of larger clustering units. In this example it would be better to have schools as the clustering unit and select a larger number of them than to cluster on the basis of education authorities, say, and have to select only a few of them.

Advantages   Geographically large areas can be studied without excessive travel and subsistence costs being involved. These are especially useful designs in cases where sampling frames for all individuals are not readily available. A listing of all pupils in the country does not exist, but lists within schools are available or can be created easily.

It is possible to create multi-stage designs by selecting clusters and then conducting random sampling (or some form of stratified sampling) within the cluster.

Disadvantages   As people within a cluster tend be more like one another than individuals in different cluster units, the standard errors associated with parameter estimates tend to be higher than with SRS designs. It is also possible to accidentally select clusters that contain no, or very few, people belonging to a certain stratum of the population. By chance, for instance, you might select schools from areas with few members of ethnic minorities in them, thus under-representing that group.

7.5.4 Quota sampling

Quota sampling attempts to create a representative sample by specifying quotas, or targets, of particular types of people that need to be included to represent the population. As an example, let us assume we know that 50% of the population in a particular age group are female and that 16% of males and 14% of females are left-handed pen users. We want a sample that is representative of both sex and handedness: we decide on a sample size, say 100, and then set quotas. We need 50 males and 50 females. We also need to balance the handedness of respondents appropriately within the sexes, so we set four quotas as follows: 8 left-handed males (16% of 50), 42 right-handed males, 7 left-handed females (14% of 50) and 43 right-handed females.

Once the sample is defined, the researcher approaches people in the relevant age group, confirms their sex and asks them about handedness when using a pen. People become sample members as long as the quotas have not been filled. Once we have our 7 left-handed females we reject any subsequent left-handed females that come along.

Advantages The great advantage of quota sampling is that a sample that looks something like the population in terms of key characteristics can be obtained very quickly and cheaply. No population listing is required; only information about the population characteristics with which to define quotas is needed.

Disadvantages All sorts of selection biases may serve to render the sample unrepresentative of the target population. People who are not physically or temporally near the sampling point could never enter the sample. The researcher might only approach people who look as if they would be polite and co-operative. People who are not easily classified as male or female just by observation may be excluded by not being approached. If you have multiple levels of controls on the quotas (e.g. male left-handers over 60 with ginger hair) filling some quotas may prove very difficult.

Most common statistical tests in psychology calculate standard errors assuming the sample is a simple random one. They are not strictly appropriate for quota sample derived data. Moser and Kalton (1971) discuss ways of assessing the representativeness of quota samples and statistical procedures that are appropriate for use with them.

7.5.5 Theoretical sampling

Where the aim is not to estimate population parameters but to develop theory it may be appropriate to sample groups of people who are most likely to provide theoretical insights. A study on the impact of unwanted pregnancies using large scale SRS surveying procedures would be rather cumbersome.

Approaching pregnant women in local clinics and self-help groups would seem a more efficient way of gaining useful insights into the problems of unwanted pregnancy. This approach is common in qualitative research (Glaser and Strauss, 1967) and where statistical inference is not required.

Advantages   You talk to the people who are likely to give you the greatest insight into the research question. Travel and labour costs are minimised.

Disadvantages   You may not end up talking to people who would provide information that contradicts your theory. Other researchers may choose to dismiss your work because their theoretical sample supported a different theoretical position.

7.5.6   Other sampling strategies

Random digit dialling (RDD) survey techniques are rapidly gaining acceptability within the social sciences. This is really a cross between a sampling strategy and a data collection technique. Put very simply, a computer randomly generates telephone numbers and the researcher conducts a simple screening procedure to see if anyone at the end of the telephone is a member of the population of interest to the study. If so, a telephone interview is carried out and indeed the answers are usually entered straight into the computer (sometimes referred to as **computer-aided telephone interviewing** or CATI). Attempts are usually made to make such procedures as random as possible, and traditional objections to the technique on the grounds that not everyone has a telephone, while still relevant, are now regarded as less serious than in the past (Marcus and Crane, 1986; Groves, 1989).

   Snowball techniques are particularly useful for inaccessible populations for which population listings will not be available (e.g. drug users, cult members). In these cases, a small number of known members of the target population are asked to introduce you to other members who, in turn, are invited to nominate other members to help you. By this means you hope your initial small sample will 'snowball' into a larger one. This procedure may often be the best available to you though it has obvious built-in biases. You will only ever get to contact people who are in the social network you tap into. People in another network or in no network at all will not be sampled.

7.6   WHERE TO GET POPULATION LISTINGS

For large scale surveys of the general population of adults the *Electoral Register* and the *Postcode Address File* are the most commonly used sampling frames. The *Electoral Register* is available in libraries and main post offices and lists people eligible to vote. Before using this list you should read one of the many sociological guides to its use (e.g. Butcher and Dodd, 1983; Arber, 1993) as it contains some known biases which may have significance for your research problem.

   The *Postcode Address File* lists addresses to which mail can be sent. This is available in computerised form which makes it convenient and it has better coverage than the *Electoral Register* (Dodd, 1987). As this is not a list of individuals you will have to conduct an initial screening survey to see if anyone in your target population lives at the address. Obviously some addresses will not be domestic residences so you might want to use the *Small User File* which lists addresses that receive a small amount of mail.

A number of commercial companies now exist that can do academically respectable sampling for you. Their services are not free but, as they are in business to provide good quality samples and enhance their reputations among both the business and academic communities, they may be able to do a better job at this than you could do. When requesting a sample it helps if you are aware of the previous discussion of sampling strategies: you will then be talking the same language.

Studies with young people may involve school registers/records to obtain population listings. Whilst such lists are not necessarily accurate, these are one of the few sources that also provide the respondents' ages. Access is best achieved by an initial approach to headteachers, though for a large study an approach to the education authority for 'in principle' agreement to release names would be advisable. Headteachers are under no obligation to provide these lists and they may reasonably ask that parental agreement is sought before any child's name is released to you. There is a degree of clerical work involved in collating such lists and permissions, so it would be appropriate to offer clerical assistance and/or money to pay for the clerical work. Most headteachers would like some feedback on the results of the study.

Access to samples based on hospital or GP records may be appropriate for studies dealing with health-related topics. An approach to the local family practitioner committee and the local hospital ethical committee will be necessary. They will need to be assured that the study has some value both to the research community and, in principle, to the eventual sample members. Ethical committees may well demand design changes to your study before they agree to let your research go ahead. One of the most common requirements is that respondents give **informed consent** before taking part in the study (see Chapter 3). While this is ethically desirable for all surveys, research on medical issues usually requires greater explanation than is the norm in other survey topics.

If you intend to keep any information on computers about people you should register as a holder of such information to comply with the Data Protection Act. Most universities and health authorities have an officer who deals with registering users. Respondents have a number of rights under this Act which they can exercise regardless of whether you register under the Act or not. Registering will make it easier for you to know what respondents can expect from you in terms of confidentiality and access to the data.

7.7 RESPONSE RATES

When reporting any study involving sampling, the response rate should be given. As you have no control over whether those approached actually help you with your work, the representativeness of your results depends on how many people finally take part.

In general, you should always seek to maximise response rates either by repeated recontacts or by the provision of face-to-face interviewers to help people complete questionnaires they are having difficulties with. Sending reminders, issuing repeat questionnaires or offering to return at a more convenient time will work up to a point but, depending on the research topic, additional contacts may serve to alienate people. In a sexual behaviour survey, endless repeated copies of an explicit questionnaire being put through people's doors may cause offence, for example.

It is good practice to report response rates in some detail by giving a breakdown in terms of types of non-response. Inevitably, some people will not be found at the address you have: they may have died or moved or the address may be wrong or the building derelict. It is reasonable to adjust the base against which response rates are calculated by removing these cases and reporting responses against an **achievable base**. These potential respondents were never really in a position to refuse to help you and reflect inaccuracies in the sample listings. Providing these inaccuracies are not systematically related to some characteristic of those incorrectly placed on the lists, this practice is acceptable. Some sample members, however, will be willing to help but unable to actually help (e.g. being ill or unable to read). Of course some will simply refuse to help you because they do not want to for some reason. Record these different types of non-response systematically.

You must be careful not to obscure **non-response biases** when reporting response rates. **Non-response biases** occur when your data collection procedure systematically excludes certain kinds of people. An example would be travelling salespeople or those who work on oil-rigs who are less likely to be at their home addresses when you call to interview them. Be aware of such potential biases and acknowledge them when reporting your findings.

Technically, it is not appropriate to calculate simple response rates for quota samples. It is good practice to give an indication of how many people approached refused to help you, however. As you took the first people you came across who represented each quota and you may have unconsciously approached people who looked as if they would help, then it is difficult to calculate a meaningful response rate.

There is much discussion about what constitutes a 'good' return rate, yet there is really no absolute answer to this since so much depends on the topic of the survey, the design and the nature of the sample. Postal surveys of the general public can achieve rates as high as 80% for some relatively innocuous topics yet they drop dramatically to below 40% if the topic is especially sensitive (e.g. sexual behaviour).

There is a general tendency for females to be more co-operative than males and for younger people to be more co-operative than older people. Interviewer-based surveys tend to get better responses (by around 10–15%) since it is easier to throw a questionnaire in the bin than refuse a nice polite person who calls at your door. Long questionnaires, those that take hours to complete, yield lower rates than those that take 20 minutes. There are always occasional exceptions to these generalisations which make attempting to define 'good' rates a very tricky business.

Too much emphasis on response rates can be misplaced particularly when it comes to the kinds of surveys conducted in psychology. Surveys of groups who are under some compulsion to comply (e.g. children surveyed in school) might produce very high rates yet this reflects the quasi-compulsory nature of the data collection method rather than the quality of the data *per se*. The same applies to surveys of students. These high rates do not mean that the resulting data are necessarily more valid or somehow 'better' than data gathered via a more voluntary strategy. Similarly, studies can achieve high response rates yet produce questionnaires that contain vast amounts of missing data.

Whilst one should not advocate an 'anything goes' approach to evaluating response rates, lower rates do not necessarily mean the data are worthless. It is possible, for example, to report **lower bound prevalence estimates** using information about the response rate to create alternative kinds of confidence limits to be associated with parameter estimates (see Breakwell and Fife-Schaw, 1992). It is also appropriate to describe the achieved sample as accurately as possible and compare it against known characteristics of the population (e.g. by using Census data) to assess just how representative the sample is. Yet another strategy is to compare parameter estimates gained with your data against those achieved by other studies which have possibly used a range of alternative sampling strategies (cf. Fife-Schaw and Breakwell, 1992).

7.8 SMALL SAMPLE ISSUES

In common with lots of textbooks on sampling and survey design I have stressed the desirability of getting a large sample. Generalisations about the population are likely to be more convincing to others when there is a well-drawn large sample. Large samples produce parameter estimates with small standard errors and increase the statistical power of your hypothesis tests (see Chapter 25). Studies done with small samples can yield ambiguous non-significant results as you cannot usually tell whether the result was because the null hypothesis was true or because your sample was too small. You cannot turn this around and conclude that because your sample was small any effect you observe must therefore be 'significant', however tempting this might seem!

The realities of doing psychological research on many topics are such that getting large samples is simply not possible. Much clinical research on patients with specific complaints/disorders cannot obtain large samples as, thankfully, such groups are not large. Research on offenders with particular criminal histories (e.g. child murderers) is usually done on small samples as, again, mercifully, there are not lots of such offenders to study. Given this and the desirability of large samples, is such research therefore a waste of time?

Obviously the answer is 'no'. Insights gained from researching such topics can be very valuable and will often have important practical implications. Indeed, studies on single cases can be particularly useful (see Chapter 5) especially when the single individual is studied intensively. What is needed is a recognition that 'research' does not just mean experiments, big samples and lots of statistics. Some useful illustrative examples of important small sample clinical research can be found in Powell and Adams (1993).

The use of inferential statistics such as *t*-tests and correlations (see Chapter 25) implies that hypotheses are being tested and that studies have been designed as 'fair' tests of these hypotheses. One of these criteria for 'fairness' is that you have a big enough sample to give you sufficient statistical power to make the results of such tests unambiguous. If you know in advance that your sample will be small then you should not place too much emphasis on statistical tests. It might be better to regard your study as exploratory or as contributing to a data base that later researchers using meta-analysis (see Chapter 28) might merge together with similar studies. This increases the effective sample size, thereby allowing more powerful statistical testing. You should also remember that the magnitude of any differences or correlations you find (the effect sizes) may be of importance separately from their statistical significance.

Studies with small samples may give indications of fruitful avenues for future research. If a phenomenon looks interesting in a small scale project, funding agencies may be more inclined to put in the resources to allow the collection of data from a larger sample, perhaps by increasing the size of the catchment area or period of time available for data collection. A clinical study, for instance, may have had to be based on clients presenting themselves at a small number of clinics in a relatively short period. Extra resources, made available because of the promise of your initial study, may allow you to go to more clinics over a much longer period, thereby permitting the sampling of much more of the population of interest. Essentially this is to view small sample work as a kind of pilot study.

Statistical inference and population parameter estimation are not everything, of course. Research using qualitative approaches such as focus groups and ethnographic methods are usually impractical on large samples and it is much more desirable to engage in theoretical sampling where the aim is to approach people who ought, on *a priori* grounds, be the most informative. Here you want to get a large amount of information from people in the hope that it will be substantively more informative than information you might have obtained from a large survey.

What is crucial is to distinguish between samples that will be small because the population is hard to access, and samples that are small because not enough effort has been put into the study. Small sample research, like any other kind, is only meaningful if it is carried out as rigorously as is reasonably possible.

7.9 CONCLUSIONS

This brief review of sampling and surveying should give you some idea of the important pitfalls of the various kinds of design. The last decade has seen a growth in the number of psychologists involved in large scale survey investigations and this trend looks likely to continue. Surveys offer the potential to answer a range of research questions that have until now remained in the realm of speculation. Surveys are now more cost effective than ever before and funding agencies are progressively more willing to invest in big surveys than at any time in the past. However, the value of such surveys will continue to depend crucially on good design and attention to the kinds of issues discussed here.

7.10 FURTHER READING

Most texts on survey and sampling issues tend to be oriented towards sociologists and other social scientists rather than specifically to psychologists. This should not prevent you reading them since the issues related to sociological data apply equally to psychological data. Moser and Kalton's (1971) text is widely admired as one of the most detailed yet accessible works on survey design and sampling. The ESRC/SCPR Centre for Applied Social Surveys (CASS) has a website devoted to survey methodology at http://www.scpr.ac.uk/cass/ and publishes regular newsletters on the latest research in survey and sample design issues.

8

Facet Theory: an Approach to Research

Jennifer Brown and Julie Barnett

Contents

8.1 INTRODUCTION

There are many sad stories of students, burning to carry out an experimental project, who end up with a completely unanalysable mishmash of data. They wanted to get on with it and thought that they could leave thoughts of analysis until after the experiment. They were wrong. Statistical analysis and experimental design must be considered together and, whilst there are broad principles of experimental design . . . they cannot easily be reduced to recipes guaranteed for every eventuality. (Robson, 1994: 2)

Whilst this admonition was issued with respect to experimental design, it can be extended to apply more generally to enthusiastic students embarking on a research project, whether hypothesis testing or hypothesis generating. Facet theory offers a set of principles and analytical techniques that will aid systematic research design, data analysis and interpretation within a conceptual framework. The approach can be used with structured, semi-structured and unstructured data which are either qualitative or quantitative. The only limit on kinds of data that can be analysed is want of imagination.

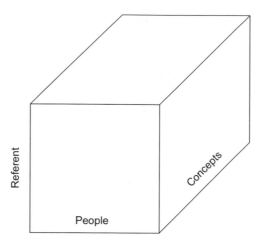

FIGURE 8.1   *The data cube (adapted from Canter et al., 1985)*

There are three broad distinctions that can be made with respect to data and the ways in which researchers attempt to examine them: aspects of people (e.g. demographic, occupational, personality characteristics) in terms of conceptualisations (e.g. thoughts, feelings, behaviour) and with respect to some referent (e.g. situations, places, times). This has been described as the data cube by Canter et al. (1985: 96) (see Figure 8.1).

This data cube shows the variety of possibilities for analysis. Each plane of the cube offers different analytic permutations. It is often extremely difficult to conduct analysis that combines all three attributes of the data. More frequently data are aggregated in some way and the analyses proceed by working through each plane of the data cube. When people are the focus of the analysis it may be required to plot individual differences with respect to a referent or a concept. Other faces of the cube can also be explored by aggregating the data across the sample. Here it is the patterns underlying the conceptualisations of the whole sample rather than the individual differences that are the focus. At yet other times the relationships between the conceptualisations and some referent may be explored.

Facet theory offers an approach in research design, analysis and interpretation of data. It can do so with novel topics for which there are no strong theoretical models and can be thought of as a kind of bottom-up approach of exploration generating conceptualisations or hypotheses. Facet theory can also be applied in a top-down mode in which the conceptualisations are well defined and verification is sought from empirical observation.

Becoming a facet theorist may require a radical shift in thinking and an eloquent personal account of such a shift is given in David Canter's introduction to his edited book on the topic (Canter, 1985). It is important to note that facet theory itself does not dictate the concepts or methods that are used. However, facet theory does offer a complete package that contains a set of tools to fashion the conceptual (**facet**) design (**mapping sentence**) and a companion set of analytical procedures (smallest space analysis or **SSA**;

multidimensional scalogram analysis or **MSA**; and partial order scalogram analysis or **POSA**) to handle empirical observations. These analytical procedures are all forms of multidimensional scaling derived from the work of Louis Guttman (1968), the architect of facet theory, and as such they all address regional hypotheses. It should be emphasised that there is little reason why facet theory cannot explore more traditional types of hypotheses (e.g. those concerning distinctions and differences between facets) (Borg and Groenen, 1997). In principle then, a facet theoretic study may utilise traditional techniques such as ANOVA. However, this is not generally the case because facet theorists tend to share Guttman's (1981) suspicion of inferential techniques. In the treatment below we will concentrate upon the use of these scaling methods in conjunction with the facet theory approach.

The research process proceeds by formulating a conceptual model and reconstructing that model from empirical reality. This is accomplished topologically. In other words the formulation is conceived in terms of a geometric structure which is retrieved from the empirical data, represented in a multidimensional space. Louis Guttman (e.g. 1981) eschewed the notion of statistical p-values which he felt to be not only arbitrary but also little understood. Rather, if the facets can successfully be retrieved, there is said to be a correspondence between the conceptual formulation and the empirical structure as revealed through analysis (Borg, 1981: 50). This would be equivalent to obtaining a statistically significant result. Thus an essential proposition of facet theory is that greater conceptual similarity will be reflected in greater empirical similarity. A **rationale** or warrant that supports the proposed correspondence is also required. In mathematical terms this correspondence is reflected in the magnitude of correlations, i.e. the greater the association the higher the correlation. In facet theory terms this is represented in terms of linear distances, i.e. the more similar any two items are the smaller the distance between them. Practical illustrations of the relationship between theoretical conceptualisations and the way in which the data are represented can be seen below.

8.2   CONCEPTUAL TOOLKIT

Facets are distinct conceptual categories that describe a discrete component in the area of research (Donald, 1995: 120). These are defined by the research investigator and are of three main types.

Background facets describe characteristics of individuals such as their age, gender and occupation. These are often used as aspects of the people face of the data cube. The research problem may address differences between people, say in terms of gender. The multivariate space of empirical observations would be expected to be made up of two distinct regions, one that contained all the women respondents and the other the male respondents. Thus a partition line can be drawn that zones the respondents by the facet of gender. If this is achieved then it satisfies the condition necessary for correspondence to have been demonstrated. **Domain facets** are the content of the theoretical formulation in the particular area of the research. In the research area of police occupational stress, Brown and Campbell (1990) proposed a domain facet describing the stressors that were likely to impinge on police officers. These comprised organisational, managerial and operational stressors. To achieve a correspondence with empirical observations, the multidimensional space should have three identifiable regions into which the different types of stressors can be placed. Finally there are **range facets** which describe the possible responses individuals may make in terms of the domain facets. This is akin to the responses in a conventional questionnaire using e.g. Likert type rating scales. Range facets may also be dichotomous.

Each facet is made up of **elements** which are 'the different values . . . that logically and completely describe the variation of the facet' (White and Mitchell, 1976: 60). Thus the background facet of gender is described by two elements, male and female. A domain facet such as the content of worries about leaving school and coming to university could have three elements: aspects of the social, work and physical environments. The range for transition worries could be couched in terms of a five-point scale of not at all worried (1) to extremely worried (5).

A system of notation is used when specifying the facets and their constituent elements. This helps to recognise redundancies in definitions and also is helpful when reconstructing the conceptual or facet structure in the multidimensional space. A capital letter is used to label the facet, and lower case with numerical subscript is used to denote the elements. For example, Payne et al. (1976) defined three facets underlying job satisfaction and organisational climate. These were: facet A, unit of analysis, with elements a_1 individual, a_2 social collectivity; facet B, aspect of analysis, with elements b_1 job, b_2 organisation; facet C, nature of concept, with elements c_1 affective, c_2 descriptive.

As well as the content of the facets and their constituent elements, the relationships within and between facets are specified. Frequently in psychological research, some conceptualisations are regarded as more salient in their influence in the processes being studied. Importance is reflected in the sequence of the facets. Decisions about this depend on the rationale, which is often derived from the theoretical literature. Moreover, within a facet the elements may be in a quantitative relationship or qualitative relationship. The former is a simple ordered sequence in which each adjacent element is more similar to its immediate neighbour than to elements further away, as in the gradations on a ruler. In the latter the relationship is non-ordered. Here adjacent elements are also most similar, to each other but now the first and last elements are also similar indicating a circular relationship like the segments of a cake.

Runkel and McGrath (1972) list the properties of facets as follows:

- Items are classified by reference to all facets in the domain.
- Each facet is divided into an exhaustive set of values or elements.
- Elements are mutually exclusive.
- Logical relationships between the facets are specified.
- Facets should exhaust the domain of concern (area of research).

Donald (1995) suggests these are somewhat ideal. In the real world of research it is unlikely that all possible categories or conceptualisations will be included,

The level of worry experienced by student x being

A Sex	B Ethnicity	C Age

$$\begin{Bmatrix} a_1 & \text{male} \\ a_2 & \text{female} \end{Bmatrix} \quad \begin{Bmatrix} b_1 & \text{white} \\ b_2 & \text{Asian} \\ b_3 & \text{Afro-Caribbean} \\ b_4 & \text{other} \end{Bmatrix} \quad \begin{Bmatrix} c_1 & \text{under 21 years} \\ c_2 & \text{21–24 years} \\ c_3 & \text{older} \end{Bmatrix}$$

D Modality	E Environment

in $\begin{Bmatrix} d_1 & \text{affective} \\ d_2 & \text{cognitive} \\ d_3 & \text{behavioural} \end{Bmatrix}$ modalities with respect to $\begin{Bmatrix} e_1 & \text{work} \\ e_2 & \text{social} \\ e_3 & \text{physical} \end{Bmatrix}$ environments

will be $\begin{Bmatrix} \text{high} \\ \text{to} \\ \text{low} \end{Bmatrix}$ worry

FIGURE 8.2   *Mapping sentence to investigate student worries*

and often for pragmatic reasons the researchers will seek to restrict some aspects of the study and thus exclude some of the facets and/or elements.

Having identified the facets, elements and order relationships, these are formally presented as a **mapping sentence**. This is 'a verbal statement of the domain and of the range of a mapping including connectives between facets as in ordinary language' (Shye, 1978: 413). Mapping sentences are extremely useful devices which impose the disciplines of rigour and precision on the research investigator to define the design and implied relationships within the study. Donald enumerates the uses and advantages of mapping sentences:

- gives a precise definition of the universe of observations to be employed in the study
- makes a succinct statement of the research design that is readily communicable
- provides a specification for the design of research questions such as items in a questionnaire
- aids the specification of relationships within and between facets
- permits modification of the research design by extending, collapsing or redefining facets and their elements
- acts as a template to engage the process of correspondence between conceptual definitions and empirical structure
- helps to develop comparative and research replication.

A mapping sentence to investigate student worries is shown in Figure 8.2. It includes three background facets (A sex; B ethnicity; C age) and two domain facets (D psychological modality; E environmental referent). Level of worry forms the range facet.

Empirical observations made in the light of the mapping sentence can be designed as questionnaire items by creating a profile (*structuple*) of one element from each of the domain facets.

8.3 ANALYTICAL TOOLKIT

In order to map the correspondence between the conceptual definitions and empirical observations, Guttman and his collaborator Lingoes devised a series of multidimensional scaling procedures.

8.3.1 Smallest space analysis (SSA)

This analysis provides a representation of data in a geometric space. This involves a series of transformations. Initially the raw data are aligned within a matrix that might comprise questionnaire items as columns and individual respondents make up the rows. Each cell of the matrix thus contains a number representing the individual's response to that item. This then is subjected to various correlational or associational analyses, dependent on the type of data, such that the higher the association between any pair of questions, the greater the magnitude of the correlation or association. A further transformation takes place in that the patterns as reflected in the correlations are converted to linear distances. Now the higher the association between any pair of questions the shorter the distance between them. The procedure operates to represent the data parsimoniously, presenting a solution that minimises the number of spatial dimensions in which to represent the best fit for the patterns of relationships. The **coefficient of alienation** is a measure that helps to judge the 'goodness of fit'. This is a measure of the rank order of the items in terms of the correlations and the corresponding rank order in terms of the linear distances. For further discussion of how to assess the acceptability of the various measures of 'goodness of fit' see Brown (1985).

Simple data might be represented in one dimension. In a study of attitudes towards nuclear power, Brown et al. (1983) asked a series of questions about the acceptability of various uses of nuclear power: offensive or deterrent weaponry, transport, electricity generation and medical application. Respondents were also classified as 'active anti', 'passive anti', 'uncommitted' and 'pro' in their attitude towards nuclear power. A one-dimensional SSA provided a neat analysis of the positioning of these applications dependent on attitudinal position. As can be seen in Figure 8.3, those classed as 'active anti' cluster all the applications at one extreme opposite the medical uses of radiation. Those holding other attitudinal positions differentiate between the applications in different ways.

More usually the solution requires two or three dimensions for an acceptable fit. An example of children's worries about moving from junior to secondary schools that illustrates this is given in section 8.4.1.

8.3.2 Multidimensional scalogram analysis (MSA)

The input data matrix for this procedure generally consists of nominal data (see Chapter 11), usually containing profiles of responses for individuals. Where the SSA plots the columns as points in space, the MSA plots the rows. The purpose is to present similarities (and differences) between profiles such

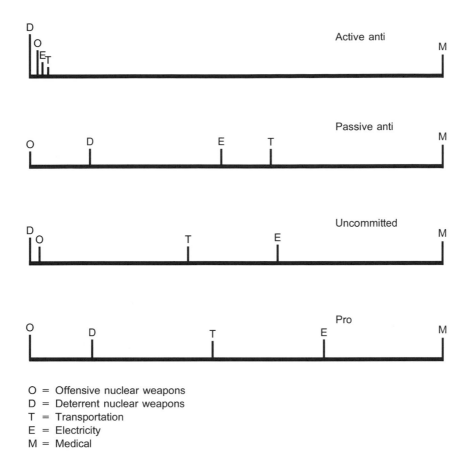

O = Offensive nuclear weapons
D = Deterrent nuclear weapons
T = Transportation
E = Electricity
M = Medical

FIGURE 8.3   *One-dimension SSA: discrimination of classes of nuclear technology*

that individuals having greater commonality will be represented as closer points in space, whereas those that are dissimilar will be presented as more distant. It is likely that the most similar individuals will form a 'centre of gravity' in the plot whilst differently dissimilar individuals will be variously located away from the main cluster depending on the nature of their shared characteristics.

Individuals are plotted as a function of comparison across all the descriptors (background and domain facets). Interpretation is aided because the points representing the individuals are anchored and each facet plot may be overlaid to see the distribution of responses for those individuals. Partition lines may be drawn on the plot that 'capture' the target items that fall into identifiable regions. There are two indexes available to indicate the efficiency of the zoning created by the lines of partition: **selectivity**, which is the exclusivity of target items appearing in the partitioned zone as a function of all the items appearing in that zone; and **sensitivity**, which is the efficiency of the partitioning in enclosing the members of the target items within the zone as a function of the total number of target items. Both indices are expressed as percentages (Shalit, 1977). See also Chapter 20.

8.3.3   Partial order scalogram analysis (POSA)

This procedure is a technique for ordering profiles on more than one dimension simultaneously. It assumes that items are ordered into discrete categories and that there is a common order. Profiles are arranged into the most compact geometric space possible that preserves the original order and can account for qualitative differences amongst them. POSA represents an extension to the classic Guttman scale. This is a symmetrical and ordered increment whereby endorsement of one item predicts the endorsement of another, e.g. if an individual indicates they have a PhD it is very likely they have an undergraduate degree and gained some kind of advanced school leaving certificate. Holding of a first degree does not predict that the person also has a doctorate. Thus it is possible to construct symmetrical profiles from having no qualifications (no PhD, no first degree and no school certificates: 000) to having specified academic achievements gathered in a particular order (PhD, first degree, school certificate: 111). The set 000, 001, 011, 111 forms a perfect Guttman scale. POSA allows for the possibility of non-symmetrical profiles, in other words an individual could have a school leaving certificate, and no first degree but hold a PhD, giving them a profile of 101.

One form of representation of a POSA is the Hasse diagram (Shye and Amar, 1985: 278). This is a geometric representation in which a profile that is greater than another is represented as a point that is higher with respect to some specified direction and with a direct line connecting the two profiles. Incompatible profiles, i.e. ones where there is not an ordered increment between the profiles, are not connected by a line. These diagrams can be constructed by hand through a process of trial and error. An example is presented in section 8.4.1. Shye and Amar describe a computerised version (POSAC/LSA) which gives a two-dimensional representation of the profiles in which numbers represent the profiles in a configuration reflecting the scores on the items making up the profiles.

8.4   EXAMPLES

8.4.1   Bottom-up heuristic approach

When the researcher is exploring a relatively new field or novel topic, there may not be an obvious formulation or set of explanatory concepts from which to draw. Muedeking and Bahr (1976) analysed the attributes of 'down and out' men in an exploratory fashion using interview material from which they constructed profiles of the men in terms of themes identified from the transcripts. This was then subjected to analysis using SSA from which three broad differentiators were retrieved that became the basis of a typology of homeless men. Brown et al. (1987) used SSA to provide an account of the structure

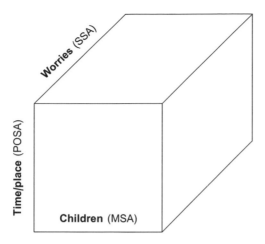

FIGURE 8.4 *Analytical procedures relationship to the data cube*

underpinning young children's conceptualisations of nuclear power as revealed through their drawings and how these changed over time. Brown and Blount (1999) drew out themes from a content analysis of the stressors experienced by sex offender treatment managers and subjected these to analysis by MSA in order to develop a questionnaire to apply to a larger respondent sample.

In a set of linked studies Brown and colleagues undertook research to determine the transition worries experienced by children when moving from primary to secondary school. There were no clear-cut conceptualisations that defined the universe of children's transition worries and little research was then available that looked at changes in worries over time. If the research problem is cast in terms of the data cube (Figure 8.4) then we can see that the task becomes the identification of worries over time as experienced by the children and perceived by the teachers. The three analytical procedures allowed the researchers to explore the underlying structure of children's worries (SSA), to map individual children in terms of their worries (MSA), and to chart the changes in the pattern of worries over time (POSA).

Brown and Armstrong (1982) asked children to indicate in an essay the worries that they had about moving from their junior to secondary school. Essays were content analysed and 22 different worries itemised. The essays were recoded in terms of the presence or absence of the 22 worries and submitted for analysis by SSA. Partition lines were drawn by visual inspection, and by reference to the correlation coefficients. These indicated three distinct types of worries: those to do with feelings and friendships; new and unfamiliar kinds of school work; and new rules, regulations and discipline regimens (Figure 8.5).

This then was the basis of the facet structure of transition worries consisting of the presence or absence of the three types of worries and formed the basis for construction of a mapping sentence (Figure 8.6).

By drawing one element from the three domain facets, one can obtain profiles that describe all possible combinations of worries. In order to determine

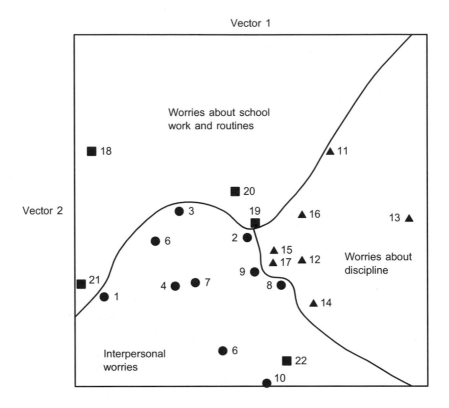

Vector 1

Worries about school
work and routines

■ 18

■ 20

Vector 2   ● 3   19   ▲ 16   13 ▲
                                ■
● 6   2 ●
                              ▲ 15   Worries about
                              ▲ 17   ▲ 12   discipline
                         9 ●
■ 21   4 ●   ● 7   8 ●
● 1   ▲ 14

Interpersonal   ● 6
worries   ■ 22
                    ● 10

1 ● feeling lonely
2 ● feeling lost
3 ● being small
4 ● not having friends
5 ● not knowing anyone
6 ● coping without best friend (from junior school)
7 ● rumours about teachers in the school
8 ● fear of 'horrible' pupils
9 ● fear of being bullied
10 ● friend paired off with someone else
11 ▲ catching wrong bus
12 ▲ detentions
13 ▲ not getting right uniform
14 ▲ being told off
15 ▲ being late
16 ▲ doing wrong
17 ▲ strict teachers
18 ■ tackling new subjects
19 ■ general fear of school routines
20 ■ doing homework
21 ■ not used to being with so many different teachers
22 ■ tests

FIGURE 8.5 *SSA of pupils' transfer worries during their first term in secondary school (reproduced with permission of the* British Educational Research Journal)

The likelihood that child x

will indicate $\left\{ \begin{array}{ll} a_0 & \text{absence} \\ a_1 & \text{presence} \end{array} \right\}$ of interpersonal

$\left\{ \begin{array}{ll} b_0 & \text{absence} \\ b_1 & \text{presence} \end{array} \right\}$ of discipline $\left\{ \begin{array}{ll} c_0 & \text{absence} \\ c_1 & \text{presence} \end{array} \right\}$ of school work

worries will be $\left\{ \begin{array}{c} \text{high} \\ \text{to} \\ \text{low} \end{array} \right\}$ likelihood

FIGURE 8.6 *Mapping sentence for children's worries when transferring from junior to secondary school*

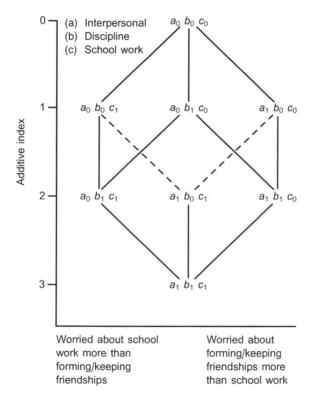

FIGURE 8.7 *Partial order scalogram analysis of children's transfer worries (reproduced with permission of the* British Educational Research Journal*)*

the change in focus of worries, a Hasse diagram representing the profiles as a partial order was constructed (Figure 8.7). The percentage of children experiencing particular combinations of worries can be plotted on to the diagram. Doing this revealed that the children switch their concerns from the interpersonal domain to school work and routines (Brown and Armstrong, 1982).

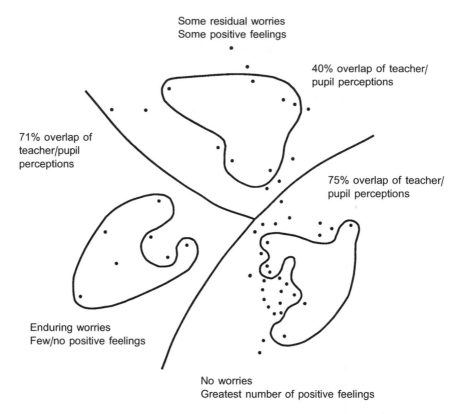

Some residual worries
Some positive feelings

40% overlap of teacher/
pupil perceptions

71% overlap of
teacher/pupil
perceptions

75% overlap of teacher/
pupil perceptions

Enduring worries
Few/no positive feelings

No worries
Greatest number of positive feelings

FIGURE 8.8   *MSA plot of individual children as a function of their expressed positive and negative expectations and feelings regarding secondary school. Each dot represents one child. Their positions relative to each other are a function of similarly expressed fears and positive feelings. Within the 'captured' circles are those children whom the teachers judge have not made a well-adjusted transfer (reproduced with permission of Routledge; currently published by NFER-Nelson)*

The final part of this series of analyses was conducted by Brown and Armstrong (1986) who wanted to show the impact of transition worries on individual children and to see the degree to which teachers concurred with the child's own assessment of their worries. The facets identified in the first study were the basis of self-assessment by the children and were also subjected to ratings by the teachers in terms of how well they thought the children had adjusted to their new school. Individual children were profiled and then plotted using MSA (Figure 8.8). The teachers' ratings were mapped on to the individual child to match teacher and child assessment.

8.4.2   Top-down hypothesis driven approach

In contrast to the exploratory approach, facet theory can also be used to generate and test hypotheses. This process will be illustrated here using the results of a class exercise in relation to the mapping sentence about student worries noted earlier (see Figure 8.2). Previous empirical and theoretical work provided the rationale for the inclusion and ordering of the facets and elements. A questionnaire was thus developed on the basis of the structuples derived from the domain facets. For example one d_1e_1 item was, 'How worried are you that you might not enjoy lectures?' Here 'enjoy' is designed to tap the affective element of the modality facet with 'lectures' being a work-related referent. A d_3e_2 item was, 'How worried are you about your ability to strike up conversations with your class mates?', which represented the behavioural element of the modality facet and the social element of the referent facet respectively. Three questions were devised to represent each structuple, thus comprising a 27-item questionnaire.

The data from the questionnaire were analysed using smallest space analysis. In the resulting plots each questionnaire item was plotted as a point. In order to begin the task of assessing the degree of correspondence between the facet structure and the way in which the questionnaire items were represented in the geometric space, the task of the researcher is initially to establish which points correspond with which structuple.

The relationship between the facet structure and the questionnaire responses would be assessed by exploring the way in which regions might be drawn on the plot to separate, for example, the d_1 items from the d_2 items and the d_3 items and so on. In the present example we hypothesised that the modality facet would form a non-ordered circular structure, that is that the elements of the facet could be partitioned as three qualitatively different 'slices of the cake'. This was not borne out in the data. Three regions corresponding to the three elements of the partition could be distinguished. However, these took the form of a modulating facet, that is, all the behavioural items were around the outside of the plot with the cognitive items within these. In the middle of the plot were all the affective items. Speculation as to the reason for this might suggest, contrary to the hypothesised relationships between the elements which gave equal weighting to each of the elements, that the affective modality is the most salient in relation to worries and the behavioural element the least salient. In this way then, the lack of the hypothesised correspondence between the facet structure and the empirical data offers the possibility of a 'conceptual iteration' which would lead to refinement in the specification of the mapping sentence.

A similar opportunity was also afforded by the results in relation to the referent facet. This had been hypothesised to form an ordered facet: that is, we hypothesised that there would be the most worry about work-related issues, with decreasing amounts of worry about social and physical issues. Evidence for such an ordered facet would be found in a partitioning that showed work items to be more similar (i.e. closer) to social items than they were to physical items. Here the task focused on identifying regions that might separate the e_1 items from the e_2 items and so on. There was evidence for an ordered facet: however, the nature of this was that worries about work issues were more similar to physical than social worries. The existence of an ordered facet can be further confirmed by mapping the mean worry score associated with each item on to the plot. Examination of the composition of the items themselves may throw some light on possible reasons for the unexpected ordering of the elements of the referent facet. It is clear that some of the 'physical' worry items, such as not being able to find your way around the campus or to the lecture theatres, have particular implications for work-related worries. This illustrates how the lack of a hypothesised correspondence between the facet structure and the profile of points in the SSA plot may lead, not only to a conceptual iteration, but also to exploring the possibility of refining the construction of questionnaire items.

In the present example, the empirical data did not offer unequivocal support for the hypothesised facet structure. However, they did provide the opportunity to demonstrate the way in which facet theory facilitates identification of the possibilities to develop both the conceptual framework and the way in which these concepts are operationalised.

8.5 CONCLUSIONS

A facet approach is a meta-theoretical framework into which a specific content theory is constructed and empirically verified. Facet theory comprises an input logic that defines conceptual formulations, a set of procedures for designing empirical observations and a package of multivariate statistics for analysing data. Ideally, these should be used *in toto*. However it is possible to use the statistical procedures without reference to facet theory, as demonstrated by Chapter 20 in this book. MSAs are a useful additional method for undertaking content analysis (e.g. Brown and Blount, 1999). Use of the mapping sentence can help to clarify a research design that may then be subjected to conventional statistical analysis of variance (e.g. Murphy, 1998). No doubt purists would be bothered by the *à la carte* advice offered here in the uses and application of facet theory, but we suggest that various aspects of the approach can be profitably employed in a flexible manner that avoids the confusions evident in the quotation from Robson presented at the beginning of the chapter.

8.6 FURTHER READING

The texts by J. Brown (1985) 'An introduction to the uses of facet theory' and Shye et al.'s (1994) *Introduction to Facet Theory: Content Design and Intrinsic Data Analysis in Behavioral Research* are both good general introductions to facet theory.

PART III

9

Research with Special Groups

John Everatt

Contents

9.1   INTRODUCTION

Almost any group of individuals could be thought of as special in some sense or other; the very act of taking part in a particular study may make a group distinct from others. We could think of children, older adults, even single cases, as special. However, for the most part, such groups will not be considered in the present chapter (reference to such cases can be found elsewhere in this book – for example Chapter 5). The term special group as used here is meant to refer to a group of individuals who comprise a cohort which is considered to differ from the norm. This could be a quantitative difference. For example, a special group could form one area of a normal distribution. A health psychologist might study those with obesity, the classification being determined by a cut-off point on a weight-to-size ratio continuum. Those above a certain point are seen as obese, those below that point are not. Such could be our way of viewing/defining the special group. However, it is often the case that these quantitative features are supplemented by qualitative aspects. Obesity is often regarded in terms of the effects of overweight on general health and life skills. Although the cut-off point on the weight-to-size continuum may be arbitrary, these additional features are regularly used as arguments for viewing the group as a distinct category. (Whether a particular group should be thought of as a distinct category is often a research question in itself and one beyond the scope of the present chapter.)

In most cases, then, a special group is considered as qualitatively different from the norm and it is usually these qualitative differences that are the features which make the special group interesting for the research psychologist. This may be due to an interest in the special group themselves: a clinical psychologist may be interested in finding better ways to help a group of clinical patients cope with life outside some institution. Alternatively, the researcher may consider special groups as telling us something about people in general: investigations involving those with language problems (e.g. aphasia) may inform cognitive or developmental models of 'normal' language processes and acquisition. However, if the latter is the reason for performing the research, we need to be sure that we can generalise our findings from the special group to the norm. Such a question is often difficult to answer and has troubled many areas of psychology.

Research into special groups can be very rewarding, both from the personal desire to perhaps assist a group of individuals, and from the theoretical questions that such research can answer. However, there are numerous methodological (both theoretical and practical) issues which need to be considered before embarking on research with special groups. For convenience, we shall divide these into sections on 'sampling and generalisation', 'internal validity' and 'ethical considerations'. The aim is not to produce an exhaustive discussion (more than a chapter would be necessary), but to highlight the main problems which may beset a researcher.

For the purposes of consistency, the examples used in the chapter will focus on educational psychology and research with one special group: those with specific reading disabilities or dyslexia. The discussion of this special group is not meant to tie the chapter to a particular theoretical standpoint regarding reading disabilities. Rather, this special group is used because it typifies most of the issues considered in this chapter. For example, dyslexia embodies the problems of defining a special group implicit in the above discussion of quantitative/qualitative features. Within the area of education, there are those who consider dyslexic individuals as being beyond some quantitative cut-off point. Dyslexia is usually considered as a deficiency in acquiring literacy skills and it is common to find educational psychologists discussing the discrepancy between a child's reading skills and their general intelligence. The child's intelligence would lead us to believe that they should reach a certain level of proficiency in their reading but their actual ability belies this. Under these circumstances, the level of the discrepancy between intelligence and reading ability determines diagnosis. However, the arbitrary nature of this level can be seen when one considers that it may vary between educational psychologists and researchers. Some might work to 2 or more years discrepancy, while others might feel that 1 or 1.5 years is a more appropriate figure to consider. This typifies the quantitative cut-off approach to defining a special group, which can lead to quite large variations in estimates of the number of individuals comprising a group and tempt some to question the unique or qualitative existence of the special group.

Contrary to the cut-off position, there is the view that those with dyslexia are distinct from the normal variation in reading/intelligence discrepancies: the dyslexic is categorically distinct from the non-dyslexic. Although discrepancies might help to distinguish the dyslexic individual, other features could be used to isolate them from the norm. The qualitative/quantitative argument has revolved around whether there is a normal distribution in reading ability or whether there is a second distribution, located at the bottom end of this scale, which comprises those with an unexpected reading problem. Which viewpoint one accepts may therefore determine whether you consider data derived from studies of this special group informative of the normal processes and development of reading skills or as potentially completely distinct from them. Those who consider that dyslexia is simply the bottom end of a normal distribution of ability would have fewer worries about making conclusions about readers in general. Those who believe that dyslexics form a distinct category would be more cautious about generalising beyond dyslexics themselves.

9.2   SAMPLING AND GENERALISATION

Issues of external validity (generalisation) rely on appropriate selection procedures. One assumption common to all research is that the sample of individuals we are studying are representative of the population of individuals we wish to generalise to. We, of course, cannot hope to select a group of individuals who are exactly the same as everyone in a population, so by representative sampling we aim to select a group who are not systematically different from the population on any important variables. The simplest way to avoid such systematic differences is to randomly select subjects from the population. Systematic biases would therefore be unlikely, particularly during replication. However, random sampling is rarely an option in psychological research and alternative sampling procedures have been developed (see Chapter 7).

Consideration of the representativeness of the sample to the target population is also an issue for research with special groups. There are times when a random sample is appropriate: we may have access to all patients of one type in a hospital and these may be our target population. For most research with special groups probability sampling is impossible. Access to the special group often determines selection. In other cases, individuals who form a special group may have been selected prior to the initiation of the research; the researcher may therefore have to rely on the appropriate selection procedures of others. A couple of examples should clarify these issues and their associated problems.

Returning to the issue of specific reading disabilities, estimates vary regarding the number of children with this learning difficulty (owing to problems of definition outlined above). However, most of these estimates consider that there is potentially at least one individual with some level of dyslexia in every class. One way to locate and study this special group would therefore be via wide-scale sampling. This could follow probability procedures: we could randomly select a local education authority within the UK and then randomly select schools covered by that authority. Although problems with gaining access to a randomly selected school might lead to systematic biases, once selected, we might test every child (within a particular age range) in each of those schools. For every state school class comprising 20 to 30 children who were assessed via an appropriate test, we would expect to find 1 or 2 with unexpected reading problems. A few individuals might be misdiagnosed because of less than perfect test reliability, but if comparisons between those with and those without reading disabilities are required, increases in sample sizes would reduce the effects of misdiagnosis to some extent. However, the amount of testing required to build the sample to a level appropriate for representativeness and statistical power would require a team of researchers. Although such research is possible, and has been performed, it is often impracticable.

The alternative to wide-scale assessments is to restrict selection to those already assessed. For some research questions this may be the more appropriate sampling procedure. Questions of the sort 'What are the effects of dyslexia?' might be better assessed by consideration of those diagnosed within the educational system rather than those identified by the research procedures. Basing selection on existing diagnoses may have the additional advantage of grouping subjects in one place. Once diagnosed the dyslexic may be given extra tuition in a special class with others with similar problems or may even move to a special school comprising large numbers of individuals with special needs. Under such circumstances, a large sample may already exist in one place, which avoids the need to test in different areas to build a sample of similar size. Alternatively, the researcher may access pre-diagnosed individuals through some form of advertisement. Often clinical/health studies will rely on notices in health centres requesting volunteers from a special group. Similar procedures have been used in studies of dyslexia.

However, this form of selection relies on others having performed an appropriate diagnosis. For example, dyslexia researchers are divided as to whether the larger incidence of dyslexia amongst males compared with females is due to an underlying sex-related biological factor or a diagnostic bias. Comparisons of dyslexics identified by wide-scale testing procedures with those selected by pre-research diagnosis highlight these differences. Usually, selection of pre-research diagnosed individuals leads to ratios of males to females with specific reading problems of 2:1 or larger. Wide-scale sampling procedures, however, may lead to equal numbers of males and females within the special group. The problem is due to different views regarding appropriate diagnosis and typifies one of the problems with research comprising such groups. The researcher is often required to perform separate diagnostic assessments of those within the special unit/school to ensure appropriate categorisation of subjects; this is certainly the case when self-selection procedures (advertisements) are used. It is only under such circumstances that an appropriate level of detail regarding diagnostic definitions can be presented to allow replication. The specific reading disabilities research literature is full of disparate findings which may simply be due to the differing diagnostic criteria used. However, even researcher-based diagnosis will not solve the problem that certain individuals may have been denied access to the special units or schools or that an advertisement attracts certain individuals and not others: differences in the literature regarding the proportions of individuals showing different types of reading problems are often blamed on self-selection biases. Unless the researcher can be confident about the pre-research diagnosis, more wide-scale testing may be the only way to avoid sampling bias.

9.3 INTERNAL VALIDITY

Few studies of special groups simply deal with members of that group. It may be the case that our researcher wishes to compare the behaviours of the special group in different conditions. For example, the researcher may be interested in assessing whether a certain regime leads to a reduction in problem behaviour amongst individuals with severe learning behaviours. Under such circumstances, we need only concern ourselves with selecting appropriate members of the special group and comparing their performance under the regime with that under some other condition – a totally within-subjects or repeated measures comparison.

However, in many other studies, conclusions may only be possible if the research includes a contrast/control group against which to assess the performance of the special group. Most research with special groups will involve some implicit or explicit comparison against some other group or norm: the usual comparison group is the general population. Research investigating the classroom disruptive behaviour of a child diagnosed as hyperactive might compare their behaviour against other children in the same class. If all children show the same level of disruptive behaviour, conclusions would be better stressing features of the class rather than the hyperactive child. A project assessing the language skills of an individual with Parkinson's disease might use a standardised assessment and compare the patient's performance against the norms (the mean and standard deviation derived from giving the test to a large number of individuals) of the test. A qualitative study profiling the life of a persistent offender might comment on the atypicality of some behaviour or refer to a response as being unusual. Implicit in such referents is some comparison group, situation or even behaviour. Such comparisons require the researcher to present a well-reasoned argument for the appropriateness of the comparison.

An understanding of the issues here will require some discussion of quasi-experimental designs and matching variables. Let us return to reading disabilities. We will consider three different research scenarios to make the points here. Project A considers whether poor reading ability, which may be linked to academic failure, is associated with emotional problems. Project B involves an assessment of the view that those with problems with the acquisition of reading skills also have problems with other language skills. Project C involves testing the idea that there is a hereditary component to reading disabilities by assessing whether there is an increased chance of a dyslexic individual having a dyslexic father.

In each project, there is the need to compare the special group against some standard: how else would we know whether factors such as emotional problems, language difficulties or paternal incidence are greater within the special group? Most research of this kind would therefore include, at least, two groups: members of the special group and a control group. We might therefore select a group of specific reading disabled children and a sample of children with no evidence of reading problems: this would, of course, require us to assess the latter group for reading problems. We would then measure both groups on the variable we are interested in (emotional wellbeing, language skills or paternal incidence of dyslexia) and perform some between-subjects comparison. The studies might even be presented as if the two groups comprised an independent variable (IV) and the measure a dependent variable (DV) (see Chapter 4).

It is not uncommon to see such studies presented as if they were an experiment with causality conclusions being derived from the findings. Just having a between-subjects variable within a study and performing analyses appropriate for independent data does not make the study an experiment. Such studies are simply measuring one variable (reading ability/disability: a subject variable) and looking for an association with a second variable. They are better thought of as simple correlational studies, though some may refer to them as quasi-experimental – suggesting that they are like experiments. Consideration of the conclusions that can be drawn from the three projects outlined above should indicate the absurdity of treating such studies as experiments. In a true experiment we manipulate an IV and investigate the effects on the DV. From an appropriately controlled study, our conclusions would argue that the IV caused a change in the DV. In project A, this may be a sensible viewpoint. Reading difficulties may lead to a change in emotional wellbeing. This may be the specific viewpoint that we are assessing. In project B, however, this seems less sensible. Would we wish to conclude that problems with the acquisition of reading lead to problems in general language? Well, it may be the case; there is some evidence that illiterates have a poorer understanding of some features of verbal language than literates. However, verbal language skills develop prior to the teaching of reading and, although some features of verbal language may require further development at the time that formal reading instruction commences, the influence should not be so great as to cause language disabilities! Project B would more likely be discussing the influence of language problems on reading acquisition, not the other way round.

Turning to project C emphasises the previous point. Would we really argue that reading problems in a child cause an increase in the incidence of paternal reading problems? Following the logic of an experiment, this would be the appropriate conclusion: the IV causes the change in the DV! Here the conclusion is obviously absurd. What we are probably looking for in project C is a potential genetic factor to be common between generations of a family. It seems more sensible to consider this common factor as leading to father and child reading problems. Note that the three studies use the same design yet imply completely different conclusions about causes: for project A, IV affects DV; for project B, DV affects IV; for project C, both IV and DV are affected by a common third variable. Yet for each study any of these three conclusions is appropriate. Although the most likely conclusion from project A is that reading problems lead to emotional problems, equally this study would be consistent with a conclusion that emotional problems lead to reading difficulties (in some cases they do!), or that both reading and emotional problems stem from a common third variable (e.g. social deprivation). Designs of this sort are not experiments and cannot make conclusions about causality with any more certainty than a correlational design. It is therefore better to think of any study with a subject variable, such as studies of special groups which require a comparison group, as comprising a correlational design and leave issues of causality to well-reasoned argument or substantive evidence. It is only when some variable is manipulated by the researcher that thoughts of experimental designs should be entertained.

So what can we do to increase our chances of making an appropriate conclusion? The arguments basically boil down to a consideration of the control of confounding variables discussed previously in this book (see Chapters 4 and 6). For example, evidence for the direction of causality might be presented by a sensible argument (general language and genetic factors precede reading problems) or the use of longitudinal studies. In the case of project A, we might assess a large cohort of children over several years prior to and following reading instruction. If those who experience problems with reading were no different on the emotion measure prior to formal reading instruction but developed emotional problems when reading instruction commenced, then we have increased evidence for the direction of the effect. However, we also need to consider third factors which may be potential alternative causes for the effects observed. One way is for our study to control these potential other explanations of the observed effects. A simple way of eliminating the potential third factor of background from project A is to match subjects in special and control groups on this factor. This could be achieved by measuring background and choosing pairs of individuals (one from the special group, the other from the control group) with identical scores: a related subjects design. Alternatively, we could ensure that the average scores (and dispersion) on the background measure for both groups were equivalent: an independent subjects design. In both cases, differences between the groups could not be produced by this third factor. Judicious choice of matching variable (or variables, since we may wish to control for several alternative explanations in our research) would increase our evidence for a particular conclusion.

Including matching variables in a project has its negative aspects, however. Matching procedures may require an increase in resources (time, test materials, etc.). Practicality states that we cannot include every possible matching variable, and research with a special group may be more restricted in its choice than other kinds of research: we may not be able reliably to determine the skills of a hyperactive child; it may be unethical to test a severely sick patient for hours on end. Clearly, we have to be selective about which matching variables we include in our research, necessitating the need for some strategy for selection.

The most obvious matching strategies require an understanding of the literature associated with a special group and/or pilot work. A pilot study is a smaller project which precedes the main study and, in this case, might assess the influence of a particular factor prior to its inclusion within the main research. Those variables which do present potential problems for the conclusions derived from our research – those which could be an alternative cause of the effects and may vary systematically between groups – would be included in the matching procedures, while those variables which do not present such threats would be ignored. Investigations of dyslexia, for example, often match special and control groups on variables such as sex, age and some measure of general ability such as non-verbal intelligence. These variables have been shown to affect performance on many of the measures used in reading research. However, which variables are matched will depend on which measures are being used in the study. We would not want to study differences between dyslexics and non-dyslexics simply on non-verbal intelligence having matched the groups for such a variable: obviously differences should not occur if our matching procedures have been rigorous. Similarly, if it has been shown that the age of the subject is independent of the measure used in our study, then matching for age is not important: any variation between groups on the measurement cannot be due to age differences. Thus matching will be based on the particular question assessed in the study and an understanding of the effects under investigation.

Matching may also require a substantial increase in numbers of subjects selected. Returning to the dyslexia example, many studies of this special group use two groups of control children. The first group is matched to the dyslexics in terms of chronological age, the second in terms of reading age. An 8-year-old dyslexic whose reading is 2 years behind expected would be matched to an 8-year-old control who has a reading age of about 8 and a 6-year-old with a reading age of 6. Obviously, the same control could not be used to match for both variables, so increasing the required number of matching variables may lead to a large increase in the number of participants – with an associated increase in test time and resources.

Now, matching dyslexic and control groups in terms of reading age may seem bizarre, particularly given the comments above about avoiding matching on a variable with which we want to show differences. Nevertheless, many questions asked by researchers may require the control of such potential confounds. An (albeit unlikely) example might make this clear. Suppose that a researcher tests the literary skills of a group of dyslexics and chronological age-matched controls from a school and finds that the dyslexics continually make errors with words containing 'qu' combinations, whereas the controls do not. The researcher concludes that dyslexics have specific problems with processing 'qu' combinations. A second researcher tests similar groups of dyslexics and controls from the same school; however, this researcher includes chronological and reading age matched controls. Consistent with the first findings, differences are found between dyslexics and chronological age-matched controls in the processing of 'qu'. However, these differences disappear when the dyslexics are compared with the reading age-matched controls. The second researcher investigates the reading books used by the school and finds that those used in the first two years of training contain no examples of the 'qu' combination. Both dyslexics and reading age-matched controls are using year 1 and 2 reading books. Chronological age-matched controls, however, are using year 3 and 4 books, which do contain examples of the 'qu' combination. Here, the difference between dyslexics and chronological age-matched controls is not due to some underlying feature of the literacy abilities of the dyslexic, it is simply a function of experience. The dyslexic's reading acquisition problems confine their experience such that they have not yet had the opportunity to master 'qu' combinations. If they had been given this chance, they may be as able as the controls to read 'qu' correctly. Although this seems an unlikely example in terms of the conclusions the first researcher might come to, similar problems can be found within the dyslexia literature. Differences are found between dyslexic and chronological age-matched controls (suggesting an underlying feature of dyslexia) which, when assessed in a group with similar reading experience, indicate that the difference could equally be a product of experience, rather than a factor indicative of the cause.

As may be deduced from the preceding discussion, matching may also require changes in the procedures for selecting participants. We cannot choose a random sample when we want to match special and control groups on a variable. The usual method is to select the members of the special group and match control individuals to them. The control would be selected based on their scores on the matching variables. Obviously, this may require a great deal of pre-testing, potentially of a larger cohort of control individuals to ensure that appropriate matches can be made. However, such procedures can lead to confounds such as that produced by regression to the mean (see Chapter 6). A couple of examples might clarify this.

Our research project suggests a need to match dyslexics and controls on a measure of non-verbal intelligence. We have a dyslexic with a non-verbal IQ of 130 – a high score for the test which has norms of 100 (mean) and 15 (standard deviation). We therefore test a number of controls and find one with the same non-verbal IQ. Any score on any test is subject to error. This means that the score obtained on a test may not be the true underlying ability of an individual. The observed score will be affected by factors internal to the subject (boredom, increased effort, fatigue, etc.) and factors external to the subject (a noisy environment for example). These random variables will influence the score produced by the subject and hence an observed score is the combination of actual ability (true score) plus these extraneous factors (error). Even a highly reliable test (one which does not suffer from extreme influences of error) will never be truly free of error (see Chapter 13). The scores produced by our dyslexic and control will also be subject to error. Regression towards the mean suggests that if (1) a test is subject to error (as they all are) and (2) an individual receives an atypical score (say, an unusually high score), then (3) the next time they are tested their score will regress towards average. This may mean that our dyslexic and control subjects are not accurately matched. Unless we are concerned with studying a single individual, this may be less of a problem; group analyses should reduce the effects of bias.

There are, however, studies where regression to the mean can be a serious problem. For example, researchers in the field of dyslexia have been interested in assessing the differences between individuals who have unexpected reading problems and those who might be expected to struggle. This research has usually compared those with poor reading skills but above average intelligence (dyslexics) with those with poor reading skills which are nevertheless consistent with their intellectual ability. We have already discussed issues to do with the sampling of a special group in the previous section; however, procedures for sampling the control group of poor readers is of particular interest here. The usual procedure is to test a large cohort of readers and compare reading and intelligence scores. A sample of non-dyslexic poor readers is then selected from those who produce low scores on both the reading and intelligence measures. Often, these subjects are matched on reading ability with the dyslexic group.

The problem here is that a whole group of subjects are selected on the basis of low scores. Within this group we are bound to get some who have just had a bad day and if they were retested would regress towards the mean. We are basically underestimating their abilities, leaving our simple one-off matching procedure inappropriate to control a potential confound within our study.

There is an alternative to the lengthy pre-testing procedures required for appropriate matching. This is to statistically control potential confounding factors within the study. Fortunately, statistical techniques have been devised for just this purpose. For example, a comparison between a special group and a control group could implement an analysis of covariance. In this case, we would measure the performance of the two groups on the research measure and the variable (the covariate) we wish to control. There is no need to match subjects or groups on the covariate; the groups would be allowed to differ. The analysis would then statistically control the covariate so that it was as if the groups scored equally on the covariate. Imagine being able to estimate the influence of one variable on another – to be able to calculate the amount of change in one variable associated with a unit of change in a second. This estimate of common variance is used in calculations of correlations r and the coefficient of determination r^2. Performing such calculations would not only tell us about the common variance between the two variables but also indicate the amount of variance which cannot be explained by the association. If the difference between our special and control group explains some of this residual variance, then we have evidence for the difference telling us something about the changes in the research measure over and above that of the covariate.

Another way of thinking about this might be to consider the effect of the covariate. Consider two groups of athletes running a 100 metre race. Each athlete has a different performance time. However, an unscrupulous trainer gives each athlete a performance enhancing drug and varies the dosage given between individuals. This drug enhances performance, but is also dependent on the original ability of the individual. However, the effects of the drug are such that there is little difference in performance between the two sets of athletes. Here we have a confounding factor which is masking the true difference between the groups in the 100 metre race. Suppose we find out about the drug-taking and we can measure how much was taken by each athlete (we measure the confounding variable). Also suppose we know the influence the drug has on performance – the change in performance produced by being given a certain unit of the drug; basically, we can estimate the association between the covariate and the performance measure. Given this information, we might be able to estimate the original performance of the athletes prior to taking the drug and reassess whether one group of athletes was outperforming the other. A similar strategy might enable us to assess whether our special group and control group differed on some research measure even if they differ on some covariate.

9.4   ETHICAL CONSIDERATIONS

One of the most important aspects of any research with a special group is the potentially sensitive nature of the topic. For some groups this may not be a problem, but for most it will. An obvious example is within clinical settings where we may be dealing with a very vulnerable group of individuals. Conducting the study in an ethically appropriate manner is vital. Within psychology there are a set of formal guidelines which, as psychologists, we must abide by. Such ethical guidelines are essential reading for the researcher interested in performing research on a special group (see Chapter 3). This is not only because we should conduct ethical research with special groups, but because we should do this no matter who the participants are. The researcher wishing to study a special group may also need to meet the ethical guidelines of another body, or explain the guidelines they are fulfilling and how they apply to their own research in detail, using non-technical terms to a group of non-psychologists. It is no use giving a parent of a dyslexic child a copy of the British Psychological Society's *Code of Conduct, Ethical Principles and Guidelines* and saying that the research will meet these. The researcher will need to understand the guidelines, recognise the concerns of the individuals involved and present a case in appropriate language – something which usually requires practice. Neglecting these issues could lead to the researcher failing to recruit participants. For example, a researcher investigating the long term effects of dyslexia might wish to recruit a group of adult dyslexics. One of the main concerns of the dyslexic adult is anonymity. The stigma attached to dyslexia is very real to the dyslexic adult: they may have gone through school being called 'thick' or 'stupid'. Avoiding the same happening in their adult career may be vital to them. Making clear assurances about anonymity will be both appropriate and necessary (remember you are recruiting individuals whose reading may still be poor).

As I mentioned above, the researcher may also have to meet the requirements of another body to gain access to a special group. Medically related research (health or clinical psychology) is an obvious example. Here the researcher may have to apply to an ethical committee for access to a patient group. This process will require the researcher to detail their study and procedures in a way that the committee will understand. Using technical jargon will rarely impress and is more likely to lead to the committee asking for further clarification. Often such a committee will meet a few times per year only. This usually means that the research will have to be prepared months prior to its start. If there is a tight deadline to meet (e.g. for a course), then such research will need to be prepared well in advance (a project could take six months to be passed by such a committee) or should be avoided. Simply because ethical approval from such a committee has been given does not mean that a process of gaining consent from participants or those caring for them will not have to be undertaken too.

Research with a special group may also lead to major ethical dilemmas. Does a researcher assessing a new teaching method which may lead to major improvements in the reading skills of a group of poor readers compare those provided with this new method with a group who are not? Ten years later we may find that one group can read whereas the other group suffers major reading problems. There are no easy answers here, although similar methods employed in other fields of research can help. For example, within the dyslexia field, procedures are often implemented to avoid the problem of withholding a potentially successful remediation method. One solution is to assess the technique over a short period of time. Gains in literacy skills can be measured in months, or assessments could be reduced to a selected set of words used in the training method. We might then be able to determine the usefulness of the method over this representative snapshot. We could even administer the remediation method to all individuals but delay its start for some. Just prior to administering the method to the remainder of the group, we would assess the skills of those who have experienced the method with those who are yet to do so. Administering the new method as an additional part of normal schooling could also reduce ethical concerns. All children would receive normal classes, but some would have extra sessions using the new technique. Experimental methods may be abandoned altogether and qualitative procedures implemented to analyse the impact of a technique given to all children; action research (see Chapter 23) is still popular in educational research, for example. Methodological issues require consideration: the snapshot needs to be representative of other periods of learning; contamination should not occur between those taking the new method and those not; interference effects between the new method and normal classes need to be avoided; action research must avoid experimenter bias and be replicable in other classes. Understanding the topic under investigation and planning the procedures carefully should lead to the research avoiding most of these potential confounds.

9.5   COLLABORATION

Gaining ethical approval for a piece of research may be the research psychologist's first contact with non-psychologists who will play a vital role in the successful completion of a project. However, practical issues may lead to necessary further collaboration with non-psychologists. This can be highly rewarding: discussions with special needs teachers can provide major insights into the problems faced by a dyslexic child; meetings with health staff might inform the researcher of changes in hospital procedures which may require modifications to the research. Such interactions can lead to increased understanding of, or a novel way of thinking about, a research topic. Nevertheless, there are also negative aspects which require pre-planning on the part of the researcher.

There are probably two basic forms of collaboration. The first requires limited involvement by others in certain aspects of the study; some of the ethical approval examples presented in the previous section might be included here. The researcher may need the co-operation of a teacher to distribute, collect and mark assessments; the health/clinical psychologist might need the assistance of a nurse to administer a drug (e.g. an injection). The role of the other party in these situations may be restricted and collaboration kept to a minimum. It may even be advisable to restrict the amount of information about the specific factors under investigation to avoid bias. There are numerous cases where a helpful teacher has sent to the researcher only those children from her class whom she knows possess the feature sought by the researcher. Unfortunately, there are also cases where dialogue has been too restrictive; a researcher performing trials of a new drug may discover that, following an advertising campaign by the company producing the drug and collaborating in the research, their placebo group are now taking as much of the drug as their experimental group. Planning the work and attempting to foresee the potential problems will help avoid many of these confounds.

The second type of collaboration is more consistent with the implicit meaning of the idea. Here there is collaboration between parties in all or most aspects of the research, from planning to dissemination. This type of research is increasing in popularity. There is a growing requirement from funding bodies for multi-group, particularly multi-disciplinary research. Again, there are advantages and disadvantages. Most of the latter can be overcome by planning.

The advantages are the increase in understanding that can come from drawing on different fields of expertise and experience, thereby shedding new light on a problem. Collaboration may allow the project to be presented in a way appropriate for other fields and so increase opportunities for funding the work and the potential audience interested in its results. Disadvantages revolve around the time required to establish a collaborative team and keep each member informed of the work's progress. Regular meetings may be necessary prior to collaboration to avoid misunderstandings about aspects of the research. A term which we think means the same to everyone may mean something completely different to someone from a different discipline. Ask someone from an education background (particularly someone from North America) what they understand by the term 'learning disability'. Then pose the same question to someone from a health background in England. They may present you with completely different definitions that refer to disparate subject populations; interestingly, both populations could be thought of as special groups. A vital aspect of collaboration between individuals from different disciplines is dialogue, despite the increase in time that this might require. It is essential first to establish and then to synthesise the goals of the group. The research psychologist's aim may be to assess a particular theoretical model of dyslexia. The educational psychologist may hope to improve diagnostic procedures. The teacher may simply wish to identify the difficulties experienced by a particular child. Failure to resolve conflicting goals will jeopardise the study.

9.6 CONCLUSIONS

We have considered many of the research issues surrounding studies of special groups. These have been intentionally focused. One of the main aims was to draw to the reader's attention the relationship between the issues raised in this chapter and the methodological problems/solutions highlighted in other sections of the book. A full understanding of the procedures available to the researcher will reduce problems for external (sampling and generalisation) and internal (control of confounds) validity. These procedures should also provide the researcher with ways to circumvent ethical difficulties which a proposed project may present. A second aim of the chapter was to highlight the need to plan a research project well in advance, particularly when dealing with a potentially sensitive topic of study such as a special group. This will be particularly the case when the involvement of others (e.g. from other disciplines) is required. Start the process early.

9.7 FURTHER READING

The diversity of the areas covered by the term 'special group' means that no single book would be able to deal with this subject in its entirety. However, a researcher interested in a particular special group will find an appropriate literature search identifying numerous books (or papers) that focus on the issues related to that group. For example: Doehring's (1996) *Research Strategies in Human Communication Disorders* (2nd edn), Dworkin's (1992) *Researching Persons with Mental Illness* and McAuley et al.'s (1987) *Applied Research in Gerontology*.

For those interested in educational research, there are a number of books which introduce the methods and issues associated with this area. For example: Cohen and Manion's (1989) *Research Methods in Education* (2nd edn), Gall et al.'s (1996) *Educational Research: An Introduction* (6th edn) and Wittrock's (1986) *Handbook of Research on Teaching* (3rd edn).

10

Cross-Cultural Research Methods

Evanthia Lyons and Xenia Chryssochoou

Contents

10.1 INTRODUCTION: INCORPORATING CULTURE INTO RESEARCH

There are a number of reasons why a researcher might consider carrying out cross-cultural comparisons. Traditionally psychologists have been preoccupied with the extent to which human behaviour is governed by universal laws and universal social processes. We might want to explore the question: are our research findings, our models and our theories universal? Could we generalise our results to the whole of humankind? Is, for example, our way of understanding and measuring intelligence, personality and stress valid globally? How can we be sure that our statements concerning psychological functioning and human behaviour apply equally to Indonesians and Londoners, to Siberians as well as to South Africans?

It is important to ask whether the psychological models developed mainly within North American and Western European cultures are relevant to and able to account for findings obtained from research carried out in other cultures (van de Vijver and Poortinga, 1982; Gergen et al., 1986; Jahoda,

1988). Such endeavours would lead to a better understanding of the nature of human behaviour and its social influences.

Furthermore, there are a number of issues that are not limited by national and cultural borders. For instance, the understanding of issues to do with perceptions of risks related to global environmental change and environmental disasters, mergers and labour mobility within the framework of a global economy, or the effects of the globalisation of the mass media on political behaviours often requires the conduct of research comparing different groups. Policy makers also ask social scientists to provide data comparing countries on issues such as economic behaviour, levels of identification with the category 'European', political and other social attitudes or health behaviours.

Culture and its relative effect on psychological functioning and social behaviour become salient issues in contemporary research. However there is no general agreement amongst researchers about how culture should be incorporated into their theorising and research practice. Underlying the differing ways psychologists incorporate culture are assumptions about the relationship between culture and psychological structures, processes and action and the extent to which we can make meaningful comparisons between different cultural populations.

On the one hand, there are those psychologists who argue that culture affects to some degree all psychological structures, processes and social behaviour. Therefore, it is important to carry out cross-cultural comparisons so that we can determine both the degree to which the psychological structures, processes and behaviours are affected by culture, and also the cultural dimensions which are likely to have an impact on them. On the other hand, there are others who argue that culture and psychological phenomena are inextricably linked. In this perspective, behaviours and cognitions acquire their meanings through social interactions in specific contexts. Cross-cultural comparisons are therefore seen to be inappropriate.

These two approaches lead to different research strategies. The former approach has led to a large body of research under the umbrella of **cross-cultural psychology**. The research strategy often adopted is underpinned by the assumption that cross-cultural studies share a lot of similarities with quasi-experiments, and the methodological considerations centre around diminishing the possible alternative explanations of any observed cultural differences that may be found. The second approach is usually known as **cultural psychology** and has its philosophical roots in phenomenology. The goal here is to understand how behaviour is embedded in particular cultural contexts. Cultural psychologists often use qualitative research methods such as participant observation, interviewing and ethnographies (Hines, 1993). Some of the methods often associated with cultural psychology are discussed elsewhere in this book.

This chapter focuses on the cross-cultural perspective. It first considers briefly some of the debates over definition and the assumptions central to cross-cultural psychology. Although these debates are covered here very briefly, it is important that the researcher who embarks on cross-cultural research is aware of them. The position taken in these debates will have consequences for both how cross-cultural research is carried out and how the findings are interpreted. Second, this chapter outlines the type of questions that can be addressed by carrying out cross-cultural comparisons. Finally, we will consider the methodological issues involved in the design of cross-cultural research, highlighting the importance of establishing comparability of constructs, method and measures.

10.2   WHAT IS CULTURE?

Culture has been defined in different ways by researchers in different disciplines and in different branches of psychology. For example, having reviewed the different ways that culture had been defined by anthropologists, Kroeber and Kluckhohn suggested that:

> Culture consists of patterns, explicit and implicit, of and for behavior acquired and transmitted by symbols, constituting the distinctive achievements of human groups, including the embodiments in artifacts; the essential core of culture consists of traditional (i.e., historically derived and selected) ideas and especially their attached values; cultural systems may on the one hand be considered as products of action, on the other as conditioning elements of further action. (1952: 181)

There are those researchers who view culture as being a set of behaviours and others who see culture as a symbolic system of meanings (Rohner, 1984). Smith and Bond suggested that 'the more important aspect of a definition of culture is that culture is a relatively organised system of shared meanings' (1998: 39), and Jahoda remarked that culture 'is embracing a wide range of phenomena, whether these be meanings or behaviours' (1984: 142), whereas Triandis accepted Kluckholm's (1954) definition that 'culture is to society what memory is to individuals . . . culture includes all that has worked in the past and become a shared perspective, transmitted from generation to generation' (1997: 334). For others culture is seen as a process: 'Culture is therefore seen as an interactive process with two main component processes: the creation of shared activities (cultural practices) and the creation of shared meanings (cultural interpretation)' (Greenfield, 1997: 303).

These are just some examples of the many ways that researchers have defined culture. From these examples one can see how difficult a concept it is to define and how all-encompassing some definitions are. Most importantly they make apparent the fact that the definitions of culture reflect different conceptualisations of the relationship between culture and psychological structures, processes and social behaviour. These conceptualisations are likely to have different implications for the research strategy adopted and to influence the choice of groups one seeks to compare.

For instance if culture is seen as the process by which shared practices and meanings are created, then research is likely to focus on understanding how actions and the participant's understandings of these actions are constructed in specific contexts. Culture is not seen as being separate and distinct from the individual. Rather this research is likely to use qualitative methods to reconstruct the shared practices and meanings of particular groups in specific contexts.

On the other hand if culture is seen as the context of psychological functioning and human behaviour, then culture should be considered as an 'independent' variable or set of variables producing differences among groups.

Now that the importance of having an explicit definition of culture has been highlighted, the following section outlines the different ways that research questions are framed within a cross-cultural perspective. These reflect the two dimensions taken into consideration in comparative research, namely the inductive or deductive nature of the research and the extent to which contextual factors are incorporated into the design (van de Vijver and Leung, 1997a).

10.3 RESEARCH QUESTIONS

There are a number of ways one can carry out cross-cultural research. For instance one can focus on the relationships between variables in different countries or the level of distribution of a particular variable, or on the effect of a particular dimension of a culture on the particular variable. Alternatively one can focus on understanding the meanings attached to specific phenomena in particular cultures.

So for example a student of recent and ongoing social changes in Europe could choose to ask the question: is the relationship between adoption of a particular political ideology and attitudes towards enlargement of the European Union the same in all member states of the EU and ex-Eastern European countries? That is, are relationships between variables the same in different cultures?

Alternatively, the researcher might ask: is the level of adoption of a particular political ideology the same in all member states of the EU and ex-Eastern European countries? Do people in all member states of the EU and ex-Eastern European countries hold positive attitudes towards enlargement of the European Union to the same extent? That is, is the same behaviour/personality trait/attitude distributed at different levels in different cultures?

Or, they may choose to ask: does a particular political institution have an effect on the extent to which people adhere to a particular political ideology or attitudes towards enlargement of the European Union? That is, how does a particular cultural/structural dimension influence psychological functioning and/or social behaviour?

In other words, cross-cultural research can focus on either differences in the relationship between variables (structure-oriented studies) or differences in the magnitude of a variable (level-oriented studies) (van de Vijver and Leung, 1997b).

As mentioned above, research questions in comparative research vary along two dimensions. First, comparative studies differ in the extent to which they are driven by theory. When no specific predictions can be made about the cultural similarities or differences that may be observed, the study is an exploratory one. When a study is designed to test specific hypotheses, it would be at the other end of the continuum, i.e. hypothesis driven. Second, cross-cultural studies differ in the extent to which they take into consideration contextual factors such as demographic or psychological variables. Some studies use context variables to explain cultural similarities or differences and others simply document differences and similarities without including these factors. Van de Vijver and Leung (1997b) suggested a typology of comparative studies by crossing these dimensions which may be useful to bear in mind when designing a piece of cross-cultural research:

- *Generalisability studies*: studies concerned with the relative generalisability of research findings obtained in one group to other groups (hypothesis driven; no contextual factors).
- *Theory driven studies*: studies concerned with validating a theoretical model which takes into account specific cultural variations. In this case *a priori* predictions are made and sampling of the cultures is carefully considered (hypothesis driven; contextual factors).
- *Psychological differences studies*: studies concerned with the application of a measurement instrument in two different cultural settings in order to establish whether there are cultural differences in the means, standard deviations, etc. No predictions concerning the nature of the differences are made. In these studies contextual variables are not included and usually *post hoc* explanations are used to interpret the differences (exploratory; no context variables).
- *External validation studies*: studies concerned with the explanation of the meaning and causes of cross-cultural differences without having *a priori* hypotheses. In this case a large number of context variables need to be included in order to determine which of these explain better the variations observed in the dependent variable by using statistical techniques such as regression analyses (exploratory; context variables).

In a cross-cultural perspective, it has to be remembered, culture is seen as the 'independent variable'. Therefore, whatever orientation one chooses to adopt to define its research question, the issue that is still to be addressed is how one could operationalise culture. The following section deals with this particular issue.

10.4   OPERATIONALISING CULTURE

As the concept of culture is so all-encompassing, 'operationalising' it is rather difficult. Often, the way culture is operationalised is reflected in the choice of the groups to be compared. Although this issue will be dealt with in more detail below, it is worth noting that certain definitions of culture invite us to use the concepts of culture, society and nation interchangeably. Over the past century the world has often been categorised in terms of nation-states: the temptation is therefore great to equate nations with cultures. This failure to distinguish between nation and culture gives rise to other issues. First, comparing two nations does not necessarily imply that we are doing a cross-cultural comparison because the nations may be closely related culturally (e.g. comparing Germans and Austrians). Although some of the methodological issues discussed later could and should be applied to this kind of comparison, cross-cultural researchers tend to exclude cross-national comparisons from the cross-cultural research definition (Berry et al., 1992). Second, choosing nation-states as the unit of analysis implies that national cultures are unitary and homogeneous systems. However, besides the different groups and categories which could form a nation (e.g. age groups, social classes, sexes), nations also often include different ethnic groups which are culturally diverse. Thus, cross-cultural research could be undertaken within the nation-state by comparing different ethnic groups.

It has been argued that as an explanatory concept culture may not be very useful. For instance, Leung remarked: 'it is generally accepted that the use of culture as an explanatory variable for cultural differences is not satisfactory and culture must be unpackaged' (1989: 703). That is, different dimensions, contextual factors that comprise culture, need to be separated and their relationship to observed cultural differences examined. This approach aims to uncover the relational rules between aspects of culture, psychological functioning and behaviour. However, some researchers consider that culture cannot be reduced to a number of isolated variables. In this perspective, culture is a complex system and it is perceived as more than just the sum of its various components. Culture as a system implies 'the presence of organisation and structure, a set of relationships linking the various components' parts' (Jahoda, 1984: 149).

Culture could be operationalised either in terms of specific dimensions/ aspects or in terms of relationships between different variables. It is important to select carefully the cultural dimensions on which comparisons are to be made. Of course the choice of these dimensions might be guided by theoretical considerations. However, even in this case there is a danger that dimensions that are important in one culture are considered as equally important in another culture. This is an assumption that cannot be made without investigation.

10.5 THE EMIC–ETIC DISTINCTION

To avoid comparing 'birds' with 'dogs' one should carefully select the dimensions which make the groups chosen comparable. To do so one should avoid using the dimensions that are important to define 'birds' to compare 'birds' with 'dogs' and thus draw conclusions about their differences. There are some characteristics that are specific to each group and there are others that are common to both dogs and birds. When we make cross-cultural comparisons it is important to ensure that we make evident the common characteristics between cultures without forgetting those that are culture specific. This idea is linked to the debate of universal- versus culture-specific investigations we presented earlier.

The differing emphasis on universal versus specific behaviours and cognitions is better known as the distinction between emic and etic studies. This distinction was introduced by Berry (1969; 1989) who, following Pike (1966), distinguished between an emic and an etic approach. This differentiation is drawn upon the linguistic distinction between phonetics and phonemics. Phonetics are linked to the universal properties of spoken sounds whereas phonemics are linked to the ways in which these sounds are produced in different languages. In the same way, etic studies are focused on universals whereas emic studies are focused on culture-specific behaviours. Berry argues that, instead of assuming that the situation has the same meaning in different settings and therefore imposing etic measures, it would be better to conduct a series of emic studies in different cultures. This will help us to reach a more valid set of derived etic generalisations. Both the emic and the etic approach are seen to be valuable. He argued that psychological science could benefit from a combined emic–etic approach which comprises a three-step process.

First, research is conducted in the researcher's cultural setting (emic A). Second, armed with the concepts and instruments derived by this research, the researcher could attempt to study the phenomenon in another culture by imposing the assumptions of the first research (imposed etic). In this perspective, research is conducted in the second culture in order to acquire familiarity with it (emic B). Third, the researcher has two conceptual systems to compare (emic A and emic B). According to Berry, if there are common features emerging, the comparison is possible. Thus, conclusions could be drawn concerning these features in an etic approach (derived etic).

This procedure gives us a starting point for conducting research without patronising other cultures. Furthermore, without assuming universality, it provides the possibility of drawing conclusions about derived etics including progressively more and more cultural settings.

However, although this approach involves both intracultural and inter-cultural comparisons, Leung (1989) remarks that it is still at an individual level of analysis. By individual level of analysis he meant that the analysis is based on the search for individual differences. According to Leung (1989), if we observe a difference at the cultural level (where averages are computed), in order to construct a valid psychological theory we need to observe the same relation at the individual level (when the individual scores are computed) within each culture.

What Leung (1989) is arguing is that it is possible that a relation found within a culture (between individuals) does not hold at a cultural level (between cultures) where structural properties of the cultures are interfering, and vice versa. Therefore we should take into account not only the individual properties involved but also the cultural properties. In order to be able to interpret differences between cultures, an approach combining an *individual* and a *culture* level of analysis is required.

10.6 DESIGNING A CROSS-CULTURAL STUDY

As is the case with all types of research, the design of a cross-cultural study should be informed by three main considerations. First, it should be informed by theory concerning the particular psychological phenomenon to be investigated and, as we have seen, by definitions of culture and assumptions about the universality or specificity of psychological functioning and social behaviour. Second, it should be informed by the research question addressed. Third, special consideration must be given to the issue of comparability. This is a crucial issue for any cross-cultural researcher because both the validity of the comparisons made and the degree of confidence with which you can attribute any observed differences to cross-cultural variation are at stake. The importance of choosing the comparative dimensions and comparison groups is difficult to underestimate. However the process of sampling raises other issues which are discussed below.

Having decided whether an emic or an etic approach should be adopted, it is important to ensure that you do indeed compare similar things, and secondly that observed differences in the dependent variable are unlikely to be attributable to methodological biases involved in either the content or the administration of the measurement instruments used.

10.6.1 Sampling

Considerations about sampling in cross-cultural research involve different stages: one should decide first which cultural groups will be compared, second which subgroups within each culture will be compared, and third which individuals within each subgroup will be sampled. These choices should be made on theoretical and practical grounds. Often we are tempted to carry out particular cross-cultural comparisons because we are familiar with certain cultures or we know somebody in that particular country. This is often called *convenience sampling* and any differences found are rather difficult to interpret. Theoretical considerations would involve whether the objective of the research is to test the universal nature of a particular behaviour or personality characteristic or whether the focus of the research is to understand a particular problem which can best be defined in international/cultural terms.

First one should decide which cultures/nations are to be compared. This decision should be based on theoretical grounds. One should decide which variables/aspects of culture are likely to have an effect on the target behaviour or psychological functioning and then choose cultures which are likely to vary along those particular dimensions. The number of countries chosen would very much depend on practical as well as theoretical grounds. Ideally one would want to involve as many cultural groups as necessary to cover the whole range of variation on the particular relevant dimension. However the resource implications of adopting such a strategy are not negligible.

Another sampling strategy is to randomly select as many cultural groups as possible. It is almost impossible to achieve a random sample because of the vast number of countries that would need to be participating in the research. However a number of studies have chosen to collect data in a large number of countries. For example, Schwartz (1992) collected data on values in 20 countries, Smith and Peterson's (1996) study on managers involved samples from 30 countries and Doise et al.'s (1999) study of social representation of human rights included samples from 35 countries. Involving such large numbers of cultural groups is likely to be costly in both time and resources However, the larger the number of countries involved the more the sample approximates to a random one (Doise et al., 1994).

Whether one chooses cultural groups which are similar or different depends on the question you try to address. For instance, in the case of systematic sampling, the more extreme that countries are as measured on the target dimension, the more likely it is that you will find differences in the dependent variable, if the differences are there. However if you find differences between cultural groups that are similar along many dimensions, it would be easier to interpret such differences. When searching for universalities, the more different the cultural groups are the more convincing the evidence would be.

The second stage in selecting your sample is deciding which subgroups within the chosen cultures would be involved in the research. If for example you are interested in looking at cultural differences in consumer behaviour, it will be bizarre if you were to compare middle class adults in one culture with working class adults in another. So wherever possible you should try to match the subgroups you compare. The same considerations that apply in the selection of individuals in any other experimental or survey design would apply here.

In cases where matching subgroups or individuals in the different cultural groups is impossible, data on demographic characteristics and other relevant variables should also be gathered so that statistical techniques such as covariance analysis could be used to control the likely impact of such differences.

10.6.2   Comparability of content of a measurement instrument

Few psychologists would disagree with the statement that different groups can attach different meanings to a particular behaviour or that a particular behaviour can have different meanings in different contexts. It is also widely recognised that particular aspects of testing would favour one group over another or that different groups may have differential response styles. For example educational research has shown that, in England, boys are likely to score higher than girls on multiple choice tests whereas girls are likely to do better on essay-based tests (Gibbs and Murphy, 1994).

When comparing two or more cultural groups, it is therefore important to make the context, the content, and the administration of tests comparable across different groups. This would enable you to rule out interpretations of cultural differences which are based on methodological biases.

Ensuring the stimulus content comparability   There are two ways in which content can be comparable or equivalent across different cultural groups. It can be semantically equivalent or functionally equivalent.

Functional equivalence is achieved when two behaviours are related to the solution of the same problem. An example often given is Field's (1960) research where visiting a priest in his shrine in Ghana was found to be very similar to visiting a psychotherapist in Europe or America. So the item 'Do you visit your shrine regularly?' is regarded as functionally equivalent to the question 'Do you have your own psychoanalyst?' in California. Another example can be seen in Topf et al.'s (1989) research on feelings of national pride when they treated monarchy in Britain as equivalent to the Basic Law in Germany.

Semantic equivalence refers to the linguistic meaning of the items. This is usually ensured by 'back and forward translation'. An instrument developed by a researcher in one cultural group should be translated by another in the other cultural group. This translated version is then translated back to the initial language. This process examines the extent to which the translation is possible and precise. Both the original and translated versions of the instruments should therefore be 'decentred' to make them more natural and fluent. Werner and Campbell (1970) have also pointed out that measurement instruments should avoid including culture-specific features.

There are a number of guidelines for wording the original instrument that should be followed in order to ensure that an instrument can be easily and accurately translated (Brislin et al., 1973):

1 Use short, simple sentences in order to minimise the cognitive load of the instrument; a simple item-per-item check whether the phrasing can be simplified can lead to considerable improvement in translatability.
2 Employ the active rather than the passive voice.
3 Repeat nouns instead of using pronouns (which in some languages may be difficult to translate).
4 Do not use metaphors and colloquialisms, which are not usually easily translated.
5 Avoid the subjunctive mood (e.g. verb forms with 'could' and 'would').
6 Add sentences when key concepts are communicated. Reword these phrases to provide redundancy.
7 Avoid adverbs and prepositions telling 'where' and 'when', such as 'beyond' and 'upper'.
8 Avoid possessive forms where possible.
9 Use specific words such as 'chickens' and 'pigs' rather than general terms such as 'livestock'.
10 Avoid words indicating vagueness, such as 'probably' and 'frequently'.
11 Use wording familiar to translators where possible.
12 Avoid sentences with two different verbs that suggest different actions.

10.6.3 Potential biases in the administration of measurement instruments

In addition to ensuring comparability in terms of the content of the measurement instruments, it is also important to pay some attention to the procedures involved in the administration of measurement instruments in cross-cultural contexts. It is necessary to try to eliminate any potential effect that such procedures may have on the data obtained. Four main sources of such biases have been identified.

First, it has been shown that interviewer/tester characteristics may have an impact on the participants' responses. If the interviewer is from a different cultural background from that of the respondent it may affect both the level of disclosure and/or the type of responses given. Different cultural groups may for example have different attitudes towards different age or gender groups which may influence what and how they respond to them. Interviewer effects are discussed in more detail in Chapter 17. It is important that the interviewers are trained to be aware of such potential biases. Alternatively, a number of different interviewers can be employed so that the effect of different characteristics such as age, sex and cultural background can be determined and if possible measured so that they can be statistically corrected.

Second, aspects of the interaction between the interviewer/tester and the respondent may potentially bias the data obtained. If the interviewer/tester does not speak the same language as the respondents or does not speak it fluently and there is a need to use interpreters, the potential interpreter effect must be assessed. This is usually done by using at least two interpreters and the results obtained by the two interpreters are compared. Also if the interviewer/tester is not fully aware of all the cultural rules guiding different kinds of social interaction, this may result in inadvertently creating a situation where the participants may feel uncomfortable or may be getting the wrong message as to what is required of them. Finally, in some situations the mere presence of the researcher may have an effect on the observed behaviour. This issue is particularly important in ethnographic or participant observation studies and is discussed in more detail in Chapter 23.

Third, the response procedure may be unfamiliar to a particular group or differentially familiar to the different comparison groups. It has been shown for example that respondents in Western societies may be more familiar with Likert type scales than other cultural groups. Another study which is often cited as an example of this source of bias is that of Serpell (1979) who showed that the response procedure had an effect on Scottish and Zambian children's scores on a pattern-copying task. Scottish children were better when they used a paper and pencil than when they used iron-wire modelling, whereas the reverse was true of the Zambian children.

Fourth, it has been shown that the degree of familiarity with the stimulus itself is likely to have an effect on responses. It is therefore important that the materials used in cross-cultural contexts are equally familiar to the comparison groups.

10.7   ITEM BIAS

In addition to the biases that may stem from inappropriate content of the measurement instrument and its administration procedures, there is another kind of bias that may operate at the item level. This is often called differential item functioning and refers to biases stemming from either poor translation, or inappropriate use, of an item in particular contexts. Item bias is shown when two individuals with the same ability or attitude do not have the same probability of responding correctly to the item.

There are a number of statistical techniques used to test item bias. Van de Vijver and Leung (1997a; 1997b) reviewed the procedures used and concluded that they can be distinguished along three dimensions. Firstly, there are tests such as analysis of variance which are based on linear models of measurement and are used when the data are interval or ratio level. Others are based on non-linear models (for example, item response theory) and are used with nominal scored items. Secondly, it is important that the bias statistical test used has a known sampling distribution if the statistical significance of the discrepancy of score patterns across groups can be assessed. Finally, a distinction can be made between those tests that compare individual scores across cultural groups per score level and those tests which are unconditional; for instance comparisons of item averages.

10.8 EQUIVALENCE

In order to be able to compare data obtained from different cultural groups in a meaningful way, it is necessary to establish their comparability. In particular, it is necessary to show that (1) data sets from different cultures have the same structure (i.e. they share the same psychometric properties: structural equivalence), (2) the scale units for a common construct are identical in the different data sets (measurement unit equivalence) and (3) that the scales used have the same origin (scalar equivalence).

Structural equivalence relates to the issue of whether observed differences in 'behaviour' are reflections of the underlying structure of, for instance, beliefs or personality traits. Is the structure of the construct(s) an instrument purports to measure in different cultures the same? Unless this level of equivalence is established, it is impossible to know whether the dimensions measured are the same. It is impossible to show that the comparisons made are meaningful.

Structural equivalence is usually established by examining the correlations of the items of an instrument or the correlations of the instrument with other measures. Different statistical techniques such as factor analysis, multidimensional scaling and structural equation modelling (SEM) are used to determine whether the same structures underlie the different data sets. For a full review of these statistical techniques refer to Malpass and Poortinga (1986) and van de Vijver and Leung (1997a; 1997b).

Measurement unit equivalence refers to the need to ensure that the scale units are identical in the two or more cultural groups. For example, if we were to measure weight in one data set in pounds and in another in kilograms, comparisons of the two cultural groups along this dimension would be meaningless even though weight is a common dimension.

Scalar equivalence requires not only that the measurement unit in the different data sets is identical but also that they have a common origin. For example, although the Islamic calendar and the Gregorian calendar both measure time in years they have different origins, which makes direct comparisons between the two measures meaningless. However, differences between two points in time in each calendar are comparable. Only when full scalar equivalence is established, that is both the measurement unit and the origins of the scales are identical, can both across- and within-cultures raw score comparisons be carried out. However, van de Vijver and Leung (1997a; 1997b) observe that scalar equivalence is difficult to establish with psychological constructs and it is much easier to disprove it than to prove it.

10.9 CONCLUDING REMARKS

This chapter has dealt with some of the conceptual and methodological issues involved in cross-cultural research. As has been argued, cross-cultural comparisons could make useful contributions to some of the fundamental debates within psychology such as the universality versus specificity of psychological structures, processes and social behaviour. At the same time it has argued against a simplistic conceptualisation of a dualistic relationship between culture and the individual. The social nature of human beings needs to be recognised. In addition, cross-cultural comparisons can make a useful contribution to our understanding of current social phenomena which are not limited by national boundaries.

Throughout this chapter there has been an emphasis on comparability, suggesting that it may be useful to conceptualise cross-cultural research in ways comparable to a quasi-experimental approach (see Chapter 6). This is not to ignore the complexities of the phenomena under study. Rather it is to emphasise the need for methodological rigour that would enable the researcher to make valid and interesting theoretical arguments.

Cross-cultural research should not be seen as a distinct methodology. It can involve a range of methods of data collection and cross-cultural data can be treated with any one of many statistical techniques. However there are a number of issues which are particularly pertinent to comparative research. It is vital to ensure comparability in terms of the comparison dimension, procedure, instruments and measurement.

Finally, a note of caution. Cross-cultural research should not be carried out because there are different cultures and nations out there. It should be conducted only when comparisons are likely to make theoretical contributions and enable us to better understand social phenomena.

10.10   FURTHER READING

Berry, J.W., Poortinga, Y.H., Segall, H.M. and Dasen, P.R. (1992) *Cross-Cultural Psychology: Research and Applications*. This is a useful textbook providing an overview of cross-cultural studies in a number of different fields in psychology as well as discussing methodological and design issues.

van de Vijver, F. and Leung, K. (1997) *Methods and Data Analysis for Cross-Cultural Research*. Thousand Oaks, CA: Sage. This book provides a comprehensive review of methodological issues in cross-cultural research and underlying theoretical assumptions. It also shows how advanced statistical techniques can be used in cross-cultural studies.

Adamopoulos, J. and Kashima, Y. (eds) (1999) *Social Psychology and Cultural Context*. Thousand Oaks, CA: Sage. This very recent book includes contributions of leading researchers in the field of cross-cultural social psychology. The book addresses major theoretical issues and discusses both in a theoretical and an applied way some of the questions addressed in the chapter.

11

Levels of Measurement

Chris Fife-Schaw

Contents

11.1 INTRODUCTION

While there are many aspects of the research process that do not involve measurement and, indeed, some fields of research where traditional measurement is avoided, the great majority of research studies will involve some form of measurement. Whether a research hypothesis stands or falls may depend on how well the key concepts have been measured, independently of whether or not it is a worthy hypothesis. What follows in this chapter is a discussion of measurement issues that have been central to the pursuit of 'positivist' psychological science. Key amongst the assumptions (cf. Cattell, 1981) is that before we can construct grand psychological theories and laws, we must first be able to measure and describe things with reasonable accuracy.

For this chapter, measurement is defined as the assigning of numbers to objects, events or observations according to some set of rules. Sometimes these numbers will be used merely to indicate that an observation belongs to a certain category; at other times these numbers will indicate that the observation has more of some property than an observation that is assigned a lower number.

In much of psychology we have to measure psychological properties indirectly because we have no direct access to the mental constructs we want to measure. It is a straightforward matter to measure length and we can do this fairly directly by offering up our measuring instrument (ruler or tape measure) to the object we want to measure. In the case of IQ, for example, we can only infer levels of intelligence from tests that ask people to solve problems of varying difficulty. We assume that people who get more of the more difficult items correct are more intelligent, but we cannot yet observe intelligence in any more direct way than this. In many respects the existence of something called intelligence is itself a hypothesis and the debate about what IQ tests *actually* measure has often been a heated one in the past. While few people would argue about what a ruler measures, the quantities measured by many psychological measurement instruments are more open to debate and much more obviously depend on the theoretical perspective of the researcher than is the case in the physical sciences.

This is not to say that psychological measurements are of little value. A great deal of effort has been expended in establishing the reliability and validity of psychological measures over the last century. There are now libraries of well-validated tests for all sorts of psychological phenomena which can be used very effectively as long as the manuals are used appropriately. Chapter 13 outlines the principles involved in test construction and development commonly used in psychology.

While many established tests exist, researchers are often confronted by the need to create their own measures to deal with the specific problems they have. This may be because nobody has yet fully developed a test for the particular kinds of observations you are interested in. It may be that you are measuring something which has not been measured before or, perhaps, that the existing tests are too cumbersome for your purposes. Here, you will have to pay particular attention to the precise meaning and nature of your new measures.

It should go without saying that the goal is always to measure things as well as possible. There are often trade-offs that have to be made, however. Measures that demand lots of time and effort from participants may induce fatigue and boredom that may simply introduce unwanted 'noise' into your measurements. On the other hand, measures that are very simple and quick for the respondents to complete are frequently crude and inaccurate. Ultimately you will have to make the judgement as to whether your measures are 'good enough' for your purposes.

11.2   CLASSIFYING MEASUREMENTS

Whether you use a ready made measure or create your own, you always need to know what class of measurement you have made. How you classify a measurement will have an impact on the kinds of numerical analyses you can perform on the data later on. S.S. Stevens (1946) proposed that all measurements can be classified as being of one of four types. This system has become dominant within psychology and no methods textbook would be complete without describing it. There are other systems of classification (see Minium et al., 1993) but Stevens's remains the best known.

11.2.1 Nominal/categorical measures

Nominal or categorical measurements (variables) reflect qualitative differences rather than quantitative ones. Common examples include categories like yes/no, pass/fail, male/female or Conservative/Liberal/Labour. When setting up a categorical measurement system the only requirements are those of mutual exclusivity and exhaustiveness. **Mutual exclusivity** means that each observation (person, case, score) cannot fall into more than one category; one cannot, for example, both pass and fail a test at the same time. **Exhaustiveness** simply means that your category system should have enough categories for all the observations. For biological sex there should be no observations (in this case people) who are neither male nor female.

A key feature of categorical measurements is that there is no *necessary* sense in which one category has more or less of a particular quality: they are simply different. Males are different from females (at least at some biological level) and northerners come from the north and southerners do not. Sometimes, however, this will seem like an odd assumption. Surely 'passing', for example, is better than 'failing'? Well, yes, in certain cases this would be so, but this would depend on what your *a priori* theory about the measure was. If you believed that 'passing' was more valuable and reflected more positively on somebody (e.g. that they were more intelligent, paid more attention, etc.) then that is a matter for you as a researcher; the use of a pass/fail category system does not inherently contain any notion of greater or lesser value.

For the purposes of using computers to help with our analyses, we commonly assign numbers to observations in each category. For instance we might assign (code) a value of 1 for males and 2 for females. The important point is that although females have a numerically larger number there is no suggestion that being female is somehow better or more worthy. Again, this can cause confusion especially as your computer deals only with numbers and not their meanings. You could, for instance, ask it to calculate the mean sex of the respondents and it might come up with a figure something like 1.54; clearly this is pretty meaningless.

Although the categories of a categorical variable do not necessarily have any value associated with them, this does not mean that they cannot reflect some underlying dimension in some instances. As an example, you might classify people you are observing in the street as 'young' or 'old' because you are unable to approach them to ask their ages directly. While this is likely to be an extremely crude and inaccurate classification, this system implies an underlying continuous dimension of age even though we place people in only two categories.

The criteria for categorical measurement do not preclude the possibility of having a category of 'uncategorisable'. If you were to have such a category you would satisfy both the mutual exclusivity and exhaustiveness criteria, but if there were a lot of 'uncategorisable' observations then the value of your categorisation system might be brought into question. How useful is it to have a variable on which the majority of observations are 'uncategorisable'? This can only truly be answered with reference to your research question.

11.2.2 Ordinal level measures

This is the next level of measurement in terms of complexity. As before the assumptions of mutual exclusivity and exhaustiveness apply and cases are still assigned to categories. The big difference is that now the categories themselves can be rank ordered with reference to some external criteria such that being in one category can be regarded as having more or less of some underlying quality than being in another category. A lecturer might be asked to rank order their students in terms of general ability at statistics. They could put each student into one of five categories: excellent, good, average, poor, appallingly bad. Clare might fall into the 'excellent' category and Jane into the 'good' category. Clare is better at statistics than Jane, but what we do not know is just how much better Clare is than Jane. The rankings reflect more or less of something but not *how much* more or less.

Most psychological test scores should strictly be regarded as ordinal measures. For instance, one of the subscales of the well-known Eysenck Personality Questionnaire (EPQ) (Eysenck and Eysenck, 1975) is designed to measure extroversion. As this measure, and many like it, infer levels of extroversion from responses to items about behavioural propensities, it does not measure extroversion in any direct sense. Years of validation studies have shown how high scorers will tend to behave in a more extroverted manner in the future, but all the test can do is rank order people in terms of extroversion. If two people differ by three points on the scale we cannot say *how much* more extroverted the higher scoring person is, just that they are more extroverted. Here the scale intervals do not map directly on to some psychological reality in the same way that the length of a stick can be measured in centimetres using a ruler.

Since many mental constructs within psychology cannot be observed directly, most measures tend to be ordinal. Attitudes, intentions, opinions, personality characteristics, psychological wellbeing, depression, etc. are all constructs which are thought to vary in degree between individuals but tend only to allow indirect ordinal measurements.

This conclusion is a point of contention for many researchers since one of the implications of assuming these measures to be ordinal is that some parametric statistical tests should not be used with them. Indeed even the humble mean is not used appropriately with ordinal measures (the median is a more appropriate measure of central tendency). This sits uneasily with what you will see when you read academic journal articles, where you will regularly find means and parametric statistics used with ordinal measures. We will deal with this issue later in this chapter (see also Chapter 25).

11.2.3 Interval level measures

Like an ordinal scale, the numbers associated with an interval measure reflect more or less of some underlying dimension. The key distinction is that with interval level measures, numerically equal distances on the scale reflect equal differences in the underlying dimension. For example, the 2 °C difference in temperature between 38 °C and 40 °C is the same as the 2 °C difference between 5 °C and 7 °C.

As we will see later, many behavioural researchers are prepared to assume that scores on psychological tests can be treated as interval level measures so that they can carry out more sophisticated analyses on their data. A well-known example of this practice is the use of IQ tests. In order to treat scores as interval level measures, the assumption is made that the 5-point difference in IQ between someone who scores 75 and someone who gets 80 means the same difference in intelligence as the difference between someone who score 155 and someone who scores 160.

11.2.4   Ratio scale measures

These differ from interval level measures only in that they have a potential absolute zero value. Good examples of ratio scales are length, time and number of correct answers on a test. It is possible to have zero (no) length, for something to take no time, or for someone to get no answers correct on a test. An important corollary of having an absolute zero is that, for example, someone who gets four questions right has got twice as many questions right as someone who got only two right. The ratio of scores to one another now carries some sensible meaning which was not the case for the interval scale.

The difference between interval and ratio scales is best explained with an example. Say we measure reaction times to dangers in a driving simulator. This could be measured in seconds and would be a ratio scale measurement, as 0 seconds is a possible (if a little unlikely) score and someone who takes 2 seconds is taking *twice* as long to react as someone who takes 1 second.

If, on average, people take 800 milliseconds (0.8 of a second) to react we could just look at the *difference* between the observed reaction time and this average level of performance. In this case the level of measurement is only on an interval scale. Our first person scores +1200 ms (i.e. takes 2 seconds, 1200 ms longer than the average of 800 ms) and the second person scores +200 ms (i.e. takes 1 second, 200 ms more than the average). However, the first person did not take 6 times longer (1200 ms divided by 200 ms) than the second. They did take 1000 ms longer, so the *interval* remains meaningful but the ratio element does not.

True psychological ratio scale measures are quite rare, though there is often confusion about this when it comes to taking scores from scales made up of individual problem items in tests. We might, for instance, measure the number of simple arithmetic problems that people can get right. We test people on 50 items and simply count the number correct. The number correct is a ratio scale measure since four right is twice as many as two right, and it is possible to get none right at all (absolute zero). As long as we consider our measure to be *only* an indication of the number correct there is no problem and we can treat them as ratio scale measures.

If, however, we were to treat the scores as reflecting ability at arithmetic then the measure would become an ordinal one. A score of zero might not reflect absolutely no ability at all as the problems may have been sufficiently difficult so that only those with a moderate degree of ability would be able to get any correct. It would also be a mistake to assume that all the items were equally difficult. Twenty of the questions might be easy and these might be answered correctly by most people. Getting one of these right and adding one point to your score would be fairly easy. The remaining items may be much more difficult and earning another point by getting one of these right might require much more ability. In other words, the assumption that equal intervals between scores reflect equal differences in ability is not met and we should strictly treat the scores as an ordinal measure of ability.

11.3 DISCRETE VERSUS CONTINUOUS VARIABLES

Many types of measurement result in indices that consist of indivisible categories. If someone scores 13 on our 50-item arithmetic test, they might have scored 14 on a better day but they could never have scored 13½. The score 13½ was not possible as the individual questions can be marked only correct or incorrect. Measures like this are called **discrete variables** since they can have only discrete, whole number values.

Some variables like height and time are referred to as **continuous variables** since they could be divided into ever smaller units of measure. We could measure height in metres, then centimetres, then millimetres, then micrometres, then nanometres and so on until we got to the point where our measuring instrument could not make any finer discriminations. There are an infinite number of possible values that fall between any two observed values. Continuous variables can be divided up into an infinite number of fractional parts. Ultimately it is the accuracy of our measuring instrument that puts limits on the measurement of continuous variables. If our ruler can measure accurately only to the nearest millimetre we must settle for that degree of precision.

When measuring a continuous variable you end up recording a single figure but this really represents an interval on the measurement scale rather than a single value. It is therefore always an **approximate value**. If we time someone doing a task to the nearest second, say it takes them 20 seconds, we are really saying that the time taken lies somewhere in the interval between 19.5 s and 20.5 s. Had it actually taken them 19.4 s we would have rounded the time to 19 s, not 20 s (note: when rounding a number that ends exactly with a numeral 5, always round to the nearest even number). Similarly, an elapsed time of 20.6 s would have been rounded to 21 s. This is shown in the diagram.

Real limits

18.5	19.5	20.5	21.5
19	20	21	

In this example we are deliberately recording times only to the nearest second but, in principle, the choice of any measurement tool carries with it a limit to the degree of accuracy that can be achieved and thus the rounding process will have to happen even if we are unaware of it. We will still be reporting a time that corresponds to an interval and not a discrete value. If our stopwatch could record times to the nearest 100th of a second, say, and we recorded a time of 20.12 s, this would still mean we were saying that the time taken lay somewhere in the interval between 20.115 and 20.125 s. These boundary values are referred to as **real limits**.

It is always appropriate to use the most accurate measure practicable. Any calculations you do using approximate values necessarily include that approximation in the final result. Use two or more approximate values in a calculation and the scope for misleading results increases dramatically. Hence it is always preferable to use approximate measures associated with the smallest intervals possible so as to minimise this problem. You should also note that, although our variables might be theoretically continuous, like time and length, the act of measurement always reduces the measure to a discrete one.

11.4 MEASUREMENT ERRORS

The goal of all researchers should be to minimise measurement errors. Put formally, these are the discrepancies between the observed value of your measurement and the 'true' value. There is a simple formula to illustrate this:

$$observed\ score = true\ score + error$$

The 'error' term may be positive or negative.

Obviously it would be nice to have the error term as small as possible. If you were measuring people's heights with a ruler marked off in inches then you could probably only measure accurately to within half an inch. Having a ruler marked off in millimetres would give rise to much more accurate measurement and finer distinctions between individuals could be made (see previous section). In a similar way, psychological measures should strive to make as fine a set of distinctions between people as possible. Assuming your measure is valid, it makes sense to have more points on your measurement scale rather than fewer.

This holds true only so long as you believe the individual points on the scale carry the same meaning for all participants. When it comes to ratio scale and interval level measures such as time, this is not a problem. You could measure time to the nearest millionth of a second, though you might find the necessary timing equipment a little expensive! For most psychological research, timing to the nearest millisecond is probably accurate enough. Things get much more difficult when you have ordinal measures, however. Problems arise when you try to label individual responses on your ordinal scale. Take the following as an example.

Let's assume you have an attitude statement about a political issue and you would like people to tell you how much they agree or disagree with it. You could provide a five-point scale as follows:

1	2	3	4	5
Strongly agree	Agree	Neither agree nor disagree	Disagree	Strongly disagree

Most respondents would know what they were required to do with such a response scale. While you could not be certain that all those who 'agreed' had agreed to the same extent, you would probably feel reasonably happy that they did not intend to tell you they had very strong views on the topic. Similarly it is probably safe to assume that they are not entirely equivocal about the issue either.

If you gave this question to several hundred people in a survey, however, you might find that so many people had the same score on the item that it did not discriminate very much between people. In this situation you might want to increase the number of response options available. A seven-point scale could be used and it would be reasonably easy to label the response options. You might even think a nine-point scale was appropriate, though labelling all the points might prove more of a challenge. Indeed you could simply label the end- and mid-points, leaving the rest unlabelled.

Why not opt for a 29-point scale instead? This would give even greater discrimination, surely? The answer is, regrettably, no. Respondents would now have trouble working out where they should indicate their response on the scale. Should it be the 18th or the 19th point or even the 20th? Such a response format increases the scope for confusion on the part of the respondent and thus will introduce, rather than reduce, measurement error. There is also the problem that we still do not know that all people responding at point 19 agree to the same extent. Such multi-point ordinal scales introduce an unfortunate illusion of precision.

11.5 CHOICES OVER LEVELS OF MEASUREMENT

In the previous and very traditional section you will have noticed that I have implicitly suggested that ratio and interval level measurement is to be preferred over ordinal or categorical measures. The reason for this is that in most cases a good ratio scale measure will contain more information about the thing being measured than a good ordinal measure. You would probably rather have temperature reported in degrees Celsius than on a scale of very cold, cold, neither warm nor cold, warm, hot, very hot. You should always strive for greater accuracy of measurement where possible.

Naturally some kinds of variable are always going to be categorical (e.g. sex) and some are always going to be ordinal (e.g. most scaled measures; but see section 11.6). In such cases you should not regard your measures as somehow inferior. Whilst it would be nice to think that ultimately we will have access to more direct measures of attitudes and personalities, for example, these are not likely for the foreseeable future.

There are, however, some common practices which should be discouraged. The most notorious of these is the collapsing of ordinal measures into categorical ones. It is quite common to see researchers take an attitude item with a seven-point agree/disagree response format and collapse the data into a simple three-point scale of agree/uncertain/disagree. This practice degrades the measurement by removing the extremity information.

There are three kinds of motive for collapsing data in this way. One is the desire to use simpler statistical procedures; a second is to make graphs and tables clearer; and the third is that you might not believe that your seven-point measure is very accurate or valid. With the ready availability of comprehensive statistics books and computer programs the first problem is easily overcome. While clarifying graphs and tables is an admirable aim it would be desirable to collapse the scores only for this purpose and conduct statistical analyses on the uncollapsed data. The third justification is also a justification for not using the measure. If you doubt the validity or accuracy of a measure then you should think twice about using it at all.

11.6   THE RELATIONSHIP BETWEEN LEVEL OF MEASUREMENT AND STATISTICS

Most good statistics texts present readers with 'decision trees' which help you select the correct statistical test to use providing you know the answers to a number of simple questions about your data and research design. These are very useful, and simple versions are provided in Chapter 25 on bivariate analyses.

These decision trees ask about the level of measurement for your data as well as the nature of the distribution of scores on the measure that you expect in the population from which your sample scores were drawn. The topic of distributions of scores is dealt with in Chapter 25 but the level of measurement issue is pertinent here, particularly at the boundary between ordinal and interval level measures.

The attraction of **parametric tests**, ones that assume something about the distribution of scores in the population (e.g. *t*-test, ANOVA), is that there are many more of them than **non-parametric tests**. They often allow you to ask interesting questions about your data that are not easily answered without using such parametric procedures. To say that your measure is only ordinal, rather than interval level, usually rules out these useful procedures. Chapter 26 outlines some of the many possibilities. Two views have developed over the appropriateness of treating ordinal measures as interval ones. Those interested in reading more on this debate should see Henkel (1975), Labovitz (1975), Davison and Sharma (1990), Townsend and Ashby (1984) and Stine (1989) among many others.

One view states that, most of the time, providing you have a good quality ordinal measure, you will arrive at the same conclusions as you would have using more appropriate tests. It is sometimes argued (see Minium et al., 1993) that while most psychological measures are technically ordinal measures, some of the better measures lie in a region somewhere between ordinal and interval level measurement.

Take a simple example of a seven-point response scale for an attitude item. At one level this allows you to rank order people relative to their agreement with the statement. It is also likely that a two-point difference in scores for two individuals reflects more of a difference than if they had only differed by one point. The possibility that you might be able to rank order the magnitude of *differences*, while not implying interval level measurement, suggests that the measure contains more than merely information on how to rank order respondents. The argument then runs that it would be rash to throw away this additional useful information and unnecessarily limit the possibility of revealing greater theoretical insights via more elaborate statistical procedures.

The more traditional and strict view (e.g. Henkel, 1975; Stine, 1989) says that using sophisticated techniques designed for one level of measurement on data of a less sophisticated level simply results in nonsense. Computer outputs will provide you with sensible-looking figures but these will still be nonsense and should not be used to draw inferences about anything. This line of argument also rejects the claim that using parametric tests with ordinal data will lead to the same conclusion *most of the time* on the grounds that you will not know when you have stumbled across an exception to this 'rule'.

The debate on this issue continues. The safest solution, advocated by Blalock (1988), is to conduct analyses on ordinal measures using both para-metric and non-parametric techniques where possible. Where both procedures lead you to the same substantive conclusion then, when reporting parametric test results, you will at least know that you are not misleading anyone. You should be guided more by the non-parametric procedures if the conclusions are contradictory.

What would be unacceptable would be to select the statistical procedure that leads to results that support your hypothesis. You should attempt consistency in reporting findings so that you decide either that your data meet the assumptions for parametric procedures or that they do not.

Ultimately, whether this issue matters will depend on the seriousness of making a mistake and who your audience is likely to be. Research on a drug or an intervention that may change people's lives demands the most strict and conservative approach to your analysis. On the other hand, if your research topic is more esoteric and your audience is researchers in a field that has regularly used (abused?) parametric techniques on ordinal data, then you may find it difficult to get a hearing if you do not report findings in the accepted way.

11.7 CONCLUSIONS

This chapter has attempted to alert you to the main issues surrounding levels of measurement. As time marches on, the research community may come to an alternative system of classifications (cf. the debate discussed above). However, the Stevens system described here remains the dominant one in psychology for the time being. Chapter 25 takes this a step further by looking at the principles of statistical inference in more detail. Be sure that you have understood this chapter before you read Chapter 25.

11.8 FURTHER READING

All good statistics textbooks explain Stevens's classification system and the relationship levels of measurement and statistics, though few books will go much beyond what has been presented here and in Chapter 25. Minium et al. (1993) has the virtue of spelling out many of the debates in a clear and accessible way. Many of the key papers on the debate about measurement and statistics have appeared in the *Psychological Bulletin* and are likely to continue to appear in that journal.

12

Questionnaire Design

Chris Fife-Schaw

Contents

12.1 INTRODUCTION

The humble questionnaire is probably the single most common research tool in the social sciences. The principal advantages of the questionnaire are its apparent simplicity, its versatility and its low cost as method of data gathering. For many research topics, questionnaires provide data which are of a good enough quality both to test hypotheses and to make real-world policy suggestions. Where people wish to make population parameter estimates, the cost advantage of questionnaires over interviews means that many more people can be sampled for a given budget than might otherwise be possible. Questionnaires are a relatively well-understood technology and there are numerous guides to designing good questionnaires (e.g. Sudman and Bradburn, 1982; Oppenheim, 1992).

Designing the perfect questionnaire is probably impossible, however. Experience shows that you can rarely design one that all your respondents, let alone your academic peers, are happy with. Similarly it is unlikely that you will complete a questionnaire study without asking yourself the 'Why didn't I ask about that?' question. This should not be seen as a failing of questionnaire methods themselves so much as an inevitable part of the research process. This is not to say that careful questionnaire design can be ignored. There have been too many questionnaires produced over the years that contain simple errors that have seriously undermined the value of the data collected. You should always strive to minimise the number of these errors and hopefully what follows will alert you to the more obvious problems.

The focus of this chapter is on self-completion questionnaires, though the section on item wording contains some ideas that apply equally to interview schedules. You should read this chapter in conjunction with Chapter 7 on surveys and sampling.

12.2   WHAT INFORMATION DO YOU WANT?

The very versatility of the questionnaire as a data gathering technique means that it is difficult to generalise about its appropriate uses. It is, however, useful to try to classify common aims since the temptation is often to milk questionnaire data to meet a number of these aims simultaneously while fulfilling none of the aims particularly well. An awareness of these general purposes should help focus the questionnaire design process.

12.2.1   Hypothesis generating

In this mode, questionnaires are useful for asking a large number of people 'what if', exploratory types of question. The intention is to get a feel for how people respond to certain issues. When attempting to elicit interesting insights in this way, it is often desirable to allow people to make open-ended responses, unconstrained by your prior expectations of what classes of response are useful to you. While this kind of information can also be obtained by unstructured interviews and group discussions, a questionnaire study can give you a feel for the range of likely responses and a rough idea of how common certain responses are.

Sometimes the goal is to see if there is any underlying dimension, or putative cause, that influences responses to a set of items. In such cases, exploratory data analytic procedures, such as exploratory factor analysis and cluster analysis, are commonly used (see Chapter 26). As there is often no established theory generating hypotheses about the items, only your hunches and intuitions, such analytic procedures are best thought of as generating hypotheses about the nature of certain items for future studies.

12.2.2   Test development and validation

A common application of questionnaires is in the realm of test development. This can take many forms. A set of items (questions on the form) may be being tested as a potential scale to measure a psychological trait. The aim is to collect responses to the items so that various psychometric procedures can be used to test reliability and/or validity. A set of items supposedly measuring some psychological construct may be administered to groups with known characteristics so as to attempt to assess the validity of the measure. Chapter 13 outlines many of the standard procedures associated with this use of the questionnaire.

12.2.3   Population parameter estimation

Once a range of measures exists, either as published tests or as the result of procedures outlined in section 12.2.2, questionnaires can be used to estimate population scores on such tests. For instance, you might be interested to estimate the levels of psychological wellbeing among police officers. After appropriate sampling, you could administer a questionnaire containing the General Health Questionnaire (GHQ; Goldberg, 1972) and treat the resulting scores as an estimate of the 'true' level of psychological wellbeing among police officers. These estimates can then be compared with norms, the responses of other groups who have taken the GHQ in the past. Parameter estimates can be made for almost any type of question you could ask.

12.2.4   Hypothesis and model testing

If measures of key constructs already exist then questionnaires can be useful for hypothesis testing purposes. Common examples would include testing causal models (e.g. the Theory of Planned Behaviour) or confirming the factor structure underlying responses to a set of pre-existing items. Hypothesised differences between identifiable groups on specified measures is another common application, as is the evaluation of an intervention (e.g. a teaching programme).

   Ideally, you should keep the above aims separate and conduct different studies to deal with each aim in turn. In reality, however, limited resources are likely to mean that you will combine some of these aims within one questionnaire study. For instance, it is common practice to specify a new measure (e.g. a set of scaled items) and then attempt hypothesis testing within the same data set. This practice tends to mean that the validity of the measure is not established and, while inter-item reliability can be assessed, the interpretation of the data necessarily requires greater caution than would be the case had established measures been used.

   There is an important distinction to be made here between dishing out lots of questionnaires and fishing through the data to find statistically significant relationships and a more theoretically driven exercise. With the advent of easy-to-use computer programs such as SPSS, there is a growing temptation to confuse exploratory, hypothesis generating uses of questionnaires with hypothesis testing. This should be avoided where possible.

12.3   OPEN VERSUS CLOSED RESPONSE FORMATS

Before looking at individual types of question it is worth saying something about possible response formats.

A major distinction lies between open-ended and closed-ended response formats. With **open-ended formats** respondents are asked to write down their response to a question in any terms that they see fit. When asking about occupations it would be prohibitive to list all possible occupations, so you would normally allow respondents to make an open-ended response and simply write down their occupation. As another example, you might ask people to give their reasons for recycling glass bottles and allow them to list as many reasons as they felt they had for recycling. **Closed-ended formats** require the researcher to have a reasonable idea of the likely responses to the items. In the recycling example, they would need to provide a list of likely reasons for recycling and ask respondents to indicate which of the reasons applied to them.

The advantages of closed-ended formats are that they clarify the response alternatives for the respondent and they reduce the number of ambiguous answers that might be given. Open-ended questions often prompt people into providing multiple responses even if these responses are substantively the same. Also, from a clerical point of view, they reduce the number of **coding errors** in the data set. Coding errors occur when an open-ended response is misinterpreted by the researcher at the stage of turning verbal responses into numbers that can be used for computer analysis. Respondents can answer closed-format items quickly, making responding to you at all more attractive if they are under time pressure.

The disadvantages of closed-ended formats are of many sorts but perhaps the most important is that they can create artificial forced choices and rule out unexpected responses. Your list of reasons for recycling may not include one that is very important for some people. Making up the response categories is often difficult as they must cover the full range of likely responses.

Another problem concerns the shared meanings attached to the words used in the questionnaires. For instance, the term 'tea' is used differently by people from different social strata and different geographical locations. Most people would recognise 'tea' as a drink, but for some people it is also a light snack in the afternoon and for others a larger meal in the early evening. This is rather a quaint example, but closed-ended response formats assume that people share the same understanding of the items and response categories as does the researcher. There are many other biasing effects that occur when using closed-ended formats; these will be discussed in more detail later in this chapter.

While it might seem that the problems with closed-ended response formats are legion, the main reason for their continued popularity lies in the difficulties of analysing open-ended responses. Open ended responses simply do not lend themselves to easy numerical analysis in the same way that closed response formats do. It is possible to turn such responses into numbers and, of course, it is possible to analyse data without recourse to numbers and statistics, but most questionnaire designers tend towards maximising the number of closed-ended items wherever possible.

To get over the problems with closed-ended items, it is essential that the items you choose to use and the response options you give are ones that potential respondents would use and understand. This means that you must go out and talk to likely respondents to find out what *they* think the key questions are and what their responses would be. Running a series of focus groups (see Chapter 22) is often very useful for this purpose. Taped interviews or focus groups, once transcribed, give useful insights that ought to be drawn upon when designing your questionnaire. Having done this it is still important that careful pilot work is done to see if respondents understand your questions and respond appropriately.

12.4 COMMON RESPONSE FORMATS

Categorical   Examples would include those in Figure 12.1. Note that with categorical response formats it is possible to have items where respondents can circle more than one response, as is the case with question 4 in the figure. Such items are referred to as **multiple response items**. Care is needed when coding the responses to such items into a computer since, for example, question 4 contains effectively three separate responses: one for whether apples were purchased, one for pears and one for oranges.

1	Have you ever attended school in the UK? *(please circle one answer)*	YES NO
2	Are you male or female? *(please circle one answer)*	MALE FEMALE
3	If there were a General Election tomorrow, which political party would you vote for? *(please circle one answer)*	CONSERVATIVE LIBERAL LABOUR OTHER PARTY WOULD NOT VOTE DO NOT KNOW
4	Which of the following items have you purchased in the past week? *(you may circle more than one item)*	APPLES PEARS ORANGES

FIGURE 12.1 *Examples of categorical response formats*

Rating scales   Examples would include those in Figure 12.2. Note that here the respondent is asked to circle one of the five alternative responses. It is perfectly possible to present the response options as in Figure 12.3. Having numbered each option respondents can be asked to write in the number that corresponds to their chosen option in a box next to the question statement or to tick boxes laid out so that the response options form columns.

Ranking formats   Examples would include those in Figure 12.4.

Please say how much you agree or disagree with the following statement *(please circle one response only)*:

Government policy on public transport will be good for the environment in the long term

STRONGLY AGREE
AGREE
UNCERTAIN
DISAGREE
STRONGLY DISAGREE

or

How important is European unification to you, personally?

EXTREMELY IMPORTANT
VERY IMPORTANT
MODERATELY IMPORTANT
NOT VERY IMPORTANT
NOT IMPORTANT AT ALL

FIGURE 12.2   *Common rating scale response formats*

Alternative A

Using the scale below, please tell us how much you agree or disagree with the following statements by placing a number in the box provided.

1	2	3	4	5
Strongly agree	Agree	Neither agree nor disagree	Disagree	Strongly disagree

1   Government policy on public transport will be good for the environment in the long term ☐

- -

Alternative B

Please tick one box for each question.

	Strongly agree	Agree	Neither agree nor disagree	Disagree	Strongly disagree
1 Government policy on public transport will be good for the environment in the long term	☐	☐	☐	☐	☐

FIGURE 12.3   *Alternative layouts for rating scale responses*

Which of the following do you feel are the most important factors to consider when choosing a new car?

Please *rank* the following in order of importance. Number them so that 1 = most important, 2 = next most important, through to 6 = least important.

Fuel consumption	____
Maximum speed	____
Quick acceleration	____
Having a safety cage/cell	____
Servicing costs	____
Status/prestige	____

FIGURE 12.4   *An example of a ranking response format*

12.5 COMMON WORDING PROBLEMS

In this section I have grouped together a range of common wording problems that you should be aware of. Oppenheim (1992) and Sudman and Bradburn (1982) among other texts provide more examples of these types of wording problem.

Vague/ambiguous terminology   If you are vague in the phrasing of your questions you cannot be sure what responses to the items mean. An example would be in the wording of frequency response options for behavioural report items, as in Figure 12.5. Just what does 'frequently' mean here? Every hour? Twice a fortnight? Such a term is sometimes referred to as a **vague quantifier**. Respondents will try to guess what you mean by 'frequently' but they may not all make the same guess, leading to hidden ambiguity in the data.

How often do you clean your teeth? *(please circle one answer)*	FREQUENTLY OFTEN INFREQUENTLY NEVER

FIGURE 12.5 *Example of vague quantifier response format wording*

Another problem under this heading concerns ill-defined terms. In sexual behaviour research, for instance, researchers were initially keen to ask people if they felt they were promiscuous or not. Unfortunately, research has shown (Spencer et al., 1988) that the public are unsure what 'promiscuous' means in terms of absolute numbers of sexual partners. Indeed some people believe promiscuity is a term that applies to anyone who has had more partners than they have. Beware inherently ambiguous terms.

Technical terminology   It might seem like a good idea to use technically correct terminology to get over problems of the ambiguity of day-to-day language. For some research topics this may be appropriate but you should pilot your form carefully to be sure that respondents will understand the terms. If appropriate you can give both a technical and a lay explanation for problematic terms in the introduction to the questionnaire. You should always seek to use plain English wherever possible.

Hypothetical questions   In many research areas you are interested to ask people 'What would you do if . . .?' types of question. Such questions about hypothetical future situations must appear reasonable to respondents if their answers are to be meaningful. If you were to ask, say, 'If it appeared that the Liberal Democratic Party could win the next election would you vote for them?', the meaning of the response would depend on the respondent accepting that the Liberal Democratic Party being in a position to win the election was a realistic premise. You might think it was, and some respondents might agree with you, but others might not. Responses from these two groups may not be comparable and there is little you could do about this unless you also asked whether this premise was acceptable first.

Leading questions   Questions such as 'Would you agree that the government's policies on health are unfair?' will suggest to some people that you would like them to agree with you. Similarly, 'Do you agree that Brand Z washes whiter?' might be harder to disagree with than a more neutrally worded item. In such cases you may be indicating something about what would be regarded by some as a 'right' response. Avoid leading questions.

Value judgements   Item wordings should not contain implicit value judgements. In a similar way to leading questions, you should not express your own views, or those of the research sponsor, in question items.

Context effects   These are somewhat more subtle effects on responses that are dependent on the nature of the rest of the questions on the form. Take the following question as an example: 'How many pints of beer did you drink last week?' In the context of a survey into young people's lifestyles and leisure activities this seems like a reasonable question and young males in particular might give relatively high figures in response. If you had asked the same question in the context of a questionnaire on health behaviours and heart disease, responses might well be lower. You should be aware of the potential impact of surrounding questions on your target item.

Double-barrelled questions   Items that involve multiple premises are to be avoided as the meanings of responses are unclear: for instance, 'Do you believe the training programme was a good one and effective in teaching you new skills?' If someone disagreed with this item it could be because they thought the programme was generally good but ineffective for them personally, or bad and ineffective, or even effective for them despite being of poor quality. Here it is not clear exactly which premise is being disagreed (or agreed) with.

Hidden assumptions   Items should not contain hidden assumptions. The classic example of this sort of problem is contained in the item: 'When did you stop beating your wife?' This assumes you used to beat your wife and, indeed, that you have a wife to beat.

Social desirability   Whilst it might seem a source of irritation to the questionnaire researcher, people like to present themselves in a positive light when answering questionnaires. If you were asked if you ever gave to charity, for instance, then saying 'no' (assuming this to be the correct answer) says something about you that you may not want to convey to the researcher. Many apparently innocuous questions have response options which, if selected, might indicate something negative about the respondent. This leads to potential biases in response patterns which you would usually wish to avoid.

Sometimes social desirability phenomena can be quite subtle. For example, Krosnik and Schuman (1988) have shown that people are more prepared to agree 'not to allow' something than to 'forbid' the same thing. Though these responses are logically equivalent the latter one is thought to carry with it undesirable authoritarian overtones, making some people in favour of forbidding things less likely to tell you, the researcher.

On some occasions it can be useful to use items with certain socially desirable responses since this is of some theoretical or analytical use to you. The Crowne–Marlowe Social Desirability Scale (1964) is sometimes used for this very purpose.

Sensitive issues   You should be wary of assuming that all your respondents find your questions as acceptable as you do. When you are engaged in research on sensitive issues (e.g. death, sex, religion) you should be aware that your items may cause offence to certain groups. It is good practice to ask about sensitive issues as directly, yet with as much sympathy for your respondents, as is possible. Do not try to get at sensitive information indirectly by attempting to deceive respondents. If you cannot ask something fairly directly then you should think about approaching the issue via an alternative method to the questionnaire.

12.6   TYPES OF INFORMATION GLEANED FROM QUESTIONNAIRES

Questionnaires can be used to gather a variety of types of information. You can ask about people's background and other factual, demographic information. You can ask about their behaviours, their attitudes or beliefs, their knowledge or their intentions and aspirations. Each sort of information is associated with particular difficulties which are discussed below.

12.6.1   Background and demographic data

Most questionnaires will ask for some information about the respondent's background. Numerous texts deal with how to ask for this demographic information (e.g. Sudman and Bradburn, 1982) and it is well worth the time consulting such books if in doubt about how to phrase certain items. Although these types of information are readily accessible to the respondent themselves, it is surprising how often people resist giving this information. You should consider some of the following issues.

Age   Do you need to know a person's age exactly? Some respondents may not want to declare their ages exactly, so it may be appropriate to ask people to indicate their approximate age in a series of age bands (e.g. 18–25, 26–35, 36–50, etc.). How many bands you need will depend on how crucial it is to distinguish between respondents on the basis of age. If you need to know ages more accurately, then you should ask directly, making it clear how accurate you want the answer to be. You can ask for ages in years, or in years and months. It is possible to ask for dates of birth as an alternative. Requesting greater precision runs the risk of some respondents failing to answer at all.

Biological sex   It is good idea to make this a forced-choice, male/female item. If you leave the response category open-ended someone will put something inappropriate in. Although social scientists draw a distinction between biological sex and gender and often wish to classify the respondent's gender, the term 'gender' is not well understood by lay respondents and may serve to confuse some people. Unless it is central to your research it is probably easiest to use an item like question 2 in Figure 12.1. A question asking 'What is your gender?' can annoy certain sections in society and thereby produce unusable responses.

Ethnicity and nationality   Ethnicity and nationality are two bits of information about respondents that you may need to ask about despite the fact that the very act of asking for this information is heavily laden with political baggage. Many people confuse nationality with ethnicity and, as a researcher, you should be absolutely clear what information you need *and why*. Remember that being 'British' is a statement about nationality not ethnicity. Respondents may reasonably want to know why their ethnicity or nationality is relevant to your study and what use you will make of this information. Research that may reveal important differences between ethnic groups may be regarded as politically suspect by whichever group is likely to come out worst in the survey. If you must ask about nationality and/or ethnicity you should be sure that such information cannot be used to systematically disadvantage any group. Indeed this applies to all demographic data. If you wish to ask about this, the items in Figure 12.6 may help reduce confusion.

What is your *nationality* (e.g. British, French)?   _____

What is your *ethnic origin* (e.g. Caucasian, Afro-Caribbean, Asian)?   _____

FIGURE 12.6   *Example questions to assess nationality and ethnicity*

Social class or socio-economic status   Social stratification is a topic on which so much has been written it is difficult to provide simple guidance on good practice. There are several systems of classification of which the Standard Occupational Classification is the best known and the one used by the UK Office of National Statistics. Most systems involve defining class on the basis of the nature of the person's occupation. This means obtaining enough information about someone's job to permit accurate classification. A common problem is that if someone says they are an 'engineer' this could mean anything from someone who repairs TVs through to someone who designs nuclear power stations. You need more information such as that provided by the items in Figure 12.7 (adapted from the ESRC 16–19 Initiative: Banks et al., 1992).

   When studying women it is difficult to know *whose* social class/status should be assessed. There is a debate (e.g. Dale et al., 1985) about how women's social class should be measured, particularly as women's jobs tend to carry a lower occupational status than men's jobs in some classification systems. Basing a

---

What is your job called?   _____

What job do you do?   _____

Where do you work?   _____

What does the employer make or do?   _____

Is the work full-time or part-time?   FULL-TIME
(please ring one answer)   PART-TIME (less than 30 hours a week)

FIGURE 12.7   *Example occupation questions*

woman's class/status on her husband's occupation is common practice but is probably unsound and ignores those who are not married.

Difficulties also occur when trying to classify young people's occupations. Occupations common among people at the beginning of their careers tend to carry low status yet they may still lead to high status careers in later life. Using parental class/status is one possible solution but it is unclear at what age a person's occupation should be regarded as a good indication of class/status. Classifying students and the unemployed also remains problematic.

When asking about social class/status you should be clear in your mind what it is you really want to know about the respondent. Sociologists have spent decades theorising about what constitutes our social status and even a cursory dip into the literature will make it clear that such concepts as 'class', 'status' and 'advantage' are complex yet very slippery things indeed: psychologists should beware the temptation to accept measures of 'status' unconditionally. For many psychological applications it might be more appropriate to simply ask about factors such as income and educational history since it may be these variables you are really interested in rather than a stratification based on occupations.

Income   A person's income is perhaps one of the most sensitive issues you can ask about in social research. Requests for exact amounts are often regarded with suspicion, and common practice in market research is to provide income bands (e.g. £0–£5000 p.a., £5001–£10,000 p.a., etc) and ask respondents to select one band only. Respondents need to be assured that their responses will not be handed over to the Inland Revenue or other government agency.

With many factual types of responses it can be useful to ask respondents to tick a box if they do not wish to provide certain bits of information. This helps you distinguish between data that are missing because people did not want to provide some information, and data that are missing because people simply neglected to fill in the form completely. Providing an option not to respond like this may help to make people feel more relaxed about providing other sorts of information. Making people feel they have to answer absolutely everything may make some feel they would rather not respond at all. Obviously, you should not do this with items that are crucial to your study's design.

There is a useful discussion of alternative ways to ask for social stratification information (including examples) at the CASS website (see section 12.10).

12.6.2 Behavioural reports

By their very nature, questions asking about past behaviours assume accurate memory for events as well as a willingness to report these to a researcher. Both assumptions need to be considered afresh for each new item you generate.

It should come as no surprise that sensitive and socially undesirable behaviours are often misreported if reported at all. Enquiries about sexual activities are thought to produce over-reporting in some groups and under-reporting in others (see Boulton, 1994). Reports of involvement (or not) in illegal practices are also likely to be prone to error.

It would be a mistake to assume that biases apply just to the reporting of private and/or undesirable acts. Sudman and Bradburn (1982) report studies that suggest over-reporting biases apply to socially desirable behaviours too (e.g. charity donations, library use). Given these problems, the best solution in the absence of corroborative data is to introduce additional items elsewhere in the questionnaire to test for consistency in reporting. If someone is going to misrepresent their behaviour to you, then if they are inconsistent at least you can have clear grounds to exclude their responses from your analyses.

In some circumstances it may be possible to make respondents believe that you will have an alternative way to find out about their behaviour. This tactic is called the **bogus pipeline**. In a questionnaire study on children's smoking behaviour, Evans et al. (1978) took saliva samples at the time of questioning and led respondents to believe that the saliva would be used to confirm their behavioural reports on the questionnaire. In fact, the cost of saliva testing was too high to permit all samples to be tested but, compared with a control group, the group who thought their behaviours could be monitored reported higher levels of smoking. Where appropriate, this strategy seems likely to improve the quality of behavioural report data though you should be wary of deliberate attempts to deceive respondents, especially if you will be unable to fully debrief them.

Assessment of the frequency with which behaviours have been done in the past is an area where there is much research activity (see Gaskell et al., 1993). What is clear is that you should avoid vague response categories (such as 'regularly') as discussed above. When asked about very regular, mundane events people may find it easier to estimate how often they have done the act in a given time period since they are unlikely to remember every time they did the act. When asking about more memorable, major life-events, more specific recall can be requested.

12.6.3 Attitudes and opinions

People's attitudes and opinions are often of great interest but there is little consensus on how measuring them is best done. The most common procedure is to present a statement and ask people to rate on a scale (usually five or seven points) how much they agree or disagree with the statement (see Figure 12.3). It is possible to use more than five or seven points. You can provide a line with the ends labelled 'strongly agree' and 'strongly disagree' and ask respondents simply to mark their preferred position on this agreement dimension with a cross. This procedure requires the researcher to use a ruler or template on each response to retrieve a usable score for computational purposes.

An alternative to the rating scale is the forced-choice design where two opposing statements are presented and the respondent must choose to endorse one or the other. This procedure is less common as it does not give information about the extremity of agreement/disagreement. However, five- or seven-point rating scales can suffer from people's over-reliance on the neutral response ('neither agree nor disagree') rather than committing themselves to expressing an opinion.

All pen-and-paper attitude measurements make a number of assumptions. The first is that people actually have attitudes towards the issues and that they have ready access to them. The second is that these can be adequately reflected in simple ratings or forced-choice judgements. Sometimes you will see the type of rating scale presented in Figure 12.3 referred to as a Likert scale. This is only technically true if the item has been developed so that it generates normally distributed data: this may not always be the case.

Given these kinds of problems it is common to ask multiple questions about the same attitude object in the hope that greater accuracy will be achieved. Multiple item measures of attitudes allow for the possibility of measuring the internal reliability of the items and thus how much 'error' there is in the measurement of the attitude (see also Chapter 13).

12.6.4   Knowledge

Quite often it would be useful to assess factual knowledge in a questionnaire survey. Such 'tests' can be carried out but the validity of responses and thus the knowledge scores has to be considered to be in some doubt. Unless you can be present at the time of testing you cannot be certain who answered the test. This could apply to the whole questionnaire, of course, but people may simply ask someone else for help with the difficult questions so that they do not appear ignorant. Tests of this sort can be used reasonably successfully in non-survey settings on populations such as school pupils and employees where you can exert some control over the testing conditions.

12.6.5   Intentions, expectations and aspirations

Many social psychological theories are concerned with accounting for intentions, expectations and aspirations which are fairly easily assessed via questionnaires. You should be careful to specify an appropriate time frame for such items as vague specifications can lead to vague responses. For instance, if you were to ask 'Do you expect to travel abroad in the future?', respondents could quite reasonably say 'Who knows'? A much better form would be to ask 'As far as you can tell, do you expect to travel abroad in the next year?'

12.7 EXISTING SCALES AND MEASURES

When using established measures it is often tempting to alter the wording of some items to make them sound better or to clarify them a little. It is quite surprising how many published and well-established measures contain wording errors like those outlined in the earlier sections of this chapter. It is also the case that scales developed in other countries can contain culturally specific phrases or assume some familiarity with cultural norms that would be somewhat inappropriate for your sample. Should you change item wordings or leave them as they are?

It is not possible to answer this with a categorical 'yes' or 'no'. One side of the argument says that any tampering with item wordings will change the nature of the scale so that it is no longer equivalent to the original. Hence, comparability of scores between your study and existing research using the scale is no longer appropriate. You might be tempted to make minor changes in the hope that scale scores will still be comparable but, in the absence of supporting validity data, this cannot be assumed.

The other side of the argument says that it is poor research practice to administer questionnaires that contain phrases or assumptions that your respondents are unlikely to be familiar with. It may alienate them or make them think the items are silly or not serious. As an example, early versions of the Wilson–Patterson Conservatism Scale (Wilson and Patterson, 1968) contained items asking people to endorse (or not) chaperones, pyjama parties and beatniks among other potential indicators of conservative attitudes. At the time (the 1960s) chaperones, pyjama parties and beatniks were topical and made sense in such a questionnaire but today these items would raise eyebrows.

The point about the latter example is that the scale would presumably no longer be particularly valid (indeed Wilson subsequently updated the scale). Even though you might wish to compare current levels of conservatism with those found in the 1960s and 1970s by using an equivalent measure, it is doubtful that such a comparative study would be very informative. You should always consider this potential lack of validity when thinking about using an existing measure that was not validated on the type of sample that you are going to study. You may need to consider attempting to establish validity yourself (e.g. via a criterion groups approach, see Chapter 13).

12.8 QUESTIONNAIRE LAYOUT

This section deals with issues in the presentation of your questionnaire. There is always a trade-off between better presentation, and thus better quality data and higher response rate, and increased cost. This is important even if you are going to be present when the questionnaire is administered.

Respondent motivation   Unless you will be present at the administration, explanatory notes should always be provided. These should spell out the broad aims of the study and why the individual's compliance is important.

The individual must be encouraged to feel that their responses are valued by you and that you will treat them with respect. Wherever possible, you should ensure anonymity for respondents. If the research design is such that you need to be able to identify individual respondents, acknowledge this and ensure confidentiality (and, of course, mean it). If you intend to keep computerised records of responses that could identify respondents, you should seek to be registered under the Data Protection Act as a holder of such information. Tell respondents that you have done this.

Provide feedback to respondents (which is always good practice), and explain how this is to be achieved. Compliance is likely to be higher if respondents can find out what happened to the research and what benefits may have come from it.

You should always thank respondents for their help in the introductory notes *and* at the end of the form.

Case identifiers   It is good housekeeping practice to be able to identify individual questionnaires (though not necessarily individual respondents, note) so that when you find problems with the data later on you can use the computer to tell you which questionnaire the problem is associated with. Fail to do this with a large survey and it will be very difficult to make valid corrections to the data.

Length   There are no rules to guide you on the optimum length for a questionnaire since this depends so much on the topic of the study, the method of distribution (e.g. postal, face-to-face) and the anticipated enthusiasm of your respondents. There are some rough guidelines that can be given, however.

The problem facing most researchers is how to ask all the questions they want to ask without tiring or boring their respondents. How long it takes to answer a questionnaire can only really be assessed via pilot work, and efforts should be made to pilot the form on people who are likely, on *a priori* grounds, to have difficulty with it. Experience would suggest that forms that take more than 45 minutes to complete are only appropriate where the respondent can be assumed to be very highly motivated to help you.

Very short questionnaires (one or two pages) have the virtue of not taxing respondents unduly though they may not be taken very seriously either. It would be rare to have a substantive research issue that could be dealt with in such a small questionnaire and some respondents may think the exercise can only be superficial and thus adopt a less than serious attitude towards answering.

Question order   There seems to be a growing convention in social research to collect information about respondent demographics (age, sex, etc.) at the end of a questionnaire. This is information that people have ready access to and, if asked appropriately, they will have little difficulty in providing it. As they tire of your questionnaire they get asked the less taxing questions.

It is also rare to place extremely sensitive questions right at the beginning of a form. People need time to get accustomed to the types of issues you are interested in, and starting off with your equivalent of 'When did you stop beating your wife?' will not make the respondent feel at ease.

Question density   You may be tempted to cram lots of questions into a small number of pages so that the questionnaire booklet does not appear too large and daunting. This is generally counterproductive as squashing lots of items into a small space makes the form look complex and raises the possibility that respondents will get confused and put their responses in the wrong places. Clear, self-evident layout will enhance the possibility of getting valid information from your sample.

Questions that do not apply to everybody   It is often the case that you are forced to use a single form to ask questions and some of these will not be applicable to some people. For instance, you may not wish to ask unemployed respondents about how many hours they work. If you cannot provide a separate questionnaire for the unemployed, you will need to use **filter questions**. An example is shown in Figure 12.8.

---

1   Are you currently unemployed?   YES
                                         NO

   If you answered YES to question 1, ignore question 2 and carry on with question 3.

2   How many hours did you work last week? _____ hours

   Everyone should answer question 3.

3   Are you male or female?   MALE
    (please circle one answer)   FEMALE

FIGURE 12.8   *An example of a filter question*

Typeface and size   Some people will find small, densely packed text difficult to read. Pick a clear font (typeface) and make it reasonably large (12 point or bigger). Use a different font or colour for instructions and bold or italic lettering for filter questions if you have such a facility.

12.9   CONCLUSION

This chapter has attempted to alert you to many common problems in questionnaire design. The solutions proposed here are intended as guides to good practice but you should not feel that these are the only possible solutions to these difficulties. A lot more inventive use could be made of questionnaires than is currently the case. Guides such as this necessarily deal with common problems but you should not limit yourself to asking about the broad general topics covered here. Breakwell and Canter (1993), for example, illustrate a number of possibilities for alternative questionnaire approaches to the social psychological topic of social representation; such experimentation should be encouraged in other research domains too.

12.10 FURTHER READING

Oppenheim (1992) is a good and clear introduction to questionnaire design, as is the older Sudman and Bradburn (1982) text. Schuman and Presser's (1996) book reports an intriguing series of experimental studies with survey data which highlight the sensitivity of respondents to quite minor wording changes in questionnaire items. Those wishing for a contemporary angle on some of these effects should take a look at the work of Gaskell et al. (1993). Information on how to ask questions about demographic issues can be found at the ESRC/SCPR Centre for Applied Social Surveys (CASS) web page at http://www.scpr.ac.uk/cass. This gives information on the way in which such questions have been asked in major social surveys and one hope is to promote best practice in this area and seek some standardisation where possible.

13

Using Psychometric Tests

Sean Hammond

Contents

13.1 BACKGROUND

One of the most widely used methods of data collection in psychological research is psychometric testing. However, it must be said that there is a plethora of suboptimal studies in the psychological research literature whose major failing is the ill-advised use of psychometric methodology. In this chapter I intend to address some of the main issues in psychometric testing in the hope that the reader should be able to make informed decisions when selecting a test for use in a research project.

There appear to be two main reasons for the popularity of psychometric tests in psychological research. Firstly, psychometric tests have been developed to measure an extremely broad range of mental characteristics including aptitudes, competencies, personality traits, mood states, psychopathology, psychosomatic symptomatology, attitudes, motives and self-concept. These developments have provided the researcher with a wide variety of measurement tools which make a large number of psychological variables accessible for research. A second reason for the popularity of psychometric methods is the relative ease with which it is possible to collect large amounts of data. A great many psychometric tests, though by no means all, allow the researcher to gather data at one sitting from large numbers of respondents.

However, one reason why so many studies based on psychometric test data remain unconvincing is because the interest in using psychometric tests is not attended by an equal interest in the technicalities and sophistication of the psychometric principles that underlie their proper use. This lack of interest in psychometrics itself, coupled with an uninformed use of psychometric methods, has burdened the psychological research literature with poorly operationalised studies with little or no potential for replication.

Psychometrics means literally 'measurement of the mind' and psychometric tests are designed to measure the intrinsic mental characteristics of a person. One of the main problems confronting the researcher in psychology is how this measurement can be effected. Almost by definition, the variables under consideration will be those characteristics of the individual that do not lend themselves to simple physical measurement. For example the degree of extroversion that an individual has or their level of numerical reasoning are characteristics that are not accessible to such measuring devices as rulers or weighing scales. Nevertheless, accurate measurement is a necessary prerequisite for any scientific exploration.

Owing to this lack of direct access to the mental characteristics under scrutiny, the discipline of psychometrics has developed a detailed set of procedures and models for statistical estimation. Essentially, these procedures rely on the presence of a large number of indicators which allow us to 'focus in' on the characteristic being measured. In most psychometric tests these indicators may be viewed as the individual items or questions of which they are composed.

13.2   TYPES OF PSYCHOMETRIC TESTS

There are many different types of psychometric test, each using a different strategy for data elicitation. The type of test is dictated by the theoretical orientation of the researcher as well as the kinds of questions being asked. For our purposes we will broadly describe the various types under four headings: projective tests, self-report inventories, objective tests and idiographic measures. Each of these types of test has a place in psychological measurement although each has its own application, advantages and limitations. It is always depressing to read an account by a researcher who believes that his or her preferred technique should be used in preference to all others. The choice of

FIGURE 13.1   *An example of a Rorschach inkblot*

test must depend entirely on the nature of the research and the theoretical framework being applied. However, the underlying psychometric issues are similar irrespective of the test form. These are that the test should be reliable, valid and appropriate for the particular study it is being used for.

13.2.1   Projective tests

Projective tests are designed to be indirect measures of an individual's mental state. The common element in all these tests is that the testee is asked to proffer an unstructured response to some form of stimuli or task. Projective tests are typically widely used in identifying personality characteristics related to abnormal psychological functioning. One primary use of such tests is to examine aspects of the person that are considered to be unconscious. The basic idea is that issues a person would not normally be able to articulate directly may be accessed by the process of projective testing.

The most widely known projective test is the Rorschach inkblot test in which the respondent is presented with a series of ambiguous stimuli in the form of inkblots (Figure 13.1) and is required to say what each brings to mind (Rorschach, 1921; Erdberg and Exner, 1984). The tester then interprets the responses according to a scoring protocol derived from some *a priori* theory (often psychoanalytic). He or she is then able to derive a score for the respondent, often leading to placing the respondent within a diagnostic category.

A wide variety of projective tests is available (Klopfer and Taulbee, 1976; Ziller, 1973). One popular form involves presenting respondents with pictures and asking them to compose a story around the image. Themes within these stories are then identified by the tester, again using an *a priori* theoretical

ework, which enables a categorical judgement to be made of the respon-
s mental state. Examples of these tests are the Blackie Test (psychoanalytic framework) (Blum, 1949) and the Thematic Apperception Tests
(Murray's Needs framework) (Atkinson, 1958).

One of the weaknesses of projective tests is that they typically operate at the
nominal level of measurement, that is, simply provide a categorical description of the respondent. Procedures for more elaborate quantification of an
individual's responses do exist for some of the most well-used projective tests
although they are nearly always complicated to learn (Exner, 1986; Atkinson,
1958). This is because of the almost infinite variety of possible responses
which need to be coded and categorised.

Projective tests are frequently criticised owing to the fact that they appear to
lack objectivity. The tester's interpretation of open-ended information is often
said to be subjective and arbitrary. While this is certainly a major issue in
projective testing it is one that can be addressed with care and the rigorous
application of objective scoring criteria. Of course, the basis of these criteria
resides in the *a priori* theoretical model upon which the test is built. This means
that projective tests are not normally appropriate in an eclectic research
context. For this reason they are not widely used in research and tend to occur
in therapeutic contexts.

13.2.2 Self-report questionnaires

The use of self-report questionnaires as a means of measuring psychological
characteristics grows out of the simple assumption that the best way of finding
out about an individual is to ask them direct questions. A huge number of
well-used self-report questionnaires exists and most of them are designed to
measure personality traits or attitudes. The reason for this abundance is their
comparative ease in administration and the almost limitless range of psychological characteristics that can be addressed.

One of the first self-report questionnaires to be developed was the Woodworth Personal Profile which was used during World War I as a means of
screening conscripts into the army; examples of some of the questions are
provided in Figure 13.2. Woodworth's questionnaire is bizarre by today's
standards but it is a useful reminder of how test items will reflect the attitudes
and values that prevailed at the time they were developed.

Do you daydream frequently?
Do you usually feel well and strong?
Do you think you have hurt yourself by going too much with women?

FIGURE 13.2 *Example items from Woodworth's Personal Profile*

It is important, therefore, that the questions or items in a self-report questionnaire are relevant to the characteristic being examined. Clearly the accuracy of the measurement depends to a great extent upon this relevance. Thus,
if we were developing a questionnaire to measure extroversion we might

include questions on social activities and impulsivity, whereas a question on a person's fondness for bicycles would have no bearing on the domain in question. This is an issue of content validity and we return to it later.

Questionnaires are often criticised as research tools owing to the problem of response bias. This describes the situation in which a respondent systematically fails to answer the questions accurately. There may be many reasons for response bias. It may be due to a deliberate attempt to present an image of themselves which is not true, a situation known as **faking good**. In addition, respondents may possess an in-built tendency to answer 'yes' or 'no' to our questions producing a response bias termed a **response set**. Alternatively, the respondents may simply not know the answer to the question either through lack of self-knowledge or because the question is posed in an ambiguous manner. Thus, an important assumption in using self-report questionnaires is the accuracy of individuals' responses.

13.2.3 Objective tests

The development of the discipline of psychometrics grew out of early attempts to measure human abilities. The social Darwinist approach of Sir Francis Galton, based on his desire to estimate intellectual potential from physical characteristics, soon gave way to the more pragmatic approach of Alfred Binet. Binet devised a series of tasks, performance on which served to indicate the intellectual level of young children. Some examples of Binet's tasks are presented in Figure 13.3. Nearly all ability tests developed since have been based on Binet's basic strategy. Thus, tests of numerical reasoning present the respondent with a series of numerical tasks (addition, division, etc.) while tests of verbal reasoning present the respondent with verbal tasks (synonyms, comprehension).

Point to various parts of face (age level 3)
Repeat five digits (age level 7)
Recite days of the week (age level 9)
Repeat seven digits (age level 12)

FIGURE 13.3 *Examples of Binet's tasks*

A distinction is often drawn between tests of **knowledge** and tests of **performance**. So the former type of test simply prompts the respondent to provide information, as in a history test with the item, 'What year was the battle of Hastings?' Alternatively, the test may ask the respondent to carry out a task, as in the numerical reasoning test with the item, 'What is 16 multiplied by 7?'

A further distinction may be made between **power tests** and **speed tests**. A power test asks the respondent to respond to each item in their own time, placing no time constraints upon them, while a speed test asks the respondent to respond to as many items as they can within a specific time frame. Obviously, the speed test is more practical to administer but it does carry the assumption that speed is associated with ability.

For the test to be useful it must be able to discriminate between respondents. Therefore, it is important that the tests are appropriate for the particular group of respondents on whom they are used. If the test is too easy a large number of the respondents may get every question correct and this will mean that the resulting measurement will not enable the tester to discriminate between respondents. In other words our research would be compromised by the existence of a **ceiling** or **floor effect**.

13.2.4 Normative, criterion referenced and idiographic tests

When we have obtained a test score, the problem remains of how to interpret it. Simply having a neuroticism score of 12 tells us nothing about the respondent unless we can refer the score to some kind of standard. Most psychometric tests in use today are **normative** or **norm referenced** which means that data exist which tell us what range of scores is expected from the population under consideration. This requires that the means and standard deviations of a large representative sample are available to the tester so that s/he can interpret the meaning of an individual's score. These descriptive statistics are termed the **norms**.

For example, most intelligence tests will be constructed so as to produce scores with a mean of 100 and a standard deviation of 15. A respondent with an IQ score of 130, therefore, is deemed to have a high IQ while a respondent with a score of 100 is deemed to be of 'average' intelligence. This means that the interpretation of the test score requires that there exists some normative information in the form of means and standard deviations relevant to the population from which a particular respondent is drawn. A vast majority of psychometric tests are developed as normative tests in which the test norms serve as a standard against which individuals are measured.

Of course, this assumes that the test score occupies a point along a continuum and that the population scores will conform to a normal distribution. Without a normal distribution the mean is not a useful measure of central tendency and so the standard deviation is meaningless as an index of variation. All norm referenced psychometric tests make this assumption of normality by definition.

It is possible to use criteria other than test norms for interpreting test scores as long as they are clearly specified in advance. This strategy is employed by a class of tests known as **criterion referenced** (Glaser, 1963). In this case an external performance criterion becomes the standard against which a respondent is judged. Typically, criterion referenced tests are used in the assessment of competencies particularly in an educational assessment context (Nitko, 1988).

For example, a set of reading problems may be given to a child. The criteria for entering a particular class is that the child will correctly solve each problem. If the child does not answer each question correctly they fail to reach the criterion and are not accepted into the class. The main point in criterion referenced tests is that the respondent either reaches a pre-specified criterion or does not. Obviously, this means that the criteria have to be established very accurately and precisely justified before the test is made

available for use. Criterion referenced tests may also be interpreted norma-
tively since the resulting score is usually a continuous, number correct, value.
The test norms may be used for interpretation as well as the criterion pass
mark as long as normative information exists.

The tests described so far rely for their interpretation upon a comparison,
either with normative or with external *a priori* criteria, so that an individual
respondent can be placed in some relative position. However, there are situations in psychological research where focus is upon the individual respondent
and placing them on a relative scale is irrelevant. An example of such a study
might be one where a researcher wishes to follow a patient over a course of
psychotherapy and attempt to measure the change in their psychological state.
In this case, the respondent may be asked to complete some form of questionnaire on a number of occasions and the changes over time serve as the
focus of interest.

This approach is known as **idiographic** since it focuses on the individual
respondent in isolation. This means that the questions that are asked of the
respondent may be unique to them, and indeed one of the most popular
strategies for idiographic measurement is the use of a repertory grid in which
the respondent generates the constructs that are of most relevance to them.
This means that the assessment device is idiosyncratic and there is no commonality between respondents in the constructs being measured. Another
example of an idiographic research strategy is to be found in Chapter 16.

The idiographic approach has the drawback that comparisons between
respondents are difficult if not impossible and the aggregation of idiographic
data is meaningless. However, the approach may be of great value when the
focus of interest is upon the dynamic processes within individuals which, of
course, is often the case in clinical evaluation research and audit.

13.3 THE PROBLEM OF RELIABILITY

As we have seen above, psychometric measurement depends upon estimation
rather than direct measurement. As a result psychologists cannot expect
perfectly accurate measurement. The role of the test developer is to produce
tests which have the greatest accuracy possible and to provide the test user
with details of the degree of accuracy they can expect when using the test in
question.

The earliest psychometric measurement theory stems from the work of
Charles Spearman and is variously called classical test theory, true score theory
or reliability theory; it remains today the most widely applied basis for psychometric measurement. A number of other psychometric models have grown
out of this classical approach, notably generalisability theory (Cronbach et al.,
1972; Shavelson and Webb, 1991) and item response theory (Hambleton et al.,
1991; Suen, 1991; Lord and Novick, 1968; Mislevy, 1993).

The **true score model** serves as the basis for classical test theory. In this
model it is assumed that the test score is influenced by two factors. Firstly,
and most obviously, the true extent of the characteristic being measured will

influence the test score. The second influence is random error. This may be represented formally as:

$$\text{observed} = \text{true} + \text{error}$$

Thus the test score, or observed score, is a function of the 'true' variance and the error variance. The error variance may be positive or negative so that when we obtain a score from a test it may be an overestimate of the true score or an underestimate. It is the job of the test developer to produce reliable psychometric tests in which the error variance is minimised. A reliable test is one where the 'true' score is close to the 'observed' score.

The error associated with a test score may be systematic or unsystematic. **Systematic error** refers to aspects of error that are built into the test itself and biases the resulting score consistently in one direction. Such error may be due to the use of ambiguous items or the situation where the test is influenced by another variable which is not being assessed. **Unsystematic error** refers to error which is external to the test itself and is assumed to be random such that it might equally result in inflated or attenuated scores. Classical test theory is built upon the assumption that the test has been constructed with sufficient care that systematic error is negligible and only unsystematic error exists.

Classical test theory also makes a number of assumptions about the nature of this unsystematic error variance:

1   Error variance is random.
2   Error variance is normally distributed with a mean of zero.
3   Error variance is completely independent of 'true' variance.
4   The error variance of different tests is not correlated.

The implications of these assumptions are that, if we test an individual on a large number of tests for a single characteristic, the mean of these 'observed' scores will equal the mean 'true' score for that individual. This is because the error variance is partialled out by the operation of adding all the test scores together. This is shown in Figure 13.4. Thus, the argument that summing the responses to each item gives a reasonable estimate of the 'true' score only holds true if we can accept the assumptions of classical test theory.

	Observed score	True score	Error
Test 1	22	21	1
Test 2	24	21	3
Test 3	18	21	-3
Test 4	19	21	-2
Test 5	22	21	1
Mean	21	21	0

FIGURE 13.4   *Simple example of the basic premise of classical test theory*

The reliability of a test is an indication of whether it measures anything at all. As we have already said, the reliability of a test is an indication of the similarity between the 'true' and 'observed' scores. One way of conceiving reliability, therefore, is to think of the correlation between the 'true' score and the 'observed' score. Similarly, it may be possible to conceive of reliability as the ratio of 'true' variance to the total test variance:

$$\text{reliability } r_{tt} = \frac{\sigma^2{}_{true}}{\sigma^2{}_{observed}}$$

In this way reliability can also be seen as the proportion of variance in test scores that is due to the variability of true scores. This is equivalent to the squared correlation between 'true' and 'observed' scores. The simple correlation between true and observed is known as the reliability index, while the squared correlation between true and observed is termed the reliability coefficient.

The greater the reliability a test has, the less the error; and the less the error, the greater the accuracy. Therefore, reliability is associated with the accuracy of the test. If we are looking at the score of one person on a test of known reliability it is possible to estimate the accuracy of that person's score by calculating what is called the standard error of measurement (SEM):

$$\text{SEM} = \sigma_{observed} \sqrt{(1 - r_{tt})}$$

The SEM allows us to generate confidence intervals for a single respondent's score. The SEM can be used to estimate the accuracy of a person's test score for two tests with differing reliability coefficients. Nunnally and Bernstein (1994, Chapter 6) give a readable account of the main issues surrounding SEM.

So far we have talked about reliability theoretically and have shown that it may be conceptualised as the correlation between true and observed scores. However, in practice we do not know the value of true scores and so the estimation of reliability is not quite as simple as this account might suggest. In order to estimate the reliability of a test psychologists have adopted the notion of consistency. The idea is that randomness is inconsistent: therefore, if we can identify consistency in our test we have the confidence of knowing that it is not simply a function of random error. There are a number of kinds of consistency that we can explore in our test but there are essentially four that are traditionally used.

13.3.1 Consistency between parallel tests

As we have seen, the idea of large numbers of parallel tests forms the basis of the development of classical test theory. The argument follows that if a perfectly parallel pair of tests exists then differences in scores must be due to measurement error since the true score will be the same for both tests. Where no error exists, the scores between the two tests will be perfectly consistent with each other. If enough parallel tests are used the average score of all the tests will equal the true score given that the error variance is random. Of course, we must assume, as with classical test theory, that the tests have equal variance and the error variances of the tests are uncorrelated. Having made this assumption we can then estimate our correlation coefficient in the case of two parallel tests by calculating the correlation between them. The correlation between the two parallel forms is equivalent to the squared correlation between the 'observed' and 'true' scores.

Despite the fact that consistency between parallel forms is theoretically directly linked to the concept of reliability (Gulliksen, 1950) there are a number of glaring practical problems with this approach to reliability estimation. Most obviously the procedure requires that we develop not one but two tests for the characteristic in question. Having done this we then have to ensure equivalence between the two forms. As we will see, test development is not a trivial procedure and requires a great deal of investment of time and resources. In addition the time of test administration is doubled because both tests must be taken by the respondents.

13.3.2   Consistency across time (test–retest reliability)

Another approach to reliability estimation involves assessing the consistency of a test over time. To assess reliability a test is given to a sample of respondents at time 1 and then is administered to the same respondents later at time 2. The interval between the two administrations may vary from a few days to a few years. The consistency of the scores between the two administrations of the test is a measure of the reliability. In this case reliability is viewed as an index of stability in which the test is thought of as parallel with itself. The assumption is that any differences across time will be due to measurement errors. The same basic assumptions can be made as with parallel tests. Therefore, the correlation of the two administrations is an estimate of the reliability coefficient.

One of the problems with estimating reliability by test–retest is deciding on the appropriate interval between administrations. If the interval is too short respondents may remember their responses to the first administration and this may distort their responses at time 2. Usually, test–retest reliability estimation requires an interval of a month or more. A second problem is that this type of reliability assessment assumes that the characteristic being measured is stable over time. It would make little sense to assess test–retest reliability for a test of mood state since we would fully expect changes in the characteristic to occur over time. Certain personality traits such as extroversion are generally held to be stable over time, as is intelligence. However, the test user should be clear that this form of reliability estimation makes assumptions, not only about measurement error, but also about the thing being measured.

13.3.3   Internal consistency

A more practical method for estimating the reliability of a test is to examine its internal consistency. This is based on the principle that each part of the test should be consistent with all other parts. An early approach based on this principle was suggested by Spearman (1907) and came to be called the split-half approach. In this procedure the test is administered to a large sample and is then divided into half. This may be done by taking even-numbered items as one half and odd-numbered items as the other half. A score is obtained for each half of the test and a correlation r between the two halves is calculated. The split-half reliability coefficient is then calculated by the following formula:

$$r_{tt} = \frac{2r}{1+r}$$

However, although the principle of split-half reliability is reasonably straight-forward, there is one fundamental drawback and this is that different ways of splitting the test can produce quite different reliability coefficients. What was needed was a procedure that gave the average of all the possible combinations of split halves. This was precisely what Kuder and Richardson (1937) provided in a formula that came to be called the KR20 (Kuder and Richardson's 20th formula):

$$\text{KR20} = \frac{N}{N-1} \frac{\sigma^2{}_{\text{observed}} - \sum pq}{\sigma^2{}_{\text{observed}}}$$

The KR20 was developed for use with dichotomous items but it is very simply generalised for use with items measured on continua or rating scales. This generalisation was due to Cronbach (1951) and came to be called Cronbach's alpha. Alpha can be estimated in a number of ways but two methods are as follows:

$$\alpha = \frac{N}{N-1} \frac{\sigma^2{}_{\text{observed}} - \sum \sigma_i^2}{\sigma^2{}_{\text{observed}}}$$

$$\alpha = \frac{N}{N-1} \left(1 - \frac{N}{N + 2\sum r_{ij}} \right)$$

where N is the number of items, σ_i^2 is the variance of item i and r_{ij} is the correlation between item i and item j. The second formula shows the relationship that alpha has to the inter-item correlations. As we would expect with a procedure designed to estimate internal consistency, alpha is related to the average of all the inter-item correlations. The higher the correlations between the items, the greater the internal consistency. This makes sense if we assume that all the items are indicators of a common characteristic. Thus each item must have variance in common with all the other variables. In other words the reliability of a test is related to the homogeneity of the items with each other.

13.3.4   Inter-rater consistency

So far we have assumed that the test score is measured on a continuum and this is usually the case. However, we mentioned earlier that some psychometric tests produce measurement at the nominal level. Clearly, the procedures for estimating reliability detailed above, relying as they do on the correlation coefficient, are not appropriate for such data. In this case it is usual to estimate reliability by examining inter-rater consistency. For this procedure, two test scorers are used to generate the categorical score for a number of respondents.

A contingency table is then drawn up to tabulate the degree of agreement between the two raters. The percentage agreement gives a rough estimate of reliability although a better estimate is obtained by calculating an index of agreement. This is usually Cohen's kappa which ranges between 0 and 1 and represents the proportion of agreement corrected for chance (Cohen, 1960):

$$\kappa = \frac{P_a - P_c}{1 - P_c}$$

where P_a is the proportion of times the raters agree and P_c is the proportion of agreement we would expect by chance. In fact, it is possible to extend kappa to take into account more than one test scorer and so achieve an even more accurate estimate of reliability. Details of these extensions are beyond the scope of this chapter but the interested reader is referred to the basic papers of Fleiss (1971) and Light (1971).

13.3.5   General considerations

Unlike the kinds of statistical coefficients psychologists commonly deal with such as t, F and r, reliability coefficients are population parameters and not sample statistics. This means that strictly speaking we should not generalise from one sample to another. However, for the sake of simplicity they are usually treated as sample statistics and this does mean that they should be estimated on very representative samples. If the test reliability was estimated on a sample that differs from the sample upon which the test is to be used there is no guarantee that it will have a similar reliability on the new sample. For example, giving an IQ test developed for the general population to a sample of university students may produce reliability coefficients markedly lower than expected because the students would produce smaller test score variance. For this reason care must be taken when choosing a ready made psychometric test for a research project.

It is also worth noting that the estimates of reliability described above are lower bound estimates. Thus, Cronbach's alpha coefficient gives us a low estimate of the reliability. The actual reliability may be slightly higher. While the type of test dictates the type of reliability estimate that is appropriate, it is generally assumed that KR20 and Cronbach's alpha are the most accurate estimates of reliability available within the classical test approach.

We should now turn to the tricky question of what is a 'good' reliability coefficient. Received wisdom (Nunnally, 1978) suggests that reliability coefficients should be greater than 0.7 before we can assume sufficient reliability for a research tool. However, if a psychometric test is being used for a diagnostic of job selection purposes, it should have a reliability of at least 0.9.

The basic principle in deciding on whether a test is reliable is to remember that the reliability coefficient is a measure of the proportion of overlapping of 'true' and 'observed' variance. Thus, a test with a reliability of 0.7 means that 30% of its variance is residual and irrelevant; a reliability of 0.6 suggests a test in which 40% of its variance is made up of error.

The reliability of a test is dependent on the number of items in the test. Providing the items are of sufficient quality, the more the items the greater the reliability. This is entirely to be expected given that items are indicators of an underlying characteristic. Obviously, the more the indicators the more accurate our estimate of the 'true' score. This has often been used as an argument to excuse poor tests. A test with, for example, five items may be found to have a reliability of 0.5; test developers have been known to argue that the reason for the low reliability is that the test has only five items and that it is a good test nevertheless. In fact, the test is not a good test on two counts. Firstly it is inadequate because it does not have enough items to describe the underlying characteristic, and secondly it is highly unreliable. A small number of items does not excuse poor reliability estimates.

13.4 THE PROBLEM OF VALIDITY

In estimating the reliability of a test we are examining its viability as a measurement device. If we find that the reliability is low we have to assume that the test does not measure anything with any degree of credibility. The reliability of a test is not specific to the characteristic being measured. In other words, we may have a highly reliable test but discover that it does not measure the thing we think it does. This leads us to the problem of validity, which may be posed as the question: how well does the test measure what it purports to measure?

As reliability asks whether a test measures anything at all, it should be apparent that reliability logically precedes validity. We may have a reliable test that is not valid but we cannot have a valid test that is not reliable. Without reliability we cannot have validity.

An example of how we may have a reliable test without validity came to the author's attention a few years ago while conducting an undergraduate research methods class. The task was to construct a personality measure of a Freudian construct and the topic chosen was penis envy. The students dutifully set to work to write a set of questions that tapped this particular domain. Eventually a 50-item questionnaire was constructed which was then distributed to about 200 young women (the theory suggests that males do not manifest penis envy). Upon analysing the responses we were pleased to note that our internal consistency coefficient exceeded 0.8, suggesting that we had constructed a reasonable measurement device. However, a small but enterprising group of students had also collected data on a group of males, the expectation being that since the domain was not relevant to this population the responses to the questions would be random and produce very low reliability. As it happened the reliability was higher for males and, disconcertingly, males appeared to manifest higher scores on penis envy than did females. The problem was one of validity. We had constructed a reliable test but it was not a test of penis envy as was supposed. In fact it was probably better described as a test of salaciousness.

Assessing the validity of a test, therefore, requires a precise knowledge of the psychological domain under consideration together with a clear operational definition of each characteristic being measured. There are essentially three approaches to test validation. These are termed **content validation**, **criterion validation** and **construct validation**. Cronbach (1971) sees them as three different methods of inquiry.

13.4.1 Content validation

Content validation simply asks the question: is the content of the test relevant to the characteristic being measured? We may check the **face validity** of a test which is simply the subjective evaluation of the relevance of the test items. This particular form of validity check does have a place although it is often not given much credence because it lacks objectivity. Let us suppose that we have a particular characteristic we wish to measure (for example degree of psychosis). We would first search through the literature until we come across a number of tests that purport to measure psychoticism. We would then need to examine the content of the test items to assure ourselves that the test does coincide with our own operational definition of the construct to be measured. In other words, is our operational definition the same as that of the test which is manifested in the content of its items? Thus, Eysenck and Eysenck's (1976) test of psychoticism measures what most people might term 'psychopathy', while the Minnesota Multiphasic Personality Inventory (MMPI) scale for 'schizophrenia' is more closely associated with the traditional use of the term 'psychotic'.

Having a test with clear face validity may also be useful in obtaining compliance from respondents since, if the items appear irrelevant, testees may become irritated. Nevertheless, in some cases face validity may be a liability since the respondent may identify the purpose of the questions and then proceed to answer them in a biased manner. Clearly, it is up to the researcher to determine whether a high degree of face validity is important for their own study.

Content validation procedures are important when developing a test as it is necessary to construct items that sample the psychological domain in question. One strategy is to ask 'expert' judges to evaluate the relevance of the items to the characteristic being measured. If the judges agree that an item is not measuring the characteristic or they disagree on its relevance, the item may be considered equivocal and its content validity is questionable.

In content validation, an important consideration is the complexity of the test item. A highly complex item may diffuse the focus of the question and result in contamination from some other characteristic that is not being measured. For example, the two questions in Figure 13.5 require the respondent to perform a simple arithmetic operation. However, (b) is far more complex than (a) and requires that the respondent has a reasonable reading ability. As a result, if item (b) was found in a test of children's arithmetic reasoning, we would have to question its content validity, since it is contaminated by the irrelevant variable 'reading ability'.

(a) $2 + 6 + 4 - 6 = ?$

(b) Bill has two apples; Jane gives him six bananas. Sam, who is trying to impress Jane
     with his generosity, gives Bill four more apples. Maggie then steals six apples from
     Bill. How many pieces of fruit does Bill have left?

FIGURE 13.5 *Two items reflecting content validity*

Content validation, then, is largely a qualitative process and it depends upon the tester having a clearly defined idea of what it is they wish to measure.

13.4.2   Criterion validation

Criterion validation involves testing the hypothesised relationship of the test with external criteria. This is a more quantitative process than content validation but it requires that the tester is able to generate a reasonable set of hypotheses as to how the test should relate to the criteria variables. Criterion validation may be carried out under a number of headings including predictive validation, concurrent validation, convergent validation and divergent validation.

Predictive validity asks the question: does the test predict later behaviour? For example, a child's IQ score may be expected to predict scholastic success; a person's score from a test of the type A behaviour pattern should predict the later development of heart disease.

Predictive validation is vital when developing tests for aptitude or job selection since these tests are designed specifically to measure the potential of a person. It is necessary that a test being used to assess a respondent's potential should have a convincing body of empirical evidence demonstrating its relevance to the characteristics under consideration. Certainly, 'off-the-shelf' tests of personality appear to be poor predictors of job performance (Blinkhorn and Johnson, 1990).

Obviously predictive validity is a very important feature of a psychometric test since our choice of a psychometric test in research is commonly informed by assumptions of its predictive quality. However, when constructing a psychometric test the practicality of predictive validation is quite difficult owing to the time involved. Many test constructors will adopt the more short term strategy of **postdictive validation** in which test scores of individuals who already own the characteristic being predicted are compared with those without it. Thus, if our test purports to predict performance in a particular job, high-fliers in the job will be compared with those who are less adept. This is not strictly predictive validation because we cannot be sure that the variables being measured by the test have not been modified by an interaction between the person and the job. If high-fliers and inept employees had been screened before they started work we may have found no difference in test scores but the experience of the job may have differentially modified the characteristics being tested.

Concurrent validation involves observing the relationship between the test and other criteria that are measured at the same time. More often than not this involves a correlation between the test in question and one or more other measures for which a hypothesised relationship is posited. Thus, for example, scores on a self-report test of extroversion may be correlated with peer ratings of sociability. Usually multiple criteria are used and the pattern of correlations between the test in question and its validating criteria is examined to assess the concurrent validity of the test. It is always a good idea to include, among the validating variables, a number of variables which are not expected to correlate with the test. In this way we can also check the specificity of the test.

13.4.3   Construct validation

It is important for multiple item tests that the internal structure of the test is examined. This often involves fitting the observed responses to some kind of measurement model. We have already seen that one way of assessing reliability is to examine internal consistency of the test items. The resulting coefficient (usually Cronbach's alpha) is based upon the homogeneity of the items, a high alpha occurring when the items correlate well together. In this way reliability evaluation may be viewed as a kind of construct validation. In this case the internal structure of the items is assumed to reveal inter-item homogeneity.

Another commonly hypothesised structure is that the items form a **unidimensional scale**. In this case the items are expected to have a particular pattern of correlations which reflects their order along a single latent trait. Some authors have confused unidimensionality with internal consistency and it is important to realise that alpha coefficients may tell us something about the average size of the inter-item correlations but it tells us nothing about their pattern. The way to assess the unidimensionality of a scale is to use multivariate data analytic methods which allow you to examine the underlying structure of the test items (see Chapter 26).

It is also common for the test developer to suggest that there may be multiple dimensions underlying the test items. In this case, a number of distinct scales are expected to be found within the item pool. A good example of this is the 90-item Eysenck Personality Questionnaire which measures four traits: extroversion, neuroticism, psychoticism and response bias. The structure of the inter-item correlations is such that all the items designed to measure extroversion correlate well together but correlate less well with items from the other scales. This is expected to be true for each of the remaining traits. The procedure that is commonly used when assessing this multidimensional measurement model is known as factor analysis (see Chapter 24).

Construct validation, then, involves testing hypotheses about the structure of the test. This often involves the use of quite sophisticated data analytic methods.

13.4.4   General issues of validation

Up to this point the reader would be excused for thinking that validity is an intrinsic feature of the test in question. In fact, one of the most widespread problems of validity in the use of psychometric tests in research relates not so much to invalid tests but rather the invalid use of tests. When scholars are casting around for a standard test to use in their research they need to be particularly careful that the test they choose is appropriate for their use.

For example, British researchers often make use of tests developed on American samples. It is important that the test user justifies his or her use of such tests on British samples. Equally, a great many tests in common use are very old and there is no particular guarantee that items constructed even 10 years ago have the same meaning as they do today. The onus is on the researcher to provide a full and informed justification of his or her choice of psychometric test.

There are essentially four points about validity that should be borne in mind:

1 There are numerous methods of validation which may be seen as different modes of inquiry (Cronbach, 1971). Their relative importance depends upon the test in question, its proposed usage and the conceptualisation of the construct it purports to measure.
2 Validity cannot be estimated by a single coefficient but is inferred from an accumulation of empirical and conceptual evidence.
3 Validation is cumulative. The validation of a test is an ongoing process which should last for as long as the test is used.
4 Validity is as much a function of the appropriate use of a test as of the test itself.

13.5 ITEM RESPONSE THEORY

In this chapter we have concentrated exclusively upon the classical test model. However, it is not possible to conclude a chapter on psychometric tests without mentioning item response theory (IRT). We can give only the briefest of introductions to this important and rapidly growing area of psychometrics here and the interested reader is referred to Hulin et al. (1983), Suen (1991) and Hambleton et al. (1991), all of whom provide excellent introductory accounts. IRT integrates early work on scaling (Guttman, 1941) and the statistical modelling of human responses (Rasch, 1960; Birnbaum, 1968) and is exemplified in the seminal works of Frederick Lord (Lord and Novick, 1968; Lord, 1980). This approach represents a radical departure from classical test theory in which the test score is the fundamental unit of interest, because it concentrates instead upon the probability of a particular item response. This is the probability that an individual with a certain ability or trait strength will respond in a given way to a particular item within a test.

In Figure 13.6 the responses of three individuals to a five-item numerical reasoning test are presented. A value of 1 means that the respondent provided a correct answer and 0 indicates an incorrect answer. As we can see the respondents have the same number of correct responses. In classical test theory terms, this means that they share the same score and thus have the same ability.

			Items			
	A	B	C	D	E	Score
Respondent 1	1	1	0	1	0	3
Respondent 2	0	0	1	1	1	3
Respondent 3	1	1	1	0	0	3

FIGURE 13.6 *Three item profiles producing equivalent scores*

However, we can also see that each of the three respondents presents a qualitatively distinct profile of item responses which indicates that they are not equivalent in their numerical reasoning. Item response theory addresses this anomaly by explicitly modelling the response profile expected from a person with a given ability. The ability of an individual is estimated statistically using information from a large data set. In IRT terminology the ability of a person is a **person parameter**. In addition, the difficulty of each item and its ability to discriminate between high and low ability respondents are estimated, and these are known as **item parameters**. It is even possible to estimate a third item parameter which describes the degree to which the answer to an item is correctly guessed (a **guessing parameter**). A large number of item response models exist but most can be described under three main headings based on the number of item parameters that are free to vary as follows.

One-parameter or Rasch-type models treat the item discrimination and guessing parameters as fixed (usually the guessing parameters are fixed at zero). This is a relatively strict model in which the only item parameter free to vary is the difficulty. This is the model most favoured among European psychometricians, perhaps because of the seminal influence of the Danish statistician Georg Rasch (1960) who developed the basic model. It may be viewed as a probabilistic extension of Guttman's (1941) scalogram approach and has the advantage of describing a cumulative scale.

Two-parameter models allow the difficulty and discrimination parameters to vary. These models appear to be favoured among American psychometricians and are slightly more relaxed in terms of model constraints than the Rasch models. However, in allowing the item discrimination to vary, this model loses the advantage of fitting data to a cumulative scale.

Three-parameter models allow difficulty, discrimination and guessing parameters to vary. These are the most relaxed of the available models but they are extraordinarily complex because of the numbers of unknown parameters that need to be estimated (Birnbaum, 1968; Lord, 1980). It is also necessary to have very large sample sizes before consistent estimates can be made and this makes these models impractical except in the case where many thousands of respondents are available.

We are painfully aware that the above descriptions of IRT models are too brief to provide a full understanding of IRT and all we can hope, given the space allotted to the subject, is that the reader is made aware of these alternative, statistically sophisticated approaches to psychological measurement. IRT modelling is fast becoming the chosen approach among psychometricians although it is only slowly being adopted in mainstream psychology as an alternative to classical measurement procedures.

The main reason for its rise among psychometricians is that it answers a number of problems in classical test theory. For example, it provides SEM estimates for each person rather than relying on general test-based estimates. Its slow acceptance in mainstream psychology probably reflects the general lack of interest in measurement and a resistance among many psychologists to statistically sophisticated procedures. It is perhaps relevant to alert the reader to the work of Joel Michell (1997) at this point, in which the scientific pretensions of psychology are cast into doubt. Michell argues convincingly that the naïveté exhibited by psychologists towards measurement militates against our discipline ever achieving a realistic scientific status.

13.6   CONCLUSIONS

In this chapter we have discussed the two main issues in the use of psychometric tests: reliability and validity. The development of a psychometric test is a long and detailed process and a full account is beyond the scope of this chapter. However, the issues that we have raised while discussing the problems of reliability estimation and validation are central to test construction. Nevertheless, the psychological literature is peppered with poorly constructed tests where even these basic principles have not been adhered to. The continuing use of such weak tests does nothing for the science of psychology and simply serves to generate more random numbers to distract us from our true purpose as researchers, the identification of replicable and stable laws that govern behaviour. It is the role of the researcher who wishes to use psychometric tests to maintain high standards in their selection of the tests they use. This requires that the researcher using psychometric tests should be aware of the major issues in psychometric methodology. This chapter has attempted to provide a basis for this awareness but its necessary brevity means that it cannot hope to provide a full account. It is hoped that researchers planning on using psychometric tests will consult further texts such as Kline (1993), Suen (1991) or Murphy and Davidshofer (1991).

13.7   FURTHER READING

Paul Kline has written a number of introductory books in the area of psychometrics. His *Handbook of Psychological Testing* (1993) is a good comprehensive introduction which should be accessible to both undergraduate and postgraduate researchers. An equally comprehensive book is Cronbach's (1990) *Essentials of Psychological Testing* (5th edn). This book goes into slightly more technical detail than Kline's tome and it serves as an authoritative reference. Another very readable account of psychometric testing issues is Anastasi's (1990) *Psychological Testing* which stands as one of the seminal works in its comprehensive treatment of the issues involved. For the complete beginner, Rust and Golombok's accessible treatment *Modern Psychometrics* (1989) offers a practical introduction.

Finally, any researcher who is seriously considering psychometric research should consult a text on test theory. An excellent starting point is Suen's (1991) *Principles of Test Theories*. This introduces the principles underlying classical test theory as well as item response theory and generalisability theory. As we have seen, IRT is a complex and sophisticated approach to psychological assessment and there are few introductory level treatments available. Suen's text certainly bears study as well as Hulin et al.'s (1983) *Item Response Theory*, which is an early and accessible treatment. A very useful concise and accessible account is to be found in Hambleton et al.'s (1991) *Fundamentals of Item Response Theory*. Excellent accounts of the Rasch model exist in Wright and Stone's (1979) *Best Test Design* and Andrich's (1990) *Rasch Models for Measurement*. A very useful Internet site is run by Benjamin Wright's group at Chicago University (www.rasch.org) which provides invaluable resources including free reports and reviews.

14

Psychophysical Methods

David Rose

Contents

14.1 INTRODUCTION

Psychophysical methods are primarily techniques for measuring the parameters of the sensory and perceptual systems, and of mental information processing in general. However, they have also found application in a wide variety of other applied and theoretical problems, including the assessment of anxiety, stress, memory, criminal behaviour, social attitudes, advertising effectiveness, and so on. Additionally, these tests are increasingly used in personnel selection, for jobs where fine sensory aptitudes are predictive of success (e.g. flying, military target recognition, and detecting tumours in X-ray clinics).

Perhaps the commonest use of these methods is for finding the minimum intensity of a stimulus that can be detected, i.e. the **detection threshold** or **absolute threshold**. Hence for most of this chapter the independent variable under discussion is **stimulus intensity**. However, the principles can be applied to many other types of variable, both sensory (e.g. line length, colour) and general (word frequency, facial attractiveness, salience, and so on).

This chapter first summarises theoretical understanding of what limits sensory detection, and then reviews the techniques available to investigate those limits. Later, procedures for measuring the strengths of percepts above threshold are considered. Finally, some general issues of experimental practicality are discussed.

14.2 PRINCIPLES OF ABSOLUTE THRESHOLDS

I have often been amused by the reactions of novice students to near-threshold stimuli. For example, in a practical in which they were required to read words presented very briefly in a tachistoscope, some students complained that the apparatus was not working properly, because sometimes they could read a word clearly but on other occasions, repeating exactly the same presentation, the word was unrecognisable.

Of course, the apparatus was functioning perfectly; it was the students who were varying from trial to trial. People are not robots (especially not students); they do not function 'like clockwork'. Their reactions to a stimulus are not exactly the same on every occasion. Instead, they fluctuate in their sensitivity. In the terminology of information theory, people are full of noise: random, apparently spontaneous factors, internal to the subject, affect human performance. Biologically based theorists ascribe this noise to the spontaneous firing of action potentials that occurs along sensory nerves; but noise can also be regarded more generally as informational garbage (or information loss) at any level in the system. Some stimuli are so weak they are drowned out by this noise, and hence are not detected at all. Stronger stimuli may be detected, but appear more or less intense, depending on the amount of noise around at the instant when the stimulus occurred.

So consider first a subject's reaction to a simple stimulus presented briefly, say a spot of light shone briefly on to a screen, or an auditory tone, a touch to the skin, or whatever. The magnitude of the sensation felt by the subject will not be constant every time we repeat the stimulus. Sometimes it will be larger, sometimes smaller. If the stimulus is extremely weak, then on some presentations the subject may not notice it at all. Stimulus detection then becomes a probabilistic affair. The weaker the stimulus, the lower the probability of it being detected.

The probability of detecting any given stimulus can be measured by presenting that stimulus repeatedly and counting the number of times the subject perceives it. We then convert that number to a percentage of the number of stimulus presentations or **trials**.

By choosing a series of stimuli that differ in strength, we can in fact estimate the amount of noise in the sensory system. Plotting the probabilities for each stimulus strength gives us a graph called the **psychometric function**. A typical example is shown in Figure 14.1. Probability of detection varies from practically zero for very weak stimuli, to 100% for strong stimuli.

The notion of absolute threshold as an all-or-none detection level is thus somewhat obsolete. Basically, it assumed that weak stimuli are not detected because they do not activate the sensory system sufficiently; only sensory events that exceed a minimum, threshold amount are able to pass on to higher levels of perception and action. The word 'threshold' is nevertheless still often used as a shorthand for the dividing line between correct and incorrect performance. In Figure 14.1, the stimulus intensity that would give us 50% detection is conventionally defined as the absolute threshold.

The slope of the psychometric function is proportional to the amount of noise in the system. Steep slopes indicate low noise (a robot with no noise

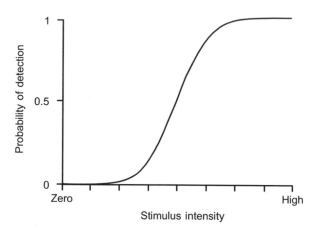

FIGURE 14.1   *The psychometric function*

would give a step function, changing sharply from no response below threshold to 100% responses above threshold), while shallow slopes reveal the presence of much noise, i.e. subject variability over time (Treisman and Watts, 1966).

A problem with the above experiment is that, if the subject knows a stimulus is actually presented on every trial, the subject will maximise the number of trials he or she gets correct by saying 'yes, I detected it' every time (or at least, 'yes, a stimulus was there'). Subjects are notoriously obstreperous in this fashion: they will regard the experiment as a test, and try to score as highly as possible, regardless of what you want them to do. So the only thing to do is to introduce some blank, 'catch' trials, on which you present a stimulus of zero intensity, and make it clear that responding 'yes' to a blank trial will incur horrific penalties, or at least a withering glare.

Nevertheless, subjects still do sometimes respond positively to blank trials, even when they are not trying to out-guess you but are genuinely trying to respond appropriately. Why does this happen? It is because the noise in their sensory system has momentarily risen to such a large extent it is mistaken for the level of activity normally evoked only by a real (but weak) stimulus.

The situation that pertains in a sensory system during such experiments is illustrated in Figure 14.2. The noise in the system fluctuates from moment to moment, so the probability of there being a given level of activity at any instant in time is described by the distribution labelled 'noise' in Figure 14.2. A Gaussian curve is usually an accurate description of the noise distribution (Green and Swets, 1966). The sensory system normally lives with this noise within it, and learns to ignore it. When however a stimulus occurs, the level of activity within the system is elevated, by an amount proportional to the stimulus's strength. Over many, repeated instances of the same stimulus, the probability distribution is shifted to the right. This is now called the **signal-plus-noise** distribution. It has the same shape as the noise distribution if (as often, but not always, occurs) the stimulus simply adds a constant amount to the level of activity in the system.

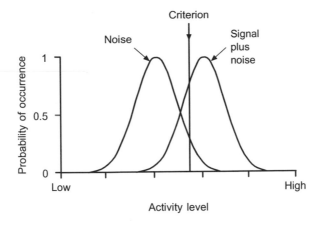

FIGURE 14.2 *The activity levels in the nervous system with and without the presence of a stimulus, expressed as probabilities*

If the stimulus is strong, the signal-plus-noise distribution is easily distinguished from the noise-alone distribution, because it constitutes much higher levels of activity. When the stimulus is weak, however, there may be considerable overlap between the two distributions. What can the sensory system do to maximise its performance? If it ignores all levels of activity that are normally present between trials due to the internal noise, it will miss many stimuli, i.e. the ones that occur when there is so little noise that the signal-plus-noise activity is still less than sometimes occurs due to noise alone. If however, it wants to detect every stimulus, it must accept lower levels of activity as indicative of stimulus occurrence; but then it will mistakenly respond on some catch trials, i.e. those when the level of internal noise is high. According to **signal detection theory**, the sensory system accepts all levels of activity above a certain criterion as indicating that a stimulus has occurred, while all levels below the criterion are rejected as due to internal noise. The criterion is normally set to an intermediate, compromise level, above the point at which all stimuli are detected, and below the point at which mistakes are made on catch trials (Green and Swets, 1966).

Four outcomes from each trial are thus possible (Figure 14.3). On catch trials, the subject may deny the occurrence of the stimulus: this is known as a correct rejection. If the subject mistakenly says a stimulus did occur, this is a false alarm. On trials with a stimulus present, denial of the occurrence of the stimulus is known as a miss, while a claim to have detected the stimulus is called a hit. The probabilities of each of these four possibilities are equal to the areas under the probability distributions in Figure 14.2, above and below the criterion.

The stronger the stimulus, the greater the distance between the means of the two distributions in Figure 14.2. The symbol used to represent this distance is d', while the criterion level of activity is known as β. As stimulus strength increases, the proportion of hits will increase, while the number of false alarms will be unaffected, if β stays the same. However, one of the important

Response

	Present	Absent
Present	hit	miss
Absent	false alarm	correct rejection

Stimulus (labels to left: Present / Absent)

FIGURE 14.3 *The four possible logical outcomes of experimental trials on which there either may or may not be a stimulus presented, and on which the subject must either respond that a stimulus was detected or one was not*

postulates of signal detection theory is that β can vary, depending on the circumstances of the experiment (see further, below). So when stimulus strength increases, it is possible for β to increase proportionately, such that the probability of scoring a hit remains constant despite the now higher intensity of the stimulus. In that case, however, the proportion of false alarms will be seen to decrease. So it is always possible to disentangle the effects of the stimulus, in creating a higher mean level of activity in the system, and the effects of changes in criterion. The two variables d' and β, can vary independently, but they are related to the proportions of hits and false alarms.

The values of d' and β can be calculated from the proportions of hits and false alarms, either by looking them up in published tables (e.g. Freeman, 1973), or by computing the integrals under the probability distributions in Figure 14.2 directly (Rose, 1988). (These assume the noise and signal-plus-noise distributions have equal variance.)

A common way of plotting the results of such experiments is in the form of a **receiver operating characteristic** or **ROC** curve (Figure 14.4). This shows the proportions of hits and false alarms in the experiment. Changes in d' or β alter the ratio between the two variables, but in a manner predictable from the theory depicted in Figure 14.2.

Changes in d' and β can be deliberately induced by the experimenter to plot a series of ROC curves. Manipulating stimulus intensity will affect d'. Changes in payoff are the commonest way of altering β; if the reward for scoring a hit is high and the punishment for giving a false alarm is low, subjects will lower their criterion, which has the effect of increasing the proportions of both hits and false alarms, at the expense of correct rejections and misses. Severely punishing any false alarms has the opposite effect. (In practical terms, if you are a radar operator watching for incoming nuclear missiles, you need to set a low criterion to avoid missing any, even though this may mean frequent false alarms. On the other hand, if you are out in a hunting party you need a high criterion for target identification, to be sure you don't shoot your companions by mistake.) β can also be altered by making the probability of stimulus occurrence (i.e. the percentage of catch trials) higher or lower. A neat way of generating an ROC curve is to get your subject to rate the confidence with which his or her judgement is made (Green and Swets, 1966). This is equivalent to asking the subject to generate and

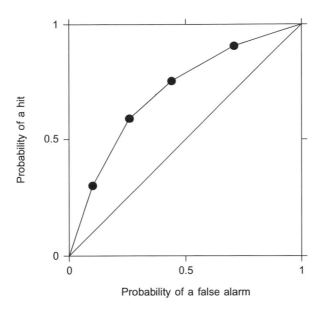

FIGURE 14.4   *A receiver operating characteristic for a constant stimulus intensity. The four points were obtained by varying β. If stimulus intensity were zero, the points would fall on the diagonal; higher intensities, and hence higher d' values, cause the points to move towards the top left corner of the graph*

maintain several different criterion levels simultaneously. For example, scores might be given on an integer scale from 0 to 5, with 5 indicating complete confidence that the signal was present. Each rating score is treated as reflecting achievement of a separate criterion level, and the analysis then proceeds as usual, by plotting a series of hit and false alarm probability pairs, each of which shows the probabilities cumulated up to one of the rating levels.

14.3   FORCED-CHOICE TECHNIQUES

On every trial there has to be a method by which the subject can tell when the stimulus may occur; on a catch trial, for example, you cannot leave your subject sitting there indefinitely waiting for something to happen. So the trial has to be demarcated in time, with the stimulus presented (if at all) during that time. One way is to allow your subject to 'self-pace', i.e. to start each trial by pressing a button, and the stimulus then occurs immediately or very soon after. (Self-pacing has the advantage of enabling subjects to rest, scratch themselves, sneeze, or whatever, whenever they like.) More common, however, is to signal the trial **interval** with another stimulus. For example in vision experiments it is usual to sound a (clearly audible) tone when the stimulus might appear. For auditory experiments the signal might be a light coming on. The subject thus knows when to attend and when to make a response.

A common variation on these techniques is to present two such demarcation indicators. These may follow one another in time, or may be located at different positions in space. The stimulus to be detected is presented on every trial, together with one of the indicators, and the other indicator accompanies a blank or catch stimulus. The subject knows that every trial contains a stimulus, but has to say with which demarcation indicator it is associated. This is know as a **forced choice**.

So in temporal forced-choice experiments there are two indicators, separated by a pause, and the subject has to say whether the stimulus occurred in the first or the second interval. In spatial forced choice, the indicators might be placed, say, to the left and right of each other, and the subject has to say in which location the stimulus was presented.

In fact, the number of demarcation indicators need not be only two (**two-alternative forced choice** or 2AFC); there can be several, but there is always only one stimulus and hence one correct answer.

The psychometric functions derived from forced-choice tasks are similar to that in Figure 14.1, except that the 'floor' is no longer 0% detection. In a 2AFC task there is a 50% chance of guessing correctly even when the stimulus is very weak, so the function increases from 50% to 100% performance as stimulus intensity rises, and the curve is compressed to fit between those limits.

14.4 METHODS FOR MEASURING ABSOLUTE THRESHOLDS

The experimental technique described above and illustrated in Figure 14.1 is known as the **method of constant stimuli**. It is the most comprehensive way of monitoring a subject's reactions to a stimulus, giving data on both threshold and noise (the slope of the psychometric function). Its main disadvantage is that many trials are required (plus some pilot trials to find which stimulus intensities to use). The probability estimates for each stimulus intensity should be based on at least 50 trials. At least four stimulus intensities need to be presented – excluding any that the subject happens to score 0% or 100%, since (1) it is then impossible to know where the function intersects with the floor or ceiling, and (2) the data are usually fitted with a cumulative Gaussian curve, and this goes to infinity at 0% and 100%. In total 300 trials should be regarded as an absolute minimum for reliable estimates of threshold (and even more trials for estimates of noise). At (typically) 5 seconds per trial, this means 25 minutes of intense concentration by the subject. Even with frequent rests, subjects are unable to maintain a constant state of alertness for such long periods: fatigue, boredom and other extraneous variables will alter their operating characteristics during the experiment. In many practical circumstances, these factors are exacerbated: testing young children, busy executives, or patients in hospital, for example. For this reason, other techniques abound that measure threshold more quickly. They do so by abandoning any attempt to estimate noise accurately, concentrating instead on collecting data near threshold.

First consider how one should collect data to give the quickest, most efficient estimation of threshold. In Figure 14.1, the threshold or 50% performance level is the point where the slope (of a cumulative Gaussian) is maximal. In general, it makes sense to collect data near the point of maximal slope, because at that point small changes in the stimulus give the biggest changes in the subject's behaviour. Stimuli that the subject gets 98% or 99% right do not tell us so much about the threshold as stimuli the subject gets 49% or 51% right.

So, many techniques attempt to present the stimuli only at those medium intensities. The subject's responses during the experiment are often used to help the experimenter adjust, from trial to trial, the intensities chosen for presentation. These are generally known as **adaptive techniques**. Sometimes, these are used in preliminary investigations to pilot the choice of stimuli to be presented later in a full-blown method of constant stimuli experiment, but nowadays they are used very often in their own right.

At one extreme, the subject may be given absolute control over stimulus intensity, and the experimenter does nothing. Thus in the **method of adjustment**, the subject alters the stimulus, by turning a knob, or pressing at will two buttons that respectively increase or decrease intensity. The instructions are to adjust the stimulus to the point of detectability (or loss of detectability). This adjustment may be repeated many times, beginning alternately from above or below threshold, and the results averaged. Alternatively, the subject may be asked to track the threshold, perhaps oscillating the setting continuously by a small amount around the threshold. This can be a useful technique in situations where the threshold may be changing, for example in the period immediately after exposure to an intense stimulus. The method of adjustment is quick and easy to do. However, one can never be certain what criterion the subject is using. Some, particularly naïve subjects, will refuse to admit they detect the stimulus unless it is clearly present, and will adjust intensity accordingly. Other subjects may move the setting to the point just below the level where the stimulus has disappeared. There is no way of finding out from the data alone what kind of strategy the subject is using. Also, the setting from an individual can be quite variable, perhaps due to the subject changing criterion during the experiment.

In the **method of limits**, the experimenter adjusts the stimulus in a more formal simulation of the method of adjustment. The stimulus is initially set well above threshold and is reduced in **steps** from trial to trial until the subject fails to detect it. The stimulus level at that point is recorded. The stimulus is then set well below threshold and its intensity is increased from trial to trial until the subject succeeds in detecting it. The point at which the subject's response changes is recorded. These descending and ascending series are repeated until enough data have been collected, and the endpoints of all the series are averaged. It is normal to find some overshoot in this system, i.e. the ascending series give higher estimates of threshold than the descending series. Also, subjects can anticipate what kind of response is expected in the next trial, since it is easy for them to work out the rules that determine stimulus intensity from trial to trial.

Another disadvantage of the method of limits is that many trials present stimuli clearly above or below threshold, and thus elicit largely predictable responses from the subject. In **staircase methods**, however, the stimuli are focused more closely around the threshold level. As before, the stimulus is

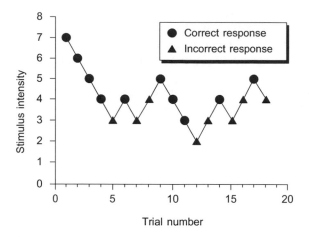

FIGURE 14.5   *Changes in stimulus level during a staircase experiment*

initially presented above threshold and then lowered in steps until the subject fails to detect it. The next step is then an increase in intensity, but starting from the point of failure, not from well below threshold as in the method of limits. The stimulus level continues to be raised from trial to trial until a successful detection is made, and then the stimulus is stepped progressively down until the subject fails to detect it again. This sequence of ascending and descending runs continues, with the stimulus level thus oscillating closely around the threshold (Cornsweet, 1962). Figure 14.5 shows the typical course of an experiment. A block of trials may continue until, say, 10 reversals of the direction of stimulus change have occurred, which would take typically 40 to 70 trials (depending how large the step size is, relative to the subject's noise level). The reversal points are noted, and are averaged at the end of the experiment to give an estimate of threshold.

Staircase techniques are very common, and there are many variations. The first is designed to cope with the possibility that the subject may anticipate the next stimulus; knowing that clear detections will lead to a reduction in stimulus contrast on the next trial, and failures to detect will lead to an increase, the subject may realise what kind of response would be expected on the next trial, and respond appropriately. This problem is removed by interleaving two or more staircases (Cornsweet, 1962). In its simplest form, the first trial begins staircase one, the second begins staircase two, the third trial is the second on staircase one, the fourth trial is the second on staircase two, and so on. The subject soon loses track of which staircase is which. Better still is to pick the staircase randomly on each trial, rather than presenting them in strict alternation. With more than two staircases interleaved, the situation is even better. Moreover, these staircases need not be identical in terms of the stimulus tested. For example if you wish to know whether red, green or blue lights are seen equally well you can present three staircases, randomly interleaved, one staircase for each colour. (Although the subject may know from the colour which staircase has just been tested, as long as he or she cannot anticipate which colour will be tested on the next trial, the results will be valid.) What is also beneficial is that the three thresholds will be assessed simultaneously, thus avoiding the possibility of subject practice, fatigue or boredom biasing the result, as they might if you tested each colour sequentially.

A popular variation is to alter the rules, so the stimulus intensity is not lowered every time the subject gets one right, but only after two (or three, or more) correct responses from the subject. (The subject still has to get only one wrong, however, to cause an increase in stimulus intensity on the next trial.) The effect of this is to converge the staircase on to a higher point on the psychometric function: for example 71% for the two-down/one-up rule, instead of 50% for the normal one-down/one-up rule (Wetherill and Levitt, 1965). This makes the staircase slightly longer to run, but has a number of advantages as follows.

First, subjects are in general much happier if they know the stimulus they are looking out for. Presenting the occasional clearly detectable stimulus helps, since it literally reminds the subject of the target. If the staircase presents stimuli that on average are detected 71% of the time, this problem is reduced, relative to those with near 50% detectability levels.

Second, some workers collect all the data from a staircase experiment and, instead of simply averaging the reversal points and ignoring the trials in between each reversal, they use all the data to build a psychometric function (e.g. Figure 14.1; Hall, 1981). Thus many stimulus levels may be presented during a staircase, most of them several times over. This enables the probability of response to be calculated for each stimulus level. A collection of these probabilities can be used to form a psychometric function. By presenting several staircases with different rules, perhaps interleaved, for example staircases that converge on the 50% level, the 71%, and so on, the data can be deliberately spread out to give a good coverage of the full range of the psychometric function. (Using the method of constant stimuli you need to find out before the experiment what that range is; with staircases, the stimulus levels adjust themselves automatically to fill the range.) From psychometric functions, it will be remembered, an estimate of the noise can be obtained as well as the threshold level.

Third, with forced-choice staircases, the threshold measure obtained is often an underestimate of the true threshold (Rose et al., 1970). This is called **bias**, and occurs because of the nature of guessing when the stimulus level is low. Consider a very weak stimulus that evokes activity below β. The subject is then forced to guess which demarcation indicator is correct, and will do so approximately 50% of the time. A correct guess has the effect of lowering the stimulus on the next trial, so the subject will likely have to guess again. The net effect is that the stimulus level drifts down well below threshold. (It is a fact that random guesses may carry on being right in an unbroken sequence more often than most people think; it takes longer than you would expect to even out right and wrong guesses.) So in the end some of the reversal points in the staircase will be much too low. The converse problem does not occur: correct guesses elevate stimulus intensity, so the subject soon detects the stimulus correctly without guessing. The problem of bias can be reduced by keeping the stimulus level up, for example near 71% detection level rather than 50%. (However, there is an even better way of avoiding this problem, which is to increase the number of alternatives in the forced-choice task to three or four, so the subject does not guess correctly so often.)

Further variations on the staircase technique are designed to converge progressively on to the threshold, by starting with fairly large step changes in the stimulus between one trial and the next, and reducing the step size as the experiment progresses. The reduction is usually made at reversal points. Thus the early trials direct the stimulus quickly to the approximate region of threshold, and subsequent trials fine-tune the stimulus closer and closer to the threshold level (Taylor and Creelman, 1967; Pentland, 1980; Tyrrell and Owens, 1988).

Staircases can, like the method of adjustment, be used to track a changing threshold, provided the rate of change is slow. If the changes are rapid, the only alternative is the **method of a thousand staircases**. For example, adaptation to an intense stimulus experienced for a minute or two usually leads to an after-effect that lasts at most a few minutes. Tracking these changes cannot be done with a conventional staircase: instead, the experiment has to be repeated many times, with sufficient time between experiments for complete recovery. In each experiment a number of trials (notionally 1000) are presented, each at strictly the same time relative to the period of adaptation (for example the first trial might be 5 seconds after adaptation, the next 10 seconds, and so on). The outcome of the first trial in the first experiment is used to determine the stimulus level that will be presented in the first trial of the second experiment. The response to the first trial in the second experiment determines the stimulus in the first trial of the third experiment. Meanwhile, the second trial in the first experiment determines the second trial in the second experiment. And so on. Each staircase consists of a series of trials, one trial in each experiment. The length of the staircase equals the total number of experiments done. Each staircase converges on the threshold at the particular instant in time its trials were all presented, relative to the time of exposure to the adapting stimulus (Cornsweet and Teller, 1965).

The most modern **adaptive techniques** use far more complicated calculations between each trial to decide which stimulus level to present next. They depend upon theoretical assumptions about efficiency and the shape of the underlying psychometric function. The computer programs are however not necessarily long; for example, the best known, Quest, contains only about 40 commands in Basic (Watson and Pelli, 1983). The number of trials needed to obtain a measure of threshold can be as few as 20–40, depending on how accurate you want your answer to be: the more trials, the more precise your estimate will be. I cannot go into numerical detail about the methods here, but merely mention that they generally concentrate upon placing the next stimulus at a level that will give most information about the location of the threshold (e.g. Harvey, 1986; King-Smith et al., 1994; Treutwein, 1995). This level is not always at the threshold, because (a) the point of maximum slope of the psychometric function is not always at the threshold (the underlying curve is not always a cumulative Gaussian), and (b) binomial sampling error is maximal at 50% response levels, which makes response probabilities near 50% less reliable than those at higher or lower values. The errors become progressively smaller above and below the 50% level. In two-alternative forced-choice experiments, a 50% response level is expected for very weak stimuli, and in this case the optimal stimulus to present is somewhat above the threshold intensity. The optimal level in any given experiment thus depends on the number of forced-choice alternatives, and on the slope of the psychometric function. Recent techniques enable the slope to be estimated adaptively during the experiment as well as the threshold (King-Smith and Rose, 1997).

14.5 DIFFERENCE THRESHOLDS

The field of psychophysics is not, thankfully, limited to studying absolute thresholds. We can also investigate what happens when clearly detectable stimuli are presented. The first question we can ask is, however, still one about thresholds: namely, what is the minimum detectable difference between two stimuli that can be noticed? This is known as the **difference threshold** or **just noticeable difference** (JND). The basic methods available to us include all those listed above: constant stimuli, adjustment, limits and staircases, with or without forced choice. For example the subject might be shown two spots of light and asked to adjust the intensity of one until it is just noticeably brighter than the other. The variable stimulus may be called the **test** or **probe stimulus** while the other, that is kept constant, is the **standard** or **comparison stimulus**.

The first parameter we can vary in experiments on difference thresholds is the intensity of the standard stimulus. In other words, we can test whether a weak but clearly detectable stimulus has to be incremented by a lesser or greater amount than a strong stimulus must be incremented, to enable a subject to detect the difference. This is the basic paradigm that led to **Weber's Law**, which states that the increment threshold is a constant fraction of the standard stimulus. So if a dim spot of light has to be increased in intensity by 2% before the subject can see the difference, an intense spot must also be incremented by 2% of its luminance before the subject will notice. Weber's Law applies to a large number of sensory situations, although the value of the **Weber fraction** varies enormously (e.g. 2% for light intensity, 3.3% for weight, 33% for sound intensity, 0.3% for sound frequency, 20% for taste intensity). The Weber fraction rises above its normal value at very low intensities, where noise becomes significant (so a standard of zero intensity has a difference threshold not of zero, but of the absolute threshold). The fraction also tends to deviate for very intense stimuli.

A second issue in difference threshold experiments is whether the standard stimulus is presented with the same time-course as the test stimulus. There are two common paradigms here. First, the standard may consist of a con-tinuously presented background while the test is a brief probe presentation superimposed on the background. Second, the background may be set to zero intensity, while the standard and test are both (equally) brief; the subject has to discriminate between the two types of brief stimulus. (A third situation is possible but rarer: stimuli may be given for the same long period and the subject has as long as desired to inspect the stimuli before responding.) The first paradigm bears on many real-world tasks, but has some disadvantages:

(1) for stable performance, the subject first has to adapt to the background, and this often takes longer than is generally thought (this problem applies to the second paradigm too); (2) brief, 'transient' test stimuli might be detected by different mechanisms from those that detect continuously presented 'sustained' background stimuli. The second paradigm can also resemble some real-world tasks, but may run into problems about what the subject is actually doing. Thus it is possible for the subject to build up in memory, over the course of many trials, a representation of an 'average' stimulus. The subject may then judge which of the two brief stimulus presentations was most clearly the greater relative to that memory trace rather than to each other. In fact, some experimenters deliberately leave out the standard stimulus and merely ask the subjects to judge whether the test stimuli are above or below average: this is the **method of single stimuli**. This can give quite good results, showing that memory for the stimulus can act as a stable reference (Woodworth and Schlosberg, 1954).

The third point to note is that difference thresholds can be measured for decrements as well as increments away from the standard. These two thresholds are not always identical. For example luminance decrements are easier to detect than increments of equal physical magnitude.

An alternative approach is to present a series of test stimuli that range both above and below the standard in the same experiment. The subject is forced to choose whether the test appears greater or less than the standard. A single curve (usually, a cumulative Gaussian) is fitted to all the data. The stimulus level where both responses are equally (50%) probable is identified and is labelled the **point of subjective equality** (PSE). The standard deviation of the Gaussian is taken as a measure of the difference threshold. This method is however used principally where the PSE is the main parameter of interest. The use of a single cumulative Gaussian rather than two such ogives, one for the increment threshold and one for the decrement threshold, shows that the theoretical underpinnings of the PSE approach are somewhat different from those used for assessing JNDs directly.

14.6 SENSATIONAL MEASUREMENTS

A major concern of the early psychophysicists was to measure the strength of sensation. The commonest technique for doing this is **magnitude estimation**. Individuals are first shown a standard stimulus and asked to associate that stimulus with a particular number, for example 100. They are then shown a test stimulus and asked to rate the strength of that stimulus relative to the standard. So if, for example, they thought the test stimulus to be half the strength of the standard, they would give the test a rating of 50. If they thought it twice as strong, the rating would be 200. And so on. A series of test stimuli of various strengths can be used to build a picture of how apparent magnitude Ψ varies with physical magnitude ϕ. Generally, it is found that the relationship is a power function, $\Psi = \phi^i$, where $i = 0.67$ for sound intensity, 0.3 for brightness, 3.5 for electric shock, and various other values for the other sensory dimensions. Magnitude estimation is a simple technique which requires little training of the subject and yet elicits reliable data from an individual. However there can be wide variability between subjects, so many have to be studied if normative statistics are required.

A variation on the response technique is **matching**. People are asked to adjust the strength of a comparison stimulus to 'match' the intensity of a test stimulus that differs in some way. The setting can be made by the method of adjustment, or by any other technique. In **cross-modal matching** the stimuli are in completely different sense modalities, for example a spot of light might be adjusted to match the perceived intensity of a touch to the skin. However, it is also common to see **intra-modal matching**, for example adjusting the intensity of a red light to match the intensity of a white light.

There are in fact two ways this procedure can be used. First, a range of different test stimuli can be adjusted to match the intensity of a standard. For example different coloured lights can be matched in apparent intensity to a standard white light. Plotting the data as a function of the wavelength of the test stimulus then gives an **iso-intensity contour**. A family of such contours can be plotted for standard stimuli of different intensities. For example if the white light is just at absolute threshold, then lights of all the other colours will be adjusted to their respective thresholds. The lowest possible contour in the family will thus be the threshold for light detection as a function of wavelength. For a comparison (e.g. white light) stimulus above threshold, lights on its iso-intensity curve will all appear equally strong. In many cases (e.g. sound intensity, black–white contrast), these curves tend to flatten out at high intensities, so perceived intensity becomes independent of the physical parameter under consideration.

Alternatively, the adjustable stimulus may remain the same, in all but intensity, throughout (in our example, it remains a white light), while the test stimuli are of different qualities (e.g. colours) but constant physical intensity. This gives measures of the apparent intensities of the test stimuli that are more akin to those obtained by magnitude estimation; in effect, the subject is adjusting the intensity of the (white) light to match the apparent intensity of the test stimulus.

Another technique for scaling the apparent intensity dimension is **fractionation**, in which subjects are presented with two stimuli that are identical in all but intensity, e.g. white lights. They are asked to adjust one of the stimuli so it appears half the intensity of the other. Subjects can be asked to quarter, or to double, the apparent intensity, but it is easier to stick to halving and build up a scale of apparent intensity by varying the intensity of the comparison stimulus. For some stimulus dimensions, **bisection** can be used. A stimulus has to be adjusted so it lies exactly half-way between two other stimuli. (This is more common for dimensions other than intensity, an obvious example being spatial distance judgements.) In effect, the subject has to decide whether the two intervals between the three stimuli are identical.

Magnitude and scaling techniques do not depend upon there being a linear relationship between perception and response. Any monotonic relationship will do. Another response that can be used under some circumstances is **reaction time (RT)**. In general, reaction times decrease as stimulus intensity rises. This effect is clearest at low intensities; RT tends to stabilise at higher intensities. Measures of RT are therefore sometimes used to assess stimulus strength. The procedure is relatively simple: subjects merely have to press a button as quickly as they can when the stimulus occurs. A warning signal is usually given first, and then a waiting period of random duration before the stimulus is presented (to prevent the subject anticipating when it might occur). A lot of trials are needed for each RT measurement (of the order of 100 repetitions at minimum), and a lot of practice trials have to be given before performance stabilises. Moreover it is problematic how to average the data, since the RT distribution is almost always positively skewed (i.e. there are more very long RTs than there are very short). Some workers transform the data non-linearly, averaging the logarithm or arcsine of the RT; others use the median, or average only the central 90% or 95% of the distribution. Finally, the procedure requires stimuli with sudden onset, so sensory mechanisms detecting sustained stimuli cannot be assessed in this fashion.

In some cases, perceptual effects can be monitored by **nulling** them with another stimulus. This method can be used in situations where the perceptual effect is illusory, or a distortion of the real stimulus. Such distortions include those induced by surrounding stimuli (simultaneous contrast; e.g. when a small stationary visual stimulus is viewed against a moving background, the stimulus appears to drift in the opposite direction). Alternatively, the distortions might be after-effects of adapting to an intense stimulus (successive contrast; e.g. the motion after-effect). There must be a clear null point along the stimulus dimension, for example stationariness in the case of movement, white in the case of apparent colour, constant intensity in the case of stimuli that appear to be increasing or decreasing in intensity, and so on. The idea is that the illusory or distorted percept will be cancelled by the perceptual effect of the real, ongoing input, yielding a percept that is at the neutral or null point. So apparent movement, for example, may be nulled by moving the test stimulus in the opposite direction and asking the subject to judge whether the stimulus appears stationary (Blake and Hiris, 1993). The dependent variable is the amount of real movement that exactly cancels the apparent movement. This technique is quite sensitive and is relatively easy for the subject to do. However, issues of interpretation arise, in that the test stimulus is not neutral, but is entering the sensory system and affecting it during the test period. There may be quite complex or unknown interactions between the system's response to the test stimulus and the processes within the system that are generating the effect you are trying to measure.

14.7   SOME GENERAL TIPS ON RUNNING EXPERIMENTS

Performance on novel tasks is not necessarily stationary over time. Practice makes subjects better, while fatigue and boredom may have the opposite effect. The number of practice trials that should be given before the data collection proper starts is an empirical matter: one should always check that performance has levelled off (or at least is minimal compared with the variability intrinsic to performance). The usual procedures of randomisation or counterbalancing of conditions should be followed to reduce the effects of residual non-stationariness on the interpretation of the results (see Chapter 4). Most psychophysical tasks are in fact extremely boring to do, involving intense concentration on a stimulus array that hardly ever varies. Motivation is therefore very important, as are frequent recreational breaks from the laboratory. Uninterrupted sequences of trials (blocks) should not exceed about 100 trials in length, or last more than 10 minutes. Successive trials may follow one another closely in time to speed things up, but subjects will be happier, and less likely to make errors, if they can pause at any time during a block for a rest. In many experiments data will need to be combined from different blocks; this involves theoretical assumptions about stationariness, but is usually unavoidable.

Other refinements allow for human fallibility. Subjects can make errors not just because of sensory limitations but also for mechanical or for other extraneous reasons. Firstly, their fingers may slip or become misaligned when pressing the response keys, so they activate the wrong one by accident. Secondly, their attention may wander during a trial, or they may sneeze or be distracted. So in vision experiments they may blink, or allow their eyes to deviate from the fixation point; in auditory experiments the telephone in the next room may ring or their stomachs may gurgle; in olfactory experiments they may fart (well, the experimenter never does); and so on. There are two ways of coping with this. One is to allow for it in the data analysis, for example by assuming that the psychometric function (Figure 14.1) will never reach 100% even for very strong stimuli, because of these errors (Hall, 1981). The curve can then be compressed so it asymptotes at, say, 99% instead of 100% (i.e. assuming 1 error in 100 trials; other figures are of course possible if your subject is more reliable – it is a matter of judgement). The second method is to give your subject a 'cancel-the-previous-trial' key, so if a problem arises that the subject is aware of, he or she can press the emergency button and the computer will reset the values of all its variables as though that trial had never occurred. The latter method can, of course, be used only if the stimulus presentation order contains some randomness, so the subject cannot cheat by simply pressing the button over and over to obtain multiple presentations of the same stimulus before making a decision.

In detection tasks, an important consideration, as mentioned previously, is the subject's knowledge or memory of the target. Knowing what the stimulus appears like aids performance and lowers threshold; uncertainty has the opposite effect. There are two ways uncertainty can arise. One is memory loss. This can be reduced by allowing the subject to see the stimulus consciously and clearly, either (1) occasionally during the experiment (for example by presenting a range of stimulus intensities that includes some well above detection threshold) or (2) deliberately at the beginning of each block of trials. Some workers present a supra-threshold stimulus before every trial in the experiment; however this is dangerous, because that stimulus could easily mask the near-threshold test stimulus that follows it, or it may cause adaptation, or it may have unknown effects on memory (Is it a sensory buffer, working memory or long term memory that needs to be activated? Will it cause retinal after-images in visual experiments?).

The second common source of uncertainty is the random mixing of different stimuli within the same block of trials. Thresholds are higher when the subject knows that the stimulus on any given trial may take one of two (or more) forms, such as different colours of lights, rather than all the stimuli being the same (apart, of course, from intensity). In fact the more uncertain the subject, the worse performance gets for each stimulus individually.

Knowledge of results, or feedback, is also important. Subjects perform better and more stably when they receive feedback. This is usually given in the form of a brief indicator as to whether they were right or wrong on the previous trial. For example in an experiment on vision, a tone may sound only after correct trials (a tone that is clearly different from the tone that demarcated the observation interval), or there may be two different tones, for correct and incorrect trials.

14.8 FURTHER READING

Matlin and Foley (1992) *Sensation and Perception* and Sekuler and Blake (2000) *Perception* are excellent introductory textbooks with chapters on psychophysical methods. The chapters by Pelli and Farell (1995) and Farell and Pelli (1998) also provide useful recent material. Gescheider (1985) *Psychophysics* gives a detailed but clear exposition, especially of signal detection theory and magnitude estimation. Finally, Macmillan and Creelman (1990) *Detection Theory: A User's Guide* is also useful for understanding the theory behind the tests.

15

Psychophysiological Methods

Paul Barrett and Paul Sowden

Contents

15.1 WHAT IS PSYCHOPHYSIOLOGY?

Specifically, the field of psychophysiology is concerned with the manipulation of psychological variables and their corresponding observed effects on physiological processes. Basically, psychophysiology is concerned with observing the interactions between physiological and psychological phcnomcna. More generally, psychophysiology can be said to encompass both the study of behavioural consequences of physiological properties of the body at a biochemical and anatomical level, and the effects of behaviour on these same physiological properties.

This chapter aims to provide the reader with an understanding of the breadth of possibilities in psychophysiological work. The tone of this chapter is less discursive and more didactic than many of the other chapters in this book. It is intended to scrve as an appetite whetter for those readers who may wish to pursue this kind of research.

Much of psychophysiological investigation is concerned with examining the concepts of emotion, behavioural states, stress, cognitive task performance, personality and intelligence. In each case, the relationships between psychological factors, stimulus perception and recognition, situational indices and physiological response are used in an attempt to shed light on the initiation, execution, maintenance and termination of behavioural events. Ultimately, the field can be partitioned into six major areas of endeavour as follows.

Social psychophysiology   Social psychophysiology is the study of the interactions between physiology and behaviour when those behaviours are involved in social processes. For example, non-verbal communication and group dynamics may be investigated by observing the interplay between various behaviours and each individual's dynamic physiological changes such as pupil size, muscle tone and skin electrical resistance (e.g. Wagner and Manstead, 1989; Birnbaumer and Ohman, 1993; Blascovich and Kelsey, 1990).

Developmental psychophysiology   This is the study of the ageing process, looking specifically at how changing properties of physiological systems and anatomical structures affect behaviour (e.g. van der Molen and Molenaar, 1994). In addition, the changing nature of the interaction between the psychological and physiological factors is also examined. For example, research may use measures of brain activity (e.g. event-related potentials) to examine ongoing brain function during early development (Steinschneider et al., 1992).

Cognitive psychophysiology   This concerns the relationship between information processing and physiology (see Jennings and Coles, 1991). That is, it examines the relationships between cognitive task performance and physiological events. For example, it looks at how perception, movement, attention, language and memory may be associated with particular features of brain electrical and magnetic activity (see Kutas and Dale, 1997).

Clinical psychophysiology   This is the study of psychological disorders and their relationship with physiological functioning and malfunctioning (e.g. Halliday et al., 1987; Magina, 1997). In addition, this area is concerned with the examination of the effectiveness of treatment regimes and drug effects on the psychological behaviour and affect of the individual. For example, in looking at chronic depression, it is sometimes useful to look at the benefits of any treatment applied in terms of both the behavioural outcomes and the changed nature of physiological parameters such as brain activity, sympathetic nervous system responsivity and biochemical substance assays (Carlson et al., 1994).

Applied psychophysiology   This area is involved with the application of psychophysiological techniques and findings to occupational, recreational, clinical and other areas of interest. For example, the monitoring of certain physiological activity within an individual, and providing instant and appropriate feedback of this activity, is known as biofeedback. This technique is used as an aid for relaxation therapy, stuttering, respiration control and a variety of other practical problems whose treatment may be amenable to self-control therapeutic techniques (Forgays et al., 1992; Schwartz, 1995).

Individual differences   This is a relatively new area that looks specifically at the relation of physiological processes and anatomical structures to measures of personality and intelligence (generally defined by psychometric measures, e.g. Gale and Eysenck, 1993). These measures may be of typically dynamic psychophysiological form, such as the relationship between the overall amplitude of brain evoked potentials to varying levels of stimulation, and introversion–extroversion (the augmenting–reducing phenomenon), or may quantify aspects of anatomical physiology and relate these to the psychometric or psychological indices. For example, from histological surveys of human cadavers, the number of dendrites and their length correlate positively with the level of education attainment within individuals.

15.2   THE PRINCIPAL AREAS OF PHYSIOLOGICAL DATA ACQUISITION

This section is a brief résumé of important facts and information surrounding the quantification of parameters describing the function of particular physiological structures and systems. It is not intended to be a comprehensive overview but rather is a snapshot of the diversity and richness of the measurement process in psychophysiology.

15.2.1   Muscle activity

Abbreviation   Electromyographic (EMG) activity.

What is measured   The electrical potentials that are associated with contractions of muscle fibres. These potentials are brief impulses lasting between 1 and 5 milliseconds (ms).

Transducers   These vary from invasive needle electrodes inserted into muscle tissue and recording individual fibre potentials, to non-invasive surface electrodes that are glued to the skin above the particular muscle of interest, recording the mass action of muscle fibre groups.

Signal properties   The amplitude of recorded signals can vary between about 1 and 1000 microvolts (μV), although recordings of less than 20 μV are difficult to obtain. The frequency of the electrical impulses can be anywhere between 20 and 1000 hertz (Hz).

Quantitative measures   These vary depending upon the focus of investigation. For example, when one is looking at the behaviour of a single nerve fibre or a homogeneous group of fibres, the single or compound (many fibres) action potential may be measured in response to a precise, targeted stimulus such as a small electric shock. Measures extracted from this potential include those of impulse amplitude and nerve conduction velocity. Alternatively, when looking at the long term activity of muscle fibres, the integrated amplitude, frequency of nerve firing (impulses) and gradients of frequency responses may be examined.

Example application   EMG recordings on the face have been used to measure emotional reactions. Such research has revealed that people show different reactions to real (Duchenne) as opposed to deliberate (false) smiles (Surakka and Hietanen, 1998).

15.2.2   Sweat gland activity

Abbreviations   Electrodermal activity (EDA) or galvanic skin response (GSR).

What is measured   The electrical properties of the skin that are associated with eccrine sweat gland activity. This activity is responsive to changes in emotionality and cognitive activity in general. Electrical activity can be recorded by measuring the voltage potential between an electrode over an 'active' site and a reference electrode on an inert site. These are called **skin potentials**. Alternatively, by imposing a constant voltage across the electrodes, across the surface of the skin, the current between these electrodes can be measured: this current is indexing the conductivity of the skin between the two electrodes. Alternatively, a constant current may be maintained between the two electrodes by constantly adjusting the voltage: this voltage adjustment is indexing skin resistivity. Both momentary fluctuations (phasic) and relatively stable measures (tonic) can be recorded.

Transducers   Two non-invasive, metallic, surface electrodes generally placed on either the palm or the fingers of one hand.

Signal properties   If measuring skin potentials, the voltage amplitude between the two electrodes may be recorded. Normally this ranges between about 1 and 6 millivolts (mV). If measuring **skin resistance**, then given a baseline level of resistance around 100 kilohms (kΩ), values ranging around this baseline level between 0.1 and 50 kΩ may be observed. That is, given a relatively stable level of resistance of about 100 kΩ to the passage of electric current through the surface of the skin, variability of resistance around this baseline value can reach up to 50 kΩ or more in magnitude (ranging between 50 and 110 kΩ). **Skin conductance** is generally measured in microsiemens (μS = Ω^{-1}). Given a baseline level of conductivity of 10 μS, conductivity can be seen to vary generally between about 8 μS and 20 μS. A typical response duration would be between about 1 and 3 seconds. Of course, these example values will be heavily dependent on the type of experimental conditions used to elicit changes in potential, resistivity and conductivity.

Quantitative measures   Basically, these are measures of response wave-form amplitude and latency, rise/fall times, and frequency of responses. In addition, gradients over time of these measures can be analysed, as in the case of habituation of response amplitude to repetitive stimuli.

Example application   Measures of electrodermal activity have been widely used to indicate level of arousal to almost any conceivable stimulus. For instance, Blair et al. (1997) recently found that psychopathic individuals show a lower electrodermal response to distress cues in others than a group of matched controls.

15.2.3   Eye movements – pupillary response

Abbreviations   Pupillary response (PR) and electro-oculography (EOG).

What is measured   Pupillography or pupillometry is the measurement of pupil diameter via low level infrared light reflected from the surface of the eye. EOG is the term that describes the measurement of eye movements, indexed by the change in voltage potential between the positive cornea and negative retinal segment of the eye. In addition to PR and EOG, eyeblink rate and duration can also be measured.

Transducers   For PR, an individual's eyes are illuminated via low level infrared light. A low light level video camera is used to record pupil size, with digital signal processing of the video images to provide a continuous meas-urement of pupil diameter. EOG uses non-invasive pairs of electrodes placed around the eye. Electrodes placed at the side of the eye record horizontal movement, those placed above and below the eye record vertical movement.

Signal properties   In PR, pupil diameter changes can be measured over a 0.5 mm to 10 mm range. Spontaneous, continuous pupil size changes vary around 1 mm or so. EOG amplitude varies between about 0.4 and 1 mV. Currently, EOG signals can record movement up to 70° from a central position with a resolution of 1.5°. Eyeblink duration is generally seen to fall between 100 and 400 milliseconds (ms), with rates heavily dependent upon specific situational factors.

Quantitative measures   For PR, measures encompass pupil diameter and rate of change in diameter in response to either a specific stimulus or a longer term emotional state. EOG measures encompass eye movement speed, direc-tion, type (smooth pursuit as in tracking tasks or fast saccades as in reading or examining a static stimulus), and eyeblink rate and duration.

Example application   Electro-oculograms are regularly used in sleep research, for instance, as one indicator of entry to the phase of sleep known as REM (rapid eye movement) sleep, which is characterised by the eyes making rapid darting movements (e.g. see Carlson, 1998).

15.2.4   Cardiac response, blood pressure and blood volume

Abbreviation   Electrocardiography (ECG) and blood pressure (BP).

What is measured   ECG is the recording of the electrical potentials generated by the heart muscles over the period of one heartbeat. The **PQRST complex** is the labelling applied to the electrical waveform produced by the sequence of contractile responses in a heartbeat. The P wave is the small change in potential caused by the initial excitation of the atrial (upper heart chambers) muscles just prior to their contraction. The QRS complex represents the contraction of the left and right ventricular (lower chambers of the heart) muscles that pump blood from the ventricular chambers to the lungs and rest of the body. The R wave is the point of maximum ventricular excitation. The T wave indicates repolarisation of ventricular muscle. The term **systole** is used to describe the atrial and ventricular contraction phases (P-S) and **diastole** to describe the relaxation phase (T-P) of the passive filling of the atria and ventricles. Blood pressure measurement is based upon the measurement of the systolic and diastolic phase wavefronts in the blood moving through the arteries. Blood volume measurement (plethysmography) assesses the amounts of blood that are present in various areas of the body during particular activities.

Transducers   For ECG, surface electrodes can be placed on the wrist, ankle, neck or chest. For the measurement of blood pressure, a **sphygmomanometer** (pressure cuff) and stethoscope are used to detect the systolic and diastolic pressures. For blood volume measurements, conventionally a photoplethysmograph is used to detect the amount of blood passing in tissue directly below the sensor (using the principle of light absorption characteristics of blood). This device is normally placed on a fingertip or an earlobe.

Signal properties   For the ECG, the cardiac cycle lasts about 830 ms (based upon a heartbeat rate of 72 beats per minute (bpm)). For a cycle of about 800 ms, the heart is in ventricular systole for 200–250 ms and in diastole for 550–600 ms. The R peak wave is as high as 2 mV in amplitude. The average heartbeat rate is about 75 bpm. Normal systolic blood pressure (measured in millimetres of mercury displacement (mmHg)) ranges from 95 to 140 mmHg with a figure of 120 mmHg as the average pressure. Normal diastolic blood pressure ranges from 60 to 90 mmHg with about 80 mmHg as the average pressure. Blood volume measures are always relative to some baseline within an individual. The signal is generally an amplified analogue voltage that indexes light absorption by the photoelectric sensor.

Quantitative measures   Within ECG, measures of heart rate (counting the number of R waves over a minute) and heart period (the duration between R waves) are the most popular descriptors of cardiac activity. However, with a multicomponent waveform as in the PQRST complex, and the physiological processes that underlie the waveform, meaningful measures can be generated from many combinations of latencies or amplitudes between and within the

PQRST complex. The measurement of blood pressure yields simple pressure indices; however, the ratio between the systolic and diastolic pressure values is of significance as is the absolute value of each pressure parameter.

Example application   Measures such as heart rate variability have been widely used to indicate the mental workload (a concept that reflects information processing demands and complexity) imposed by a variety of tasks, such as those involved in flying aircraft (e.g. Backs, 1998; Sammer, 1998).

15.2.5   Respiration

Abbreviation   None.

What is measured   The breathing and gas-exchange process. More specifically, oximetry examines the arterial blood oxygen (O_2) levels and infrared capnometry examines the lung carbon dioxide (CO_2) levels. Abdominal and thoracic respiration rate and depth may also be measured.

Transducers   For oximetry, a specially calibrated photoplethysmograph is used, with output calibrated as percentage of saturated haemoglobin. For capnometry, a nasal catheter is inserted about 6 mm into a nostril and held in place with some tape on the upper lip. CO_2 expiration pressure (PCO_2) and end-tidal CO_2 (the concentration of CO_2 in expired air) pressure (PCO_2) or percentage volume of expired air ($PETCO_2$) can be measured. For abdominal and thoracic breathing measurement, pneumography and strain gauges are most often used.

Signal and quantitative measures   Generally these are analogue voltages, digital values or direct pressure manometer readings that index the gases or strains being measured. There are up to 50 measures that can be extracted from an examination of the output from oximetry, capnography and pneumography. These vary from measures of volume displacement, frequency and pressure, to proportionate fractionation of gases in expired air and oxygenation of the blood. The analysis of respiration has inexplicably been neglected in psychophysiology. However, the book by Fried and Grimaldi (1993) is a remarkable testament to the richness of relationships between respiration and psychological factors, and to the theoretical importance of respiration to conventional models of arousal and physiological functioning.

Example application   Capnometry has been used to examine breathing patterns in individuals suffering from panic disorder, a condition that has been linked to the physiological effects of hyperventilation (e.g. Hegel and Ferguson, 1997).

15.2.6   Electrical potentials of the brain

Abbreviation   Electroencephalography (EEG), averaged evoked potential (AEP), magnetoencephalography (MEEG).

What is measured The electrical activity of the mass action of neurons within the cortex and midbrain structures. In addition, since electrical currents generate magnetic fields, these can also be measured (MEEG).

Transducers For EEG, these can vary from invasive needle electrodes, placed directly into the exposed cortex or deeper structures, to non-invasive electrodes placed upon the surface of the scalp. These electrodes are used to record voltage differences between one or more cortical sites and a *relatively* electrically inactive area (such as an earlobe). For MEEG recording, super-conducting quantum interfering devices (SQUIDS) are used to detect the minute magnetic fields within the brain. These are basically extremely sensitive superconducting electrodes that can detect the dynamic fluctuations of minute magnetic fields underneath their surface. Unlike EEG electrodes, SQUIDS do not have to be in contact with the scalp or cortical tissue as there is no reliance on electrical conductivity of electrons through body tissues.

Signal properties The electrical signals emanating from the brain are of the order of microvolts. Spontaneous EEG is the term used to describe the continuous stream of activity that is always present within the brain. This activity can be characterised as patterns of oscillatory waveforms that have conventionally been subdivided in terms of their frequency into four main bands:

delta: low frequency, 0.5–4 Hz   amplitude 20–200 μV
theta: low frequency, 4–7 Hz   amplitude 20–100 μV
alpha: dominant frequency, 8–13 Hz   amplitude 20–60 μV
beta: high frequency, 13–40 Hz   amplitude 2–20 μV

If, instead of recording the spontaneous activity of the brain, a brain response is evoked by a quantifiable stimulus, then it is possible to examine the change in electrical activity in direct response to a known stimulus. This technique is known as **evoked potential EEG**. Some of these evoked potentials can last less than 10 ms (such as the brain-stem auditory evoked potential generated by subcortical brain tissues) or up to a second or longer as in the case of the *Bereitschaftspotential* or readiness potential (a slow shift in voltage that is observed as preceding voluntary or spontaneous movement within an individual). Generally, because of the low level of brain response over and above the normal background EEG activity, many evoked responses are collected and then summed to produce an average evoked response (AER), also known as an AEP. The basis for this summation is that activity in the waveform that is not generated in response to the stimulus will be almost random and hence sum to near zero over occasions, while activity that is related to the stimulus will be enhanced by adding these stimulus-generated signals together.

Quantitative measures Within spontaneous EEG data, the most popular method of analysis is based around Fourier decomposition of the waveform into cosine and sine wave components (i.e. the number and type of oscillatory components of a particular frequency and magnitude that can account for the complex waveform). From these components, the power spectrum (the amount of electrical energy accounted for by each particular frequency that could possibly make up the complex waveform) provides direct, quantitative measures that index signal power at certain frequencies. More recent methods of analysis have re-expressed multi-electrode output as a spatial contour map – the topographical EEG map. This is a method of interpolating activity between electrodes in order to produce a set of smoothed gradients that can be 'mapped' over the surface of the scalp, encompassing all electrode positions and the intervening spaces between electrodes. In addition, chaos theory (non-linear dynamic analysis – fractal dimensionality analysis) has very recently been applied to the background EEG as a method for determining the 'complexity' of the EEG. This methodology basically computes the number of differential equations that are required to generate a segment of EEG. If few equations are required, then the EEG is said to be low dimensional (note that a totally random waveform would require an infinite number of such equations and would thus have infinite dimensionality). For AEP research, measures invariably focus on peaks and troughs in the waveform, characterising these components by their amplitude and latency from the point of stimulation. Some work has also focused on the spectral composition of the AEP but, because of the brief duration of the waveform, such analyses tend to be error-prone. (A new method of displaying instantaneous power at frequencies within short impulse functions is now available in the engineering world – the wavelet transform. However, as yet, very little work with this transform has taken place in the area of human biosignal research.)

Example application   Electroencephalography has frequently been used to study levels of arousal from deep sleep, where delta activity predominates, through to alert attentiveness, where beta activity predominates. More specifically, evoked potentials have been widely used to study attentional mechanisms in the brain and their anatomical loci (e.g. Hillyard, 1993).

Finally, nuclear imaging, endocrinology and neuroimmunology have been ignored in the above résumé. This is not because they lack importance, far from it: some of the most exciting results in the study of the biological bases of behaviour are now emanating from these three areas of research. However, the facilities (and finance!) required by these methodologies are such that only a few centres in the UK and worldwide can offer a postgraduate student access to these technologies. Some references for further reading in these areas is provided in section 15.4.

15.3   QUANTIFYING BIOSIGNAL DATA

15.3.1   The level of measurement

As can be seen from the information presented in section 15.2, the measures made from psychophysiological data are at true ratio level measurement (see Chapter 11). That is, a constant unit of measurement is used that enables differences between any two sets of parameter values to be considered equal, if their differences are also equal. Additionally, unlike most psychological data/parameters, there is a true zero in nearly all biosignal data. Zero voltage means exactly that: no voltage at all.

15.3.2   Hardware, signal processing and data volume

Therefore, having established that the scale of measurement is superior to nearly all psychological data, it is apparent that many issues in the quantification of parameters that bedevil psychology fade into insignificance in this area. However, the cost of this philosophical simplicity is the price of computational and methodological complexity. The measures made are invariably electrically based, exact to a predetermined level of accuracy defined by the properties of the sensors and any amplification used, and prone to levels of noise that can utterly distort any parameter or signal. So, in order to attempt to measure any physiological parameter from any part of the human body, fairly detailed knowledge is required of the underlying physiology to be assessed, the physical properties of the sensors/transducers to be applied, the properties of the signals thus generated (electrical engineering and digital signal processing techniques) and the plethora of possible methods of analysis (both bivariate and multivariate methods of waveform analysis, periodicity analysis, event detection, pattern recognition and clustering techniques).

A simple measure such as heart rate (counted in bpm) seems a trivial parameter to acquire, until you ask yourself how you are going to measure the heart rate (HR). Having found out that two electrodes placed say on each wrist will enable the acquisition of the information, your next problem is to work out how you are going to extract the HR parameter itself: that is, how you record the electrical signals. Assume next you are provided with an amplifier, a chart recorder, and a device which outputs a number every 10 seconds or so which indicates beats per minute. Looking at the number, you see the HR is alternating between 50 and 70 beats per minute. Is this acceptable? The individual being assessed is sitting quietly. Your local expert happens by and notices that the 50 Hz hardware notch filter is off. In addition, checking the earth electrode shows that very poor electrical contact is being made between this and the individual. By improving this contact and switching the notch filter in-line, the HR stabilises around 70 bpm. To understand what has happened requires knowledge of the expected HR, the properties of metallic electrodes, earthing problems, the operation of a notch filter, and the appreciation of how an HR monitor works. This is all *before* you begin to manipulate a single psychological variable. Note also that here you were dealing with a relatively large biological signal. Imagine attempting to measure high frequency EEG of maybe 5 μV in amplitude with amplifiers that have background, self-generated electronic noise of about 1 μV, and where mains noise can be of a magnitude of 10–20 μV. The knowledge required to ensure that the signal you are seeing is actually biologically generated and not some property of the hardware in use, or of bad measurement technique, is quite considerable.

Unlike much purely psychological research, it is possible to generate quantitative physiological data that are literally pure error. This is a problem in some topographic EEG systems that provide maps of brain electrical activity computed from many electrodes placed upon the scalp. Most systems have automated filtering such that only frequencies between 0 and 40 Hz are displayed. However, if an electrode becomes detached from the scalp or its connecting wire breaks (inside the insulating plastic), this electrode will pick up large amounts of background mains noise (and any other stray frequencies present in the environment). Depending upon the efficiency of the filters, this electrode position will be seen as producing either very low amplitude signals across the signal spectrum or high frequency beta of moderate amplitude (where beta activity was defined as being from 20 Hz upwards). In this latter case, the filter does not remove *all* 50 Hz activity and, owing to spectral smearing (given a low sampling speed and short segment of EEG), this gets mapped as high frequency activity in your EEG records. Experienced EEG technicians and researchers can invariably detect this. For a novice researcher, it poses a serious problem. Once again, only knowledge of the measurement process and the characteristics of the hardware can guard against this incorrect interpretative process.

15.3.3   Designing the experiment and choosing parameters to measure

If you set up an experiment protocol, and have acquired some electro-physiological data, your next problem is deciding what parameters to extract from these data. This stage of the measurement process *must* be decided on the basis of *a priori* measurement and psychological hypotheses. Data dredging (extracting every conceivable parameter and attempting to relate them to the psychological parameters) in the hope of finding something is virtually impossible to implement in this area. So many parameters can be computed that attempting to sift through your data in this manner is a recipe for disaster. You will run out of time, computing facilities and energy! The best modern laboratories keep all physiological data on some form of archive medium (whether magnetic or CD-ROM). However, only certain hypothesis-specific parameters are extracted from this archive for use in the examination of psychological relationships. Should other hypotheses evolve over time, the archive data can then be reanalysed (where relevant) in order to permit the extraction of the new parameters.

One major problem you may face is that the system you are using to acquire psychophysiological data may permit only certain forms of analysis or, more rarely, provide no parameters at all. That is, you may have access to a skin conductance meter, amplifier and computer which will acquire and store the continuous conductance levels. However, if you don't have a program that analyses this output in terms of response latency and amplitude, then the data are practically useless. Your only options are to write all the incoming data to a chart recorder and carry out all such measures by hand, or obtain or write a computer program yourself that implements the procedures necessary to extract these parameters. This highlights another global feature of psychophysiological data acquisition: the collection of data can take a few minutes, but the volume of data generated can tax the computer system and the analysis of one participant's data by hand can take days! For example, digitally acquiring data from 16 EEG electrodes, sampling and acquiring the voltage value at each electrode 1000 times a second for a duration of 1 second, yields 16,000 numbers per second, invariably stored as two computer bytes (words) per number which thus generates 32,000 computer bytes per second. If, say, you are recording the 1 second segments 30 times (in response to 30 discrete stimuli prior to averaging), you will have to store 480,000 numbers, or 960,000 bytes (almost 1Mb) of data, for each participant tested. Thus, you can easily appreciate the problems of duration of analysis and computing equipment requirements for EEG research!

Of course, returning to the HR example above, it may be that only five such measures are made throughout an experiment, where say the only focus of interest is the effect of difficulty of task problem on HR. The drawback to such simple experiments is that the explanatory power of any results is limited by the paucity of variables analysed! As Fried and Grimaldi (1993) also point out in their discussion of pulmonary (respiration) research, using observable movements of the chest or abdomen (pneumography) alone as indicators of respiration activity is not to be recommended, as $PETCO_2$ activity demonstrates that such movement can be quite unrelated to actual airflow into and out of the lungs. Thus to use respiration rate or depth as an indicator of increasing or decreasing airflow is liable to be prone to error. In the same way, the use of HR alone is not of much practical use except as a simple descriptor of one particular feature of cardiac activity.

15.4 FURTHER READING

Andreassi's (1995) *Psychophysiology: Human Behavior and Physiological Response* (3rd edn) is an excellent introductory text. It is probably the best general textbook for students who are completely new to the area. This book is mandatory for any student wishing to study psychophysiology at a basic level. Cacioppo and Tassinary's (1990) *Principles of Psychophysiology: Physical, Social, and Inferential Elements* should be the second book to be read after Andreassi's text. This is a remarkably comprehensive book that would serve as a reference source for both undergraduate and graduate students. This book is mandatory for any student seriously interested in psychophysiology.

Dempster's (1993) *Computer Analysis of Electrophysiological Signals* is a good introductory text on the analysis of psychophysiological data – excellent for students who already have some knowledge of basic statistical methods. Since electroencephalography is one of the largest research areas in psychophysiology, it is useful to take a look at Fisch's (1991) *Spehlmann's EEG Primer* (2nd edn). It is written at an introductory level suitable for students who have no prior knowledge of psychophysiology. For students who wish to undertake projects involving EEG, this is an essential handbook that provides much practical as well as some theoretical information. Finally, Fried and Grimaldi's (1993) *The Psychology and Physiology of Breathing* is an absolutely brilliant book. It contains an excellent introductory section on psychophysiological measurement and provides a masterful description of respiratory functions and processes. In addition, the provocative and challenging hypotheses in the book make this probably one of the best 'specialist' books in this area. If you are to study psychophysiology at any level, you must read this book.

16

Direct Observation

Jill Wilkinson

Contents

Observation is a fundamental aspect of any science and has played an essential part in the development of psychology as a scientific discipline. The major strength of direct observation is precisely that it is direct. There is virtually no time delay between the occurrence of the responses in question and their recording, by either the observer or some recording device. Observations are also more direct than interviews or questionnaires in that they do not require the subjects to respond in word representations to stimuli presented in word representations.

Observation was the most important method of data collection in the early years when psychology was involved in establishing itself on a par with the natural sciences and keen to dissociate itself from its earlier 'unscientific' origins in introspection and philosophy. Psychology accordingly came into the laboratory. Here the subject is in a controlled environment in which conditions can be held constant and the individual components of the situation manipulated. In this way the effect of each variable can be examined in turn. One of the main problems with this approach was that it took us farther and farther away from what people actually did in their lives and how, in reality, they behaved in the situations they encountered. In its haste to progress, psychology seems to have rather rushed through what, in the natural sciences, is the basis of scientific research: the systematic and rigorous observation and description of phenomena in its natural state, before attempting to exert any form of manipulative control.

As the discipline progressed, the emphasis shifted from the observation of overt events, to an interest in the covert, cognitive aspects of human functioning and the subsequent decline in the role of observation in experimental psychology. This has coincided with, and to some extent been compensated by, the emergence of interest in very different approaches to observation, noticeably **ethology**, which tends to focus on behaviour in natural settings and which aims to exert little or minimum experimental control over the subjects under observation.

Regardless of the ebb and flow of interest in the various approaches, direct observation remains one of psychology's most important research tools. It has long been, and remains, the assessment of choice in the evaluation of behavioural training in areas such as teaching (Rose, 1998) and parenting (Danforth, 1998). It is also of particular value to those studying the behaviour of populations who cannot give accounts of themselves. For example, studies using direct observation have examined the effects of sensory stimulation on patients in prolonged coma (Wilson et al., 1991), how a history of exposure to interparental aggression relates to children's behaviour during conflict (Gordis et al., 1997) and the concordance between staff ratings and direct observations of behaviour of nursing home residents with Alzheimer's. There are also some behaviours or situations on which subjects would be unable to report with any degree of accuracy, such as non-verbal behaviour which often takes place outside our conscious awareness (e.g. Beattie, 1983) or domestic situations where there is a high level of emotion (e.g. Gordis et al., 1997). Observation is also useful in situations where there may be some investment in impression management or a 'correct' way of responding. For example junior doctors may know theoretically how they should 'break bad news' to a patient and this may influence any self-report of their responses in such situations.

These are just some of the areas of investigation in which direct observation might be the preferred method or one of several methods of collecting data for a particular study. Clearly what is observed will depend on the goals and purpose of the study in question, but the examples do highlight the wide range and variation of possible target behaviours from a discrete non-verbal response to a highly complex social interaction. This chapter will outline the main approaches to observation and then discuss some of the practical and theoretical issues and the various stages in planning and implementing observational research.

16.1 OBSERVATIONAL APPROACHES TO THE STUDY OF BEHAVIOUR

A knowledge of the various approaches to direct observation is particularly important when considering using observation as a means of collecting data. The two possibly most influential trends come from very different theoretical perspectives: experimental psychology and ethology. Other important influences include ecological psychology and ethnography. The kinds of data each approach yields are quite different and will be discussed in section 16.7.

Systematic observation was developed in the context of experimental psychology and has traditionally been the mainstay of behavioural theory and research. Here the methods of observation are systematic and standard procedures for obtaining data and can be considered as extensions of measurement theory and methods. In order to conduct this type of systematic observation, the researcher needs to define the categories and units of behaviour to be observed and to work out ways of measuring them. This usually involves timing, counting or rating them. This may necessitate a period of informal observation of the behaviour in its natural state, but this will involve nothing like the detailed recording characteristic of the ethogram described below.

Ethology is a very different approach to observation. It is an interdisciplinary science combining zoology, biology and psychology in the study originally of animal but more recently of human behaviour, usually in the natural rather than the laboratory environment. The ethological approach is characterised by a particular method of direct observation which aims to record the behaviour completely impartially in all its detail, correlating it with the stimuli which evoke it. No evaluations are made, nor are attempts made to infer the motivations, intentions or emotions of the subjects under observation. The resulting account is called an **ethogram**. Only when the ethogram is complete will ethologists consider formulating hypotheses which can form the basis of experiment and analysis, and only when the ethologist knows what behaviour there is to modify will any attempt be made to modify it. On the whole though, ethologists prefer to leave their subjects alone.

Another area that has developed and employs its own observational procedures is **ecological psychology**. This approach has aims similar to those of ethology, that is, to describe and analyse the life-systems of individuals in their natural environments, and detailed commentaries are made of all activities and stimuli with which the person comes into contact. There are, however, some fundamental differences between the two approaches, the most crucial being that whereas ethological reports must be purely descriptive, ecological psychologists are concerned with making inferences about the attitudes, motives and intentions of their subjects.

Ethnography is an approach to research which employs observation as one of a range of methods of collecting and analysing data. This is dealt with in Chapter 23.

16.2 TYPES OF OBSERVATION

Casual observation often takes place at the planning stage of research. Observing a situation with relatively open eyes, ears and mind can provide valuable insights and yield information indispensable for subsequent meaningful data collection. Casual observation is helpful for making decisions about the best location in which to make the observations and for developing the categories to be used in systematic observation. It is essential to make notes of casual observations as first impressions are usually the most vivid and are most useful when written down immediately.

Formal observation is the planned and systematic application of a system of procedures for conducting the observations or gathering the data, usually from one or a combination of the theoretical approaches discussed above. It usually involves an unintrusive observer who makes field notes and/or times, counts or rates behaviours or events. Sometimes a video camera will replace the observer in the field or laboratory and the tape will be subsequently analysed. The rest of this chapter is concerned mainly with these kinds of formal observations.

Participant observation, as the name implies, differs from casual and formal observation in that the observer is part of the events being studied. There are a number of advantages to this approach. It enables access to possibly more private events which subjects would not allow an outsider to observe; it can give access not only to behaviours but to the attitudes, opinions and feelings and it gets over the problem of observer effects (see section 16.8). The main criticisms are that it is impossible for the participant observer to be objective; the observations will be subject to fluctuations in the attention of the observer; there are ethical and procedural problems in becoming an observer if the person has a role in the setting; and not inconsiderable personal demands are made on the researcher by the dual role and the possibility of role conflict.

16.3   WHAT TO OBSERVE

It would clearly be impossible to observe everything. What situations, events, behaviours or actions are selected for observation will depend on factors such as the nature of the research problem/question, the hypothesis to be tested, the specific relationships being examined and the underlying theoretical framework. Data must ultimately be reduced to a form where they can be analysed and this is usually achieved by classifying, rating and/or measuring the duration and frequency of behaviours or events. This can be done at the time of the original observations and the data recorded in a pre-coded form (the standard behavioural approach); or a selection can be made from written objective non-evaluative narrative accounts (the ethological approach); or classification may start in the field and be developed and refined 'back home' (ecological and ethnographic approaches). Responses can also be recorded on audiotape or videotape and subsequently analysed in the laboratory.

Usually the first stage in deciding what to observe is to conduct some informal observations and to identify the broad categories of behaviours to be studied. Examples of categories might be 'assertive behaviour', 'pupil initiative', 'temper tantrums'.

Decisions also need to be made not only about what to observe but about *who* to observe, and this may have a bearing on the choice of categories. For example, in examining the conversational behaviour of someone suffering from a psychiatric disorder, is he or she the only person targeted for observation or would you be interested in the effect that person's behaviour might have on others involved in the interaction? In a study exploring the connection between emotional expression in the child's family environment and children's social competence with peers, Boyum and Parke (1995) chose to observe the target child and the parents, but included the other family members to the extent it was practically possible.

Another very important consideration at this stage relates to the breadth of information sought within the broad categories, usually referred to as **units of behaviour**. Small segments of behaviour such as short phrases, expressive gestures, looking at, face touching are known as **molecular** units and are relatively easy to define and measure reliably. However, molecular units of behaviour taken out of context may have little meaning in the real world and thus validity is reduced. There are some exceptions where individual behaviours are pertinent to the research problem; for example, in research examining specific aspects of social behaviour such as repetitive actions and mannerisms in those suffering from Alzheimer's disease (McCann et al., 1997).

The **molar** approach takes larger behavioural wholes as units of behaviour. The size of the molar units can vary considerably depending on the subject of the research and the theoretical orientation of the researcher. Ecological molar units can be quite long sequences of behaviour lasting several minutes and include events such as going to school or walking with a friend. Other examples of molar units might be 'buys sweets at the newsagents', 'does homework'. These types of molar units are usually defined as occurring within the conscious awareness of the individual. That is, the person knows what he or she is doing.

Molar units can also be qualitative and might include such categories of behaviour as 'blame' (e.g. Gordis et al., 1997), 'co-operativeness', 'friendliness', 'discomfort' or 'openness'. Molar categories of this type tend to be more psychologically meaningful (and therefore more valid) than discrete molecular units of behaviour. They are, however, likely to require a fair degree of inference on the part of the observer and data are often in the form of ratings, which are, of course, subjective. This may therefore reduce the reliability and validity of this sort of data.

Attempts have been made to define operationally molar constructs like 'friendliness' by trying to identify and list the behavioural components. This can achieve a high degree of precision and reliability. The problem is that in doing this, often the whole flavour of what is being observed is also reduced.

Clearly, there is no 'ideal' solution to the problem. Both molecular and molar units have their advantages and disadvantages in terms of reliability and validity. The size and type of the unit of observation chosen will depend on the type of study undertaken. The most important thing is to choose the size of unit which makes sense in terms of the aims of the research, to be aware of the limitations associated with the size of unit and to be as rigorous as possible in overcoming them.

16.4 DEFINING BEHAVIOURS

Examples were given above of the kind of units of behaviour which are often the subject of observation in psychological research. But what is meant by, for example, 'looking at (the other person in the interaction)'? Is looking at the person's kneecaps counted as 'looking at him'? Clearly the answer from a common-sense view is 'No'. But what about looking at his neck or chin? This is not so clear-cut. Similarly we all know a smile when we see one. Or do we? When does a smile become a grimace? What about 'nervous' smiles? It gets worse when we get on to the qualitative molar behaviours in the example. We use constructs like openness in our everyday communications and people seem to know what we mean. But do they always agree with you? If not, is this because you have different perspectives on the person in question, maybe see them in different contexts, or is it because your idea of openness is not quite the same as the other person's? This is all right in everyday life. People can argue about and hopefully resolve their differences. This is one of the fundamental ways in which everyday and scientific observations differ. The behavioural scientist needs to be able to measure behaviour reliably, and in order to do this, the measurement of the constructs needs to be valid. There is no point in having a list of seemingly quite specific behaviours unless people can agree on precisely what is meant by the various labels employed to describe them.

Where responses are being classified and possibly measured at the time of the observation, definitions of the behaviours need to be constructed and evaluated in advance of the period of observation. Where the data are recorded on videotape or by detailed narrative, decisions about units of behaviour and their definitions can be made with reference to these taped or written records. The observer using narrative would nevertheless need to have some idea of the size of unit in order to record the observations at a level of detail required for subsequent analysis.

Definitions of the units of behaviour should be clear, complete, unambiguous and couched in terms of observable characteristics. Danforth (1998), in his study of the outcome of parent training, defines the unit of behaviour 'command' as 'direct orders that specified the child behaviour. Presented in imperative structure, not as questions.'

It is usually more straightforward when the unit is expressed in behavioural terms, as in the preceding example. When the unit involves a quality of behaviour, such as 'friendly', 'aggressive' or 'open' behaviour, it is rather more complex but attempts should be made at an operational definition in order to tell others what *you* mean by the term. For example, 'By "openness" I mean readily gives information about self when asked. The information should include more than that demanded by the question and should be at a level of self-disclosure similar to or only slightly deeper than the preceding content.' It can be seen that this still involves the observer having to make inferences from the subject's behaviour and using judgements about self-disclosure, although some guidelines are given to the observer in this respect. Whilst this may not be acceptable to a behavioural 'purist' it may, in the interest of collecting some data, be permissible. Ideally, a complete definition should be constructed to include the descriptive name, the definition and elaboration (rather like in a dictionary) and typical examples, borderline examples and examples of what would not be included. These definitions should then be tested out on a pilot study and modified accordingly.

The above procedure is very time-consuming and, unless the scope of the observations is fairly narrow, would probably be out of range for most postgraduate students working on their own. What often happens in practice is that researchers use and modify categories, behavioural units and definitions developed by other researchers working in the same or a related area. You cannot assume, however, that because the work has been published you can accept uncritically other people's definitions. They are not always as rigorous as they should be and may need further refinement. Because this level of information is usually not published in research papers, you will probably need to write to the researchers yourself requesting the information and explaining your reason for doing so.

16.5 SAMPLING

Having decided on the broad categories and possibly on the more specific units of behaviour and their definitions you need to think about how you are going to sample the situations, events or behavioural units in question. There are a number of methods of sampling behaviour, the most relevant being event sampling, time sampling and the use of simulated situations.

Event sampling is used when studying a particular type of event, such as temper tantrums, fights, playground games, marital rows. It is extremely important to have very clear definitions of the class of event in order to be sure that what is being observed is what you call a 'temper tantrum' and also that you don't miss the event whilst trying to decide if it is one! One of the main strengths of event sampling is that there is an inherent validity in studying a 'complete' phenomenon from beginning to end rather than the more 'piecemeal' behavioural acts which are often the focus of time sampling. Event sampling also enables the observation of events that are relatively rare and would probably not be picked up by time sampling. Clearly, though, with event sampling the researcher needs to know when the event is likely to occur or to be prepared to wait until it does occur.

Time sampling is the selection of periods of observation at different points in time. Observation units can be chosen in a systematic way, say two 5-minute observation periods at specified times during each of the three nursing shifts on a ward; or randomly, say four 5-minute observation periods selected at random from a universe of 5-minute periods. There are many ways in which time samples can be set up and selected, but how many periods and for how long and whether they are systematic or random will be influenced by the research problem. With time sampling the researcher is assured of obtaining representative samples of behaviour, but only behaviour that occurs relatively frequently. The main drawback to time sampling is that it lacks continuity and the quality of completeness found in event sampling.

Event sampling and time sampling assume that the behaviour in question is going on 'out there' somewhere; but what happens if you want to sample responses which take place only rarely or not at all in the subjects' natural environment, such as conversational skills of schizophrenics living fairly isolated lives in the community, or people's behaviour when confronted by the threat of fire? Sometimes behaviour can only be, or is best, sampled by constructing **simulated situations** in which the subjects knowingly or unknowingly take part. A particular type of simulated situation called a **role-play** is often used in clinical research and studies evaluating the effects of various types of training programmes and procedures. Role-plays offer highly standardised situations which allow for comparisons to be made between subjects or groups and usually take place in laboratory settings. An example of a role-play set up for the purpose of observing conversation with strangers in a semi-social setting might involve constructing a situation with a stooge who would have been instructed to respond in various prearranged ways, such as asking particular questions or responding to the subject in a friendly or cool way. The subject would be informed of the context of the interaction and instructed to behave in particular ways, such as to start a conversation with the stooge, or to try to make the stooge feel 'at home'. One of the main problems with using this sort of simulated situation concerns the ecological validity of such procedures: that is, the degree to which the behaviour of the subjects in the laboratory corresponds to their behaviour in the natural environment. Results of studies of generalisability of behaviour in role-played interactions are equivocal, but it has been found that longer role-played interactions have greater ecological validity than role-played scenes which require only brief responses. Ecological validity, however, is not always an issue. You might be interested not in what subjects actually *do* in their natural environments but in what they *can* do. It is important to remember that subjects cannot produce behaviours in the laboratory that are not in their repertoires. Conversely, because they do not exhibit a behaviour in a simulated situation, this does not necessarily mean it is not present in other situations.

One way to increase the ecological validity of simulated situations is not to let on to the subject that they are taking part in the experiment. There are many examples of people being invited to a laboratory to be the subject of one experiment, unaware of the fact that they are taking part in another one. For example, conversational skills of subjects have been observed in a waiting area whilst they were waiting to take part in the 'real' experiment (e.g. Gutride et al., 1973), and subjects' responses to (simulated) epileptic seizures have been studied whilst they were ostensibly involved in a project about student problems (e.g. Latane and Darley, 1970). This sort of deception clearly has ethical implications and these must be fully explored before undertaking any research employing such procedures.

16.6 THE ENVIRONMENTAL SETTING

There is a vast range of possible environmental settings that could be used for conducting research involving direct observation. In practice however most observational data are collected in clinics or hospitals, in people's own homes, in schools and in laboratories. Whether the observations take place in the laboratory setting or in the field will depend on considerations such as sampling (discussed above), the theoretical approach adopted and the degree of environmental control desired.

As ethology is primarily concerned with the precise observation of organisms in their natural habitat and ecological psychology with the interaction of the environment with the behaviours of the organisms in it, observations from these perspectives take place almost exclusively in the field. Behavioural research, on the other hand, is frequently conducted in the laboratory where it is possible to have a higher degree of environmental control, often considered desirable in experimental psychology. It would be necessary, however, to make the observations in the natural environment when the target behaviours occur only in the presence of other events which cannot be duplicated in an analogue setting, such as playground fights, behaviour at football matches and marital arguments (although there are undoubtedly some couples who could produce the behaviour in question of any time, in any place, including in the laboratory).

Although there is considerable ecological validity in observing behaviour in its natural setting there are some drawbacks other than those discussed in relation to sampling. You will probably require the consent and co-operation of others in the environment; your schedule for observing could be disrupted by factors beyond your control; naturalistic observation is time-consuming; and you may encounter ethical, legal or practical problems if you want to use videotape or audiotape. For a discussion of the ethical problems of observing private behaviour see Middlemist et al. (1976) on personal space invasion in the lavatory and also Koocher (1977) on bathroom behaviour and human dignity.

16.7 METHODS OF COLLECTING AND RECORDING OBSERVATIONAL DATA

Observations can be recorded in a narrative form or on audiotape or video-tape and subsequently transformed into data by classifying or measuring the various elements of behaviour. Alternatively, data can be collected at the time of observation by a similar process of classifying and measuring. If data are being collected directly from the observations as they occur, then the categories and measurement strategies, as discussed above, will have been pre-determined and no permanent record is kept of the sequence or details of the actual responses other than can be inferred from the data themselves.

Narrative data are accordingly a form of 'raw' data in that they only take on any meaning when translated into categories or numerical form. Typically narrative accounts aim to reproduce behavioural events in a written form in much the same way, and in the same sequence, as they originally occur, often aiming for little or no interpretative content. In reality, observers are selective in their observations (see section 16.8) so not everything that happens can be recorded; and many researchers find that, without some inference, interpretation of narrative data is difficult.

Usually, narrative is used to describe particular episodes, or anecdotes, where there is a beginning, a middle and an end. You will already have made decisions about what constitutes the class of episode in question (see section 16.5), and the size of the units of behaviour, whether molar or molecular or a combination (see section 16.3). You need also to decide on the level of inference you are going to allow in your written account.

There is no 'correct' way or set pattern to writing up anecdotal reports but they should always be as complete as possible. It is better to include too much at this stage than too little. Material can always be discarded in the analysis. There is usually a main person under observation in the episode and reports should include the basic actions and statements (using direct quotations wherever possible) of this person and the responses and reactions of the others involved. Enough details of the setting should also be included and should indicate when and where the behaviour occurred and under what conditions.

Reports should also be as objective and accurate as possible. It is better to say 'she left the room, fists and jaw clenched, slamming the door noisily behind her' than 'she left the room angrily'. Notice how it is description at a molecular level that gives clues about the emotional tone. Sometimes it is more difficult to communicate meaning without evaluative labels. 'She handed her the letter in an offhand way' could be described in objective behavioural terms, but some of the flavour of the action would undoubtedly be lost. It should be noted, however, that this is one person's *interpretation* of what happened and, where interpretations are included or inferences made, they should be differentiated from the main description by the use of inverted commas or some other marking device.

It is important to write up the report as soon as possible after the period of observation, during which notes can be made of key words or essential features of the incident. Writing and observing at the same time is quite a skill in itself and audio tape recorders are often used to supplement the observations. When undertaken with due rigour, anecdotal descriptions can be valuable research tools as well as fascinating to construct. They are useful for recording behaviour in a variety of contexts such as classrooms, hospital wards and the home environment.

Field notes are a type of narrative data often used in ethnographic studies and by other participant observers. Like anecdotal reports, they aim to present the sequence of action and interaction but they are less concerned with describing behaviours and events and more with interpreting aspects of the situation which are of particular interest to the researcher. The transformation of the observations into data therefore starts in the field and is an ongoing process which, in turn, influences the subjects of subsequent observations.

Videotaped data could also be described as narrative data, but similarly, only become 'real' data when converted into a form which can be subsequently analysed. With the development of the now ubiquitous video camera many researchers and students alike envisaged a transformation in observational procedures and the possibilities seemed endless. Video recordings offer a relatively cheap and semi-permanent record (that is, unless you accidentally record over it) which can be played back repeatedly, allowing for analysis at a level of detail and reliability not previously possible from observations made directly in the laboratory or field.

There are a number of factors to be taken into account when thinking of using video recordings. Subjects are often moving targets unless instructed to remain seated, or in a situation, like a meeting, where you can anticipate that they will remain seated. In the natural environment other people can get between the camera and the subject resulting in the loss of maybe quite important information. Therefore what you are hoping to record and how you are going to follow the actions of your subjects need careful consideration. Where the scene involves people other than the main subject, you will need to decide in advance who to include in the recording. So, for example, Boyum and Parke (1995), when observing families at meal-times, asked the families to sit in their usual places and positioned two cameras to best film the subject child and the parents, with additional family members included to the extent possible. If you decide that the responses of others are important and should be included, this will reduce the amount of data available to you from the actual subject. You might not, for example, have the face in sufficient close-up to observe the subtleties of facial expression, or the direction of eye gaze. If you try to overcome this when filming by using the zoom, it should be used only at fixed, predetermined times during the filming, otherwise you will be adding your own interpretation to the 'raw' data, thereby threatening its validity.

These days most people are well used to being filmed: by security cameras, by their relatives, by film crews on location and by anthropologists! Nevertheless using a camera in a public place or even in an institution can cause quite a stir. This can interfere both with the process of collecting the data and also with the behaviour of the subjects. (Reactivity of subjects to being observed is discussed in section 16.8.) Filming in public places also has ethical and legal implications, particularly if the people you are filming are unaware that they are the subjects of your research or if you are filming in a potentially 'sensitive' area, such as where drugs are sold. These complications are less likely to arise if you are filming in an institution, where issues of access will probably be the responsibility of the organisation, but this is something you need to check carefully with them. Getting permission to film in an institution might also involve negotiating with a large number of people and this could be extremely time-consuming and frustrating (see Chapter 3).

Filming in the laboratory is usually much easier. Because you can have a great deal more environmental control in the laboratory than in the natural setting, you can position cameras and instruct subjects in order to optimise your chances of recording the behaviours in question. In the laboratory cameras may be placed unobtrusively or positioned in such a way as to provide recording from several angles, or of different people in an interaction, if you have access to split-screen facilities.

Many cameras have in-built facilities for recording the time, date or other numbers or letters. It is usually a good idea to use these and also the coded number of the subject so that the recordings are readily identifiable. Some systems also have timing devices which will display the running time on the screen and which can be zeroed at the start of each recording. This can be very useful for timing or pinpointing particular behaviours or sequences when transforming the recordings into data.

Considerable care needs to be taken at the filming stage as the data into which the tapes are transformed will only be as valid as the recordings themselves. As with any form of narrative data the recordings should be as complete as possible. Redundant material can always be discarded at a later stage.

Checklists are used for classifying and measuring the frequency and/or the duration of behaviours during the observation period itself and can also be used for converting video-recorded material into data. Checklists usually consist of a number of behavioural units or categories with clear descriptions of each unit (see sections 16.3 and 16.4). Then, depending on the characteristics of the units of behaviour and what the researcher wants to know, the observer can note the existence or non-existence of the behaviours on the checklist, can count the number of occurrences of the behaviour (the frequency) or can take various measures of duration in relation to the behaviours in question. Where the units of behaviour are molar, frequency and duration measures can be made directly from observations. With molecular units, such as glances or posture shifts, it is easier if the observations are recorded on videotape. This also has the advantage of making it possible to code any number of behaviours, rather than the limited number it is possible to observe in the field.

Frequency data are obtained by counting the number of times a behaviour occurs during an observation period. This can then be expressed as a rate per minute, per hour or per day to allow for comparisons to be made between observation periods of different lengths. Frequency measures can be recorded on a simple mechanical counter and are relatively easy to obtain providing you can actually see them, that you have clear, unambiguous definitions and descriptions of the behaviours you are attempting to count and that the behaviours have a clearly discernible onset. If you cannot identify when a behaviour starts, then you cannot code it reliably. Frequency measures, however, cannot give any information on duration, intensity or quality of behaviour.

There may be particular reasons why you might want to collect frequency data which are to do with the subject of the research. It is also the case that some behaviours lend themselves to counting, others to timing and some to both. Where the behaviour is relatively brief and clearly defined, such as a head-nod, a major posture shift or asking for information, then frequencies are probably the most appropriate measures. When there are longer sequences of behaviour, such as responses to questions or 'nervous' self-touching behaviour, then it may be better to use **duration** measures. As with frequencies, you need to be able to tell when the behaviour starts and also when it ends. Response duration measures can be transformed into frequency data, percentage of total time and average response duration. In addition to measuring the duration of the response itself, you might be interested in measuring the time between a specific stimulus and the response or 'latency', for example, the time between the end of a question and the beginning of the response, or the inter-response time. Stop watches or the running clocks on videotaped material are the simplest way of recording duration times. Event recorders can also be used if available. These usually consist of a number of buttons, corresponding to behavioural categories, on a control board which are electrically connected to pens. The observer depresses the appropriate button when the behaviour begins and holds it down until the behaviour terminates. Pens mark on continuous paper and provide a permanent record over time.

Frequency and duration measures in themselves do not give information about when the events occurred unless you record the time which elapses during and between the responses. Another way of doing this is to record your observations using some type of **interval recording** system. With interval recording, the observation period is divided into usually quite brief intervals of time, say 10 seconds, which are indicated by some sort of cueing device such as bleeps on a tape recorder. In **whole interval** recording the behaviour is recorded only if it occurs throughout the whole interval, and in **partial interval** recording if it occurs during a portion of the interval, which can be specified. **Frequency within interval** is where the behaviours occurring within each interval are counted, and in **momentary time sampling** the behaviour is recorded only if it is observed at a specified moment within the interval, usually at the beginning or end. There are several advantages to interval recording systems in addition to providing some idea of the sequence in which the behaviour occurred: by dividing the time into units, any disagreements between observers can be pinpointed, thereby increasing the possibility of obtaining reliable data; estimates of both frequency and duration can be made; it is possible to observe several behaviours at the same time; and, with the exception of 'frequency within interval', it can be used for recording behaviours that do not have clear onsets or endings, such as the sort of head and upper body movements that are often visible during conversations. Part of the difficulty with using the various systems of interval recording is that the estimates are often biased. Mathematical formulae, however, have been produced which estimate the error produced by partial interval, whole interval and momentary time sampling procedures when used to estimate duration (Ary, 1984).

Ratings can be used for measuring the qualitative aspects of behaviour, such as 'appropriateness of verbal content' in the speech of schizophrenic patients, or 'degree of anxiety' shown by students giving presentations. Whereas with checklists the only judgement the observer has to make is whether or not a particular behaviour belongs in a predetermined category, ratings require the observer to make a subjective evaluation about the behaviour in question. There are a number of ways of reducing the subjectivity of qualitative ratings: points along an evaluation continuum can be explicitly defined to provide evaluation guidelines; ratings can be made 'blind' by observers who do not know the subjects, and preferably do not know the aims of the research; and, of course, clear, comprehensive descriptions should be supplied.

Advances in microcomputer-based technology have made assessment and data collection less time-consuming. One such system is the Direct Observation Data System (DODS) (Johnson et al., 1996), a series of microcomputer programs designed to simplify the task of assessing student progress in special education and inclusive settings and 'to facilitate the collection, summation, graphing and reporting of assessment data' (1996: 256). This program also claims to be 'user-friendly' and will hopefully encourage those involved in teaching or therapy with such populations to become scientist-practitioners, thereby contributing to the development of their discipline.

16.8   THE OBSERVER

The very fact that someone knows they are being observed, either by another person or by a camera or tape recorder, can affect the way in which they would normally behave in a given situation. This is known as **observer effect** or **reactivity** and can present a threat to the validity of the data. It is necessary to be aware of this when planning to use observational methods as there are a number of things that can be done to reduce reactivity. Observers and/or equipment can be placed as unobtrusively as possible; you can even try to hide. If you cannot hide you could at least try to make sure your dress and behaviour attract as little attention as possible; blend in with the surroundings. You may be able to get your subjects to habituate to your presence so they no longer take any notice of you, and it has been found that the initial day of observation is more reactive than subsequent days (Gittelsohn et al., 1997). Subjects may also behave differently if they know precisely what you are observing and why. It is probably better to tell them only in the broadest terms. You could also tell your subjects that you are going to observe them but not tell them exactly when or why. So in a study attempting to identify those attributes of human behaviour which affect growth and reproduction in pigs, in which stockpersons' interactions with pigs were classified as positive in nature, which included pats and strokes, or negative, which included slaps, pushes and hits, the stockpersons were told that it was the relationships between sexual behaviour in pigs and reproductive performance that were being studied (Coleman et al., 1998). Finally you could resort to deception and not tell your subjects you are observing them at all, but this approach may have serious ethical implications which should be thoroughly explored and considered before deciding to go ahead with it.

Reactivity can not only modify the behaviour of the subjects under observation. It can have an effect on the observers as well. This often takes the form of **observer bias**. If you are committed to the experimental hypothesis of the project (which you may well be if it is your own project) this may influence your perceptions of events. You may, quite unwittingly, 'see' events that conform to your theory and miss others that do not. Bias is even more likely to creep in if you are making ratings of qualitative aspects of behaviour which call for observer interpretation. Observer bias therefore clearly reduces the reliability of the data and every attempt should be made to minimise it.

One way of doing this is to get someone else, who does not have the full details of the project and is 'blind' to your hypothesis, to observe with you for a proportion of the observations. (This is obviously much easier if you are observing from video recordings.) Inter-observer agreement can then be calculated and there are a number of statistics available for this purpose. Cohen's kappa is probably the most commonly used index of inter-rater reliability (see Bellack and Hersen, 1998). It should be noted, however, that when observers know that this sort of reliability check is being made on them, they tend to reach a higher level of agreement than when they are unaware that checks are being made. If you are using ratings perhaps you could get an independent observer to make them or, better still, a panel of say three people which could, depending on how they were selected, reduce the possibility of cultural or sex bias. This would probably be feasible only with recorded material.

A rather more straightforward threat to reliability of observational data comes from the understandable limitations of the observers themselves. They get tired. They may have other things on their minds. Boredom may set in. This is not such a problem with recorded observations. You can always come back to them. You can also check on the reliability of your observations yourself by taking measures of the same subject at different points in time, this time calculating intra-rater reliability. If you are observing in the field, then it is important that you are not tired and that the period of observation is consistent with your attention span. Concentration does improve with practice so, if you can, have a few 'practice runs' which can act as training sessions. Observers employed on large scale projects usually undergo a period of training during which reliability checks are made which act as feedback. Finally, if you are designing you own (or working on someone else's) project using observational data, try to make sure it is something that interests you and has some meaning for you. Your interest will then be sustained and you will hopefully be rewarded by a supply of rich and high quality data.

16.9   CONCLUSIONS

Systematic observation may seem a good deal more complicated, time-consuming and challenging than some other forms of data collection. It can also be a good deal more interesting. In this chapter the methods have been presented and discussed with reference to quite complex lengthy sequences of behaviour. You may, however, be interested in only one or two behaviours or units of behaviour emitted during a short time period. This makes it much more manageable and possible in terms of a student project. The methods and principles are exactly the same.

16.10   FURTHER READING

Bellack and Hersen's (1998) *Behavioural Assessment: A Practical Handbook* is a good general guide to assessing behaviour and Chapter 5, in particular, expands on what is presented here. Hutt and Hutt's (1970) *Direct Observation and Measurement of Behaviour* is another good guide that takes a more ethological approach to observation.

17

Interviewing

Glynis M. Breakwell

Contents

17.1 WHEN TO USE INTERVIEWS

Interviewing is an essential part of most types of social research. This chapter describes how interviewing is done in a research context. The skills needed are similar to those required when interviewing is used in other contexts such as selection or appraisal procedures but there are differences. Research interviews require a very systematic approach to data collection which allows you to maximise the chances of maintaining objectivity and achieving valid and reliable results.

Interviews can be used at any stage in the research process. They can be used in the initial phases to identify areas for more detailed exploration. They can be used as part of the piloting and validation of other instruments. They can be used as the main vehicle of data collection. They can be used once findings have been compiled to check whether your interpretations of other data make sense to the sample which was involved. The interview is a virtually infinitely flexible tool for research. It can encompass other techniques (for instance, as part of an interview, a self-completion questionnaire can be administered or psychophysiological measurements can be taken). Also it can be placed alongside other data elicitation procedures (for example, it can be used in tandem with ethnography or participant observation).

No method of collecting information is free of pitfalls. This chapter will present both the strengths and weaknesses of the interview method. When all the problems surrounding question construction, the biases introduced by the researcher and the interviewee, and the inadequacies of the available media of communication and recording mechanisms are taken into account, the method still has much to recommend it. Like any method, it has to be used with care and in the full knowledge of its limitations.

17.2 ASKING QUESTIONS

Having specified the research questions, you need to translate them into a form that can be used with your interviewees. This translation process is often troublesome because the way that the research question can be operationalised in a series of questions posed to a sample is severely limited by the level of the capacities and co-operation of the respondents. In its entirety, the series of questions asked in an interview is usually called the **interview schedule**. Interviews use many question-and-answer formats which range from the totally structured to the totally unstructured. Few real interviews fall at either of the poles of this continuum between fixed and absent structure.

Structured interviews involve a fixed set of questions which the researcher asks in a fixed order. Commonly, respondents are asked to choose an answer from a fixed series of options given by the researcher. The options may include ratings scales. This type of interview structure yields information which is easily quantified, ensures comparability of questions across respondents and makes certain that the necessary topics are included. However, like all pre-structured data elicitation techniques it leaves little room for unanticipated discoveries. People often feel constrained because they are not free to give the information which they feel is important. You may miss very salient issues in this way.

In **unstructured interviews**, the researcher has a number of topics to cover but the precise questions and their order are not fixed: they are allowed to develop as a result of the exchange with the respondent. Open-ended answers allow interviewees to say as little or as much as they choose. Comparability across respondents is sacrificed for the sake of personal relevance. It would be wrong, however, to think that the flexibility of the unstructured interview of necessity permits a deeper analysis than the structured interview. In both cases, the richness of the data is determined by the appreciation that the researcher has of the topic.

Analysis of unstructured interviews is time-consuming and difficult but not inevitably qualitative. Content analysis will provide categorical data which are open to quantification. There are now sophisticated software packages which, given the word-processed transcript of an interview, will count the incidence of certain phrases or words for you, taking the pain out of content analysis. However, many people who use unstructured interviews shun all quantification. They believe that by immersing themselves in the data they can understand the key themes which emerge. These they believe can be illustrated through taking direct quotes from transcripts and linking these in a coherent description of the themes. Ideally, the quotes allow the interviewees to speak for themselves, telling their own story. The researcher acts as the editor only in so far as quotes must be chosen. Chapter 19 describes some of these approaches further.

Whether you use structured or less structured interviews there are a number of guidelines to follow in formulating questions and in asking them. Questions *should not*:

- Be double-barrelled, for example: 'Do you think whaling and seal culling should be banned?' A 'no' answer could mean no to either whaling or seal culling or both.
- Introduce an assumption before going on to pose the question, for example: 'Do you think that the terrible cruelty of whaling has been adequately reported in the press?' This question assumes that whaling is seen to be cruel by the respondent. The assumption may or may not be true and makes interpretation of any response indeterminate.
- Include complex or jargon words, for example: 'Do you think you are eco-conscious?' This might be inadvisable unless you checked that the respondent shared your definition of eco-consciousness.
- Be leading, for example: 'I suppose you know what eco-consciousness is?' Some people might say no to the question in that form but the pressure is on them to say yes.
- Include double negatives, for example: 'Do you think now that not many people would not understand the term eco-consciousness?' Could you be sure what a 'no' response meant?
- Act as catch-alls, for example: 'Tell me everything you know about the Green movement and how it has influenced you?' After the silence, it is unlikely you will get anything useful without a series of further prompt questions.

Avoiding these traps in formulating the questions may seem relatively easy. However, a surprising number of experienced researchers fall into them. There is a further set of problems which also need to be tackled. An interview schedule needs to be looked at in its entirety. Getting the individual questions right is vital but they also have to be ordered appropriately. A good interview schedule has a rhythm to it which takes the respondent through what appears to be a set of issues which are sensibly related. Interviews cannot jump, without explanation, from one topic to another. Even if it is not the real rationale for the research, the respondent has to be given some notion of why the questions are being asked and must feel that the sequence of questions makes sense. If the schedule fails to do this, respondents can become confused, suspicious and sometimes belligerent. Jumps between topics can be covered by short but apparently reasonable explanations. For instance, often at the end of an interview it is necessary to get data which will allow socio-economic status to be calculated, and respondents sometimes fail to see why this is relevant to the views they have just been offering you. The switch to questions about their occupational status or educational qualifications can be made if you use a link explanation such as: 'As a matter of routine we collect information on what jobs our interviewees do, I hope you do not mind me asking you . . . .' If the respondent then queries the relevance of the questions, it can be helpful just to add: 'Occasionally, we find differences between the views of people who have different jobs.' The key thing in constructing link explanations is that they should not suggest what you expect people to say in answer to the next set of questions.

When designing the interview, you should also include clear guidelines to the interviewer on how to conclude the interview. Some debriefing may be needed. If a cover story has been employed, this may need to be explained. Often respondents want the interviewer to tell them immediately what their answers reveal about them. The interviewer has to be ready with a response which is non-committal and not likely to cause offence. It is best to anticipate this request for immediate analysis by stating at the end that you cannot say anything about individuals or that the findings will take a long time to produce. Whatever strategy you choose to adopt at the end of the interview, it is good practice to be consistent across respondents.

Since there are so many problems in getting the individual questions, the order in which they are asked and the links between them absolutely right, interview schedules need to be piloted. In the same way that you would pilot a questionnaire (see Chapter 12), an interview schedule must be tested and refined. There is no required routine for piloting an interview schedule. The following stages are, however, frequently used.

Stage 1   Test whether your explanation for the interview is understood by a small sample drawn from the same population as people you intend to interview. Normally, understanding in this context is ascertained by having this pilot sample explain the interview back to you in their own words. They can also be asked to tell you about any doubts or queries they might have about the interview. Getting the explanation for the interview right is fundamentally important. Not only will it influence the data you get from the people you manage to interview, it is very likely to have a big impact upon whether people are willing to be interviewed at all. The most successful explanations are those which emphasise the significance of the research, the significance of the particular individual's participation in it, the confidentiality of all data, and the possibility of withdrawing from the interview if at any point the person wishes to do so. At the pilot stage, you may wish to try alternative types of explanation in order to test if they will influence response rates.

Stage 2   Use the same pilot sample to test comprehension of particular questions which you know have not been used with this population before or which you feel are difficult (e.g. possibly ambiguous, lacking relevance, advanced vocabulary, etc.).

Stage 3   Amend introduction and questions in the light of stages 1 and 2. Surprisingly, researchers often go through the motions of piloting and then ignore what they find. This is a form of intellectual arrogance and research hypocrisy. There is no point in doing the pilot work if you do not respond to the information it gives you and then check by further piloting that your changes were the right ones.

Stage 4   With a new subsample, test the revised explanation and all questions for comprehension. This should be a complete run through of the entire interview schedule. It is still possible to make changes at this point. It is better to fine-tune the questions in the course of the pilot work at this stage than to get into a never-ending cycle of resampling in order to test out small refinements of the schedule.

Stage 5 With a new subsample, use the interview schedule to establish whether the answers which you are getting are the ones which interest you. This stage moves away from testing comprehension to being genuine data collection. Nevertheless, even if the schedule is working as you wished, the data from this stage should not be collapsed with data later collected from the main sample since this would change the sample structure (obviously, this warning matters only if your sample structure is important to you). Assuming that the schedule is performing as you expected, it is possible at this point to proceed to the main study.

Properly conducted pilot work pays off: it minimises the chances of finding midway through the study that a vital issue has been ignored or that certain components of the sample cannot understand batches of questions. Of course, to be maximally useful, the pilot work must be conducted on a subsample which is thoroughly representative of the sample you will ultimately use. Rigour in choosing the subsample for pilot work is important and often missing. It should be noted that piloting is just as important for unstructured interviews as it is for structured interviews. The unstructured interview, despite not having a fixed list of questions in a fixed order, must be informed by a thorough appreciation of which routes of questioning are likely to be productive, what sorts of questions make sense, and so on. It is impossible for the researcher to achieve that understanding without preliminary pilot work (or its equivalent). In the absence of good piloting, unstructured interviews can all too easily lose sight of the main research issue they were addressing.

There are traps lurking for you when you formulate questions but there are also traps waiting for you when you ask them. In order to avoid them, there are a few golden rules which should be followed. First, be thoroughly familiar with the interview schedule before you start. Second, ask all questions of all respondents, even if you think you know what some of them will say. Give all respondents an equal hearing. Third, know what each question is meant to tap and, if you are failing to get relevant material, probe further. Probes (e.g. non-committal encouragements to extend answers using eye contact, glance, repetition of the answer, gentle queries like 'I'm confused here') should be non-directive. Prompts (which suggest possible answers to the interviewee) should be used only if they are deployed consistently to all. In pursuing a point it is important not to seek or give unrelated or irrelevant information. It is essential to avoid offering advice or counselling as part of a research interview unless this has been explicitly agreed in advance. If the interviewee does become upset or aroused the researcher should ensure that this is acknowledged and should not leave until the interviewee is calmed. The researcher handling sensitive subject matter should be sure to have information ready which will tell the interviewee where advice can be found. Fourth, whatever technique you use, be consistent in recording answers. Fifth, an answer in a face-to-face interview has both verbal and non-verbal components. It is sometimes useful to encode non-verbal aspects of the answers even when visual recording is not used. They can change the underlying message substantially.

Of course, interviews do not have to be face-to-face. Increasingly researchers are using telephone interviewing. Telephone interviewing seems to yield similar data to face-to-face interviews. Telephone interviewing is cheaper and faster than other methods. Computer-assisted telephone interviewing (CATI) can be used. This involves the interviewer being linked to a computer which cues the questions to be asked and allows answers to be inputted directly. There is no evidence that the vocal characteristics of the interviewer influence refusal rates, but more experienced interviewers do have better success rates. Since interviewers can be all located in one place using a bank of telephones, it is easier to monitor their performance and to assess problems with the interview schedule.

The telephone interview does have its drawbacks. It is difficult to predetermine who in a household will answer your call. Women are more likely to pick up the phone at most times of the day and this results in telephone interview samples containing more women unless steps are taken to ensure gender equality in the sample. 'Cold calling' for interviews (i.e. without any prior warning or agreement) is likely to mean that the interviewee is pulled away from some other activity to answer your questions. When this happens, it is difficult to ascertain whether the context (for instance, what they were doing immediately previously) is important in determining their responses. People are unwilling to talk on the telephone for very long periods. A maximum of 15 minutes has been suggested for the standard interview. Anything longer needs to be timetabled in advance. Answers to open-ended questions also seem to be truncated on the telephone. People are faster in their responses and silences seem to be avoided. Complex questions (or those with a large number of response options) prove more difficult to understand on the telephone and this means that question structuring needs to be tailored for the telephone administration specifically. Response rates are lower (on average 7–10% lower than face-to-face approaches) and are worse on evening and weekend calls (perhaps because people who are at home are busier at these times). Now that the vast majority of households in industrial societies have telephones, one of the problems that used to militate against the use of telephone interviewing, namely the exclusion of lower income households from the sampling frame, has been removed. On balance the scales weighing the pros and cons of telephone interviewing seem nowadays to be tipping increasingly in its favour – particularly for short, well-structured interview schedules. With the increasing availability of online electronic access (through the Internet) it might be expected that researchers will seek to move beyond telephone interviewing to Web interviewing. Indeed, the Web is already regularly used for surveys involving questionnaires.

It should be acknowledged that interview questions do not have to be addressed to one person at a time. It is possible to conduct group interviews. Chapter 22 addresses some of these issues with regard to focus groups and the peculiarities of group interviewing consequently will not be considered here.

17.3 INTERVIEWING DIFFICULT PEOPLE

There are some categories of people who are particularly difficult to interview effectively (some of the issues of dealing with special groups discussed in Chapter 9 are pertinent here). These include children and the very elderly. There are a number of hazards to watch out for, especially when dealing with children. Some of them clearly apply when dealing with other respondents who may feel themselves to be in a less knowledgable or powerful position relative to the researcher.

Young children are often unwilling to assert themselves or to contradict an adult. They will, therefore, answer questions in a way they think you want them answered. Of course, teenagers may relish contradicting adults, which results in a totally opposite bias in information derived from interviews. Either way, it is important to guard against giving them clues about what you expect them to say. They have to be encouraged to disclose their own opinion. This can be achieved by reassuring them that you are really only interested in what they think and that there are no right or wrong answers. Any approach which looks like a test should be avoided since this will either silence them or release a store of responses which they think adults would like to hear. There is a strong **acquiescence response bias** in children: children tend to say 'yes', irrespective of the question or what they think about it. Questions should be posed so that they are not open to a yes–no response. For instance, 'Did you want to do that?' would become 'How did you feel about doing that?'

Besides the acquiescence bias which is most marked when they are eager to please, children exhibit a preference for 'don't know' responses. Children say 'don't know' for a variety of reasons: they aren't interested in answering; they don't understand the question either conceptually or in its vocabulary; they think you expect them not to know; they do not wish to admit what they know; they are too shy to say more; they don't know how to explain what they know; and, they really do not know. Consequently, 'don't know' is a response which need cautious treatment. It is sensible never to base a conclusion on 'don't knows', especially the conclusion that children 'don't know'.

Children, like elderly people, are relatively easily distracted. They pay attention to unpredictable aspects of the interview situation or the questions. They can become fascinated by your pen, the lorry loading outside the window or an itch in their nose. Besides being disconcerting to the interviewer, this can result in time-wasting and irrelevant information. To retain their attention, an interview must be full of different topics and changes of pace, with verbal questions giving way to visual materials (e.g. cartoons or objects) and responses perhaps being in the form of some physical activity (e.g. the child illustrates what she did in the situation you are talking about or draws a picture which depicts her feelings). A quiet location, not overlooked, and free of strong emotional connotations (e.g. not the headteacher's office where the child was recently severely reprimanded), can improve concentration. However, it would be foolishly optimistic to expect to get more than 15 minutes worth of good answers from young children even in optimal conditions. Therefore, it is important to keep the interview short.

Young children, like any novice to a linguistic community, tend to interpret questions literally. Metaphors, similes and analogies should all be excluded from questioning. Any phrasing of the question which relies upon an underlying set of assumptions about cultural or social mores must be carefully checked so as to ensure that children of the age group actually understand these assumptions. Essentially, any question such as 'When do you think your sister has been as good as gold?' tell you as much about what the child knows of the aphorism as what she thinks about her sister's activity.

Children have quite different priorities from those of adults. They may not understand that the implicit rule of the interview is that one person asks questions and the other person answers. They may wish to ask as well as answer questions. Particularly, they are likely to be curious about you, whether you are new, why you are there, all sorts of personal details. Responding to these questions briefly, without showing any exasperation, is the best tactic. For children who gets into the infinite regress of 'Why?' questions, the best strategy is to distract them with a new topic.

Very often children explain what other people do in terms of their own feelings or characteristics. They find it difficult to see the world through another person's eyes (what is called taking the role of the other). This is one aspect of childhood egocentricity (something which returns in another form in some very elderly people). It means that it is important that you check when accepting an answer that the child is actually focusing upon the right subject. For instance, you might ask a child 'Why did your mother shout at you last night?' The child might say 'She was sad.' It would be necessary to check whether the sadness mentioned referred to the feelings of the mother or the feelings that the child experienced.

Children, and other categories of people who have some vocabulary deficits, may hesitate in answering questions. The pauses which ensue introduce a pressure upon the researcher to jump in to offer suitable words. In essence, this means that the researcher answers for the respondent. This is a temptation which must be resisted.

Some groups of people, and children and the elderly are amongst these, are often interviewed in an institutional setting (for instance, the school or hospital). This entails taking them away from the normal activities of the institution, interviewing them, and then returning them. Once back, they are liable to talk about the interview with other inmates who will subsequently be interviewed. This introduces the possibility of a feedback loop with early interviewees acting as informants for later interviewees. There is a very real prospect of the gossip about the interview resulting in rumour and in a distorted expectation of what the interview entails. The later interviewees may develop a distorted picture of what you are doing. This needs to be controlled. You can ask later interviewees what they have heard and what they expect and then clarify any misconceptions.

It can be especially difficult to keep accurate records of what an interviewee is saying if you are reliant upon note-taking when the responses are perhaps self-contradictory and the interviewee requires coaxing. The note-taking is also disruptive since a child interviewee may lose interest in the moments it takes you to get your notes in order. It is best to have someone else record the interaction or, if possible, use audiotaping.

The chief hazards in interviewing children, amongst other difficult types of people, can be summarised: the tendency to say 'yes'; the tendency to say 'don't know'; susceptibility to distraction; literal-mindedness; different priorities; egocentricity; the urge to prompt; feedback loops; and recording problems.

17.4 VALIDITY AND RELIABILITY OF INTERVIEW DATA

There is no evidence to suggest that in any generic manner interviews as a data elicitation technique yield data which are less valid or reliable than other methods. There are artefacts intrinsic to the interview method which affect the validity and reliability of the data it produces but these tend to be common to many methods.

Like any self-report method, the interview approach relies upon respondents being able and willing to give accurate and complete answers to questions posed no matter what their format. Yet respondents may be motivated to lie. They may dislike or distrust the researcher. They may wish to sabotage the research. They may be too embarrassed to tell the truth. Even if they wish to co-operate, they may be unable to answer accurately because they cannot remember the details requested or because they do not understand the question.

You can overcome some of these difficulties by constructing a systematic set of questions which, at the same time as helping the respondent to remember or to understand, will provide evidence of consistency (or not) across responses. Having a pattern of questions which allows for internal consistency checking offers you one way of assessing the validity of the data. If a respondent is inconsistent in the pattern of answers, you may wish to extend the questioning to achieve clarification or you may choose to exclude those data from the analysis. Of course, consistency of response does not guarantee accuracy but inconsistency certainly entails some inaccuracy. The other way to establish the validity of interview data is by complementing it with other types of data. You might use observation, diary techniques, or experimental procedures in addition to the interview. Collecting such ancillary data may not be necessary for the entire sample. To assure you that the interview is effective it may be sufficient to take additional evidence from only a subsample of respondents.

There is a common belief in the research community that the validity of data collected in interviews improves if you can talk to the person repeatedly. It is thought that interviewing someone on several occasions increases their openness and honesty. Of course, since only people who have a positive attitude towards the research are likely to agree to be interviewed repeatedly it is possible that the apparent power of repeated interviewing to induce frankness is an artefact of the sample bias which develops in any panel study because of differential dropout.

Like any method where the researcher is an overt participant in the data collection process, interviewing involves **researcher effects** (elsewhere labelled experimenter effects). In an interview the characteristics of the researcher (e.g. demeanour, accent, dress, gender, age, and so on) will influence the respondents' willingness to participate and to answer accurately. Various effects have been catalogued: people engage in more self-disclosure to an interviewer who they think is similar to themselves; people of both sexes and of all ages are more likely to be willing to talk to a middle aged woman rather than a man, irrespective of his age, about sexual matters; people are more likely to comply with requests for information from someone who speaks with a received pronunciation accent than a regional accent; and so on. It is evident from the research which has focused on interviewer effects that the characteristics of the interviewer interact with the subject matter of the interview to determine how the interviewee will respond. An interviewer characteristic which is not salient in one interview will become important in another. For instance, the fact that the interviewer and interviewee are of different religious backgrounds may be unimportant when the topic of the interview concerns responses to traffic noise, but the religious differences may encroach if the topic is responses to the conflict in a province torn apart by religious rivalry.

Such **interviewer effects** cannot be eliminated but steps can be taken to control for them. One way to do this entails having the same interviewer conduct all interviews. This serves to hold the stimulus provided by the interviewer constant. This will not wipe out the possibility that the same interviewer has different effects across interviewees as a result of some complex interaction between their characteristics and those of the interviewer. In any case, using a single interviewer may be impractical in any large scale study. Another way to tackle the problem is to use many interviewers and randomly allocate them to respondents. This way allows you to eradicate any strong effects of any one interviewer. It also allows you to analyse the extent of interviewer differences. The interview data collected by each interviewer are compared with those collected by others. Any systematic differences can be identified and attributed to some characteristic of the interviewer, and, if sensible, some weighting procedure can be used to moderate the data. Sometimes, interviewer effects are countered in a different way which uses matching procedures. For instance, if interviewer gender is thought to be the biggest potential bias, the research director might use a pool of interviewers who were all female or all male. Alternatively, in such a situation, interviewer gender might be matched to interviewee gender. The matching approach can only be used if you know which interviewer characteristics are likely to have a significant effect upon the interviewees.

Interviewer effects do not simply occur because the respondent reacts to some attribute of the interviewer. It is also possible that they occur because the interviewer reacts to some characteristic of the respondent and this influences how questions are asked or how responses are recorded. Since the interviewer may be completely unaware that this is happening, controlling it is notoriously difficult. Clearly, following the guidelines described above which emphasise consistency in question presentation will reduce the problem, but in unstructured interviews the effect can be considerable. In large samples, with large numbers of interviewers and assuming the bias is randomly distributed relative to the research question, the effect could become important statistically. It is where the bias introduced by the interviewer is pertinent to the research issue or where the interviewer conducts large parts of the study that the problem is significant. Good initial training of the interviewers will serve to heighten their awareness of their own prejudices, etc. that are relevant to the research topic. This may reduce the likelihood that they will be completely oblivious to biases which they are introducing. Therefore, it makes sense, when using a team of interviewers, to include a procedure for debriefing the interviewers. This would include a component which allowed them to express any doubts which they had about their conduct of particular interviews in a systematic manner (perhaps as a written comment required after each interview). Where any doubt was expressed by the interviewer, that interview or set of interviews could be compared with data from interviews with other similar individuals in the sample to explore if there were apparent inconsistencies. This process might result in some interviews being excluded from subsequent analysis.

The best way to exclude interviewer bias from the recording of responses is to use some mechanical method for recording them. Audiotaping is cheap and easy. Videotaping captures the fuller range of information (e.g. non-verbal communication). Either way, the record is permanent and open to verification by other researchers. There is no good evidence to show that audiotaping constrains what respondents are willing to say. Even video recording has now lost its power to intrude as many people have access to the technology.

17.5 ANALYSING INTERVIEW DATA

People using interviews as a research tool often find that they collect an enormous amount of information and then do not know how to interpret it. The problem is obviously less acute if you use fully structured interview schedules, since then the response variety is constrained. In a structured interview the data are usually already framed ready for analysis. With unstructured or semi-structured interviews, there are some guidelines which could focus your activity.

First, allow your research questions to act as a prism through which you view the data collected. Content analysis (described in Chapter 19) can be used to reduce the data to manageable proportions. Content analysis can be supplemented with systematic quotations from the interviews to illustrate conclusions. There will be problems in deciding what categories to use in the content analysis. You are trying to generate slices of meaningful information and knowing where to cut into the flow of information is tricky. It may be necessary to try out several cutting positions before you find one which reveals interesting results. Also, remember that some of the best researchers rely on spotting what is omitted from what the respondent says in order to draw conclusions. It is sensible to stand back occasionally from the attempt to impose order (which is essentially what a content analysis does) and search for the disorderly elements, the discord which shows important differences. Look for themes which you expected to find but which are surprisingly absent. This may guide you to a new perspective. Sometimes people fail to say what they treat as common knowledge or very obvious. Many of the most central understandings in a community are unspoken because they are taken for granted. If you are driven by a simplistic approach to your content analysis you will misinterpret these apparent absences.

Second, your analysis should be open to verification as far as possible. You should provide a description of the data on which you base your conclusions which is good enough for someone else to repeat what you have done and check your conclusions. You may wish to include estimates of **inter-rater reliability** (Chapter 13) to establish that your interpretations of the data are not idiosyncratic. In the interests of verification, you should always keep raw data for a significant period after you publish or report on it.

Where interviews are recorded (audio or video) it is possible to transcribe the tapes and use these transcriptions as the basis for analysis. Usually, it is easier to content analyse from the transcripts since moving backwards and forwards in the text is easier than doing so on the tapes. The transcripts can include systematic records of the non-verbal communication involved (a system of notation is available). Transcription is sadly a slow and expensive business and it may be necessary to be selective about which elements of the interviews you choose to get transcribed fully (7 hours for 1 hour of speech). Selection can be driven by theoretical concerns. Initial selections can always be revised later. The tapes are available as the complete and permanent record; they can always be re-examined.

'Authenticate interpretations' is a dictum which has helped many researchers. Taking the conclusions back to the interviewees (or some subset of them) to check whether they make sense has become a popular pastime. There are, of course, difficulties in knowing what to do when the interviewees do not agree with your conclusions. Who is right and at what level becomes an interesting issue.

Following these guidelines will help you to produce a relevant and focused analysis of the interview material. If there is a single thing to remember when using interviewing, it is that it is a data elicitation technique which can deliver the broadest possible variety of data types. The analysis you choose must match the measurement level of the data and be sensitive to your sample structure but there is usually more than one way to examine the data. Try multiple techniques in the analysis. See whether they lead you to the same conclusions. Stop the analysis only when you are satisfied that you understand the data fully.

17.6 FURTHER READING

Arksey and Knight's (1999) *Interviewing for Social Scientists*, Breakwell's (1990) *Interviewing* and Kvale's (1996) *Interviews* are all worth looking at for more thorough overviews of interviewing techniques.

18

Discourse Analysis

Adrian Coyle

Contents

18.1 INTRODUCTION

Discourse analysis is a field of inquiry that traces its roots to various domains such as speech act theory, ethnomethodology, conversation analysis and semiology. It owes a particular debt to post-structuralism which holds as a central tenet that meaning is not static and fixed but is fluid, provisional and context dependent. However, discourse analysis does not fit easily within any particular disciplinary boundaries. Indeed, it does not even fit within a unitary framework, as the term 'discourse analysis' has been applied to diverse analytic approaches that are often based upon different assumptions and have different aims. This makes it difficult to provide an account of the commonalities of discourse analysis except in the broadest terms and any representation of the field will inevitably satisfy some and irritate others.

The popularisation of discourse analysis within social psychology can be dated to the publication in 1987 of Potter and Wetherell's classic text *Discourse and Social Psychology: Beyond Attitudes and Behaviour*. This work urged a radical reformulation of the issues that social psychology has traditionally addressed. Social psychologists have long worked with linguistic and textual material in the form of spoken responses within interview settings and written responses to questionnaire items. The question then arises as to what status should be accorded to this material. It is generally assumed that language is a neutral, transparent medium, describing events or revealing underlying psychological processes in a more or less direct, unproblematic way. The possibility of self-presentational and other biases occurring within this material may be acknowledged but it is assumed that these can be eradicated or at least minimised by refining methods of generating and collecting data.

18.2 DISCOURSE ANALYSIS: ASSUMPTIONS, APPROACHES AND APPLICATIONS

Within a discursive approach to psychology, language is represented not as reflecting psychological and social reality but as *constructing* it. There are no objective truths existing 'out there' that can be accessed if only the appropriate scientific methods are employed. Instead, language in the form of **discourses** constitutes the building blocks of 'social reality' (note that it is common practice to use inverted commas to draw attention to the constructed nature of taken-for-granted 'things'). The analysis of discourse emphasises how social reality is linguistically constructed and aims to gain 'a better understanding of social life and social interaction from our study of social texts' (Potter and Wetherell, 1987: 7).

Discourse analysis can therefore be classed as a **social constructionist** approach to research. The social constructionist perspective adopts a critical stance towards the taken-for-granted ways in which we understand the world and ourselves, such as the assumption that the categories we use to interpret the world correspond to 'real', 'objective' entities (Burr, 1995). These ways of understanding are seen as having been built up through social processes, especially through linguistic interactions, and so are culturally and historically specific. For example, the categories 'gay man', 'lesbian' and 'homosexual' are now a taken-for-granted part of how we talk about sexualities. It is easy to forget that defining people in terms of their preference for sexual partners of the same gender as themselves only began in the eighteenth century. Prior to this, there were terms that referred to sexual *activity* involving people of the same gender but these terms did not denote a particular kind of *person*. Furthermore, the ways in which these behaviours were socially organised, regulated and responded to varied across cultures. The term 'homosexual' was not coined until the mid nineteenth century with the increasing medicalisation of sexuality. Terms such as 'gay man' and 'lesbian' were adopted only in the 1960s and 1970s in line with the political concerns of the gay liberation and women's movements (for detailed analyses of the social construction of 'the homosexual' see Plummer, 1981). And with the post-modern trend within lesbian and gay studies, concepts of 'the gay man' and 'the lesbian' are now being called into question (Simpson, 1996). So, from this one example, it can be seen that there is nothing fixed or inevitable about what may appear to be common-sense ways of representing the world: they are socially constructed.

The emphasis on language as a constructive tool is one of the core assumptions of discourse analysis and it is what makes discourse analysis more than just another method of analysing qualitative data. The approach cannot be separated from its **epistemology**, i.e. its core assumptions about the bases or possibilities for knowledge. The language user is viewed as selecting from the range of linguistic resources available to them and using these resources to construct a version of events, although not necessarily in an intentional way. The person may not be able to articulate the constructive process in which they are engaged but this does not mean that it does not exist. It simply highlights the extent to which the constructive use of language is a fundamental, taken-for-granted aspect of social life.

Discourse analysis does not use people's language as a means of gaining access to their psychological and social worlds. As Burman and Parker have contended, 'Psychological phenomena have a public and collective reality, and we are mistaken if we think they have their origin in the private space of the individual' (1993a: 1). Instead, discourse analysis focuses on this 'public and collective reality' as constructed through language use. It examines how people use language to construct versions of their worlds and what they gain from these constructions. With such an explicitly social focus, a discursive approach helps to counteract the cognitive reductionism that characterises much of what passes for social psychology and offers the possibility of a truly *social* psychology.

It can be difficult to specify exactly what discourses are because, although they are generally represented as broad patterns of language use within spoken or written material, a variety of meanings have been ascribed to the term 'discourse'. It may be useful to consider various definitions of 'discourse' and of related concepts in order to divine some basic commonalities. Parker (1992: 5) has emphasised the constructive potential of discourses and defined a discourse as 'a system of statements which constructs an object'. Potter and Wetherell (1987) prefer the term 'interpretative repertoires' rather than 'discourses' because the idea of 'repertoire' implies flexibility in the ways in which the linguistic components of the repertoire can be put together. They regard these interpretative repertoires as linguistic phenomena which have a certain coherence in terms of their content and style and which may be organised around one or more central metaphors. In a similar vein, Burr has defined a discourse as 'a systematic, coherent set of images, metaphors and so on that construct an object in a particular way' (1995: 184). This definitional survey is hardly exhaustive but, amalgamating these and other related ideas, discourses can be defined as sets of linguistic material that have a degree of coherence in their content and organisation and which perform constructive functions in broadly defined social contexts. Different discourses can be invoked to construct any object, person, event or situation in a variety of ways.

Discourses are identified through the examination of **texts**. All spoken and written material (and indeed the products of every other sort of signifying practice too) can be conceptualised as a text and subjected to discourse analysis, in the same way that within traditional scientific paradigms, almost anything can be construed as data and analysed. This means that discourse analysis can be applied in a wide range of research settings.

Discourse analysis assumes that all linguistic material has an **action orientation**, i.e. language is used to perform particular social functions such as justifying, questioning and accusing, and it achieves this through a variety of rhetorical strategies. Key tasks that discourse analysts set themselves are to identify what functions are being performed by the linguistic material that is being analysed and to consider how these functions are performed. This entails a close and careful inspection of the text. In this process, some discourse analysts are concerned with the fine grain of talk. These writers tend to adopt and adapt the approaches of conversation analysis in their work (see Atkinson and Heritage, 1984), recursively moving between a micro-level focus on textual detail and a global consideration of the rhetorical functions to which the text is oriented. Generally, though, discourse analysis is more concerned with the social organisation of talk than with its linguistic organisation. This approach involves looking at what discourses are shared across texts and what constructions of the world the material can be seen as advocating, rather than focusing on the details of how utterances relate to the conversational sequences to which they belong and the interactional work accomplished by these utterances and sequences.

Exploring this issue of different approaches further, and returning to a point made at the start of the chapter, it is worth noting that there are two main approaches to the study of discourse in the UK (Burr, 1995). The approach focused upon in this chapter addresses the social functions of talk and writing and considers how these functions are achieved through the construction of accounts. This approach characterises the work of writers such as Jonathan Potter, Margaret Wetherell, Derek Edwards and Michael Billig (for example, Billig, 1987; 1991; Edwards and Potter, 1992; Potter, 1996; Potter and Wetherell, 1987). Work conducted within this tradition often adopts an extreme social constructionist position and contends that there is nothing that is not text, i.e. that is not constructed through language.

This approach has been represented as politically limited by other practitioners who have grappled with the question of realism within discourse analysis (Parker, 1998) and who are more concerned with issues such as identity, selfhood, social change and power relations. This tradition informs the work of writers such as Ian Parker, Erica Burman and Wendy Hollway (for example, Burman, 1992; 1995; 1997; Burman and Parker, 1993b; Hollway, 1989; Parker, 1992). Some writers within this tradition, such as Hollway, have drawn upon particular versions of psychoanalytic theory to introduce into their analyses a notion of the person as motivated and as having agency, i.e. as acting upon their environment. The adoption of psychoanalytic theory for this purpose has been justified on the grounds that current Western cultural representations of the self draw heavily upon psychoanalytic principles (Parker, 1994). Furthermore, it could be argued that psychoanalytic theory and discourse analysis are compatible in that they both represent the person as nonunitary and the version of psychoanalytic theory used by these discourse analysts has a linguistic focus. Nevertheless, the incorporation of psychoanalytic concepts increases the risk of slipping back into the 'mentalist' discourse of traditional psychology, with its talk of individual drives and motivations. Even when adopting approaches which do not use psychoanalytic concepts, it is difficult to avoid such slippage because of the cultural pervasiveness of mentalist discourse. Also, given that psychoanalytic theory has been invoked in the pathologisation of women (Chodorow, 1989) and lesbians and gay men (see Bieber et al., 1962; Socarides, 1978), it is politically puzzling why it should be dusted off and put to use in discourse analysis, even though Parker (1997) has acknowledged its dubious history and oppressive applications and has pointed to radical versions of psychoanalytic theory.

To the newcomer, discourse analysis can seem far removed from 'real-life' concerns and nothing more than a form of intellectual navel-gazing. Yet, because 'Language (organised into *discourses*) . . . has an immense power to shape the way that people . . . experience and behave in the world' (Burman and Parker, 1993a: 1, original emphasis), discourse analysis does have considerable practical potential. For example, the title of Willig's (1999) edited volume *Applied Discourse Analysis: Social and Psychological Interventions* makes this point explicitly and the contributors apply discourse analysis to diverse practical topics such as the investigation of crime, human reproductive technologies and psychiatric medication. Within clinical psychology, Harper (1995) has identified the ways in which discourse analysis can contribute to the mental health field: for a critical discursive analysis of the modern 'crisis' in male mental health, see Coyle and Morgan-Sykes (1998), and for a discourse analysis of material from psychotherapy sessions, see Heenan (1996) and Madill and Barkham (1997). Within health psychology, Middleton (1996) has used discourse analysis to examine how common experiences are constructed through talk in a support group for parents caring for children with chronic renal failure. However, the possibility of a turn to discourse within that field has met with resistance on the grounds that it has been said to mark 'a retreat from practical concerns' and to threaten 'the applied aspirations of health psychologists to influence practices and policies outside research psychology' (Abraham and Hampson, 1996: 226). This raises the question of the extent to which discourse analysis can act as a force for change.

With its focus on the socially constructed nature of reality, discourse analysis can point to the constructed nature and the implications of problematic and oppressive discourses and can indicate that alternative discourses could be constructed in their place. Given this potential, it is not surprising that discourse analysis has been taken up with enthusiasm by those who wish to give psychology a radical, political edge. Some analysts choose to focus on discourses which reproduce social relations of dominance and oppression: see, for example, Wetherell and Potter's (1992) extensive study of racist language and practice in New Zealand. Indeed, some researchers have subjected aspects of psychology itself to discourse analysis and have drawn attention to the political processes (defined in a broad sense) operating in this domain. For example, Harper (1994a) interviewed mental health professionals about diagnosing 'paranoia' and pointed out that, within the same interviews, sometimes appeals were made to 'objective' criteria for diagnosis and at other times the social and personal influences on diagnosis were acknowledged. Similar analytic work has been conducted by Parker et al. (1995) on the practices of 'psychopathology' generally. This body of analysis suggests that diagnostic categories of psychopathology are problematic and need to be interpreted in the light of the socio-political context in which they have been produced and are maintained: they cannot be naïvely represented as 'objective'. The discursive examination of such categories shifts the emphasis away from using them as an explanatory resource (e.g. 'he is doing that because he is suffering from paranoia') and towards exploring them in their own right (e.g. 'what interests are served by the concept of "paranoia" in this context?') (Harper, 1995). Given such an agenda, it is easy to see why McLaughlin (1996), also working in the area of 'psychopathology', has described his research approach as 'emancipatory discourse analysis'.

However, there is some debate as to whether discourse analysis is *inherently* political (see Burman, 1990; Gill, 1995). Indeed, Burr's (1995) assessment of the field points to inadequacies in the discursive analysis of how social change may be brought about. The supplanting of oppressive discourses is a complex and lengthy process and there is no way of predicting with confidence what the social implications of discursive change might be.

18.3 SAMPLING DISCOURSE

In this and subsequent sections the practicalities of conducting discourse analysis are explored, taking as an example a study conducted by the author which examined an attempt to construct an alternative to the traditional condemnatory Christian discourse on homosexuality in a workshop for members of a predominantly lesbian and gay church. In order to conduct an analysis of discourse, texts are required in which discourses may be discerned. These texts may take many forms. For example, the analyst may use recordings of interactions in natural settings, transcripts of interviews conducted on the research topic or excerpts from writing on the topic. In the study under consideration, the text was obtained through tape recording and transcribing workshop proceedings, having obtained the permission of the workshop facilitator and participants. Accurate transcription is a lengthy process which is made even more laborious if the transcriber wishes to include every 'um' and 'uh' uttered by the speakers and to measure pauses in speech production. This sort of detailed approach is less often seen in discourse analysis than in conversation analysis.

Within traditional approaches to sampling in psychological research, the emphasis is placed on securing as large and representative a sample as possible. Within discourse analysis, if interview material is used as a source of data, there is no necessity to sample discourse from a large number of people. If newspaper reports of a particular event are to be used, it is not necessary to collect all reports from all newspapers on that event. The analysis stage of qualitative data is almost always more laborious and time-consuming than the analysis of structured data so the researcher must beware of ending up with a mountain of unstructured data to sift through. What is important is to gather sufficient text to discern the variety of discursive forms that are commonly used when speaking or writing about the research topic. This may be possible from an analysis of relatively few interview transcripts or newspaper reports, especially where common discursive forms are under consideration. In this case, larger samples of data add to the analytic task without adding significantly to the analytic outcome. Where an analysis is purely exploratory and the analyst has little idea in advance of what the analytic focus might be, larger samples of data are required. Hence, in the study that will be considered here, the entire workshop proceedings were transcribed because the specific analytic focus had not been determined in advance.

18.4 TECHNIQUES OF DISCOURSE ANALYSIS

While it is relatively easy to expound the central theoretical tenets of discourse analysis, specifying exactly how one goes about doing discourse analysis is a different matter. On being asked how to do discourse analysis, a colleague once replied: 'discourse analysis is what you do when you say you're doing discourse analysis'. A perusal of the range of approaches adopted to discourse analysis suggests that there might be some truth in her jesting comment. There is no rigid set of formal procedures to guide discourse analysis. It has been contended that the key to analysing discourse is scholarship rather than adherence to a rigorous methodology (Billig, 1988). The emphasis is placed upon the careful reading and interpretation of texts, with interpretations being backed by reference to linguistic evidence in the texts. The first step is said to be the suspension of belief in what is normally taken for granted in language use (Potter and Wetherell, 1987). This involves seeing linguistic practices not as simply reflecting underlying psychological and social realities but as constructing and legitimating a version of events. The key to analysis is held to be the development of an 'analytic mentality' which takes the form of 'a repertoire of craft skills acquired through practical experience' (Wooffitt, 1993: 291).

As discourse analysis has a radically different epistemology from most other approaches to psychological research, it is not surprising that it also has a very different way of proceeding methodologically. At times, however, one cannot help feeling that a more systematic approach would be enormously beneficial to those entering the field for the first time. It is all very well to suggest that to conduct discourse analysis, one needs to develop 'a sensitivity to the way in which language is used', especially to the 'inferential and interactional aspects of talk' (Widdicombe, 1993: 97). However, it is unclear exactly how this sensitivity is developed and systematised. While understanding the desire of discourse analysts not to be tied to a rigid set of analytic procedures, Henwood and Pidgeon (1994) have suggested that greater specificity on method does not have to place discourse analysis in a methodological ghetto.

In an attempt to provide some pointers, Potter and Wetherell (1987) have suggested a loose 10-stage approach, with two stages devoted to the analytic process. This process begins with what is termed **coding**. By this is meant the process of examining the text closely. If the research focus has been specified in advance, instances of the research focus are identified at this point. It is worth being as inclusive as possible and noting what appear to be borderline instances of the research focus. This makes it possible to discern less obvious but nonetheless fruitful lines of inquiry. The coding process is more complex if the research focus has not been determined in advance. In this case, it is necessary to read and reread the text, looking for recurrent discursive patterns shared by the accounts under analysis. It is at this stage that Widdicombe's (1993) notion of sensitivity to the way in which language is used is important. Hypotheses about which discourses are being invoked in the text are formulated and reformulated. This can be a very frustrating stage as hypotheses are developed, revised or discarded as the linguistic evidence needed to support them proves not to be forthcoming. It is important that the analyst should remain open to alternative readings of the text and to the need to reject hypotheses that are not supported by the text.

A useful strategy for the next stage of analysis involves reading the text mindful of what its **functions** might be. Any text has an action orientation and is designed to fulfil certain functions, so the question is, what functions is this text fulfilling and how is it fulfilling them? The formulation of hypotheses about the purposes and consequences of language use is central to discourse analysis. However, identifying the functions of language is often not a straightforward process because these functions may not be explicit. For example, when someone asks you to do something, they may phrase it not as an order or command ('do the washing up') but as a question to which the expected answer is 'yes' ('would you like to do the washing up?').

In seeking to identify discursive functions, a useful starting point is the discursive context. It can be difficult to divine function from limited sections of a text. A variety of functions may be performed and revisited throughout a text so it is necessary to be familiar with what precedes and follows a particular extract in order to obtain clues about its functions. Furthermore, as Parker and Burman (1993) have noted, the analyst needs to be aware of broader contextual concerns such as cultural trends and political and social issues to which the text alludes. As they put it, 'If you do not know what a text is referring to, you cannot produce a reading' (1993: 158).

Another analytic strategy that may be helpful is to examine a text mindful of what version of events it may be designed to counteract. Any version of events is but one of a number of possible versions and therefore must be constructed as more persuasive than these alternative versions if it is to prevail. Sometimes alternative versions will be explicitly mentioned and counteracted in a text but on other occasions they will be implicit. If analysts are sensitised to what these alternative versions might be, they may be well placed to analyse how the text addresses the function of legitimating the version constructed therein.

In analysing function, it is useful to become acquainted with the ways in which various features of discourse are described in the discourse analytic and conversation analytic literatures. These discursive features are frequently employed to perform specific rhetorical functions. Therefore, if analysts are able to identify these features, they can examine the text mindful of the functions that these features typically perform. For example, the use of terms such as 'always', 'never', 'nobody' and 'everyone' may represent what have been called 'extreme case formulations' (Pomerantz, 1986). These take whatever position is being advocated in the text to its extreme and thereby help to make this position more persuasive. For those interested in becoming acquainted with these technical features of discourse, Potter (1996) has outlined a wide range, but the best strategy is to examine studies which have used discourse analytic and conversation analytic approaches.

According to Potter and Wetherell (1987), one means of elucidating the functions of discourse is through the study of variability in any discourse. The fact that discourse varies appears a common-sense statement. If we were analysing discourse from different people about a particular object, we would expect variations related to whether individuals evaluated the object positively or negatively. However, variation also occurs within an individual's discourse, dependent upon the purposes of the discourse. Indeed, this was a key feature of Harper's (1994a) study of mental health professionals' talk about diagnosing 'paranoia', which we considered earlier. It has been claimed that, in their search for individual consistency, mainstream approaches to psychology have sought to minimise or explain away intra-individual variation (Potter and Wetherell, 1987). Discourse analysis, in contrast, actively seeks it out. As variability arises from the different functions that the discourse may be fulfilling, the nature of the variation can provide clues to what these functions are. The process of discourse analysis therefore involves the search for both consistency (in the identification of discourses) and variability (in the analysis of discursive functions).

A final feature that can often be discerned in texts is **positioning**. This concept comes not from the Potter and Wetherell tradition of discourse analysis but from Davies and Harré (1990) and represents a discursive interpretation of the social psychological concept of identity. When an individual is constructed through discourses, they are accorded a particular subject position within that discourse, which brings with it a set of images, metaphors and obligations concerning the kind of response that can be made. In their linguistic response to that positioning, the individual can accept it (and fulfil the obligations of their position) or they can resist it. Of course, the person can also position themselves within a discourse and their audience can accept or reject this positioning. Any individual may assume some positions consistently within their talk while other positions are more temporary, giving rise to variability. Identity is thus understood as 'the totality of subject positions, some permanent, some temporary and some fleeting, that we take up in discourse' (Burr, 1995: 146).

18.5 WORKING WITH DATA

To examine these principles and techniques in practice, a broad preliminary analysis will be presented of some aspects of the proceedings of a workshop which attempted to challenge the traditional Christian discourse on homosexuality. This discourse is grounded in interpretations of Biblical texts and centres around notions that same-sex sexual activity is sinful and unnatural. One denomination that has tried to counter and reinterpret it has been the Metropolitan Community Church (MCC). The majority of MCC's clergy and congregations in Europe and North America are lesbian or gay. This denomination has reinterpreted those Biblical passages that are customarily seen as referring to and condemning homosexual activity and, by extension, gay men and lesbians. The essence of the alternative discourse it offers is that the Bible contains no unequivocal prohibitions against same-sex sexual activity and that a belief in God, the authority of the Bible and homosexuality are entirely compatible. MCC has attempted to propagate its alternative discourse through its congregations and publications and by offering courses and workshops on its Biblical reinterpretations. The following analyses are based on a transcript of one such workshop conducted at MCC in East London by a senior figure in MCC's theological college in Europe, an American who will be referred to as 'David'.

Given that the workshop ran for an entire day, the transcript of the proceedings was very lengthy. This transcript was read and reread closely, looking for broad recurrent discursive patterns. One which was discerned was the establishment of legitimacy or warrant by the facilitator for his reinterpretation of the traditional discourse. As we have noted, the attempt to ensure that one's version of events prevails against competing versions is a common feature of accounts. This aspect of the proceedings was therefore selected as a potentially interesting analytic focus. The analysis that follows is not designed to be comprehensive but rather to demonstrate some basic aspects of the analytic process in simple terms. For examples of more complete, complex and polished analyses, the reader is referred to the journal *Discourse & Society* and to the discourse analytic research articles and chapters that have already been cited. Note that in the extracts of text that are cited in the following analysis, empty square brackets indicate where material has been omitted.

The principal strategies that David used during the workshop to establish warrant were positioning himself as an expert through expositions of his scholarship; positioning himself as a benign teacher or guide; tales of his personal experiences with the traditional discourse; and assurances of his honesty. These were juxtaposed and interwoven to create a powerful cumulative warranting effect.

At several points during the workshop, David emphasises his Biblical scholarship, particularly his skills in Biblical languages. For example, at different points he says:

> What I'm going to say to you has very sound academic structure, foundation. I don't intend to overwhelm you with the academics of it, which can be quite boring. I do have the academic background and the study in the original languages to support what I'm going to say.

> The Bible was written in ancient languages. The Old Testament is written in Hebrew with some Aramaic in the Book of Daniel and one of the other prophets. The New Testament is written in Greek, in koine Greek which was the common language of the people. Greek is a very complex language with balanced clauses and classic literary Greek is great fun to translate which is where I started my Greek studies. The New Testament Greek is sort of common street slang language sometimes and is great fun – the koine Greek.

The use of this strategy establishes credibility and validity specifically for the reinterpretations of Biblical passages that he will expound later and generally for any other pronouncements that he will make. If his views are regarded by his audience as informed opinions, underpinned by scholarship and expertise, they are more likely to prevail than if they are seen as uninformed speculation. However, a heavy emphasis on scholarship may risk alienating the audience if they are made to feel inadequate in comparison or if they assume that what will be said will be 'over their heads'. This possibility is counteracted by the way in which David constructs his learning. He reassures his audience that 'I don't intend to overwhelm you with the academics of it, which can be quite boring.' One could fill in the implied 'to the layperson' at the end of this utterance, which positions David as an expert, the possessor of privileged insight into the material he is about to address.

Within the second extract ('Greek is a very complex language . . . the koine Greek'), he also creates the impression that he wears his learning lightly and points to the enjoyment he derives from it. The juxtaposition of the account of the complexity of classic literary Greek (complete with the introduction of the quasi-technical term 'balanced clauses') and the description of it as 'great fun' further stresses David's scholarship. Note how the notions of complexity and fun are accompanied by terms of emphasis ('very complex'; 'great fun'). Their presence draws attention to the possibility that these notions are carrying out important work in this extract. Whatever the public perception of classic literary Greek might be, it is unlikely that fun features significantly. While it takes a high level of intellectual capacity to become proficient in as complex a language as Greek, one would imagine that an even more rarefied level of operation would be required to find it 'fun'. Note also how the range of David's learning is stressed here. He is skilled not only in 'classic literary Greek' but also in the 'common street slang language [ ] the koine Greek', which is again described as 'great fun'. Mark the judicious use of the technical term 'koine Greek'. David provides a description of what this means, so one could ask what function the use of the technical term serves. It adds nothing in terms of meaning and could easily have been omitted, so it may be seen as performing an explicitly rhetorical function. This is an example of an occasion when the analyst needs to be mindful of potential alternative versions of the text. It may be that the use of the term again stresses David's expertise by giving an example of the privileged knowledge to which he has access. So we can see that in these extracts, David positions himself as an expert and subsequently reinforces that positioning.

Although David bases his warrant largely on his scholarship, he appears to belittle this scholarship at one juncture. However, the way in which he elaborates his point means that he ends up emphasising his scholarly skills and further reinforcing his position as expert. He says:

> At that point there came in hand [ ] a book by an Anglican clergyman called *Homosexuality and the Western Christian Tradition* by Derek Sherwin Bailey. He wrote this as a part of the Wolfenden report and it was published as you see in 1955 and he was saying, only with all the basic academic apparatus that I didn't have and with all of the scholarly qualifications, the very same thing that I had discovered and I was quite bowled over by it.

This is a clear instance of variability in the account that David is providing of himself. We have seen how earlier he assiduously emphasised his scholarship, yet here he actively denies it. What clues does this variability provide to the function of this description? Although he underplays his 'academic apparatus' and 'scholarly qualifications', he claims that, independently, he reached the 'very same' conclusions (note the emphasising 'very') as Bailey. He exalts Bailey's standing by associating him with the Wolfenden report, on which was based the 1967 law reform decriminalising consensual private sexual activity between men aged over 21 years. This interpretation is founded on an understanding of the context which David is evoking, which underlines how important it is for the analyst to be familiar with the context in which the text under analysis is located. The rhetoric in the extract implies that, underlying whatever formal academic training David has, is an inspired mind that enabled him to reach the same conclusions as such an intellectually esteemed figure as Bailey. His humility at this discovery is conveyed by his reaction to it ('I was quite bowled over by it'). That this reaction is expressed in folksy terms again underlines his construction of himself as an ordinary person. He is thus simultaneously positioned in conflicting ways. The function these positionings serve is to reassure the audience that David possesses the formal scholarship and the creative thinking necessary for the expression of informed opinions, while downplaying any threat that this scholarship may present.

The theme of not overwhelming the audience with scholarship recurs at several points in the text. Having constructed himself as gatekeeper to a privileged realm of knowledge, David proceeds to represent himself as cutting a careful path through academic irrelevancies for the workshop participants. For example, while distributing handouts on principles of Biblical interpretation, he says:

> These are just some basic, a basic approach for example. It's very helpful to have access to the original languages either directly or through the work of others. There are very fine books where they are attempting to – to interpret the Greek and the Hebrew in a popular way without overwhelming you with technical things and to have access to that scholarship is very helpful if you can't do it yourself.

This extract constructs the audience as lacking knowledge of and scholarship in Greek and Hebrew and so they need to be directed to popularised texts that will not overwhelm them. Such a positioning is not without risk, as it may appear condescending to the audience who may subsequently resist it. This possibility is offset somewhat by the use of the phrase 'if you can't do it yourself'. Although the audience's lack of knowledge and competence is strongly implied, the use of this conditional phrase hedges the implication to some extent. The extract also implicitly positions David as a knowledgeable and benign teacher or guide, furnishing his audience with the tools necessary for reinterpreting the traditional discourse but not overwhelming them. The way in which a previous extract was constructed tallies with this interpretation of David as teacher:

> The Bible was written in ancient languages. The Old Testament is written in Hebrew with some Aramaic in the Book of Daniel and one of the other prophets. The New Testament is written in Greek, in koine Greek which was the common language of the people.

The extract is constructed in a didactic fashion. It begins with a straightforward statement of 'fact'. David then elaborates this statement in a more specific way, incorporating technical terms ('Old Testament', 'Hebrew', 'Aramaic', 'Book of Daniel') and introducing and explaining a more inaccessible term ('koine Greek').

As Gergen put it, 'one may justifiably make a claim to voice on the grounds of possessing privileged . . . experience' (1989: 74). David invokes this warranting strategy when he uses various powerful rhetorical devices to construct an emotive testimony of his personal involvement in the arguments that he will advance, saying:

> I have a very personal stake in this material. I came out of a church which taught me that God does not love gay and lesbian people, that God condemns us out of hand, and it was a very conservative church in the United States. I was married. I have three children. When my wife and I separated, the minister who succeeded me at that church used the scriptures to take my children away. I mean to take their minds away, convincing them that I was going to go to hell because I'm gay and I haven't seen two of my three children in twelve years and I have a very personal stake in what the Bible says.

The deeply personal emphasis within this extract acts as a counterbalance to any connotations of objectivity that the emphasis on scholarship may have created. This extract sees David's first explicit statement of his sexual identity which may be viewed as another convention of warrant. He establishes warrant for his deconstruction of the traditional Christian discourse on homosexuality and for the need to offer an alternative discourse because he, as a gay Christian, has suffered personally and grievously at the hands of those who wield the traditional discourse. Furthermore, David's disclosure of his sexual identity positions himself alongside his audience, most of whom had earlier presented themselves as gay or lesbian. This positioning is achieved through the statement 'I came out of a church which taught me that God does not love gay and lesbian people, that God condemns us out of hand'. The clause 'that God condemns us out of hand' restates and emphasises the point made in the clause 'that God does not love gay and lesbian people'. However, its more important function is that, in replacing 'gay and lesbian people' with 'us', David explicitly presents himself as gay and constructs a commonality of oppression between himself and his audience. The workshop participants are thereby incorporated into his personal testimony of having been oppressed by the traditional discourse, which imparts legitimacy to the need to rework it, not just for David's sake but for the sake of all present.

Powerful though the relating of personal experience may be as a warranting device, it may also have the opposite effect. As a gay Christian, David may be seen as having a vested interest in seeking to alter the traditional Christian discourse on homosexuality. This unspoken version of events is counteracted by a fourth strategy that he uses to establish warrant, namely his self-construction as 'honest David'. He employs this device at the beginning of the workshop and again when discussing a gospel text. At the outset, he says:

> Whatever your questions are, if I don't have an answer, I won't try to bluff you. I'll tell you I don't know, cos I'm not in the business of trying to sell you a bill of goods that I can't support.

Later, he examines two verses from Matthew's gospel and two from Isaiah which refer to eunuchs. He talks of how these passages have been unjustifiably used by gay apologists to assert that sexual outcasts in general and gay men and lesbians in particular will have their place in the Kingdom of Heaven. He claims that there is insufficient evidence to support such an assertion, saying:

> It's far more honest to say we're not really sure than to try to sell a bill of goods or try to read into it [ ] If we could make a case that based on the Isaiah prophecy that these people who were sexual outcasts would be gathered in and we could make that connection and jump to Matthew and then to us it would be wonderful [ ] but if we're really going to be honest, it's not there, and I don't I don't see an honest connection.

The strategy of taking material that appears to support his argument and rejecting it on the basis of its unjustified interpretation is a powerful warranting device. It suggests that he has not simply amassed material regardless of how tenuously it supports his argument. Rather, it suggests that he has applied his scholarship to Biblical material and has selected those passages that can justifiably be interpreted as indicating that same-sex sexual activity is not prohibited by the Bible. The Biblical interpretations that he will offer are thus warranted in advance. David is positioned as a rigorous and honest interpreter, thereby offsetting any accusation of bias in the interpretations that he will provide.

18.6 EVALUATING DISCOURSE ANALYTIC WORK

The discourse analyst is sometimes accused of 'putting words into the mouths' of those whose discourse is being analysed and of unnecessarily complicating apparently straightforward speech acts. Yet, post-structuralist writers, with their contention that meaning is not fixed or stable, have noted how language use may have consequences that the speaker did not intend. The speaker's rhetoric may invoke discourses and ideologies of which they may not even have been aware. For example, in their analysis of talk about community care policies, Potter and Collie (1989) have pointed out how the notion of 'community care' invokes a reassuring community discourse, centred around images of neighbourliness, close ties and social support. This poses problems for those who wish to criticise community care, as, in naming it, they end up invoking these positive associations and thereby undermining their arguments. For this reason, Potter (1996) has suggested that discourse analysis is and should remain agnostic on the issue of intention in language use. As individuals may not be aware that their language creates such effects, the method sometimes advocated for evaluating qualitative analyses which involves asking those who produced the data to comment on the analyses is inappropriate for discourse analysis. Those who produced the texts that have been analysed may complain 'we never meant that' but this does not invalidate the analysis. The analyst is engaged in elaborating the perhaps unintended consequences of the language that was used, tracing the ripples that discourses create in the pool of meaning into which they are tossed.

This does not mean that analysts are free to posit whatever interpretations they please. For discourse analysis to be taken seriously, there must exist criteria which allow the quality of an analysis to be evaluated. Discussions about the evaluation of psychological research generally focus on success in hypothesis testing and concerns about reliability and validity. For example, commenting on Harper's (1994a) identification of legitimation themes in interviews with mental health professionals about the diagnosis of 'paranoia', Walkup (1994) reported difficulty in imagining how the interviews could not have involved legitimation. In his reply, Harper (1994b) constructed this criticism as implicitly invoking a notion of hypothesis testing based on a traditional discourse of science. It is inappropriate to evaluate discourse ana- lytic work within such a framework because discourse analysis is located outside this tradition. Criteria such as reliability and validity are based on the assumption of scientific objectivity, which in turn assumes that researcher and researched are independent of each other. With discourse analysis, this cannot be the case. Analysts who demonstrate the contingent, socially constructed, rhetorical nature of the discourse of others cannot make an exception for their own discourse (Potter, 1988). Like the person whose talk or writing they are analysing, analysts construct a purposeful account of their texts, drawing upon their available and acknowledged linguistic resources and ideological frameworks in what has been called 'passionately interested inquiry' (Gill, 1995). In the analysis offered in this chapter, factors such as my training as a psychologist, my familiarity with existing work relevant to the research topic and my position as a gay man all influenced the ideological framework which I brought to bear on the analysis, what has been termed my 'speaking posi- tion' (Burman, 1994). Acknowledging this should not be seen as undermining the analysis because no one can adopt a perspectiveless, utterly 'objective' stance on the world. Instead, it should be seen as part of a process of making research more accountable, more transparent and easier to evaluate.

This reflexivity bridges the chasm that more traditional research approaches create between researcher and researched and makes it impossible to assess an analysis of discourse using traditional evaluative criteria. Potter and Wetherell (1987) suggest four alternative criteria. The most convincing are that an analysis should impart coherence to a text – showing how the discourse fits together in its content, functions and effects – and should be fruitful, i.e. should provide insights that may prove useful in the analysis of other discourses.

This evaluative aspect of discourse analysis and indeed of qualitative research in general requires further development and greater specificity (but see Elliott et al., 1999). However, the method of reporting discourse analytic studies potentially provides a useful means of evaluating them. Alongside interpretations, the analyst should try to present as much of the relevant text as possible, demonstrating how analytic conclusions were reached with reference to the text. Readers can then judge for themselves whether the interpretations are warranted. They can offer alternative readings of the text so that, through debate, coherent and persuasive interpretations can be achieved. The only problem with this is that the submission guidelines of most academic psychology journals make it difficult to present large amounts of raw data in research reports (although researchers may now be able to make interview transcripts available on the Internet). At present, relatively few journals cater exclusively or primarily for discourse analytic work, the notable exceptions being *Discourse & Society* and *Discourse Studies*. As the acceptability (or at least the tolerance) of discourse analysis increases within psychology, it is to be hoped that journals adopt a more open attitude to discourse analytic research and that it becomes easier to access and disseminate this work.

18.7 PROBLEMS WITH DISCOURSE ANALYSIS

In the relatively short space of time since it was formally introduced to social psychology, discourse analysis has made tremendous strides in terms of its epistemological development and its influence on the discipline. However, as with any evolving field, it is not without its problems. Parker and Burman (1993) identified no fewer than 32 problems with discourse analysis, some of them more commonly encountered and more serious than others. For example, while they agree with the emphasis on the linguistic construction of social reality, they also believe that there is a need to hold on to some idea of language representing things that have an existence independent of language (see Parker, 1998). Otherwise, they fear, the focus of interest shifts away from what is being accounted for and towards the account itself. In a similar vein, they point out that, in analyses of power, discourse analysis encourages an over-attention to how unbalanced power relations are reproduced in language and an under-emphasis on the endurance of such power relations independent of language. To address these issues, Parker (1992) has suggested that 'things' should be represented as having different statuses as objects. Some objects are said to exist independently of thought and language, i.e. those that are needed for thought to occur (such as our brains and bodies) and around which thinking can be organised (such as the physical and organisational properties of the environment). Yet, we do not have direct knowledge of these objects because thinking is a constructive, interpretative process. Other objects are constructed through language but are treated in language as if they had an enduring reality.

However, those working within the extreme social constructionist tradition resist the idea of there being any 'reality' beyond language. It has been contended that, without such a concept of reality, there can be no criteria for evaluating the validity of particular discourses, leading to a problem of relativism (Burr, 1995). Indeed, it could be argued that accounts of the assumptions and procedures of discourse analysis can have no essential 'truth' status. Instead they must take their place alongside other accounts of the nature of knowledge and methods of attaining it, with no one account being privileged over another. Despite this, the insistence that there is nothing beyond the text has been strenuously defended by Edwards et al. (1995).

Another problem within discourse analytic literature is that there is a tendency to reify discourse. One sometimes gets the impression that discourses are somehow embedded in the text and that the analyst plays the role of the linguistic archaeologist, simply chipping away the surrounding linguistic material to excavate and reveal the discourses (and, in the case of interview texts, often ignoring their role as interviewer in constructing the texts). As Parker and Burman (1993) have noted, this reifying tendency leads to discourses being represented as static and unchanging. To counteract this, they urge discourse analysts to study the fluctuations and transformations of discourses. Furthermore, the archaeological model of discourse analysis is inappropriate because any discourse analysis involves interpretation by the analyst and is constructed from the analyst's reading of the text. As has already been noted, this means that a discourse analytic report can itself be seen as a text which attempts to construct a particular view of social reality and which can itself be subjected to discourse analysis (to practise using discourse analysis, consider how my analysis of David's language use is itself legitimated). While the constructed and reflexive nature of discourse analysis and related pursuits has been acknowledged and indeed celebrated (see Ashmore, 1989), there is a sense in which discourse analysts (and others working within a social constructionist framework) are not too sure what to do about it. This may be due to the potential for a serious consideration of reflexivity to unsettle, destabilise and subvert social scientific inquiry, as taken-for-granted 'truths' are exposed as arbitrary (Pollner, 1991). However, once the constructed nature of all texts has been highlighted, it is not enough for discourse analysts to bracket this insight and carry on as if their analyses are somehow exceptions to the rule.

The discourse analytic stance on personal agency, motivation and intention has also been subject to criticism. As was noted earlier, some writers have used psychoanalytic concepts to allow for a view of the person as agentic and motivated. Madill and Doherty (1994) have, however, claimed that, despite the refusal of discourse analysis to speculate about what might be going on inside a person's head, the approach is based on an implicit model of the person as an active, creative and strategic user of language, thereby connoting motivation and intention. The idea that language has an action orientation and is performing particular social functions could be interpreted as implying a language user who is motivated to have these functions performed. Yet, these criticisms could be seen as a reflection of the difficulty of escaping from culturally pervasive mentalist discourse when reading a text. Madill and Doherty (1994) have themselves noted that, because discourse analysis says nothing about the 'inner life' of the speaking subject, audiences may tend to fill this gap using familiar mentalist discourse. Also, when presenting discourse analytic research, it is difficult for researchers to avoid producing a text that could not be read as having mentalist implications. It is therefore a relatively simple matter to trawl through studies which lay claim to an agnostic stance on the possibility of an 'interior world' and find passages which can be read as contradicting this, as Madill and Doherty (1994) have done with the work of Wetherell and Potter. Indeed, in the analysis offered in this chapter, an attentive reader could find many instances where motivation, intention and other mental states and qualities seem to be implied. Pointing this out is not a criticism of discourse analysis *per se*. Rather it acts as a reminder of the continual need to convey clearly the epistemology of the approach and the way in which it constructs the speaking subject. However, Parker (1997) sees such slippage into agency-related talk as an inevitable consequence of refusing to theorise subjectivity and he uses this to justify the use of psychoanalytic theory to address subjectivity in discourse analysis.

These problems are not life-threatening for discourse analysis. They merely represent the developmental troubles of a domain which, while no longer in its infancy, still has work to do on its theory and practice. As discourse analytic specialists within psychology extend and refine their ideas and as the body of research work grows as more psychologists from various branches of the discipline turn to discourse, there is every reason to believe that this developmental work will be forthcoming. Indeed, in the relatively short time between the first and second editions of this book, advances have been made, positions clarified and new debates initiated within the field. During this process, it is to be hoped that discourse analysis will continue to develop and to offer a radical challenge to mainstream approaches to psychology.

18.8 FURTHER READING

Potter and Wetherell's (1987) very readable and broad-ranging text *Discourse and Social Psychology: Beyond Attitudes and Behaviour* remains the obvious starting point for anyone interested in discourse analysis. Potter's (1996) *Representing Reality: Discourse, Rhetoric and Social Construction* offers a clear and comprehensive account of the history, epistemology and practicalities of discursive approaches, with many clarifying examples. For an outline of the principles of the other major discourse analytic tradition in the UK, see Parker's (1992) *Discourse Dynamics: Critical Analysis for Social and Individual Psychology*. Readers interested in a critical engagement with discourse analysis will find much food for thought in *Feminism and Discourse: Psychological Perspectives*, edited by Wilkinson and Kitzinger (1995).

19

Qualitative Data Analysis: Data Display Model

Evanthia Lyons

Contents

19.1 INTRODUCTION: DEFINING QUALITATIVE RESEARCH

This chapter is concerned with the strategies that can be adopted to deal with qualitative data. Qualitative data usually refers to verbal rather than numerical data. Some researchers have also argued that visual images can lend themselves to similar kinds of analysis (Harper, 1989; Ball and Smith, 1992). Observations, interviews or examining documents are some of the common methods of collecting qualitative data and these data are most often collected in naturalistic contexts.

Qualitative research is increasingly becoming more accepted in psychology. Its appeal perhaps lies both in being able to meet some of the limitations of quantitative research which has traditionally been the dominant paradigm in psychology and on the assumptions it makes about the nature of social phenomena and the basis of scientific knowledge. For instance, qualitative research considers meanings to be negotiable and variable rather than fixed; it is often concerned with understanding the uniqueness and particularity of human experience rather than seeking to establish general regularities; and it avoids overwriting internally structured subjectivities with externally imposed systems of meaning (Henwood and Pidgeon, 1992; Henwood, 1996).

A variety of techniques are now being used to analyse qualitative data. These are based on a range of theoretical perspectives that make different assumptions about the basis of scientific knowledge, use different procedures and have different aims. Defining qualitative research is therefore rather difficult. However, it is characterised by certain features which have been summarised succinctly by Flick (1998). Henwood and Pidgeon (1994) have also produced a framework locating different approaches to qualitative research using their epistemological and methodological positions.

First, qualitative research is concerned with the ability/potential of the method used to study a particular object of research and do justice to its complexity. The object of the study determines the choice of method used. Furthermore, the aim of qualitative research is to develop theories which are relevant to the participants and are grounded in the data obtained. This contrasts with the goals of quantitative research which often aims to test existing theories and, in an attempt to model clear cause–effect relationships, loses the complexity of the object of study.

Second, qualitative research puts emphasis on explicating the perspectives of the participants in a given social situation, highlighting their diversity. For example, suppose you are interested in studying how disruptive behaviour is dealt with in schools. Instead of seeking to establish causal relationships between school ethos and teachers' response to disruptive behaviour, a qualitative researcher is likely to focus on understanding teachers' and pupils' perceptions of, and meanings attached to, activities (which are defined by them) as disruptive, the activities they engage in to deal with such behaviour, and the interactions which are likely to precede and follow disruptive behaviour. In other words, a qualitative study of school disruptive behaviour will seek to understand the participants' perspectives and practices and the interactions and rules that guide them and will locate these in concrete contexts.

Third, the researcher is seen as an important part of the process of knowledge production, bringing to it their own understandings, conceptual orientations and a stock of cultural knowledge. Qualitative researchers are therefore expected to reflect on their actions and reactions during all the stages of the research process. These reflections then become part of the data and play a role in the interpretation of the data.

Fourth, as mentioned above, qualitative research is based on a variety of theoretical and methodological approaches. These inform what research questions are asked as well as the research practice. Henwood and Pidgeon (1994) and Henwood (1996) have showed that different theoretical choices link together particular epistemologies (assumptions about the basis for knowledge), methodologies (theoretical analyses defining a research problem and research practice) and methods (specific techniques). By conceptualising these links they identified three main strands of inquiry. The first strand is based on an empiricist epistemological position: the main methodological principle is that of a discovery of valid representations by using inductive reasoning, and it evaluates qualitative research by using criteria analogous to reliability and validity. Examples of this strand are traditional content analysis (e.g. Krippendorf, 1980; Holsti, 1969) and the 'data display' model (Miles and Huberman, 1994). The second strand is based on contextualism. The main methodological principle involved is the construction of intersubjective meaning (or *Verstehen*), and the usefulness of qualitative research is argued on the basis of generating new theory which is firmly grounded in participants' own meanings in concrete contexts. Examples of this strand are grounded theory (Glaser and Strauss, 1967; Strauss and Corbin, 1990) and ethogenics (Harré and Secord, 1972). The third strand is based on constructivism and its main methodological principle is that of interpretative analysis. This strand focuses on 'the reflexive functions of language, which construct representations of "objects" in the world and which have material-discursive effects' (Henwood, 1996: 31). Examples of methods used in this strand are discourse analysis (Potter and Wetherell, 1987) and narrative analysis (Gergen, 1988; Riessman, 1993).

Fifth, most qualitative approaches start by analysing a single case in depth before new cases are used for comparison purposes. By this process of comparison a typology, or a wide a range, of either subjective theories or courses of conversations or discourses or structures of cases is produced.

Sixth, qualitative research is based on the premise that reality is not objective and given. Rather it is socially constructed either by the participants' accounts of their experiences, or through social interaction.

Seventh, and finally, text is most often the empirical material on which the reconstruction of a social situation and its associated meanings and their interpretation is based.

Having discussed some of the features which characterise qualitative research, it might have become obvious that certain research questions and problems lend themselves more readily than others to qualitative research. However, the decision whether to carry out a qualitative or quantitative study can also be either taken on 'technical' grounds or based on the epistemological position of the researcher (Henwood and Pidgeon, 1992; Henwood, 1996). Qualitative research is best undertaken when there is no very well-developed theory to enable the researcher to make specific hypotheses; when one cannot obtain an adequate sample so as to be able to use quantitative statistical techniques; and when one has the appropriate resources (as qualitative research requires a lot of time and incurs high costs). However, Henwood and Pidgeon (1992) have claimed that researchers need to be aware that the choice of the approach they adopt carries with it a baggage of epistemological assumptions. Doing qualitative research is based on beliefs about what is legitimate scientific inquiry and warrantable knowledge which are incompatible with the analogous beliefs underlying quantitative research.

This chapter will describe the **data display** approach to qualitative data analysis. This approach has been developed by Miles and Huberman (1994) and contrasts starkly with discourse analysis which is discussed in Chapter 18. It has three main advantages. It attempts to apply rigour and transparency to the process of qualitative data analysis; it places emphasis and value on the role played by theory in qualitative research; and it urges the researcher to go beyond description to explanation.

Before we consider some of the analytic tools and principles provided by this approach, some of the considerations of sampling in qualitative research will be discussed.

19.2 SAMPLING

A qualitative researcher is faced with sampling decisions at different stages of the research. First, they need to make sampling decisions at the time of data collection. What cases should be included? And which groups should the cases be selected from? Second, at the data analysis stage, the researcher may have to sample the material obtained. Which of the materials selected can be excluded from the analysis? Also, should the material obtained from each case be analysed in its entirety? For instance, are there any sections of an interview or of any written material collected that can or should be excluded from the analysis? Finally, when the researcher presents her findings, she faces the decision which extracts to include in her account of the research.

To start with, it is important to note that whilst in quantitative research most often cases are considered to be individuals, in qualitative research a case is defined in a much more diverse way. A case can be an individual, a role, a group, an organisation or a culture. Thus, sampling within a case is also necessary. It may be required that sampling decisions have to be made with regard to activities, events, times, locations and role positions.

In general, qualitative researchers do not seek to establish a random sample. As qualitative research is concerned with studying particular phenomena and social processes embedded in specific contexts in-depth, qualitative samples tend to comprise a small number of cases chosen on a theoretical basis. One of the many dilemmas confronting qualitative researchers is to what extent they should limit the scope of the research by setting boundaries on what is to be studied whilst they have a sampling frame that allows them to understand the whole range of concepts and processes involved in the phenomenon under study. Often the purpose of qualitative research is to understand different ways of making sense of and experiencing things. In some instances, it may be important to be able to represent the diversity of as wide a range of experiences in a particular field as possible whilst at other times it may be important to understand a particular field in considerable depth. The research question, the adopted approach to qualitative research, and practical considerations such as financial and time resources available usually determine the sampling strategy used.

A number of different sampling strategies have been identified. For example Miles and Huberman (1994) presented a list of 16 different types of sampling strategies (Figure 19.1). These differ in terms of the extent to which the sample is determined prior to the data collection or whether it is gradually selected during the data collection stage.

An important issue to consider is what a case in the sample is meant to represent. For example, does it represent the views of a particular individual or the views of a group that the individual is a member of? Suppose you were studying how disruptive behaviour was dealt with in a school and you inter-viewed teachers, students and administrative staff. What would each interview represent? Flick (1998) suggests that in such circumstances, each case can be representative in five ways. Firstly, a case would represent itself. That is, it represents the individual's subjective views and experiences which are the result of the person's biographical experiences against the background of cultural

Type of sampling	Purpose
Maximum variation	Documents diverse variations and identifies common patterns
Homogeneous	Focuses, reduces, simplifies, facilitates group interviewing
Critical case	Permits logical generalisation and maximum application of information to other cases
Theory based	Finding examples of a theoretical construct and thereby elaborating and examining it
Confirming and disconfirming cases	Elaborating initial analysis, seeking exceptions, looking for variation
Snowball or chain	Identifies cases of interest from people who know people who know what cases are information thick
Extreme or deviant case	Learning from highly unusual manifestations of the phenomenon of interest
Typical case	Highlights what is normal or average
Intensity	Information-rich cases that manifest the phenomenon intensely, but not extremely
Politically important cases	Attracts desired attention or avoids attracting undesired attention
Random purposeful	Adds credibility to sample when potential purposeful sample is too large
Stratified purposeful	Illustrates subgroups; facilitates comparisons
Criterion	All cases that meet some criterion; useful for quality assurance
Opportunistic	Following new leads; taking advantage of the unexpected
Combination or mixed	Triangulation, flexibility, meets multiple interests and needs
Convenience	Save time, money and effort but at the expense of information and credibility

FIGURE 19.1   *Sampling strategies (Miles and Huberman, 1994: 28)*

changes. In our example, a teacher's interview would represent their own opinions, views and attitudes towards disruptive behaviour and ways of dealing with it in their school against the general background of changes of governmental and societal attitudes towards education. Secondly, the case can represent the institutional context in which they have to operate. For example, the teacher's views and activities are likely to be influenced by the whole school's goals and the way he/she makes sense of and reacts to them. Thirdly, the case can represent a particular group that they are a member of, and which is relevant to the field under investigation. For example, the case can represent the teaching profession, or headteachers, or pupils and so on. Fourthly, the case can represent a subjectivity which is developed by acquiring certain bodies of knowledge and developing ways of acting and making sense of the world. Fifthly, the case can represent the context of a particular activity such as dealing with disruptive behaviour which is constructed in a dynamic way through social interaction.

19.3   DATA DISPLAY APPROACH

This approach to dealing with qualitative data is based on *transcendental realism* (Bhaskar, 1978; Harré and Secord, 1972). It is based on the belief that 'social phenomena exist not only in the mind, but in the objective world as well, and that there are some lawful, reasonably stable relationships to be found among them' (Huberman and Miles, 1994: 429). It also acknowledges 'the historical and social nature of knowledge, along with the meaning making at the centre of phenomenological experience' (1994: 429). Therefore the aim is to construct explanations that would account for these relationships as well as providing a full descriptive account of each instance of that explanation. They adopt an inductivist position that lawful relationships can be discovered from detailed qualitative data obtained in naturalistic contexts.

Although the data display approach is discussed mainly in relation to large scale research in specific contexts involving collecting data from a number of participants and sources, it can easily be adapted for use in smaller projects where the data are collected by semi-structured interviews.

The 'data display' approach stipulates a number of operations to be used to manage data so that (a) data are always accessible and of high quality, (b) the analyses carried out are carefully documented and the documentation is kept in an accessible manner, and (c) data and the analyses are kept after the end of the study. This is particularly important when data are collected by a number of different researchers and at different times, but it applies equally to smaller projects run by a single researcher. Five general issues need to be considered in relation to data management. The first is concerned with issues to do with the **formatting** and organisation of written-up fieldwork notes. The second is **cross-referral**. Each file should contain information about where other relevant information can be found. For example, a file on a teacher's interview can have information about where data on the class she teaches can be found. The third issue has to do with **indexing**, recording the category system. This should include clear definitions of the categories, a codebook showing the structure of the category system, and cross-referencing between the codebook and the data base. Fourthly, **abstracting**: a summary of longer material should be included in the file with clear links to the longer material. Finally, some thought should be given to **pagination**. Material in field notes should be given unique numbers to locate it in the file. For example, each interview with a teacher will be given a combination of digits and letters so that the school, the teacher and the time of the interview can be located.

Miles and Huberman (1994) produced a checklist of what information needs to be stored, retrieved and kept after the project is complete so that the risk of **miscoding**, **mislabelling**, **mislinking** and **mislaying** data is minimised and the findings can be verified or replicated (see Figure 19.2).

Within the data display model, data analysis is seen as comprising three processes: data reduction, data display and conclusion drawing and verification. Data reduction refers to the process by which the potential universe of data is summarised and reduced. This inevitably involves selection and takes place at all stages of the research. At the design stage of the research, data reduction occurs by the researcher choosing a particular conceptual framework, specific cases and instruments. Also what research questions are asked is likely to place boundaries on the data collected. At the analysis stage, data reduction is achieved through coding, identifying themes, clustering and writing up reports.

1	*Raw material*: field notes, tapes, site documents
2	*Partially processed data*: write-ups, transcriptions; initial versions, and subsequent corrected, 'cleaned', 'commented-on' versions
3	*Coded data*: write-ups with specific codes attached
4	*The coding scheme or thesaurus*, in its successive iterations
5	*Memos or other analytic material*: the researcher's reflections on the conceptual meaning of the data
6	*Search and retrieval records*: information showing which coded chunks or data segments the researcher looked for during analysis, and the retrieved material; records of links made among segments
7	*Data displays*: matrices or networks used to display retrieved information along with the associated analytic text; revised versions of these
8	*Analysis episodes*: documentation of what you did, step by step, to assemble the displays and write the analytic text
9	*Report text*: successive drafts of what is written on the design, methods and findings of the study
10	*General chronological log or documentation* of data collection and analysis of work
11	*Index* of all of the above material

FIGURE 19.2 *What to store, retrieve from, and retain (adapted from Miles and Huberman, 1994)*

Data display is defined as 'a visual format that presents information systematically, so the user can draw valid conclusions and take needed action' (Miles and Huberman, 1994: 91). Data displays are supposed to facilitate the work of the researcher by presenting all of the data in a condensed and focused way in the same location. They should be focused and arranged in such a way as to allow the researcher to interrogate the data and carry out careful comparisons so that she can identify differences as well as patterns and themes in the data. These can take the form of *structured summaries, synopses, vignettes, matrices* and *networks.*

The process of **conclusion drawing and verification** involves the researcher interpreting and making sense of displayed data by using a wide range of tactics in an iterative manner. These tactics include comparing and contrasting, examining negative cases, clustering, and identifying themes and patterns.

19.4 DATA ANALYSIS

The process of qualitative data analysis is an iterative one and starts in the early stages of the research process. Data analysis starts before the completion of data collection. Miles and Huberman (1994) suggested a range of methods that help the researcher to reduce data and draw meaning from them.

At the early stages of a project, they recommend that the researcher produces **contact summary sheets**, detailing their initial thoughts and reflections on each contact with the participants.

Coding should also begin early on in the research process. Qualitative data can soon become overwhelming. A way of dealing with the large amounts of material usually collected is by developing coding categories. 'A code is a symbol applied to a group of words to classify or categorize them' (Robson,

1993: 385). Coding categories can be created prior to data collection on the basis of the research question and the theoretical framework within which the study is conceived. Alternatively, the codes can be generated by examining the data themselves in an inductive way. As new data are collected and examined it is likely that the codes would need to be revised. Miles and Huberman (1994) distinguish between first- and second-level codes. The first-level coding is descriptive; labels are attached to groups of words. The second-level coding is called **pattern coding** and involves grouping initial codes together as themes and patterns are identified.

It is also important to keep a record of the researcher's thoughts and interpretations of the codes as the analysis goes on. This is usually achieved by writing **memos**. Glaser defined a memo as 'the theorising write-up of ideas about codes and their relationships as they strike the analyst while coding . . . it can be a sentence, a paragraph or a few pages . . . it exhausts the analyst's momentary ideation based on data with perhaps little conceptual elaboration' (1978: 83–4). Memos are used to show how codes are distinguished from each other, or how they are linked to each other. They are also used to indicate how the analysis can elaborate on existing concepts or how it can develop new ones. Memos can be revised as the interpretation goes on; they are the tools that enable the analyst to make sense of the data.

In order to ensure that the data collected are relevant to the focus of the research and are likely to result in interesting and useful findings, it is important to produce an **interim case summary** at an early stage of the research. This would include a summary of the findings so far, an examination of the quality of the data obtained and an outline of the next waves of data collection.

Once the data collection is completed, the analysis continues with the aid of a wide range of data displays. The list includes partially ordered displays, time ordered displays, role ordered displays, conceptually ordered displays, explanatory effects matrices, case dynamics matrices and causal networks. These are tools that the researcher has available to her in order to understand what happens within a case. Some of these enable a descriptive analysis of a case (e.g. time ordered displays or conceptually ordered displays) whilst others help the researcher to clarify why things happen the way they do. They provide the researcher with tools which can take her beyond description into explanation.

It is beyond the scope of this chapter to provide examples from each of these types of data displays. Two examples will be given, however, to illustrate what a descriptive data display might look like and what a causal network might be like. For more illustrations see Miles and Huberman (1994).

A conceptually clustered matrix is designed to bring together items that are expected to cluster together on a theoretical or an empirical basis. For example, interviewees themselves may answer different questions in a similar way or their responses may show a tendency to link them to each other. The example of the matrix given in Figure 19.3 is designed to examine whether the participants' initial attitudes towards an innovation were related to their motives for adopting the innovation, in this case a new educational practice.

Another powerful tool available to the researcher is a **causal network** display. This is usually generated towards the end of the analysis and is a representation of the relationships of the most important independent and

Research questions

	Motives (types)	Career relevance (none/some)	Centrality (low/medium/ high)	Initial attitude (favourable, neutral, unfavourable)
Informants	*Users* *U₁*				
	U₂ etc.				
	Administrators *A₁*				
	A₂ etc.				

FIGURE 19.3   *Conceptually clustered matrix: motives and attitudes (Miles and Huberman, 1994: 128)*

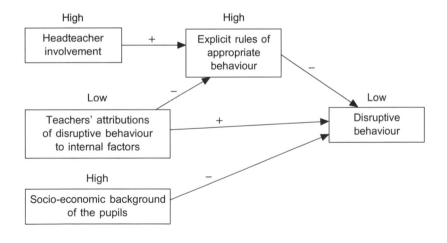

FIGURE 19.4   *An example of a causal network*

dependent variables. The direction of these relationships is illustrated by an arrow. The example in Figure 19.4 shows a causal network of the relationship between some important independent variables and the incidence of disruptive behaviour in a particular school.

There a number of steps that need to be taken in order to generate a causal network. These are summarised by Miles and Huberman (1994: 156) and are as follows:

- Consider a *specific case* for which you've reviewed a lot of data.
- Translate the pattern codes into *variables*, that is something that can be scaled (high to low, big to little, more to less).
- Rate the variable (e.g. high, moderate, low). How much of it is in the case?
- Draw a *line* between pairs of variables that *co-vary*, that is, that appear together consistently in the case, that have some kind of relationship – for example, more of one variable goes with less of another.
- Draw a *directional* arrow between each variable that comes first (temporally) and those later ones it appears to influence. *Influence* here means that more or less of one variable determines to some extent the rating of another. The rating of the second variable might have been different had the first not been there: a reasonable 'mechanism' is involved.
- If two variables co-vary but seem to have only a tepid or oblique influence on each other, probably another, latent variable needs to be invented to join the two (tactic: finding intervening variables). Review the full list of codes to see whether one fits here.

The notion of causality is central to this approach and will be discussed in some detail below.

Sometimes a research project can involve collecting data in more than one setting (e.g. more than one school). In such instances a single case analysis is followed by cross-case comparisons. This can be achieved by bringing together the matrices generated for each of the cases in order to identify similarities and differences. Cross-case analyses often result in a clarification of patterns by identifying themes across cases. For example by examining teachers' attitudes towards, and ways of dealing with, disruptive behaviour in different schools, one could find that the theme of rule-breaking tolerance cuts across all schools. This may be concluded by looking at data on how decisions about how and when to respond to disruptive behaviour are taken, implicit theories of why disruptive behaviour occurs and so on.

19.5 CAUSALITY

The data display model approach to qualitative research differs from most other approaches to qualitative data analysis in that it explicitly tries to establish causality. It provides a way of thinking about causality and argues that qualitative analysis is a powerful method for assessing causality, despite the dominant belief that qualitative research can be used only as an exploratory study to develop hypotheses.

First, causality involves a temporal dimension. Events happen over time and preceding events are thought to have a link with subsequent events. Secondly, causality is local. Suppose you want to establish why a pupil is engaged in a disruptive behaviour: you can evoke distant causes such as something to do with his/her upbringing or the hierarchical structure of the school and so on. However, even if these have an effect, such an effect happens in a concrete setting at a specific time. It is therefore important to understand the local network of causal relationships which may have to do with teacher/pupil or pupil/pupil interactions and how the participants made sense of them. Thirdly, causality can be established by means other than following Hume's criteria of temporal precedence (if A precedes B), constant conjunction (when A always B) and contiguity of influence (a plausible mechanism links A and B). Causality can be inferred by examining observed associations between two events or variables, if there is:

- strength of association (much more B with A than with other possible causes)
- consistency (A is found with B by many studies in different places)
- specificity (a particular link is shown between A and B)
- temporality (A before B, not the reverse)
- biological gradient (if more A, then more B)
- plausibility (a known mechanism exists to link A and B)
- coherence (A–B relationship fits with what else we know about A and B)
- experiment (change A, observe what happens to B)
- analogy (A and B resemble the well-established pattern noted in C and D) (Miles and Huberman, 1994: 146)

Fourthly, causes are always complex and multiple and influenced by conditions in the specific context in which they take place. Causes combine in different ways and influence each other in varying ways in different contexts. Moreover, different combinations of causes can have the same effect. It is therefore important to take this complexity into account and conceptualise causal relationships as embedded in networks of relationships between events and/or variables that have the potential to change over time and from situation to situation. Finally, it is argued that establishing causality is always a retrospective process and therefore explanations always follow causal actions. 'The report is retrodictive rather than predictive . . . a retrospective gathering of events into an account that makes the ending reasonable and believable . . . more than a mere chronicling . . . It configures the events in such a way that their part in the whole story becomes clear' (Polkinghorne, 1988: 171).

If such a view of causality were to be adopted, then qualitative research becomes a powerful way of establishing it. For it allows us to provide rich, context specific and in-depth data in order to identify possible and plausible mechanisms by which one event/variable leads to another. Qualitative research also allows us to deal with the temporal dimension and does justice to the complexity of the networks of actions and processes in concrete contexts.

19.6 CRITERIA FOR EVALUATING QUALITATIVE RESEARCH

There are a number of ways of giving credibility to the findings of a qualitative research study which are different from those of validity and reliability used within positivism. These include:

- *Keeping close to the data*: the analysis and conclusions should closely reflect the data.

- *Documentation*: as discussed above, there are a number of documents which record the decisions taken through the process of the research and analysis that should be kept and made accessible so that other researchers can either follow the steps of the initial researcher or attempt to replicate the research in another setting.
- *Transparency of the process of analysis*: the process of analysis should be made transparent in the reporting of the research and through documentation as described above.
- *Reflexivity*: given that in qualitative research the investigator is part of the research process, it is important that they reflect on and discuss explicitly the likely impact of their own beliefs, theoretical orientation, and involvement with the object of the study on both the process of data collection and the process of analysis.
- *Transferability*: this is a substitute for the concept of generalisability. The latter seems to be inappropriate given that sampling decisions in qualitative research are not made on statistical grounds. Transferability refers to the idea that one can speculate on the likely applications of the data to other similar but not identical, conditions.
- *Fruitfulness*: qualitative research can also be judged in terms of its usefulness at both a theoretical and an applied level. To what extent does the research account contribute to the development of theory? To what extent is the particular interpretation of the data useful to the participants themselves as an engine of change or to policy makers in engineering change?
- *Triangulation*: the credibility of the findings is enhanced by comparing data obtained from different sources or from different investigators or different methods of collecting data. If such comparisons show that the findings hold, then one can have more confidence in their interpretation. However, if the findings obtained by different methods of data collection differ, one must be careful in rejecting the usefulness of the findings. The differences may be the result of the methods used to obtain the data rather than the result of misinterpreting the data.

19.7 FURTHER READING

John Richardson's (1996) *Handbook of Qualitative Research Methods for Psychology and the Social Sciences* is a useful introduction to a wide range of qualitative methods. Miles and Huberman's (1994) *Qualitative Data Analysis* is another helpful textbook that is rapidly becoming one of the classics in this area.

20

Structuring Qualitative Data Using a Scaling Procedure

Margaret Wilson and Sean Hammond

Contents

20.1 QUALITATIVE DATA AND CONTENT ANALYSIS

Qualitative data are descriptive material. They can be written, as in accounts in newspapers; verbal, such as what people say in interviews; or visual, for example drawings or photographs. Qualitative data for psychological research may already exist in the form of records, publications and so on, or they may be collected by researchers from interviews or observations.

The first step in dealing with qualitative data is to set up some type of classification scheme. The classification of open-ended material is known as 'content analysis' (e.g. Krippendorf, 1980). It may often appear that content analysis is simply a matter of counting the number of times a certain thing occurs. However, most theorists are adamant that content analysis should be viewed as a process of theory development and hypothesis testing. Developing a framework for categorising qualitative data is a time-consuming process, and requires a sound theoretical basis for the results to be meaningful.

20.1.1   Non-verbal behaviour

The first example is based on the non-verbal behaviour of candidates being interviewed for a job. It would be possible to video the candidates and develop a coding scheme which classified aspects of their non-verbal behaviour. In order to do this, the researcher would need to have hypotheses about the types of behaviour which were relevant to what they were studying. If they were interested in how nervous the candidates were, they might hypothesise about those behaviours which might be indicative of 'nervousness'. From the literature they might hypothesise that scratching one's nose indicated nervousness. They could also hypothesise that the candidate touching their hair was a nervous reaction. Once the types of behaviours have been established, the researchers would watch the candidates and see whether each behaviour occurred. They might be interested in whether or not the behaviour occurred regardless of the frequency, or they might be interested in the number of times a certain behaviour occurred. The coding of behaviours turns the descriptive visual material into numbers, representing whether or not, or how many times, something occurred for each candidate.

20.1.2   Children's drawings

The second example examines the way in which children's experiences of war are reflected in their drawings. It would be possible to take two samples of children, one who had and one who had not experienced war in their country. The children might be asked to draw a picture about war. The pictures could then be content analysed to see what features were and were not represented in them. It could be hypothesised that while both sets of children would include guns or other weapons in their pictures, children with real experiences of war would include other, quite different features. For example, war-experienced children might include more realistic images such as blood and dead bodies. It could also be hypothesised that children of war would include references to themselves or people known to them, whereas children who have not experienced war would be unlikely to include representations of themselves or people close to them. In this way the researcher would set up a classification scheme to include the features to be classified in the children's drawings.

20.1.3   Careers in the police force

The final example illustrates the use of existing data in the form of records of people's job histories. Using this type of data it would be possible to assess the different career paths followed by a group of individuals in a particular area, for example, the police force. The researcher might hypothesise that different career experiences may be related to outcomes, such as success. The classification scheme would require hypotheses about what aspects of a person's career history might be related to their success in the job. The researcher might hypothesise that the police officers' educational background was important, along with the types of work they had been involved in, how long they had spent in certain departments, and how many job changes they had made during their career in the police force. Identifying the categories on each variable which distinguish between the different career paths would provide the researcher with a framework for classifying each of the individuals being studied. It would then be possible to identify what characterised those police officers who had been promoted to senior positions.

20.2   INTER-RATER RELIABILITY

Once the classification scheme has been established it is very important that a second, independent rater classify the material in addition to the researcher. This procedure is designed to establish the reliability of the classification scheme. If the scheme is reliable, it is sufficiently unambiguous that two people will be able to classify the material in the same way. Unless the scheme is tested by another rater, it may be that the classifications are open to individual interpretation, and the first rater may be imposing their own view of the material on to its classification.

Once a second person has classified the descriptive data, it is possible to calculate the reliability by simply assessing the number of times the raters agree as a percentage of all possible observations. The strategy for quantifying rater agreement reliability is to use Cohen's kappa coefficient (see Chapter 13). When results are presented it is important to state what the inter-rater reliability of the coding scheme is.

20.3   USING THE DATA

Once the researcher has established a reliable way of classifying the material, there are a variety of ways of using the data. If it is a descriptive or 'normative' study, the classification process may well be the endpoint of the research. So, referring to the hypothetical examples described above, the researcher might conclude that a certain percentage of all interview candidates display some non-verbal behaviour hypothesised to be indicative of nervousness. Or in the second example, children who have experienced war might portray different images in their drawings from children who have not experienced war. In the final example, it might be possible to indicate whether the career paths of senior officers in the police force were characterised by consistency or variability in terms of the number of qualitative job changes. These kinds of results are certainly interesting in their own right, and in much qualitative research this is as far as the analysis goes.

However, if the study is more complex, the researchers might want to use the qualitative data further. For example it would be possible to correlate the number of nose scratches in an interview with an independent measure of nervousness, in order to confirm that nose scratching is a valid measure of anxiety in an interview. Similarly, one might suggest that children who represented members of their own family in their drawings of war may have experienced greater trauma as a result of the situation in their country. It would then be possible to relate the content of their drawings to their psychological assessment, or their progress in coming to terms with their experiences. In the final example, it would be of interest to relate the features of police officers' career histories to background characteristics in order to identify, for example, whether successful female officers follow a different career path from successful male police officers. It would also be of interest to establish which features of the officers' career histories were most predictive of fast promotion.

20.4 MULTIDIMENSIONAL ANALYSIS

Whether the researcher stops at the point of the descriptive study, or whether they use the results to examine other issues, the qualitative data described above are being used at their simplest level. It may be very interesting that most people scratch their nose when they are nervous, or that English children do not represent death in pictures of war, or that most senior police officers have a degree. But the data have so much more potential when they are analysed multidimensionally. For example, say 60% of the interview candidates scratched their noses, and 60% of the candidates touched their hair. Are they the same people? There may be some candidates who do both, and then there may hair touchers and nose scratchers. What makes these people different? Perhaps hair touchers are more likely to be female, while nose scratchers are male. The important issue is how each of the variables (classifications) relates to one another, and how each combination of variables relates to the items themselves, in this case the people.

Multivariate analysis becomes even more important if the researchers are intending to use the descriptive categories to take the study further. If a researcher managed to find a relationship between any one feature of a drawing and a child's psychological state they would be very lucky indeed. Similarly, it would be very surprising if any one feature of a police officer's background could be used to predict success in the force. For example, just having a degree, or just having experienced a range of police work, would be unlikely to predict their future career prospects. However, if the officer had a degree, and had experienced many types of police work, and had risen through the ranks in a comparatively short period of time, then it might be more likely that they would be promoted to the most senior ranks of the force.

By taking a multidimensional approach to qualitative data it is possible to look at the relationship between the variables, and the way that they overlap. This chapter describes one particular type of multidimensional analysis which allows the researcher to examine all the relationships in the data, between the items, between the variables, and between the variables and the items in the analysis. This complex set of relationships is known as the structure of the data.

There has been a relatively recent growth in the availability of techniques for analysing multivariate qualitative data (see Agresti, 1996; von Eye, 1990). However, the technique to be illustrated here is particularly useful in revealing the underlying structure in qualitative data. It is called multidimensional scalogram analysis (MSA) and is derived from the work of Louis Guttman (1941) and James Lingoes (1968). In an earlier chapter of this book (Chapter

8), MSA was briefly described in relation to an approach named facet theory. While facet theory may be useful in allowing *a priori* order to be imposed upon a structure, the present chapter attempts to present a more general use of the MSA technique.

20.5 MULTIDIMENSIONAL SCALOGRAM ANALYSIS

Multidimensional scalogram analysis (MSA: Lingoes, 1968) is a technique which can be used to examine the structure of qualitative data. It allows the relationship between each of the variables or classifications, and the items themselves with respect to those variables, to be represented in one coherent visual summary.

Although MSA is only one of a number of multidimensional scaling (MDS) techniques it has special properties which make it ideal for understanding qualitative data relationships. In order to explain the way that MSA works and how it can be used in qualitative research, this section presents a very simple worked example. The description of MSA is intended to explain how the analysis works conceptually. Those interested in the technical background to the technique are particularly referred to Lingoes (1968). Suffice it to say that MSA is related to a family of techniques known generally as correspondence analysis (Greenacre, 1993; Nishisato, 1993; Gifi, 1990). Other related mathematical developments may be found in the work of Saporta (1979) and Kiers (1989).

20.5.1 The data

The example describes the similarities and differences between a number of different occupations. In order to illustrate the use of MSA, this example will consider only six occupations, which form the 'items' for this analysis. It is therefore a very simple example which will serve to illustrate the way the analysis works. The six jobs being considered are police officer (I1), nurse (I2), psychologist (I3), surgeon (I4) barrister (I5) and teacher (I6).

First, the researcher would need to decide what the key concepts are which distinguish between the different occupations. Whilst there could be many of these distinguishing concepts, this example will work with just four. These concepts will be the 'variables' in the analysis. The concepts or classifications used in this example are salary (V1), contact with people (V2), uniforms (V3) and training (V4).

Each of the variables will describe the differences between the occupations on that concept. The concepts can have as many categories as are required to describe the differences between the items. However, this example will keep the classifications very simple to illustrate the technique.

Salary (V1) has been assigned three categories:
1 well paid
2 quite well paid
3 badly paid.

Contact with people (V2) also has three categories:
1   much contact with people
2   some contact with people
3   little contact with people.

Uniforms (V3) is simply classified into:
1   wears a uniform
2   does not wear a uniform.

Amount of training (V4) each job requires is classified into:
1   a lot of training
2   little training.

The next stage requires the classification of the occupations on each concept to form a data matrix. The matrix has each occupation as a row of data, and each concept or variable as a column. The cells of the matrix show which category each occupation has been assigned to on each of the four variables. So for example:

		Variables		*(concepts)*	
		V1	V2	V3	V4
	Police officer	2	1	1	2
	Nurse	3	1	1	2
Items	Psychologist	2	2	2	1
	Surgeon	1	2	1	1
	Barrister	1	3	1	1
	Teacher	3	1	2	2

Each occupation has been classified as to which characteristic it possesses according to the four variables. Thus, reading down the column corresponding to V1 it is possible to see that nurses and teachers have been classified as badly paid (3), psychologists and police officers have been classified as quite well paid (2), and surgeons and barristers have been classified as well paid (1). The same applies to column V2 which shows that in terms of their contact with people, nurses, police officers and teachers have been classified as having much contact with people (1), psychologists and surgeons as having some contact with people (2), and barristers as having little contact with people (3). The third column V3 shows whether they wear a uniform (1) or not (2). Finally, column V4 shows whether each job has been classified as requiring a little (2) or a lot (1) of training.

Having classified the occupations, the resulting data matrix summarises the distinctions between the jobs which are hypothesised to be important and shows the similarities and differences between the occupations. Reading along a line of data it is possible to see a profile of scores which summarises the qualities which each occupation possesses. Compare the nurse and the police officer. The nurse is (3112) and the police officer is (2112). This shows that they scored the same on three out of four of the criteria, and that they are therefore quite similar in terms of the classifications used. The thing that makes them different is the salary: police officers are quite well paid whereas nurses have been classified as badly paid. Now compare the psychologist with the nurse. The two profiles show that the psychologist (2221) and the nurse (3112) have different codings on all four variables.

20.5.2 The analysis

Multidimensional scalogram analysis (MSA) plots each item (in this case an occupation) as a point in geometric space. It attempts to find a configuration of points so that the plot can be divided into clear regions which distinguish the items on the basis of each of the variables. In effect this means that the more qualities two items have in common, the closer together they are in the plot.

Since this sounds quite complex, this example will work through this process of finding a configuration of points step by step. First it is necessary to visualise the plot as a square 'box', and in that box are six points, one representing each of the six occupations. At this stage the points could be placed anywhere in the plot and can be visualised as 'floating' or moveable in the space (see Figure 20.1).

In order to demonstrate how regions representing each variable can be established, the example will consider each variable separately. First MSA needs to separate the occupations into three regions in the plot so that they are distinguished in terms of our first variable, that is salary. The points can be moved around so that the plot is divided into three regions, each one containing the items coded as possessing that characteristic (see Figure 20.2).

Next the MSA needs to arrange the points again, so that the space can be divided for variable V2. Once it has distinguished the occupations on variable

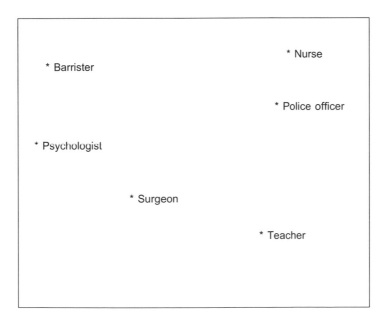

FIGURE 20.1 *Imaginary starting point*

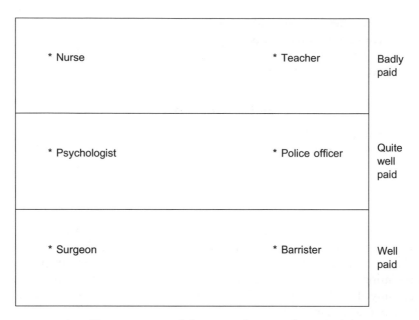

FIGURE 20.2   *Possible partitioning of the MSA plot according to salary*

V1, these boundaries cannot be crossed. So whilst keeping the distinctions between the occupations on variable V1, the points must be rearranged so that distinctions can be made on variable V2. Variable V2 requires that the nurse, the teacher and the police officer are in the same region of the plot because they all have a lot of day-to-day contact with people. So at this stage the existing configuration of points does not need to be changed as it is possible to draw a line diagonally, as in Figure 20.3.

Variable V2 also requires that the psychologist and the surgeon are in the same region because they both have some contact with people. In order to do this the points need to be rearranged to swap the positions of the surgeon and the barrister. This does not alter the distinction made on variable V1, but allows the partition to be made on variable V2 (see Figure 20.4).

This means that the partitions generated to distinguish the occupations on variable V1 are still the same, but that now we can make a distinction on variable V2 at the same time. Variable V3 requires that a distinction be made between those occupations where people are required to wear a uniform of some kind, and those where they are not. Since this is a dichotomous variable it does not present too many problems for MSA: it requires two regions, one that contains those occupations where uniforms are worn and one that contains those where they are not. Again it is necessary to maintain the distinctions that have already been made, but still move the points about until the third variable can be represented as regions in the space.

Taking the existing regions in Figure 20.4, the plot can be divided again, only this time for uniforms. Looking at the data matrix, the psychologist and the teacher (no uniforms) need to be in a different region from the police officer, the barrister, the surgeon and the nurse (uniforms). This partition can

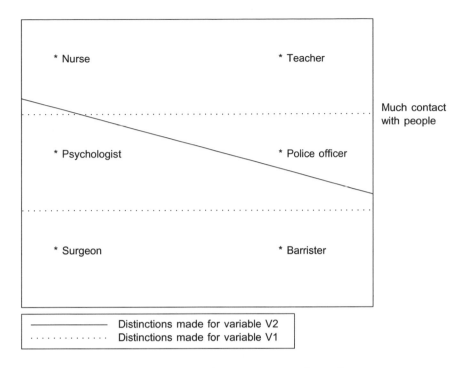

FIGURE 20.3   *The first partition according to contact with people*

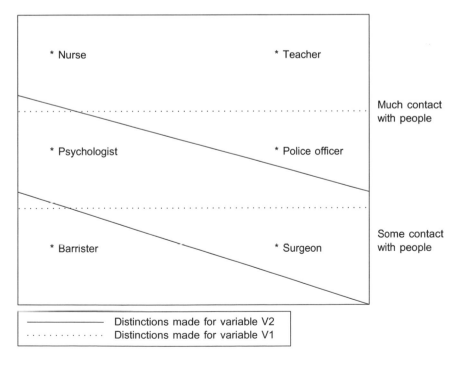

FIGURE 20.4   *Partitioning of the MSA plot according to contact with people (note: barrister and surgeon rearranged)*

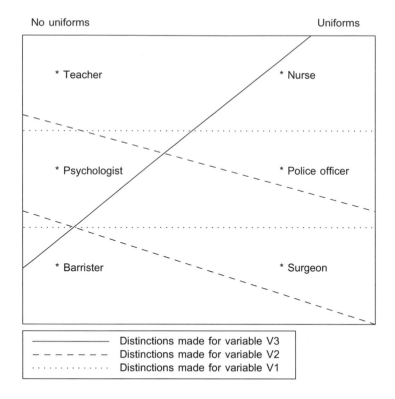

FIGURE 20.5 *Partitioning of the MSA plot according to uniforms (note: teacher and nurse rearranged)*

be done by simply swapping the position of the nurse and the teacher. This does not alter the regions of the plot for variables V1 and V2 but allows the partition to be made for variable V3, shown in Figure 20.5.

Finally, the MSA plot needs to represent the final variable V4, which distinguished between occupations requiring a lot of training and occupations requiring less training. This variable does not require any further alterations to the position of the points, as the teacher, police officer and nurse (little training) can be distinguished from the other occupations (a lot of training) as demonstrated in Figure 20.6.

20.5.3 The coefficient of contiguity

This example has broken down the partitioning of the space into stages, one for each variable, in order to describe what the analysis does. This is not the way the analysis works mathematically, but it helps to understand the analysis conceptually. In this simple example, it was possible to rearrange the points to partition the space by hand. It was possible to find a configuration of points which satisfied the ideal requirement of the analysis. That is, that the distinctions on every variable can be represented as overlapping regions in the same geometric space.

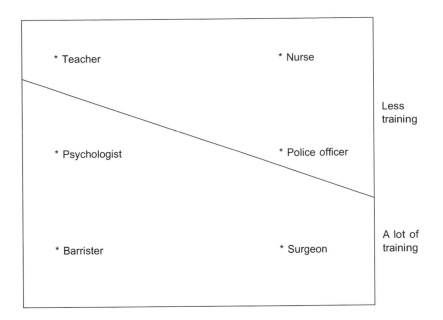

FIGURE 20.6 *Final MSA configuration with partitioning according to amount of training*

Obviously, when real data are involved it is much more complex, and less likely that all the different variables can be represented in the same space. A measure of how well the analysis has been able to achieve this solution is the coefficient of contiguity. A perfect solution would have a coefficient of +1. Most researchers using this technique would accept a coefficient of contiguity of 0.9.

20.5.4   Interpreting the plot

The output of the MSA provides the researcher with two types of plot. First, the overall plot shows the final configuration of points which summarises the relationships between items in the analysis (see Figure 20.7). The more similar two items are according to the classifications across all the variables, the closer together they will be positioned in the plot. This plot is comparable to the type of representations available from other MDS techniques. However, using other, more traditional techniques, it is possible to see that two items are similar across all the variables, but it is not easy to identify exactly what makes two items similar or different.

The second type of plot which MSA provides is called an item plot. The analysis derives one item plot for each variable. Each plot indicates the regions which correspond to the categories on each variable (see Figure 20.7). The item plots can be compared with the overall plot and with one another. In this way MSA preserves all the reasons for the similarities and differences between the items, so that it is possible to show not only that two items are similar or different, but the reasons why they are similar and different.

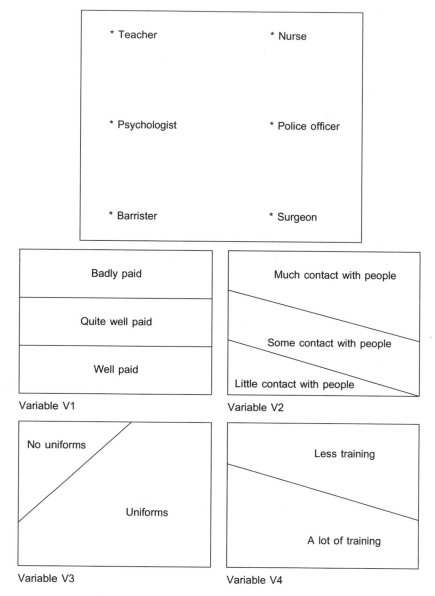

FIGURE 20.7   *Final configuration and item plots for the worked examples*

The results allow four important constituents of the structure of the data to be revealed:

1   The overall plot shows the similarities and differences between the items according to the variables in the analysis. This plot summarises the relationships between the items.

2   The item plots show what characteristics each of the items possesses, thus maintaining all of the original data. Comparison of the item plots with the overall plot reveals why two items are similar or different.

3   The item plots show the relationship of each variable in the analysis to the others. By comparing the way in which each item plot partitions the space it is possible to draw conclusions about the relationships between the variables themselves.

4   The most complex set of relationships portrayed by the analysis is revealed by combining all of the information from both the plots. Combinations of overlapping variables can be used to interpret the overall meaning of the similarities and differences between the items.

20.6 PRESENTATION OF THE RESULTS

There are no hard and fast rules for presenting the findings, and the reader may come across many different ways of representing the results in the published literature. It is possible to present the overall plot, along with each of the item plots partitioned schematically, as in Figure 20.7. In this way the data relationships can be discussed and any findings of interest elaborated. The reader may be left to visualise the way in which variables combine and relate to the items, or further schematic diagrams may be presented.

The second type of presentation is to summarise the data relationships in one diagram, where the variable partitions in the item plots are used to interpret the similarities and differences between the items. The researcher would then draw partitions on to the plot to express the meaning of the similarities and differences between the items being studied. This approach is popular with authors using facet theory (see Chapter 8), and should be treated with some caution until the researcher is familiar with the different types of partitioning and their interpretative implications (see Levy, 1981).

20.7 FURTHER READING

Berelson (1971) and Krippendorf (1980) are some of the most widely cited books on content analysis. However, Bainbridge (1985) and Mostyn (1985) provide more readable accounts of the procedure (see also Chapter 18).

A methodological account of MSA is provided by Zvulun (1978). Brown (1985) and Canter (1983a) discuss MSA in relation to facet theory. The use of MSA in conjunction with the multiple sorting procedure is outlined by Canter et al. (1985), and applications in the study of conceptual development in education and group decision making are illustrated in Wilson and Canter (1990) and Wilson and Canter (1993) respectively.

21

Diary Techniques

Glynis M. Breakwell and Peter Wood

Contents

21.1 WHAT ARE DIARY TECHNIQUES?

Any data collection strategy which entails getting respondents to provide information linked to a temporal framework is essentially a diary technique. The record of information in relation to the passage of time is referred to as the diary. In fact, this record may be unlike anything that would be recognised as a traditional diary purchased in a stationery shop and would not necessarily involve a *daily* record of events: the frequency of entries differs according to the research purpose. Diaries can involve various media of report (most obviously verbal or written records but also photographic or video descriptions). Nowadays, researchers might use multimedia diary records. The diary techniques allow the medium of the record to be chosen so as to best suit the topic and the type of respondent studied. One recent study, for example, used the original idea of a *postcard* diary for tracking health care utilisation (Reuben et al., 1995).

The reports required can differ substantially in the amount of structure imposed by the researcher and the flexibility permitted the diarist. Some demand very detailed accounts of one type of behaviour. For instance, consumer researchers may wish to know how often certain groups of people purchase eco-labelled products. They can find out something about this by asking samples from those groups to keeping shopping diaries in which they simply have to tick against a checklist what they purchase on a daily or weekly basis. In such diaries, entries are carefully pre-structured. If, however, the object was broadly to understand more about eco-friendly behaviour, the research might ask each individual to describe in the diary what they thought they had done during that period which had some bearing on environmental conservation.

Diary studies can use reports which are specially elicited or can be analyses of spontaneously generated records of information over time. So, for instance, a researcher attempting to identify the way military leaders make decisions under stress may ask a sample of such leaders to produce diaries during an operation specifically for the study or may consider it more useful to analyse the published diaries of senior army commanders. The value of historical diary material has recently been more accepted by psychologists who now recognise that it is one way to test claims that psychological processes are socio-culturally specific.

Since it is simply a data collection strategy, the diary can be used as part of any type of research design. Diary techniques have been used in experimental and quasi-experimental research designs as well as in single case studies, large scale surveys and ethnographies.

The time period over which the diary is drawn can vary widely from a few hours to several years and this is echoed in variability in the periodicity of entries, which can range from every few minutes to every few months.

21.2 WHAT SORTS OF DATA ARE SUITABLE?

Diary techniques can be used with virtually any type of data. The breadth of subject matter is as large as the imagination of the researcher. They may entail reports of actions, thoughts or feelings as well as accounts of physical or social context. An interesting example of unusual subject matter for a diary comes from the work of Freud on the interpretation of dreams. He compiled records of his own dreams by writing down what he remembered of them as soon as he awoke each morning. Dream researchers still use this method. More conventional early uses of diaries tended to concentrate on such issues as consumer buying patterns, household work activities or TV viewing patterns. However their usage has spread to a much greater range of psychological issues. Recent examples drawn from the psychological literature utilised the technique to study social interaction (Nezlek, 1991), cognitive therapy (Campbell, 1992), illness behaviour (Dworkin and Wilson, 1993), mood or emotional states (King and Wilson, 1992), stressful events and HIV/AIDS (Coxon, 1995).

In addition, diaries are now often used in combination with other psychological methods, such as questionnaires (see Chapter 12) or structured observation (see Chapter 16), to provide a more rounded picture, or as part of the process of triangulation. This diverse list is by no means comprehensive, but clearly illustrates how ubiquitous the diary technique has become.

We might assume that the diary technique would be restricted to a single individual making self-reports about some aspect of themselves or their life. However this is not necessarily the case. Numerous studies involve respondents completing diaries on themselves and others (in studies of social interaction for example), or pairs of respondents completing diaries about the same events (husband and wife for instance) (Dunn et al., 1993).

21.3 THE PROS AND CONS OF THE DIARY APPROACH

Since diary techniques have no simple uniform guise, it is not easy to draw up simple lists of the pros and cons associated with them as a research method when exploring psychological processes. Some forms of diary technique have some types of advantage and disadvantage; other forms have different costs and benefits. It is, however, possible to give general indications of the strengths and weaknesses of this approach to data collection.

The diary approach can be used to great effect because respondents are typically familiar with the notion of what a diary is. When you ask someone if they will keep a diary of activities of a specific kind every day over a fortnight, the person understands the task. You may need to refine that understanding through careful instructions, but you have the advantage of the respondent having some initial appreciation of what you want. This may be very helpful if you are dealing with individuals who are especially anxious, suspicious or ignorant about psychological assessments. Having said this, one should bear in mind that when we draw a sample for any type of psychological study, the characteristics of the volunteers may differ from those of the non-volunteers. There is some evidence that even when using essentially non-threatening diaries, those who volunteer are likely to be more stable and have less anxious personalities than those who do not (Waite et al., 1998).

The diary approach can be particularly useful, and cost-effective, when you want data from the same person over a considerable period of time and/or very frequently. Given appropriate instructions, respondents can be generating information often for long periods without the need for the researcher to be in contact. They can be given the diary to complete and only recontacted at the end of the study.

Of course, the greatest advantage of the diary approach is that it yields information which is temporally ordered. It tells you the sequence of events, giving you the profile of action, feelings or thoughts across time. There are other ways of doing this but they tend to involve greater intervention by the researcher and consequently higher potential interference with the sequence under consideration.

Diaries are often used in order to access so-called 'intimate' information (for example, about sexual behaviour), in the belief that iterative self-reporting, mostly without any interpersonal interaction, will engender self-revelation and honesty. Whether this assumption is valid or not has not been fully established: however, it seems likely that respondents may be prone to **under-reporting** events/behaviour they believe may be disapproved of, and conversely **over-reporting** things they think people will approve of. In some cases this common social desirability bias can be allowed for and it remains the case that the range and variety of personal information elicited in a diary can be very great. This makes it a valuable tool when first formally exploring an area of psychological processes.

Diaries can be used to map the variety of human experiences salient in a domain. In doing this, it is sometimes useful to use spontaneously generated diaries. Just because a diary was not produced specifically for your research does not mean that it is not useful to your research. There are essentially two

types of spontaneously generated diaries: those produced for private consumption and those produced for public consumption. There is some evidence
that women are more likely to keep private diaries than men. It has been
suggested that the act of diary-keeping may be interpreted as a self-initiated
coping strategy for life's hassles, involving reflection and aiding the management of emotions.

Both types can be useful for the psychological researcher. They differ significantly in two ways: their accessibility and their veracity. The accessibility
difference is evident. Getting hold of diaries which have not been produced for
publication can be difficult for obvious reasons: you are unlikely to know of
their existence and, even if you do, you are unlikely to get permission to use
them. The veracity difference is more contentious. Diarists writing for public
consumption are subject to a variety of pressures which may lead to misrep-
resentation of events or their sequencing. In the simplest terms, diarists who
seek publication of their diaries are unlikely to wish to represent themselves
negatively. They will wish, most probably, to justify or excuse themselves.
Questions concerning their accessibility and veracity obviously limit the real
usefulness of spontaneously generated diaries for psychological researchers.
However, it must be added that published diaries are one of the few sources of
data giving a historical perspective on psychological processes. If, for instance,
a researcher wishes to examine whether questions of identity processes which
were pertinent in the late twentieth century were salient in the nineteenth
century, one of the rare ways of tackling the question will be through a
systematic analysis of diaries produced in that period.

The advantages of the diary approach can be summarised therefore in a few
key words: familiarity; cost-effective sampling of information; sequencing
data; intimacy; exploration; spontaneity; and historicity.

The potential disadvantages of the diary approach can be ameliorated and
are not inevitable. They should nevertheless be summarised before examining
the ways to overcome them. Control over the data elicited is always difficult
to achieve. Clearly, if you use spontaneously generated diaries you have no
real control over what data are provided. These diaries inevitably involve **self-
selection of material** by the diarist. Even if you use diaries which you request,
your level of control is suspect. You can, of course, ask for specific categories
of information. However, getting people to remember to make entries at
the right time about the right things can be difficult, even when they have
goodwill towards the research and every intention of complying with your
instructions.

The diary technique is plagued by a further lack of control. Diary studies
suffer significant problems with dropout: respondents do not continue to provide information throughout the designated period. This problem of **sample
maintenance** often can be exacerbated by poor initial recruitment into the
study. Completing a diary (especially over any lengthy period) can be seen as
onerous and will result in people being unwilling to join the study in the first
place. This combined with subsequent potentially high dropout rates is likely
to mean that the sample is highly biased by the end of the study.

Another disadvantage of the diary approach harks back to the issue of
veracity. Getting the respondent to tell you the truth may be difficult but,

more importantly, you may never be able to ascertain whether they did or not. It may be necessary, if you are very concerned with verifiability of data, to use other methods alongside the diary approach. A number of such studies have been conducted to establish the validity of diary data by comparing them with such methods as checklists, interviews, questionnaires, observation and mechanical recording methods. By and large the results have been encouragingly positive, although reporting biases have been shown to occur in some cases, as mentioned earlier.

Like any intrusive research technique, the diary when initiated by the researcher may produce data affected by 'reactance'. The very fact of having to produce the diary may alter the behaviour, thoughts, feelings and so on which are recorded. An example of this effect comes from Freud's dream diaries. As he got into the habit of recording the dreams, he found that he 'dreamed more often' (i.e. tended to wake at a point in the sleep cycle when he was more likely to recall his dreams). The extent of reactance is essentially unassessable and may vary over time throughout the period of the research, thus influencing results in a non-constant fashion. It is clear, however, that if we require individuals to make large numbers of entries, or write extensively about events, then the action 'diary filling in' becomes a significant element of everyday behaviour. Whilst in general we look for psychological methods to have low reactance, occasionally the process of conducting the study can be deliberately planned so as to have positive effects. At least one such study involving the diary technique has used this approach. In this case, the research was concerned with the management of information systems development, and it was found that the act of filling in the diaries supported reflection and changed work habits by the respondents.

The disadvantages of diary techniques can be summarised in a few key words: control of content; dropout; poor recruitment; veracity and verifiability; and reactance.

21.4 GETTING THE BEST OUT OF DIARY TECHNIQUES

The advantages of the diary approach can, obviously, be enhanced and the disadvantages minimised by careful construction of the research.

First, it is obviously important to choose the right recording medium for your type of respondents. Respondents lacking the necessary level of literacy should not be asked to produce written diaries (this might include the young, the ill-educated, and anyone who for physical reasons – e.g. poor eyesight – might find the task impossible). Alternative recording forms such as audio-taping should be considered.

Second, respondents should be given very comprehensive and comprehensible instructions on how to complete the diary. Pilot work should be used to establish that the instructions are understandable. These instructions should emphasise the importance of accuracy and offer assurances of confidentiality and anonymity where appropriate. They should indicate that entries need to be made regularly at the times specified and explain that entries made retrospectively, relying on memory, are subject to distortions which detract from

MONDAY

Please enter today's date here:

Please enter in the table below how much time (in minutes) you spent in the 24 hours
between 12 midnight Sunday and 12 midnight Monday doing each of the things listed.

Number of minutes

Sleeping
Physical exercise (e.g. walking, football)
Doing housework (e.g. cooking, cleaning
   the house, washing clothes)
Looking for a job
Watching TV
In the pub
House maintenance (e.g. painting, decorating)
Gardening

FIGURE 21.1   *Example page of a diary*

the value of the information. The possibility of reactance should be described
to the respondents in simple terms so that they are on guard against it.

Third, the diary format should be straightforward and uncluttered. With
written diaries the print quality of the booklet is important as a cue to the
professionalism of the research. Layout is vital for the written diary.
Respondents have to be given enough room to provide their answers. Figure
21.1 is an example of a diary layout which might be used in a piece of
research designed to establish how unemployed men spend their time. The
format imposes a clear structure on the record, indicating which types of
activity should be reported and what the unit of report is to be (i.e. length
of time).

Fourth, no matter how clear the diary format and instructions are, there
will be respondents who fail to understand. It helps to give respondents an
example of a completed entry to the diary so that they can see what they are
supposed to be doing. Also part of the procedure for diary administration,
whenever possible, should include talking the respondent through the diary.
This will allow you to cue and target appropriate recording. As a general rule,
therefore, diary placement would normally involve a personal contact by a
member of the research team, rather than sending diaries by post.

Fifth, problems with sample maintenance are reduced if you can ensure
relatively frequent contact with respondents. This is particularly important in
the early stages of a diary study. As with direct observation (see Chapter 16)
there will inevitably be queries about category definitions (what, for example,
constitutes a 'leisure activity'?), questions about the boundaries between
various activities, the level of detail required and so on. It may be useful to
provide respondents with a telephone number, so that they can contact you
to resolve such queries fairly quickly. If this is not done then they may abandon
the recording because they are in a state of uncertainty about what to record,

or perhaps even worse, make up their own decisions about what should be recorded and thus provide large numbers of entries that are useless for your analysis.

A postcard or telephone call occasionally (e.g. birthday or Christmas cards) for long term diary studies has been shown to improve sample retention. Requiring diaries to have frequent entries also seems to improve sample maintenance. Material incentives (such as small payments) tend to have a good effect upon retention. Along these lines, researchers have used lotteries to encourage both joining and remaining in studies. The prospect of winning something has been shown to incite initial interest but, once the outcome of the lottery is known, some researchers have found large scale dropout. One answer seems to be to operate with repeated lotteries but this practice is less effective now as the general public have become sensitised to the technique.

Sixth, in order to maximise initial response rates and to retain the sample subsequently, it has been shown that it is best to start with relatively brief diaries. If you need to collect lengthy diaries, it seems to be most effective to introduce the respondent to the process first using a short diary. They can be weaned from the short to the long version more easily than persuading them to start from scratch on a lengthy diary.

Finally, there have been various ingenious techniques used to ensure that people remember to make entries when they are supposed to do so. It is now not uncommon to give respondents electronic paging devices and ask them to make their entries when the devices bleep. Alternatively, researchers may enlist the help of other members of the family to remind the respondent at meal times. Some recent studies have used computer-assisted diaries (Baumann et al., 1996), whilst others have used electronic devices for a time-use diary (Kalfs and Willem, 1998)

21.5 ANALYSING DIARY DATA

Since the forms of data yielded from diary studies vary widely, many analytic approaches are possible. The decision that you take concerning the amount of structure which you impose upon the record will affect all subsequent decisions. If you leave the diarist free to choose what is recorded you are virtually sure to need to conduct a content analysis before doing any further data processing. The procedures involved in content analysis are described in Chapter 19. Having done the content analysis, you can subject the data to either a qualitative or a quantitative description.

Content analysis, when tied to simple quantification, is most likely to result in a matrix which tells you how many people report each category of behaviour or event and how often these occurred. This may be all you need to do but that is unlikely. A major feature of a diary technique is that it gives you data which are ordered over time. To take advantage of this you need to use analyses which allow you to map sequences or patterns in the data across time.

One way to do this with non-parametric data is to use an analysis which identifies whether within the sample there are groups of respondents whose sequences of entries are similar to each other and different from the patterns of other groups. So for instance in a sample of 25 men completing diaries for the first 3 months of a period of unemployment, there might be 10 who spend most of their time in job search for the first month, house maintenance for the second and watching TV for the third. Another 10 might focus on housework in month 1, job search in month 2 and TV watching in month 3. The remaining 5 might concentrate on TV watching in month 1, job search in month 2 and TV watching again in month 3. The analysis would show the range of profiles that exist in the sample. It would also show whether the distribution of individuals across the profiles is not statistically significant and might be expected by chance. Profiles exemplified by either more or less of the sample than would be expected by chance are worth exploring further since these may be indicative of 'types' or 'anti-types' of response. The task of the psychologist would then be to explain the origin of these 'types'. One statistical technique which will allow you to identify these profiles is called configural frequency analysis (e.g. von Eye, 1990). There are, of course, many other mechanisms for structuring qualitative data (see for example Chapter 20).

When you use highly structured entry formats in the diary the range of analytic approaches available is very broad. There is no reason why the diary should not include standard questions with response categories such as those used in a questionnaire. In this case, you would be able to use all of the techniques described in Chapter 12.

In choosing analytic approaches the vital thing to remember is that you are using them merely as tools that will give you answers to the questions you posed at the start of the research. Amid the flood of data which a diary technique can generate, it is easy to lose sight of your original objectives for the research. You can get lost in the minutiae of the specific life stories. The process of analysis should be one which allows you to see genuine patterns within these data. Thus it is vital to choose analytic tools which give you relevant answers and which are appropriate for the type of data you have.

21.6 CONCLUSIONS

It should be clear that the diary technique is potentially extremely useful as a means of collecting psychological and behavioural data. As with other methods it has both advantages and disadvantages. Before embarking on a diary study you should ask yourself a number of questions. Firstly, a blindingly obvious one: 'Do I *really need* to collect data on a continuous basis over time?' Secondly, although we should always have a clear idea of our research objectives, this is particularly so when using diaries. The reason for this was mentioned earlier. Diaries can be a very rich source of data, and unless we have a clear view of the purpose of the study, the unwary researcher can be overwhelmed by the volume of data generated. Finally, do not be seduced by the apparent simplicity of the technique. The quality of the data will be directly related to the amount of time which has been spent in the development of the instrument and the care which is invested in its subsequent placement and maintenance.

21.7 FURTHER READING

Perhaps not surprisingly, given the novelty of diaries in psychological research, there are few general texts on the topic; most discussion of the technique is associated with particular instances of diary research. Two books which give some broad coverage to the technique are: Bryant and Edwards (eds) (1992) *Methodological Issues in Applied Social Psychology: Social Psychological Applications to Social Issues* and Montgomery and Duck (eds) (1991) *Studying Interpersonal Interaction*. If you come across a diary study in your chosen research area, by all means be guided by precedent; however, you should not feel obliged to copy existing procedures.

22

Focus Groups

Lynne J. Millward

Contents

22.1 INTRODUCTION

The focus group is a discussion-based interview that produces a particular type of qualitative data. It involves the simultaneous use of multiple respondents to generate data and it is the 'focused' (i.e. on an 'external stimulus') and relatively staged (i.e. by a 'moderator') nature of the focus group method that separates it from other types of group interviewing strategy. According to some, a focus group is no more than a well-targeted and designed meeting. Yet the implications of this for psychology are not quite so simple. Whilst the study of group processes has a rich and substantial research history, the focus group challenges the epistemological assumptions underlying much research in psychology. This lends it a rather controversial flavour.

The focus group has historical roots in sociology, being associated with research into the effectiveness of wartime propaganda (Merton and Kendall, 1946) and the social effects of mass communication generally. Yet its methodological evolution is attributable not to sociologists but to marketing consultants for whom focus groups have become central to answering the question of 'why' consumers behave as they do. For decades, the use of focus groups within the marketing context has relied on the untested assumption that generating group data is the quickest and most cost-efficient means of obtaining consumer relevant information. Currently, the focus group method – at least in the marketing domain – has largely evolved as a 'quick and dirty' means of fulfilling client needs rather than as a sophisticated research tool. The substantial literature on how to conduct focus groups was thus mainly tied to the marketing arena (see section 22.13) rather than set within a framework of social science.

In 1988 Morgan noted that 'the contribution of focus groups to social science research at present is more potential than real' (p. 75). At that time few focus group studies had been published indicating that the method could be successfully transported beyond marketing boundaries into the social sciences generally. Since then there has been an exponential rise in the number of studies employing focus group methodology, as witnessed by the increased number of social science textbooks devoted to the topic (e.g. Greenbaum, 1998; Krueger, 1994; Morgan and Krueger, 1997). Within psychology alone, the method has gained a substantial foothold since 1988. Between 1991 and 1997, 210 papers were identified in PsycLit, all of which use the focus group method as either their primary or their secondary data gathering technique, compared with only 10 recorded between 1974 and 1991. The method is seen to be especially popular within applied psychology, particularly consumer psychology and health psychology.

Morgan went on to warn that 'social scientists will have to work hard to adapt the focus group technique to their purposes' (1988: 77–8). How far have we come since then? Have we managed to integrate the method into our repertoire of research techniques? What kind of data can and does it yield? What potential does the technique have for refinement and/or elaboration? Until recently, the focus group method has been primarily used to elicit information about consumer needs, desires/preferences and responses to products or services with a view to developing more appropriate products, services or interventions and/or more effective marketing strategies. It is only now that the method is being harnessed from a distinctly psychological rather than socio-logical or marketing perspective. For instance, the focus group is beginning to be used as a forum in which to develop and/or operationalise constructs (e.g. Strong and Large, 1995), elicit a uniquely different perspective on an issue (e.g. Michell and West, 1996) and generate dialogue worthy of analysis in its own right (e.g. Lunt, 1996). However, uses of this kind are still few and far between. Secondary uses of the focus group with a 'psychological edge' to them (e.g. for decision making, intervention, collective empowerment and social change), and of which there are many, do not fall within the same remit. In these instances, the focus group is used as a strategic tool for obtaining some end other than research (e.g. attitude change, problem solving).

As in the chapter written for the first edition of this book, I hope to demonstrate that focus groups can not only enhance the ability of psycho-logists to answer their research questions but more importantly generate questions from new angles and perspectives. Some additional practical issues will also be addressed later in this chapter: in particular, the tendency of participant employees to cast the facilitator in the role of 'organisational therapist', and also issues of confidentiality. It will be argued that the future of focus group research in psychology depends not only on the quality and rigour of its use (Krueger, 1993) but also on political and interpersonal acumen in many instances (Asbury, 1995).

22.2 THE APPROPRIATENESS OF THE FOCUS GROUP METHOD

Used alone or in combination with other methods, the aim of focus groups is to get closer to participants' understandings of and perspectives on certain issues. It is not geared to the formal testing of hypotheses in the traditional hypothetico-deductive sense, although it can be used for hypothesis formu-lation and/or construct development. The focus group can be used either as a self-contained means of data collection (i.e. a primary research technique) or as a supplement (i.e. a supplementary research technique) to other methods depending on how it fits into the overall research plan, and also its epi-stemological basis (i.e. qualitative, quantitative).

Used as a primary research technique, the focus group method is a forum in which to explore people's opinions, attitudes, beliefs, values, discourses and understandings of things, as valid in their own right. Exploration of this kind may be of particular interest to researchers operating within the qualitative epistemological tradition like discourse analysts (e.g. Lunt, 1996) or advocates of the phenomenological approach (e.g. Michell and West, 1996). For instance, Lunt (1996) used the focus group to elicit and unpack discourses of 'savings', which he observed to be extremely complex (e.g. tension between discourses of cash and credit, between budgeting and borrowing, between necessity and luxury, and between prudence and pleasure) and linked to discourses of social and economic change.

On a different note, Michell and West (1996) obtained 'phenomenological' evidence from focus group research suggesting that children are more self-determined during their teenage years than they have been given credit for, being actively involved in the decision to smoke or not. This evidence challenges the findings of previous research using conventional techniques demonstrating that young people are more often than not coerced or bullied into smoking by their peers. The potential for focus groups to yield an alternative and equally valid perspective on an issue than that afforded by other more traditional techniques is thus illustrated.

Alternatively, the focus group as a primary tool may be used as a first step in the process of construct development and/or questionnaire development. For instance, Strong and Large (1995) explored the 'coping' construct in the context of chronic pain using the focus group method, whilst Hyland et al. (1991) used it to derive issues and themes pertinent to coping with asthma as the basis for questionnaire construction (e.g. The Living with Asthma Questionnaire). Some work has also been conducted demonstrating the potential for focus groups to yield data pertinent to testing the viability of a conceptual model. Specifically, Stanton et al. (1993) used constructs provided by 'protection motivation theory' to examine risk protection in the context of adolescent sexual behaviour. In this case the theory was used to 'focus' and also 'frame' the discussion. Here the emphasis was on understanding risk protection practices using the developmental, socio-historical and cultural concepts afforded by the theory rather than on offering a formal test of the theory and its validity.

As a supplement to other more traditional methods, the focus group method may be used to provide a more in-depth look at the issue in question. Probably the most common use of the focus group method is supplementary to the large scale survey (Asbury, 1995). An example of this is provided by Winborne and Dardaine (1993) who used the focus group to supplement survey data, using it as the means for generating a dialogue around issues arising from the survey, with a view to identifying 'common ground' in representations of the child 'at risk' in an educational setting.

22.3 WHAT TYPE OF EVIDENCE DO FOCUS GROUPS YIELD?

From a social psychological perspective, the focus group is 'by definition an exercise in group dynamics and the conduct of the group, as well as the interpretation of results obtained must be understood within the context of group interaction' (Stewart and Shamdasani, 1990: 7). Two interrelated forms of evidence are therefore derived from focus groups: the group process (the way in which people interact and communicate with each other) and the content around which the group process is organised (the focal stimulus and the issues arising from it).

The group process can be understood on two different levels: (1) intrapersonal, i.e. the thoughts, feelings, attitudes and values of the individual; (2) intragroup, i.e. how people communicate and interact with each other within the group. Considerations of the group process are integral to the role of the moderator who will require very different skills from those of one-to-one interviewing. This is dealt with later on in the chapter. Here we need to consider the implications of the group process for the form of evidence elicited. Basically, focus groups afford rich insight into the realities defined in a group context and in particular the dynamic effects of interaction on expressed beliefs, attitudes, opinions and feelings.

One advantage of using the group as opposed to the individual as the medium of investigation is its 'isomorphism to the process of opinion formation and propagation in everyday life' in so far as 'opinions about a variety of issues are generally determined not by individual information gathering and deliberation but through communication with others' (Albrecht et al., 1993: 54). Focus groups are communication events in which the interplay of the personal and the social can be systematically explored. This alludes to the potential of the focus group method in the investigation of social representations – their structure and processes, and identity-related phenomena (Breakwell, 1993). Social representations originate in communication and interaction processes. They are forged in particular by people attempting to make sense of their lives. As such, social representations reflect and communicate identity issues and provide a basis for action.

Gervais (1993), for instance, used focus groups (among other qualitative methods) involving Shetlanders to analyse their processes of social representation in the wake of an oil spill. Each focus group comprised a natural social unit (a family, a fisherman crew, fish farmers, local council members and a group who had got together after the spill to act on behalf of the community). Evidence revealed the evolution of a collective rhetoric which maintained community integrity by minimising the impact of the crisis despite it being experienced 'like a death in the family' (engendered by the intimate relationship that Shetlanders have with their land). The rhetoric was derived from Shetlanders representations of their identity as 'resilient' and of the archipelago as 'The Old Rock'. The focus groups thus provided the ideal forum in which the collective mobilisation of community resources and traditions could be captured and analysed in the face of crisis.

The assumption is that people will become more aware of their own perspective when confronted with active disagreement and be prompted to analyse their views more intensely than during the individual interview. Attempts to resolve differences are one of several mechanisms whereby participants build comprehensive accounts to explain their various experiences, beliefs, attitudes, feelings, values and behaviours. Jarrett (1993), for instance, describes how, in her study involving low-income black Americans, participants were inclined to 'perform for each other'; a climate was established in which they were encouraged to discuss things with greater licence than they would otherwise. The reality created within this forum was tempered by peer pressure to 'tell it like it is' whenever idealism prevailed. In this way group pressure inhibited people from providing misleading information.

Few have taken up this potential within focus group contexts for examining communication processes *per se* and the impact of these on the way a topic is constructed *in situ*. Most uses of the focus group are focused on eliciting 'content' (i.e. opinions, attitudes, feelings, etc.) rather than investigating focus group 'processes' and their influence on how content comes about. One rare example of the latter is provided by Delli-Carpini and Williams (1994) who used the focus group technique to examine the relationship between television and the formation of public opinion. The focus group was seen as a vehicle (a 'conversational metaphor') for examining the way opinions are formed via discourse generated by television. This conversational metaphor for examining the influence of the media contrasts radically with the idea that the media operate like a 'hypodermic' syringe, 'injecting' people with opinions. Instead it fosters a view of people forming opinions through dialogue, in the way described by Moscovici (1976). It is this kind of research that reveals the true potential of focus groups in social science research.

22.4   THE FOCAL STIMULI

The 'focusing' component of focus group research – i.e. its distinguishing characteristic – refers to the concrete and specific character of the discussion in relation to a particular stimulus object, event or situation. Originally the stimulus object was a form of mass media communication (e.g. a film or a pamphlet). In marketing, the focus of research might be people's reactions to a particular advertising campaign or consumer product. In the social sciences, the stimulus might be a behavioural scenario (e.g. a sexual encounter as a way of accessing attitudes towards safer sex: O'Brien, 1993), a concrete event (e.g. driving and young people's risk taking: Basch, 1987), or even a concept (e.g. household crowding and its effects on psychological wellbeing: Fuller et al., 1993). The range of possible stimuli is in fact quite extensive, extending to the use of projective techniques, role-play scenarios, word association exercises, sentence completion and fantasy themes – which have proved especially effective in eliciting responses from children.

One suggestion put forward by Stanton et al. (1993) is to use 'theory' as the focusing vehicle. Where the topic of conversation or issue is complex and/or potentially sensitive (personally or politically), 'theory' can afford some useful constructs or questions around which to anchor the dialogue. Stanton et al. (1993) invited young adolescents to talk about their sexual behaviours for instance by using risk-protection constructs from 'protection motivation theory' as the means to guide them. Moreover, they say, the use of constructs to frame focus group discussion in this way can help 'translate theory' into practice. Hilder (1997) used Schein's model of organisational culture – an otherwise complex and multi-faceted construct – to frame employee discussion in a series of focus groups conducted in organisational settings. Culture is a topic that employees may not have thought much about before, and even if they had, may not easily be able to comment on it without being provided with some kind of discussion context. The researcher is thus faced with a dilemma. If the discussion is framed using constructs from a model, there is an obvious risk of prejudicing the information gained. 'Advance organisers' of this kind may eliminate other avenues that would otherwise be explored by participants with respect to the topic of culture, which thus risks loss of useful information. On the other hand, participants may not know where to start or what to say, and may end up talking endlessly about quite superficial aspects of culture giving them most cause for grievance (e.g. lack of office space, poor air conditioning). Since some kind of 'focus' is necessary and limitless time is not available, it may be more sensible, Hilder (1997) recommends, to scene-set so as to gain quality input on the preferred topic within an agreed time-span.

Providing focus by framing the discussion in some way, using theoretical constructs or a conceptual model, raises issues of whether the research objectives should be communicated to the focus group. In general, research objectives guided by substantive issues (i.e. theoretical concerns) are not likely to be exactly the same as the aims presented to participants and which are used to frame the discussion process. In the research conducted by Stanton et al. (1993) it is unlikely that the participants were told that the aim of the focus group was to enable the researchers to 'explore developmental, socio-historical and cultural concepts' influencing sexual behaviour! Participants would be informed more concretely that the aim is to find out what they think or how they feel about particular sexual behaviours. The aim of the focus group is the research objective translated into a concrete operational form. Thus, if the purpose of the research is to 'get inside the consumer mind' (e.g. Cooper and Tower, 1992), the onus is on the researcher to translate this into an aim that will both focus and facilitate group dialogue (e.g. 'the aim of the discussion is to find out what your feelings are about . . .'). Where focus groups are guided purely by pragmatic rather than substantive concerns (e.g. to find out what clients think about the quality of a particular hospital service), the aims are rather more translucent.

The issue of what to tell participants about the research aims generally is likely to become particularly salient in an organisational context where political sensitivities may arise. For example, in focus groups to discuss organisational culture, the objective may be to articulate a particular model of culture, or to test an approach for eliciting employees' understandings of culture, or simply to attempt an analysis and understanding of organisational culture. In each of these cases the topic for discussion is the organisation's culture, which is made clear, but the actual objectives of the focus group may remain opaque as far as participants are concerned. Yet at the same time, participants may become suspicious and defensive, apt even to withhold information or to say only what they feel is expected of them, if they perceive that they are not being properly informed. Participants may suspect a 'hidden agenda' and will need to be reassured that this is not so. Gaining participation in defining the nature and scope of the subject for discussion is one way of achieving a sense of group ownership of a topic (and thereby opening people up to further discussion) especially if the definition is then employed as an *aide-mémoire* throughout the session (Hilder, 1997).

22.5 THE USE OF FOCUS GROUPS IN SURVEY DESIGN AND INTERPRETATION

Although surveys and focus groups originate from different research paradigms, there is nothing inherent in the methods themselves that should prevent them from being integrated into one research design. The survey method is not designed to investigate phenomena in any great depth and yet its design must be built on some assumptions about the meaning of certain things for a particular population of people. The focus group method provides a forum in which some of these assumptions can be tested. Moreover it can yield information about an issue, or indeed raise issues that have never been considered in relation to the topic at hand.

Specifically, the researcher can become acquainted with the phraseology and concepts used by a certain population of respondents. They can establish the variety of opinion concerning a topic, establish relevant dimensions of attitudes and identify relevant indicators for the constructs being measured. Focus groups are helpful in cross-cultural survey research where they can clarify the relevance of certain concepts and redefine them using common vernacular (e.g. Harari and Beaty, 1990). They can be used to test various questionnaire items for readability, comprehension, wording, order effects and response variation.

There are other ways that focus groups might be used once the survey has been conducted. The first is to assess respondents' reactions to the survey and in particular to trace the cognitive and social processes involved in answering, and the second is to aid in the interpretation of survey findings by exploring in greater depth the implications of certain quantitative patterns and relationships (e.g. Cooper and Tower, 1992).

22.6   FOCUS GROUP DESIGN AND PLANNING

The very first step in the design and planning process is to define and clarify the issues to be investigated in terms of the exact nature of the evidence required. Both substantive and practical considerations will influence this.

22.6.1   Sampling and recruitment of subjects

It is not the intention of focus group methodology to yield generalisable data so random sampling is not necessary. Nonetheless, it is important to employ a systematic strategy when deciding on group composition. The sample should be chosen on theoretical grounds as reflecting those segments of the population who will provide the most meaningful information in terms of the project objectives. Moreover, the participants should have something to say about the topic of interest.

The recruitment strategies employed have important consequences for the degree of co-operation and commitment generated amongst respondents. The time and energy invested in meeting with 'local' people and making personal contact with potential participants at the outset can facilitate group rapport and contribute substantially to this.

Focus group researchers disagree on whether it is necessary to use screening procedures during the recruitment process. One argument in favour of screening alludes to differences in participant background and/or lifestyle that might inhibit the flow of discussion due to lack of common ground. Others argue to the contrary that if all participants were to share virtually identical backgrounds the discussion would be flat and unproductive. The general rule of thumb is that group members should exhibit at least some common characteristics (e.g. same socio-economic class, same age group) to facilitate the sharing of experiences.

Another argument in support of screening is based on the principle of reactivity. Ordinarily, the reactivity arising from the screening process is seen as a liability: participants are given the opportunity to familiarise themselves with the research issues and may therefore enter the focus group situation with prejudice and bias. However, the reactivity created by screening procedures may also afford people the opportunity to mull over the topic in advance. Effectively, the attention given to the topic may enhance rather than undermine the validity of the content generated by the discussion.

Ultimately the decision rests on determining the composition of the group which will maximise the probability of obtaining the most theoretically relevant information. Research identifying how best to construct focus groups is lacking. There is some evidence that males and females interact differently in mixed-sex as opposed to same-sex groups, and this has prompted some to suggest that focus group sessions should be homogeneous in terms of gender (Stewart and Shamdasani, 1990).

Knodel (1993) advocates conducting separate focus group sessions with homogeneous but contrasting subgroups defined in terms of break characteristics. Break characteristics are selected on substantive grounds and involve the subdivision of groups according to their potentially contrasting views and experiences concerning the issues being investigated. For example, the sample may comprise females who are subdivided by role – e.g. 'housewife and mother' and 'career woman' – in an investigation of social representations of women in connection with female identity. Another pertinent break characteristic might be socio-economic class. There is a limit to the number of break characteristics that can be incorporated into any one study. Knodel suggests that they should be kept to a minimum otherwise both the sampling and the analysis process will become unwieldy and also very costly given, at the very least, one focus group conducted for each combination of break variables.

It has become conventional in the marketing context to ensure that the focus group is composed of strangers. Acquaintanceship can indeed inhibit the flow of discussion in certain instances. Social scientists however would argue that there are many occasions when the fact of a shared history is of interest from the point of view of the research objectives. Indeed, there are many examples of focus groups being successfully conducted with naturally occurring communities of people (e.g. Gervais, 1993; Taylor et al., 1991). Taylor et al. (1991) for instance used 'natural' focus groups to examine the psychosocial impact of solid waste facilities within exposed communities. Ultimately, the decision rests on determining the composition of the groups which will maximise the probability of obtaining the most theoretically relevant information. In the Taylor et al. (1991) investigation, it was the community response to potential environmental hazard that was of interest.

22.6.2　Sample size

Sample size (not group size, note) varies widely from as small as 21 (e.g. occupational therapy practitioners in Llewelyn, 1991) to one rare exception of

744 (e.g. parents, adolescents and educators in Croft and Sorrentino, 1991). The number of focus group sessions conducted will be a function of both sample and group size. Some researchers have noted that the data generated after about 10 sessions are largely redundant. The decision rests on the type of evidence required and from whom, as well as considerations of cost in terms of time and resources.

22.6.3   Group size

A systematic review of recent focus group research in psychology yields an average of nine participants per session as conventional, with a range of six to twelve, which on the whole is consistent with the figures quoted in the focus group literature, although some would advocate between six and eight participants as ideal (Albrecht et al., 1993; see also Asbury, 1995). The latter is based on evidence showing that group size is inversely related to the degree of participation fostered.

There are several reasons why it is advisable to keep the groups as small as possible whilst still being able to elicit the breadth of responses required. Large groups are unwieldy to manage, afford free-riding and can be apt to fragment as subgroups form. Also it may be hard to obtain a clear recording of the session: people talk at different volumes and at different distances so the discussion may be difficult if not impossible to track. It is common practice to over-recruit for each session by 20% since it is inevitable that not all will actually turn up. The group size on the day will therefore vary.

22.6.4   Location and setting

Choice of location will need to balance the needs of the research with those of participants. It should set the tone of the research as professional and where possible on neutral ground, although there are times when the sample will be hard to reach unless the research is conducted on home territory (e.g. a hospital). Two prime considerations for participants are convenience and comfort. The location should be easy to reach and the research schedule should not pose any difficulties for them (e.g. child care and transportation problems). Once there, the conditions of the room itself should be conducive to a smooth-flowing discussion and basically comfortable (e.g. appropriate ambience of informality, availability of refreshments, nearby toilets, suitable seating and table arrangements). It is also usual to supply name tags.

22.6.5   Length of session

Most focus group researchers agree that between 1 and 2 hours is the standard duration for each session involving adults, and up to a maximum of 1 hour for sessions involving children.

22.7 FOCUS GROUP IMPLEMENTATION

22.7.1 Moderator style and skills

The skills of the moderator are fundamental to the effectiveness of the focus group. In the social science context it is preferable for the moderator to be someone directly involved in the project who is sensitive to the research issues and the need for methodological rigour even if their group management skills are not especially polished. Moreover, instances may arise where the moderator must be someone with whom the participants can identify in order to gain their trust and commitment (e.g. members of low-income ethnic minority groups). The issue is whether the moderator is able to obtain theoretically useful information. This will require more than just the ability to manage a group: the moderator will need to be someone who can maximise self-disclosure by balancing the 'requirements of sensitivity and empathy on one hand and objectivity and detachment on the other' (Stewart and Shamdasani, 1990: 69). In practice people will talk surprisingly freely about a wide variety of personal topics so long as the climate is permissive and non-critical. Figure 22.1 shows four types of moderator style.

The art of moderating can be termed 'process facilitation'. Central to this is the concept of participant empowerment. Basically this means that the moderator is the facilitator of someone else's discussion. A pose of 'incomplete understanding' but not ignorance (which will appear insincere) is recommended; the moderator makes it clear that (s)he is there to learn from the participants.

The best facilitator guides the proceedings in an unobtrusive and subtle way, intervening only to the extent of maintaining a productive group. For example, one or two of the more dominant group members may be engaged in a heated exchange at the expense of others in the group who are obviously experiencing some discomfort. In this case the moderator would need to take active steps to defuse the situation, refocus the group and balance out the discussion process (segment 3, Figure 22.1).

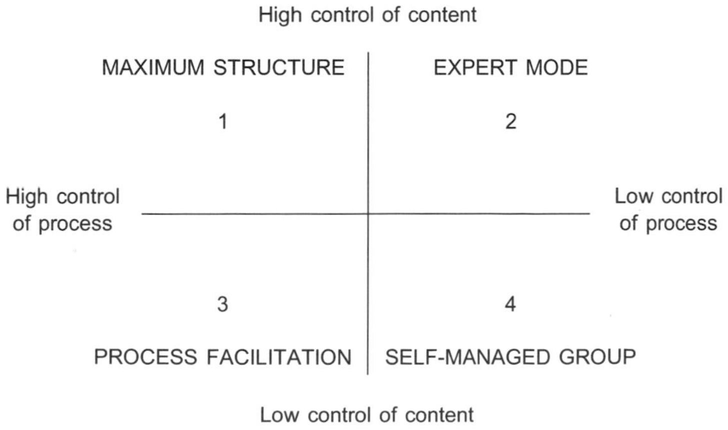

High control of content

MAXIMUM STRUCTURE	EXPERT MODE
1	2

High control of process ─────────────────── Low control of process

3	4
PROCESS FACILITATION	SELF-MANAGED GROUP

Low control of content

FIGURE 22.1 *Four types of moderator style*

There are some instances where group members may themselves take responsibility for the flow as well as the content of the discussion. This would occur when, say, someone in the group tries to reorient a discussion that has gone off track or who frequently asks others for clarification. Jarrett (1993) describes how the low-income African-American women in her study challenged each other's 'idealised accounts' (e.g. as strong women who have to manage errant husbands, disobedient children and meddlesome mothers) of their housewife role. The extent to which self-management of this kind occurs depends on the climate established by the moderator at the very outset (segment 4, Figure 22.1).

Segment 1 of Figure 22.1 maximal direction and control of content and process. This type of moderator style is characterised by a standardised exchange of questions and answers – best suited to the highly structured one-to-one interview.

Segment 2 shows high content control and low process control. This moderator style would befit only the 'expert mode' (e.g. doctor–patient, teacher–pupil). It affords little if any scope for participant involvement. A norm of passivity rather than interaction is created, or one of only talking when asked. Without participant-centred interaction there is no focus group.

Segment 3 shows low content control and high process control. This is the 'process facilitation' moderator style most appropriate for the conduct of focus groups. The moderator facilitates interaction amongst the participants by ensuring that the discussion is productive (i.e. all the relevant issues are covered and in sufficient depth), Control over content is minimal; only the issues to be focused on are determined in advance. However there will be occasions when the research objectives are revised in accordance with the findings derived from focus group sessions, in which case the moderator should allow mainly the participants to determine the agenda.

Segment 4 shows minimal direction and control of content and process. This segment characterises the self-managed group. The moderator may introduce the focus group session in the process facilitation mode and then work to empower the participants to take progressively more responsibility for the process as well as the content of the discussion (movement from segment 3 to segment 4). It therefore provides the opportunity to see how participants naturally organise their discussions of certain issues. The climate is also ripe for the discussion of controversial or sensitive topics that would otherwise threaten rapport if the researcher introduced them. The main disadvantage of course is the complete absence of standardisation, thus rendering it impossible to compare findings across different focus groups within the same research project. Without prompting, some topics may never come up.

The degree of control over the structure in any one focus group session will vary along the central continuum. The less the degree of external control, the less opportunity for moderator biases to operate (e.g. unwittingly leading participants into a particular area of discussion that provides validation for previous work), thereby increasing the validity of the information derived.

As well as the criterion of minimal direction, there are three additional criteria for ensuring that 'focus' is maintained: specificity, range and depth. The first requires that minute detail is sought in people's responses and reactions to the stimulus object or event. It is the moderator's task to elicit meanings and differential responses. The second concerns coverage, the issue for the moderator being one of facilitating transitions from one area of a discussion to another. The third concerns the personal context of the response or reaction elicited by the stimulus. Eliciting in-depth responses involves expanding on responses beyond limited reports of 'positive' or 'negative', 'pleasant' or 'unpleasant' reactions. The moderator's task is to diagnose the level of depth at which participants are operating (i.e. ranging from superficial description to detailed elaboration) and where necessary to shift it towards a 'deeper' level. All these criteria can be met by the moderator who is skilled in listening and questioning techniques.

22.7.2 Topic guide

A topic guide is necessary only to the extent that it prompts the moderator to recall the key issues to be discussed. The guide should be no more than suggestive, affording the moderator considerable latitude to improvise fruitful questions and pursue unanticipated lines of inquiry as the discussion progresses. Do not use the guide in the form of a questionnaire or interviewing straitjacket. Reliance on fixed questions may undermine the ability of the moderator to listen analytically to the content of the discussion, thereby overlooking the implications of what is said. Sometimes the feelings being expressed in people's comments are cloaked in abstractions and rationalisations. The moderator might form a hunch about the nature of the undercurrent and raise it in the form of tentative questions, thus creating a climate in which people are encouraged to articulate their feelings. To ward against using the guide as a script, some have advocated that the issues to be covered are instead committed to memory. The number of issues raised will depend on the extent to which the group identifies with the topic as a whole and the type of thinking they are required to engage in (e.g. highly sensitive topics may lead quickly to emotional fatigue). It may be advisable to pre-test the 'tone' of the discussion to derive clues about the appropriateness of the focus group method for how easily or openly a topic is discussed and the range of emotions elicited.

22.7.3 Listening and questioning skills

The listening and questioning style of the moderator is key to determining the nature of the discussion. This will reflect in the sequence of questions as well as how the questions are worded. Leading questions – ones that prompt people to agree or confirm something that they have not actually said (e.g. 'Would you agree that . . .?') – are likely to provoke people into reacting against the flow of the discussion, engendering a climate of defensiveness and/or withdrawal. Some people may need help articulating a response (e.g. 'Are you saying that you feel . . .?') but it is important not to actually lead them into saying something that they did not really mean for the sake of a response. Leading questions give the impression of being uninterested in listening to what the respondent really thinks and feels. The wording should facilitate openness.

Closed questions, for example, direct people to say either 'yes' or 'no' without elaboration ('Are you happy with . . .?') whereas open questions – ones that invite a response without specifying the particular nature of the response (e.g. 'What are your thoughts about . . .') and probing questions – designed to elicit more specific information (e.g. 'Tell me more about . . .', 'Why do you feel that way?') – help create a climate of attentiveness and listening where people feel able to respond in any way they like.

Merton and Kendall (1946) distinguish questioning styles according to their degree of structure: unstructured, semi-structured and structured. The unstructured question is one which is free of stimulus and response; the respondent is not guided either on which stimulus or aspect of a stimulus to respond to or on the type of response that is required (e.g. 'What are your thoughts on recent health education campaigns emphasising safer sex?'). There are two types of semi-structured questions: stimulus structured and response free; and stimulus free and response structured. In the former, the particular focus of the question is specified but the nature of the response is left completely open (e.g. 'How do you feel about the emphasis on condom use in campaigns on safer sex?'). In the latter, the focus of the question is unspecified but a particular kind of response is requested (e.g. 'What did you learn from the campaigns on safer sex?'). In the structured question, both the stimulus and the response components are rigidly specified (e.g. 'Do you think that sticking to one sexual partner is a better means or as good a means or a poorer means of practising safer sex than the regular use of condoms?'). From this you can see that the structured question exerts complete control over the respondent to answer in a particular way.

Silence is also a powerful way of getting people to talk, allowing them time to think about and formulate a response. Moderators should not be tempted to fill every single void with a question.

Different combinations of questions can be used that 'funnel' people into responding at a more concrete and specific level, i.e. generally provide a series of openers which orient them into thinking about a particular issue (e.g. 'Tell me about . . .') and progress to using more focused but not leading types of questions in order to obtain information in minute detail. If there is some initial reluctance to talk, 'inverted funnel' tactics can be used whereby a very specific 'factual' question is asked, the response to which is then used to motivate people to gradually talk more freely about the issue (e.g. open questions).

Skilled use of questions also requires double hearing. This means that the moderator should be able to read between the lines of a discussion in order to 'ferret' out what is only implied rather than relying totally on what is made explicit. By explicating the implied (e.g. tentatively playing it back to respondents in the form of a clarificatory question), it is rendered legitimate (e.g. it is acceptable to talk about this) and respondents may thus feel able to elaborate.

22.7.4 Managing transitions in the discussion

There are two types of transitions: respondent initiated and moderator initiated. Respondent-initiated transitions can be informative in that they may reflect an unwitting attempt to escape from talking about something uncomfortable. Whilst people should never be forced to pursue something they obviously feel uncomfortable about, the moderator can at least try to uncover the reasons for and the spread of the discomfort (e.g. is the discomfort shared by others and if so what is the basis of this?).

Moderator-initiated transition may be cued by something said or alluded to by a respondent or by a more strategic desire to revisit an issue that was sidestepped, superficially discussed or not mentioned at all. Cues originating from the respondents help maintain the flow of the discussion whereas the more stylised kind of moderator-initiated moves can interrupt the flow if not managed carefully.

22.7.5 Managing difficult people

- *The self-appointed expert*: use assertive techniques to undermine the tendency of self-appointed experts to state opinions as fact. In particular, make it a rule that the basis for strong opinions must be explained to the group, thereby using the group process to deal with them.
- *The hostile member*: if someone is hostile to the extent of intimidation it may be advisable to discreetly ask him or her to leave at the most opportune time (e.g. at coffee break).
- *The silent member*: a skilful use of questioning can encourage otherwise silent members to contribute.
- *The talkative member*: lever the energy of this person by playing the reactions of the group against him or her.

22.7.6 The facilitator as 'organisational therapist'

One of the major difficulties with focus groups taken from organisations is their desire to treat the facilitator as a therapist (Hilder, 1997). Problems with the company and management are raised in the focus group, and this is particularly the case if the topic for discussion is the company itself (e.g. organisational culture, corporate identity, group commitment, etc.). Dealing with this can be a problem and presents a number of concerns. (a) Has the focus group itself caused this discussion, and thus opened up grievances that might not otherwise have been considered, thus creating a culture of discontent? (b) Are the problems raised relevant to the topic under discussion? (c) What are the expectations of the group in talking about the problems with you? (d) What is the state of mind of the group at the end of the discussion?

There are no ready answers to these concerns although the following pointers should be borne in mind. Firstly, a focus group that is managed in a truly facilitative fashion is unlikely to actually create discontent; if problem issues are raised, in the main they can be assumed to be real. It is however the facilitator's job to ensure by gentle questioning that problems raised gain adequate context and perspective. It may also be necessary to play devil's advocate, so that the session does not become a general moan. Secondly, it usually becomes quickly apparent if the problems are relevant to the topic under discussion. If they are not, firm handling and a shift back to the subject is required. If they are relevant it is still important that the discussion takes place in a positive fashion; again this may require firm handling. Thirdly, the group's expectations of the facilitator will have been set out at the start of the session. It may be worth reminding them at the end of the aims of the focus group so that false expectations are not taken away. Equally important is the mood of the group at the end. It is important to try to wind up the focus group with a feel-good session so that the group disperses on a relative high, not in a state of discontent (Hilder, 1997).

22.8 COLLECTING THE DATA

Focus groups usually generate qualitative data in the form of transcripts produced from audiotape or videotape. By videotaping the focus group sessions, observational data can be extracted (e.g. non-verbal communication) as well as the content of the discussion. However, this might be outweighed by the effects on the interaction and communication process created by the presence of CCTV equipment. The latter may render the situation more formal than is conducive to relaxed and open discussion, especially if two sets of equipment are used to capture it from different angles. The audiotape limits the form of data to the content of the discussion but can be supplemented by observations of process made by the moderator. It is unlikely however that the moderator will be in a position to observe, take notes and concentrate on facilitating the process of discussion unless co-moderation is possible. The presence of a separate observer/co-moderator may, however, have the same alienating consequences as CCTV equipment. It also adds to the cost of running the focus groups. Most researchers rely on audiotaped recordings of the discussions supplemented by a few general field notes.

Whatever the type of recording used it is crucial to first obtain the consent of the participants, having explained the purpose of the recording and assured them of confidentiality. Once agreed, the logistics of using the tape recorders needs to be considered (i.e. how many and where best positioned). The larger the group the less easy it is to get a clear recording using one tape recorder alone. The ground rule established at the outset that everyone should speak loudly and clearly enough to be picked up by the microphone does not always work.

22.9 TRANSCRIPTION

It has been said that the analysis of transcriptions is one of the most challenging aspects of the focus group method. If each session lasts about 2 hours, 40–50 pages of transcription are yielded. If 20 sessions are conducted overall, that's 1000 pages of transcription to analyse.

Transcription is a purely mechanical task. Its time-consuming and laborious nature, however, has often led researchers to analyse the content directly from the tape which entails transcribing only the most illustrative comments. Since the purpose of a focus group is to gain insight into how respondents represent a particular issue as a whole and on a collective rather than an individual basis, it is important to capture the entire character of the discussion, warts and all. Any form of editing during transcription is therefore undesirable.

22.10 CONTENT ANALYSIS

This discussion of content analysis as it is used to analyse transcription data is equally applicable to other types of data that can be reduced to textual form (e.g. discourses and historical materials). Content analysis can even be used to analyse non-textual data such as works of art and architecture. However, most psychological applications are concerned with analysing material that can be presented to content analysts as texts (Holsti, 1969).

Content analysis comprises both a mechanical and an interpretative component (Krippendorf, 1980). The mechanical aspect involves physically organising and subdividing the data into categories whilst the interpretative component involves determining what categories are meaningful in terms of the questions being asked. The mechanical and interpretative are inextricably linked in a cycling back and forth between the transcripts and the more conceptual process of developing meaningful coding schemes.

There are three main forms of content analysis: qualitative, quantitative and structural content analysis.

22.10.1 Qualitative content analysis

This type of content analysis tends to be more subjective and less explicit about the processes by which interpretation of the target material occurs. The emphasis is on meaning rather than on quantification.

Initially the system of classification may be derived from the research question and the topic guide used by the moderator during process facilitation. Additional conceptual codes may arise from a closer examination of the data as a whole. Coded segments may include long exchanges, phrases or sentences. The transcripts are cut and then sorted. Codes can also be developed to signal useful quotations. Following this a grid which tabulates code on one axis and focus group identifier on the other is developed that provides a descriptive overview of the data. The aim is to be able to find quotations to illustrate particular themes or strands of meaning within the transcript. With this form of content analysis the aim is not normally to put numbers to the data.

Computer-assisted approaches to data reduction which are designed to organise textual data can make at least the mechanics of the task much more manageable. The most well known of these is a software package called The Ethnograph (Seidel et al., 1988). Coding is performed on the data base and the segments coinciding with each code are then sorted so that all units of data relating to a particular theme can be readily assembled and retrieved.

Chapter 18 on discourse analysis also deals with many related issues so they will not be dealt with further here.

22.10.2   Quantitative content analysis

This type of content analysis can be used to generate numerical values from the target material. These might be frequencies, rankings or ratings. However, the process by which these values are generated may include elements of qualitative analysis, so the qualitative/quantitative distinction is far from clear-cut. Quantitative content analysis is slightly mislabelled anyway, as it is less a type of analysis than a way of producing data which can then be statistically analysed, i.e. the output of the content analysis is not the end of the analysis as a whole.

The first stage involves the selection of the material to be analysed – the universe of material. Clearly, in the case of transcripts of focus groups this will be all the material that has been collected while running the groups. More generally, the universe of material refers to all the material that is potentially available for analysis. Indeed, the initial definition of the universe of material is common to all forms of content analysis.

The second stage involves the selection of some unit of analysis. The units of analysis are the discrete bits of information that will be assigned to categories in the subsequent analysis. A unit of analysis (or coding unit) can be a word, a theme, a character, an item, time spent on a topic, etc.

When the unit of analysis is a word then content analysis may become a relatively simple exercise of counting the occurrences of particular words or types of words (e.g. active versus passive constructions). Although this approach has some advantages, in particular that it can be easily computerised, it is limited in that the meaning of a word can change depending upon the context. A more subtle, though potentially less reliable, approach is to identify themes.

A theme is a statement or proposition about something. Sometimes themes can be identified by the presence or absence of specific words (e.g. self-referential statements may be identified by the presence of 'I' and 'me'). However, the identification of themes will often require some interpretative action on the part of the coder(s).

In order to conduct a thematic content analysis one needs to generate a coding frame. The coding frame is a set of categories into which instances will be allocated. The categories should be exhaustive (i.e. all instances can be assigned to a category) and exclusive (i.e. all instances should be assigned to only one category). The coding frame can be developed either on the basis of the substantive content of the target material (e.g. categories could be different types of environmental issue) or on the basis of theoretically determined categories (e.g. internal and external attributions). To some extent, a theoretically derived coding frame is more analytic whilst a content derived coding frame is more descriptive. Of course, different coding frames can be applied to the same material.

Thematic content analysis requires an assessment of the reliability of the coding. This is typically done by using more than one coder to code the same material. Inter-rater reliability is then assessed by computing an agreement index such as Cohen's kappa.

In respect of quantification of the material, the output of a content analysis is often the frequency of occurrence of the different coding categories, e.g.

how many times a particular coding category appears in a transcript (or text, etc.). Comparisons between different source materials may then be assessed. However, it is possible to evaluate the content along an ordinal dimension(s). This increases the scope for statistical analysis of the data. Ranking may be used when a number of instances are being analysed, e.g. one could rank focus groups on the degree to which group members used personalised examples to illustrate points in their arguments. Rating scales may also be used in some cases.

22.10.3 Structural content analysis

This type of content analysis involves the development of a representation of the relationships between elements in the target material. In order to do this both qualitative and quantitative aspects of the data have to be considered.

Structural content analysis is appropriate for the analysis of complex systems of which naturally occurring focus groups are an excellent example. Variants of this approach, such as cognitive mapping (Axelrod, 1976), have often been applied to aspects of decision making. As well as being relevant to decision making this approach is useful for investigating belief systems and social representations. Structural content analysis involves some of the same processes and techniques as are used in quantitative (and qualitative) content analysis. However, the rules governing the relationships between response categories also need to be defined. This allows both qualitative and quantitative aspects of the target material to be represented.

These relational rules will vary depending upon the research aims. Research on political decision making for example, might examine belief systems about crime and what should be done about it. As well as being able to examine the effects of group contexts on the expressed beliefs one can compare the belief systems of members of different parties (or other groups), and explore change in the belief systems over time. Relational rules would relate to covariation and potential causality, e.g. does the political make-up of the group influence the way crime is discussed? Do expressions of particular policies tend to come from people who believe in certain classes of causes of crime? And so on.

Content analysis is not without its problems. It is heavily reliant on the multiple judgements of a single analyst. As the analyst may be (unknowingly or otherwise) keen to find support for a particular view of the data, it is advisable to independently involve two or more people in the coding of the transcripts so that the reliability of the analysis can be systematically assessed.

Other problems include concentrating only on what is mentioned. Sometimes what is not mentioned or strategically sidestepped by the group may be as important. If it doesn't appear in the transcript it cannot be content analysed. Also, talking about themes in the data in isolation may sidestep the complex totality in which 'themes' are embedded. In the focus group the content is generated by communication and interaction in the collective sense. Structural content analysis may go some way to dealing with this problem, though the techniques of structural analysis are relatively underdeveloped and where they are developed they tend to be tailor-made to deal with very specific problems.

22.11 OTHER FORMS OF ANALYSIS

Researchers working within the framework of discourse analysis have established specific procedures for handling textual data, which are beyond the scope of this chapter. From this perspective the focus group method is a particularly apt medium for the analysis of the collective functions of discourse generated therein (see Chapter 18).

Fantasy theme analysis is a form of discourse analysis but which is based on an entirely different set of epistemological assumptions (Bormann, 1972). It is concerned with how communication affords dramatisation (e.g. story telling) which in turn creates social realities for people. Dramatisation is of interest only in the collective sense as providing insights into the cultural, emotional and motivational style of a particular community or population of people. The focus group method provides the ideal forum for the investigation of 'dramatised communication'. A detailed consideration of how to conduct fantasy theme analysis can be found in Bormann (1972).

22.12 FEEDBACK OF RESULTS/FINDINGS

Some focus groups may express a desire to find out the results of the research exercise overall, particularly those conducted in organisational settings. Focus group participants will for instance express interest in what other groups in the company say, in similarities and differences and in analyses and interpretations. Hilder (1997) recommends that the facilitator is careful not to give anything away that might prejudice the confidentiality of the information between a group and the facilitator. Any feedback that is promised to the group should be such that it is easily provided. The time-consuming nature of the analysis of focus groups means that there is more than enough to do without promising additional and unnecessary reporting. However, it is important to remember that people gave time and input, and notes of thanks as follow-up are appreciated, as well as making sure that people will continue to have time for you.

Feedback to a company raises more of a dilemma for the researcher. It is unusual for access to be granted within a company without some expectation by the company of benefit gained, and some form of feedback to the company sponsor will be expected. Some of the information arising out of the focus group may not be what the sponsor wants to hear and may even be personally compromising. One has to consider that what people have talked about in the group may be: (1) not what they would wish to pass on, and (2) not pleasant to receive. The decision as to how much if any information and analysis are discussed with the company sponsor has to be an individual one. Clearly no attributable information should be given: the confidentiality agreed with the group members must be absolute. However, if the focus groups are part of a potentially long term relationship between you, the researcher and the company, then the relationship with the sponsor is also an important one. Thus while diplomacy in the analysis given may be appropriate there is little point in hiding non-attributable information which will form part of the longer term study. Honesty is (as in consultancy) the best policy, even if this means a lost corporate access (Hilder, 1997).

22.13   FUTURE DEVELOPMENTS IN FOCUS GROUP RESEARCH – THE 'GLOBAL FOCUS GROUP'

Advances in technology, and the 'globalisation' of real-time communication in the conversational sense of the word, open up the possibility for focus groups to be run 'on-line'. Greenbaum (1998) has coined the term 'global focus groups' to describe on-line discussion groups that cross cultural, spatial and temporal boundaries. Two types of on-line global focus groups can be envisaged: real-time focus groups who log on to the network at a set time for a set period to discuss a topic or issue, and ongoing focus groups whose members sign up and sign off whenever they wish, and contribute whenever convenient and/or they feel appropriate. In the real-time version, a focus group could be run in the traditional fashion with a facilitator keeping the discussion on track and probing wherever necessary and so on. In the ongoing version, a discussion is not easily managed or facilitated, the group itself being responsible for determining the shape and direction of the dialogue that ensues. Real-time 'virtual' focus groups are staged whilst ongoing focus groups are not and exist irrespective of whether all their members are signed on at any one time. Whether the unmanaged and ongoing aspects of on-line discussion groups mean that they can no longer be called focus groups is yet to be contemplated.

The concept of 'global focus groups' opens up a whole realm of research possibilities but also brings with it considerable logistical problems and issues of 'virtual' facilitation. One problem is ensuring that everyone knows what time to sign up and that the timings are co-ordinated exactly across time zones. The interested reader should consult Greenbaum (1998) for more on this. One advantage of on-line discussion is that the issue of transcription is sidestepped. Greenbaum (1998) also talks about the impact of technology on focus group research generally.

22.14   FURTHER READING

There is now an ever more burgeoning literature on the focus group method. Recently published books include Greenbaum's (1998) *The Handbook for Focus Group Research* (2nd edn) which introduces the idea of 'global focus groups' and also examines the relevance of technological advances for the focus group method, and Morgan and Krueger's (1997) *Focus Group Kit* comprising a set of six books each devoted to a particular aspect of the focus group method, from design and planning through to implementation and analysis. Krueger (1994) *Focus Groups: A Practical Guide for Applied Research* (2nd edn) has also revised and updated his book first published in 1988. This addresses all the issues and problems likely to be encountered during focus group research, and moreover provides a down-to-earth and pragmatic handbook on how to optimise the potential of the focus group method. Other recommended books include Stewart and Shamdasani's (1990) *Focus Groups: Theory and Practice* which provides a more theoretical slant on the focus group method than the other books, and Morgan's (1993) *Successful Focus Groups: Advancing the State of the Art.*

PART IV

23

Ethnographic and Action Research

David Uzzell

Contents

23.1 INTRODUCTION

Most psychological research has the goal of getting as close as possible to the mental processes and products which structure and guide human action and give it meaning. Psychological research methods try to minimise the distance and distortions between what is in the head and its representation to the researcher. In our choice of research method we are often presented with many dilemmas. One such dilemma is: do we use a nomothetic or an idiographic methodology? A **nomothetic methodology** is one in which we collect data from a large number of people (for example, through questionnaire surveys) and by some process of averaging purport to generalise with some degree of confidence to a larger population and thereby imply a wider validity. An **idiographic methodology** (for example, in-depth interviews), on the other hand, often captures the richness and complexity of the phenomenon under investigation but at the risk of basing conclusions on a small number of potentially atypical cases.

The use of a nomothetic methodology such as questionnaire surveys on, say, attitudes to the environment allows the collection of a large quantity of data but at the expense of a detailed insight into the complex and often contradictory ways people think about issues. A questionnaire, for example, channels responses along a predetermined route with very little opportunity for the individual to say 'Yes, but . . .', to elaborate on exactly what they mean or to contextualise their responses. When asked, for example, how concerned they are about environmental problems, many people may respond positively. They may be concerned, but what does this mean in terms of their behaviour? We know from research that attitudes are not always a predictor of behaviour: what people say they do and what they do are often very different things. Would this information in any case lead to usable and actionable conclusions for policy and decision makers? This type of problem raises a rather more fundamental issue which serves to distinguish ethnography from many other approaches in psychology: the meaning and significance of the social world being investigated is defined by the researcher, not the respondent.

It should be emphasised from the outset that ethnography is not a single method. Many of the methodologies described in this book could be used by the ethnographic researcher: direct observation (Chapter 16), interviewing (Chapter 17), discourse analysis (Chapter 18), diary techniques (Chapter 21) and even questionnaire surveys (Chapters 7 and 12). What distinguishes ethnographic research is its purpose – **cultural description**. Spradley defined ethnography as a 'culture-studying culture. It consists of a body of knowledge that includes research techniques, ethnographic theory, and hundreds of cultural descriptions. It seeks to build a systematic understanding of all human cultures from the perspective of those who have learned' (1979: 10–11). This last point is crucially important for it stresses that, unlike other areas of social science research where the researcher attempts to explain human action in terms of psychological theories such as attribution theory, ethnographic research lays emphasis on the actor's understanding and theorising about their actions. In other words, the view is not the outsider looking in, but the insider looking around.

It might also be useful to think of the distinction between the ethnographic approach and other types of research in psychology and the social sciences as a distinction between a quest for questions and a quest for answers. Within psychology, we know (or we think we know) what questions we are trying to answer. In ethnographical research we are interested in the questions people are answering themselves about their life, their relationships and their environment by their actions. They may be questions which are unarticulated because they are part of the taken-for-granted world. Nevertheless, by their actions people are responding to the situations, rules and relationships in which they find themselves. Ethnographic research often starts with observation and description, for it is in the process of observing that situation-specific questions emerge. In Spradley and Mann's (1975) closely observed study of life in Brady's Cocktail Bar, they found that cocktail waitresses learn very quickly that a good waitress is not one who serves customers well but one who knows how to please the bartenders. Not only is making the bartenders' job easy essential to ensure a trouble-free life, but because of the status hierarchy the waitresses need the approval and praise of bartenders.

23.2   WHAT IS ETHNOGRAPHY?

Werner and Schoepfle propose that 'Ethnography is description' and that 'description must closely resemble the original cultural reality. The resemblance must be good enough that the natives are able to recognise in it familiar features of their own culture' (1987: 24). Goetz and LeCompte have defined ethnography as the 'analytic descriptions or reconstructions of intact cultural scenes and groups. Ethnographies recreate for the reader the shared beliefs, practices, artefacts, folk knowledge, and behaviours of some groups of people' (1984: 2). Goetz and LeCompte (1984) suggest that ethnography is a process, a way of studying human behaviour, and that ethnographic methodologies have four characteristic features. First, they aim to elicit phenomenological data – that is, they aim to represent the world-view of those individuals or groups under investigation. Although other methodologies in psychology seek to do this, where ethnography differs from other methodologies is that the representations of the world are structured by the participants, not by the researcher. It is the participants' structuring of the world in which the researcher is interested.

In an **ethogenic approach**, the researcher is interested in how participants theorise about their own behaviour, rather than imposing theory on to the behaviour. Marsh et al. write that the ethogenic approach 'is based on the idea that human social life is a product of an interaction between sequences of actions and talk about those actions. Everything can be redone by talk' (1978: 21). They argue that since the same skills and social knowledge are involved in the creation of both action and accounts of that action, then the researcher has two mutually supporting and confirmatory ways of revealing the underlying system of social knowledge and belief. Marsh et al. go on to argue that the best (but not the only) authorities as to what action is and means are the actors themselves. This is not to say that such accounts are in any sense 'true'. Marsh et al. demonstrate quite clearly in their multi-method study of football hooligans that the rhetoric and ritualization of aggression do not reflect 'reality' in any documentary sense, but the accounts by the football supporters serve to confer meaning and status on their world structure. 'Hooliganism', rather than being seen as mindless and irrational aggression, can be reinterpreted as rational and rule-bound from the perspective of the 'hooligans'.

Another important aspect of Marsh et al.'s (1978) study is that it demonstrates that the social and environmental situation or context in which action takes place is fundamental to the analysis of the behaviour, illustrating Spradley's comment above. The socio-environmental context is not ignored as if it were irrelevant or interfering noise but is crucial to the explanation of behaviour by both the researcher and the actors themselves.

Second, ethnographic techniques are empirical and are almost without exception employed in naturalistic settings. The researcher is interested in how individuals and groups behave in their own real-world setting unmanipulated by the researcher. Ethnographic research has been undertaken in an extensive range of settings (Hobbs and May, 1993) and has been concerned with a substantial number of social issues (Burawoy et al., 1991).

Third, ethnographic research attempts to present the totality of the phenomenon under investigation. The context is as important as the action. The temporal and environmental factors and the social/cultural and economic context are not noise but fundamental contributory explanatory variables. Behaviour is seen to have a history and an anticipation of the future. Finally, given the kind of picture painted here of ethnographic research, it will not come as a surprise to find that not only is a variety of methods and techniques used in ethnographic research but any one study will invariably be multi-method.

23.3   ETHNOGRAPHY: JOURNALISM OR SCIENCE?

An accusation sometimes levelled at psychology is that so much psychology is just 'common sense' (Wegner and Vallacher, 1981). A criticism that is similarly directed at ethnography is that it is just journalism. Perhaps its extensive use of qualitative data, its employment of illustrative quotations, and the strong 'human interest' focus make such a misunderstanding inevitable. But there are important differences between ethnographic research and journalism. Any social scientific account of human action, if it is to be of worth, has to be based on sound research, systematic data collection, and reliable and valid data. Perhaps most importantly, it has to be theory-driven. In the case of ethnography the emphasis may, at least in the early stages, be descriptive but even description is theory-driven however slightly articulated the theory. One aim of collecting ethnographic data is to assist in the development and verification of theory in order to account for human behaviour. This is not the aim of journalism.

There is a long tradition of ethnographic research in the social sciences, with many notable studies dating back to the 1920s and the Chicago school of human ecology: Zorbaugh's (1929) *The Gold Coast and the Slum*, Wirth's (1928) *The Ghetto*, and later Whyte's (1993) *Street Corner Society*. Park (1967) believed that urban areas and communities constitute large scale social laboratories and could be studied like any scientific phenomena. Thomas argues that 'Ethnography . . . respects the same basic rules of logic, replication, validity, reliability, theory construction, and other characteristics which separate science from other forms of knowledge' (1993: 16).

A further distinction between journalism and ethnography is that journalism is typically concerned with news, with the reporting of the atypical events of everyday life: the unusual, the non-routine, the breaking of tradition. Much ethnographic research is concerned with precisely the opposite: revealing the routine and the 'paramount reality' of the everyday world of individuals and groups (Berger and Luckmann, 1971).

23.4   PROBLEMS IN ETHNOGRAPHY

So much of what is cultural is hidden and is rarely made explicit. It exists between the lines and in the assumptive world of both the researcher and the researched. Murray Parkes, describing the concept of the **assumptive world**, writes: 'A man is tied to his assumptive world. By learning to recognise and act appropriately within his expectable environment a man makes a life space of his own . . . the assumptive world not only contains a model of the world as it is . . . it also contains a model of the world as it might be' (1971: 104). Young and Kramer describe the assumptive world as 'multidimensional; it includes perceptions of the world, evaluations of its aspects, a sense of relatedness to them, and recurrent demands that they are acted upon. These dimensions interact to generate preferred states of the world and "calls to action"' (1978: 239).

Ethnographic approaches present a particular set of problems for the researcher. In the process of trying to understand the assumptive world of individuals and groups we have to try to break free from our own assumptive world. In the process of description and interpretation there is always a danger that our viewpoint will be ethnocentric. However hard we try, it is difficult to describe or analyse outside our own cultural references and world-view. Werner and Schoepfle (1987) suggest that we should keep two separate records: the **journal**, which is the ethnographer's account (i.e. texts that are the product of the ethnographer's mind); and the **transcript** text, which is the product of the respondent's mind. Although the term 'respondent' is used here, it denotes the person providing ethnographic data in whatever form. They are not necessarily interview data as typically implied by that term: they could be text material. Some psychologists often use the generic term 'subjects' but this implies a certain relationship between researcher and researched which is questionable. Some ethnographers use the label 'natives', but outside certain contexts this may be equally inappropriate.

Allied to this problem is the reduction of what Werner and Schoepfle (1987) call **semantic accent** – the confusion of respondents' meanings with the ethnographer's meanings. One word may be the same but the meanings may be different. Therefore we think we know what an individual means when in fact they may mean something very different.

It was suggested at the beginning of this chapter that the attraction of the ethnographic approach is that it reduces the distance from respondents' meanings, understandings and world-views to our own understandings. With each description and analysis we inevitably translate others' meanings and world-views into our language – the language of the social scientist. However hard we try to retain the fidelity and verisimilitude of the original there is a mutation not only in meaning, but probably also in richness and complexity. This can be illustrated if we think of the problem of research methods which attempt to understand the past.

No historical account can ever capture what is the infinite content of an event. Most of the information generated by an event – whether it is at the individual or group level, or whether it is cognitive, affective or behavioural information – is not recorded. That which is recorded is also only a record of the past and can be verified only through other accounts of the past. Lowenthal (1985) argues that what is now known as the past was not what anyone experienced as the present. There is a sense in which we know the past better than those who experienced it. We have the benefit of hindsight and we know the outcome of the story: 'Knowing the future of the past forces the historian to shape his account to come out as things have done.' Historical knowledge, however well authenticated, is subjective and subject to the biases of its chronicler who in turn is subject to the psychological processes of selective attention, perception and recall. Finally, there is the temporal equivalent of the problem of ethnocentricity. It is very difficult to view and understand the world outside the framework of our twenty-first century beliefs, values and attitudes.

The touchstone of scientific endeavour is reputedly the replicability of the investigation. When one is working within a naturalistic setting with social groups engaged in everyday actions, one cannot guarantee that a research exercise and its results can be repeated. Reality is not stable. As the Greek philosopher Heraclitus argued 2500 years ago, the essence of the universe is change: you cannot step into the same river twice, for the second time it is not the same river. It is doubtful whether you can even step into the same river once as it changes while one is stepping. This would suggest that a thing never is because it is always changing into something else. Although this is particularly relevant to ethnographic methodologies it ought to be seen as no less of a problem in all psychological research.

In ethnographic research it is impossible to duplicate naturally occurring events in all their complexity and their history because the river has flowed on, but this does not necessarily invalidate the findings. One should remember that many important events take place on unique occasions and for this reason one must separate statistical or scientific significance from behavioural significance. The significance of an event is independent of its probability of occurrence. Events are behaviourally significant when something happens which makes a difference to the values and behaviour of the individuals or groups affected, or when behaviour departs significantly from a previous steady state. There have been many one-off events which have brought about behavioural changes for individuals and the communities in which they live. In the absence of replication, multi-method and confirmatory data sources (Chapter 2) become all the more important.

In experimental psychology the researcher attempts to control as many of the experimental variables as possible. Any change in the dependent variables can be attributed to purposeful manipulation of the independent variables. But in naturalistic or field settings the researcher has only limited opportunities to manipulate the independent variables. Furthermore, not only are the contextual variables such as place and time (what in many experimental situations would be called 'noise') equally likely to have an effect, but also one is interested in them in their own right. They may be an important source of data contributing to the explanation of behaviour.

23.5 ACTION RESEARCH

In the traditional model of research, the researcher is often conceptualised as a dispassionate chronicler of social activity akin to what Bannister and Fransella described as the 'stereotypical Victorian physicist who seems to be our current ideal' (1971: 193). Furthermore, we like to believe that the researcher is an invisible filter allowing through information which they perceive to be important and relevant. At least two objections can be raised to regarding the researcher simply as a chronicler of social activity.

First, research methods such as questionnaire surveys serve to distance the researcher from the very people to whom they are trying to get closer in order to understand their world. In the process by which researchers collect information they move through a number of stages which increasingly serve to distance them from the individuals and communities they are studying. For example, hypotheses about communities and the activities of social groups will be formulated. The decisions social scientists then take as to how they will test these hypotheses are crucial, because they will have an important influence on everything else that follows. If a survey approach is to be used, *what* questions are asked and *how* those questions are phrased and structured will be conditioned by the subsequent statistical analysis. Therefore, the nature and form in which information is collected will be determined not by their meaningfulness to the respondents but by the way the information is to be treated statistically. For this reason, once the questionnaire is designed we are talking to processed people, that is, people who are answering our questions on our terms. Furthermore, the way in which we collect data will also have a highly significant effect on the degree to which the research will allow a critical analysis of the phenomenon under investigation (Habermas, 1979).

Second, the researcher's role, especially those researchers working in the community and on issues of public policy, is a political one. However objective we try to make research techniques, the researcher will always be there with their values, perceptions and interventions. The researcher is an intermediary as they stand amid the research methods on the one side and the individual, the community and society on the other. The researcher's position is essentially a political one because the techniques used will affect the relationships they have with the community. In addition to the implications of the research for public policy which will have political implications in a more conventional sense, the relationships formed in the course of the research raise questions of power, influence, control, responsibility, accountability and even 'the public interest'.

Some have argued that the relationship between researcher and researched can become mechanistic, authoritarian, if not ethically highly suspect (Argyris, 1970; Haney et al., 1973). The goals and methods of the research are defined almost totally by the researcher. The 'subject' is seen to be able to offer little or nothing to the research design because the researcher is seen as a skilled technician who knows how best to collect information. The 'subject' is expected to conform to the goals of the researcher and unquestioningly comply with all instructions (Milgram, 1974).

Warr (1977) maintains we have to earn the right to become involved in people's lives. There are costs in all research, and if a researcher is to intervene in an individual's life, then that person must see that the research has relevance for them. Warr amplifies this point when he writes: 'I have quite often met objections to a research proposal on the grounds that the potential participants are tired of University researchers taking up their time and then disappearing to their ivory towers: nothing has changed and the participants have gained nothing' (1977: 4).

It is doubtful whether researchers are seen by groups as the dispassionate unbiased observers we have deceived ourselves into believing for so long. Because we have been inculcated with a natural science model of research, we have deluded ourselves into believing that our role is a neutral one (Murphy et al., 1984). For many groups, our role is not neutral, however hard we try to suggest that it is. One only has to read Roy's (1965) account of his attempted study of industrial conflict, in which he mistakenly assumed interviewees understood his role, to see the disturbing result of such a misunderstanding.

One way in which research can benefit the communities that it is intended to serve is by the researcher giving psychology away, as George Miller (1969) suggested over a quarter of a century ago. This might be achieved in any number of ways. Research in community psychology has for many years sought to devise ways in which people, organisations and communities can mobilise psychological theory and practice to take control over their own affairs. The community self-survey may be one way whereby communities, with the assistance of social scientists, are made responsible for the collection and analysis of information about their community and which in turn might lead to a more insightful understanding of the phenomena we are trying to study. Fetterman (1993) suggests that through 'empowerment evaluation' evaluators can teach people to conduct their own evaluations, thereby demystifying and desensitising evaluation and making it an accepted part of programme planning.

There has been a renewed interest in action research in recent years. Partly this has been in response to the particular considerations mentioned above. It has also, however, reflected a concern to acknowledge and act upon the critiques of research philosophy and practice which have emerged from post-modern, feminist and critical theory in recent years.

23.6   THE RESEARCHER AS AN AGENT OF SOCIAL CHANGE

Action research is not just an alternative way of collecting data. The premises and relationships upon which the methods are based are very different from conventional social research techniques. Action research has its origin in the writings of Kurt Lewin (1952) who believed that in order to gain insight into a process one must create change and then observe its variable effects and new dynamics. The use of this approach in research probably reached its apogee in the 1960s and 1970s when government research funding and policy were more liberal and participatory. Action research methodologies have been employed in many different areas of social investigation such as public policy (Lovett, 1975), police management (Horton and Smith, 1988), industrial organisation and management (Whyte, 1991) and community development (Lees and Smith, 1975). One area where it continues to be influential is education (Elliot, 1991; Zuber-Skerritt, 1992).

There are many different styles of undertaking action research. Rapoport identifies four types of action research (diagnostic, participant, empirical, experimental), but what is common to each is that, 'Action research is a type of applied social research differing from other varieties in the immediacy of the researcher's involvement in the action process' (1972: 23). Carr and Kemmis (1986) distinguish between three types of action research – technical, practical and emancipatory – with the authors arguing that only the last is 'true' action research.

Central to all though is the idea that the researcher moves from the role of being solely a chronicler of social activity to that of an agent of social change. Doing the research is integral to taking action, because action is part of the research and research is part of the action: they are two sides of the same coin. Action research can take many forms including education and training, facilitation, advocacy and decision making. The researcher becomes part of the decision making machinery, so that research findings are in the form of shared experience which creates a knowledge which may not be so readily communicable in conventional academic terms.

Zuber-Skerritt (1992) identifies five defining characteristics of action research which serve to distinguish it from orthodox social science methodologies. First, it is practical in that the research not only should lead to theoretical and disciplinary advances but also will have practical consequences for all the participants. Second, it is participative and collaborative, thereby attempting to overcome the unequal power relationship between researcher and researched to which reference was made earlier. Third, it is emancipatory: those who have traditionally been referred to as subjects in psychological research are regarded as active and equal participants in the research process, holding positions of influence both in respect of the research and subsequently in terms of their actions and daily lives. Fourth, it is interpretative whereby the perspectives and interpretations of all the participants have validity, rather than just seeing the researcher's expert opinion as dominant and 'correct'. In this respect it makes an important link with ethnographic research. Finally, it is critical as all the participants engage in a critical analysis of their situation, possible courses of action and constraints on action, which may as a consequence lead to a change in both their situation and themselves.

Action research has some features in common with participant observation (see Chapter 16), but the relationship between researcher and researched is different in several important respects. In participant observation, those being observed reveal themselves to the observer, but the observer does not reveal himself to them. In action research the researcher acts as a fully participating member of the group, and so the relationship is more honest and open. As Rowan states, the participant observer 'can often remain unchanged and unchallenged by his experience which thus becomes of one-way benefit to him and his sponsor' (1974: 93). The sort of role outlined here has the flexibility to accommodate changes in the research, researcher and the community which inevitably and unavoidably take place in the life history of a research project.

One implication of using a technique such as action research in, for example, a community context is that the researcher can become actively involved and help shape the future of voluntary and community groups. One might be able to help them towards an effectiveness they might not otherwise have achieved, or which could have taken much longer. Such groups may well give the researcher insights into the research problem and an understanding which might never have emerged had they adopted more conventional research practices. It is a two-way interaction with mutual benefits.

One important issue concerns **interviewer effects** or **contamination**. It is sometimes argued by critics of this approach that by being involved one will influence not only community group activities but also any attitudinal or behavioural information which one is collecting as part of the research. Ultimately this would mean that the researcher does little more than monitor themselves. The type of researcher described here is an activist who is most effective when they are only an encourager, and not adopting manipulative or doctrinaire positions. It also has to be recognised that whatever type of study is being undertaken there will always be experimenter effects. The important point is to be aware of them and, if possible, control for them.

23.7 CHANGE

One of the first things to strike the newcomer to action research is that a significant amount of space in books describing action research methodology is given over to discussing the role of the researcher in the research process. Normally the researcher does not warrant consideration because the assumption is that they will be transparent to the research process. In action research this is not the case because the researcher is an integral part of the research whose task is 'to provide leadership and direction to other stakeholders in the research process' (Stringer, 1996). The researcher is not an expert who *does* the research (as implied in the experimenter–subject relationship), but is a resource person who initiates and guides. Stringer suggests that the researcher becomes a facilitator or resource who acts as a catalyst to assist stakeholders in defining their problems clearly and providing information which helps those making decisions come to an informed choice over alternative courses of action. While in essence this is true, strictly speaking the action researcher is not a catalyst because the catalyst within any change process remains unchanged by the change process. It is inevitable and desirable that the researcher will be changed by the research process because it is only by recognising the dynamic nature of shared knowledge and multiple interpretations of reality that the researcher will develop their understanding of the situation.

Consequently, a common theme running through accounts of both ethnographic research and action research is the idea of change. One aim of ethnographic research is to record processes of change – not stability. Conventional approaches to social science invariably take people's behaviour at a static moment in time with little regard to the fact that people are constantly changing in response to changing situations. The researcher who takes a static view of a social group's activities would surely not fail to realise that in their own research they are continually developing and refining their ideas and theories about those whom they are studying. As the social scientist is continually developing, so too is the community he or she is studying. In understanding change, action research is a particularly apposite strategy as development is part of the research process. At the same time, the researcher plays an active role in becoming a change agent by informing, encouraging and supporting the community group, and studying and interpreting their actions in the light of their interventions. The important point to make about the researcher's role as an agent of social change is that they are still researchers, but fully participating ones.

Data collection methodologies such as questionnaire surveys and interviews can be planned with a relatively high degree of precision in terms of time management. The process of designing, piloting, modifying and administering a questionnaire can be planned to take place over a set number of weeks or months. Likewise, the processing of the data in terms of cleaning, coding and analysing can also be anticipated with a reasonable degree of accuracy. This is less the case for action (and ethnographic) research where one is following the life history of events.

Some events may take place over a day, a week, a month or even several years. For example, one event in which the author participated took over two years to play itself out (Uzzell, 1988). This involved an attempt by a community group to receive statutory recognition in local government by becoming a parish council. The application for parish council status involved organising a community-wide survey of attitudes towards local government and the establishment of a parish council, the analysis and interpretation of the data with community leaders, presenting the findings to the local authority and lobbying for change. Initially the application was rejected and so an appeal was made to the Boundary Commissioners who instituted an inquiry at which barristers representing local commercial interests, trades organisations and senior local authority officers opposed the community group. Throughout the two-year period the author was involved at every stage from the design and analysis of the community survey to making representations to the Boundary Commissioners' inquiry.

23.8 CONCLUSIONS

Having read this far the reader should be alert to the dangers of assuming that there is only one appropriate model of scientific activity and one appropriate role for the researcher. The question is *not* how flawed is action research because of the researcher's involvement, or how reliable is ethnographic research because of the 'noise' and confounding variables, but rather, are we not deluding ourselves into believing these same processes are not operating in other, more conventional research strategies?

Some researchers will feel unhappy with the roles implied by these types of research methodologies, either for professional or for personal reasons. It is not everyone's preference to make these kinds of interventions or to engage in these kinds of relationships. Likewise, it should be emphasised that both ethnographic and action research strategies are not appropriate for all types of research. The goals and objectives of the research as well as the constraints which inevitably operate in any research situation should determine the type of research strategy adopted. But in coming to any decision about the most appropriate methodology to use it should be remembered that as there is not one model of science, so there is not one model of the researcher.

23.9 FURTHER READING

Whyte's (1991) *Participatory Action Research* and Stringer's (1996) *Action Research: A Handbook for Practitioners* both provide an excellent introduction to action research. For detailed 'how to do' accounts of ethnography the books by Hammersley and Atkinson (1995) *Ethnography: Principles in Practice*, Fetterman (1989) *Ethnography Step by Step* and Werner and Schoepfle (1987) *Systematic Fieldwork. Volume 1: Foundations of Ethnography and Interviewing* are worth consulting. Hobbs and May's (1993) *Interpreting the Field: Accounts of Ethnography* provides examples of the varied contexts in which ethnographic strategies have been used, but also highlights the difficulties and dilemmas which may emerge when undertaking ethnographic research.

24

Using the Computer to Define and Explore Theories in Psychology

Peter Simpson

Contents

24.1 INTRODUCTION

Training in the use of the computer forms an essential part of most contemporary degree courses. In psychology the computer is most often used to carry out statistical analyses. Computers can also be used to present words, text, graphics, sounds, etc. They can be used in experimental procedures, psychometric testing, questionnaire studies, psychophysics and physiological measures.

In these applications it is possible to integrate the control and presentation of material with response recording and data analysis. Of course it remains possible to carry out a significant range of statistical analyses using pencil, paper, a calculator and graph paper. But access to a computer-based resource enables the user to conduct a range of analyses, and especially those which are complicated and arduous to perform, on data stored in magnetic form within the computer or on removable disks.

During the last 40 years computers have also been used to test models of psychological and neural processes expressed in the form of computer programs. This work has been carried out to specify and test the viability of a number of theories of psychological and neural functions and to create systems which display artificial intelligence. This chapter describes the role of simulation in scientific investigation and what is involved in using a computer to carry out this process. The argument is illustrated by reference to studies using the computer which have extended our understanding of psychological processes and neural systems.

24.2 UNDERSTANDING THROUGH SIMULATION

In the seventeenth century, the philosopher Descartes proposed that scientific inquiry involves the analysis and synthesis of phenomena. In the case of psychology, the term 'phenomena' encompasses the concept of behaviour exhibited by humans and other animals. The behaviour of interest to the psychologist could involve the occurrence of a co-ordinated motor response or the appearance of a syntactic feature in language. It might entail the expression of an attitude or knowledge within or in response to a language statement. It might involve the generation of a solution to a problem or task which allows us to infer states of understanding or misunderstanding.

Within Descartes's scheme, the first step is analysis. This involves the creation of a simplified description of a phenomenon and identification of the variables that produce the phenomenon. If the phenomenon of interest is still present in the simpler model, then you have identified the key variables contributing to it. This assumption can be tested through the process of synthesis which will test the adequacy of our understanding. There are three types of synthesis. In the physical sciences it has proved possible to test by means of **direct synthesis**. The chemist can synthesise compounds, for example penicillin, solvents, hormone preparations, etc., which were originally extracted from natural sources. If the synthetic compounds produce the same effects as the original natural products we can take that as evidence of the acceptability of the original analysis.

In those parts of psychology which can use the experimental method, the test by synthesis takes the form of a **synthesis by prediction**. If our analysis of the important variables is correct, then the behaviour of interest will change as the variables are manipulated. In practice our analysis may have led to proposals not only about what variables are controlling the phenomena but also about the independence, or lack of independence, of the variables in controlling the phenomena. These relationships can be tested or explored by use of the synthesis by prediction procedure.

A third type of synthesis involves the creation of a **model**. In this case we test our understanding of a phenomenon by constructing a model. We build into the model the elements we think are important and also our conception of the way these elements interact to produce the phenomenon. This approach is especially attractive when the phenomenon of interest reflects the action of a number of variables and component processes linked to subsystems in, for example, models of weather patterns, economic processes and engineering systems. In cognitive science and psychology, artificial intelligence systems capable of language understanding, reasoning and planning and neural networks which learn and categorise have been investigated.

Since the 1950s computers and programming languages have become generally available which lend themselves to describing and testing theories in psychology. Using this kind of method potentially involves two of the types of synthesis described by Descartes. Using a simulation procedure embodied in a computer program it is possible to carry out synthesis by prediction and synthesis by model.

The origins of work on computer simulation arose in the context of engineering rather than psychology. One stimulus for this work was the need to design computers which could carry out symbolic manipulation tasks which matched the capacity of humans (Minsky, 1968). The criterion for evaluating their design and content was the degree to which the performance of the computer program could match the performance known to arise from the human cognitive system.

Whether or not the means by which the artificial intelligence program achieved its performance parallels the processes underlying human performance remains a key question for some philosophers (Searle, 1990). From the perspective of the engineer and systems analyst, the important part of the hypothesis under test relates to the specification and organisation of the functional elements involved in a system. These properties are independent of how the functions are embodied in a biological or electronic substrate (Simon, 1981). It remains open to critics of work on artificial intelligence to argue that the behaviour and performance of these systems do not match their criteria for intelligence. However, these criteria reflect social attitudes and they change over time with development and innovation in the fields investigated (Collins, 1992; Ford and Hayes, 1998).

24.3　COMPUTER SIMULATION: METAPHOR, ANALOGY OR HYPOTHESIS?

Craik (1943) presented a 'Hypothesis on the nature of thought' which argued that mechanical and psychological systems share properties which make them capable of reasoning. The key element is the generation of an internal representation which forms the basis of reasoning, deduction, inference, etc. The symbols or states in this internal representation can be realised in mechanical, electromechanical, solid state physics or biochemical form.

Craik's argument may not find easy acceptance because at a concrete level the appearance and performance of mechanisms, electronic systems and biological systems are obviously different. However, Simon (1981) has argued that the success of scientific thought arises from the creation of an abstract account of the phenomena of interest. This account can be independent of an understanding of the detailed processes which cause those phenomena. Thus we accumulated a great deal of knowledge of the gross physical and chemical behaviour of matter before we had knowledge of molecules. Similarly we had a great deal of knowledge about molecules before we had an atomic theory, and so on. These developments were possible because the behaviour of a system at each descriptive level depended on only a very approximate, simplified, abstracted characterisation of the system at the level beneath it.

According to Simon, artificial systems and adaptive systems, which include both psychological and biological systems, have properties which make them particularly susceptible to simulation via simplified models. Resemblances in the behaviour of these systems without identity of the inner (i.e. underlying) systems is particularly likely if the aspects of behaviour which we are interested in arise from the organisation of the parts making up the inner system, independently of all but a few properties of the individual components. For example, in structural engineering we may need to know only about the tensile and compressive strength of a material and not its chemical properties or origins to predict its behaviour and design a structure.

Given these considerations, taken together with the abstract character and symbol manipulation capacity of the computer and the ease with which it is possible to generate functional descriptions, the computer provides a powerful medium in which to express and test theories.

24.4 THE PRACTICE OF COMPUTER SIMULATION

Thus far emphasis has been placed on the use of the computer as the medium for defining and testing theory and understanding. In this role the computer is used as a tool in the process. Thinking and imagination are essential in the generation of schemes of understanding and theories relating to the phenomena of interest. Indeed investigation through simulation may be achieved through the process of a thought experiment alone in combination with externalised reasoning aids – schematic diagrams, flow diagrams, logical formulae, etc.

If thought experiment can be considered as a form of simulation, why do we need to resort to simulation using a computer ? How can a simulation ever tell us anything that we do not already know? Surely a simulation is no better than the assumptions built into it and the computer can do only what it is programmed to do. Simon (1981) considers that while both these assertions are true, they distract from the fact that simulation can provide new knowledge. Even if we start from the correct premises, it may be difficult to discover what they imply. This problem is especially marked when the system under investigation involves a number of variables which may interact. Constructing and running a simulation is a means to uncovering these details.

Miller et al. (1984) have described stages in the construction of theory in cognitive science. This is a discipline which draws on the techniques of linguistic and semantic analysis, psychological experimentation and artificial intelligence. They suggest that computer simulation is a technique best used at the midpoint between initial theory formulation and the development of explicit process models. Both Miller et al. and Simon suggest that clarification of the scope and problems of a theory can be achieved in the middle stage even though the system underlying the theory is poorly understood. Simon's account of the role of abstraction in theory formation, reviewed earlier, provides a rationale for this view.

24.5 UNDERSTANDING CASE STUDIES IN SIMULATION

The principles underlying investigations using computer simulation have now been described. It is appropriate to consider specific case studies. Unfortunately we now encounter a significant communication problem with respect to computer models. Miller et al. (1984) argue that it is very difficult to understand how a simulation model works without gaining experience in constructing models of this type. Having access to appropriate computing resources and training may also be necessary.

The problem is compounded by dialect variations in computer languages, even if they nominally are the same language, e.g. LISP. Furthermore it is generally very difficult to infer the properties of the theory which is embodied in the program code from the listing of the code. This problem arises from the nature of the relationship between the surface form of a computer language and its meaning in relation to the processes they refer to (Strachey, 1966). This point is amplified in section 24.6 on communicating with computers.

One solution to this communication problem is for the author of a computer model to explain the theory underlying its construction in verbal form – that is, by using natural language. But this medium for explanation is open to lack of clarity and imprecision, and fuzzy thinking. Moreover, the means by which elements of a theory are implemented can use procedures which are *ad hoc* and independent of any theoretical principles which guide the construction of the model under investigation.

Miller et al.'s (1984) observations suggest that it is crucial to learn about simulation and the use of programming languages in relation to concrete tutorial examples. Clocksin's (1987) and Scott and Nicolson's (1991) accounts of the use of the language Prolog use this tactic. Similarly in Winston and Horn's (1984) textbook, explanations of the features of the language LISP are linked to worked examples. Naylor (1983) presents a number of programming case studies which model expertise using the Basic programming language. It should be noted, however, that teaching materials designed to develop skills in using a programming language are not explicitly concerned with promoting skills in the use of computer simulation as a research tool.

24.6 COMMUNICATING WITH COMPUTERS

In order to use a computer as a medium for computer simulation, the user must learn to use the operating system and an appropriate language to specify the actions required of the computer. Computer languages can vary in their complexity and their expressive power. Languages can also differ in their semantics. For example Prolog is a **declarative language**. A program can be built by writing down statements in formal logic which specify facts and relationships. The language is best suited to applications that require symbolic computation. Prolog contrasts with **procedural languages** like Basic, Fortran and Algol 68. The writing of a program in Prolog is not like specifying an algorithm. Another language built for symbol manipulation is the language

LISP. Advocates of this language argue that many psychological functions are easily realised in LISP (Winston and Horn, 1984: 5–7).

Strachey (1966) reviewed the skills required to become an effective programmer. He argued that it was necessary for the user to understand the meaning, i.e. the semantics, of the instruction language as well as its form, i.e. the syntax. Statchey's perspective is further clarified by Winston's (1984: 252) commentary on the properties of language representations. A language representation is a set of syntactic and semantic conventions that make it possible to describe things – with a particular interpreter in mind of course. The syntax of a representation specifies the symbols that may be used and the way those symbols may be arranged. The semantics of a representation specifies how meaning is embodied in the symbols and the symbol arrangements allowed by the syntax.

With this perspective in mind, the programmer must translate the description of the theory relating to the system or process under investigation into instructions in a computer program. This operation will involve consideration of how the elements in theory can find expression in the semantics and syntax of the programming language. The form of the programming language may have its origins in mathematics, logic or symbolic information processing. Thus the choice of the computer language used to create the simulation can play a major role in the translation of the theory into program form and the results obtained from the simulation.

The hope is that the initial stage of analysis leads to an account of the phenomena at a level of abstraction (Simon, 1981) which allows the theory to be expressed in a veridical form within the programming medium for investigation by simulation.

24.7 STUDIES IN REASONING AND LANGUAGE UNDERSTANDING

Two investigations will now be described to illustrate the form that a computer simulation can take. Both studies are relatively old since they date from 1968 and 1972. However the time since their first publication has allowed the ideas they contain to be assimilated and evaluated. Both studies have explored concepts which are relevant to psychological issues.

The first study to be considered is Evans's (1968) study which involved the generation of a program to solve geometric analogy test questions. The test material was taken from an educational testing context. It involved the use of a restricted set of geometric objects and relationships combined in figures presented in a standardised format. Scores on geometric analogy test items have long been used as an index of intellectual performance. In consequence Evans could compare the program's performance with the performance levels and errors observed with human solvers. The stimulus for the study, however, was the need to devise an artificial intelligence program which could reason with visual representations.

The system described by Evans (1968), and summarised by Minsky (1968), involved four stages. After the initial 'perception' of the individual test figures, descriptions of the geometric figures (taken singly and in pairs) were generated at three levels. At the first level the description specifies the object's properties and the relationships of each element in the test figures. At a later stage, descriptions are generated which represent the differences, transformations and equivalences existing between the various test figure pairs. The transformation rules governing the changes which occur between pairs of figures are systematically compared to determine the best answers for each analogy problem.

Evans's investigation suggests that solving geometric analogy test problems depends on the ability to form (i.e. generate) and compare abstract descriptions. This insight emerged in the context of generating a theory about the representations and process leading to the choice of the analogous pairs. Some of the programming techniques and representations used to achieve a working program seem unlikely candidates for a psychological theory of task performance. However, the overall organisation of the program and characterisation of the intermediate representations are independent of the programming medium used. The principles used in the program were sufficiently compelling for Sternberg (1977) to draw on the Evans model for his work on modelling geometric analogies performance. Subsequent work by Winston (1984) on a model of inductive concept learning with pictorial concepts shared a number of organisational and process features found in the Evans program.

By working with a computer simulation technique, Evans was able to formalise aspects of a process of visual reasoning which it is difficult to formalise from direct experience on this kind of task. The work carried out by Evans, Winston and others suggests that common processes underlie performance on tasks which are traditionally regarded as distinct and separate. These investigations show that pattern recognition, inductive learning and simple analogy involve common processes and representations. The insight gained from this family of programs indicates the possibility of shared principles and processes. Thus a number of distinct phenomena can be explained within a common framework.

Later investigations of analogy and analogical reasoning have been extended to consider their contribution to language understanding, learning and instruction (Vosniadou and Ortony, 1989). DeJong (1989) has reviewed a number of attempts to extend our understanding of the analogy process which use 'computationally oriented' theories. He argues that uncertainty about the definition of analogical relationships and incomplete details of the proposed computational models makes evaluation difficult. Gentner's (1989) study, which combines an experimental investigation of children's performance with an exploration of a process (computational) theory, shows how effective a dual research strategy can be in advancing understanding.

The figures used in the traditional geometric analogies test utilise a small set of geometric figures and relationships in their construction. The task is primarily concerned with the perception of relationships rather than the perception of the meaning or the significance of the stimuli. However, investigations of language understanding using computer simulation have modelled the processes underlying the perception of meaning and significance. Obermeier (1987) has summarised the various approaches to natural language processing.

One very significant study was conducted by Winograd (1972). His work integrated a number of elements to create a model and a system which carried out an integrated process utilising syntactic, semantic and pragmatic knowledge. His program had three components: a **syntactic parser** which embodies a large scale grammar of English; **semantic routines** which interpret the meaning of words and sentence structure; and a **cognitive deductive** system to explore consequences, plan and carry out commands and find answers to questions. When interpreting sentences Winograd's system works from the analysis of syntax to semantics to action. However, the system allows inter-action between representational domains to, for example, resolve structural and referential ambiguity.

The criterion used by Winograd to evaluate the system's capacity to understand language was based on an operational definition of understand-ing. The system's capacity was tested in terms of its ability to answer ques-tions and carry out actions in a simulated blocks world. On these criteria, the program proved an impressive performer.

Following its initial publication, Winograd's model was subject to scrutiny and comment. Objections were raised with regard to the type and scope of the model of grammar used in the system. Others have considered that the blocks world in which the program acted placed serious limits on the generality of the study and Winograd's demonstration. It is evident that the scope of the 'real-world knowledge' available to the system was limited. In effect the program operated in a very specific and concrete conceptual 'world'. Thus it was not capable of the elaborative inferences which contribute to our com-prehension of language.

Winograd has continued to develop his ideas about language understand-ing, in particular with regard to communication between persons and the issues of shared knowledge and understanding. For details see Winograd's (1980) article reproduced in Aitkenhead and Slack's (1994) collection of papers. Widening the range of issues considered increases markedly the com-plexity of the problems involved in developing a framework for language understanding.

As noted earlier, a number of detailed criticisms were made of Winograd's (1972) work. Unlike many accounts of traditional psychological theories, the description provided by Winograd was sufficient to allow detailed analysis and commentary to occur. This feature can be considered as one of the strengths of the method of investigation through simulation. However, it is easy to get distracted by the details of the implementation and forget the overall principles and organisation which guided the design of Winograd's scheme. Simon (1981) would of course argue that these features are the key aspects to consider.

Winograd (1980) lists four features of his model which involved conceptual and technical innovations in modelling the language understanding process. The model used a reasoning formalism based on the 'procedural embedding of knowledge'. Knowledge of language form, semantics and pragmatics was expressed as procedures. The states of knowledge involved are implicit in the processes carried out. At any point in the interpretative process, the particular sequence of steps in the procedure which operate on a sentence will reflect the general syntactic properties of language and the particular structure and lexical content of the sentence under interpretation. The adaptive quality of this process is illustrated in the case of morphemic analysis in Winograd (1971).

Within Winograd's model, meaning was based on an imperative as against a declarative process. The meaning of a sentence was represented as a command to the program to do something rather than a fact about the world. Thus a statement about ownership of an object was represented as a program which added information to the data base of the system. In effect language statements result in the initiation of action within the system. The representation for the meaning of words and idioms was also based on procedures which operate to build representation structures corresponding to the sentence. This feature enabled the program to deal with features like pronouns.

Finally, the program included an explicit representation of the cognitive context. In order to resolve the reference for a phrase, the program must decide on the basis of a representation of conceptual focus or a recency criterion specific to the context of the sentences preceding the current phrase. This knowledge obviously lies outside the category of general facts about the objects within the domain considered.

The significance of these features for the development of a process model of language understanding can only be assessed in relation to theory and findings in this area. A number of specific aspects of Winograd's (1972) implementation have proved difficult to extend to other language understanding phenomena. Nevertheless the range of the phenomena his system exhibited is impressive. The clarity with which he was able to describe the properties and operation of the elements included in the system make it possible to specify how the model might be extended. This is not always the case for verbal descriptions of a theory.

An account of how work on natural language understanding has developed during the last 20 years can be found in Gazdar (1993). He describes how the definition of the 'problem to be solved' with regard to language understanding and the heuristics used to guide theories and solutions have changed during this period. Along with changes in the theoretical framework, the power of computers has dramatically increased relative to their cost. This development has changed the technological possibilities for storing information and accessing it through a natural language interface. The problem of defining and organising the common-sense knowledge which humans use in language understanding has been addressed (Lenat, 1995). This work has led to the construction of systems which exhibit properties of artificial intelligence with respect to language comprehension and knowledge and provide frameworks for understanding natural intelligence.

24.8 NEURAL NETWORKS AND CONNECTIONISM

The two areas of study considered above have made use of a 'mind as a computer' framework in order to explore how computational processes can be organised to exhibit 'intelligent' behaviour (Ford and Hayes, 1998). In parallel with the development of this type of investigation, the computer has been used to investigate how the properties of the neural systems making up our brains may operate to categorise stimuli, learn and represent information in memory. The starting point for this work is usually linked to McCulloch and Pitts's (1943) paper entitled 'A logical calculus of the ideas immanent in nervous activity'. As the title suggests, the authors considered how neural structure and function could provide a system which embodied logical operations to provide a substrate for reasoning and thought. This work was then developed to investigate how systems made up of interconnected elements with attributes based on selected properties of neurones, including their synaptic and integrative properties, would become organised and behave under the impact of stimulation designed to simulate a learning cycle.

Simulating processes which incorporate the properties discovered by neurophysiological studies of the brain together with concepts taken from engineering and cybernetics has proved very appealing. One factor in the popularity of this approach could be that the hypotheses which are investigated are **reductionist**. Investigations of neural network models explore how the properties and behaviours which we regard as being part of psychology could arise from the properties and processes defined in terms of a lower and perhaps more fundamental level of description. Another important factor is that work in this area has led to the development of a neural network technology and the production of systems capable of carrying out recognition and classification. These systems have been used for auditory analysis, visual recognition in the quality control of manufactured components, speech recognition, medical image screening, and the development of decision support systems for medical diagnosis (Churchwood, 1993; Giger and Pelizzari, 1996; Economou et al., 1996). Thus the investigation and development of artificial neural networks has led to the design of systems which exhibit behaviour which many would regard as reflecting intelligence. These achievements lend strong support for this kind of work.

Accounts of the basic concepts of neural networks and connectionism can be found in many published sources. When setting out to understand work in this area it is necessary to cope with mathematical functions. It is possible to described the general properties of simple neural networks using words and diagrams but the detailed aspects of the properties of the network elements and connections can be expressed only in mathematical forms which is how they are defined in the simulation. However, describing the properties of elements and connections does not allow us to directly deduce what the behaviour of a network will be. This point was considered earlier when reviewing Simon's (1981) account of what we gain by carrying out investigations using simulation techniques.

Finding an account of neural networks, and their use in exploring hypotheses, which is compatible with a reader's conceptual resources, can require persistence and patience. Some authors provide only a general outline. Others address the problem of mathematical understanding and set out to describe and explain the properties which emerge from a network when the network is trained in a non-mathematical form. The general strategy involved in using simulation as a means of investigation in cognitive science, including neural networks, is considered by Green (1996). Churchwood's (1993) argument in favour of explanation within a neurocomputing framework includes a non-mathematical treatment of neural networks and changes in performance which follow training. Anderson's (1998) account offers a gentle mathematical treatment of neural networks and considers how this approach could help our understanding of aspects of mathematical knowledge. Hinton (1992) provides a concise and well-illustrated account of ideas in the neural network field.

24.9   CRITICISMS AND RESERVATIONS

During the long development of the ideas underlying neural networks, objections have been frequently voiced about the impact of the simplifying assumptions which have been made with respect to the properties of artificial neural networks. Dawson and Shamanski (1994) believe that these simplifications markedly reduce the value of these investigations when attempting to understanding the operations of real brains. They argue that while there have been great achievements in the development of artificial neural network technology, work in this area has not led to illumination of actual brain function since the work is based on implausible assumptions. Thus the neural networks may not model appropriate physiological processes. However, Anderson (1988) has argued that by understanding the relationships between the properties of the artificial neural networks and their associated 'psychologies' or behaviours, we will be in a better position to understand the properties exhibited by biological systems. In a similar vein, Ford and Hayes (1998) have argued, using as an example the development of the aeroplane, that technological developments will often occur which are well ahead of current scientific thinking and knowledge. The need to refine the technology leads to new knowledge which enhances scientific understanding and stimulates investigation. In the case of powered flight this knowledge led to improvements in the design of aircraft and enhanced our understanding of the basis of flight in biological systems.

24.10   CONCLUSIONS

Using a computer to test and explore theory in psychology forces the investigator to express the theory in a form compatible with the programming medium, i.e. language, to be used. That language must have a semantics structure which is compatible with the states and processes envisaged in the theory. In practice the need to express the theory in program form may shape and hopefully clarify the theory. This aspect of creating and using simulation programs has elements of the chicken and egg problem! In the case of neural network simulations, the language for expressing a theory or model is mathematics. This representation is precise and offers a powerful medium in which to model states, interactions and change. Nevertheless, simplification and idealisation of the phenomena under investigation may be required to achieve the simulation. The choice of the simplifying assumptions can have a major impact on the validity of the simulation.

As Miller et al. (1984) have argued, the use of simulation for investigation becomes appropriate only when sufficient facts about a phenomenon have been accumulated and a theory or theories have been formulated. If the theory predicts that a phenomenon reflects interactions between subcomponents of a system, then simulation can provide a powerful investigative technique. Working with a simulation technique brings the user into contact with concepts from computing, mathematics, theory of representations and systems analysis. These ideas can be fruitful additions to psychological theory.

24.11 FURTHER READING

An inexpensive set of edited readings in cognitive science which includes both papers in psychology and classic studies in artificial intelligence can be found in Aitkenhead and Slack (1994) *Issues in Cognitive Modelling*. Part of the material on artifical intelligence can also be found in Waltz's (1982) well-illustrated article entitled 'Artifical intelligence' in *Scientific American*, 247(4): 101–22. Detailed discussion of the theory and method used in work carried out within a computational framework is presented in Kintsch et al. (1984). Herbert Simon provides a clear account of investigation through simulation in *The Sciences of the Artificial* (1981). A collection of essays covering neuro-physiological, computational and philosophical aspects of understanding and simulating intelligent behaviour can be found in Broadbent (1993) *The Simulation of Human Intelligence*. James Anderson provides a tutorial account of using a neural network framework to understand aspects of mathematical knowledge in Scarborough and Sternberg (1998) *An Invitation to Cognitive Science*, Volume 4 (2nd edn).

25

Bivariate Statistical Analyses

Chris Fife-Schaw

Contents

25.1 INTRODUCTION

In a book on research methodology it is not possible to avoid a discussion of statistical techniques or approaches to data analysis. Teachers of statistics around the world know how the topic strikes fear into the hearts of many a psychology student, yet most of the ideas underlying these analyses are very straightforward. Many people see statistical formulae and assume that they will not be able to understand them, yet the vast majority involve little more than being able to add, subtract, multiply or divide numbers.

In this chapter I will attempt to explain the ideas underlying some commonly used tests with reference to as few formulae as is possible. There is not enough space in this book to provide full explanations of all bivariate tests so you will need to look at a statistics book at some point. However, the aim is to explain the logic of common bivariate statistical tests in the hope that when you do look at the statistics text it will make more sense to you. You should make sure you have read Chapter 11 on levels of measurement first as I will assume you are familiar with these issues. Before looking at any bivariate analyses you should be aware of some key concepts that many texts take for granted that you understand.

25.2 SOME BASIC DEFINITIONS

Population The collection of all individuals of interest in a particular study. More abstractly it is the set of all 'units' of analysis defined by your problem area: for example, all people resident in the UK, all people with a particular disease, all females, etc.

Unfortunately, the term 'population' is also used in a more specific way to refer to a population of scores. The sample of people you draw upon will provide you with a sample of scores from the population of scores. This can be confusing since the population of scores probably does not exist in any real sense: for example, you get test scores from your sample but as the rest of the population has not taken the test their scores exist only at a kind of abstract, 'as if' level.

Sample A set of individuals selected from a population and intended to represent the population under study. Usually it is impractical to study everybody in your target population so you have to draw a sample. See Chapter 7 for a discussion of sampling issues.

The case or unit of analysis As psychologists we are interested in people and this means that for many applications the case or unit of analysis is the individual respondent or participant. We assign individuals to conditions, say, and measure their responses. You should be aware that statistical tests do not require that the case be a person. The case could be a household or a rat or a stick or anything that could reasonably have data associated with it.

Data Measurements or observations. A **data set** is a collection of measurements.

Raw score An original measurement or observed value (a datum). A value before some form of manipulation has been done.

Variable A characteristic or condition that changes or has different values for different individuals (e.g. height, hair colour, score on a test).

Parameter   A value that describes a population. It could be a single measurement (e.g. mean score on a mathematics ability test) or derived from a set of observations *drawn from the population* (e.g. mean maths score of all females who are above average on an English test). There is a convention in textbooks that population parameters are indicated by using Greek characters (e.g. μ, σ).

Statistic   A value that describes a sample. This can be a single measurement (e.g. mean maths score of the people in your sample) or derived from a set of observations (e.g. mean score of the females in your sample). Often a statistic is the best estimate you have of a population parameter since you may not be able to 'test' everybody in your target population. All sorts of numerical values that summarise your sample data are statistics. These could be means, medians, percentages, correlations, t-values, F-ratios, etc.

Descriptive statistics   These summarise raw scores, e.g. average, percentage, variance, etc.

Inferential statistics   These are techniques for using sample data to make statements about the population that the sample came from. Most of the time you are interested in using inferential statistical techniques to tell you how justified you are in concluding something about the population based on the data provided by your sample.

Most psychologists collect data from samples of people. We rarely have access to the total population of people who we might have been interested in studying. Say, for instance, you were conducting an experiment to assess the impact of two teaching methods on mathematical ability in children. The chances are you would set up the two teaching schemes in local schools and test the children's ability before and after the schemes were put in place. Obviously, in the long term you would like to be able to recommend one scheme as being more generally useful than the other, as you would like your research to have an impact on children's education generally. However, you cannot test all children in the country on one or other of the methods; you have to draw a sample of children and then extrapolate the findings from your sample to what you think you would have found if you had tested all children.

This process of extrapolating from findings based on sample data is referred to as **statistical inference**. You try to infer something about the population from your sample. Analytical procedures that allow this sort of extrapolation are called inferential statistics.

Test statistic   Most inferential statistical tests produce a number which has to be compared with some criterion value to determine its **statistical significance**. A t-test produces a t statistic, a Kendall's tau correlation produces a τ statistic, etc. These summarise something about the *relationship* between your variables.

Statistical significance   This is the probability of having observed a test statistic as large as you have if there was in fact no relationship between the variables in question. Statistical significance, probability and hypotheses are considered later in more detail.

Substantive significance   This is not to be confused with statistical significance. Psychology journals are packed with statistically significant findings but this does not necessarily mean that the findings are psychologically or theoretically important. As we will see later, it is possible to get a statistically significant result associated with a relationship between variables that is so small it is of no substantive, practically important, significance at all.

Effect size   We use test statistics when considering, say, whether two groups' scores are statistically significantly different. The probability value (p-value) we get will tell us how likely it was that we would have observed a difference between the groups' scores as big as we did if there really were no differences between the groups in the population. This depends to a large degree on the size of the sample but tells us nothing about *how different* the two groups' scores are. We could just say what the difference was expressed in the units of our scores (e.g. IQ points, number of 'correct' responses) but it is often helpful to express the differences in terms of an established effect size metric. Common effect size metrics include Cohen's d, eta-squared (η^2) and R^2. There are more but they all share in common the ability to say how big a difference or relationship has been found in a study and there are conventions for saying whether an effect is 'small', 'medium' or 'large'. It is becoming common for journals to require authors to report effect sizes since traditional statistical significance tests do not tell us how big an effect has been revealed by a study (see also Chapter 28).

Measurement error   As discussed in Chapter 11, all measures of psychological constructs contain errors that are attributable to the measurement process itself. With the exception of a small class of sophisticated multivariate analyses (see Chapter 27), common inferential statistical procedures do not allow for this kind of error. Even if a statistical test is highly appropriate for the data you have, poor quality measures with unknown amounts of measurement error could invalidate any conclusions you might wish to draw from your test. You must always seek to minimise measurement errors.

Sampling error   When you calculate a statistic based on data from a sample it is likely that your sample isn't absolutely representative of the population. In fact, it is highly unlikely that any sample statistic will exactly match the population parameter. So, there is something called sampling error which we need to know about whenever we want to make general statements about the population. Most of the time, the bigger your sample in relation to the size of population, the smaller the size of the sampling error.

Random sampling   The way you draw your sample from the population of interest should be by true random selection if at all possible. Non-random selection processes are likely to introduce biases into your parameter estimates.

Most inferential statistical techniques (see section 25.7) assume that you have obtained your sample via random sampling procedures.

In practice, psychologists often use non-random samples for convenience (e.g. students, attendees at the local clinic, etc.) or implicit quota designs (see Chapter 7). Much has been written on the relationship between inferential statistical procedures and sampling procedures and those interested in the techniques of estimating the impact of sample designs, known as **design effects**, should consult Moser and Kalton (1971).

25.3   WHAT ARE BIVARIATE STATISTICAL ANALYSES?

In the remainder of this chapter the focus is on the use of inferential statistical procedures since, as researchers attempting to explain human behaviour generally, we are rarely interested in merely describing our sample. We would like to make theoretical claims that apply to all people in a given population.

This chapter deals with analyses that involve two variables. These analyses can be broken down into two broad categories: (1) tests that look for *differences between groups*, as defined by one variable, on scores on another variable; and (2) tests that detect an *association* or correlation or relationship between scores on two variables. Chapter 26 will discuss analyses that deal with more than two variables at a time, which are called **multivariate analyses**.

25.4   CLASSICAL BIVARIATE DESIGNS

Much of this book has been concerned with explaining common research designs and, at the risk of repeating material you may already have read, the following prototypical approaches commonly require bivariate analyses. It is important to understand the relationship between research design and the types of statistical procedures which are appropriate for use with them.

25.4.1   Experimental designs

In experiments an independent variable is changed or altered while changes in a **dependent variable** are observed. To be sure of a cause and effect relationship between the two variables, the experimenter tries to exclude the effects of all other variables by randomly assigning people to **conditions** or **treatments** (values of the independent variable) and by controlling or holding constant other things that might affect the results. It is possible to have more than one independent variable but we will deal with that in Chapter 26.

The **independent variable** is a variable that is controlled or manipulated by the experimenter. Usually it is a categorical/nominal level variable and normally you have an expectation that the independent variable causes changes in the dependent variable. Levels of the independent variable are often referred to as conditions or treatments. For example, no drug treatment vs. low dose treatment vs. high dose treatment; teaching method A vs. teaching method B.

The dependent variable is the variable that is affected by changes in the independent variable. It is *never* thought of as influencing the independent variable. Chapter 4 discusses experimental designs in more detail.

In its most basic form an experiment will randomly allocate people to one of two conditions of the independent variable, say, people taught statistics by method X and a control condition of people who are exposed to no statistics teaching. We let a period of time elapse so that method X can have some impact and then we test both groups on statistics, our dependent variable. This is referred to as an **independent groups** or **between-groups** design since none of the participants appear in both groups and we are interested in differences between groups.

This design is acceptable but there may be problems if, by chance, when randomly allocating people to the two groups, we allocate people who are already better at statistics to the method X group. This would make it more likely that we would get higher scores for the method X group. To get over this we could simply measure everyone's statistics ability first, then expose them to method X, and then retest their ability. This is called a **repeated measures** or **within-subjects** design. This latter design does not get over the problem that statistics ability might improve over time without help from method X (though data from a control group would help), but it does get over the problem of randomly allocated participants being different before the experiment took place.

It is important to know whether you have an independent (between-group) design or a repeated measures (within-subjects) design when selecting an appropriate statistical test. You should also be aware that it is now regarded as more appropriate to call experimental subjects 'participants' even though the terminology to describe designs has yet to change: we do not yet have 'within-participants designs'.

25.4.2 Quasi-experimental designs

These are similar to true experiments except that the levels of the independent variable are not under the control of the experimenter. For example, if you want to see whether school-based anti-smoking campaigns had an effect on smoking behaviour you could not randomly allocate children to the schools that either would, or would not, have the anti-smoking intervention.

Quasi-experiments are often the best you can hope for as you do not always have any real ability to control the independent variable. There is always a possibility that any effects you show are due to unforeseen **confounding variables**. For example, smoking rates might already be different in the schools you studied; your campaign might have no effect but schools will show a difference in smoking rates after the intervention. Your 'control' school may choose to run its own anti-smoking campaign which would be another kind of confounding variable (see Chapter 6 for more on quasi-experimentation).

Relationships between supposed independent and dependent variables in most questionnaire surveys are tested only within this quasi-experimental framework. If you conduct a survey and want to see what effect various background factors (e.g. social class, amount of education, etc.) have on test scores, again you cannot randomly allocate people to different levels of class or educational experience. This is important because some survey analyses are written up to read *as if* they were true experiments.

25.4.3   Correlational and observational designs

These look to see if there is any systematic relationship between two variables. The aim is only to show that levels of one variable are associated with levels of another. There are no independent and dependent variables as such, as no causal relationship can usually be inferred from correlational analyses even if you have a good hunch that there is one.

For example, if you found that the size of car engines seemed to increase with the aggressiveness of their owners, as measured on a personality test, you could draw at least the following three conclusions: (1) it could be that aggressive people buy fast cars to express themselves; (2) it could also be that owning a fast car gradually makes you more aggressive; or (3) something else that you have not measured causes both the buying of fast cars and the development of aggressive personalities. You cannot sort this out with a correlational or observational study but you can at least show that there is a relationship and that it is not zero.

A notable exception to this is when the temporal ordering of events is not in question. For instance, the number of cigarettes smoked when someone was 20 might be highly correlated with levels of tar found in the lungs at age 50. It seems *unlikely* that levels of tar at age 50 *caused* levels of cigarette smoking at an earlier age (though even here, the possibility of a third, unmeasured variable influencing both variables still cannot be ruled out).

Note that all three of these general approaches concern the relationship between two variables. These designs can be made multivariate by incorporating additional variables, but for the present purposes we will deal with these prototypical cases. The experimental, and to a lesser extent, quasi-experimental designs tend to require analyses that look at differences between groups or conditions (defined by the independent variable) in scores on some outcome (the dependent variable). Correlational or observational approaches require analyses that detect associations between variables where neither variable is necessarily the dependent or independent variable (they could be but it is not necessary that they are).

25.5   THEORIES AND HYPOTHESES

This section spells out some aspects of classical hypothesis testing. This perspective on the conducting of good research is only one of a number of views but it is still the dominant view in psychology. It owes a lot to the theorising of Karl Popper (1959) and is sometimes called the hypothetico-deductive model. It is also a form of positivism and assumes that there is a reality and some form of truth out there waiting for us to find it. Chapters 1 and 2 discuss this and alternative perspectives and if you are in any doubt about what is said here, refer back to those chapters.

25.5.1 Theories

These are statements about the underlying mechanisms of behaviour: the 'how' and 'why' of behaviour. To satisfy Popper it is essential that these are stated in such a way as to allow the potential of them being shown to be wrong. Theories that could never, in principle, be shown to be wrong are not part of good science. They become acts of faith. Theories should generate specific **hypotheses** that can be tested. If these prove false then the theory can be questioned, modified or rejected.

25.5.2 Hypotheses

These are predictions about the outcomes of experiments or studies. Usually one does this by formally expressing a theoretically generated prediction, or an educated guess, about how an independent variable will affect a dependent variable. Conventionally we deal with two sorts of hypothesis when we do any inferential statistical tests. These are as follows.

25.5.3 The null hypothesis

This is what we actually test and it appears slightly odd at first sight. The null hypothesis in an experiment is the statement that: the independent variable has *no effect* on the dependent variable at all *in the population*. In a correlational study the null hypothesis would normally be that two variables are not associated, or correlated, with one another *in the population*. Note that what happens in the *sample* is not what we are really interested in. The null hypothesis is often referred to as H_0.

25.5.4 The alternative hypothesis

This is usually our 'hunch' hypothesis: that the independent variable does indeed affect the dependent variable *in the population* or that two variables are correlated with one another *in the population*. However, this is only one hypothesis in a range of possible alternative explanations about what really affects the dependent variable and we cannot treat our preferred alternative hypothesis as absolutely true. This is in part because we normally draw on data from a sample rather than from the whole population.

For example, say you wanted to prove the hypothesis that 'all people have two hands' and you draw a sample of one person. If that person had two hands that would not prove that all people had two hands. Some people that you have not sampled might have more hands or, more likely, fewer. If the sample person had one or none, however, then you would have to throw out your hypothesis; it would definitely be wrong.

It is easier to show that a hypothesis is false than it is to show that a hypothesis is true. Indeed, there is a philosophical argument that we can only ever prove that something is not true: we can never show that something is always absolutely true. The alternative hypothesis is referred to as H_1.

25.6   TYPE I AND TYPE II ERRORS

25.6.1   Type I error

This type of error has occurred when you reject a true null hypothesis. This is where you conclude that the independent variable did affect the dependent variable when, in fact, it didn't. This can happen when, for instance, by chance you allocate people who were already high scorers to one condition and low scorers to another. When you measure the dependent variable, the difference between the conditions is due to the fact that the people were different before you started, *not* because the independent variable had any effect. In terms of correlational analyses, Type I errors occur when you say that the two variables were related to one another when, in fact, they were not.

Publishing findings with Type I errors in them could mislead people into doing more research on a dead-end topic or making serious life threatening decisions based on the inaccurate conclusions from your work.

25.6.2   Type II error

This occurs when you fail to reject a false null hypothesis. You conclude that the independent variable has no influence on the dependent variable when it actually does. This happens sometimes because the size of the treatment effect is very small and hard to notice in your sample. It can also happen when you get the opposite of the example given for Type I errors. Here, by chance, you allocate people who were already high scorers on the dependent variable to the treatment condition that actually lowers scores and vice versa. The effect of the experiment is to level up the two groups so that there is now no difference between treatment groups on the scores and you accept the null hypothesis of 'no differences' between groups. In fact, the independent variable had a big effect but your sampling obscured this. One solution for this example is to adopt repeated measures designs so that you know how people scored before and after the experiment.

With correlational designs Type II errors have occurred when you conclude that there is no relationship between your two variables when, in fact, there is. If you can publish such 'non-findings' at all, then it may discourage people from investigating a potentially important effect.

The aim is always to minimise the probability of these two types of error occurring.

25.7   PROBABILITY

25.7.1   Basic definitions

Probability p is the likelihood or chance that something will happen. Where a number of possible outcomes A, B, C, D, etc. could occur, the probability of any particular outcome is a proportion based on the following:

$$\text{probability of outcome A} = p(A) = \frac{\text{number of possible A outcomes}}{\text{total number of outcomes}}$$

Probabilities always vary between 0 and 1. The sum of the probabilities of all possible events (A, B, C, D, etc. above) must always add up to 1. Some probability examples are as follows:

$p = 1$ if something *always* happens: for example, the probability of picking a joker out of a pack of 52 jokers.

$p = 0$ if something *never* happens: for example, the probability of picking a joker out of a pack of cards with no jokers in it.

$p = 0.5$ e.g. the chance of an unbiased coin coming up heads: another way of saying this is a '1 in 2 chance'.

$p = 0.25$ e.g. the chance of picking a diamond card from a pack of 52 playing cards: another way of saying this is a '1 in 4 chance'.

The most common application of probability notions in psychology is to decide how likely it is that your *sample-based* test statistic is found to be as big as it is by chance, assuming that your null hypothesis was, in fact, true. As an example, if there really was no real difference between people who had received a medical treatment and those who had not, then could it be (or rather, how likely is it) that the observed improvement in the treatment group was as big as it was just by chance?

Let us say we have a new treatment under test, and our null hypothesis is that the mean score of our cognitive test (the dependent variable) will be no different from that found in untreated people. In other words, our null hypothesis is that the population mean for treated people is the same as that for untreated people. Figure 25.1 is a frequency distribution of all the possible differences between treatment and control group means that would be obtained if you repeatedly drew new samples and calculated the means for each new sample. This is called a **sampling distribution**. You do not have to create this distribution yourself: this is simply shown here to explain the logic of hypothesis testing.

The shaded areas, known as **critical regions**, contain 'extreme' or very unlikely outcomes. They are still possible differences in means even if our null hypothesis is true. The proportion of mean differences falling into the critical regions gives you the probability of observing a difference that extreme if H_0 is true.

By convention, if the probability of observing means as different from that predicted by the null hypothesis (under the assumption that the H_0 is true) is less than $p=0.05$ (alternatively, 1 in 20 or 5%), then you reject the null hypothesis. If the probability is not less than 0.05 then you do not reject the null hypothesis. This $p=0.05$ figure, called an **alpha criterion**, is the maximum probability of making a Type I error.

In the above example we have looked at the difference between group/ treatment means observed in your sample and what would have been predicted

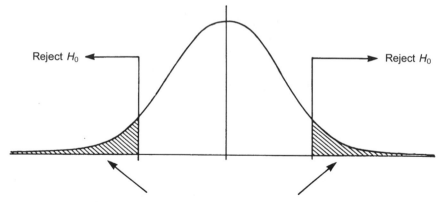

Extreme differences (probability = alpha) if H_0 is true.
Possible but quite unlikely group differences.

FIGURE 25.1   *A sampling distribution of differences between group means under the assumption that the null hypothesis is true*

under H_0. The same logic applies to designs concerned with associations between variables, too. When you are interested in correlations your null hypothesis is usually (though not always) that there is no (zero) correlation between the variables. As with the means, you look to see how likely it is that, via sampling, you would have observed a correlation that big between the two variables if H_0 were actually true. Again you could create a sampling distribution of correlations and look to see if your observed correlation fell into the critical region where you would reject the null hypothesis.

Most inferential statistical techniques, whether concerned with means or correlations or some other test statistic, use sampling distributions to determine whether the observed value falls into a critical region. Sometimes these sampling distributions make reference to population parameters and assume you have drawn random samples from the population, and sometimes the sampling distributions are constructed out of the range of possible outcomes given the particular experiment or study you are doing (see section 25.8).

The 0.05 probability figure is not a magical figure. It is only a convention and there are times when you would not be happy to reject the null hypothesis at this level. When people are conducting particularly controversial research, like trying to establish the existence of clairvoyance (if true it would undermine some well-established laws of physics), it is usual to adopt a more strict alpha criterion. This has the effect of making all your analyses more conservative.

You are free to set the alpha criterion at any value you like but you must declare it and be prepared to have to convince others that you are justified in doing this. This is an example of how some of the relativist and socially conventional processes discussed in Chapter 2 creep into a part of the research process which, from the outside, might appear concrete, highly rigorous and uncontroversial. Many would argue (e.g. Kirk, 1996) that the undue focus on *p*-values has actually hampered science rather than promoted it.

25.7.2   One-tailed versus two-tailed tests

When hypothesis testing you must decide whether you are going to make a one- or two-tailed test of the null hypothesis. In a one-tailed test, you reject the null hypothesis if the difference between the observed mean, say, and that predicted under H_0 is relatively small but is in a *previously specified direction*. A two-tailed test requires a somewhat larger difference but is independent of the direction of difference.

This distinction is best illustrated by an example. Say you had a wonder drug that was supposed to influence cognitive performance. If you had a strong theory about the action of this wonder drug which said that it would increase scores on the cognitive test, then if you observed no difference between treatment and control groups *or* you found that the drug group scored less, you would have disconfirmatory evidence for your theory. In this case your *null hypothesis* would be that drug treatment scores would be the same or less than those of the controls. This would be a one-tailed test.

In most psychological research, our theories are generally less well specified and we would be interested in differences in either direction. Big drops in score would be just as interesting as big gains. We would not wish to ignore a big drop in scores by doing a one-tailed test. This time our null hypothesis would be that treatment and control group means would be the same. Figure 25.2 illustrates the point. In this figure we can see that the shaded areas in the tails of both distributions occupy 5% of the total areas under the curves and thus 5% of all sampling means. In this hypothetical example, the one-tailed critical value is 26 so any observed mean for the drug group greater than 26 would lead us to reject H_0. For the two-tailed test any value greater than 27 or less than 13 would lead us to reject H_0. Notice that when doing a two-tailed test you have to get a bigger difference between the two group means to reject H_0. This makes the two-tailed test inherently more conservative (less prone to Type I error) and this is partly why psychology journal articles contain more two-tailed probability values.

The same logic applies to tests of hypotheses of association. If you have a strong hypothesis that two variables will be positively (or, alternatively, negatively) correlated then you can specify a one-tailed test. In most psychological applications you will be interested in strong relationships regardless of whether they are positive or negative and so two-tailed tests may be more appropriate. Use the less conservative one-tailed test only when you have a very strong hypothesis that specifies the direction of the expected effect. Do not swap between a two-tailed and a one-tailed probability just to get a 'significant' result: the decision about which to look at must be made before conducting the test.

25.7.3   Statistical power

The point of all hypothesis testing is to reach the correct conclusion about the hypotheses. The previous sections looked at the Type I and Type II errors and the probability of making type I errors. Statistical power is associated with the tests you use and is the probability that the test will correctly reject a false

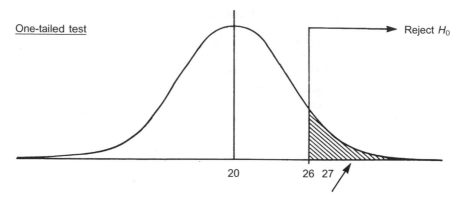

5% of extreme differences in one direction only

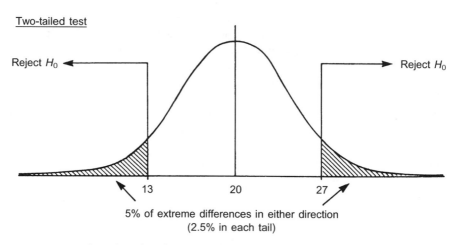

5% of extreme differences in either direction
(2.5% in each tail)

FIGURE 25.2 *Sampling distributions of differences between group means:*
critical regions for one-tailed vs. two-tailed hypothesis tests

null hypothesis. This is the test's power to detect an effect when there really is
one there to detect.

Most textbooks refer to the probability of making a Type II error (the
probability of accepting a false null hypothesis) as β (Greek letter beta). Since
the sum of the probabilities of all possible events must add up to 1, the
probability of rejecting a false null hypothesis, the power of your test, is:

$$\text{power} = p(\text{rejecting a false } H_0) = 1 - p(\text{accepting a false } H_0) = 1 - \beta$$

While this formula is very simple, settling on a single value for β is not
straightforward. Although people often talk of this or that test as being more
powerful than another, power depends on a number of factors that vary for
each application. There is no single figure that always applies to each particular type of test.

One factor is the size of the **treatment effect** or the **effect size**. Put simply, if your independent variable has an effect on the dependent variable (i.e. H_0 is false) but the size of this effect, the treatment effect, is small, it is going to be harder to detect this effect. Thus you will need a more powerful test to detect the effect (with a given size of sample) than would be the case if the treatment effect was strong. If the treatment effect is large, detecting it will not be difficult. A second factor is the level you set for the alpha criterion. Setting a smaller level will make it less likely that you will reject a true null hypothesis but it will also now be harder to reject a false hypothesis, all other things being equal.

A third factor is sample size. As the sample size gets larger and approaches the size of the population, so you will increase the statistical power of your test. If there really is a treatment effect (H_0 is false) in the population, you are more likely to find it in a larger sample than with a small one. Note, however, that power is about the ability to reject a false H_0 and is not about the size of the treatment effect. You might add more and more participants to your study to increase statistical power but this will not change the absolute magnitude of the treatment effect or its substantive significance.

As an example, you might have invented an expensive intervention programme to improve scores on IQ tests. Let us assume that it does work, though you do not know it yet, but it improves IQ by only 1 point (IQ scores often have a mean of 100 and a standard deviation of around 15). You set up a controlled experiment with 10 participants getting your programme and 10 control participants. You find the treatment programme group have an IQ score 1 point higher than the controls. You carry out the appropriate test and you fail to reject the null hypothesis and you make a Type II error.

Disappointed but not deterred, you realise that you did not have enough statistical power, so you rerun the study with a sample of 1000 in the treatment and control conditions. Again you find the treatment programme group have an IQ score 1 point higher than the controls. You now have a lot of power and your test correctly leads you to reject the null hypothesis. The intervention programme has a statistically significant effect on IQ scores. However, in practical terms, this effect is too small to justify the expense of the programme and people may well question the importance of being able to improve IQ by a single point. Beware confusing statistical significance with substantive, 'real-world' significance.

It is possible to use **power tables** to estimate the size of sample you would need to achieve a test with a given power as long as you can make some reasonable estimate of the likely size of the treatment effect (effect size). When designing a study it is highly desirable to use power tables to work out how many participants you need in advance, rather than to run the study only to find out that you had little chance of detecting the effect because you didn't have enough power as you had not approached enough people. Ethical committees and grant awarding bodies are highly likely to ask you to do a power analysis before agreeing to let you conduct a study, as studies that lack sufficient power are seen in some quarters as essentially unethical. Non-significant findings will be inherently ambiguous, as you will not know whether the failure to get a significant result is a result of the null hypothesis being true or it being false and you having insufficient power to detect the effect you are looking at.

Computer programs are now available to do power calculations (e.g. G*POWER) and as some are free there is little excuse for not using them.

25.8   PARAMETRIC VERSUS NON-PARAMETRIC TESTS

The final major distinction you need to be aware of before selecting a statistical test is whether you can do parametric or non-parametric statistical tests. A good number of the well-known statistical tests such as the *t*-test, the Pearson product moment correlation and analysis of variance (ANOVA) make assumptions about the distribution of scores in the populations. The most common assumptions are that the scores are normally distributed (have the classic 'bell-shaped' curve) in the population or that the distribution of (hypothetical) sample means is normally distributed. Also they assume that you have drawn a random sample from this population of scores. Some parametric tests assume that the variances of population scores are the same in your treatment and control groups. Tests that involve these assumptions are called **parametric tests**: they make use of assumptions about the distribution of scores in the population (i.e. information about population parameters).

If, as is often the case, your own data do not satisfy these assumptions then you should use the **non-parametric** alternatives to the parametric tests. These do not make the same assumptions about the distributions of scores in the population and so violating these assumptions is not a problem. Sometimes you will see these tests called **distribution-free tests**. These sorts of test are also especially appropriate for use with ordinal and categorical measures where the mean is not an appropriate measure of central tendency. To truly establish the normality of a distribution you would need to be able to estimate its mean and variance and thus it is difficult to establish this assumption with ordinal and categorical data. This is not to say that there are no parametric procedures appropriate for such measures but these require additional special assumptions to be met and will not be considered here.

Hypothesis testing with non-parametric tests proceeds by creating sampling distributions that apply specifically to your study. In essence, most work by calculating all possible values of the relevant test statistic given your study's data, design and null hypothesis. Then they look to see whether your observed value of the test statistic is relatively extreme and therefore unlikely to have occurred by chance if your null hypothesis were true. Whilst the procedures are not identical to those used with parametric tests, I hope you will appreciate that the basic logic of hypothesis testing remains the same as described earlier in this chapter. Statements about differences in the population can be made only if you have used random sampling procedures.

Parametric tests, if appropriate for your data, should be chosen in preference to their non-parametric equivalents since they tend to be more powerful and are thus better able to detect treatment effects if they really exist. See Chapter 11 for a discussion of violations to the levels of measurement assumptions of parametric tests.

25.9   CHOOSING A STATISTICAL TEST

Most statistics textbooks give you tree diagrams like the ones at the end of this chapter that help you decide which statistical test you should use. You need to know the following before you can use such trees.

First, you need to decide whether you are interested in looking for relationships (e.g. correlations, associations) or differences (e.g. between groups).

Second, if you are interested in differences then you should identify which variable is the dependent (outcome) measure and which is the independent variable.

Third, if you are interested in tests of association and you have normally distributed interval or ratio scale measures, produce a scatterplot (a graph) of scores on one variable against scores on the other. Figure 25.3 shows some hypothetical scatterplots. You should decide whether the relationship between the two variables looks linear or monotonic. Graphs (a) and (b) in the figure show linear, 'straight line' relationships between the X and Y variables. Graph (a) shows a positive linear relationship: increases in X seem to be associated with increases in Y. Graph (b) shows a negative linear relationship; increases in X are associated with decreases in Y.

A relationship is considered to be linear if you could reasonably draw a straight line through the points. Straight lines have been added to graphs (a) and (b). If there was a perfect relationship between X and Y then all the points would lie on a straight line. As the relationships are not perfect you observe an elliptical distribution of observations around the 'best-fit' straight lines.

I hope you can see that it would not be possible to do this with graph (c) since changes at higher scores on variable X do not seem to be associated with big changes in Y. Lower down the scale, changes in X are associated with bigger changes in Y. This is a monotonic relationship. Monotonic relationships are ones where increases in one variable are always associated with increases (or, if a negative relationship, decreases) in the other variable but the rate of change is not constant or linear. Graph (c) shows a positive monotonic relationship.

If the scatterplot looks U-shaped or n-shaped or has several peaks, you will not have a simple relationship between the two variables. You will have to consult a statistics text and look at the possibility of carrying out a mathematical transformation of one or both of your variables.

Fourth, what is the level of measurement of each variable? When testing for an association the choice of test will depend on the levels of measurement of both variables. When testing for differences between groups or conditions, the level of measurement of the *dependent* variable is crucial for test selection.

Fifth, if you have interval level or ratio scale measures and you think you may be able to do a parametric test, you must ask whether the variables are likely to be normally distributed in the population and whether you have been able to sample at random from the population.

As noted earlier, many psychological studies rely on convenience samples so, in such cases, you will not have met the random sampling assumption. In practice, the use of parametric tests such as the t-test is acceptable as long as

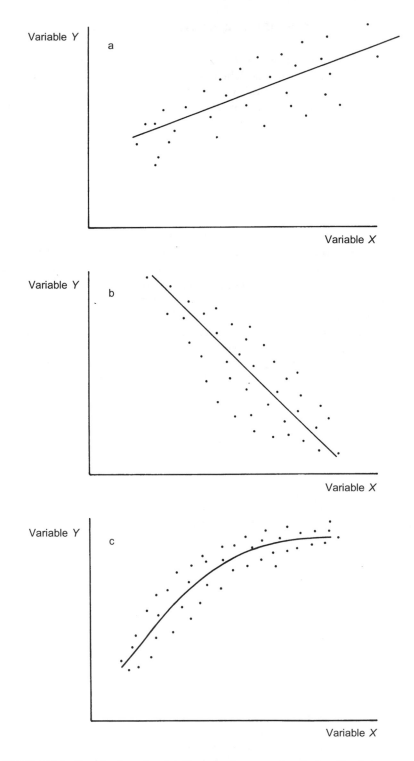

FIGURE 25.3   *Scatterplots showing linear and monotonic relationships between two variables*

participants are *randomly assigned* to treatment conditions (see Minium et al., 1993). The justification of this is technically complex but boils down to the fact that, in most cases, the conclusion drawn from the *t*-test is the same as would have been achieved if the most appropriate statistical model had been used. However, the results from your convenience sample are not sufficient for making generalisations about the population; you will need further evidence to support those conclusions.

In practice you are also unlikely to have access to information about the distribution of scores in the population so you will be able to look only at the distributions of scores in your sample data. There is much written about how **robust** parametric tests are to violations of the normality assumption (see Blalock, 1988). Although there are dissenting voices, there is now some consensus that minor deviations from normality will not unduly undermine the value of many common parametric tests.

If you have access to a statistics computer package you can look at diagnostic statistics that tell you how much your sample's data deviate from what would have been expected if they were normally distributed. Skewness is a figure which indicates the degree to which the distribution of scores is skewed to the left or the right. Kurtosis indicates the degree to which the distribution is more peaked or flatter than would be expected. Both figures should be zero and have known standard errors (see Chapter 7) so confidence limits can be calculated. As a rule of thumb only, skew and kurtosis figures within the range +1 to –1 with medium to large samples are probably sufficiently close to normality to allow the use of parametric tests.

So, if your sample data appear normally distributed then it is probably safe to assume you have satisfied the normality assumption. If, however, you have multiple modes ('peaks') in your sample data or the distributions look severely non-normal, then use the non-parametric equivalent test. When in doubt, do both types of test and rely on the non-parametric test if the two tests do not lead to the same conclusion.

Sixth, when group difference testing you must know if independent (separate) samples provide scores or whether the samples are matched so that either; (1) each respondent (case) is paired off with another respondent assumed to be alike on some basis, or (2) each respondent provides more than one score on a measure. This simply refers back to your research design. If you have two or more separate groups or conditions and each respondent (case) provides a single score you have what is often referred to as **independent groups**. If your respondents provide two or more scores on a measure, say before and after an intervention, the design is a repeated measures one. In this example, each respondent's before and after scores are matched together for the purposes of the test. Studies involving matched samples are possible but relatively less common.

Unfortunately, statistical texts have yet to reach a consensus on the terminology to be used to deal with this dichotomy. This is partly because authors want to provide decision trees that are appropriate for all possible applications of tests and thus they need to use abstract terms. Here, since this chapter has discussed only the two most common types of bivariate test (tests of difference and tests of association), we can hopefully adopt more simple terminology.

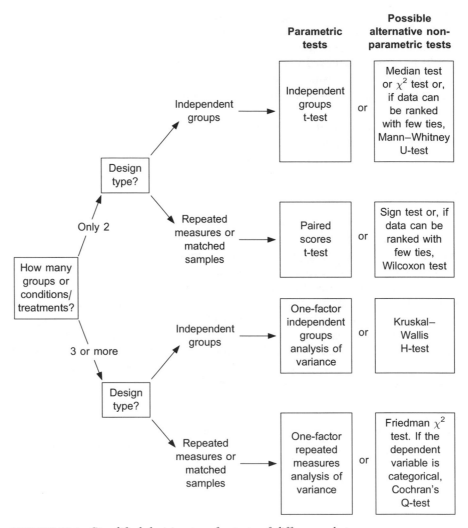

FIGURE 25.4   *Simplified decision tree for tests of differences between groups or treatments/conditions*

Figure 25.4 should be used when you wish to look for differences between groups or differences between conditions/treatments. Figure 25.5 should be used when you are looking at the relationship between two variables.

Let us assume you had two groups of people, those with maths GCSE and those without, and you wanted to see if their scores on a statistics test were different. This is a quasi-experimental research design. Let's assume the scores are on a ratio scale (number of items correct), and in your sample data the scores appear to be normally distributed in both groups (i.e. their distributions look like the one in Figure 25.1). This requires a test of differences so you would look at Figure 25.4.

The first question you are asked is how many groups or conditions/treatments you have. You have two, so you move up the tree to the next

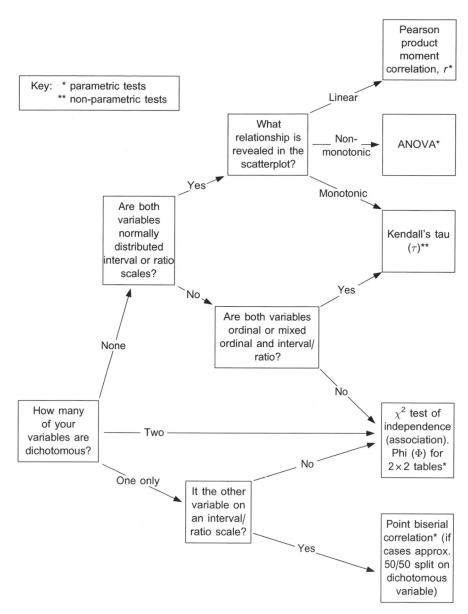

FIGURE 25.5 *Simplified decision tree for tests of association or relationship between two variables*

question which asks what type of design you have. Here, your two groups are independent of one another (you cannot both have and not have maths GCSE) so you move along and up again. This leads you to the independent groups *t*-test which is a parametric test. As you have normally distributed interval-level data you can use the *t*-test. Were you unable to satisfy these parametric assumptions you could use the Mann–Whitney U-test providing there were not too many people who had the same score on the test.

Using another example, let us assume you had measured attitudes towards death metal music on a seven-point, 'strongly in favour' to 'hate it' scale, and you had asked people to tell you how many times they had been to church in the last month. You want to know if church-going is associated with a dislike of death metal. Using Figure 25.5 you are first asked how many variables are dichotomous (have two categories only). Neither of your measures is dichotomous so you move up to the question, which asks if both variables are on interval or ratio scales. Your church attendance measure is, but strictly speaking the attitude measure is an ordinal one so you move down the 'no' branch. The next question asks if both variables are ordinal or you have a mix of ordinal and interval/ratio. Here the answer is 'yes', which leads you to the box containing Kendall's tau, a non-parametric correlation coefficient.

Both decision trees have been much simplified for the sake of clarity and there are a range of tests that could also have been included. However, for most basic bivariate tests of either difference or association, these decision trees will lead you to an appropriate analysis.

25.10 CONCLUSIONS

The aim of this chapter was to describe the logic underlying hypothesis testing with simple bivariate statistical tests and give some guidelines on how to select appropriate tests. In the space of one chapter it is not possible to describe individual tests but I hope you now have a better understanding of what they can do for you. To keep matters simple I have dealt with the two most popular classes of bivariate tests: those that test hypotheses about differences between samples and those that test for associations between variables. There are other kinds of bivariate test such as tests for trends or tests of differences in dispersion, for example. These are less common applications within psychology but most standard texts deal with these issues. It is always important to remember that the statistical tests are a research tool and not an end in themselves. They are not uncontroversial and, as explained in Chapter 2, need to be understood for what they are if psychological research is to progress productively.

25.11 FURTHER READING

Minium et al.'s (1993) *Statistical Reasoning in Psychology and Education* is very good for explaining the reasons behind various statistical procedures and is clear and accessible. Kirk's (1996) 'Practical significance: a concept whose time has come', *Educational and Psychological Measurement*, 56(5): 746–59 gives a useful discussion of how statistical tests ought to be used and how, if abused, can prove a hindrance to the advancement of psychology. Kraemer and Thiemann's (1987) *How Many Subjects? Statistical Power Analysis in Research* is an easy-to-understand text on how to calculate statistical power and thereby estimate the numbers of participants that will be needed for a study. Of the books available on this topic this is by far the easiest to use.

G*POWER is a power calculation program freely available on the Internet from the following address: http://www.psychologie.uni-trier.de:8000/projects/gpower.html. Please cite the G*POWER authors if you use it.

26

Introduction to Multivariate Data Analysis

Sean Hammond

Contents

26.1 BACKGROUND

When we collect information based upon a large number of variables such data are termed **multivariate**. This is in contrast to data from one variable (univariate) or two variables (bivariate) (see Chapter 25). By convention data from more than two variables are known as multivariate data.

Obviously, multivariate data can convey more information about a sample of people than univariate or bivariate data. As undergraduates most of us learn the standard univariate and bivariate statistical approaches to data analysis but we are rarely taught the more sophisticated methods of multivariate data analysis in any great detail. This is a shame because most of the more interesting research questions we might ask in the social sciences are multivariate by nature.

A common problem that faces research psychologists is the one where we are interested in looking at the differences between two or more groups of people and we have a number of measures (dependent variables) on which to compare them. The temptation is to carry out a separate statistical test of group difference for each dependent variable. This commonly involves the multiple use of the *t*-test or one-way ANOVA. There are two major problems with this approach.

First, we have the problem of 'weighing the odds' in favour of a significant result. As discussed in Chapter 25, statistical tests are commonly interpreted by probability estimates. What this means is that if we carried out 100 *t*-tests using random data, we would expect to obtain five *t*-values with an estimated probability less than or equal to 0.05. In other words the more tests we carry out the greater the chance we have of obtaining a statistic that will be interpreted as significant. This will lead us to a Type I error (see Chapter 25).

One way around this problem is to apply an adjustment to the probability level that we use to signify a significant statistic. A commonly used method is known as **Bonferroni adjustment** and simply involves dividing the traditional probability level by the number of dependent variables. Thus, if you were looking for a probability of 0.05 or less before deciding that the result was significant, and if you had five dependent variables, you would divide 0.05 by 5 giving you the probability 0.01. You would then describe only statistics with a probability of 0.01 or less as significant. Other methods of adjusting the probabilities for multiple statistical tests exist (Sidak, 1967; Holm, 1979) but the Bonferroni method is the simplest to apply.

However, this gets around only one of the problems of multiple statistical tests. Another, more difficult problem is the one of relationships between the dependent variables. Let us consider a simple example in which an educational psychologist is comparing persistent truants with non-truant children on three variables: IQ, scholastic achievement and reading ability. Suppose that the psychologist decides to calculate three *t*-tests to examine the difference between truant and non-truant children on the three dependent variables. They find that each test produces a statistically significant result at the 0.01 level. This may lead to the conclusion that the two groups of children differ on three distinct variables. However, another interpretation may be that the two groups differ significantly on only one of the variables (say, reading ability) and the other two dependent variables reflect this because reading is fundamental to both scholastic achievement and the successful completion of an IQ test. Thus, the IQ measure and the achievement ratings may be highly correlated with the reading test and the fact that they also show significant *t*-tests is an artefact of this relationship. What is needed in this situation is a method of data analysis that takes the relationships between the variables into account. We will return to this example later when we describe the technique known as discriminant function analysis.

It should be apparent from the preceding chapters that the nature of the research question will dictate the data analytic strategies used. Multivariate data analysis techniques can be grouped according to the research question being posed. For the purposes of this chapter we will categorise available methods under the following headings:

1 predicting outcomes
2 examining differences between groups
3 exploring underlying structure
4 fitting our measurements to theoretical models.

Some of the methods appropriate for each type of question will be discussed and then we will look at the special case of categorical data. Clearly, in the space of one chapter it will not be possible to give a comprehensive review of multivariate methods; a number of books that attempt to do this are reviewed at the end of the chapter. What this chapter aims to do is to act as an initial pointer to the new researcher who is looking for a data analytic method to fit his or her research questions.

26.2 MAKING PREDICTIONS

One common question that is often asked is, 'How can we use our data to make predictions?' For example, we may have carried out a piece of research showing that self-efficacy is related to recovery time after a hospital operation. We may need to answer the question, 'How can we predict recovery time if we know a patient's self-efficacy level?' Typically, this kind of question is addressed by a class of multivariate methods known as **regression procedures**. We will describe the most common form of regression analysis, starting with the special bivariate case where we have one predictor and one dependent variable. We will then develop our arguments to include the multivariate situation.

26.2.1 Simple regression

As an example of simple regression we will consider the problem of predicting scholastic achievement from IQ. In Figure 26.1 we see the relationship between IQ score and reading ability represented in a scatterplot. We can see that the relationship is a positive one such that an individual with a high IQ will tend to have a high scholastic achievement. Thus if we know an individual's IQ score we can make a guess at their likely scholastic achievement score. In fact, we can do better than that: we can estimate the scholastic achievement score statistically.

To do this we first calculate the position of the regression line. This is the straight line that passes through the scattered points such that the distance from the points to the line is minimised. The slope of the line is calculated as the parameter beta (β) and the intercept (that is the point at which the line cuts across the X-axis) is estimated as parameter alpha (α). Given a new individual with a known IQ X, we can then estimate the achievement score Y by using the following formula:

$$Y = \beta X + \alpha \qquad\qquad (26.1)$$

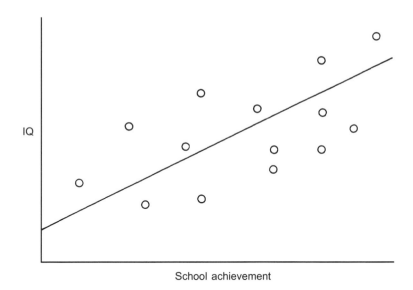

FIGURE 26.1   *Scatterplot of IQ against school achievement*

Thus, β is a weight which is applied to our predictor variable to optimally predict our dependent or criterion variable. The parameter α is simply a scaling parameter to transform the scale of the predictor variable to that of the criterion variable (IQ score to scholastic achievement score). This estimate is accurate only if the points in the scatterplot are close to the regression line since we are using this line as our 'model' of how the two variables are related. If all the points in the plot lie on the regression line we will have an absolute correlation coefficient of 1.00 and we will have a perfectly accurate estimate. The product moment correlation coefficient refers to a relationship represented by the product of the moments around the regression line. Thus, whenever the correlation is less than 1.00 and greater than -1.00 we have some inaccuracy in our prediction.

Let us think of this correlation between IQ and scholastic achievement in another way. Figure 26.2 shows a schematic representation of the relationship in which each variable is conceptualised as a ball of variance. Where a correlation exists two variables are said to co-vary; this is represented by an overlap between the two variables. In Figure 26.2 we see that the correlation between IQ and scholastic achievement is 0.60; the squared correlation (0.36) represents the proportion of covariance or overlapping variance between the two variables. This tells us that 36% of the variance of scholastic achievement is shared with IQ and the remaining 64% is unique or residual.

Note that where correlations are concerned we assume that each variable has been standardised to have a mean of zero and a variance of 1.00. This is done automatically when we calculate the product moment correlation. Thus, if two variables have a perfect correlation of 1.00 or -1.00, they will be represented as two perfectly overlapping spheres in which 100% of the variance is shared.

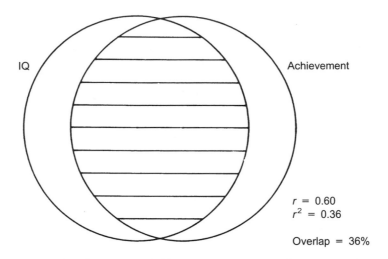

FIGURE 26.2 *Schematic representation of a correlation between two variables*

26.2.2 Multiple regression

From this analysis we might be tempted to say that scholastic achievement is a function of IQ. However, we have to be very careful about making causal judgements. Causality can be shown only if three features are true:

1 A is related to B.
2 A precedes B.
3 The relationship between A and B is not due to their joint relationship with C.

We have demonstrated point 1 and we may use theoretical argument to assert that point 2 holds, but point 3 remains a problem. This latter point tells us to beware of confounding variables. Let us consider one such variable, reading ability. Figure 26.3 shows a schematic representation of the relationships between the three variables of scholastic achievement, IQ and reading ability. The first thing is that when we look at IQ and reading ability together we notice that we have accounted for a greater proportion of scholastic achievement than with IQ alone. We also note that some of the covariance between IQ and achievement is also shared by reading ability. If we were to take only the covariation unique to IQ and achievement and exclude that (cross-hatched) part we would be partialling out the effect of reading ability. This would result in what is known as the **partial correlation**. Note that since we are talking about proportions of variance, of course, we are describing the squared partial correlation. Thus, while the correlation of IQ with achievement is 0.60 when we partial out the effect of reading ability, we may find that the resulting partial correlation becomes 0.50.

The multiple regression method utilises this notion of partitioning of variance to find the optimal prediction of one variable (achievement) given a

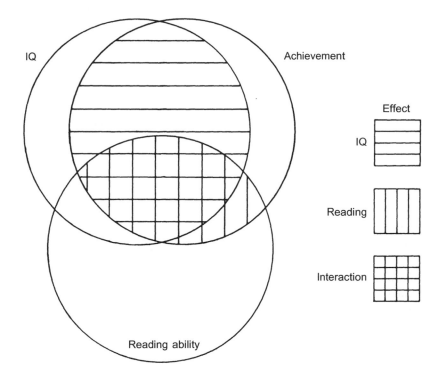

FIGURE 26.3   *Schematic representation of a correlation between three*
variables

number of predictors (IQ, reading ability). The fundamental idea is to
account for as much of the variance of the criterion variable as possible. We
have seen that the variance of the criterion variable, achievement, can be
partitioned into that which is accounted for by IQ, reading ability and the
interaction or overlap of the two, and that which remains, which is commonly
termed the residual or unique variance.

Of course, these schematic representations of the process are rather simple.
In practice we do not use such graphical methods for analysing our data but
rather resort to sophisticated mathematical estimation methods. This essentially involves the generation of a composite variable consisting of the relevant
parts of the predictor variables plus a rescaling coefficient. This composite
is constructed in order to produce a maximal correlation between it and
the criterion variable. This composite variable represents the estimate of the
criterion variable given the predictor variables. Beta weights for the predictor
variables are calculated as in the bivariate case. The predicted value is then
calculated by:

$$Y = \alpha + \beta_1 X_1 + \beta_2 X_2 + \ldots + \beta_n X_n \qquad (26.2)$$

The size of the beta weight indicates the relative weight of the standardised
predictor variable in question. Variables with greater weights are more relevant

Predictor	r	Beta
IQ	0.60	0.45
Reading	0.60	1.34
Multiple r = 0.80		
Multiple r^2 = 0.64		

FIGURE 26.4   *Multiple regression with two predictors*

to the prediction equation. For our example, the results of the regression analysis are given in Figure 26.4. Here we see that reading ability is the most important variable in predicting achievement.

It is possible to carry out a **stepwise regression** in which the computer program (no one does multiple regression by hand any more) will select the best combination of predictors for accounting for the criterion variance. One procedure is to use all the possible predictors and take them out one at a time until a more parsimonious but almost equally accurate solution results (**step-down method**). Alternatively, the program could select the predictors one at a time to build up the solution (**step-up method**). Most programs now include a method that combines both strategies (**stepwise method**). Personally, I have always found the step-down method to be most useful although it is really a matter of individual preference.

The multiple regression analysis also provides a multiple correlation coefficient which represents the correlation between the composite of predictor variables and the criterion variable. The composite is simply an estimate of the criterion variable estimated by formula (26.2). Thus, if we manage a perfect prediction, Y (from (26.2)) will be identical to the criterion score for every individual. The multiple correlation between Y and the criterion variable will be perfect and will produce a coefficient of 1. The statistical significance of the multiple r is estimated by carrying out an analysis of the ratio of accounted variance over residual variance. This is exactly equivalent to the ANOVA test which provides an F-statistic.

26.2.3   Further issues in regression

The procedures we have been talking about here have a number of strict assumptions. Firstly, they are parametric methods. The use of the product moment correlation always assumes that the variables in question have a relatively normal distribution and that the relationships between the variables are assumed to be linear. If the variables cannot be assumed to be normally distributed it may be appropriate to use a non-parametric correlation coefficient as a starting point. The non-parametric **product moment** correlation is **Spearman's rho** which is essentially a Pearsonian correlation on the data after they have been transformed into ranks. However, if this is done it is important that the researcher realises that they are simply predicting the **rank order** of the criterion variable and not the actual value.

In addition, it is important that a relatively large sample size is used so that the sampling error, which inflates the correlation coefficient, is minimised. This would normally mean that a multiple regression should be attempted only with a sample size in excess of 100 (Kerlinger and Pedhazur, 1993). If the sample size is smaller the reliability of the result may be open to question. However, in the research process there may be times where it is interesting to carry out the analysis on smaller samples. When reporting a regression analysis it is important to indicate the sample size.

Another problem with the multiple regression method is that it loses accuracy when the predictor variables are highly correlated with each other. This situation is known as **multicollinearity** and it causes difficulty when estimating the beta weights. In order to mitigate this problem, techniques exist such as **ridge estimation** or **Stein type estimation**. These are not commonly available on the most widely used computer packages so it is a good policy to take care that your predictors are reasonably independent of each other by examining the simple correlations between your variables before proceeding.

Other methods of regression analysis exist for cases where non-linear relationships are assumed although these non-linear methods are theoretically and mathematically complex. Methods also exist for categorical data: these methods include **logistic regression, logit** and **probit analysis**. Detailed discussion of these methods is beyond the scope of this chapter but the interested reader is referred to Clogg and Stockley (1988) and Haberman (1978; 1979). Tabachnick and Fidell (1996) give an excellent introduction to logistic regression which is used when the criterion variable is categorical, and a more detailed coverage may be found in Hosmer and Lemeshow (1989).

One situation that we have not touched upon is the case where the researcher has more than one criterion variable as well as a number of predictor variables. In this case, one set of variables is being used to predict responses on another set of variables. The method used in this case is known as **canonical variate analysis**. Again this brief chapter cannot do justice to this method and the interested reader is referred to the excellent introductory treatment in Hair et al. (1992: chapter 5) or Tabachnick and Fidell (1996: chapter 6). For more detail try Tacq (1997: chapter 10).

26.3 EXAMINING DIFFERENCES BETWEEN GROUPS

We now turn to the second of the research questions we may need to ask. The focus of this question is the difference between two or more groups. Typically, this question demands that we specify a particular representative parameter of each group and compare that. More often than not this parameter is the mean, although tests exist to compare medians and variances as well. Traditionally, when we are faced with the question of group difference we will look to the set of techniques known as the analysis of variance in which means are compared (see Chapter 25). In this case we have at least one variable that is measured on the nominal level. The nominal variable represents the group membership. For example, we may be interested in truancy from school and one of our variables will be coded 1 if the child in question is a regular truant and 2 if not. The number we give to each group is arbitrary since all we are conveying by this level of measurement is the group membership for each individual and the number simply serves as a name (hence nominal).

As with regression we will begin by describing how group differences may be viewed in the simple bivariate situation and show how this can be generalised to the multivariate case. We will then turn to the situation where we have one independent variable and a number of dependent variables.

26.3.1 Analyses of variance

Let us assume that we have one dependent variable and one independent variable and that the independent variable is categorical. For the purpose of demonstration we will look at the case where the dependent variable is IQ score and the independent variable is truancy. We are interested in group differences and group membership is represented by the categories of the independent variable (1 = a truant, 2 = not a truant).

In order to see whether the two groups are different in IQ we would normally perform a t-test in which the two means are compared. The t-test is actually a special case of the one-way ANOVA when there are just two groups to compare. If we carry out an ANOVA on this data the resulting F-statistic will equal the square of the t-statistic obtained by a t-test. This approach to testing group differences appears quite straightforward and entirely different in concept and approach to the correlational methods we have just discussed. However, this difference is more apparent than real.

In Figure 26.5 we see a schematic diagram of the problem. Note that it looks almost identical to Figure 26.1 where we were discussing correlation. In fact, the principles are essentially the same. We are interested in finding out how much of the dependent variable's variance can be accounted for by variation in the independent variable. This partitioning of the variance is where analysis of variance gets its name.

The terminology differs somewhat from that of correlation. We talk in terms of the mean squares rather than variance but the concepts are essentially the same. In Figure 26.6 we show the ANOVA summary table.

This tells us a few things about Figure 26.5. The mean square (MS) column informs us that a large amount of the variance of IQ has been accounted for by truancy. This **accounted-for variance** is greater than the residual or error variance. The statistic F, which tells us whether there are differences between the mean scores of the two groups, is a ratio of accounted-for variance and the residual variance represented by the truancy MS and residual MS respectively. Because this example involves just two groups, the resulting F-statistic of 16.00 is exactly equivalent to a t-test statistic of 4.00.

Let us now move on to consider the multivariate situation where we have more than one independent or 'group' variable. To illustrate this let us assume that we have simply added the independent variable of sex into the study. We are now interested in seeing whether IQ differs between truants and non-truants as well as females and males. We may also be interested in the additional information of the interaction between sex and truancy in respect to IQ.

Figure 26.7 represents this situation schematically. Here, we have two independent variables accounting for a substantial amount of the IQ variance.

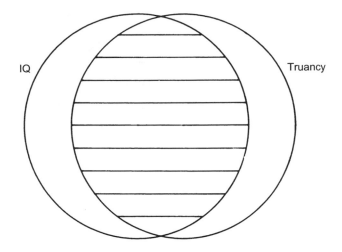

FIGURE 26.5   *Schematic representation of the effect of IQ on truancy*

Source of variation	SS	Degrees of freedom	MS	*F*
Truancy	40.00	1	40.00	16.00
Residual	120.00	48	2.50	
Total	160.00	49		

FIGURE 26.6   *Summary table for a one-way ANOVA*

The part at which they both intersect represents the interaction between truancy and sex. The results may look something like Figure 26.8.

The largest effect is that of truancy and this is statistically significant at the 0.05 level (we know this by looking up the value of F with 1 and 46 DF in statistical tables). Neither the sex effect nor the interaction between sex and truancy account for a statistically significant amount of IQ variance.

The ANOVA procedures are extremely flexible and they can be adapted to analyse data derived from a very wide variety of research designs (see Chapters 2, 5 and 6). It is beyond the scope of this brief chapter to go into all the possible design variations and the interested reader is referred to the comprehensive treatment of Winer (1978).

26.3.2   Discriminant analysis

So far in this section we have discussed the situation where there is one dependent variable and a number of independent variables. At the beginning of this chapter we alluded to this situation in discussing multiple significance tests where we have a large number of dependent variables and we wish to see how our groups differ on them. This is essentially a problem of group discrimination. In other words we are using our dependent variables to allow

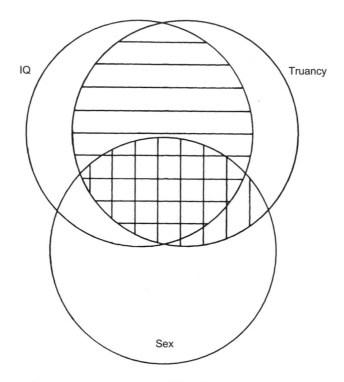

FIGURE 26.7   *Schematic representation of the effect of IQ and sex on truancy*

Source of variation	SS	Degrees of freedom	MS	F
Truancy	33.60	1	33.60	13.60
Sex	6.20	1	6.20	2.51
Truancy by sex	6.40	1	6.40	2.59
Residual	113.80	46	2.47	
Total	160.00	49		

FIGURE 26.8   *Summary of a two-way ANOVA*

us to discriminate between the groups. The method most often employed in this case is multiple discriminant function analysis. Our treatment here must be very brief but, should it whet a reader's appetite for more information, the short book by Klecka (1980) is a more comprehensive though very readable account.

Let us take the example mentioned at the beginning of this chapter. We are interested in seeing how truants and non-truants differ on the three variables of IQ, scholastic achievement and reading ability. The technique of discriminant function analysis begins by forming a composite of the dependent variables such that this composite variable will maximally discriminate between the groups. This composite variable (or function), as in the case of multiple _t_-tests

	Control group mean	Truant group mean	
IQ	101.23	94.20	$t = 3.56$
Reading	100.83	82.63	$t = 5.62$
Achievement	104.10	88.55	$t = 5.44$

Discriminant function weights

	Raw	Standard
Reading	1.342	0.723
Achievement	0.344	0.251
IQ	−0.033	−0.116

Group means

Phobic	−1.562
Control	1.621

FIGURE 26.9   _Discriminant analysis on data from the school example_

regression, is made up by weighting the dependent variables. A simple analysis of the group differences on this composite variable is then carried out. If there are just two groups this analysis is equivalent to a simple _t_-test and, as developed by Harold Hotelling, is known as Hotelling's _t_-test. Where there are more than two groups a large number of alternative tests are possible but they mostly use the chi-squared statistic to test for significance.

The result of our example may look like Figure 26.9.

Here we see that the multiple _t_-tests suggest that all of the variables differentiate the two groups significantly (the _t_-values all exceed 1.96). The multivariate test tells us that the two groups can indeed be discriminated but when we look at the weights on the discriminant function it is apparent that reading ability is the important variable and that the other two have little or no relevance. This tells us that the discriminant function (composite) is essentially one of reading ability. When we look at the group means on this function we see that the truant group has a low score while the non-truant group has a high score (we have already observed that this difference is statistically significant).

However, IQ and scholastic achievement also have significant bivariate _t_-test statistics and we are now saying that they have no relevance. This is because we can now see that they are largely made up of reading ability. In other words reading is necessary to perform well on the IQ test and it is also an essential part of scholastic achievement. The discriminant analysis has shown us that it is reading problems that discriminate the truant group from the non-truant group. This gives us the potential for remedial intervention which may not have been the case had we assumed that truancy was largely a function of IQ.

This is a very simple example of discriminant function analysis and it is often the case that we are trying to discriminate between more than two groups. In this case, the analysis will generate more than one function. The maximum number of functions will be one less than the number of groups or one less than the number of dependent variables whichever is the smaller. Each function can be assessed for statistical significance, usually by a chi-squared statistic, and they are always presented in descending significance. When multiple functions exist they must be interpreted by examining which variables have been weighted the most in forming them. The group means (sometimes called **centroids**) on the function are then examined to see how they discriminate the groups.

One of the uses that discriminant analysis is sometimes put to is to classify new cases where the group is unknown. Suppose we have a new child at our school; we have their IQ, reading ability score and scholastic achievement record and we wish to predict whether s/he will become a truant or not. We can use the weights generated in our discriminant function analysis to estimate this child's score on the function. This allows us to estimate the probable group that the child belongs to. In this way we can see that discriminant function analysis serves the function of a multiple regression analysis when the criterion variable is a nominal group membership variable.

Discriminant function analysis is a very useful method but it does have a number of strict assumptions. Most importantly, an assumption of normal distributions among the discriminating variables is made. This is also true for the traditional ANOVA procedures but it is rather more critical with discriminant function analysis.

As with multiple regression, the larger the sample size the more reliable the results. There are no easy 'rules of thumb' in discriminant analysis as there are with regression. Certainly, each group should be large enough to enable us to argue that they are representative of the population of such people. As a general rule it would be inadvisable to carry out a discriminant function analysis with fewer than 30 subjects in each group although much larger samples should be aimed for.

The discussion so far has assumed that the discriminating variables are measured at the interval level. Procedures for carrying out discriminant analysis on categorical data do exist but they are not readily available in existing computer packages. The interested reader might consult Anderson (1972) for a mathematical description. Alternatively, a technique mentioned later in this chapter – named correspondence analysis – might prove useful.

One situation that we have not mentioned is the one in which we have a number of independent variables as well as multiple dependent variables. The typical method of data analysis in this case is the **multivariate analysis of variance (MANOVA)**. MANOVA is simply a generalisation of ANOVA and discriminant function analysis, combining the generation of composites with variance partitioning. The procedure is extremely complex and general and it can be shown that multiple regression and canonical variate analysis are also special cases of the MANOVA model. Most psychological researchers come across MANOVA when they are trying to carry out a simple ANOVA analysis with repeated measures using a computer package such as SPSS. This simply shows that nearly all ANOVA designs are a special case of MANOVA, which in this case is just the name of the program subroutine and not the specific analysis method.

For any reader who has an interest in the statistical models underlying these methods the MANOVA is a fascinating model and an excellent introductory account is provided in Marascuilo and Levin (1983).

26.4 EXPLORING UNDERLYING STRUCTURE

A very common research question concerns the underlying structure of our data. Often in multivariate research we are interested in finding out whether our variables imply the existence of some superordinate structure. For example, questions in a scale designed to measure extroversion and neuroticism are assumed to have a structure comprising two underlying traits. Alternatively, a group of 20 symptoms from a checklist might be expected to be clustered into two groups relating to psychological and physical symptomatology. In each of these cases we are interested in examining the underlying *structure* of our observed variables.

One of the main reasons for examining the underlying structure of our data is so that we can describe what is being observed in a more parsimonious way. Thus, we can describe the 20 symptoms mentioned above in terms of only two superordinate variables, psychological and physical symptomatology.

The underlying structure of a group of variables is implied by the inter-relationships that exist between them. This means that for nearly all of the methods described below the first step is the calculation of inter-variable associations. These are usually, but not always, correlation coefficients. The table of all inter-variable correlation coefficients is known as the correlation matrix and it is the structure implied by this matrix that is to be explored.

Although we are addressing the exploration of underlying structure, it is important to realise that no good research is entirely exploratory. The selection of the variables will have been informed by some theoretical position. The fact that we are looking at the structure implies that we have reasoned grounds for such a tactic. In other words, we will usually have some *a priori* expectation, at least in broad terms, of what we will discover. This expectation need not be formally stated but it will be useful to use as a yardstick when we have to interpret our analyses.

In this section, I will briefly describe three methods for analysing multivariate structure: these are factor analyses, cluster analyses and multidimensional scaling analyses. We will then turn to the issue of **confirmatory** or **restricted analyses**.

26.4.1 Factor analysis

One of the most widely used approaches for exploring the underlying structure of a set of variables is factor analysis. Factor analysis is a global term describing a wide variety of different techniques developed primarily as a means of examining the existence of underlying latent traits. This means that the use of factor analysis cannot ever be said to be purely exploratory since the most basic assumption of this method is that the structure may be described in terms of one or more bipolar constructs.

As with nearly all methods for examining structure, factor analysis begins with the calculation of the inter-variable correlation matrix. It is most important to note that almost all factor analysis methods require that these correlations are product moment estimates or direct estimates of covariation.

The analysis proceeds to identify the set of underlying linear traits that are best implied by the inter-variable relationships. In fact, the analysis generates underlying composite variables in much the same way that regression and discriminant analysis do. These composites are then identified and interpreted by observing their correlations or regression weights with each variable included in the analysis.

The factor analysis treats the correlation matrix as a ball of inter-variable variance and it extracts chunks of variance to representing each underlying factor sequentially. These 'chunks' get smaller as each factor is extracted. The mathematical terminology for these chunks is the **eigenvalue**. Thus, the first factor extracted has a relatively large eigenvalue and each successive factor is built around a smaller chunk of variance or eigenvalue than the preceding one.

As an example, let us look at a questionnaire study on environmental concern. A short 20-item checklist taken from Ashford (1994) was administered to 311 university students. Each item concerned an environmental issue such as 'global warming' and 'threat to sea mammals', and the respondents were asked to indicate the degree of concern they felt for that issue on a five-point rating scale. It was expected that the resulting 20 variables would be described by three underlying factors relating to global, local and wildlife concerns. A 20×20 correlation matrix was generated and a factor analysis was performed. The three eigenvalues extracted were 8.76, 2.93 and 1.71. The resulting structure is reported in Figure 26.10. Here we see that each factor is represented as a column of numbers. Each number is known as a loading and describes the weight that each item has on the factor in question. What we can immediately see is that the large (or salient) loadings on factor 1 belong to items associated with global issues. Factor 2 has high loadings from items relating to wildlife, while factor 3 appears to be associated with local issues.

Note that some items have quite large loadings (here we take 0.35 or above as salient) on more than one factor. Thus, 'transport congestion' is seen as relevant to both local and global issues. These items are known as **factorially complex**.

Factor analysis is essentially a descriptive method. This means that the usefulness of the technique is a function of how interpretable the solution is. However, there are a number of pitfalls in factor analysis that this simple example has not highlighted.

The first problem is deciding how many factors to extract. In this example we extracted three factors because we had good reason (from Ashford's work) to expect this solution. Often, we do not have an *a priori* expectation of the appropriate number of factors. Indeed, the technique allows the researcher to extract as many factors as there are variables, which would be unhelpful. The researcher has to have some broad expectation of the number of potential factors before embarking on a factor analysis. A number of strategies for deciding on the number of factors has been proposed but none are without limitations.

Variable	Factors		
	I	II	III
Global warming	**0.88**	0.01	−0.26
Ozone layer	**0.91**	0.03	−0.28
Water pollution	**0.61**	0.17	0.12
Air pollution	**0.69**	0.12	0.14
Factory farming	0.29	**0.49**	0.09
Endangered wildlife	0.17	**0.81**	−0.12
Threat to forests	0.11	**0.45**	−0.15
Overpopulation	**0.45**	0.17	0.15
Acid rain	**0.60**	0.17	0.21
Threat of nuclear power	**0.53**	−0.02	0.28
Fossil fuels	**0.48**	−0.13	0.37
Cruelty to animals	−0.12	**0.81**	0.09
Trade in rare animal products	−0.06	**0.89**	0.01
Litter	−0.20	0.26	**0.71**
Transport congestion	**0.51**	0.02	**0.36**
Waste disposal	**0.47**	0.03	**0.43**
Building on green belt land	0.12	**0.41**	**0.40**
Food contamination	0.22	0.01	**0.69**
Noise nuisance	0.01	0.03	**0.81**
Threat to sea mammals	0.05	**0.78**	0.02
Factor correlation matrix:			
Factor 1	1.00		
Factor 2	0.40	1.00	
Factor 3	0.30	0.31	1.00

FIGURE 26.10   *The factor structure of 20 pro-environment behaviours*

One of the most commonly used criteria is also one of the worst and this is to extract only as many factors as have eigenvalues greater than or equal to one. This method will usually extract more factors than appropriate and so it has some value as a means of identifying an upper bound. Despite its use in common practice and its occasional recommendation in the literature, the researcher is strongly advised to avoid the use of this criterion for deciding the number of factors. The advice we present here is to use **interpretability** as the criterion for selecting the number of factors. This means that the researcher identifies the minimum and maximum number of factors and carries out an analysis for each potential solution. The solution which makes the most theoretical sense is the most appropriate. Clearly, this method involves an element of subjective interpretation but it assumes that the researcher is in tune with the theoretical underpinnings of the data and that the interpretation is properly detailed in the dissemination of results. To find out more about alternative methods to aid in deciding the number of factors the researcher is referred to works by Cattell (1978), McDonald (1985) and Harman (1976).

Another bone of contention in factor analysis is the issue of rotation. This is where the initial factor-loading matrix is transformed to aid in interpretation. Essentially, this involves moving the variance around to overcome the artefact where successive factors contain less variance than those preceding them. There are two types of rotation (although there are many techniques) termed **orthogonal** and **oblique**. Orthogonal rotation involves a transformation that forces the underlying factors to be uncorrelated with each other. Oblique rotation, on the other hand, allows the factors to be correlated. Some authors advise the researcher to use orthogonal rotation (Child, 1990) because it is supposed to be 'simpler'. Indeed, orthogonal rotation, using the VARIMAX technique, is the default option on many computer programs. However, psychologists rarely deal with constructs that are unrelated to each other. In our example, it would be odd if concern for global issues was not correlated with concern over other environmental issues. If we were to use orthogonal rotation in this case we would be imposing an unnecessary artefactual restriction on our data. In Figure 26.10 we also see the correlations between the factors which indicate a high degree of relationship.

Factor analysis is a huge topic but anyone wishing to use the method should take the time to find out about the various controversies and pitfalls that attend it. The method is widely used but it is also very widely misused and many poor factor analytic studies succeed in being published which makes it difficult for the young researcher to identify best practice from the literature. However, one rule of thumb is that if a study reports a factor solution in which the number of factors is decided by eigenvalues greater than one and it is then rotated by the VARIMAX criterion without justification of the orthogonal structure, the chances are that it is an ill-considered and opportunistic analysis simply availing itself of canned computer program default options. When writing up a factor analysis the author should justify the use of the method, the choice of the number of factors extracted and the rotational strategy employed.

A final point worth highlighting is the need for a good sample size. Since the factor analysis is a variance partitioning method we need a sample size that minimises sampling error. To produce a reliable factor solution it is advisable that a sample size of 200 plus is used where possible. As a general rule it is also recommended that there are at least four times as many subjects as variables. Of course, smaller samples can be used although the reliability of the solution may be questionable; however, there is one very definite requirement of sample size and that is that there are more subjects than variables. This latter stipulation is necessary to justify the matrix algebra that underlies the method.

26.4.2   Cluster analysis

Factor analysis is widely used but, as we have seen, it is not without limitations. An alternative method of exploring underlying structure which may be more supportable with the data psychologists often handle is termed cluster analysis (Blashfield and Aldenderfer, 1988).

The basic premise of cluster analysis is that the variables can be grouped into discrete clusters. Thus in our environmental concerns example we might expect the variables to group into three discrete groups representing global concerns, local concerns and wildlife concerns. Unlike factor analysis, we do not expect these clusters to represent an underlying bipolar trait ranging from high to low concern but simply understand them as a descriptive set of categories. These clusters can be represented as simple nominal categories or as hierarchical arrangements in which all variables belong in one superordinate (general concern) cluster which may be broken down into more and more clusters.

Cluster analysis is often used to cluster people rather than variables. Commonly, this involves a variety of clustering methods termed **partitioning** or **non-hierarchical** methods. These methods usually require the user to tell the program how many clusters are expected. The program then places objects (people or variables) into the relevant clusters according to the similarity they have with each other. The idea is that objects within a particular cluster will be more similar to each other than to objects in other clusters.

The hierarchical methods generally start by placing each object into its own unique cluster and then, by examining the similarity of the objects, merging the two most similar into a new cluster. The resulting $N-1$ clusters are then examined and another merger occurs. This continues until only one cluster remains.

Unlike factor analysis, cluster analysis does not place a great many demands upon the researcher and it is accessible to a wider range of data types. Like factor analysis it relies upon the relationships between the objects to describe the underlying structure. However, factor analysis is a variance partitioning method which means that the measure of the inter-variable relationship must be a measure of covariance or correlation. Cluster analysis, in contrast, can start from any symmetric measure of association. This means that it may be carried out using data which do not allow the use of product moment correlations. For example, Kendall's tau (τ) or Goodman–Kruskal's gamma (γ) for ordinal variables may be used and, if skewed dichotomies exist, non-parametric association coefficients such as Jaccard's index or Yule's Q. More commonly, cluster analysis uses the simple Euclidean distance coefficient.

As an example of a hierarchical cluster analysis we will use the data already used in the factor analysis above. A summary of the results is presented in Figure 26.11. This figure presents a dendogram showing the hierarchical structure of the 20 environmental concerns. It is clear immediately that there are three distinct clusters that appear to overlap well with the factor solution of Figure 26.10.

As with factor analysis, cluster analysis presents the user with the problem of specifying the number of clusters to use in describing the data structure. Again, the best way to address this problem is to develop a sound theoretical justification for the solution chosen. A number of less subjective methods have been developed but, as with factor analysis, these operate outside the substantive context of the research. One strategy that I have employed with some success is to generate a series of cluster solutions using different methods of clustering. The solution which shows the most agreement across methods is the solution that may have greatest reliability. However, this procedure still requires that the researcher has some idea of the upper and lower bound for numbers of clusters.

Another problem with cluster analysis is the interpretation of the clusters. This is particularly a problem when people rather than variables have been

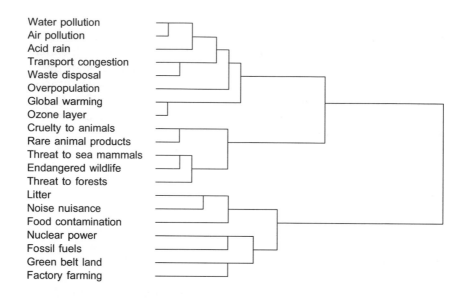

FIGURE 26.11   *Hierarchical cluster analysis dendogram of 20 pro-environmental behaviours*

clustered because we do not necessarily have a simple label we can apply to each person in our sample as we do for the variables.

A common strategy in identifying clusters of people is to carry out a non-hierarchical partitioning cluster analysis and then to treat the cluster membership as a criterion variable in a subsequent discriminant function analysis. In this way each cluster may be defined by the composite functions that discriminate them. When clustering people in this way the usual focus of the study is to identify some kind of typology and this is perhaps the simplest way of distinguishing between factor analysis and cluster analysis. Factor analysis assumes an underlying trait model while cluster analysis assumes a simple type model.

26.4.3   Multidimensional scaling

We now move on to briefly describe another method that offers yet another way of examining data structures. Parametric methods for multidimensional scaling (MDS) grew originally out of early work on factor analysis. However, in the 1960s and 1970s a series of non-parametric methods became available and it is these so called non-metric methods that we commonly refer to when using the term MDS.

The basic idea of MDS is to represent data spatially by plotting variables as points in *n*-dimensional space. The distance between the points represents the similarity of the variables. Thus, if variable X is highly correlated with variable Y then these two variables will be situated close together on the plot. The advantage of MDS is that the structure of the data can be examined in a number of ways. For example, we can examine the regionality of the space by

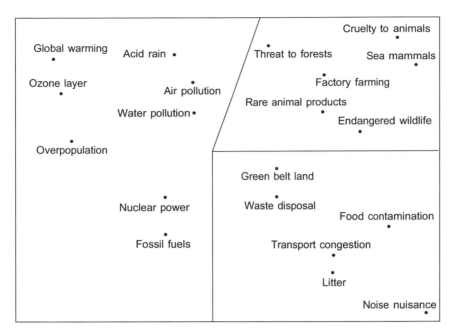

FIGURE 26.12   *Multidimensional scaling analysis of 20 environmental concerns*

identifying regions occupied by a particular group of variables. Alternatively, we can examine the shape of the plot; for example, whether the variables arrange themselves in a straight line or a circle.

Non-metric MDS has very few assumptions and is appropriate for most forms of data (Chapter 20 describes a variation of this method for use with qualitative data). Because MDS solutions may be interpreted very broadly it makes them an ideal choice when carrying out entirely exploratory work. They are particularly effective for theory building since the method does not tend to impose a model on the data that may influence the interpretation as the linear factor model does. However, this may also be seen as a problem because it means that interpreting MDS solutions is often a somewhat arbitrary and subjective affair. As we have stated above there is no replacement for some kind of *a priori* expectation in interpreting structure, but when these expectations do not include underlying linear traits or discrete groupings, MDS is a useful method. The combination of facet theory (see Chapter 8) and MDS is a very potent research strategy since it merges the strict conceptualisation of the research topic with a flexible and open-ended data analytic technique.

In order to demonstrate an MDS analysis the same environmental concern data were used. A two-dimensional plot is reported in Figure 26.12. In this plot we can see the three regions of global, local and wildlife concern emerging. It is also worth noting the almost circular structure that emerges.

Apart from the necessary subjectivity in interpretation, MDS has a problem in common with factor analysis and cluster analysis: that of choosing the number of dimensions to present the data in. It should be apparent that the

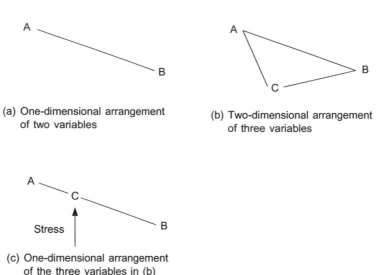

FIGURE 26.13 *The dimensionality of three variables*

maximum dimensionality we can expect will be one less than the number of variables. Thus, two variables need only one dimension (a straight line) to represent them (Figure 26.13a), while three variables need only two dimensions (Figure 26.13b) although they can be represented in one (Figure 26.13c).

When we have 20 variables the maximum dimensionality is 19: however, it would be impossible for most researchers to conceptualise a 19-dimensional space. Even the most able of researchers cannot think in terms of more than four dimensions and even that is not simple. Three dimensions is about all any of us can hold in our heads spatially. This means that MDS, in order to be readily interpreted, must squash the variables down into at most four dimensions. This 'squashing' results in pressure as our recalcitrant variables want to express their true dimensionality and push against the constraints imposed by the MDS. This pressure is measured by an index known variously as the **stress** or **alienation** coefficient. This ranges between 0 and 1 and the smaller this coefficient is, the less the pressure, and the better the data fit the MDS solution. Unfortunately, there is no hard and fast rule which says what is a 'good' stress measure. In our example the stress was 0.15 which would normally be considered reasonable for 20 items. Advice on the size of the stress ranges widely from the very strict (Kruskal, 1964) to the more *laissez-faire* (Shye, 1988).

The only advice I can give here is to suggest that interpretability is the first and most important criterion. Clearly, if you find you can interpret a solution but the stress is very high, say 0.60, then you will need to question the tenets of your interpretation since the data do not appear to fit very well.

One drawback with MDS is the dearth of readily accessible texts describing the methods for the beginner, exceptions being Kruskal and Wish (1978) and Schiffman et al. (1981). Indeed, the techniques are still relatively new and are being developed and improved all the time for both general and specific research contexts. An excellent account of MDS developments to date can be found in Borg and Groenen (1997).

26.4.4 The myth of confirmatory methods

So far we have been concerned to describe three methods for exploring the underlying structure of your data. It should be clear that, despite the use of the term 'explore', the effective use of these methods requires that the researcher has some theoretical expectations of what they might find. Indeed, carrying out a factor analysis without understanding that the result will suggest underlying linear structure would be a waste of time and may result in the researcher thinking that they have discovered something that they themselves imposed on the solution. Nevertheless, these methods may still be used in an exploratory way since the researcher may not have a formalised set of hypotheses but rather a number of broad expectations.

There now exists an increasing interest in approaches claiming to be confirmatory as opposed to exploratory. Essentially, what this means is that the researcher is asked to generate a formal model of the relationships between the variables. This model is then tested for fit to the empirical data, resulting in a statistic evaluating the degree of misfit to the model. This statistic is usually chi-squared. The most useful of these approaches grew out of factor analysis and came to be called variously linear structural relations analysis or covariance structure analysis. A number of computer programs now exist for carrying out these analyses (LISREL, COSAN, EQS). It should be mentioned that a number of 'confirmatory' methods have also grown out of MDS (see Borg and Groenen, 1997), but it is the factor analytic methods that have seen the most widespread use.

The most immediate limitation with these methods is that they are generally built around a strict linear model. This means that if we wanted to test the hypothesis of a circumplex model of our data (meaning that the variables form a circle in an MDS plot) we would have to formally represent it in linear form. The second limitation is that the statistics which supposedly tell us whether the data fit the model are severely problematic and are sample size dependent. This suggests that a large sample size will almost inevitably produce an inflated chi-squared statistic which means that the data do not fit the model. A number of coefficients for fit which do not have this drawback have been proposed but they generally do not allow statistical inference to be made, so they take on the status of the stress coefficient in MDS.

A third and altogether more important limitation with these methods is that although they are termed confirmatory methods, they confirm nothing. Simply finding that the data do not contradict a model does not confirm that model. Note that these methods work by constraining the freedom of the solution parameters to emerge in a way that contradicts the model. Remember too, that for each model there is a large number of competing models that may fit the data as well or better. Typically, these models are not tested. This, coupled with the weakness of the 'confirmatory' statistics, docs not support the extravagant claims that are sometimes made about the use of these methods.

I do not wish to appear to be advising against the use of these methods since they can be extremely useful in the appropriate context. I have found them especially useful when examining measurement models. However, a better term to describe such methods is as *restricted* rather than *confirmatory*. This is because the data are constrained to fit, as best as possible, the model in question. Once this terminological problem is resolved we can get back to the basic issue in the multivariate analysis of inter-variable relationships. This is to apply a method which is appropriate to the nature or the research question and is justifiable for the data being analysed. Certainly, in many cases a restricted analysis is appropriate. Confirmation, on the other hand, comes with replication and the cumulation of research findings (see Chapter 2).

26.5   THE SPECIAL CASE OF NOMINAL DATA

So far we have been concentrating our description on variables derived from continuous measures. However, psychological researchers commonly have to deal with categorical data. Increasingly, with the growth of the content analysis of qualitative data there is a demand for multivariate procedures for handling categorical measures.

Traditionally, group differences with categorical variables have been analysed by chi-squared methods. In fact, these methods can be readily generalised to the multivariate situation as long as there are not too many variables. The result is a nominal equivalent of the ANOVA termed **interaction structure analysis** (ISA) which derives from the partitioned chi-squared model of Lancaster (1969). However, there is very little about the technique in the literature and very few computer programs exist to help the researcher. Interested readers are referred to Lautsch and von Weber (1990) or von Eye (1990).

A more common strategy is to apply the more general **loglinear methods**. These methods allow the researcher to test differences between groups analogously to ANOVA and also to test predictive models analogous to regression models. A treatment of loglinear methods is beyond the scope of this chapter and the interested reader is referred to Everitt (1977).

When the research question involves the examination of underlying structure, special methods exist for categorical variables. However, these techniques are not widely available on computer packages as yet although SPSS now contains a package of routines specifically designed for such data. The interested reader is refered to Gifi (1990) for a full and excellent coverage of these routines.

One useful technique is known variously as **correspondence analysis** or **optimal scaling**. This is essentially a **principal component analysis** (similar to factor analysis) of categorical data but it produces a graphical output much like MDS. In addition to exploring structure it may also be used as a form of discriminant analysis for categorical data. Interested readers should consult Greenacre (1984), Nishisato (1980) or Weller and Romney (1990) or, for a more comprehensive mathematical account, Gifi (1990). The MDS methods described in Chapter 20 are based on a similar mathematical premise as correspondence analysis (Lingoes, 1968).

A number of methods also exist for examining typologies of respondents measured on categorical variables. The interested reader should look up references to **latent class analysis** (Clogg and Stockley, 1988) and **configural frequency analysis** (von Eye, 1990).

26.6 CONCLUSIONS

None of the methods reported here are typically carried out by hand with the exception of the ANOVAs, although even these are rarely carried out without the use of a computer. The use of computer programs for data analysis has liberated researchers from the toil of data analysis and so, presumably, generated more time for thought and consideration of the research process. Unfortunately, the other side of this situation is that researchers have been provided with a host of very sophisticated methods for analysis of their data and there is a temptation to throw the data into the computer in the vague hope that the analysis will tell us something. There is certainly emerging a class of research in which the researcher has taken very little time to understand the basic principles and logic of the methods they use. Such work is increasingly managing to emerge in the research literature despite the best efforts of journal reviewers, and its presence at best fails to add much to the body of psychological knowledge, and at worst sets a precedent for the rest of us to misuse the powerful and often mathematically complex techniques that are increasingly available.

This chapter is certainly neither sufficiently comprehensive nor sufficiently detailed to convey the full range and limitation of multivariate data analytic methods. The purpose here has been to give the new researcher some feel for the basic classes of methods that exist. It is fervently hoped that the student researcher will seek out more detailed and critical sources before embarking on their analysis. I finish on a plea that if you are considering a multivariate analysis you will make the acquaintance of the method, its logic, its assumptions, its controversies and its theoretical underpinnings. The unquestioning use of user-friendly computer programs with their host of default options is becoming a significant source of suboptimality in psychological research.

26.7 FURTHER READING

An excellent treatment of multivariate data analysis and, in my opinion, the one book that all student researchers should have at their fingertips is Tabachnick and Fidell's (1996) *Using Multivariate Statistics*. This is written in an easy and accessible style and contains many examples in which the various computer packages are compared. Another useful text that makes effective use of examples is Hair et al.'s (1992) *Multivariate Data Analysis*. This provides detailed examples of a number of the most commonly used techniques. Another very useful reference book is Nesselroade and Cattell's (1988) *Handbook of Multivariate Experimental Psychology*. This is now in its second edition and provides a series of review chapters by different authors on a variety of data analytic methods.

If the reader is looking for a reasonably accessible introduction to the statistical background to the methods discussed here, then I would recommend Marascuilo and Levin's (1983) *Multivariate Statistics in the Social Sciences* and Tacq's (1997) *Multivariate Analysis Techniques* as good starting points. However, at the more technical end of the continuum it is hard to beat Gifi's (1990) *Nonlinear Multivariate Analysis*.

27

Introduction to Structural Equation Modelling

Chris Fife-Schaw

Contents

27.1 INTRODUCTION

Though it might seem like quite an esoteric topic to include in a general research methods textbook, we have included a chapter on structural equation modelling (SEM) because it is an approach that is growing in popularity and one that encourages the organisation of systematic research programmes. The chapter has two broad aims. One is to give an overview of the ideas underlying SEM so that articles using it, of which there are an ever increasing number, can be better understood. The second is to encourage researchers to adopt some of these ideas in the hope of promoting greater rigour in quantitative psychological research. I will try to keep the use of jargon to a minimum but some is inevitable, I am afraid.

SEM is a set of statistical procedures that can be applied to quantitative data that allow the researcher to: (1) test theoretically specified 'models' of the relationships between **observed variables** (e.g. test scores) and unobserved **latent variables**, these models are sometimes called **measurement models**; and

(2) test theoretical models of the relationships between sets of latent variables, which are called **structural models**.

SEM offers immense potential for psychologists since, by and large, most of psychology's key constructs are unobserved latent variables even though we may not think of them as such. Personality traits, for instance, cannot be observed directly and we have to infer a person's level of extroversion, say, from their answers to personality test items (observed variables). We do not know what units extroversion should be measured in and we have no direct way of measuring extroversion other than by inferring it from indirect measures such as test responses, peer reports or behaviours, etc. The same applies to attitudes, beliefs, stress, intelligence, depression, anxiety, job satisfaction and a whole host of other popular psychological constructs.

Although it is becoming more popular, SEM remains a mystery for many people. It has its origins in the 1960s (Jöreskog, 1970) and some of the ideas date back much further and are shared with other procedures such as path analysis, factor analysis and loglinear analysis (see Chapter 26). Much of the problem has been that the literature on SEM, and early SEM computer programs, were unduly mathematical and tended to assume that the reader/ user possessed a university-level knowledge of matrix algebra. This had the effect of restricting SEM to a highly numerate and motivated elite and it is only in the last few years that these techniques and principles have been made readily accessible to the rest of us via more user-friendly computer packages.

SEM differs from many forms of statistical analysis in that to do it you have to make explicit your theories or **models** of the relationships between your observed measures and latent variables and the relationships you expect between the latent variables. Doing what is pejoratively called data mining (or 'fishing') in the hope of finding something 'significant' in your data can be done within SEM but is massively time-consuming and unrewarding. SEM pushes you to be more rigorous in your approach to data analysis and therefore has to be seen as a good thing, as I hope you will see.

Popular computer packages to conduct SEM include LISREL/SIMPLIS (Jöreskog and Sörbom, 1993), EQS (Bentler, 1995) and CALIS (Wilkinson and Hill, 1994) and the list is growing all the time. As this chapter is not intended to be an introduction to any particular software package I will not refer to command syntaxes directly. A good general guide to the range of packages available and the differences between them is given by Ullman (1996).

You should be aware that SEM is known by a number of alternative names such as **analysis of covariance structures**, **covariance structure modelling**, **simultaneous equation modelling** and (inappropriately as we will see) **causal modelling**, but these all refer to the same family of procedures.

27.2   THE IDEA OF MODEL FITTING AND MODEL COMPARISON

Underlying SEM is a set of ideas about what constitutes good scientific practice. These lean heavily on the hypothetico-deductive principles discussed in Chapter 2 and assume that you already have a theoretical model about how your measurements/observations are related to latent constructs and how the latent constructs themselves are related to each other. The name of the game is to confront your theoretical model with some hard data and see to what degree your model is consistent with these data. We will see how this is done later, but if your model is not consistent with the data then (assuming the data are good) the model must be wrong and therefore either rejected or modified by respecifying the relationships in the model. If the model is consistent with the data then you can tentatively proceed with it: *you have failed to disconfirm it.* Regrettably, finding a model consistent with the data does not mean you have found 'the True Model'; there may be alternative models out there that you have not tested which are as good as or better than your model.

SEM assumes that the goal of research is to generate and test a theoretical model that will allow the accurate prediction of existing and, hopefully, future data points. A theory that cannot make such predictions is not really a theory in the SEM framework. As you might expect there are some competing pressures in this enterprise. On the one hand you want a theoretical model that provides accurate predictions, but on the other you also want to settle on a simple and parsimonious model. In general, there is little point in making a model so complex that it becomes as complex as the data it is trying to explain. The SEM analyst's task is to decide how best to strike this balance.

An example might help. Suppose you want a theory that will account for why some children get more GCSE exam passes at grade 'A' than others. In SEM terms you want a simple but accurate model that will predict each individual child's exam performances. Assuming we knew nothing about these children as individuals, our best guess at the performance of any given child would probably be the average performance of all children in the population. This would be a very simple model with one bit of information and a relationship, or **parameter**, in it (strictly, a **parameter** is a numerical quantity that describes some aspect of your model in the population). This would not be a very helpful model though, since it would make the same prediction for each child.

We could make the model more predictive of exam performance by adding extra information about each child to the model. We could add information on their IQ scores and we might reasonably expect that adding this parameter (the relationship between IQ and exam performance) would improve the accuracy of our predictions. If we know a child's IQ we can make a guess at their exam performance because these variables tend to be correlated with each other. Put another way, we would predict that children who score above average on IQ tests would also tend to do better than average in formal exams.

It is possible to go on adding variables and relationships to the model. We could add information about each child's socio-economic status (SES), for example, since research suggests that greater socio-economic advantage tends to be associated with greater success at school and that this effect is probably independent of the effect of IQ on performance. Clearly we could go on adding information about each child to the model until it contained as many parameters as there were children whose performances we wanted to predict.

At this point it would be more efficient to simply say Joe Blogg's score was X, John Brown's score was Y, etc.

Each time we add a new parameter, accuracy will go up (or stay the same) at the expense of making the model more complicated. Ultimately, however, needing to ask for thousands of bits of information from each child to predict performance does not make much sense. We need to find a way to decide whether adding a parameter will produce a worthwhile increase in predictive power. Here we apply the principle (sometimes referred to as Occam's razor) that if two models predict something equally well then we will conclude that the more simple and parsimonious model is more likely to be the correct one.

Conceptually it helps to think about this in the following way:

$$\text{data} = \text{model} + \text{error}$$

The data are the basic observations, the model is your theoretically derived neat and compact explanation or representation of the data, and the error is the amount by which the model fails to represent the data. The error is best thought of as the degree to which the predictions made by the model are inaccurate. In our example above the (very simple) model says that exam performance is caused by IQ and SES and we can make a prediction about each child's performance based on knowledge of these two variables. However, it is unlikely that our model's predictions for each child will be 100% accurate and the degree to which we get each child's scores wrong is the error. The error is often referred to as **residual variance** in SEM since it may not truly be error but variability in the outcome that is caused by something you have not accounted for (school teaching quality, for example). It follows from this that:

$$\text{error} = \text{data} - \text{model}$$

We need to reduce the error when we build theoretical models and we can do this by collecting better quality data, data with less measurement error, using better research designs and adopting better data collection strategies. The error can also be reduced by making the model's predictions conditional on additional information about each case (here a case is a child): this means changing the model by adding parameters such as teaching quality and its relationship to exam performance in the example.

How do you know if a more complicated model with more parameters is 'better' than a simple one? If we start off with a simple model, model C (called a **compact model** in the jargon), and then create a model with more parameters in it, model A (referred to as an **augmented model**), then model A should have the same or less error than model C, so:

$$\text{error(A)} < \text{error(C)}$$

We can work out the **proportional reduction in error (PRE)** we have achieved by:

$$PRE = 1 - \frac{error(A)}{error(C)}$$

PRE is an index that ranges between 0 and 1. Deciding whether a PRE of, say, 0.40 is worthwhile will depend on inferential statistics (more on this later). However, we would be more impressed by a PRE of 0.40 when it involved adding only one more parameter to the model than we would if we had had to add 10 new parameters to achieve the same level of improvement. Also, as the number of data points/observations is usually the upper limit on the number of parameters that can be added to a model, a PRE of 0.40, say, will be more persuasive and impressive when the difference between the number of parameters added and the number that could have been added is big. SEM researchers have developed a whole range of more sophisticated alternative indices to PRE that take this into account.

The endpoint of this kind of approach is to make two decisions. The first is whether the model, even in its augmented form, makes good enough predictions (i.e. it is consistent with the data). The second is to decide whether the improved accuracy (predictive power) of an augmented model has warranted making the original compact model more complicated. Both decisions have to be based on statistical criteria but they must also meet theoretical criteria. It is possible, for instance, to improve predictive power by adding a parameter that makes no theoretical sense. In our example we could try to predict GCSE exam performances (which are usually taken at age 16 in the UK) by using information about A level exam performance at age 18 and the chances are that these two bits of information will be highly correlated with each other and the predictive power will be high. A theory for understanding academic performance at age 16 that uses information collected after the age of 16 is hardly of much use theoretically or practically, however.

This is the broad logic of what is going on in SEM. In practice, rather than trying to predict raw scores for cases, SEM tries to predict the variances of, and covariances (or correlations) between, observed variables. Though this sounds (and is) different from predicting a raw score it is ultimately the same idea. When trying to account for a variance we are essentially trying to explain why a particular case's score deviates from the mean score: why does child F score X more exam passes than the average child?

27.3 MEASUREMENT MODELS AND CONFIRMATORY FACTOR ANALYSIS

SEM approaches are primarily used to test two sorts of models: (1) models of the relationships between observed and unobserved (latent) variables; and (2) models of the relationships between latent unobserved variables. In this section I will deal with the former, which are often called **measurement models**, and a particularly popular form of measurement model testing called **Confirmatory Factor Analysis (CFA)**. The principles involved in model fitting that are discussed below apply equally to structural models: however, before you start to worry about testing an impressive structural model you must establish that you can measure the main latent variables of interest well.

In CFA, scores on observed variables (e.g. responses to questions) are thought to be 'caused' by unobservable common factors and some **uniqueness** (a factor or an error unique to the variable). SEM deals with a matrix of the relationships between variables rather than the raw scores themselves, so this becomes a question of asking whether the patterns of covariation in the observed variables are 'caused' by variation in the unobservable factors. These unobservable factors are referred to as **latent variables** since they cannot be observed directly but are nonetheless thought to exist and to cause the manifestations of variables you can observe. The researcher must come up with a substantively motivated model that imposes clear **constraints**. These are to decide:

1   how many common factors or latent variables there are
2   which pairs of common factors or latent variables are correlated with each other
3   which observed variables are affected by which common factor or latent variable
4   which observed variables are affected by a unique factor (usually error)
5   which pairs of unique factors or errors are correlated.

Notice that you are not asking the SEM package to tell you the answers to these questions: you think you know the answers already but are testing these out against the data.

Figure 27.1 gives a much abbreviated example based on a study of 235 young people in Swindon conducted as part of the ESRC's 16–19 Initiative. This study was concerned with the attitudes and lifestyles of young people and how these were related to occupational and political aspirations. In this simple measurement model there are six questions from the questionnaire. Three of these (questions Q8, Q9 and Q10) are questions from the Hammond (1988) Estrangement Scale and are thought to tap feelings of psychological estrangement. The remaining three (questions Q12, Q13 and Q14) are thought to tap a negative attitude towards new technology. In this example I have used the convention that latent variables (factors) are denoted by ellipses and observed variables by squares. Do not worry about the Greek letters and subscripts for now; these are included only because they are the conventional symbols used in what is known as LISREL notation.

Each observed variable has an arrow entering it from a latent variable or factor and an arrow indicating that some of the variability is 'caused' by some other source (uniqueness) of error. It is possible to specify that these sources of error are correlated with one another if this makes some substantive sense (e.g. the errors are 'caused' by the same thing) but it does not in the present example.

The important idea here is that some relationships (parameters) are constrained to have particular values (usually, but not always, zero). It is not the case, for instance, that every observed variable is related to both latent variables. Some observed variables are constrained to have no (zero) relationship

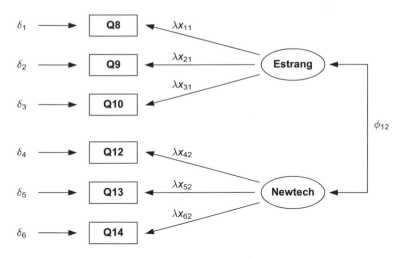

FIGURE 27.1 *A simple two-factor model*

with particular latent variables (e.g. Q10 and the factor Newtech). Conventionally these zero relationships are not drawn in: the absence of an arrow indicates no proposed relationship.

The input into the analysis is a correlation or covariance matrix that shows how scores on each observed variable are related to every other observed variable in your sample. This sample correlation or covariance matrix is known as **S**. Remember the point of your model is to explain why the data are the way they are (i.e. to be able to predict them) and you want your model to be relatively simple and parsimonious. Here you want to explain why variables are correlated with each other in the way they are, and the model proposes that the reason is that the observed scores are 'caused' by certain specific latent variables or factors (two in this case).

In essence, and at the risk of oversimplifying matters greatly, the analysis package takes **S** as a starting point and asks what the correlation (or covariance) matrix would be like in the population if the constraints in the model were imposed (i.e. the model is 'right'). The covariance (or correlation) matrix generated by the model is known as Σ. The procedure makes estimates of the parameters in the model (the λ loadings, δ errors and ϕ factor correlations, etc.) to do this and gradually refines these until it cannot do any better. At each stage in estimating the parameters the program compares **S** and Σ and tries alternative parameter values in order to increase the similarity between these two matrices. Eventually it stops doing this when it cannot increase the similarity any further.

If there were no constraints imposed by the model, **S** and Σ would be exactly the same. Almost any set of parameter estimates would work and you would have achieved nothing. It is analogous to having a theoretical model that says everything is related to everything else – not a very helpful model. The constraints in your model mean that Σ will not be exactly the same as **S** and you can then ask how different Σ and **S** are and whether this difference is

Name		Desired value for good fit
χ^2	Chi-squared	Small and non-significant or, if $n > 500$, $\chi^2 < 3$ DF
GFI	Goodness of fit index	> 0.95
AGFI	Adjusted goodness of fit index	> 0.9
RMR	Root mean squared residual	< 0.05
RMSEA	Root mean square error of approximation	< 0.05
NFI	Normed fit index	> 0.9

FIGURE 27.2 *Commonly seen fit indices*

so big that your model must be wrong or badly misspecified. If the difference between **S** and Σ is acceptably small then the parameter estimates (λs, δs, ϕs, etc.) are probably good and tell you something meaningful about the relationships between the latent and observed variables.

A number of what are known as **fit indices** can be calculated to indicate how badly Σ fits **S**. The best known of these is χ^2. Importantly, and contrary to what people normally expect when doing inferential statistical analyses, you want a *non-significant and small* χ^2 value which indicates that what you observe in your data (the matrix **S**) is not significantly different from what you would expect to be the case in the population if the model were true (Σ).

There are a number of shortcomings to the fit index χ^2 (see Ullman, 1996 for an overview) so it is common to see researchers report a range of additional fit indices in the hope that, as a whole, they suggest the model fits the data well. Each has its own technical limitations but if you have a good model then the majority of indices should be telling you that it is good; if not, you need to investigate the indices further. Figure 27.2 gives some of the better known indices and what is regarded as indicative of a 'good' fit: there are others but these are probably the best known.

In our present example the fit indices are as follows: $\chi^2(8) = 12.37$ ($p = 0.14$), GFI = 0.98, AGFI = 0.95, RMR = 0.046, RMSEA = 0.048, NFI = 0.96. All of these indices suggest that our proposed two-factor model is consistent with the data and that we have distinct measures of the two latent constructs. The correlation between the Estrang (Estrangement) and Newtech (Negative attitudes to new technology) latent variables or factors is 0.22. This is the estimated correlation after measurement errors in the observed variables have been removed and suggests a moderate tendency for estranged young people to have negative attitudes towards new technology (Figure 27.3).

27.3.1 Identification

Before you can start to estimate the parameters in a model you must ask whether the parameters are **uniquely determined** or **identified**. If a model (or part of it) is not identified it would be possible to find an infinite number of values for the parameters that would produce a population correlation/covariance matrix Σ that fitted the sample correlation/covariance matrix **S** and your model's constraints. This is obviously not a desirable state of affairs

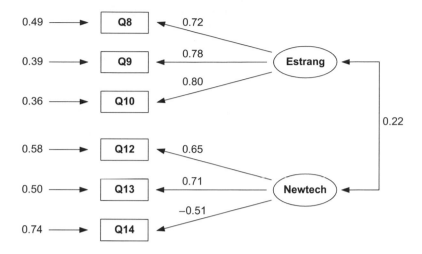

FIGURE 27.3 *The simple two-factor model after LISREL has estimated the*
unconstrained parameter values

and arises because your model requires the estimation of more parameters
than you have data points (correlations or covariances) on which to base the
estimates. The problem is analogous to trying to solve the following equation:

$$x + y = 10$$

An infinite number of combinations of values for x and y will satisfy this
equation and it cannot be uniquely solved until you have additional information. If you also know that:

$$2x + y = 14$$

it is a simple matter to work out that x must be 4 and y must be 6.

Establishing that a model is identified is potentially quite complicated (see
Long, 1983) and unfortunately computer programs will sometimes estimate
parameters for unidentified models, so you need to be aware that this may
happen. This problem is gradually declining in importance as computer
packages become better able to detect under-identified models and warn the
user that there are difficulties. Nonetheless if you get a warning that your
model or parts of it are under-identified this usually means that the model is
misspecified and/or that you do not have enough observed variables to estimate all the specified parameters.

27.3.2 Estimating parameter values

Working out the values of the parameters and thence the values for Σ can be
achieved in a number of ways. The most commonly used are maximum
likelihood (ML), unweighted least squares (ULS), generalised least squares

(GLS) and weighted least squares (WLS). There are others but these will do for the time being. Each of these methods (algorithms) produces a **fitting function** which is an equation that generates a value to indicate how different Σ is from **S**. The program iterates (keeps doing) its estimation procedure until it cannot reduce the value of the fitting function any more.

The way these work and the reasons for choosing one method over another are beyond the scope of this chapter (see Ullman, 1996 and/or program manuals) but there are a number of pitfalls that are common to all algorithms.

The first of these is known as finding a **local minimum**. Here the program finds a value for the fitting function that it cannot make smaller by making minor adjustments to the parameter estimates. However, were it to have started its search for the smallest value of the fitting function from somewhere else (different starting values) it might actually have found a better fitting set of parameters. It is not easy to tell whether this has happened, though Long (1983) claims this may not be a common problem in practice.

A second kind of problem in estimating parameters concerns 'silly' parameter estimates. Sometimes a good fit can be achieved but the values of the parameters don't make sense. For instance, it is possible to get negative variances or correlations with an absolute value greater than 1, even though such figures are meaningless. If this happens your specified model may simply be wrong or some of your variables may not meet distributional assumptions (important when using certain estimation algorithms). This can also happen when your sample size is very small and the asymptotic (big sample) assumptions that drive the estimation algorithms may not be justified.

Another potential cause of silly estimates is missing data. Researchers tend to prefer to use correlation (or covariance) matrices that are generated by 'pairwise' deletion of missing values since this maximises the number of cases contributing to each correlation. However this means that different parts of the matrix **S** are generated by samples of different sizes, leading to a matrix that may not be internally consistent with itself. Sometimes the program will detect this, sometimes it won't. The newer versions of software packages are better at detecting this and warning the user.

27.3.3 Modification indices (MIs) and specification searches

If you find that the model doesn't fit, how should you change it? Trying to change a model to get a better fit is called a **specification search**. One way to do this is to look at the **modification indices** (MIs) (sometimes called **Lagrange multiplier tests**). These indices tell you what might be expected to happen to the value of the χ^2 goodness of fit index if you freed a previously constrained path to be estimated. Freeing one constrained (not estimated) path to be estimated loses one degree of freedom and the MI then becomes a test of the hypothesis that the parameter to be freed is equal to its former fixed value. If this is significant, then the model would fit better than it did before and the freed parameter was probably not equal to its former fixed value.

The freeing of parameters should not be done at random but should be theoretically acceptable. Often high MIs suggest that the model is substantially misspecified. Freeing up any old parameter just because it has a large

MI can result in a much better fitting but substantively meaningless model. Your original model may not fit the data but, generally, you should not let the data dictate the form of your model.

In some senses the opposite kind of problem occurs when you have specified that a parameter should be estimated in your model but, in fact, the parameter is so close to zero that the model might have been better specified with the parameter fixed at zero. This would make the model more simple and is generally desirable *unless* fixing the parameter at zero would be theoretically inappropriate.

One of the most straightforward approaches to finding parameters that are probably best constrained to be zero is to compare the values of estimated parameters with their standard errors (provided by the software). This amounts to doing a *t*-test to test the hypothesis that the parameter estimate is actually zero. If a *t*-value suggests that a parameter is not different from zero it might make sense to respecify your model constraining that parameter to be zero, thus reducing the number of parameters to be estimated and simplifying the model at the same time. If you remember, simple is generally better in SEM.

In our two-factor CFA model all the parameter estimates are theoretically reasonable (remember that the Newtech factor is *negative* attitudes towards new technology) and have values significantly greater than zero. The modification indices suggest that the χ^2 fit would be improved by 4.61 ($p<0.05$) if we allowed the errors of Q8 and Q10 to be correlated. However, since there is no theoretical justification for doing this (there is nothing about the questions which might suggest why the errors might be correlated) and the model fits adequately anyway, this modification is not made.

If you respecify a model using your sample data then, strictly speaking, you should not test the model on the same data set: obtain a new data set and test the revised model on that. This is the orthodox view, but you will see revised models retested on the same sample data. The issue is whether the revision remains theoretically coherent and consistent or is just a fishing exercise that capitalises on chance relationships in your sample. Replication is always desirable.

27.4 STRUCTURAL MODELS

In psychology we are often interested in predicting the outcome of some sort of process. In the traditional jargon of experimental psychology we want to know which **independent variables** 'cause' or predict scores on our **dependent variable**. In SEM terms (it would have been too simple to stick with the same terminology) the independent variables are called **exogenous variables** and the dependent variables are called **endogenous variables**. The real advance of structural equation modelling is that we can deal with many dependent, or endogenous, variables at the same time. The other great advance, and one which we have already dealt with, is that we can ask about the relationship between the *un*observed latent factors that we are normally really interested in.

Looking at the relationship between exogenous and endogenous variables is conceptually similar to doing multiple regression (when there is a single

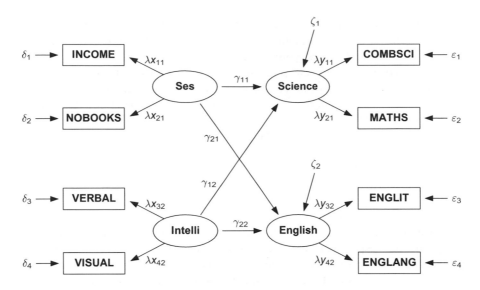

FIGURE 27.4 *A tentative structural model of factors influencing exam performance*

endogenous variable) and path analysis (when there are many endogenous variables).

When we do traditional regression or path analysis we are implicitly assuming that the observed variables are perfectly reliable and contain no error. If we were measuring height or age these measures would still contain error but probably not enough for psychologists to worry about. We could carry on treating the observed variables as 'perfect' indicators of height and age and carry on as before. With most psychological variables the measures we have are imperfect indices of latent constructs that *in principle* we could never measure perfectly accurately. SEM offers us the chance to try to take this error in measurement into account when estimating our model parameters.

This is important for a number of reasons. Measurement errors usually serve to bias parameter estimates and this tends to be in the direction of underestimating the effects of one variable on another (though not always). If we want to know how strong a relationship is between two constructs it would be desirable to estimate the size of this relationship after errors have been 'controlled' for. A second reason for wanting to eliminate errors is that the fit of our model to the data is usually bad in part because of measurement errors. Again, controlling for errors should allow a less biased assessment of our model's fit.

To illustrate this I have expanded on the example used earlier about predicting academic ability. In Figure 27.4 I have two latent exogenous variables, Intelli (intelligence) and Ses (socio-economic status). These are both thought to cause two observed variables each. I am assessing Ses by counting the number of books in the household (NOBOOKS) and asking about household income (INCOME). Intelli is measured by getting scores on verbal (VERBAL) and visuo-spatial (VISUAL) primary ability tests.

The endogenous latent factors are slightly more refined in this example. Here I am trying to predict academic ability rather than raw examination scores and I am interested in trying to predict general ability in science (Science) and English (English) which are conceived of as latent variables here. The interesting feature here is that I am recognising that ability in science, for example, might be measured with error if I just looked at a single exam score (people might feel unwell on the day of one of the science exams, for example). By having two indicators of ability in science (COMBSCI and MATHS) I hope to get a more accurate assessment of ability in science than I might otherwise have got.

All the principles of model comparison we have discussed so far apply to this more complex situation. We will specify a model with parameter constraints and see how well the population covariance matrix generated by the model fits the sample covariance matrix. I can ask whether the two types of academic ability are independent of one another (uncorrelated) as specified here. As the model already states that both abilities are caused by Ses and Intelli, I am asking whether they are independent after these sources of shared variation are accounted for. If the model fits well enough then I can continue with the model. If it does not fit, and the modification indices suggest that I should add a path from Science to English (or vice versa), then my hypothesis that the two types of ability are independent will have to be abandoned.

There are some basic rules that (currently) have to be obeyed when looking at structural models. Firstly, the sources of error for the x variables (the δs) must not be correlated with the errors for the y variables (the εs). Also, these errors in the observed variables must not be correlated with the errors in the latent variables (the ζs). Though these sound like unduly limiting restrictions they are in practice not difficult to apply and are being relaxed in some software packages.

A possibility offered by SEM is the testing of models containing **reciprocal** (or sometimes **simultaneous**) causal links. These are models where one endogenous latent variable is thought to 'cause' another and this endogenous variable is, in turn, thought to 'cause' the first latent variable. This is perfectly acceptable statistically though many people have objections to models containing such relationships. This is a philosophical matter really and depends on what you regard to be necessary for something to be caused by something else.

Most formulations of causation require that the cause is temporally prior to the effect, and saying that two factors simultaneously cause each other necessarily violates this requirement. An example might suggest classes of problem where being able to test models with reciprocal causation might nevertheless be very useful.

Suppose you had measured people's levels of depression and social activity. It is probably the case that when people become depressed they go out and socialise less often. The absence of social activity also adds to the level of depression, and increased depression and lowered activity reinforce each other in a spiral. Because you were not in a position to assess depression and social activity at the point at which the cycle started, and you cannot monitor levels of these variables constantly throughout the day, it is not possible to say unambiguously which cause came first. Here, essentially the time gap between the 'cause' and the 'effect', and the subsequent influence of the 'effect' on the 'cause', is shorter than the gap between possible measurements. We still believe a temporal gap existed but we are not in a position to collect data within that time gap to work out which 'cause' came first.

Models which contain elements of mutual causation and/or feedback loops are called **non-recursive** models; those that do not are called **recursive** models.

27.5 ANALYSIS STRATEGY

It is unlikely that, in an introduction such as this, I will be able to set out an uncontroversial SEM strategy that will be applicable to every problem. What is presented here is more of a set of guidelines based on some fairly clear principles.

First, you must be able to state what latent variables you are interested in. Second, you must be able to measure these well; if you cannot then there is little point in continuing. Third, you must have a theory which clearly states how your latent variables are related to each other. Any modifications made to the model must be theoretically justifiable and any resulting model must have legitimate parameter values. Finally, you must retest your model on fresh data.

What follows is an idealised strategy for SEM:

1 Start with a theoretically generated initial compact model (your model C). The model should be the simplest one possible, with few parameters in need of estimation. Start with a simple model that you may have to make more complex rather than a complex model that you hope to simplify. You should have some ideas about what modifications of the model would not make sense for your theory.
2 Pilot your key measures on samples drawn from your target population. Check that the measurements you are making are based on good measurement models by conducting CFAs. If these models are weak or misspecified then there is little chance that your structural model will fit well.
3 Collect your main sample data using the best possible data collection strategies available to you.
4 Test conceptually distinct subparts of your initial model. If these are *not* OK then go to step 5, otherwise go to step 6.
5 Respecify the submodel(s) by relaxing constraints to make an augmented submodel(s). Only relax constraints that are conceptually OK to relax. Relax them singly or in small numbers: don't radically respecify the original model unless you have good grounds for doing this.
6 Combine the submodels into one overall global test. Again modify this only if it makes some theoretical sense.
7 Confirm the specification of the final model on a new sample of data.

In practice you probably won't have the resources to do what is essentially (at least) three data collections. This is a fact of life but you should beware of testing your measurement models and the structural models in the same data set. Using only one sample necessarily makes any of your conclusions sample specific.

27.6 OTHER THINGS THAT CAN BE DONE WITH SEM

Firstly, SEM packages will deal with models that contain only observed variables which can be a useful alternative to conventional regression-based path modelling packages. You do not have to have any latent variables to go model testing and this is useful if you believe your measures contain no error (i.e. are perfect indices of the key constructs).

Secondly, it is possible to do what is called **bootstrapping** when you have doubts about variable distributions. This involves taking lots of random samples of a given size k $(k<N)$ from your sample data and estimating the parameters many times over. Doing this allows you to make estimates of the standard errors associated with each parameter (and, usefully, the fit indices) which, in turn, lets you draw up confidence intervals for each parameter estimate. This is a relatively specialised statistical technique but one which is gradually becoming more common in the psychological literature.

Thirdly, one of the most promising areas that developments in SEM allow is the testing of measurement and structural models in more than one group at a time. This is called **multi-group modelling**. A common application is in the development of psychometric tests for use in other cultures. For example, a test developed in one country, say the UK, might be translated into another language and the researcher wants to know whether the underlying measurement model has remained the same as it was in the UK. You can collect sample data from both countries and ask the SEM package to test whether the measurement model (a CFA model) is exactly the same in both places. 'Exactly the same' would mean that the item loadings, inter-factor correlations and errors were constrained to be identical in both countries. The analysis will give a single set of fit indices that tell you whether the model fits well simultaneously in both countries. If it does not you can relax constraints (e.g. perhaps allow item loadings to be different between countries) and see whether the revised, less strictly equivalent model, fits.

This can be extended to substantive structural models too. You might develop a theory of factors influencing political identification among males and then see whether the model holds for females too and was therefore equally applicable to both sexes.

Fourthly, so far the discussion has been about measurement and structural models which are conceptually extensions of factor analysis and multiple regression/path models. SEM can be used to conduct analyses that we might previously have thought of doing using group difference tests such as t-test and ANOVA procedures. As we have already seen, one of the virtues of SEM procedures has been the ability to estimate relationships between variables with measurement errors removed. This can be transferred to group difference testing so that you end up testing whether there is a difference in scores on the latent variable even though, necessarily, you have data only on the observed variables. This is an important possibility, since when you find a group difference using a traditional t-test, say, you are unsure whether this difference is a difference attributable to differences in measurement errors or in the 'true' latent variable you are interested in.

Regrettably, conducting the equivalent of a humble t-test even with the friendlier computer packages is still quite difficult to do and, indeed, understand! Hopefully, more user-friendly implementations will come along soon.

27.7 CAUTIONARY NOTES

The most common objection raised by critics is that SEM analysts often claim to be testing causal models even though the input data are correlations/ covariances. Since correlation does not imply causation, claims made that causal relationships have been established cannot be supported. At best SEM can show only that a suggested causal model is consistent with observed correlations.

When doing SEM it is very encouraging to believe that when your pet theoretical model seems to fit the data you have somehow proved your model to be correct. Regrettably, since you will not have tested all possible alternative models, some of which might fit the data even better, all you can really conclude is that until other models have been tested, yours will have to be regarded as the currently 'least bad' model rather than the 'best' or 'true' model. A related criticism is levelled at the use of the term 'confirmatory', particularly when SEM is used for confirmatory factor analysis (CFA). It is often pointed out that nothing is actually 'confirmed' in CFA but rather that models are not disconfirmed. Sean Hammond's suggestion in Chapter 26 that the term *restricted* is used seems like a good compromise.

SEM and related model fitting approaches have often been criticised for their emphasis on prediction at the expense of real explanation. It is quite possible to produce a model to predict something well without really having been able to explain the phenomena of interest. For example, we might find that socio-economic status (SES) is a good predictor of academic attainment without really knowing what it is about having a high SES that causes children to perform better. I am sure the reader can probably make some good guesses as to what these aspects of SES might be, but a well-fitting model might nevertheless be achieved by simply stating that SES predicts academic performance.

While prediction is clearly not the same thing as explanation, theories that claim to explain phenomena but cannot predict them are of limited utility in SEM terms. If no predictions can be made it becomes difficult to see in traditional hypothetico-deductive terms how such theories are to be tested.

SEM currently deals primarily with linear relationships between variables. Because SEM analyses are based on correlations and/or covariances which assess only the degree of linear relationships between variables, they cannot easily deal with data that contain true non-linear relationships. Some transformations of data are possible (see Ullman, 1996) and specialist packages for non-linear problems are gradually appearing on the market, but in the meantime it is incumbent on researchers to be clear about whether they expect linear relationships between variables before embarking on an SEM analysis.

Finally, this is still a developing field and many problems remain to be addressed. Frustratingly, advice in the specialist texts naturally reflects current wisdom and this changes all the time as this is an area of considerable research activity. Fit indices that were once hailed as the best thing since sliced bread are soon shown to be flawed and applicable only in special cases which your own data never seem to be an example of. Estimation algorithms that are claimed to be capable of dealing with strangely distributed variables are suddenly found to require sample sizes of several thousand before they will produce good parameter estimates; and so on. All this means that a certain willingness to learn about the field is necessary if you are to become an effective user of SEM.

27.8 CONCLUSIONS

In this chapter I hope to have given you some idea of what is going on when people apply SEM approaches to data analysis. It may seem a bit dry but SEM really does offer a lot to psychology. The ability to estimate relationships between unobservable latent variables after measurement errors have been excluded is a major advance for psychologists whose research interests are primarily about constructs that are fundamentally unobservable. Coupled with this, SEM brings with it a more overtly rigorous approach to hypothesis testing and model building which must be viewed as a good thing in a political climate where psychology is struggling to be recognised, and to maintain its status, as a 'real' science.

27.9 FURTHER READING

An introduction to the whole SEM area that includes references to software packages is Ullman (1996) 'Structural equation modeling', in Tabachnick and Fidell, *Using Multivariate Statistics* (3rd edn). It is a large chapter in a very well-written and generally useful multivariate statistics book and there are not many better explanations around. Other good introductions include Hoyle (1995) *Structural Equation Modelling: Concepts, Issues and Applications* and Maruyama (1997) *Basics of Structural Equation Modeling*.

If you have access to the Internet you can look up the web page of the SEMNET interest group http://www.marketing.gsu.edu/semsite/ which contains details of how to join its e-mail discussion group. If you join you can send queries to this group and contribute to the very lively debates that seem to be conducted at a frenetic pace.

28

Meta-Analysis

Peter Wood

Contents

28.1 LITERATURE REVIEWS AS 'META-ANALYSIS'

Take one step forward, all those people who have ever had to write a research report, a thesis or a dissertation. Few people who have studied or worked in the behavioural sciences will be left unmoved by such an order. Conducting and writing up research is considered by all educationalists to provide training in numerous valuable skills which go far beyond the exercise itself.

So we've all done it – so what? Well you may be surprised to learn that if you have 'done it,' then you've also conducted a 'meta-analysis'. In its most general sense, meta-analysis is no more nor less than the business of describing, synthesising and analysing research findings in a particular field. So, that second chapter of your dissertation, which was probably headed 'previous research' or 'literature review', and which involved you spending hours in the library and wading through all those expensive photocopies, was a meta-analysis.

28.2 OBJECTIVES OF REVIEWING RESEARCH

When you've stopped congratulating yourself for something you didn't know you'd done, ask yourself a simple question: why did you do a literature review? Well, leaving aside the trite answer ('because my supervisor told me to'), the reasons which spring to mind include:

1   to ensure that your chosen research problem is clearly defined and set within an established context
2   to examine what researchers have previously found about the chosen topic
3   to try to draw some broad, overall conclusions from previous research
4   to derive a theoretical stance, based either on earlier findings or on the current most successful theory.

None of these activities is easy. Although data bases have made access to references wonderfully simple, the choice of key words and search strategy have become crucial. Thoughtless use of either can lead to the novice researcher deciding to pursue a different career. (Use 'stress' as a key word in PsycLit and it will come up with more than 27,000 references!)

Let's suppose we don't have the problem of too many references, but that our chosen topic has generated a 'reasonable' number. What a reasonable number is will depend mainly on how narrowly we have defined our topic and also upon the context. An undergraduate dissertation for example would be expected to look at the major papers in the area, whereas a PhD thesis would attempt a comprehensive review. There is no answer to the unspoken question, 'How few papers can I use in my literature review?'

28.3   DIFFICULTIES INHERENT IN REVIEWING

There is no getting away from the fact that if you're going to achieve any of the goals set out in section 28.2, you're actually going to have to *read* all this previous research. We're all prone to that sense of glowing achievement that stems from successfully photocopying a core article, brought on no doubt by the belief that by some magical process of osmosis, the very act of photo-copying has imparted knowledge of the contents. No, that won't do: we have to read and inwardly digest what researchers have done. We have to know what variables have been used, how they have been defined, what measures were employed, the context of the research, the sample used, the method of analysis.

The reason we must go through this procedure is that all of these things (and others not mentioned) may have a profound effect on the findings and conclusions. In this respect the social and behavioural sciences stand in con-trast to the physical sciences, where in many cases research is based upon standardised techniques and measures conducted on well-established samples under controlled conditions.

If the object of a literature review were merely to describe research which had previously been conducted, then the process we have described so far sounds fairly straightforward. This is hard work, but not intrinsically difficult. Description, however, is not what it's all about. Our goal is to synthesise, to draw together results from disparate sources, to interpret their findings and to integrate them into broad conclusions. This is where it all gets a bit tricky, for even a cursory review of the literature in a given field will often find it littered with contrasting and contradictory findings. Explanations for differing results may seem equally reasonable and the theoretical implications drawn may appear equally attractive. In such circumstances, how can we go about integration? Or draw general conclusions? The strategy adopted by many researchers is simply to sidestep the issue and conduct a 'pseudo-synthesis'. Such reviews are peppered with such phrases as, 'in contrast, Strabismus and Myopia (1982) found', or 'on the other hand, Toast-Rack (1976) concluded that', or 'contrast this result with Proboscis et al. (1989)'. Such reviews, whilst not valueless, are really little better than annotated bibliographies.

If this approach exemplifies the 'could do better' end of the scale, what does a 'proper' reviewer do that is different? Perhaps the most important thing is to offer *reasons* why findings may differ, and to suggest research which may help *resolve* such differences. They will also identify why some research findings are more significant (in the non-statistical sense) than others and which ones make important theoretical contributions. It will be readily appreciated that reviews of this type are immensely valuable, not only in saving time and effort for less gifted researchers, but also in summarising the current state of knowledge, and stimulating fresh directions for research. It will also be appreciated why not everyone is good at this exercise. Synthesis and integration of this nature demand the highest levels of cognitive ability. You will find literature reviews which achieve these standards in prestigious journals across the psychological literature.

Even the best literature reviews, as just described, are not above criticism however. Inevitably the interpretation of findings, the insights derived, the manner in which conclusions are drawn, are all dependent on the judgements of a single individual, the reviewer (or at best a small group of reviewers). In other words, such opinions fall squarely into the category of **subjective judgements**. If we disagree with a viewpoint, we may quite validly say, 'my (subjective) opinion is as good as their (subjective) opinion'. It is of no help to counter this statement with the indisputable fact that many major literature reviews are published by researchers who are exceedingly eminent in their field. Sadly, the history of science teaches that these individuals are no less prone to bias, selective inclusion of evidence, and misinterpretation of research findings. Indeed, since most eminent researchers often have a long-standing association with a particular theoretical standpoint, or line of research, it could be argued that they will have to work *harder* to maintain a suitable unbiased view. The foregoing is not intended, in any sense, to question the academic standards of any literature reviewer, but merely to illustrate the fact that even the best literature reviews are *subjective*.

28.4 QUANTIFYING THE REVIEW PROCESS

So far we have talked exclusively about literature reviews in their most familiar form. We have discussed their aims, their value and their disadvantages. Because of this, the reader may be assuming that 'literature review' and 'meta-analysis' are the same thing. This is not the case. What we have described up to this point should more accurately be called **narrative literature reviews**, and these form only one of a range of meta-analysis techniques. All the alternative meta-analysis techniques have been developed in an attempt to bring the same standards of scientific rigour to the literature review as exist for individual studies (Wolf, 1986): in other words, to move away from the possible biases and subjectivity which are acknowledged to be present in narrative reviews. Guzzo et al. (1987) suggest that we may think of meta-analysis techniques as being on a **continuum of quantification**. At one end (least quantified) rests the narrative review in the form already discussed. Moving along the scale we may conduct what is often called a 'box score' review. To do this one constructs a table in which counts are made, based upon the frequency with which studies in the research literature support (or refute) a particular finding.

Yet further along our scale we could include techniques for combining and cumulating significance levels reported in individual studies. Using these methods it is possible to estimate the probability associated with research findings (Guzzo et al., 1987).

At the 'most quantified' end of the continuum are a group of statistical techniques which have, over the last 15 or so years, become known by general usage as **meta-analysis**. It is these techniques which we will concentrate on for the remainder of this chapter.

28.5 THE RATIONALE OF META-ANALYSIS

That meta-analysis has become associated with one particular set of techniques is largely due to a seminal paper by Glass (1976). In this, he categorised three levels of analysis:

1 *Primary analysis*: the original analysis of the data from a research study.
2 *Secondary analysis*: the re-analysis of original data from a research study using different statistical techniques, perhaps to examine alternative questions or explanations.
3 *Meta-analysis*: the statistical analysis of results from a large number of individual research studies so as to integrate their findings.

The word 'statistical' is important here. It is Glass's position that 'The findings of multiple studies should be regarded as a complex data-set, no more comprehensible without statistical analysis than would be hundreds of data points in a single study' (Glass et al., 1981). So each *study* in a meta-analysis is equivalent to a subject in a primary analysis. The requirement for statistical meta-analysis techniques was in response to the perceived subjective nature of traditional narrative reviews. An additional consideration was the very large number of studies which have been conducted. Hunter et al. suggest that, 'In many areas of research the need today is not additional empirical data but some means of making sense of the vast amounts of data that have accumulated' (1982: 27). Not only were statistical meta-analysis techniques seen as offering a more objective means of integrating the findings of previous research, but in doing this they move literature reviews closer to the standards of scientific enquiry and repeatability which are applied to the individual study.

More specifically, meta-analysis is thought to address a number of particular problems to which narrative reviews are prone:

1   It is suggested that narrative reviews are often not comprehensive. There is a danger that a reviewer may, for a variety of reasons, include only a subset of studies in the review.
2   There is a tendency in narrative reviews to concentrate on whether particular hypotheses are supported by significance tests in each individual study. In so doing, such reviews overestimate the accuracy and importance of significance tests on small samples, and underestimate the importance of the *size* of any effect.
3   We have already noted that there are many conflicting results in psychology. Narrative reviews have great difficulty in dealing with these differences. Elaborate explanatory frameworks may have to be constructed to synthesise such results. Meta-analysis suggests that in the majority of cases the results of primary research studies are distorted by many artefacts (Hunter and Hirsh, 1987). It is failure to take these errors into consideration which leads to the wide discrepancy in findings within a given topic area.
4   Because the procedures for integrating research findings have not been agreed or made explicit, the conclusions from narrative reviews may be difficult to replicate.

28.6   GENERAL PRINCIPLES UNDERLYING THE STATISTICAL PROCEDURE

Meta-analysis incorporates a wide variety of statistical techniques which vary in complexity. All, however, follow similar principles and offer a quantitative method of cumulating research findings. Having first collected the relevant studies, the findings of each analysis are then treated so that they may be expressed as a common statistic. It thus becomes possible to examine this statistic across the range of studies. In the most commonly used meta-analytic techniques, the common metric selected is an **effect size** measure, in other words an index of how important or powerful the relationship between the variables is. In addition to using a common metric, the most frequently used meta-analytic techniques use further statistical treatments so as to correct for major artefacts which will include sampling error, error of measurement and range restriction.

At this point it is worth while describing the procedures involved in meta-analysis. The best known are those by Glass et al. (1981) and Hunter and Schmidt (Hunter et al., 1982). Both are presented below.

The stages involved in Glass's procedure are as follows:

1   Select the independent and dependent variables of interest.
2   Identify, locate and obtain all relevant and usable studies containing information of interest.

3   Code each study for characteristics which might be predictors of study outcomes, i.e. might relate to the size of effects obtained. Typically these might include differences in subject's age, sex, length of treatment, etc.
4   Calculate estimates of the effect size for the variable pairs (independent–dependent) of interest. (Glass, 1977 has derived formulae for converting statistics used in primary analysis to a common effect size metric).
5   Calculate the mean and standard deviation of effect size across studies.
6   Examine those study characteristics identified in stage 3 which correlate with study effects.

Hunter and Schmidt's method may be regarded as an extension of Glass's in that it incorporates steps to correct for study artefacts. The first four stages are essentially the same and are not repeated.

5   Calculate the mean effect size across studies. The effect size for each study is then weighted by its sample size.
6   Calculate the variance of effect size.
7   Determine the extent to which differences in variance of effect size are due to sampling errors, errors of measurement and range restriction.
8   If a large percentage of the variance across studies can be attributed to the artefacts above, it is concluded that the average effect size is an accurate estimate of the relationship between the variables.
9   If, on the other hand, a large proportion of the variance is unaccounted for, then study characteristics are examined to determine their correlation with effect size (as with Glass's procedure).

It will be noted that the procedures are similar in terms of the emphasis they place on the importance of effect size, but differ in relation to correcting for study artefacts. In fact the central importance of these corrections to the Hunter and Schmidt method would lead them to recommend not undertaking stage 3 (coding for study characteristics) *before* estimating the proportion of variance attributable to the artefacts. The procedures described are of course a simplification, and the reader should consult Hunter et al. (1982) for a full description.

Although the methods outlined are not in themselves intrinsically difficult, the reader may be unfamiliar with the manipulations at some of the stages.

28.7 SIGNIFICANCE LEVELS, EFFECT SIZE AND COMMON METRICS

Hypothesis testing by assessing significance levels is one of the most familiar procedures in primary analysis of psychological data. Having decided *a priori* upon the acceptable level, calculated the appropriate statistic, and consulted the relevant table, we can report the significance level associated with the particular result. If our test statistic reaches or exceeds our set level then 'a significant relationship' can be reported; if not, then we must accept the null hypothesis. It is clearly important to know whether or not any difference we may discover between, say, control and experimental groups could have arisen by chance. However, it has been appreciated for many years that significance level alone is an inadequate study outcome. This is particularly true in areas of applied psychology, where the findings of research studies may have policy implications. So, for example, in human factors it is insufficient to know that workstation A is 'significantly better' than workstation B at the 5% level, or in personnel psychology that selection method 1 is significantly better than selection method 2, or in clinical psychology that two treatments provide significantly different outcomes. In such settings what may be of more importance is the *magnitude* of the effect between the two. It's not difficult to see why this should be so. In the real world, resources are always finite. Policy decisions must be made on the basis of utilitarian and efficiency considerations. Clearly, a Rolls-Royce might be assessed as 'a significantly better' car than a Mini, but if our purchasing decision is based on rational considerations, the important factor is 'how much better?' If the purchase–price ratio is 20 to 1, is it 20 times better? Clearly the effect size, i.e. the magnitude of the difference, assumes considerable importance in policy situations.

Whilst effect size is universally used in meta-analysis, there is some general debate concerning whether effect size or significance level is the more meaningful (Chow, 1988). However, as Mullen (1993) points out, the two aspects are mutually dependent. Any significance level can be expressed as a function of effect size, and vice versa. The relationship is as follows:

$$\text{significance level} = \text{function of (effect size} \times \text{sample size)}$$

$$\text{effect size} = \text{function of (significance level/sample size)}$$

Clearly, if we are intending to compare findings across many studies, which will inevitably report different statistics, we need a 'common currency' as the basis for calculation.

Different meta-analysis techniques may utilise different common metrics. Glass et al. (1981) calculate an effect size statistic d, where

$$d = \frac{\text{mean of experiment group} - \text{mean of control group}}{\text{standard deviation of control group}}$$

Robust strategies for estimating means and standard deviations may need to be applied in certain circumstances. These might involve the 'jackknife' (Miller, 1974), the 'bootstrap' (Efron, 1979) or subsampling procedures (Hartington, 1969). Hunter and Schmidt on the other hand consistently use the Pearson product moment correlation r as the expression of effect size. Alternatively some researchers suggest the use of Fisher's Z as a measure of effect size (Mullen, 1993). Wolf (1986) provides useful tables of formulae for converting the most common test statistics, t, F and X to r and d. Care must be exercised when making such conversions to include only those test statistics which compare pairs of variables, i.e. only for comparing two group means, or statistics with one degree of freedom.

28.8 THE EFFECT OF STUDY ARTEFACTS

Hunter and Schmidt's meta-analytic procedures are firmly rooted in the conceptual approach that unaccounted-for errors in individual research studies are the underlying reason for the many conflicting results in psychology. Their analysis procedures correct for three major sources of error – sampling error, measurement error and range restriction – although they have identified nine artefacts which may distort study findings (Hunter and Hirsh, 1987).

Sampling error is present in all studies, although the larger the sample the less the error. It arises because the sample sizes used in individual research studies are small in relation to the population. This is particularly true in psychological research, where sample sizes are most often in the range 50– 500. When we average effect size measures (correlations) in a meta-analysis, we also average sampling errors. Thus if we cumulate 40 studies each with a sample of 100, then the averaged correlation will have sampling error as if our sample had been 4000.

Correcting for the variance in our cumulated effect size measure is a little more complex. In calculating variance we must first calculate deviation scores. Some will be positive and some negative. Squaring the deviations to calculate variance eliminates the sign, and therefore stops errors from cancelling themselves out. The effect of this of course is to increase the magnitude of the variance (since negative deviations will not be represented). So in cumulating across studies we will produce a variance which is greater than the 'true' variance for our cumulated sample. Hunter and Schmidt, however, point out that this is a systematic change, and the effect of sampling error on variance is to add a known constant, which they call the **sampling error variance**. This constant can be subtracted from the observed variance, and the difference is then an estimate of the required variance of the effect size measure for the cumulated sample.

As with sampling error, measurement error is endemic in psychological research. Many psychological constructs may be measured in a variety of ways. For any given subject, measurement error is randomly distributed. Our observed score will be made up of the 'true' score plus error:

$$\text{observed score} = \text{true score} + \text{error}$$

Error can of course be a negative value, so for an observed score of 100, error might be +1 or −1, yielding a true score of 99 or 10l. The true score is unknowable. When we correlate scores across subjects, the previously random effects of measurement error have a systematic effect, in that they cause the correlation to be lower than it would have been if we could correlate 'true' scores. By utilising the reliability for each measure, Hunter and Schmidt have developed a formula for **correction of attenuation**, i.e. correcting for error of measurement.

Similarly with **range restriction**: that is, where the range of values presented on the independent variable vary between studies, this will also affect the correlations produced. Given that one has the standard deviation of the independent variable, Hunter and Schmidt use a range correction formula to project all correlations to the same reference standard deviation.

Of necessity the above explanations are considerably oversimplified and many aspects have been omitted. The reader is referred to Hunter et al. (1982) for a full description of the rationale and methods used.

Whilst providing a simple description of these artefacts we have not yet answered the question implied in the heading to this section. Hunter et al. observe that: 'In many [meta-analysis] studies we have found no variance in results across studies once artefacts such as sampling error have been eliminated' (1982: 164). Over a series of 152 meta-analyses, the average amount of variance accounted for by the three statistical artefacts discussed above was 72%.

28.9   SOME CRITICISMS OF THE PROCEDURE

This chapter began by discussing narrative reviews and the criticisms which may be levelled at them. The statistical methods of meta-analysis which have been described clearly offer an alternative, quantitative method of achieving the same objectives. We may validly ask whether this new methodology answers the criticisms or, indeed, has problems of its own.

Since all such reviews begin by definition with the research literature, this is a good place to start. The first stage is to define 'the relationship of interest'. Guzzo et al. (1987) have pointed out that whilst narrative reviews may be open to accusations of reviewer bias, meta-analytic procedures may fare no better. Whilst meta-analysis emphasises that *all* studies relevant to a particular topic should be included, this leaves unspecified how to define the boundaries of this domain. Decisions about which studies to include are what Guzzo et al. label 'judgement calls', i.e. subjective. The requirement to include all studies has certainly led to some earlier meta-analyses being criticised for lack of focus, and the charge that 'apples were being counted with oranges' (Eysenck, 1978). More recently emphasis has shifted to a more careful definition of the relationship to be tested. It is unlikely that such boundary questions are capable of satisfactory resolution. However, reviews of *all types* should include an explicit definition of the **inclusion criteria** on which studies have been selected.

Meta-analysis, of course, concerns itself with cumulating research findings. However, it is widely acknowledged that published work represents only a proportion of the research studies which are conducted; many potentially useful studies never get published and remain stored in people's offices. This problem is often referred to as the **file-drawer problem**. Does this matter? It has, in the past, been argued that journal reviewers are more likely to favour not only research which is methodologically sound, but also studies which show significant results. Rosenthal (1979) has attempted to address this problem by deriving formulae for assessing how many non-significant studies you would need to find in order to show that there was actually no relationship between the variables. Hunter et al. (1982) suggest that any difference in findings between unpublished and published research is mainly due to differences in methodological quality. Recent meta-analyses have begun to include explicit descriptions of the **retrieval strategies** adopted. These will include obvious data bases, abstracts, citation indices and bibliographies. In addition, eminent researchers in the field will be approached to inquire if they are aware of additional, possibly unpublished work in the area. Cooper (1998) provides a list of numerous retrieval procedures.

Considerable debate has surrounded the issue that, even within the domain of published research, not all studies will be methodologically sound. The question arises as to how methodologically flawed research should be treated. It has been argued that narrative reviewers, on detecting weak studies, may tend to exclude them; whilst meta-analysis, with its injunction to include *all* studies, may include them. Hunter et al. suggest caution in deciding whether or not to exclude studies, since it is impossible to know when such flaws may lead to biased findings. Others adopt the view 'garbage in, garbage out' (Eysenck, 1978). The issue is not resolved.

A category of studies which will be completely excluded by meta-analysis is those which have collected qualitative research data. The nature of meta-analysis demands that research findings be expressed in terms of a quantitative statistic, which can thus be converted into an effect size estimate. This is probably not a serious restriction since the areas of psychology where meta-analysis has had most impact, particularly organisational psychology, are primarily based on quantitative measures. In other areas of psychology where a mix of quantitative and qualitative measures are used, this may prove a more fundamental limitation, since meta-analysis could be applied only to a restricted, non-representative, subset of studies.

It must be clear from the procedures outlined in section 28.6 that the techniques used in meta-analysis demand the presence of particular descriptive statistics in the reported results of each individual study. In a perfect world this would, of course, be the case. However, in the real world of research literature it is far from true. Whilst higher standards of result reporting may in future be insisted on, it is an unfortunate fact that much research conducted prior to 1976 does not report appropriate statistics. This means that even quantitative studies of this type will be excluded from the analysis.

Guzzo et al. (1985) and Stone (1986) both report having to exclude some 50% of studies in a meta-analysis for this reason. In some cases it may be possible to make estimates of the required statistic based upon those results which are reported; however, this cannot be regarded as a defensible procedure.

Whilst correction for artefacts, as proposed by Hunter et al., may be impossible, the majority of primary analyses will provide a statistic from which an effect size estimate may be calculated. There is, however, no agreed procedure as to how this should be done, although the range of methods appear conceptually similar. One potentially more serious problem which can arise is how to calculate effect size in a research study which produces multiple results (longitudinal data for example). The formulae used for cumulation assume that values are statistically independent. Hunter et al. discuss this application and suggest ways of dealing with it. However, their explanations go beyond the scope of this chapter.

Some critics have suggested that meta-analysis produces a spurious simplification of results by its concentration on overall effects, at the expense of possible interaction or mediating variables. It is of course a fundamental precept of the Hunter et al. method that such interaction effects should only be explored once statistical artefacts have been corrected. In contrast, Glass's method prescribes utilising pre-coded characteristics once mean effect size has been calculated. The problem remains, however, that decisions must be made as to which characteristics should be coded, i.e. which might reasonably be considered as possible interaction variables. Yet another 'judgement call' arises here, since by coding for very large numbers of possible interaction variables and exhaustively testing against each one, we naturally increase the likelihood of throwing up interaction effects which have occurred by chance. On the other hand, the perhaps more defensible approach of using relevant theory and specific hypotheses as a means of selection, whilst minimising the chance of type I errors (false positives), is also less likely to uncover new and unsuspected relationships. This difficulty is not restricted to meta-analysis however.

28.10 CONCLUSIONS

This chapter has given a brief and perforce simplified overview of the place of meta-analysis in psychological research. The stance is adopted that meta-analysis is a generic term for all types of formal research literature review. Over recent years, the term 'meta-analysis' has come to be used as a shorthand for the statistical meta-analysis techniques which have been described here. Terminological confusion is not eased by the fact that Hunter and Schmidt's methods were originally labelled **validity generalisation**, which is now considered to be a special application of meta-analysis.

As a conceptual approach and set of statistical techniques, meta-analysis has had a meteoric rise in popularity since 1976. A large range of psychological journals now publish articles based on such analyses. A comprehensive bibliography would run to many pages.

It is probably sensible to group our concluding remarks under a number of points:

1   There is still a place for narrative reviews of the psychological literature. Although quantitative meta-analyses call for a comprehensive inclusion of research studies, the number of studies which 'include themselves out' (to misquote Samuel Goldwyn) because they do not report suitable statistics, or because they provide qualitative data, means that for some topics meta-analysis would be operating on only a restricted subsample of research findings.

2   Meta-analysis is an important and powerful technique when properly applied which may have a far-reaching impact in psychology. In applied fields of psychology – education, clinical, organisational – validity generalisation results may come to have important policy implications.

3   Many of the early criticisms of meta-analysis were based on misconceptions of how it worked. For an informative and interesting debate on many of the issues the reader should consult Schmidt et al. (1985).

4   Whilst adopting quantitative statistical methods for reviewing research literature, meta-analysis is not devoid of 'judgement calls', i.e. steps where subjective judgement is required.

5   Although it is early days, meta-analysis may have more utility in synthesising research findings and identifying gaps in knowledge, than in theory generating and testing.

6   Quantifying the previously unquantified can confer a spurious validity in the mind of the reader. This is not a criticism of meta-analysis but a general comment on the bias many people have when confronted by numbers (Strube and Hartmann, 1982). When new statistical techniques are developed we must learn to be 'consumers' of them.

7   This chapter was written and based on a (non-quantitative) review of the literature.

Finally, the most apposite comment would seem to be that by Green and Hall: 'Data analysis is an aid to thought, not a substitute' (1984: 52).

28.11 FURTHER READING

Four inexpensive books provide a particularly clear exposition of meta-analytic techniques. Wolf (1986) *Meta-Analysis: Quantitative Methods for Research Synthesis* gives a broad introduction to the range of research synthesising methods and supplies the relevant formulae for all the common procedures. Hunter et al. (1982) *Meta-Analysis: Cumulating Research Findings across Studies* introduces the concepts underlying validity generalisation and provides numerous worked examples. Rosenthal (1991) *Meta-Analytic Procedures for Social Research* is a particularly well-balanced account of the advantages and disadvantages of using a variety of research-synthesising procedures. Cooper (1998) *Synthesizing Research: A Guide for Literature Reviews* provides a clear and up-to-date review of the procedures.

References

Abraham, C. and Hampson, S.E. (1996) 'A social cognition approach to health psychology: philosophical and methodological issues', *Psychology and Health*, 11: 223–41.

Agresti, A. (1996) *An Introduction to Categorical Data Analysis*. Chichester: Wiley.

Aitkenhead, A.M. and Slack, J.M. (1994) *Issues in Cognitive Modelling*. Hillsdale, NJ: Erlbaum.

Albrecht, T.L., Johnson, G.M. and Walther, J.B. (1993) 'Understanding communication processes in focus groups', in D.L. Morgan (ed.) *Successful Focus Groups: Advancing the State of the Art*. London: Sage.

American Psychological Association (1992) *APA Ethics Code*. American Psychological Association, 750 First Street, NE, Washington, DC 20002–4242, USA.

Anastasi, A. (1990) *Psychological Testing*. New York: Macmillan.

Anderson, J.A. (1972) 'Separate sample logistic discrimination', *Biometrika*, 59: 19–36.

Anderson, J.A. (1988) 'Concept formation in neural networks: implications for evolution of cognitive functions', *Human Evolution*, 3(1–2): 81–97.

Anderson, J.A. (1998) 'Learning arithmetic with a neural network: seven times seven is about fifty', in D. Scarborough and S. Sternberg (eds) *An Invitation to Cognitive Science* (2nd edn), Volume 4, *Methods, Models and Conceptual Issues*. Cambridge, MA: The MIT Press.

Andreassi, J.L. (1995) *Psychophysiology: Human Behavior and Physiological Response* (3rd edn). Hillsdale, NJ: Erlbaum.

Andrich, D. (1990) *Rasch Models for Measurement*. Beverly Hills, CA: Sage.

Arber, S. (1993) 'Designing samples', in N. Gilbert (ed.) *Researching Social Life*. London: Sage.

Argyris, C. (1970) *Intervention Theory and Method: A Behavioural Science View*. Reading, MA: Addison-Wesley.

Arksey, H. and Knight, P.T. (1999) *Interviewing for Social Scientists*. London: Sage.

Ary, D. (1984) 'Mathematical explanation of error in duration recording using partial interval, whole interval, and momentary time sampling', *Behavioral Assessment*, 6: 221–8.

Asbury, J.E. (1995) 'Overview of focus group research', *Qualitative Health Research*, 5(4): 414–20.

Ashford, P. (1994) 'Proenvironmentalism: identity and the media'. PhD thesis, University of Surrey.

Ashmore, M. (1989) *The Reflexive Thesis: Wrighting Sociology of Scientific Knowledge*. Chicago: University of Chicago Press.

Atkinson, J. and Heritage, J. (eds) (1984) *Structures of Social Action: Studies in Conversation Analysis*. Cambridge: Cambridge University Press.

Atkinson, J.W. (1958) *Motives in Fantasy, Action and Society*. New York: Van Nostrand.

Axelrod, R. (ed.) (1976) *Structure of Decision*. Princeton, NJ: Princeton University Press.

Backs, R.W. (1998) 'A comparison of factor analytic methods of obtaining cardiovascular autonomic components for the assessment of mental workload', *Ergonomics*, 41(5): 733–45.

Baer, D.M., Wolf, M.M. and Risley, T.R. (1968) 'Some current dimensions of applied behaviour analysis', *Journal of Applied Behaviour Analysis*, 1(1): 91–7.

Bainbridge, L. (1985) 'Inferring from verbal reports to cognitive processes', in M. Brenner, J. Brown and D. Canter (eds) *The Research Interview: Uses and Approaches*. London: Academic Press.

Ball, M.S. and Smith, G.W.H. (1992) *Analyzing Visual Data*. Newbury Park, CA: Sage.

Bandura, A. (1997) *Self-Efficacy: The Exercise of Control*. New York: Freeman.

Bandura, A. and Walters, R.H. (1963) *Social Learning and Personality Development*. New York: Holt.

Banks, M., Bates, I., Breakwell, G., Bynner, J., Emler, N., Jamieson, L. and Roberts, K. (1992) *Careers and Identities*. Milton Keynes: Open University Press.

Bannister, D. and Fransella, F. (1971) *Inquiring Man: The Theory of Personal Constructs*. Harmondsworth: Penguin.

Barlow, D.H. and Hersen, M. (1973) 'Single case experimental designs: uses in applied clinical research', *Archives of General Psychiatry*, 29: 319–25.

Barlow, D.H. and Hersen, M. (1984) *Single Case Experimental Designs*. New York: Pergamon.

Bates, P. (1980) 'The effectiveness of interpersonal skills training on the skill acquisition of moderately and mildly retarded adults', *Journal of Applied Behavior Analysis*, 13: 237–48.

Basch, C.E. (1987) 'Focus group interview: an underutilized research technique for improving theory and practice in health education', *Health Education Quarterly*, 14(4): 411–48.

Baumann, U., Laireiter, A.R. and Krebs, A. (1996) 'Computer-assisted interaction diary on social networks, social support, and interpersonal strain', in J. Fahrenberg and M. Myrtek (eds) *Ambulatory Assessment: Computer Assisted Psychological and Psychophysiological Methods in Monitoring and Field Studies*. Goettingen, Germany: Hogrefe and Huber.

Beattie, G. (1983) *Talk: An Analysis of Speech and Non-Verbal Behaviour in Conversation*. Milton Keynes: Open University Press.

Bechtel, W. (1988) *Philosophy of Science: An Overview for Cognitive Science*. Hillsdale, NJ: Erlbaum.

Bechtel, W. and Richardson, R.C. (1993) *Discovering Complexity: Decomposition and Localization as Strategies in Scientific Research*. Princeton, NJ: Princeton University Press.

Bellack, A.S. and Hersen, M. (1998) *Behavioural Assessment: A Practical Handbook* (4th edn). New York: Pergamon.

Bellack, A.S., Hersen, M. and Himmeloch, J.M. (1983) 'A comparison of social skills training, pharmacotherapy and psychotherapy for depression', *Behaviour Research and Therapy*, 21: 101–7.

Bentler, P.M. (1995) *EQS: Structural Equations Program Manual*. Encino, CA: Multivariate Sotware Inc.

Berelson, B. (1971) *Content Analysis in Communication Research*. New York: Free Press.

Berger, P.L. and Luckmann, T. (1971) *The Social Construction of Reality*. Harmondsworth: Penguin.

Bergin, A.E. and Strupp, H.H. (1972) *Changing Frontiers in the Science of Psychotherapy*. New York: Aldine.

Berry, J.W. (1969) 'On cross-cultural comparability', *Journal International de Psychologie*, 4(2): 119–28.

Berry, J.W. (1989) 'Imposed etics–emics–derived etics: the operationalisation of a compelling idea', *International Journal of Psychology*, 24: 721–35.

Berry, J.W., Poortinga, Y.H., Segall, M.H. and Dasen, P.R. (1992) *Cross-Cultural Psychology: Research and Applications*. Cambridge: Cambridge University Press.

Bhaskar, R. (1978) *A Realist Theory of Science*. London: Verso.

Bieber, I., Dain, H.J., Dince, P.R., Drellich, M.G., Grand, H.G., Gundlach, R.H., Kremer, M.W., Rifkin, A.H., Wilbur, C.B. and Bieber, T.B. (1962) *Homosexuality: A Psychoanalytic Study*. New York: Basic.

Billig, M. (1987) *Arguing and Thinking: A Rhetorical Approach to Social Psychology*. Cambridge: Cambridge University Press.

Billig, M. (1988) 'Methodology and scholarship in understanding ideological explanation', in C. Antaki (ed.) *Analysing Everyday Explanation: A Casebook of Methods*. London: Sage.

Billig, M. (1991) *Ideologies and Beliefs*. London: Sage.

Birnbaum, A. (1968) 'Some latent trait models and their use in inferring an examinee's ability', in L.F. Lord and M. Novick (eds) *Statistical Theories of Mental Test Scores*. Reading, MA: Addison-Wesley.

Birnbaumer, N. and Ohman, A. (eds) (1993) *The Structure of Emotion*. Berlin: Hogrefe and Huber.

Blair, R.J.R., Jones, L., Clark, F. and Smith, M. (1997) 'The psychopathic individual: a lack of responsiveness to distress cues?', *Psychophysiology*, 34(2): 192–8.

Blake, R. and Hiris, E. (1993) 'Another means for measuring the motion aftereffect', *Vision Research*, 33: 1589–92.

Blalock, H.M. Jr. (1988) *Social Statistics* (rev. 2nd edn). Singapore: McGraw-Hill.

Blascovich, J. and Kelsey, M. (1990) 'Using electrodermal and cardiovascular measures of arousal in social psychological research', in C. Hendrick and M.S. Clark (eds) *Research Methods in Personality and Social Psychology*. Newbury Park, CA: Sage.

Blashfield, R.K. and Aldenderfer, M.S. (1988) 'The methods and problems of cluster analysis', in J.R. Nesselroade and R.B. Cattell (eds) *Handbook of Multivariate Experimental Psychology*. London: Plenum.

Blinkhorn, S.F. and Johnson, C. (1990) 'The insificance of personality testing', *Nature*, 348: 671–2.

Blum, G.S. (1949) 'A study of psychoanalytic theory of psychosexual development', *Genetic Psychology Monographs*, 39: 3–99.

Bollen, K.A. (1989) *Structural Equations with Latent Variables*. New York: Wiley.

Borg, I. (1977) 'Some basic concepts in facet theory', in J.C. Lingoes, E.E. Roskam and I. Borg (eds) *Geometric Representations of Relational Data*. Ann Arbor, MI: Mathesis.

Borg, I. (ed.) (1981) *Multidimensional Data Representations: When and Why*. Ann Arbor, MI: Mathesis.

Borg, I. and Groenen, P. (1997) *Modern Multidimensional Scaling*. New York: Springer.

Bormann, H. (1972). 'Fantasy and rhetorical vision: the rhetorical criticism of social reality', *Quarterly Journal of Speech*, 58: 396–407.

Boulton, M. (ed.) (1994) *Challenge and Innovation: Advances in Social Research on HIV/AIDS*. Brighton: Falmer.

Boyum, L.A. and Parke, R.D. (1995) 'The role of family emotional expressiveness in the development of children's social competence', *Journal of Marriage and the Family*, 57: 593–608.

Breakwell, G.M. (1990) *Interviewing*. London: BPS/Routledge.

Breakwell, G.M. (1993) 'Integrating paradigms', in G.M. Breakwell and D.V. Canter (eds) *Empirical Approaches to Social Representations*. Oxford: Oxford University Press.

Breakwell, G.M. (1994) 'The echo of power: an integrative framework for social psychological theorising', *The Psychologist*, 7(2): 65–72.

Breakwell, G.M. and Canter, D.V. (1993) *Empirical Approaches to Social Representations*. Oxford: Oxford University Press.

Breakwell, G.M. and Fife-Schaw, C.R. (1992) 'Sexual activities and preferences in a UK sample of 16–20 year olds', *Archives of Sexual Behavior*, 21: 271–93.

Breakwell, G.M. and Fife-Schaw, C.R. (1994) 'Using longitudinal cohort sequential designs to study changes in behaviour', in M. Boulton (ed.) *Challenge and Innovation: Advances in Social Research on HIV/AIDS*. Brighton: Falmer.

Breakwell, G.M., Hammond, S. and Fife-Schaw, C. (1995) *Research Methods in Psychology*. London: Sage.

Brenner, M., Brown, J. and Canter, D.V. (eds) (1985) *The Research Interview: Uses and Approaches*. London: Academic.

Brislin, R.W., Lonner, W.J. and Thorndike, R.M. (1973) *Cross-Cultural Research Methods*. New York: Wiley.

British Psychological Society (1993) *The BPS Code of Conduct, Ethical Principles and Guidelines*. Leicester: BPS.

Broadbent, D. (1993) *The Simulation of Human Intelligence*. Oxford: Basil Blackwell.

Brooker, D.J.R., Snape, M., Johnson, E., Ward, D. and Payne, M. (1997) 'Single case evaluation of the effects of aromatherapy and massage on disturbed behaviour in severe dementia', *British Journal of Clinical Psychology*, 36(2): 287–96.

Brown, J. (1985) 'An introduction to the uses of facet theory', in D.V. Canter (ed.) *Facet Theory: Approaches to Social Research*. New York: Springer.

Brown, J.M. and Armstrong, M. (1986) 'Transfer from junior to secondary: the child's perspective', in M. Youngman (ed.) *Mid Schooling Transfer: Problems and Proposals*. Slough: NFER-Nelson.

Brown, J.M. and Armstrong, R. (1982) 'The structure of pupils' worries during transition from junior to secondary schools', *British Educational Research Journal*, 8: 123–32.

Brown, J.M. and Blount, C. (1999) 'Occupational stress among sex offender treatment managers', *Journal of Managerial Psychology*, 14(2): 108–20.

Brown, J.M. and Campbell, E.A. (1990) 'Sources of occupational stress in the police', *Work and Stress*, 4: 305–18.

Brown, J.M., Henderson, J. and Armstrong, M. (1987) 'Children's perception of nuclear power stations as revealed through their drawings', *Journal of Environmental Psychology*, 7: 189–99.

Brown, J.M., Henderson, J. and Fielding, J. (1983) 'Differing perspectives on nuclear related risks'. Paper presented to the Annual Conference of the Operational Research Society, University of Warwick, 27–30 September.

Bryant, F.B. and Edwards, J. (eds) (1992) *Methodological Issues in Applied Social Psychology: Social Psychological Applications to Social Issues.* New York: Plenum Press.

Bryant, P. and Bradley, L. (1985) *Children's Reading Problems.* Oxford: Blackwell.

Bryant, P.E. (1990) 'Empirical evidence for causes in development', in G. Butterworth and P.E. Bryant (eds) *Causes of Development.* New York: Harvester Wheatsheaf.

Burawoy, M. et al. (1991) *Ethnography Unbound: Power and Resistance in the Modern Metropolis.* Berkeley, CA: University of California Press.

Burman, E. (1990) 'Differing with deconstruction: a feminist critique', in I. Parker and J. Shotter (eds) *Deconstructing Social Psychology.* London: Routledge.

Burman, E. (1992) 'Feminism and discourse in developmental psychology: power, subjectivity and interpretation', *Feminism & Psychology,* 2: 45–59.

Burman, E. (1994) 'Experiences, identities and alliances: Jewish feminism and feminist psychology', *Feminism & Psychology* 4: 155–78.

Burman, E. (1995) '"What is it?" Masculinity and femininity in cultural representations of childhood', in S. Wilkinson and C. Kitzinger (eds) *Feminism and Discourse: Psychological Perspectives.* London: Sage.

Burman, E. (1997) 'Telling stories: psychologists, children and the production of "false memories"', *Theory & Psychology,* 7: 291–309.

Burman, E. and Parker, I. (1993a) 'Introduction – discourse analysis: the turn to the text', in E. Burman and I. Parker (eds) *Discourse Analytic Research: Repertoires and Readings of Texts in Action.* London: Routledge.

Burman, E. and Parker, I. (eds) (1993b) *Discourse Analytic Research: Repertoires and Readings of Texts in Action.* London: Routledge.

Burr, V. (1995) *An Introduction to Social Constructionism.* London: Routledge.

Butcher, B. and Dodd, P. (1983) 'The Electoral Register: two surveys', *Population Trends,* 31: 15–19.

Cacioppo, J.T. and Tassinary, L.G. (1990) *Principles of Psychophysiology: Physical, Social, and Inferential Elements.* Cambridge: Cambridge University Press.

Campbell, D.T. and Fiske, D.W. (1959) 'Convergent and discriminant validation by the multitrait–multimethod matrix', *Psychological Bulletin,* 56: 81–105.

Campbell, D.T. and Stanley, J. (1966) *Experimental and Quasi-Experimental Designs for Research.* Chicago: Rand McNally.

Campbell, J.M. (1992) 'Treating depression in well older adults: use of diaries in cognitive therapy', *Issues in Mental Health Nursing,* 13(1): 19–29.

Canter, D.V. (1983a) 'The purposive evaluation of places: a facet approach', *Environment and Behavior,* 15(6): 659–98.

Canter, D.V. (1983b) 'The potential of facet theory for applied social psychology', *Quality and Quantity,* 17: 33–67.

Canter, D.V. (ed.) (1985) *Facet Theory: Approaches to Social Research.* New York: Springer.

Canter, D.V., Brown, J. and Groat, L. (1985) 'A multiple sorting procedure', in M. Brenner, J. Brown and D.V. Canter (eds) *The Research Interview: Uses and Approaches.* London: Academic.

Carlson, J.G., Seifert, A.R. and Birnbaumer, N. (1994) *Clinical Applied Psychophysiology.* New York: Plenum.

Carlson, N.R. (1998) *Physiology of Behavior* (6th edn). Boston, MA: Allyn and Bacon.

Carr, W. and Kemmis, S. (1986) *Becoming Critical: Education, Knowledge and Action Research.* London: Falmer.

Carroll, J.S., Wiener, R.I., Coates, D., Galegher, J. and Alibrio, J.J. (1982) 'Evaluation, diagnosis, and prediction in parole decision making', *Law and Society Review,* 17: 199–228.

Cattell, R.B. (1978) *The Scientific Use of Factor Analysis.* London: Plenum.

Cattell, R.B. (1981) *Personality and Learning Theory,* Vols I and II. Berlin: Springer.

Chalmers, A. (1982) *What Is This Thing Called Science?* (2nd edn). Milton Keynes: Open University Press. (3rd edn, 1999).

Child, D. (1990) *The Essentials of Factor Analysis.* London: Cassell.

Chodorow, N. (1989) *Feminism and Psychoanalytic Theory*. New Haven, CT: Yale University Press.

Chow, S.L. (1988) 'Significance test or effect size?', *Psychological Bulletin*, 103(1): 105–10.

Christensen, L.B. (1988) *Experimental Methodology* (4th edn). Boston: Allyn and Bacon.

Churchwood, P.M. (1993) 'On the nature of theories: a neurocomputational perspective', in R.G. Burton (ed.) *Natural and Artificial Minds*. Albany, NY: State University of New York Press.

Clocksin, W. (1987) 'A Prolog primer', *BYTE*, 12(9): 147–58.

Clogg, C.C. and Stockley, J.W. (1988) 'Multivariate analysis of discrete data', in J.R. Nesselroade and R.B. Cattell (eds) *Handbook of Multivariate Experimental Psychology*. London: Plenum.

Cohen, J. (1960) 'A coefficient of agreement for nominal scales', *Educational and Psychological Measurement*, 20: 37–46.

Cohen, L. and Manion, L. (1989) *Research Methods in Education* (2nd edn). London: Routledge.

Coleman, G.J., Hemsworth, P.H. and Hay, M. (1998) 'Predicting stockperson behaviour towards pigs from attitudinal and job-related variables and empathy', *Applied Animal Behaviour Science*, 58: 63–75.

Collins, H. (1992) 'Will machines ever think?', *New Scientist*, 134, no. 1826.

Cook, T.D. and Campbell, D.T. (1979) *Quasi-Experimentation: Design and Analysis Issues for Field Settings*. Chicago: Rand McNally.

Coombs, C. (1983) *Psychology and Mathematics*. Ann Arbor, MI: University of Michigan Press.

Cooper, H.M. (1998) *Synthesizing Research: A Guide for Literature Reviews*. Beverly Hills, CA: Sage.

Cooper, P. and Tower, R. (1992) 'Inside the consumer mind: consumer attitudes to the arts', *Journal of the Market Research Society*, 34(4): 299–311.

Cornsweet, T.N. (1962) 'The staircase-method in psychophysics', *American Journal of Psychology*, 75: 485–91.

Cornsweet, T.N. and Teller, D.Y. (1965) 'Relation of increment thresholds to brightness and luminance', *Journal of the Optical Society of America*, 55: 1303–8.

Coxon, P.M. (1995) 'Diaries and sexual behaviour: the use of sexual diaries as method and substance in researching gay men's response to HIV/AIDS', in M. Boulton (ed.) *Challenge and Innovation: Methodological Advances in Social Research on HIV/AIDS. Social Aspects of AIDS*. London: Taylor and Francis.

Coyle, A. and Morgan-Sykes, C. (1998) 'Troubled men and threatening women: the construction of "crisis" in male mental health', *Feminism and Psychology*, 8: 263–84.

Craik, K. (1943) *The Nature of Explanation* (2nd edn 1967). Cambridge: Cambridge University Press.

Croft, C.A. and Sorrentino, M.C. (1991) 'Physician interaction with families on issues of AIDS: what parents and youth indicate they desire', *The Journal of Health Behavior, Education and Promotion*, 15(6): 13–22.

Cronbach, L.J. (1951) 'Coefficient alpha and the internal structure of tests', *Psychometrika*, 16: 297–334.

Cronbach, L.J. (1971) 'Test validation', in R.L. Thorndike (ed.) *Educational Measurement*. Washington, DC: ACE.

Cronbach, L.J. (1990) *Essentials of Psychological Testing*. New York: Harper and Row.

Cronbach, L.J., Gleser, G.C., Nanda, H. and Rajaratnam, N. (1972) *The Dependability of Behavioral Measurements: Theory of Generalizability for Scores and Profiles*. New York: Wiley.

Crowne, D.P. and Marlowe, D. (1964) *The Approval Motive: Studies in Evaluative Dependence*. New York: Wiley.

Dale, A., Gilbert, G.N. and Arber, S. (1985) 'Integrating women into class theory', *Sociology*, 19: 384–409.

Dancer, L.S. (1990) 'Introduction to facet theory and its applications', *Applied Psychology: An International Review*, 39: 365–77.

Danforth, J.S. (1998) 'The outcome of parent training using the behaviour management flow chart with mothers and their children with oppositional defiant disorder and attention-deficit hyperactivity disorder', *Behaviour Modification*, 22: 443–73.

Davies, B. and Harré, R. (1990) 'Positioning: the discursive production of selves', *Journal for the Theory of Social Behaviour*, 20: 43–63.

Davis, A.M. (1991) 'The language of testing', in K. Durkin and B. Shire (eds) *Language and Mathematical Education*. Milton Keynes: Open University Press.

Davison, M.L. and Sharma, A.R. (1990) 'Parametric statistics and levels of measurement: factorial designs and multiple regression', *Psychological Bulletin*, 107: 394–400.

Dawson, M.R.W. and Shamanski, K.S. (1994) 'Connectionism, confusion and cognitive science', *Journal of Intelligent Systems*, 4(3–4): 215–62.

DeJong, G. (1989) 'The role of explanation in analogy; or, The curse of an alluring name', in S. Vosniadou and A. Ortony (eds) *Similarity and Analogical Reasoning*. Cambridge: Cambridge University Press.

Delli-Carpini, M. and Williams, B.A. (1994) 'Methods, metaphors and media research: the uses of TV in political conversation', *Communication Research*, 21(6): 782–812.

Dempster, J. (1993) *Computer Analysis of Electrophysiological Signals*. London: Academic.

Dobson, V.G. and Rose, D. (1985) 'Models and metaphysics: the nature of explanation revisited', in D. Rose and V.G. Dobson (eds) *Models of the Visual Cortex*. Chichester: Wiley.

Dodd, T. (1987) 'A further investigation into the coverage of the postcode address file', *Survey Methodology Bulletin*, 21: 35–40.

Doehring, D.G. (1996) *Research Strategies in Human Communication Disorders* (2nd edn). Austin, TX: Pro-Ed.

Doise, W., Spini, D. and Clemence, A. (1999) 'Human rights as social representations in a cross-national context', *European Journal of Social Psychology*, 29(1): 1–30.

Doise, W., Spini, D., Jesuino, J.C., Ng, S.H. and Emler, N. (1994) 'Values and perceived conflicts in the social representations of human rights: feasibility of a cross-national study', *Swiss Journal of Psychology*, 33(4): 240–51.

Donald, I.J. (1985) 'The cylindrex of place evaluation', in D.V. Canter (ed.) *Facet Theory: Approaches to Social Research*. New York: Springer.

Donald, I.J. (1987) 'Place evaluation', in D.V. Canter, D. Stokols and M. Krampen (eds) *Ethnoscapes: Transcultural Studies in Action and Place*. Aldershot: Gower.

Donald, I.J. (1995) 'Facet theory: defining research domains', in G.M. Breakwell, S. Hammond and C. Fife-Schaw (eds) *Research Methods in Psychology*. London: Sage.

Dunn, J. (1988) *The Beginnings of Social Understanding*, Oxford: Blackwell.

Dunn, J. and Kendrick, C. (1982) *Siblings: Love, Envy and Understanding*. Cambridge, MA: Harvard University Press.

Dunn, N.J., Seilhamer, R.A., Jacob, T. and Whalen, M. (1993) 'Comparison of retrospective and current reports of alcoholics and their spouses on drinking behavior', *Addictive Behaviors*, 17(6): 543–55.

Dworkin, R.J. (1992) *Researching Persons with Mental Illness*. Newbury Park, CA: Sage.

Dworkin, S.F. and Wilson, L. (1993) 'Measurement of illness behavior: review of concepts and common measures', in P.M. Conn (ed.) *Paradigms for the Study of Behavior*. New York: Academic Press.

Economou, G.-P., Goumas, P.D. and Spiropoulos, K. (1996) 'A novel medical decision support system', *Computing and Control Engineering Journal*, 7(4): 177–84.

Edgington, E.S. (1996) 'Randomized single-subject experimental designs', *Behaviour Research & Therapy*, 34(7): 567–74.

Edwards, D. and Potter, J. (1992) *Discursive Psychology*. London: Sage.

Edwards, D., Ashmore, M. and Potter, J. (1995) 'Death and furniture: the rhetoric, politics and the theology of bottom line arguments against relativism', *History of the Human Sciences*, 8: 25–49.

Edwards, D., Potter, J. and Middleton, D. (1992) 'Toward a discursive psychology of remembering', *The Psychologist*, 5: 441–6.

Efron, B. (1979) 'Bootstrap methods: another look at the jackknife', *Annals of Statistics*, 7: 1–26.

Elliot, J. (1991) *Action Research for Educational Change*. Milton Keynes: Open University Press.

Elliott, R., Fischer, C.T. and Rennie, D.L. (1999) 'Evolving guidelines for publication of qualitative research studies in psychology and related fields', *British Journal of Clinical Psychology*, 38: 215–29.

Erdberg, P. and Exner, J.E. (1984) 'Rorschach assessment', in G. Goldstein and M. Hersen (eds) *Psychological Assessment*. New York: Pergamon.

Evans, R.I., Rozelle, R.M., Mittelmark, M.B., Hansen, W.B., Bane, A.L. and Havis, J. (1978) 'Deterring the onset of smoking in children: knowledge of immediate physiological effects and coping with peer pressure, media pressure and parent modelling', *Journal of Applied Social Psychology*, 8(2): 126–35.

Evans, T.G. (1968) 'A program for the solution of geometric-analogy intelligence test questions', in M. Minsky (ed.) *Semantic Information Processing*. Cambridge, MA: MIT Press.

Everitt, B.S. (1977) *The Analysis of Contingency Tables*. London: Chapman and Hall.

Exner, J. (1986) *The Rorschach: A Comprehensive System* (2nd edn). Chichester: Wiley.

Eysenck, H.J. (1978) 'An exercise in mega-silliness', *American Psychologist*, 33: 517.

Eysenck, H.J. and Eysenck, S.B.G. (1975) *Manual for the Eysenck Personality Questionnaire*. London: Hodder and Stoughton.

Eysenck, H.J. and Eysenck, S.B.G. (1976) *Psychoticism as a Dimension of Personality*. London: Hodder and Stoughton.

Farell, B. and Pelli, D.G. (1998) 'Psychophysical methods', in R.H.S. Carpenter and J.G. Robson (eds) *Vision Research: A Practical Guide to Laboratory Methods*. Oxford: Oxford University Press, pp. 129–36.

Fetterman, D.M. (1989) *Ethnography Step by Step*. London: Sage.

Fetterman, D.M. (1993) *Speaking the Language of Power: Communication, Collaboration and Advocacy*. London: Falmer.

Field, M.J. (1960) *Search for Security: An Ethno-Psychiatric Study of Rural Ghana*. London: Faber and Faber.

Fife-Schaw, C.R. and Breakwell, G.M. (1992) 'Estimating sexual behaviour parameters in the light of AIDS: a review of recent UK studies of young people', *AIDS Care*, 4(2): 187–202.

Fisch, B.J. (1991) *Spehlmann's EEG Primer* (2nd edn). Amsterdam: Elsevier Science.

Fisher, R.A. (1935) *The Design of Experiments*. Edinburgh: Oliver & Boyd.

Fleiss, J.L. (1971) 'Measuring nominal scale agreement among many raters', *Psychological Bulletin*, 76: 378–82.

Flick, U. (1998) *An Introduction to Qualitative Research*. London: Sage.

Ford, K.M. and Hayes, P.J. (1998) 'On computational wings: rethinking the goals of artificial intelligence', *Scientific American Presents*, 9(4): 78–83.

Forgays, D.G., Sosnowski, T. and Wrzeniewski, K. (1992) *Anxiety: Recent Developments in Cognitive Psychophysiological and Health Research*. New York: Hemisphere.

Foucault, M. (1972) *The Archaeology of Knowledge*. London: Tavistock.

Franklin, R.D., Allison, D.B. and Gorman, B.S. (1997) *Design and Analysis of Single Case Research*. Hillsdale, NJ: Erlbaum.

Freeman, P.R. (1973) *Table of d' and β*. Cambridge: Cambridge University Press.

Fried, R. and Grimaldi, J. (1993) *The Psychology and Physiology of Breathing*. London: Plenum.

Fuller, T.D., Edwards, J.N., Vorakitphokatom, S. and Sermsri, S. (1993) 'Using focus groups to adapt survey instruments to new populations: Experience from a developing country', in D.L. Morgan (ed.) *Successful Focus Groups: Advancing the State of the Art*. London: Sage.

Gage, N.L. (1963) *Handbook of Research on Teaching*. Chicago: Rand McNally.

Gale, A. and Eysenck, H.O. (eds) (1993) *Handbook of Individual Differences: Biological Perspectives*. Chichester: Wiley.

Gall, M.D., Borg, W.R. and Gall, J.P. (1996) *Educational Research: An Introduction* (6th edn). White Plains, NY: Longman.

Gaskell, G., Wright, D. and O'Muircheartaigh, P. (1993) 'Reliability of surveys', *The Psychologist*, 6(11): 500–3.

Gazdar, G. (1993) 'The handling of natural language', in D. Broadbent (ed.) *The Simulation of Human Intelligence*. Oxford: Basil Blackwell.

Gentner, D. (1989) 'The mechanisms of analogical learning', in S. Vosniadou and A. Ortony (eds) *Similarity and Analogical Reasoning*. Cambridge: Cambridge University Press.

Gergen, K.J. (1989) 'Warranting voice and the elaboration of the self', in J. Shotter and K.J. Gergen (eds), *Texts of Identity*. London: Sage.

Gergen, K.J., Gulerce, A., Lock, A. and Misra, G. (1986) 'Psychological science in cultural context', *American Psychologist*, 51(5): 496–503.

Gergen, M. (1988) 'Narrative structures in social explanation', in C. Antaki (ed.) *Analysing Everyday Explanation: A Casebook of Methods*. London: Sage.

Gervais, M.-C. (1993) 'How communities cope with environmental crises: the case of the Shetland oil spill'. Paper presented at the BPS Social Psychology Section Annual Conference, Jesus College, Oxford, September.

Gescheider, G.A. (1985) *Psychophysics* (2nd edn). Hillsdale, NJ: Erlbaum.

Gibbs, C. and Murphy, P. (1994) *A Fair Test? Assessment, Achievement and Equity*. Milton Keynes: Open University Press.

Gibson, K. and Peterson, A.C. (1991) *Brain Maturation and Cognitive Development*. Chicago: Aldine de Gruyter.

Gifi, A. (1990) *Nonlinear Multivariate Analysis*. Chichester: Wiley.

Giger, M.L. and Pelizzari, C.A. (1996) 'Advances in tumour imaging', *Scientific American*, 275(3): 76–8.

Gilbert, G.N. and Mulkay, M.J. (1984) *Opening Pandora's Box: A Sociological Analysis of Scientists' Discourse*. Cambridge: Cambridge University Press.

Gill, R. (1995) 'Relativism, reflexivity and politics: interrogating discourse analysis from a feminist perspective', in S. Wilkinson and C. Kitzinger (eds) *Feminism and Discourse: Psychological Perspectives*. London: Sage.

Gittelsohn, J., Shankar, A.V., West, K.P., Ram, R.M. and Gnywali, T. (1997) 'Estimating reactivity in direct observation studies of health behaviours', *Human Organisation*, 56: 182–9.

Glaser, B.G. (1978) *Theoretical Sensitivity: Advances in the Methodology of Grounded Theory*. Mill Valley, CA: Sociology Press.

Glaser, B.G. and Strauss, A.L. (1967) *The Discovery of Grounded Theory*. Chicago: Aldine.

Glaser, R. (1963) 'Instructional technology and the measurement of learning outcomes', *American Psychologist*, 18: 519–22.

Glass, G. (1976) 'Primary, secondary and meta-analysis of research', *Educational Research*, 5: 3–8.

Glass, G. (1977) 'Integrating findings: the meta-analysis of research', *Review of Research in Education*, 5: 351–79.

Glass, G., McGraw, B. and Smith, M.L. (1981) *Meta-Analysis in Social Research*. Beverly Hills, CA: Sage.

Goetz, J.P. and LeCompte, M.D. (1984) *Ethnography and Qualitative Design in Educational Research*. London: Academic.

Goldberg, D. (1972) *The Detection of Psychiatric Illness by Questionnaire*. London: Oxford University Press.

Gordis, E.B., Margolin, G. and John, R.S. (1997) 'Marital aggression, observed parental hostility, and child behaviour during triadic family interaction', *Journal of Family Psychology*, 11: 76–89.

Gratch, H. (1973) *Twenty Five Years of Social Research in Israel*. Jerusalem: Jerusalem Academic Press.

Green, B. and Hall, J. (1984) 'Quantitative methods for literature review', *Annual Review of Psychology*, 35: 37–53.

Green, D.M. and Swets, J.A. (1966) *Signal Detection Theory and Psychophysics*. New York: Wiley.

Green, D.W. (ed.) (1996) *Cognitive Science: An Introduction*. Oxford: Blackwell.

Greenacre, M.J. (1984) *Theory and Application of Correspondence Analysis*. New York: Academic.

Greenacre M.J. (1993) *Correspondence Analysis in Practice*. London: Academic.

Greenbaum, T.L. (1998) *The Handbook for Focus Group Research*. London: Sage.

Greenfield, P.M. (1997) 'Culture as a process: empirical methods for cultural psychology', in J.W. Berry, Y.H. Poortinga and J. Pandey (eds) *Handbook of Cross-Cultural Psychology* (2nd edn). Boston: Allyn and Bacon.

Gronwall, D.B. and Wrightson, P. (1974) 'Recovery after minor head injury', *Lancet*, ii: 1452.

Groves, R.M. (1989) *Survey Errors and Survey Costs*. New York: Academic.

Gulliksen, H. (1950) *Theory of Mental Tests*. New York: Wiley.

Gutride, M.E., Goldstein, A.P. and Hunter, G.F. (1973) 'The use of role-playing and modeling to increase social interaction amongst asocial psychiatric patients', *Journal of Consulting and Clinical Psychology*, 40: 408–15.

Guttman, L. (1941) 'The quantification of a class of attributes: a theory and method of scale construction', in P. Horst et al. (eds) *The Prediction of Personal Adjustment*. New York: Social Science Research Council.

Guttman, L. (1953) 'What lies ahead for factor analysis?', *Educational and Psychological Measurement*, 18: 497–515.

Guttman, L. (1968) 'A general nonmetric technique for finding the smallest coordinate space for a configuration', *Psychometrika*, 33: 469–506.

Guttman, L. (1981) 'What is not what in theory construction', in I. Borg (ed.) *Multidimensional Data Representations: When and Why*. Ann Arbor, MI: Mathesis.

Guttman, L. (1991) *Chapters from an Unfinished Textbook on Facet Theory*. Jerusalem: Hebrew University Press.

Guttman, L. and Guttman, R. (1976) 'The theory of generality and specificity during mild stress', *Behavioral Science*, 21: 469–77.

Guzzo, R.A., Jackson, S.E. and Katzell, R.A. (1987) 'Meta-analysis analysis', *Research in Organizational Behaviour*, 9: 407–42.

Guzzo, R.A., Jette, R.D. and Katzell, R.A, (1985) 'The effects of psychologically based intervention programs on worker productivity', *Personnel Psychology*, 38: 275–92.

Haberman, S.J. (1978) *The Analysis of Qualitative Data*, Vol. 1. New York: Academic.

Haberman, S.J. (1979) *The Analysis of Qualitative Data*, Vol. 2. New York: Academic.

Habermas, J. (1979) *Communication and the Evolution of Society*. Boston: Beacon.

Hair, J.F., Anderson, R.E., Tatham, R.L. and Black, W.C. (1992) *Multivariate Data Analysis*. New York: Macmillan.

Hall, J.L. (1981) 'Hybrid adaptive procedure for estimation of psychometric functions', *Journal of the Acoustical Society of America*, 69: 1763–9.

Halliday, A.M., Butler, S.R. and Paul, R. (1987) *A Textbook of Clinical Neurophysiology*. Chichester: Wiley.

Hambleton, R.K., Swaminathan, H. and Rogers, H.J. (1991) *Fundamentals of Item Response Theory*. London: Sage.

Hammersley, M. (1990) *Classroom Ethnography*. Milton Keynes: Open University Press.

Hammersley, M. and Atkinson, P. (1983) *Ethnography: Principles in Practice*. London: Tavistock.

Hammersley, M. and Atkinson, P. (1995) *Ethnography: Principles in Practice* (2nd edn). London: Routledge.

Hammond, S. (1988) 'The meaning and measurement of adolescent estrangement'. Unpublished PhD thesis, University of Surrey.

Haney, C., Banks, C. and Zimbardo, P.G. (1973) 'Interpersonal dynamics in a simulated prison', *International Journal of Criminology and Penology*, 1: 69–97.

Harari, O. and Beaty, D. (1990) 'On the folly of relying solely on a questionnaire methodology in cross-cultural research', *Journal of Managerial Issues*, 2(3): 267–81.

Harman, H. (1976) *Modern Factor Analysis*. Chicago: University of Chicago Press.

Harper, D. (1989) 'Visual sociology: expanding sociological vision', in G. Blank et al. (eds) *New Technology in Sociology: Practical Implications in Research and Work*. New Brunswick, NJ: Transaction.

Harper, D.J. (1994a) 'The professional construction of "paranoia" and the discursive use of diagnostic criteria', *British Journal of Medical Psychology*, 67: 131–43.

Harper, D.J. (1994b) 'Celebrating a diversity of voices in the arena of discourse: response to Garety and Walkup', *British Journal of Medical Psychology*, 67: 151–3.

Harper, D.J. (1995) 'Discourse analysis and "mental health"', *Journal of Mental Health*, 4: 347–57.

Harré, R. and Secord, P. (1972) *The Explanation of Social Behaviour*. Oxford: Blackwell.

Hartington, J.A. (1969) 'Using subsample values as typical values', *Journal of the American Statistical Association*, 64: 1303–17.

Harvey, L.O. Jr (1986) 'Efficient estimation of sensory thresholds', *Behavior Research Methods, Instruments and Computers*, 18: 623–32.

Heath, C. and Luff, P. (1993) 'Explicating face-to-face interaction', in N. Gilbert (ed.) *Researching Social Life*. London: Sage.

Heenan, C. (1996) 'The war, my mother, lots of individual things – a discursive psychodynamic reading of psychotherapy text', *Changes*, 14: 208–12.

Hegel, M.T. and Ferguson, R.J. (1997) 'Psychophysiological assessment of respiratory function in panic disorder: evidence for a hyperventilation subtype', *Psychosomatic Medicine*, 59(3): 224–30.

Helmholtz, H. von (1866) *Treatise on Physiological Optics*. New York: Dover, 1962.

Henkel, R.E. (1975) 'Part–whole correlations and the treatment of ordinal and quasi-interval data as interval data', *Pacific Sociological Review*, 18: 3–26.

Henwood, K. (1996) 'Qualitative inquiry: perspectives, methods and psychology', in J.T.E.

Richardson (ed.) *Handbook of Qualitative Research Methods for Psychology and the Social Sciences*. Leicester: BPS Books.

Henwood, K. and Pidgeon, N. (1992) 'Qualitative research and psychological theorising', *British Journal of Psychology*, 83: 97–111.

Henwood, K. and Pidgeon, N. (1994) 'Beyond the qualitative paradigm: a framework for introducing diversity within qualitative psychology', *Journal of Community & Applied Social Psychology*, 4: 225–38.

Hilder, J. (1997) 'Notes on the use of focus groups in organizational settings'. Unpublished manuscript, Social Psychology European Research Institute, University of Surrey.

Hillyard, S.A. (1993) 'Electrical and magnetic brain recordings: contributions to cognitive neuroscience', *Current Opinion in Neurobiology*, 3: 217–24.

Hines, A.M. (1993) 'Linking qualitative and quantitative methods in cross-cultural survey research: techniques from cognitive science', *American Journal of Community Psychology*, 21(6): 729–45.

Hinton, G.E. (1992) 'How neural networks learn from experience', *Scientific American*, 267(3): 104–9.

Hobbs, D. and May, T. (1993) *Interpreting the Field: Accounts of Ethnography*, Oxford: Clarendon Press.

Hollway, W. (1989) *Subjectivity and Method in Psychology: Gender, Meaning and Science*. London: Sage.

Holm, S. (1979) 'A simple sequentially rejective multiple test procedure', *Scandinavian Journal of Statistics*, 6: 65–70.

Holsti, O.R. (1969) *Content Analysis for the Social Sciences*. Reading, MA: Addison-Wesley.

Horton, C. and Smith, D. (1988) *Evaluating Police Work: An Action Research Project*. London: Policy Studies Institute.

Hosmer, D.W. and Lemeshow, S. (1989) *Applied Logistic Regression*. Chichester: Wiley.

Hoyle, R.H. (1995) *Structural Equation Modelling: Concepts, Issues and Applications*. London: Sage.

Huberman, A.M. and Miles, M.B. (1994) 'Data management and analysis methods', in N.K. Denzin and Y.S. Lincoln (eds) *Handbook of Qualitative Research*. Thousand Oaks, CA: Sage.

Hulin, C.L., Drasgow, F. and Parsons, C.K. (1983) *Item Response Theory*. Homewood, IL: Dow Jones-Irwin.

Hull, D.L. (1988) *Science as a Process*. Chicago: University of Chicago Press.

Hunter, J.E. and Hirsh, H.R. (1987) 'Applications of meta-analysis', in C.L. Cooper and I.T. Robertson (eds) *International Review of Industrial & Organizational Psychology*. Chichester: Wiley.

Hunter, J.E., Schmidt, F.L. and Jackson, G.B. (1982) *Meta-Analysis: Cumulating Research Findings across Studies*. Beverly Hills, CA: Sage.

Hutt, S.J. and Hutt, C. (1970) *Direct Observation and Measurement of Behaviour*. Springfield, IL: Thomas.

Hyland, M.E., Finnis, S. and Irvine, S.H. (1991) 'Living with Asthma Questionnaire', *Journal of Psychosomatic Research*, 35(1): 99–110.

Israel, J. (1972) 'Stipulations and construction the social sciences', in J. Israel and H. Tajfel (eds) *The Context of Social Psychology*. London: Academic.

Jahoda, G. (1984) 'Do we need a concept of culture?', *Journal of Cross-cultural Psychology*, 15(2): 139–51.

Jahoda, G. (1988) 'J'accuse', in M.H. Bond (ed.) *The Cross-Cultural Challenge to Social Psychology*. Newbury Park, CA: Sage

Jarrett, R.L. (1993) 'Focus group interviewing with low-income minority populations', in D.L. Morgan (ed.) *Successful Focus Groups: Advancing the State of the Art*. Newbury Park, CA: Sage.

Jaskowski, P. (1993) 'Selective attention and temporal-order judgement', *Perception*, 22: 681–9.

Jennings, J. and Coles, M.G. (eds) (1991) *Handbook of Cognitive Psychophysiology: Central and Autonomic Nervous System Approaches*. Chichester: Wiley.

Johnson, H., Brady, J.S. and Larson, E. (1996) 'A microcomputer-based system to facilitate direct observation and data collection and assessment in inclusive settings', *Journal of Computing in Childhood Education*, 7: 253–69.

Jöreskog, K.G. (1970) 'A general method for analysis of covariance structures', *Biometrika*, 57: 239–51.

Jöreskog, K.G. and Sörbom, D. (1993) *LISREL 8: Structural Equation Modeling with the SIMPLIS Command Language*. Hillsdale, NJ: Scientific Software International/Erlbaum.

Kalfs, N. and Willem, S. (1998) 'Large differences in time use for three data collection systems', *Social Indicators Research*, 44(3): 267–90.

Kazdin, A.E. and Hartman, D.P. (1978) 'The simultaneous treatment design', *Behaviour Therapy*, 9: 912–22.

Kelly, G.A. (1955) *The Psychology of Personal Constructs*, Vols 1 and 2. New York: Norton.

Keppel, G. and Saufley, J.R. (1980) *Introduction to Design and Analysis: A Student's Handbook*. San Francisco: Freeman.

Kerlinger, F.N. (1973) *Foundations of Behavioural Research* (6th edn). London: Holt, Rinehart and Winston.

Kerlinger, F.N. and Pedhazur, E.J. (1973) *Multiple Regression in Behavioural Research*. London: Holt, Rinehart and Winston.

Kiers, H.A. (1989) *Three-Way Methods for the Analysis of Qualitative and Quantitative Two-Way Data*. Leiden: DSWO.

King, R.M. and Wilson, G.V. (1992) 'Use of a diary technique to investigate psychosomatic relations in atopic dermatitis', *Journal of Psychosomatic Research*, 35(6): 697–706.

King-Smith, P.E. and Rose, D. (1997) 'Principles of an adaptive method for measuring the slope of the psychometric function', *Vision Research*, 37: 1595–604.

King-Smith, P.E., Grigsby, S.S., Vingrys, A.J., Benes, S.C. and Supowit, A. (1994) 'Efficient and unbiased modifications of the QUEST method: theory, simulations, experimental evaluation and practical implementation', *Vision Research*, 34: 885–912.

Kintsch, W., Miller, J.R. and Polson, P.G. (1984) *Methods and Tactics in Cognitive Science*. Hillsdale, NJ: Erlbaum.

Kirchner, R.E., Schnelle, J.F., Domash, M.A., Larson, L.D., Carr, A.F. and McNees, M.P. (1980) 'The applicability of a helicopter patrol procedure to diverse areas: a cost benefit evaluation', *Journal of Applied Behaviour Analysis*, 13: 143–8.

Kirk, R.E. (1996) 'Practical significance: a concept whose time has come', *Educational and Psychological Measurement*, 56(5): 746–59.

Kitcher, P. (1993) *The Advancement of Science*. New York: Oxford University Press.

Klecka, W.R. (1980) *Discriminant Analysis*. London: Sage.

Klee, R. (1997) *Introduction to the Philosophy of Science*. New York: Oxford University Press.

Kline, P. (1988) *Psychology Exposed: Or, The Emperor's New Clothes*. London: Routledge.

Kline, P. (1993) *Handbook of Psychological Testing*. London: Routledge.

Kling, J.W. and Riggs, L.A. (eds) (1972) *Experimental Psychology* (3rd edn). London: Methuen.

Klopfer, W.G. and Taulbee, E.S. (1976) 'Projective tests', *Annual Review of Psychology*, 27: 543–68.

Kluckhohn, C. (1954) 'Culture and behaviour', in G. Lindzey (ed.) *Handbook of Social Psychology (vol. 2)*. Cambridge, MA: Addison-Wesley.

Knodel, J. (1993) 'The design and analysis of focus group studies: a practical approach', in D.L. Morgan (ed.) *Successful Focus Groups: Advancing the State of the Art*. London: Sage.

Koocher, G.P. (1977) 'Bathroom behaviour and human dignity', *Journal of Personality and Social Psychology*, 35: 120–1.

Kraemer, H.C. and Thiemann, S. (1987) *How Many Subjects? Statistical Power Analysis in Research*. Newbury Park, CA: Sage.

Krippendorf, K. (1980) *Content Analysis: An Introduction to its Methodology*. Beverly Hills, CA: Sage.

Kroeber, A.L. and Kluckhohn, C. (1952) *Culture: A Critical Review of Concepts and Definitions*. Cambridge, MA: Peabody Museum.

Krosnick, J.A. and Schuman, H. (1988) 'Attitude intensity, importance and certainty and susceptibility to response effects', *Journal of Personality and Social Psychology*, 54: 940–52.

Krueger, R.A. (1988) *Focus Groups: A Practical Guide for Applied Research*. Newbury Park, CA: Sage.

Krueger, R.A. (1993) 'Quality control in focus group research', in D.L. Morgan (ed.) *Successful Focus Groups: Advancing the State of the Art*. London: Sage.

Krueger, R.A. (1994) *Focus Groups: A Practical Guide for Applied Research* (2nd edn). London: Sage.

Kruskal, J.B. (1964) 'Nonmetric multidimensional scaling: a numerical method', *Psychometrika*, 29: 1–27.

Kruskal J.B. and Wish, M. (1978) *Multidimensional Scaling*. Beverly Hills, CA: Sage.

Kuder, G. and Richardson, M. (1937) 'The theory of the estimation of test reliability', *Psychometrika*, 2: 151–60.

Kuhn, T.S. (1962) *The Structure of Scientific Revolutions*. Chicago: University of Chicago Press.

Kutas, M. and Dale, A. (1997) 'Electrical and magnetic readings of mental functions', in M.D. Rugg (ed.) *Cognitive Neuroscience*. Hove: Psychology Press.

Kvale, S. (1996) *Interviews*. London: Sage.

Labovitz, S. (1975) 'Comment on Henkel's paper: the interplay between measurement and statistics', *Pacific Sociological Review*, 18: 27–35.

Lakatos, I. (1970) 'Falsification and the methodology of scientific research programmes', in I. Lakatos and A. Musgrave (eds) *Criticism and the Growth of Knowledge*. Cambridge: Cambridge University Press.

Lamiell, J.T. (1995) 'Rethinking the role of quantitative methods in psychology', in J.A. Smith, R. Harré and L. Van Langenhove (eds) *Rethinking Methods in Psychology*. London: Sage.

Lancaster, H.O. (1969) *The Chi-Squared Distribution*. New York: Wiley.

Latane, B. and Darley, J.M. (1970) *The Unresponsive Bystander: Why Doesn't He Help?* New York: Appleton-Century-Crofts.

Lau, R.R. and Russell, D. (1980) 'Attributions in the sports pages', *Journal of Personality and Social Psychology*, 39: 29–38.

Lautsch, E. and von Weber, S. (1990) *Konfigurationsfrequenzanalyse*. Berlin: Volk and Wissen.

Lees, R. and Smith, G. (1975) *Action Research in Community Development*. London: Routledge and Kegan Paul.

Lenat, D.B. (1995) 'Artificial intelligence', *Scientific American*, 273(3): 62–4.

Leung, K. (1989) 'Cross-cultural differences: individual-level vs. culture-level analysis', *International Journal of Psychology*, 24: 703–19.

Levy, S. (1976) 'Use of the mapping sentence for coordinating theory and research: a cross cultural example', *Quality and Quantity*, 10: 117–25.

Levy, S. (1981) 'Lawful roles of facets in social theories', in I. Borg (ed.) *Multidimensional Data Representations: When and Why*. Ann Arbor, MI: Mathesis.

Levy, S. (1990) 'Values and deeds', *Applied Psychology: An International Review*, 39: 379–400.

Levy, S. (1994) *Louis Guttman on Theory and Methodology: Selected Writings*. Aldershot: Dartmouth.

Lewin, K. (1952) *Field Theory in Social Science*. London: Tavistock.

Light, R.J. (1971) 'Measures of response agreement for qualitative data: some generalisations and alternatives', *Psychological Bulletin*, 76: 175–81.

Lingoes, J.C. (1963) 'Multiple scalogram analysis: a set theoretic model for analysing dichotomous items', *Educational and Psychological Measurement*, 23: 501–24.

Lingoes, J.C. (1968) 'The multivariate analysis of qualitative data', *Multivariate Behavioral Research*, 2(1): 61–94.

Lingoes, J.C., Roskam, E.E. and Borg, I. (eds) (1977) *Geometric Representations of Relational Data*. Ann Arbor, MI: Mathesis.

Lipton, P. (1991) *Inference to the Best Explanation*. London: Routledge.

Llewellyn, G. (1991) 'Adults with an intellectual disability: Australian practitioners' perspectives', *Occupational Therapy Journal of Research*, 11(6): 323–35.

Long, J.S. (1983) *Confirmatory Factor Analysis*. Newbury Park, CA: Sage.

Lord, F.M. (1980) *Applications of Item Response Theory to Practical Testing Problems*. Reading, MA: Addison-Wesley.

Lord, F.M. and Novick, M. (1968) *Statistical Theories of Mental Test Scores*. Reading, MA: Addison-Wesley.

Lovett, T. (1975) *Adult Education, Community Development and the Working Class*. London: Ward Lock.

Lowenthal, D. (1985) *The Past is a Foreign Country*. Cambridge: Cambridge University Press.

Lunt, P. (1996) 'Discourse of savings', *Journal of Economic Psychology*, 17(6): 677–90.

Macmillan, N.A. and Creelman, C.D. (1990) *Detection Theory: A User's Guide*. Cambridge: Cambridge University Press.

Madill, A. and Barkham, M. (1997) 'Discourse analysis of a theme in one successful case of brief psychodynamic-interpersonal psychotherapy', *Journal of Counseling Psychology*, 44: 232–44.

Madill, A. and Doherty, K. (1994) '"So you did what you wanted then": discourse analysis, personal agency, and psychotherapy', *Journal of Community & Applied Social Psychology*, 4: 261–73.

Magina, C.A. (1997) 'Some recent applications of clinical psychophysiology', *International Journal of Psychophysiology*, 25(1): 1–6.

Malpass, R.S. and Poortinga, Y.H. (1986) 'Strategies for design and analysis', in W. Lonner and J.W. Berry (eds) *Field Methods in Cross-Cultural Research*. Beverly Hills, CA: Sage.

Marans, R.W and Spreckelmeyer, K.F. (1986) 'A conceptual model for evaluating work environments', in J.D. Wineman (ed.) *Behavioral Issues in Office Design*. New York: Van Nostrand Reinhold.

Marascuilo, L.A. and Levin, J.R. (1983) *Multivariate Statistics in the Social Sciences*. Monterey, CA: Brooks/Cole.

Marcus, A.C. and Crane, L.A. (1986) *The Validity and Value of Health Survey Research by Telephone: A Review of the Literature Concerning Four Methodological Issues about Health Survey Research*. Jonsson Comprehensive Cancer Center, University of California, Los Angeles/ The Commonwealth Fund, New York.

Marin, L. (1983) 'Discourse of power – power of discourse: Pascalian notes', in A. Montefiore (ed.) *Philosophy in France Today*. Cambridge: Cambridge University Press.

Marsh, P., Rosser, E. and Harré, R. (1978) *The Rules of Disorder*. London: Routledge and Kegan Paul.

Maruyama, G.M. (1997) *Basics of Structural Equation Modeling*. London: Sage.

Matlin, M.W. and Foley, H.J. (1992) *Sensation and Perception* (3rd edn). Boston: Allyn and Bacon.

McAuley, W.J., Bliezner, R., Bowling, C.A., Mancini, J.A., Romaniuk, J-G. and Shea, L. (1987) *Applied Research in Gerontology*. New York: Van Nostrand Reinhold.

McCann, J.J., Gilley, D.W., Hebert, L.E., Beckett, L.A. and Evans, D.A. (1997) 'Concordance between direct observation and staff ratings of behaviour in nursing home residents with Alzheimer's disease', *Journal of Gerontology*, 52B: 63–72.

McCulloch, W.S. and Pitts, W.H. (1943) 'A logical calculus of the ideas immanent in nervous activity', *Bulletin of Mathematical Biophysics*, 5: 115–33. Reprinted in M.A. Bowden (ed.) *The Philosophy of Artificial Intelligence*. Oxford: Oxford Unversity Press, 1990.

McDonald, R.P. (1985) *Factor Analysis and Related Methods*. Hillsdale, NJ: Erlbaum.

McGrath, J.E. (1967) 'A multifacet approach to classification of individual, group, and organisation concepts', in B.P. Indik and K.F. Berrien (eds) *People, Groups, and Organizations*. New York: Columbia University Press.

McKee, S.P., Klein, S.A. and Teller, D.Y. (1985) 'Statistical properties of forced-choice psychometric functions: implications of probit analysis', *Perception and Psychophysics*, 37: 286–98.

McLaughlin, T. (1996) 'Coping with hearing voices: an emancipatory discourse analytic approach', *Changes*, 14: 238–43.

Merton, R.K. and Kendall, P.L. (1946) 'The focused interview', *The American Journal of Sociology*, 51(6): 541–57.

Michell, J. (1997) 'Quantitative science and the definition of measurement in psychology', *British Journal of Psychology*, 88: 355–83.

Michell, L. and West, P. (1996) 'Peer pressure to smoke: the meaning depends on the method', *Health Education Research*, 11(1): 39–49.

Middlemist, R.D., Knowles, E.S. and Matter, C.F. (1976) 'Personal space invasion in the lavatory: suggestive evidence for arousal', *Journal of Personality and Social Psychology*, 33: 541–6.

Middleton, D. (1996) 'A discursive analysis of psychosocial issues: talk in a "parent group" for families who have children with chronic renal failure', *Psychology and Health*, 11: 243–60.

Miles, M.B. and Huberman, A.M. (1994) *Qualitative Data Analysis*. London: Sage.

Milgram, S. (1974) *Obedience to Authority*. New York: Harper and Row.

Mill, J.S. (1874) *A System of Logic*. New York: Harper, 1950.

Miller, G.A. (1969) 'Psychology as a means of promoting human welfare', *American Psychologist*, 24: 1063–75.

Miller, J.R., Polson, P.G. and Kintsch, W. (1984) 'Problems of methodology in cognitive science', in W. Kintsch, J.R. Miller and P.G. Polson (eds) *Methods and Tactics in Cognitive Science*. Hillsdale, NJ: Erlbaum.

Miller, R.G. (1974) 'The jackknife: a review', *Biometrika*, 61: 1–15.

Minium, E.W., King, B.M. and Bear, G. (1993) *Statistical Reasoning in Psychology and Education*. New York: Wiley.

Minsky, M. (ed.) (1968) *Semantic Information Processing*. Cambridge, MA: MIT Press.

Mislevy, R.J. (1993) 'Foundations of a new test theory', in N. Frederiksen, R.J. Mislevy and I. Bejar (eds) *Test Theory for a New Generation of Tests*. London: Erlbaum.

Montomgery, B.M. and Duck, S. (eds) (1991) *Studying Interpersonal Interaction*. New York: Guilford Press.

Morgan, D.L. (1988) *Focus Groups as Qualitative Research*. Newbury Park, CA: Sage.

Morgan, D.L. (ed.) (1993) *Successful Focus Groups: Advancing the State of the Art*. London: Sage.

Morgan, D.L. and Krueger, R.A. (1997) *Focus Group Kit*. London: Sage.

Morley, S. and Adams, M. (1989) 'Some simple statistical tests for exploring single-case time series data', *British Journal of Clinical Psychology*, 28: 1–18.

Morley, S. and Adams, M. (1991) 'Graphical analysis of single-case time series data', *British Journal of Clinical Psychology*, 30: 97–115.

Moscovici, S. (1976) *Social Influence and Social Change*. London: Academic.

Moser, C.A. and Kalton, G. (1971) *Survey Methods in Social Investigation*. London: Heinemann.

Mostyn, B. (1985) 'The content analysis of qualitative research data', in M. Brenner, J. Brown and D.V. Canter (eds) *The Research Interview: Uses and Approaches*. London: Academic.

Muedeking, G. and Bahr, H. (1976) 'A smallest space analysis of skid row men's behaviours', *Pacific Sociological Review*, 19: 275–90.

Mullen, B. (1993) 'Meta-analysis', *Thornfield Journal*, 16: 36–41.

Murphy, E. (1998) 'Exploring gender role identities and attitudes towards offenders among men and women within three occupational settings'. MSc dissertation, Department of Psychology, University of Surrey.

Murphy, J., John, M. and Brown, H. (1984) *Dialogues and Debates in Social Psychology*. London: Erlbaum.

Murphy, K.R. and Davidshofer, C.O. (1991) *Psychological Testing: Principles and Applications*. London: Prentice-Hall.

Naylor, C. (1983) *Build Your Own Expert System*. Cheshire: Sigma.

Nesselroade, J.R. and Cattell, R.B. (eds) (1988) *Handbook of Multivariate Experimental Psychology* (2nd edn). London: Plenum.

Newell, R. (1993) 'Questionnaires', in N. Gilbert (ed.) *Researching Social Life*. London: Sage.

Nezlek, J.B. (1991) 'Self-report diaries in the study of social interaction', *Contemporary Social Psychology*, 14(4): 205–10.

Nishisato, S. (1980) *Analysis of Categorical Data: Dual Scaling and its Applications*. Toronto: University of Toronto Press.

Nishisato S. (1993) *Elements of Dual Scaling: An Introduction to Practical Data Analysis*. Hillsdale, NJ: Erlbaum.

Nitko, A.J. (1988) 'Designing tests that are integrated with instruction', in R.L. Linn (ed.) *Educational Measurement*. New York: Macmillan.

Nunnally, J.C. (1978) *Psychometric Theory*. New York: McGraw-Hill.

Nunnally, J.C. and Bernstein, I. (1994) *Psychometric Theory*. New York: McGraw-Hill.

Obermeier, K.K. (1987) 'Natural-language processing', *BYTE*, 12(14): 225–32.

O'Brien, K. (1993) 'Improving survey questionnaires through focus groups', in D.L. Morgan (ed.) *Successful Focus Groups: Advancing the State of the Art*. London: Sage.

Oldroyd, D. (1986) *The Arch of Knowledge: An Introductory Study of the History of the Philosophy and Methodology of Science*. New York: Methuen.

Oppenheim, A.N. (1992) *Questionnaire Design, Interviewing and Attitude Measurement*. London: Pinter.

Papineau, D. (1996) 'Philosophy of science', in N. Bunnin and E.P. Tsui-James (eds) *The Blackwell Companion to Philosophy*. Oxford: Blackwell.

Park, R.E. (1967) *On Social Control and Collective Behaviour: Selected Papers*. Chicago: University of Chicago Press.

Parker, I. (1992) *Discourse Dynamics: Critical Analysis for Social and Individual Psychology.* London: Routledge.

Parker, I. (1994) 'Reflexive research and the grounding of analysis: social psychology and the psy-complex', *Journal of Community & Applied Social Psychology,* 4: 239–52.

Parker, I. (1997) 'Discourse analysis and psychoanalysis', *British Journal of Social Psychology,* 36: 479–95.

Parker, I. (ed.) (1998) *Social Constructionism, Discourse and Realism.* London: Sage.

Parker, I. and Burman, E. (1993) 'Against discursive imperialism, empiricism and constructionism: thirty-two problems with discourse analysis', in E. Burman and I. Parker (eds) *Discourse Analytic Research: Repertoires and Readings of Texts in Action.* London: Routledge.

Parker, I., Georgaca, E., Harper, D., McLaughlin, T. and Stowell-Smith, M. (1995) *Deconstructing Psychopathology.* London: Sage.

Parkes, C.M. (1971) 'Psycho-social transitions: a field for study', *Social Science and Medicine,* 5: 101–15.

Payne, R.L., Fineman, S. and Wall, T.D. (1976) 'Organizational climate and job satisfaction: a conceptual synthesis', *Organizational Behaviour and Human Performance,* 16: 45–62.

Pelli, D.G. and Farell, B. (1995) 'Psychophysical methods', in M. Bass (ed.) *Handbook of Optics,* Vol. I (2nd edn). New York: McGraw-Hill, pp. 29.1–29.13.

Pentland, A. (1980) 'Maximum likelihood estimation: the best PEST', *Perception and Psychophysics,* 28: 377–9.

Piaget, J. (1952a) *The Origins of Intelligence in the Child.* New York: Basic Books.

Piaget, J. (1952b) *The Child's Conception of Number.* London: Routledge and Kegan Paul.

Pike, R. (1966) *Language in Relation to a United Theory of the Structure of Human Behaviour.* The Hague: Mouton.

Plummer, K. (ed.) (1981) *The Making of the Modern Homosexual.* London: Hutchinson.

Polkinghorne, D.E. (1988) *Narrative Knowing and the Human Sciences.* Albany, NY: State University of New York Press.

Pollner, M. (1991) 'Left of ethnomethodology: the rise and decline of radical reflexivity', *American Sociological Review,* 56: 370–80.

Pomerantz, A.M. (1986) 'Extreme case formulations: a new way of legitimizing claims', in G. Button, P. Drew and J. Heritage (eds) *Human Studies,* Special Issue on Interaction and Language Use, 9: 219–29.

Popper, K.R. (1959) *The Logic of Scientific Discovery.* London: Hutchinson.

Potter, J. (1988) 'What is reflexive about discourse analysis? The case of reading readings', in S. Woolgar (ed.) *Knowledge and Reflexivity.* London: Sage.

Potter, J. (1996) *Representing Reality: Discourse, Rhetoric and Social Construction.* London: Sage.

Potter, J. and Collie, F. (1989) '"Community care" as persuasive rhetoric: a study of discourse', *Disability, Handicap & Society,* 4: 57–64.

Potter, J. and Wetherell, M. (1987) *Discourse and Social Psychology: Beyond Attitudes and Behaviour.* London: Sage.

Powell, G.E. and Adams, M. (1993) 'Introduction to research on placement'. Paper presented at the Clinical Psychology Forum, 12–16 March, British Psychological Society.

Powell, G.E. and Wilson, S.L. (1994) 'Recovery curves for patients who have suffered very severe brain injury', *Clinical Rehabilitation,* 8: 54–69.

Rapoport, R.N. (1972) 'Three dilemmas in action research', in P.A. Clark (ed.) *Action Research in Organisational Change.* London: Harper and Row.

Rasch, G. (1960) *Probabilistic Models for Some Intelligence and Attainment Tests.* Copenhagen: Danish Institute for Educational Research.

Reuben, D.B., Wong, R.C., Walsh, K.E. and Hays, R.D. (1995) 'Feasibility and accuracy of a postcard diary system for tracking healthcare utilization of community-dwelling older persons', *Journal of the American Geriatrics Society,* 43(3): 550–2.

Richardson, J.T.E. (ed.) (1996) *Handbook of Qualitative Research Methods for Psychology and the Social Sciences.* Leicester: BPS Books.

Riessman, C.K. (1993) *Narrative Analysis.* Newbury Park, CA: Sage.

Robson, C. (1993) *Real World Research: A Resource for Social Scientists and Practitioner-Researchers.* Oxford: Blackwell.

Robson, C. (1994) *Experiment, Design and Statistics in Psychology* (3rd edn). Harmondsworth: Penguin.

Roethlisberger, F.J. and Dickson, W.J. (1939) *Management and the Worker*. Cambridge, MA: Harvard University Press.

Rohner, R.P. (1984) 'Toward a conception of culture for cross cultural psychology', *Journal of Cross-Cultural Psychology*, 15(2): 111–38.

Rorschach, H. (1921) *Psychodiagnostics*. Berne: Huber.

Rose, D. (1988) 'ZSCORE: a program for the accurate calculation of *d'* and *β'*, *Behavior Research Methods, Instruments, & Computers*, 20: 63–4.

Rose, D. and Dobson, V.G. (1985) 'Methodological solutions for neuroscience', in D. Rose and V.G. Dobson (eds) *Models of the Visual Cortex*. Chichester: Wiley.

Rose, D. and Dobson, V.G. (1989) 'On the nature of explanation and the generation of models of the circuitry of the primary visual cortex', in J.J. Kulikowski, C.M. Dickinson and I.J. Murray (eds) *Seeing Contour and Colour*. Oxford: Pergamon.

Rose, D.J. and Church, R.J. (1998) 'Learning to teach: the acquisition and maintenance of teaching skills', *Journal of Behavioural Education*, 8: 5–35.

Rose, J. (1998) 'Measuring quality: the relationship between diaries and direct observation of staff', *British Journal of Developmental Disabilities*, 86: 30–7.

Rose, R.M., Teller, D.Y. and Rendleman, P. (1970) 'Statistical properties of staircase estimates', *Perception and Psychophysics*, 8: 199–204.

Rosenthal, R. (1979) 'The "file drawer" problem and tolerance for null results', *Psychological Bulletin*, 86: 638–41.

Rosenthal, R. (1991) *Meta-Analytic Procedures for Social Research*. Beverly Hills, CA: Sage.

Rowan, J. (1974) 'Research as intervention', in N. Armistead (ed.) *Reconstructing Social Psychology*. Harmondsworth: Penguin.

Roy, D.F. (1965) 'The role of the researcher in the study of social conflict', *Human Organisation*, 24: 262–71.

Runkel, P.J. and McGrath, J.E. (1972) *Research and Human Behaviour: A Systematic Guide to Method*. New York: Holt, Rinehart and Winston.

Rust, J. and Golombok, S. (1989) *Modern Psychometrics*. London: Routledge.

Sammer, G. (1998) 'Heart period variability and respiratory changes associated with physical and mental load: non-linear analysis', *Ergonomics*, 41(5): 746–55.

Saporta, G. (1979) 'Pondération optimale de variables qualitatives en analyse des données', *Statistique et Analyse des Données*, 3: 19–31.

Schaie, K.W. (1965) 'A general model for the study of developmental problems', *Psychological Bulletin*, 64: 92–107.

Schiffman, S.S., Reynolds, M.L. and Young, F.W. (1981) *Introduction to Multidimensional Scaling*. New York: Academic.

Schmidt, F.L., Hunter, J.E., Pearlman, K., Hirsh, R.H., Sackett, P.R., Schmitt, N., Tenopyr, M.L., Kehoe, J. and Zedeck, S. (1985) 'Forty questions about validity generalization and meta-analysis (plus commentary)', *Personnel Psychology*, 38: 697–798.

Schuman, H. and Presser, S. (1996) *Questions and Answers in Attitude Surveys: Experiments on Question Form, Writing and Context*. London: Sage.

Schwartz, M.S. (1995) *Biofeedback: A Practitioners Guide* (2nd edn). New York: Guilford.

Schwartz, S.H. (1992) 'Universals in the content and structure of values: theoretical advances and empirical tests in 20 countries', *Advances in Experimental Social Psychology*, 25: 1–61.

Scott, P. and Nicholson. R. (1991) *Cognitive Science: Projects in Prolog*. Hillsdale, NJ: Erlbaum.

Searle, J.R. (1990) 'Is the brain's mind a computer program?', *Scientific American*, 262(1): 20–5.

Seidel, J.V., Kjolseth, A. and Seymour, J.A. (1988) *The Ethnograph: A User's Guide*. Littleton: Qualitative Research Associates.

Sekuler, R. and Blake, R. (1994) *Perception* (3rd edn). New York: McGraw-Hill. (4th edn, 2000).

Selltiz, C., Wrightsman, L.S. and Cook, S.W. (1976) *Research Methods in Social Relations* (3rd edn). New York: Holt, Rinehart and Winston.

Serpell, R. (1979) 'How specific are perceptual skills?', *British Journal of Psychology*, 70: 365–80.

Shalit, B. (1977) 'Structural ambiguity and limits to coping', *Journal of Human Stress*, 3: 32–46.

Shaughnessy, J.J. and Zechmeister, E.B. (1994) *Research Methods in Psychology*. New York: McGraw-Hill.

Shavelson, R.J. and Webb, N.M. (1991) *Generalizability Theory*. London: Sage.

Shye, S. (ed.) (1978) *Theory Construction and Data Analysis in the Behavioral Sciences*. San Francisco: Jossey-Bass.

Shye, S. (1988) *Multiple Scaling*. Amsterdam: North-Holland.

Shye, S. and Amar, R. (1985) 'Partial-order scalogram analysis by basic co-ordinates and lattice mapping of the items by their scalogram roles', in D. Canter (ed.) *Facet Theory: Approaches to Research*. New York: Springer.

Shye, S., Elizur, D. and Hoffman, M. (1994) *Introduction to Facet Theory: Content Design and Intrinsic Data Analysis in Behavioral Research*. Thousand Oaks, CA: Sage.

Sidak, Z. (1967) 'Rectangular confidence regions for the means of multivariate normal distributions', *Journal of the American Statistical Association*, 62: 625–33.

Simon, H.A. (1981) *The Sciences of the Artificial*. Cambridge, MA: MIT Press.

Simpson, M. (ed.) (1996) *Anti-Gay*. London: Freedom.

Skinner, B.F. (1953) *Science and Human Behaviour*. New York: Macmillan.

Smith, P.B. and Bond, M.H. (1998) *Social Psychology across Cultures* (2nd edn). London: Prentice-Hall.

Smith, P.B. and Peterson, M.F. (1996) 'In search of the "Euro-manager": convergences and divergences in event management', in G.M. Breakwell and E. Lyons (eds) *Changing European Identities: Social Psychological Analyses of Social Change*. Oxford: Butterworth-Heinemann.

Socarides, C.W. (1978) *Homosexuality*. New York: Jason Aronson.

Spearman, C. (1907) 'Demonstration of formulae for true measures of correlation', *American Journal of Psychology*, 18: 161–9.

Spencer, L., Faulkner, A. and Keegan, J. (1988) *Talking About Sex*. London: Social and Community Planning Research.

Spradley, J.P. (1979) *The Ethnographic Interview*. New York: Holt, Rinehart and Winston.

Spradley, J.P. and Mann, B.J. (1975) *The Cocktail Waitress: Women's Work in a Man's World*. New York: Wiley.

Spreen, O. and Strauss, E. (1991) *A Compendium of Neuropsychological Tests*. New York: Oxford University Press.

Stanton, B., Black, M., Laljee, L. and Ricardo, I. (1993) 'Perceptions of sexual behaviour among urban early adolescents: translating theory through focus groups', *Journal of Early Adolescence*, 13(1): 44–66.

Steinschneider, M., Kurtzberg, D. and Vaughan, H.G. (1992) 'Event-related potentials in developmental neuropsychology', in I. Rapin and S.J. Segalowitz (eds) *Handbook of Neuropsychology*, Vol. 6. Amsterdam: Elsevier Science.

Sternberg, R.J. (1977) *Intelligence, Information Processing and Analogical Reasoning*. Hillsdale, NJ: Erlbaum.

Stevens, S.S. (1946) 'On the theory of scales of measurement', *Science*, 103: 677–80.

Stewart, D.W. and Shamdasani, P.N. (1990). *Focus Groups: Theory and Practice*. Newbury Park, CA: Sage.

Stine, W.W. (1989) 'Meaningful inference: the role of measurement in statistics', *Psychological Bulletin*, 105: 147–55.

Stone, E.F. (1986) 'Job-scope satisfaction and job-scope performance relationships', in E.A. Locke (ed.) *Generalisation from Lab to Field Settings*. Lexington, MA: Heath-Lexington Books.

Strachey, C. (1966) 'Systems analysis and programming', *Scientific American*, 215(3): 112–24.

Strauss, A.L. and Corbin, J. (1990) *Basics of Qualitative Research: Grounded Theory Procedures and Techniques*. Newbury Park, CA: Sage.

Stringer, E.T. (1996) *Action Research: A Handbook for Practitioners*. London: Sage.

Strong, J. and Large, R.G. (1995) 'Coping with chronic low back pain: an idiographic exploration through focus groups', *International Journal of Psychiatry in Medicine*, 25(4): 371–87.

Strube, M.J. and Hartmann, D.P. (1982) 'A critical appraisal of meta-analysis', *British Journal of Clinical Psychology*, 21: 129–39.

Sudman, S. and Bradburn, N.M. (1982) *Asking Questions: A Practical Guide to Questionnaire Design*. San Francisco: Jossey-Bass.

Suen, H.K. (1991) *Principles of Test Theories*. London: Erlbaum.

Sunderland, A. (1990) 'Single-case experiments in neurological rehabilitation', *Clinical Rehabilitation*, 4: 181–92.

Surakka, V. and Hietanen, J.K. (1998) 'Facial and emotional reactions to Duchenne and non-Duchenne smiles', *International Journal of Psychophysiology*, 29(1): 23–33.

Tabachnick, B.G. and Fidell, L.S. (1996) *Using Multivariate Statistics*. New York: Harper Collins.

Tacq, J. (1997) *Multivariate Analysis Techniques in Social Science Research: From Problem to Analysis*. London: Sage.

Taylor, M.M. and Creelman, C.D. (1967) 'PEST: efficient estimates on probability functions', *Journal of the Acoustical Society of America*, 41: 782–7.

Taylor, S.M., Elliot, S., Eyles, J., Frank, J. et al. (1991) 'Psychosocial impacts in populations exposed to solid waste facilities', *Social Science and Medicine*, 33(4): 441–7.

Thomas, J. (1993) *Doing Critical Ethnography*. London: Sage.

Thurstone, L.L. (1951) 'Psychological implications of factor analysis', in M.H. Marx (ed.) *Psychological Theory*. New York: Macmillan.

Tizard, B., Blatchford, P., Burke, J., Farquar C. and Plewis, I. (1988) *Young Children at School in the Inner City*. Hove: Erlbaum.

Topf, R., Mohler, P. and Heath, A. (1989) 'Pride on one's country: Britain and West Germany', in R. Jowell, S. Witherspoon and L. Brook (eds) *British Social Attitudes Special International Report*. Aldershot: Gower Publishing.

Townsend, J.T. and Ashby, F.G. (1984) 'Measurement scales and statistics: the misconception misconceived', *Psychological Bulletin*, 96: 394–401.

Treisman, M. and Watts, T.R. (1966) 'Relation between signal detectability theory and the traditional procedures for measuring sensory thresholds: estimating d' from results given by the method of constant stimuli', *Psychological Bulletin*, 66: 438–54.

Treutwein, B. (1995) 'Adaptive psychophysical procedures', *Vision Research*, 35: 2503–22.

Triandis, H.C. (1997) 'A cross-cultural perspective on social psychology', in G. McGarty and A.S. Haslam (eds) *The Message of Social Psychology*. Oxford: Blackwell.

Tyrrell, R.A. and Owens, D.A. (1988) 'A rapid technique to assess the resting states of the eyes and other threshold phenomena: the modified binary search (MOBS)', *Behavior Research Methods, Instruments, & Computers*, 20: 137–41.

Ullman, J.B. (1996) 'Structural equation modeling', in B.G. Tabachnick and L.S. Fidell (eds) *Using Multivariate Statistics* (3rd edn). New York: Harper Collins.

Uzzell, D.L. (1988) 'Four perspectives on political participation in the city', *Psicologia*, VI(3): 377–84.

van de Vijver, F. and Leung, K. (1997a) 'Methods and data analysis of comparative research', in J.W. Berry, Y.H. Poortinga and J. Pandey (eds) *Handbook of Cross-Cultural Psychology*, Volume 1 *Theory and Method* (2nd edn). Boston: Allyn and Bacon.

van de Vijver, F. and Leung, K. (1997b) *Methods and Data Analysis for Cross-Cultural Research*. London: Sage.

van de Vijver, F and Poortinga, Y.H (1982) 'Cross-cultural generalization and universality', *Journal of Cross-Cultural Psychology*, 13(4): 387–408.

van der Molen, M.W. and Molenaar, P.C.M. (1994) 'Cognitive psychophysiology: a window to cognitive development and brain maturation', in G. Dawson and K.W. Fischer (eds) *Human Behavior and the Developing Brain*. New York: Guilford.

Van Dijk, T.A. (1993) 'Principles of critical discourse analysis', *Discourse & Society*, 4: 249–83.

von Eye, A. (1990) *Introduction to Configural Frequency Analysis*. Cambridge: Cambridge University Press.

Vosniadou, S. and Ortnoy, A. (1989) *Similarity and Analogical Reasoning*. Cambridge: Cambridge University Press.

Wagner, H. and Manstead, A. (eds) (1989) *Handbook of Social Psychophysiology*. Chichester: Wiley.

Waite, B.M., Claffey, R. and Hillbrand, M. (1998) 'Differences between volunteers and nonvolunteers in a high demand self-recording study', *Psychological Reports*, 83(1): 199–210.

Walkup, J. (1994) 'Commentary on Harper, "The professional construction of paranoia and the discursive use of diagnostic criteria"', *British Journal of Medical Psychology*, 67: 147–51.

Waltz, D. L. (1982) 'Artificial intelligence', *Scientific American*, 247(4): 101–22.

Warr, P. (1977) 'Aided experiments in social psychology', *Bulletin of the British Psychological Society*, 30: 2–8.

Watson, A.B. and Pelli, D.G. (1983) 'QUEST: a Bayesian adaptive psychometric method', *Perception and Psychophysics,* 33: 113–20.

Wayne, W. (1998) 'Pressure, major life events, and psychological symptoms', *Journal of Social Behavior and Personality,* 13(1): 51–68.

Wegner, D.M. and Vallacher, R.R. (1981) 'Common-sense psychology', in J.P. Forgas (ed.) *Social Cognition: Perspectives on Everyday Understanding.* London: Academic.

Weller, S.C. and Romney, A.K. (1990) *Metric Scaling: Correspondence Analysis.* London: Sage.

Werner, O. and Campbell, D.T. (1970) 'Translating, working through interpreters and the problem of decentering', in R. Naroll and R. Cohen (eds) *A Handbook of Method in Cultural Anthropology.* New York: Natural History Press.

Werner, O. and Schoepfle, G.M. (1987) *Systematic Fieldwork. Volume 1: Foundations of Ethnography and Interviewing.* London: Sage.

Wetherell, M. and Potter, J. (1988) 'Discourse analysis and the identification of interpretative repertoires', in C. Antaki (ed.) *Analysing Everyday Explanation: A Casebook of Methods.* London: Sage.

Wetherell, M. and Potter, J. (1992) *Mapping the Language of Racism: Discourse and the Legitimation of Exploitation.* Hemel Hempstead: Harvester Wheatsheaf.

Wetherill, G.B. and Levitt, H. (1965) 'Sequential estimation of points on a psychometric function', *British Journal of Mathematical and Statistical Psychology,* 18: 1–10.

White, O.R. (1972) *A Manual for the Calculation and Use of the Median Slope: A Technique of Progress Estimation and Prediction in the Single Case.* Eugene, OR: University of Oregon Regional Resource Center for Handicapped Children.

White, S. and Mitchell, T. (1976) 'Organisation development: a review of research content and research design', *Academy of Management Review,* 1: 57–73.

Whyte, W.F. (1991) *Participatory Action Research.* London: Sage.

Whyte, W.F. (1993) *Street Corner Society: The Social Structure of an Italian Slum.* Chicago: University of Chicago Press.

Widdicombe, S. (1993) 'Autobiography and change: rhetoric and authenticity of "Gothic" style', in E. Burman and I. Parker (eds) *Discourse Analytic Research: Repertoires and Readings of Texts in Action.* London: Routledge.

Wilkinson, L. and Hill, M. (1994) *SYSTAT for DOS: Advanced Applications, Version 6 Edition.* Evanston, IL: SYSTAT Inc.

Wilkinson, S. and Kitzinger, C. (eds) (1995) *Feminism and Discourse: Psychological Perspectives.* London: Sage.

Willig, C. (ed.) (1999) *Applied Discourse Analysis: Social and Psychological Interventions.* Buckingham: Open University Press.

Wilson, G.D. and Patterson, J.R. (1968) 'A new measure of conservatism', *British Journal of Social and Clinical Psychology,* 7: 264–90.

Wilson, M.A. and Canter, D. (1990) 'The development of professional concepts', *Applied Psychology: An International Review,* 39(4): 431–55.

Wilson, M.A. and Canter, D. (1993) 'Shared concepts in group decision making: a model for decisions based on qualitative data', *British Journal of Social Psychology,* 32: 159–72.

Wilson, S.L. and McMillan T.M. (1993) 'A review of the evidence for the effectiveness of sensory stimulation treatment for coma and vegetative states', *Neuropsychological Rehabilitation,* 3(2): 149–60.

Wilson, S.L., Powell, G.E., Brock, D. and Thwaites, H. (1996a) 'Vegetative state and responses to sensory stimulation: an analysis of 24 cases', *Brain Injury,* 10(11): 807–18.

Wilson, S.L., Powell, G.E., Brock, D. and Thwaites, H. (1996b) 'Behavioural differences between patients who emerged from vegetative state and those who did not', *Brain Injury,* 10(7): 508–16.

Wilson, S.L., Powell, G.E., Elliott, K. and Thwaites, H. (1991) 'Sensory stimulation in prolonged coma: four single case studies', *Brain Injury,* 5(4): 393–400.

Wilson, S.L., Powell, G.E., Elliott, K. and Thwaites, H. (1993) Evaluation of sensory stimulation as a treatment for prolonged coma – seven single experimental case studies', *Neuropsychological Rehabilitation,* 3(2): 191–201.

Winborne, D.G. and Dardaine, R.P. (1993) 'Affective education for "at risk" students – the new urban principles', *Urban Review,* 15(2): 139–50.

Winer, B.J. (1978) *Statistical Principles in Experimental Design.* New York: McGraw-Hill.

Winograd, T. (1971) *An AI Approach to English Morphemic Analysis.* Artificial Intelligence Memo 241, February 1971, Cambridge, MA: MIT AI Laboratory.

Winograd, T. (1972) *Understanding Natural Language.* Edinburgh: Edinburgh University Press.

Winograd, T. (1980) 'What does it mean to understand language?', *Cognitive Science*, 4: 209–41.

Winston, P.H. (1984) *Artificial Intelligence* (2nd edn). Reading, MA: Addison-Wesley.

Winston, P.H. and Horn, B.K.P. (1984) *LISP Second Edition.* Reading, MA: Addison-Wesley.

Wirth, L. (1928) *The Ghetto.* Chicago: University of Chicago Press.

Wittrock, M.C. (ed.) (1986) *Handbook of Research on Teaching* (3rd edn). New York: Macmillan.

Wolf, F.M. (1986) *Meta-Analysis: Quantitative Methods for Research Synthesis.* Beverly Hills, CA: Sage.

Woodworth, R.S. and Schlosberg, H. (1954) *Experimental Psychology* (rev. edn). London: Methuen.

Wooffitt, R. (1992) *Telling Tales of the Unexpected: The Organization of Factual Discourse.* Hemel Hempstead: Harvester Wheatsheaf.

Wooffitt, R. (1993) 'Analysing accounts', in N. Gilbert (ed.) *Researching Social Life.* London: Sage.

Worthington, A.D. (1995) 'Single case design experimentation', *British Journal of Therapy & Rehabilitation*, 2(10): 536–57.

Wright, B. and Stone, A. (1979) *Best Test Design.* Chicago: MESA.

Young, K. and Kramer, J. (1978) 'Local exclusionary policies in Britain: the case of suburban defence in a metropolitan system', in K. Cox (ed.) *Urbanization and Conflict in Market Societies.* London: Methuen.

Yule, W. (1987) 'Evaluation of treatment programmes', in W. Yule and J. Carr (eds) *Behaviour Modification for People with Mental Handicaps.* London: Chapman and Hall.

Ziller, R.C. (1973) *The Social Self.* Oxford: Pergamon Press.

Zorbaugh, H.W. (1929) *The Gold Coast and the Slum: A Sociological Study of Chicago's Near North Side.* Chicago: University of Chicago Press.

Zuber-Skerritt, O. (1992) *Action Research in Higher Education.* London: Kogan Page.

Zvulun, E. (1978) 'Multidimensional scalogram analysis: the method and its application', in S. Shye (ed.) *Theory Construction and Data Analysis in the Behavioural Sciences.* San Francisco: Jossey-Bass.

Index